ROME IN AMERICA

ROME IN AMERICA

Transnational Catholic Ideology
from the Risorgimento to Fascism

Peter R. D'Agostino

The University of North Carolina Press
Chapel Hill and London

Set in Quadraat
by Tseng Information Systems, Inc.
Manufactured in the United States of America

Portions of Chapter 8 originally appeared in "The Scalabrini Fathers,
the Italian Emigrant Church, and Ethnic Nationalism in America,"
Religion and American Culture: A Journal of Interpretation 7 (Winter 1997): 121–59.

Portions of Chapter 10 originally appeared in "The Triad of Roman Authority:
Fascism, the Vatican, and Italian Religious Clergy in the Italian Emigrant Church,"
Journal of American Ethnic History 17 (Spring 1998): 3–37.

The publication of this book was supported by a generous contribution
from the Institute for the Humanities in the College of Liberal Arts and Sciences
of the University of Illinois at Chicago and by the subvention accompanying the 2002
Frank S. and Elizabeth D. Brewer Prize of the American Society of Church History.

∞ The paper in this book meets the guidelines for permanence
and durability of the Committee on Production Guidelines for
Book Longevity of the Council on Library Resources.

Library of Congress Cataloging-in-Publication Data
D'Agostino, Peter R., 1962–
Rome in America: transnational Catholic ideology from the Risorgimento
to fascism / Peter R. D'Agostino.
p. cm.
Includes bibliographical references (p.   ) and index.
ISBN 0-8078-2842-4 (cloth)—ISBN 0-8078-5515-4 (paper)
1. Catholic Church—United States—History. 2. United States—Church history.
3. Roman question. I. Title.
BX1406.3.D34   2004
282'.73—dc22
2003021776

cloth 08 07 06 05 04   5 4 3 2 1
paper 08 07 06 05 04   5 4 3 2 1

There is no Rome without the Pope.
—Bishop John Hughes, 1850

Rome is our spiritual center,
the District of Columbia for Christianity.
—Rev. F. P. Garesché, SJ, 1872

The good Catholics of all the world consider Rome
as the second country of each and every one of them.
—Pius XI, 1931

We were content . . . to climb about the dark
living room examining the glassed-in paintings in
their huge gilt frames, the fruits of European travel: dusky
Italian devotional groupings, heavy and lustrous grapes,
Neapolitan women carrying baskets to market, views of
Venetian canals, and Tuscan harvest scenes—secular themes
that, to the Irish-American mind, had become tinged with
Catholic feeling by a regional infusion from the Pope.
—Mary McCarthy, *Memories of a Catholic Girlhood*

In whatever way we estimate the relative merits and
virtues of the European form of democracy in comparison
with our own, it is evident that the original conception of a
sharp distinction between a virtuous new democratic world
and a vicious tyrannical older world was erroneous.
—Reinhold Niebuhr, *The Irony of American History*

Contents

Preface
ix

Introduction:
Whose Rome? Whose Italy?
1

PART I. INTRANSIGENCE, 1848–1914

Chapter 1
The Roman Question: The Battle for Civilization, 1815–1878
19

Chapter 2
The Transnational Symbolic Contest for Rome, 1878–1914
53

Chapter 3
The Mayor of Rome Is an "Atheist Jew," 1910–1914
84

PART II. TRANSFORMATION, 1914–1929

Chapter 4
The Great War: "Keep the Roman Question Alive," 1914–1920
103

Chapter 5
The Church Encounters the Order Sons of Italy in America, 1913–1921
132

Chapter 6
Catholics Meet Mussolini: "The Chosen Instrument in
the Hands of Divine Providence," 1919–1929
158

PART III. REALIZATION, 1929–1940

Chapter 7
The Lateran Pacts of 1929 and the Crisis of 1931:
Defending "The Holy Island"
197

Chapter 8
Preaching Fascism and American Religious Politics
230

Chapter 9
Stubborn and Lonely: American Catholic Anti-Fascists
258

Chapter 10
Parish Conflicts: The Church and Fascist Italy Manage
"All Spirit of Rebellion"
282

Epilogue
304

Notes
317

Bibliography
361

Index
383

MAPS

1. Italy before Unification
21

2. The Process of Italian Unification
22

3. Modern Italy
107

Preface

On 14 November 2002, John Paul II entered the Palazzo di Montecitorio in Rome and became the first pope in history to address the Italian parliament. In his forty-five minute speech, he asked authorities to show clemency for prisoners through reduced sentences, and he urged Italians to have more children to reverse a declining birthrate, one of the lowest in the world. The *papa polacca* was keenly aware of the tortuous (and torturous) relationship between modern Italy and St. Peter's successors. "Truly deep is the bond that exists between the Holy See and Italy! We all know that this association has gone through widely different phases and circumstances, subject to the vicissitudes and contradictions of history. But at the same time we should recognize that precisely in the sometimes turbulent sequence of events that bond has had highly positive results, both for the Church of Rome, and therefore for the Catholic Church, and for the beloved Italian Nation." John Paul reminded parliament, "Italy's social and cultural identity, and the civilizing mission it has exercised and continues to exercise in Europe and the world, would be most difficult to understand without reference to Christianity, its lifeblood." In conclusion, he implored "the Redeemer of man to grant that the beloved Italian Nation will continue, now and in the future, to live in a way worthy of its radiant tradition, and to draw from that tradition new and abundant fruits of civilization, for the material and spiritual progress of the whole world. God bless Italy!" John Paul's appearance in the Palazzo di Montecitorio inspired little comment in the United States. It was an Italian event of little import to Americans.[1]

This book explains why American indifference to the Holy Father's relationship to modern Italy is relatively novel, a luxury of the last fifty years. It demonstrates how, in John Paul's words, the "association" between Italy and the Holy See that "has gone through widely different phases and circumstances, subject to the vicissitudes and contradictions of history," has had profound importance for modern Catholicism and for social relations among American Catholics and their neighbors. The "turbulent sequence of events" from 1848 to 1940, I argue, was not merely an Italian or even a strictly European matter. It shaped American Catholic identity and conditioned how Protestants, Jews, and liberals understood Roman Catholics in the United States.

This book explores one of three interrelated historical problems I have been investigating since my first research trip to Rome in 1990. First, what has been the significance for both Italian and American history of the sisters and clergy of the Italian diaspora who worked as extensions of the Italian Church in the United States? Second, how has the Italian state shaped U.S. politics and culture, particularly Italian American life and representations of Italy among American intellectuals and in popular culture? Finally, how has the papacy's distinctive relationship to modern Italy shaped U.S. history? This book takes up the last question, even as I draw upon ongoing research related to the first two questions to illuminate this analysis. Since graduate school, I have taken the advice of a wise historian of Italy who urged me to collect as much as possible in foreign archives during research sojourns before familial commitments made extended residence in Rome difficult. This was excellent advice, although I have often found myself working on too many incomplete projects at once. I am happy now to clear space from my desk.

This book then is the culmination of twenty-six months of archival research in Roman ecclesiastical and state archives over a period of thirteen years, as well as visits to a variety of more easily accessible U.S. archives. Along the way I accumulated many debts. I wish to thank the Giovanni Agnelli Foundation for a dissertation fellowship that funded research during the 1990–91 academic year in Rome and then another Agnelli grant that supported summer research at the Immigration History Research Center in St. Paul, Minnesota. I spent six months in 1996 as a Fulbright Junior Faculty research fellow in Rome. Since then, grants from Stonehill College, where I taught for six years, and the University of Illinois at Chicago have funded repeated summer trips to Rome. The University of Illinois at Chicago also granted support for Marek Suszko to scan Polish American newspapers for me. I was fortunate to be a PEW fellow in American religious history during the 1998–99 academic year. Jon Butler and Harry Stout were wonderful hosts when the fellows gathered for a conference at Yale University.

Archivists everywhere have been most helpful. I cannot list them all, but some went well beyond the call of duty, particularly Stephania Ruggiero and Michele Abbate at the Archivio Storico Diplomatico in the Italian Foreign Ministry, Tim Meagher at the Catholic University of America, Roman Godzak at the archdiocese of Detroit, and Christine Krosel at the diocese of Cleveland.

I have presented early drafts of this book and received wise feedback. I wish to thank the Stonehill College History Group for reading chapter 1; Stephen Stein, as well as Deborah Dash Moore at the American Academy of Religion, for their comments on chapter 3; Martha Hanna for her remarks on chapter 4 at the American Catholic Historical Association; Phil Cannistraro for reading chapters 4 and 5 and for inviting me to speak at the City University of New York; Jim O'Toole for comments on chapter 5 at the Massachusetts Historical Society's Seminar in Urban and Immigration History, and Conrad Wright for hosting me at that forum; R. Scott Appleby for inviting me to present half of chapter 10 at the University of Notre Dame; Martin E. Marty, John Paul Russo, Fred Turner, and Michael Coogan, for commenting upon my book proposal; Larry Moore and Colleen McDannel for reading drafts of chapters that never actually made it into this book; and Donna Gabaccia, Jim O'Toole, and especially Mary Mapes, for reading the entire manuscript.

Friends and colleagues in Rome have been remarkable guides and mentors. Particularly, I wish to express gratitude to Matteo Sanfilippo, a constant source of inspiration, and Giovanni Pizzorusso. Together they have compiled exceptionally useful inventories of the holdings on Canada and the United States in Roman ecclesiastical archives. Their spadework and many rich historical essays made the research for this book possible, and their friendship and encouragement have made my Roman sojourns all the more rewarding. The late Father Gianfausto Rosoli, my host when I was a Fulbright fellow at the Centro Studi Emigrazione in 1996, monitored my progress for many years and generously shared his time and expertise before his untimely death. Archbishop Silvano Tomasi has offered encouragement and direction, and he opened the archives of the Pontifical Council for Migrants, Refugees, and Tourists to me in 1996. Finally, Franco Brugnano has welcomed me into his home during my many research trips and taught me more than anyone about life on the streets in contemporary Rome.

Back in the United States, I want to thank Sandra Yocum Mize for sharing her dissertation with me; and Patrick Allitt for tracking down a couple of sermons at Emory University's library. Elaine Maisner and her colleagues at the University of North Carolina Press have helped me bring this project to completion.

I owe a special debt of gratitude to Martin E. Marty, my mentor at the University of Chicago, and Kathleen Neils Conzen, for their patience with a pig-headed graduate student who still won't leave them alone. Over many years, Phil Cannistraro and Donna Gabaccia have both generously read my work and guided me through thickets in Italian history and migration studies. Philip Gleason and Rudolph Vecoli have been helpful teachers. Tom Clarke at Stonehill College has been exceptionally generous in his support. Greg Shaw, at Stonehill College, and now Eric Arnesen and Paul Griffiths, at the University of Illinois at Chicago, have been terrific "bosses." Craig Prentiss and I have run up phone bills sharing ideas. My extraordinary parents, Rita and Vincent, have always encouraged me to pursue happiness and excellence. My siblings and their spouses and children learned to stop asking when this book would be finished. I dedicate this book to my wife, Mary Mapes, whose warm spirit and keen mind inspired me to finish and to nurture all that is good.

ROME IN AMERICA

Introduction

Whose Rome? Whose Italy?

In 1848 Rome erupted in revolt. Liberal nationalists throughout the politically fragmented Italian peninsula rose up to topple oppressive rulers and expel Austrian overlords. Frightened and bewildered, Pope Pius IX fled his Eternal City and went into exile. Although French arms restored the pope-king's rule over his Papal States in central Italy, liberals soon realized their dream of Italian unity and in 1861 proclaimed a constitutional monarchy. On the 20th of September 1870 the young kingdom conquered Rome itself, and the Papal States disappeared from the map of Europe. This time Pius chose an internal exile. For the next sixty years, he and his successors on Peter's throne cloistered themselves in the Vatican and hailed themselves "prisoners" of the evil Kingdom of Italy. Catholics throughout the world made these papal protests their own. They embraced popular devotions that cultivated heartfelt affections for their embattled Holy Father. Liberal barbarians, a new breed of pagans, vandalized the Eternal City and crucified Christ's Vicar, humanity's suffering servant, on a Calvary called the Vatican. Deceitful proponents of modern civilization peddling illusions of false liberty were in revolt against God. Apocalyptic broodings rattled the lost remnants of papal Rome.[1]

The Kingdom of Italy, conventionally called "Liberal Italy" from 1861 to 1922, insisted Rome's status had been settled after the conquest of 1870. The prisoner popes, however, never acquiesced to the loss of the temporal power. Christ's Vicar broadcast dramatic lamentations of this "Roman Question," the abnormal status of the pope as a prisoner of Liberal Italy without a territorial sovereignty to guarantee his spiritual autonomy. The Holy Father called upon Catholic states and his faithful children in non-Catholic states to participate in his incessant rituals of protest. Liberal Italy, on the other hand, had the backing of liberals, Protestants, and Jews the world over. It denied the existence of a Roman Question and contended the pope was a spiritual leader who did not need to rule land in order to carry out his religious mission. The temporal power of the pope was a medieval anachronism in a world of progress. Liberal Italy assured the pope a secure place in the new liberal world order that granted his church freedom from state interference, even if it denied his legitimacy as a territorial prince. Wisdom dictated that he halt his violent denunciations.

This conflict between Catholic and liberal conceptions of papal sovereignty was not an abstract debate. It was inseparably linked to the contest over the meaning of Italy as a nation and a state. Catholics throughout the world contended Italy was a Catholic nation whose greatest individuals were saints, whose most beautiful monuments were Catholic in inspiration, and whose center was the Holy Father in papal Rome. Village festivals to patron saints that marked the many *patrie*, or homelands, on the peninsula and its islands fused family, village, and municipality into Catholic Italy, the *patria*, the land of the popes. In the Catholic understanding of history, St. Peter's successors in Rome had always protected this beloved nation from foreign domination. Through God's Providence, the Roman Empire had fallen, and the bishop of Rome had become an Italian ruler and the moral arbiter of Europe. From papal Rome all civilization emanated. It assimilated barbarians and taught natural and divine law to the nations. God had chosen Italians to be the pope's champions and agents of civilization.

Before 1848 Catholics had proposed a variety of formulas to expel Austrian power and unite Italy into a confederation that honored the pope as its head and preserved his Papal States. The European revolutions of 1848 shattered this dream. When the Kingdom of Italy became a reality in 1861, Pius IX intransigently condemned the new state as an evil invention of bloodthirsty radicals, Freemasons, secret societies, and pseudoliberals who used nationalism as a pretext to attack the pope, the Church, and God. Awaiting the collapse of this demonic monarchy, Pius IX forbade Catholic participation in the political system of this degenerate state. A masterful manipulator of public opinion, he cultivated the affective loyalties of Catholics throughout the world to support his intransigence.

This high drama became a lens through which Catholics perceived the modern world and through which Protestants perceived Catholics. The meaning and status of Rome, the Italian nation, and the Italian state became the focal point of an international contest. Catholics fought liberalism and its unrelenting rejection of the papal claim to temporal sovereignty. Throughout Europe and America, journalists, scholars, and politicians debated the significance of the Roman Question. Thousands of American Catholics took to the streets in snowy frontier towns and genteel eastern cities to march against the symbols and holidays of Liberal Italy, to communicate solidarity with their Holy Father, and to keep the Roman Question alive. Their activism marked Catholic identity and inspired among their Anglo-Protestant foes a great love of Italian liberal nationalism.

The Roman Question never disappeared from public discourse, much to Liberal Italy's disgust. It persisted as a theological, cultural, and political rupture from 1848 until 1929, when the pope attained a small temporal sovereignty, the State of the Vatican City. During the interim, the Roman Question conditioned European and American Catholic life on the diplomatic plane right down to the parish level and helped shape how Protestants understood their own ecclesiopolitical positions.[2] Catholics responded to the Risorgimento—the movement to unify Italy—and the concomitant loss of the Papal States, by creating what I call the *ideology of the Roman Question*, a constituent element of Catholic culture that, in the United States, generated boundaries separating Catholics from other Americans.

The ideology of the Roman Question had two parts. First, it argued that the pope required the temporal power for spiritual independence and for the health of civilization itself. Thus, it condemned the liberal legislation the Italian state unilaterally imposed upon the pope, the Law of Guarantees (1871), which acknowledged his spiritual, but denied his temporal, sovereignty. Second, the ideology of the Roman Question ferociously cudgeled Liberal Italy as an illegitimate polity. The "movement" of these two parts of the ideology in relationship to one another, in particular their uncoupling in the twentieth century, constitutes *the transformation of the ideology of the Roman Question*. Although the intensity of the Catholic condemnation of the Italian state diminished in the early decades of the twentieth century, the popes still rejected the Law of Guarantees and called for the restoration of the temporal power. Finally, in 1929 decades of Catholic perseverance paid off in *the realization of the ideology of the Roman Question*. Fascist Italy and the Holy See signed the Lateran Pacts, which established the State of the Vatican City. At each stage the Roman Question shaped the American Church and the social relations between Catholics and others.

The problematic historical relationship of Catholicism and modern liberalism in the United States and Europe cannot be understood when it is manicured too neatly, abstracted out of the Italian and Roman contexts where conflicts broke out most vociferously and colored how the papacy reacted to tensions elsewhere. In light of that conviction, I tell the story of the creation, transformation, and realization of the ideology of the Roman Question in a narrative that is largely a contest over the status of Italy as a nation and a state.[3]

Transnational Perspectives on American Religious History

Students of religion in the United States are not accustomed to a story whose center pivots around myths and symbols of Rome. We know that Israel has a potent place in the life of American Jews and Protestant premillennialists and that

Ethiopia triggers deep associations in the African American religious imagination. However, the symbolic significance of the pope, Rome, and Italy after 1848 remains conspicuously unexplored.

The Vatican before the pontificate of John XXIII (1958–63) usually appears in American historiography as a prosaic gathering site of deteriorating Italian men. They intrude, discipline, misunderstand "American life," and stifle the creativity of "American Catholicism." This trope, for lack of a better word, has undermined historical understanding. In fact, most American Catholics stumbled over each other trying to display loyalty and love for their Holy Father, and they consistently invited the authority of the Vatican into U.S. affairs to adjudicate conflicts and discipline opponents. This may sound strange to American ears today. But the story told in this book demonstrates how a three-generation battle between the Kingdom of Italy—a second-rate power—and five aged occupants of the papal throne, an anomalous ecclesiastical office in a southern European city, preoccupied millions of Catholic Americans, inflamed their passions, mobilized their resources, and deeply troubled their Protestant, liberal, and Jewish neighbors.

Rome, not Jerusalem, Washington, Baltimore, or Dublin, was the center of the American Catholic world from 1848 to 1940. There were, of course, lesser centers, from home altars to statues in parish churches, from lay societies to the many episcopal cathedrals that jutted across the skyline of dreary industrial cityscapes. However, papal Rome—the source of juridical and dogmatic authority and a rich reservoir of history and symbolism—made possible whatever unity existed among disparate American Catholic classes, ethnic groups, and regions. Rome and the pope also defined Catholics in the imagination of other Americans. Furthermore, to invoke the Holy Father or papal Rome after 1848 was tantamount to inviting a discussion of the Roman Question and the meaning of Liberal Italy, and if non-Catholic Americans joined the conversation, a brawl inevitably ensued.

Historians have erroneously assumed that the Roman Question was an irrelevant diversion in a distant Europe about which Americans remained indifferent.[4] However, U.S. newspapers, sermons, books, lectures, devotional practices, public rituals, and diplomatic activities tell a very different story. Vague references to the French Revolution and the apostasy of Father Felicité de Lamennais usually stand in among American historians for an explanation of why the papacy turned against liberalism. But when Americans actually debated the Vatican's troubled relationship to liberalism after 1848, they discussed the status of Rome and the Vatican within Liberal Italy. I have followed this lead in my research.

This book finds a comfortable place in the scholarship on American religion. Historians have identified three periods of American religious pluralism. In the colonial and early national era, Protestants maintained denominational distinctions through confessional commitments and symbolic activity. As denominational boundaries weakened, a pan-Protestant cultural consensus emerged in the mid–nineteenth century. By the 1840s this Protestant "righteous empire" contended with growing communities of Jews and Catholics who resisted assimilation into the Protestant majority. It was not until after World War II that cultural divisions separating "Protestant-Catholic-Jew" began to wane. This "restructuring of American religion" created new social cleavages. Conservative and liberal axes within Judaism, Protestantism, and Catholicism increasingly structured religion in America. The new lines of conflict, liberal against conservative, cut through the historic faith traditions and, in the most aggressive (and simplistic) formulation, generated contemporary "culture wars." Although social historians could poke holes in, and enumerate exceptions to, this grand model, it provides a helpful starting point to our story, which falls squarely within the second period.[5]

The creation, transformation, and realization of the ideology of the Roman Question fortified the considerable ramparts that separated Catholics from other Americans. This is not to say that the status of the pope in Rome was the only marker of Catholic identity, but it was pervasive and provocative, a recurring source of tension between Catholics and others. For three generations it contributed to Catholic distinctiveness, boundary maintenance, and survival in Protestant America. Protestants, liberals, and Jews, in turn, helped to strengthen the ideology of the Roman Question as they condemned it and tendered their own beliefs about Rome and Italy. This book is about them as well as Catholics.

American Catholic scholarship, which I analyze briefly in the epilogue, is often frustratingly internalist. It frequently deploys history as ammunition in contemporary intra-Catholic debates about Church governance—the Church should be more democratic, the Church should not tolerate so much dissent, and so on. This internalist scholarship emphasizes public sparring among a minority of U.S. bishops from 1880 to 1900 and suggests these conflicts hardened into a "liberal" versus "conservative" divide that anticipated today's Catholic culture wars. Historian R. Laurence Moore, outside of this intra-Catholic fray, has dissected this story line of good-guy "liberals" versus bad-guy "conservatives." His deconstruction of this internalist narrative has gone largely ignored. So has his call to bring "American Catholics to the center of American religious history where they belong" and to demonstrate how the massive Catholic presence in the United States shaped Protestant understandings of the role of religion in society.[6]

If an internalist narrative driven by a presentist agenda obfuscates the relevance of American Catholic history for nonspecialists, it also engages in an unproductive polemic with "European Catholicism," a straw man that serves as a monolithic, static symbol of ecclesiastical absolutism and a foil to an imagined democratic "American Catholicism." For instance, a recent volume explores how "minority faiths" such as Judaism and Catholicism adopted "strategies for survival" to maintain their identities in the face of a hegemonic "American Protestant mainstream." The essay on Catholicism insists that true American Catholics in the nineteenth century wished to create an "American Catholicism" that was "modern and democratic," the opposite of "European Catholicism," which was "feudal and monarchical." This simplistic and awkward nod toward a comparative history that never actually investigates Europe ignores the many Catholics in European society who have fought and suffered for democratic and liberal values. Likewise, this reading of the past ignores the intense affection American Catholics harbored for the monarchical nineteenth-century papacy and its indiscriminate condemnations of every variety of European liberalism.[7]

Most students of American religion rarely tread upon this treacherous Catholic turf. They accept a story line churned out by "Americanist" Church historians and use it to whitewash Catholicism in the United States of its distinctiveness. In so doing, they assimilate the Church in a way that Catholics themselves struggled so passionately and successfully to avoid. American historians and sociologists make aggressive claims for uniformity across religious traditions. Catholic parishes in America are "de facto" Protestant congregations; Counter-Reformation parish missions mimicked Protestant revivals; Catholic immigrants understood their migration to the United States within a biblical Exodus paradigm, like the Puritans; the engagement of American Catholics, like Protestants, with biblical criticism and Darwinism inspired a "modernist impulse"; "American Catholicism" is just another "denomination." Notwithstanding the insights offered in these analogical studies of Catholics, a selective rendering of the national context inevitably takes an unexplained priority over the transnational one. Catholicism appears as a quirky Protestantism, divorced from its international matrix, the original and enduring context that preserved its distinctiveness and ensured its survival as a minority faith in the United States. The exercise of papal power among American Catholics appears as a vindictive bolt of lightning from an unenlightened foreign despot for mysterious Latin reasons, a "holy siege."[8]

This quest for uniformity of organizational forms across religious traditions has distorted our understanding of institutions such as parishes and made distinctively Catholic institutions invisible altogether. Religious orders, missionary societies, Catholic juridical and financial structures, episcopal diplomatic activities, the Vatican's apostolic delegation in Washington, and the papacy—Catholic institutions without obvious Protestant correlates—rarely appear in the indexes of works culminating in "models" and "paradigms" of "American religion." The Methodist Church simply does not have a secretary of state. This study hopes to recover the particular nature of Catholicism in the United States through attention to transnational factors and its dialectical relationships to Protestantism and liberalism.[9]

Since I completed the final draft of this book, two relevant works have appeared that I hope will enrich the historiographical debates that I address in *Rome in America*. John T. McGreevy's *Catholicism and American Freedom*, primarily an intellectual history, demonstrates how American Catholics, often in dialogue with Europeans, clashed with liberals repeatedly over the true meaning of freedom. Matteo Sanfilippo's *L'Affermazione del cattolicesimo nel Nord America*, a comparative study of Catholicism in the United States and Canada that draws extensively upon Roman ecclesiastical archives, covers the period from 1750 to 1920.

American History in a Global Age

It has become popular in the last decade to declare that U.S. history is an aspect of "international history" and to proclaim the value of placing U.S. history within a global or transnational context.[10] In some instances international history employs a comparative method in which the unit of analysis is the nation-state. While I make brief national comparisons of discrete events, this work is not a comparative history of Catholics in the United States with, say, Italy or Austria. And although this work contributes to a growing scholarship of an internationalized history of modern Italy, that is not the primary focus.[11]

The contemporary interest in transnationalism has arisen at a time when observers claim the nation-state grows weaker. But even during the heyday of the nation-state system, modern Catholics within states forged an "imagined community" with myths, shared symbols, and a calendar of prescribed rituals. The Holy See in the Eternal City was the center of this community. The Holy Father communicated his suffering, frequently through disapproval of events in Italy, a Catholic nation within a state established against his will. He won the unprecedented affection of Catholics everywhere, including the United States, with significant consequences for American social relations. The international frame of reference to this story makes it no less a part of U.S. history. It is a study akin to what historian Akira Iriye calls "cultural internationalism," but the focus is upon the implications of this particular papal internationalism for U.S. history.[12]

The ideology of the Roman Question, in all of its stages, was an international structure, but one that cannot be understood without special consideration of events in nineteenth- and twentieth-century Italy. The conquest of the Papal States created an anomaly within the concert of nations—a national capital with two legitimate sovereigns. Both had active diplomatic corps, denied the other's claims to temporal sovereignty, and deployed their resources to undermine the other's prestige. U.S. historians, however, have adopted liberal premises in their confrontation with (or avoidance of) this odd Roman phenomenon. They have considered the papacy an Italian domestic matter, and since the Kingdom of Italy was never a "great power," the Holy See rarely appears in their accounts of Euro-American diplomatic relations.

But European and American Catholics did not abandon their Holy Father to the Kingdom of Italy, and they never accepted the liberal solution to the Roman Question imposed upon the papacy. Although reactions varied by nation, region, and class, the Roman Question preoccupied Catholics everywhere, generating conflicts between Catholics and other citizens (or subjects) and provoking anxiety among nation-building statesmen. During international crises, foreign offices and state departments, with good reason, wondered whether their Catholic populations or those of their allies could be trusted. This was surely the case during the Great War when President Woodrow Wilson, his advisers, and his allies, tracked papal diplomacy with angst and wondered whether the American Catholic population—not merely Irish or German Americans—was all aboard for the war to end all wars. "Nativism" was an international phenomenon, and Catholic ghettos emerged within many modern states, even those that were ostensibly Catholic.[13] During the Fascist period (1922–43), American Catholics qua Catholics were perceived to be aligned with Fascist Italy or at least to support many of its illiberal policies. I set this international Catholic factor in relief in the hope that specialists in politics and foreign relations might begin to pay greater attention to Catholicism as a form of internationalism. Still, I maintain an American focus in this study in order to explore the political, cultural, and social implications of this international story for the United States.

Social Theory and Ideology

In this discussion of theory and method, I hope it becomes clear that the dichotomy between Europe and America, applied with normative implications to matters in Catholic history, can be artificial and misleading. As the subtitle of this book suggests, this is a historical study of ideology. It is neither a church history in the theological sense nor a community study of a Catholic social group. I track neither an institution nor a cohort of people through time. Instead, I have chosen to narrate the rise, transformation, and realization of an ideology and how it worked in American society.[14]

In the stories they tell, historians find a balance between impersonal structures that facilitate and limit human behavior and the agency of people who create their own lives. Structures, however, are also human creations, made and remade through social action. With each re-creation of these patterns of symbols in social life, with each reproduction of cultural schemas that generate human action, resources are mobilized and new situations arise in which structures are remade once again. Each application of inherited rules of behavior leaves room for innovation, that is, for human agency. Social theorist Anthony Giddens captures this dialectical quality: "Social structures are both constituted by human agency, and yet at the same time are the very medium of this constitution." As one of his interpreters puts it, structures "are both the medium and the outcome of the practices which constitute social systems."[15]

Structures are not all alike. Language, for example, is a particularly deep structure, one that is persistent and pervasive over time and space. Deep structures cannot be easily changed or eliminated. They set the foundation for enduring institutions because they can organize human behavior into a social system. The capacity of structures to mobilize resources determines their power. A dictatorship, with its ubiquitous police force and repressive mechanisms, exemplifies a powerful (but not very deep) structure. Needless to say, structures do not necessarily respect political borders. Catholic juridical codes and capitalism, for example, are both deep structures and relatively immune to national borders.

Ideologies, as sociologist Gene Burns has explained, "are actually special types of social structures." They comprise verbal or written utterances capable of communicating beliefs and duties. According to Robert Wuthnow, an ideology "may also include visual representations (objects such as flags or pictures), symbolic acts (salutes and genuflections), and events (sets of related acts such as a parade or religious service). In this sense ideology obviously blends with and subsumes much of what is usually referred to as ritual." As a structure that both facilitates communication and behavior as well as limits and directs thought and action, ideology requires constant social interaction to preserve its structure, which can change as historical agents transpose cultural schemas or symbolic patterns to new cases or contexts.[16]

The ideology of the Roman Question took a plurality of forms. Variations resulted from its replication on different social levels. Not every ideology appears as a propositional statement that coheres into a totalistic, all-encompassing worldview. Theorists draw helpful distinctions between "lived" and "intellectual" ideological forms. Unstable and incomplete, lived ideologies are likely to communicate assumptions or emotions, not reasoned argument. Popular forms of media —newspapers, parish bulletins, sermons, devotional tracts, letters to editors— most effectively communicated the ideology of the Roman Question. Group exegesis of these media in churches, offices, barbershops, and taverns further generated popular expressions of ideology.[17]

Changes in the political and social environment tend to transform existing ideologies or generate new ones. This often happens quite rapidly. The conquest of the Papal States and the establishment of Liberal Italy gave rise to the ideology of the Roman Question. It restructured preexisting cultural forms to challenge the existence of the Kingdom of Italy and the liberal understanding of religion as a purely "spiritual" affair. A transformation in this ideology resulted from the rise of socialism and the massive upheaval brought about by World War I. The collapse of Liberal Italy after the Great War frightened Catholics, many of whom feared a socialist revolution, but it also created an opportunity for ideological change. In this new environment, tension with Liberal Italy was relaxed and disengaged from the enduring quest for the restoration of the temporal power. After 1922,

Catholics both facilitated and exploited the rise of Fascist Italy, accelerating this ideological transformation.

Ideologies have modes of operation. Popular modes analyzed in this study were the deployment of symbols, artful gestures of protest, and implicit threats of retaliation. Repeated to the point of tedium, they constructed an interpretation of the past. Within a generation after 1848, the ideology of the Roman Question had become integrated into Catholic processes of socialization, securing broad dissemination. The expansion of print media, increased literacy, and technological developments in communication and transportation enhanced the power and depth of the ideology of the Roman Question. A voluminous transatlantic Catholic correspondence and the establishment of the Vatican's apostolic delegation in the United States in 1893 did the same. As this work shows, American Catholics participated in an international "imagined community"—the Church—of Catholic peoples in a world dominated by nation-states suspicious of all forms of internationalism.[18]

Ritual is a powerful medium to communicate ideology. Wuthnow explains that a ritual is "a symbolic-expressive aspect of behavior that communicates something about social relations, often in a relatively dramatic or formal manner." It is not a special type of activity set apart from others but the expressive dimension of all social activity. It need not be a face-to-face event; mass media also facilitate ritual. Our story describes a variety of Catholic rituals: marches and sermons of protest; tedious reiterations of key words and phrases that triggered affective associations; parliamentary speeches, public letters, and papal allocutions to cardinals. The back-and-forth polemics between American Protestants and Catholics, or between the pope and Italian statesmen, over the meaning of Italian symbols had a dramatic and formal character—they too were rituals.[19]

Competition is an important element of ideological analysis. The Roman Question instigated intra-Catholic competition. Many Catholics were committed to mixing liberalism and Catholicism. But the "intransigents"—Catholics committed to the restoration of the Papal States, the necessity of the temporal power, and an unequivocal condemnation of Liberal Italy—had the backing of the papacy, a powerful resource. Commitment to intransigence became a marker of loyalty to the Church during the nineteenth century and had a profound impact on Catholics in the United States, even those who absorbed other values from liberalism.[20]

Some historians use "ideology" to designate illusory ideas or collectively shared values that facilitate state domination. As I have defined it, the ideology of the Roman Question means something else. It is what impassioned Catholics to struggle toward a goal and mobilized resources in that struggle. Catholic cultural producers employed the ideology of the Roman Question to heighten Catholic consciousness, preserve collective memories, and act to regain the temporal power. Notwithstanding failures along the path from 1848 to 1929, the Holy Father did in the end acquire sovereignty over an autonomous and theocratic state. The State of the Vatican City exists today for all to see. It serves as an effective launching pad for papal intervention in international affairs. Before 1929, the papacy lacked that political legitimacy.

The ideology of the Roman Question affected Catholics in different ways. Bishops, editors, and priests, for example, exercised greater power than others. As cultural producers in the public sphere, they had the power to communicate their ideas. On the other hand, they had little autonomy to deviate from prescribed Catholic positions. While a bishop could author a circular letter read to thousands of Catholics at Sunday mass, this very power assured that ideological deviation in the content of that circular letter would trigger punishment from the Vatican. Conversely, lay people had less power (as Catholics). They did not fill a recognized office in the Church, and they lacked easy access to Catholic communication media to broadcast their ideas. This absence of power, however, was also a form of "negative autonomy." If a lay woman could not publicize her views, she nevertheless did have autonomy in her home, or corner grocer, or reading circle, to voice heterodoxy safely. In addition, she could more easily avoid active participation in Catholic ideology. Thus, the ideology of the Roman Question, like all ideologies, embodied mechanisms of power and discipline, which we explore in depth.[21]

Chronology and Overview

The ideology of the Roman Question falls into three periods: intransigence (1848–1914), transformation (1914–29), and realization (1929–40).

My examination of the period of intransigence in Part I describes how the Risorgimento—the movement to unify Italy—led to international Catholic condemnations of Liberal Italy as a "usurper" state controlled by evil forces who used nationalism as a pretext to attack the pope, the Church, and the Catholic nation of Italy. Catholics adopted an alternative, Catholic idea of the Italian nation that was at odds with the state's promotion of a liberal national identity. Catholics rejected Liberal Italy's unilaterally imposed legislation—the Law of Guarantees—to regulate the position of the Holy See within the Italian kingdom and expressed solidarity with their suffering Holy Father, a Christ figure redeeming the world on a crucifix constructed by plundering revolutionaries.

This study demonstrates how American Catholics, particularly of Irish and German descent, participated in the intransigent expressions of the ideology of the Roman Question (Chapter 1). They protested the Risorgimento and communicated solidarity with their Holy Father through public rituals that separated Catholics from their American neighbors. By contrast, American liberals and

Protestants celebrated the unification of Italy as the progressive realization of liberal and millennial hopes. Garibaldi, Cavour, and Mazzini, who were marauding degenerates from the Catholic point of view, in the Protestant mind were latter-day Washingtons, Jeffersons, and Franklins who liberated the Italian nation from papal tyranny.

In the generation after the Risorgimento, almost all Catholics in the United States—those dubbed both "liberal" and "conservative" in Catholic scholarship—supported intransigent expressions of the ideology of the Roman Question (Chapters 2 and 3). They condemned Liberal Italy and demonized its leaders. They insisted that the liberalism behind the U.S. political order was radically different from Europe's pseudoliberalism that had imprisoned the pope. American liberalism, they insisted, was in perfect harmony with the restoration of the temporal power. Put another way, the Roman Question inspired an American Catholic version of "American exceptionalism." I describe the importance of this Catholic version of American exceptionalism for memory and history in the epilogue.[22]

Immigration created an Italian diaspora in America. Representatives of the Italian state (the embassy and consulates) and the Italian Church (the clergy) followed migrants to the United States. The presence of Italian Americans forced Catholics from all national groups to confront the symbols and rituals of both Catholic and Liberal Italy with great frequency. Catholics, Protestants, and liberals from all national backgrounds participated in the ideological contest that erupted within and about this Italian diaspora. Catholics turned to the Vatican for instructions, welcoming its authority into U.S. affairs to adjudicate the proper behavior in this contest. Protestant home missionary societies, settlement houses, and liberal activists compelled Catholics to mobilize their resources. Migration thus intensified the ideology of the Roman Question and forced Catholics in the United States to participate in it.

The Great War initiated the transformation of the ideology of the Roman Question, examined in Part II. A cataclysm that rocked the foundations of civilization, World War I reawakened Catholic hopes to regain the temporal power (Chapter 4). The Holy See sought to arbitrate a treaty during the war, gain entrance into the peace conference, and compel the European Powers to resolve the Roman Question on Catholic terms. I demonstrate how the United States and American Catholics had an important role in papal diplomacy during the Great War. Their potential influence on President Woodrow Wilson, the Democratic Party, and the Allied states was central to the Holy See's strategy to resolve the Roman Question.

A change within the structure of the ideology of the Roman Question marked this period of transformation. The Holy Father continued to condemn the usurpation of the Papal States, decry his loss of temporal power, and withhold formal recognition of Liberal Italy. However, the Vatican for the first time permitted unrestricted Catholic political participation within Liberal Italy. The pope instructed clergy to act as Italian war chaplains and did not censure Catholic politicians actively supporting the war effort. Furthermore, in 1919 the papacy allowed Italian Catholics to create a nonconfessional but Catholic political party.

This rejection of intransigence also transformed the relationship between Italian Americans' liberal nationalist organizations and the Church (Chapter 5). Intense intra-Catholic ideological competition broke out among Italian priests in the United States during the Great War regarding the significance of ethnic organizations within the Italian diaspora. Just as the Holy See eased opposition to Liberal Italy, the Vatican and American bishops eased intransigent resistance to the Order Sons of Italy in America, a powerful fraternal organization. The Vatican permitted Catholic institutional links with the Order and similar organizations that had previously been prohibited.

The collapse of Liberal Italy after the Great War and the rise of Benito Mussolini's Fascist dictatorship in the 1920s intensified the transformation of the ideology of the Roman Question (Chapter 6). Important strands of Catholicism and Fascism shared notable affinities, particularly a disdain for liberalism, socialism, and political democracy. Fascist Italy, in contrast to Liberal Italy, acknowledged the Catholic character of the Italian nation and held out promise that the Kingdom of Italy could finally become a legitimate home for the Catholic nation. Mussolini celebrated Italy's Catholic heritage and awarded privileges to the Church. The Vatican applauded and rewarded these developments.

American Catholics participated in this ideological transformation. As the world watched Pope Pius XI (1922–39) and Mussolini perform unprecedented gestures of reconciliation, American Catholics reiterated the Vatican's position, embraced the symbols of Fascist Italy, and accepted the legitimacy of Italy's official state representatives. American Catholics supported the U.S. government's financial policy of stabilizing Fascist Italy during its vulnerable years while Mussolini consolidated his dictatorship. When debates over the religious policies of Fascist Italy surfaced, Catholics clashed with liberals and Protestants, who feared the religious liberties Italians had known under Liberal Italy were at risk. Debates about the nature of Fascism were central to religious tensions in the 1920s, when Mussolini became a protean American icon with different meanings for Catholics and Protestants. I contend that American Catholics participated in important ways in the reconciliation leading up to the Lateran Pacts of 1929, when the Holy See and Fascist Italy resolved the Roman Question and formally recognized one another. The pope became the temporal ruler of the State of the Vatican City, what G. K. Chesterton called "The Holy Island." Catholic ideology had demanded nothing less.[23]

In Part III I explore the implications of the realization of the ideology of the Roman Question for American life. This realization, most significantly the establishment of the Vatican City, instigated polemics and apologias in the United

States (Chapter 7). The American Catholic defense of the Lateran Pacts in the face of liberal and Protestant critiques intensified preexisting hostilities toward Catholics that had surfaced during Al Smith's 1928 presidential campaign. Some Catholic thinkers stubbornly insisted the Lateran Pacts created in Fascist Italy an environment of religious liberty analogous to that in the United States. Others claimed that a Catholic confessional state was appropriate for the Italian people, a Catholic nation.

American Catholics, like their Holy Father, participated in rituals legitimating Fascist Italy's religious policies and, in many instances, the Fascist regime itself. The Italian embassy and consulates promoted Fascist propaganda within U.S. society. They forged excellent relations with American Catholics and received cooperation from the apostolic delegation, U.S. bishops, clergy, and both English-speaking and Italian-speaking laity (Chapter 8). The same consulates, however, now representatives of a Catholic confessional state, found the Lateran Pacts a liability in their encounters with Protestant Americans who had committed resources to evangelizing Italians.

Among American Catholics, there was never an anti-Fascist movement. The experience of two stubborn and lonely Catholic anti-Fascists demonstrates the transnational networks of authority and discipline that linked Fascist Italy and the Holy See after the Lateran Pacts (Chapter 9). No less a figure than the Vatican secretary of state, Cardinal Eugenio Pacelli, the future Pius XII (1939–58), and his office disciplined Fathers James Gillis and Giuseppe Ciarrocchi for their anti-Fascist journalism.

After the Lateran Pacts, the links forged among American bishops, Fascist consulates, and the Holy See facilitated cultural activism to improve the image of Italian Americans during a period in U.S. history when popular movies and fiction smeared their character. I analyze two conflicts in Italian American parishes that generated mass protests in order to reveal how American bishops turned to Fascist consulates to help negotiate their difficult relationships with Italian American parishioners (Chapter 10).

The epilogue explains how American Catholics entered into polemics with liberals and Protestants over the fate of postwar Italy. Catholics staunchly defended their anti-Fascist credentials against accusations that the papacy and the American Church had no moral authority to participate in Italian reconstruction. Catholic elite argued (unsuccessfully) that the Italian monarchy that had supported the Fascist regime for twenty years ought to be maintained and that Italian republicans were untrustworthy red revolutionaries. I suggest that the American Catholic relationship to Fascism between the wars helps explain why midcentury liberals looked upon Catholicism as an authoritarian culture with affinities to reactionary politics.

In 1948, one century after Pius IX fled papal Rome and condemned the Risorgimento, the Christian Democrats, essentially a Catholic party, took the mantle of the new Italian republic and claimed the heritage of the Risorgimento as their own. The Church in America mobilized resources to bring the Christian Democrats to power against its competitor, the Communist Party. These efforts, however, no longer clearly distinguished Catholics from other Americans. American Catholic and Vatican policies toward republican Italy during the Cold War did not generate clear social boundaries between Catholics and other Americans. The Roman Question ceased to exist in the new environment. This is not to say that the pope has not remained an important symbol to Americans, but his status is no longer linked to debates about the nature of the Italian nation and state. Furthermore, while the debate about Catholicism and liberalism continues, Italy has no privileged place in these reflections.

I use several writing conventions in the text that follows. Some Italian words that have become standard in English-language writings, such as *patria* (homeland), *italianità* (Italianness), *Statuto* (the Italian kingdom's constitution), *fuoruscito* (anti-Fascist exile), and "Risorgimento" (literally, the resurgence), appear without translation. I use the term "Fascism" to refer to Italian Fascism and never to mean a generic authoritarian regime (like Spain under Francisco Franco) or Nazism or anything else. The term "Church" serves as shorthand (without theological implications) for the Roman Catholic Church. "America" is often a shorthand for the United States.

PART I

Intransigence, 1848–1914

CHAPTER ONE

The Roman Question

The Battle for Civilization, 1815–1878

On 29 November 1847, several thousand New Yorkers gathered at the Broadway Tabernacle to honor Giovanni Maria Mastai-Ferretti. His popular "enlightened policy and liberal measures" boded well for champions of the movement to unify Italy. Mayor William Brady presided as Protestant clergy rubbed shoulders with Gotham's redoubtable Roman Catholic bishop John Hughes. An ebullient audience applauded letters celebrating Mastai-Ferretti. Former president Martin Van Buren heralded the "patriotic head" of the people of Italy. Vice President George Dallas admired the "sublimity of his genius; . . . the unassailable purity of his life; . . . [his] rare combination of intellectual and moral excellences, fitting him for the love and leadership of a reviving people." Secretary of State James Buchanan discerned in Mastai-Ferretti "an instrument destined by Providence to accomplish the political regeneration of his country." Horace Greeley waxed nonnativist as he read the address to this "Heaven-appointed instrument" of a "wise and beneficent policy." It was a remarkable sight, indeed, this Anglo-Protestant embrace of the man who had ascended the papal throne in 1846 and taken the name Pius IX.[1]

The first eighteen months of Pius IX's pontificate (1846–78) inspired dreamy hopes for a new dawn in the interwoven stories of liberty and of Italy. The possibility that the Vicar of Christ might baptize the liberal-national struggle to oust Austrians from Italy captivated Europeans and Americans. The Risorgimento, the movement for Italian unity and independence between 1815 and 1870, mediated the Church's rendezvous with progressive ideas in the nineteenth century. Pius did not encounter liberalism in abstract theological manuals or philosophical disputations but in the blood-drenched collision of armies that determined the earthly destiny of his sacred home.

During Pius's long pontificate, the ideology of the Roman Question took shape. After Napoleonic Europe crumbled, monarchs reclaimed their losses at the

Council of Vienna (1815). Over the next three decades, Italian Catholics nurtured visions of Italian unification under the auspices of the papacy. But the revolutions of 1848 that erupted throughout Europe ended this flirtation between liberal nationalism and Catholicism and set the Church on a course of reaction. Radical democrats struggled unsuccessfully against moderate liberals for leadership of the Risorgimento, which culminated in the proclamation of the Kingdom of Italy in 1861. In the process Pius lost most of his Papal States, a territory that stretched across the center of the Italian peninsula from Rome to Ancona and as far north as Bologna. He condemned the Italian kingdom, Liberal Italy, with reckless fury. Finally, on the 20th of September in 1870, Italian troops broke through the ancient wall near the Porta Pia, conquered papal Rome, and transferred Italy's capital from Florence to the Eternal City. Pius dramatized his intransigent protest, proclaimed himself a "prisoner in the Vatican," and awaited the downfall of the demonic state that had incarcerated him and the "real Italy," the Catholic nation.

Americans participated in these events. The Roman Question, the contested status of the papacy in Liberal Italy, generated an ideology of protest and subversion against the usurper state throughout the Catholic world. American Catholics, like Catholics elsewhere, demanded the restoration of the Papal States. The pope's temporal power was a necessary precondition to his spiritual autonomy, argued Catholics who denounced Liberal Italy as an evil and monstrous injustice. In addition, the restoration of papal Rome held the key to the preservation of civilization. In contrast, American Protestants and Jews celebrated Italian liberty, unity, and independence. For them the blow struck against papal tyranny was evidence of the millennial march of progress from the New World to the Old. Consequently, the conquest of the Papal States strengthened boundaries separating Catholics from other Americans. The explosion of Catholics' communication media from 1848 to 1878—newspapers, periodicals, devotional texts, transatlantic correspondence—facilitated the dissemination of the ideology of the Roman Question and the rise of a popular cult to Pius, a suffering Christ figure crucified on the modern Calvary called the Vatican.

The Neoguelf Origins of the Ideology of the Roman Question

Catholics created the ideology of the Roman Question out of ideas and symbols prevalent during the Restoration (1815–48), when Catholic romantics embraced the great themes of the Risorgimento—liberty, unity, independence. Italy, they believed, was a Catholic nation with a universal mission. Influenced by liberal ideas their French rulers had impressed upon them, Italian Catholics harmonized romantic and liberal values into suggestive histories of how downtrodden Italy might revive past glories through reform of state and Church. However, even

Map 1. Italy before Unification

as romantics prophesied an Italian resurgence, despots backed with the force of arms kept Italy divided.[2]

Pope Gregory XVI (1831–46) ruled his Papal States without a constitution, and his encyclical "Mirari vos" (1832) did not hide his disgust for the new ideals animating Europe. He condemned liberalism, freedom of thought, and freedom of the press and supplied American nativists with evidence of Catholic hostility to

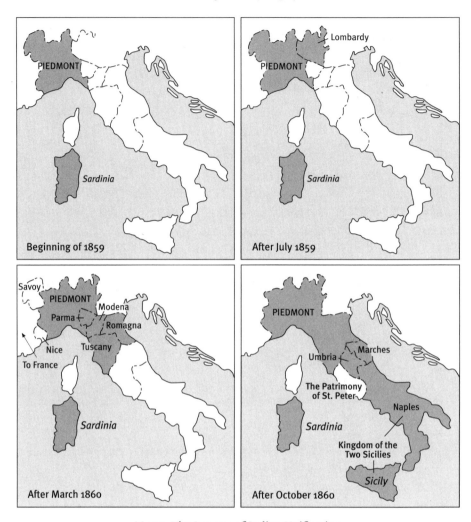

Map 2. The Process of Italian Unification

democracy. Austrian military dominance over the Italian peninsula may have in-spired romantic musings about barbarian invaders of late antiquity, but realists scoffed at the idea that an independent or liberal Italy was in the making. Aus-tria ruled over Lombardy-Venetia and had close ties to the Grand Duchy of Tus-cany, the Duchies of Parma and Modena, and the Kingdom of the Two Sicilies. The House of Savoy's stranglehold over the Kingdom of Piedmont-Sardinia (here-after, the Kingdom of Piedmont) further ensured division and absolutism.[3]

Still, dreamers wrote, preached, and painted a national past. Where did they turn for paradigmatic precursors for this most unlikely national resurgence? An-cient Rome, an obvious repository of Italian greatness, lost appeal after the Napoleonic interregnum tainted the propaganda value of classicism. Few doubted Italian preeminence in the Renaissance, but its political failures had ushered in foreign servitude. Consequently, advocates of the national idea plundered the Middle Ages in their search for Italy. Even if reaction reigned in Gregory's Papal States, papal Rome had once been a source of Italian unity and civilization. Catholic ideologues for a united Italy, the "neoguelfs," who took their name from the Guelf supporters of the medieval papacy against northern European imperial intrusions into Italy, envisioned a reinvigorated papacy at the center of European civilization and Italian national history. On the theological level, neoguelf writers debated the nature of papal and national sovereignty. On the ethico-civic plane, they highlighted the centrality of Catholicism as the source of civilization. Appealing to history, neoguelfs contended that the papacy was the center of any proper rendering of the Italian past.[4]

Historian Francesco Traniello explains how neoguelfism took both liberal-nationalist and absolutist formulations during the Restoration. In *Du pape* (1819) Joseph-Marie Compte de Maistre argued that the sovereign gave the nation "its social existence and all of its resulting goods." Medieval popes, he contended, had defended the liberty of Italian princes from Germanic imperial domination. The pope, in fact, was the custodian of the very idea of sovereignty. To attack the pope's temporal sovereignty over the Papal States was to assault all sovereigns and civilization itself. Alessandro Manzoni, by contrast, opposed de Maistre's theocratic ideal. In *Discorso sopra alcuni punti della storia longobardica in Italia* (1820), Manzoni claimed national identity existed independently of political power. When the Lombard invaders subjugated the Latin people on the Italian peninsula after the fall of the Roman Empire, the conquered nation did not assimilate. While de Maistre portrayed the pope as the defender of Italian princes, Manzoni depicted the pope as "an object of veneration" to the oppressed Italian nation suffering under the Germanic heel. Manzoni likened Italy to Israel in bondage inside Egypt. The Italian nation had turned to the pope as a religious symbol of hope, not as a temporal ruler.[5]

Neoguelfs improvised creatively upon such formulations before 1848. They called for a confederation of existing Italian states under the presidency of the pope, and they accepted the idea of a constitution. Most neoguelfs aligned themselves with moderate liberals (henceforth, the "moderates") and remained stalwart enemies of republican democrats (henceforth, the "democrats") like Giuseppe Mazzini. Deeply concerned for the freedom of the Church, neoguelfs criticized state control over Church property, ecclesiastical appointments, and papal communication networks. In the eighteenth century, such Erastian arrangements had interfered with the Church, undermined Catholic morality, and led ecclesiastical leaders to neglect spirituality. Thus, neoguelfism proposed Church reforms that would trigger the renewal of Italian society.

Neoguelfism shared affinities with "ultramontanism," an international movement that rallied Catholics to the pope as the source of Church liberty and independence against the absolutist state. For a brief moment during the Restoration, some ultramontanes called for a separation of Church and state as a way to
free the Church from the state. But after repeated papal condemnations of liberalism and the separation of Church and state, ultramontanism in the late nineteenth century grew into a mass phenomenon perpetuated through popular devotions that cultivated affections for the Holy Father, his absolute authority over the
Church, and the restoration of the Papal States.

During the 1840s, neoguelfs inspired hope for the Risorgimento as both a
political and spiritual awakening. In The Five Wounds of the Church (1848), Father
Antonio Rosmini lamented divisions within the Church as well as state influence
over bishops and priests. He believed a vernacular liturgy would enhance lay participation in the mass, and he called for laity and clergy to select bishops. Rosmini
urged clergy to withdraw from temporal concerns and for the Church to reject
state privileges and make itself accountable to the laity, not to the state. Once liberty permeated the Church, Rosmini hoped it would revitalize the nation, which
would thrive within a united federation of Italian states.[6]

In 1843, famous Piedmontese priest and statesman Vincenzo Gioberti published On the Moral and Civil Primacy of the Italians, an 800-page neoguelf manifesto.
He exalted papal Rome as the center of civilization and the Italian nation. Catholicism, with the papacy as its universal guide, had created the Italian nation, the
papacy's vehicle to spread civilization. "The Italians, humanly speaking, are the
Levites of Christianity; being specifically chosen by Providence to have among
them the Christian Pontificate." And "if in the proper religious sphere the Pope
no longer belongs to Italy alone among the nations, . . . in the civil sphere he
was the creator of Italian genius." Gioberti linked the resurgence of Italy, "a
nation of priests," to Christian themes of redemption and resurrection. There
were no racial overtones to Gioberti's idea of the nation, a people forged in history through God's Providence. The nation grew organically out of family, village,
and province and was not the last point of providential social development. Just
as war had aggregated nations under the umbrella of the Roman Empire, in the
Christian era the papacy linked nations into a spiritual imperium, without negat-
ing national aspirations for independence. Gioberti called for a confederation of
Italian states under the presidency of the pope who would initiate liberal reforms
within the confederation without limiting the autonomy of existing rulers.[7]

During the first two years of Pius's pontificate, neoguelf ideas seemed prophetic. Wishful Catholics, liberals, and Protestants fantasized how Pius would
bless a national war against Austria. When the consecration was not forthcoming, the 1848 Italian revolution quickly took an antipapal turn. The moderates'
search for national leadership shifted from the papacy to the monarchy of Pied-

mont. After 1848, neoguelfism laid the foundation for the Catholic "anti-Risorgimento," and its root ideas became building blocks of the ideology of the Roman Question. Thereafter, neoguelfism offered a Catholic alternative to both the moderate and democratic imaginings of an Italian nation, and American Catholics embraced neoguelfism in their blistering anti-Risorgimento crusade for three generations.[8]

Before the revolution of 1848, the *United States Catholic Magazine* endorsed Gioberti's *Moral and Civil Primacy* and the myth of Pius IX as an Italian Moses. "Pius IX is . . . destined to be in the hands of divine Providence the restorer of Italian nationality and the saviour of Italy." Pius had "lately recognised — at least virtually — the democratic principle of popular representation," while Austria stubbornly remained "the avowed enemy of all reform." The *Catholic Magazine* framed the events in terms pilfered from Italian neoguelfs. "The old struggle between the Guelfs, . . . the ardent friends of Italian liberty, and the most uncompromising champions of Italian nationality," and the Ghibellines, who "had secretly or openly advocated the cause of the German emperors, and had sought to establish a foreign despotism on the ruins of Italian freedom," was again unfolding. The *Catholic Magazine* backed Gioberti's moderates against the democrats, "revolutionists," who were "the greatest curse to Italy" and "the greatest pests of any well organized society." Although "we dearly . . . prize republican institutions, we do not suffer our enthusiasm to betray us into the absurd belief that such institutions are adapted to the temperament and character of every people."[9]

The *Catholic Magazine*, captive to the myth of Pius IX, described Gioberti's work as if it represented the pope's mind. Pius was enacting a "LEGAL revolution, . . . a confederation similar to that of the Swiss cantons, or of our own glorious union." The *Catholic Magazine* thoroughly endorsed Gioberti's neoguelfism. "Why should not Italy be free and independent? . . . Is she not the mother of empire, the fountain of civilization, the land of genius, the home of the fine arts, the parent of inventions, the birth-place of Dante, of Tasso, of Galileo, of Columbus, of Michael Angelo? . . . Why should she, who has ever been the greatest benefactress of the human race, be herself deprived of the blessings she has so freely communicated to others? . . . She must and will rise again."[10]

In 1848, Catholics in America were not alone in their support for a Risorgimento led by moderates against Italian democrats. All Americans reacted with ambivalence to the European conflagrations of 1848. They feared social anarchy, the loss of commerce, and the immigration of reckless revolutionaries fleeing bloody European paroxysms. But after 1848, Catholics exited from American debates comparing the merits of democrats and moderates in the struggle for Italian redemption. American Catholics instead clung to the Vicar of Christ, their Holy Father, who condemned moderates and democrats alike as conspirators against the pope and Catholic Italy.[11]

Roman Revolution, Republic, and
Reverberations in America, 1848–1850

Pius IX, bishop of Rome, successor of the apostle Peter, exercised spiritual sovereignty over the Church and reigned absolutely over the Papal States as the *papa-re*, the pope-king, like his predecessors had since the early Middle Ages. Except for a brief diplomatic mission to Chile as a young priest, Pius lived his entire life within the Papal States, serving as archbishop of Spoleto and bishop of Imola before he, the ninth child of a count, became the pope in 1846. In the first eighteen months of his pontificate, Pius raised expectations that he might baptize Lady Liberty. He granted amnesty to political prisoners and selected a popular secretary of state. He established commissions to enact administrative reforms, relax press censorship, and study economic and judicial modernization. He relaxed harsh restrictions against Jews. Laymen took significant positions in his government, and he granted his admiring subjects a constitution with a two-house parliament. These concessions accompanied Pius's heartfelt proclamations of Italian patriotism.[12]

As the bombast at the Broadway Tabernacle suggested, hopes ran high. From Rome in May 1847, Margaret Fuller, transcendentalist and feminist, described the "present Pontiff" as "a man of noble and good aspect, who . . . has set his heart on doing something solid for the benefit of Man." On 7 December, President James Polk recommended U.S. diplomatic relations with the Papal States, noting "the interesting political events now in progress [there]." After completion of his tour as consul in Genoa, Charles Edwards Lester, the great-grandson of Jonathan Edwards, felt himself "in the presence of a man Heaven seemed to have chosen to lead the human race out of the house of bondage" when he had a private audience with Pius.[13]

American Catholics relished their leader's liberal credentials. Alongside fellow citizens, they disparaged evil Austria and "illiberal ecclesiastics and laymen" in Rome who dared to obstruct Pius's reforms. Catholics boasted how Louisiana's legislature applauded "the noble efforts of Pius IX to reform ancient abuses and to promote the happiness of his people." His "kindness to the poor outcasts of the Ghetto has made him almost an object of worship to the Jews," Cincinnati's *Catholic Telegraph* assured its readers. "Some even imagine that he is their long expected Messiah." Catholics welcomed the Sicilian uprisings in January 1848, certain a papal endorsement would follow. On 10 February, Pius's ambiguous blessing of Italy gave them reason to fantasize. "It is a great blessing among the many which Heaven hath imparted to Italy, that scarce 3,000,000 of our subjects have 200,000,000 brothers of every nation and of every tongue. This will ever be her defense, so long as the Apostolic See shall reside in her centre. Oh then, Great God, shower thy blessings on Italy and preserve for her this most precious boon of all, Faith!"[14]

The Sicilian revolt inspired liberal demands elsewhere. Rulers of the Kingdom of the Two Sicilies, Tuscany, and Piedmont and Pius in his Papal States granted constitutions. King Charles Albert of Piedmont accepted the *Statuto*, which would become the Constitution of the Kingdom of Italy and remain in force until 1947. Conservative by any lights, its first sentence read: "The Catholic Apostolic and Roman religion is the sole religion of the State." But it still granted equality to religious minorities and freedom of the press and assembly. The *Statuto* created an elected Chamber of Deputies and a Senate of life peers appointed by the king. Its property restrictions limited the franchise to 2 percent of the population. Under the *Statuto* the monarch was both the head of state and of government who appointed and dismissed ministers. He could veto legislation, make war, forge treaties, and issue royal decrees. The king also retained the power to choose the prime minister, who selected a cabinet.[15]

Constitutions, however, did not quell the revolutionary impulse. In February, Parisian insurgents brought down King Louis Philippe, and Louis Napoleon became president of a French republic. In March, Prince Klemens von Metternich, the towering symbol of Restoration absolutism, fled an uprising in Vienna, and the Hungarians clamored for their liberty. Exploiting Austrian vulnerability, Milan and Venice revolted and demanded independence. Lombard priests fought alongside their people with the backing of Milan's archbishop. Provisional governments controlled parts of Lombardy and Venetia when Charles Albert, ambitious to annex Lombardy, led his army to drive out the Austrians. Pius blessed papal troops under General Giacomo Durando as they left Rome to protect the northern border of the Papal States. Durando, however, rallied his 12,000 volunteers to aid their "Lombard brothers" in a "war of civilization against the barbarians" of Austria.[16]

Jesuit historian Giacomo Martina, Pius's most distinguished biographer, describes the pope's tormented equivocation at this fateful moment. A genuine patriot who was eager for Italian independence, Pius was also aware of his duties as the Vicar of Christ. "How could the head of the Church," Martina asks, "launch a war against a Catholic nation that had neither attacked the Papal States nor brought any harm to religion?" On 29 April 1848, Pius delivered his famous allocution that stunned liberals and provoked the resignation of his cabinet. He denounced the scheme to place the pope at the head of an Italian confederation and withheld support for a national war against Austria. Interpreting the allocution as a repudiation of an independent Italy, the revolutionaries turned on Pius. His expression of sympathy for designs "to form from Italy a nation more united and compact" on 2 May and his request to Austria to withdraw from Italy fell on deaf ears.[17]

As the national forces faltered on 25 July when the Austrians defeated King Charles Albert at the battle of Custoza, unrest grew in Rome. Democrats lost faith in the moderates who controlled Pius's government. On 15 November, a demo-crat had Minister of the Interior Pellegrino Rossi assassinated. Under the advice of Cardinal Giacomo Antonelli, the Vatican secretary of state for the next quar-ter of a century, the pope fled to Gaeta, a fortress near Naples in the Kingdom of the Two Sicilies, where he remained until April 1850. King Ferdinand II, an ardent opponent of reform, welcomed Pius and promised to aid in his restoration.[18]

Democrats from all over Italy flocked to Rome. On 9 February 1849, a Constitu-ent Assembly proclaimed the Roman Republic, with executive power invested in a triumvirate comprised of Giuseppe Mazzini, Aurelio Saffi, and Carlo Armellini. The Republic declared the end of the pope's temporal power, secularized Church property, and instituted freedom of worship. Pius condemned the sacrilegious regime and called upon Catholic powers to restore him to his throne. Notwith-standing Giuseppe Garibaldi's courageous military leadership, the Republic fell in July. Austrian forces secured the northern Papal States, and Louis Napoleon, dependent upon French Catholic support at home, betrayed his fellow republi-cans and ordered his army to conquer Rome. After Pius returned from exile to his Eternal City, French troops remained to preserve order while Austrian forces patrolled the rest of the Papal States.[19]

Catholics in America learned of Pius's travail through newspapers, sermons, circular letters, and mass meetings as the ideology of the Roman Question began to take shape. The Catholic press impassioned its readers, whose inchoate com-mitments became pointed propositions. Reporting on European events, the press articulated shibboleths that crystallized into familiar symbols and communicated partisan readings of history. It awakened in Catholics a familial consciousness. They belonged to a global family; they were children united under their suffering Holy Father.

Pius's allocution of 29 April and exile to Gaeta provoked an American Catholic rethinking of Roman events. The *Catholic Telegraph* defended Pius's decision not to lead a war against Austria. The pontiff "has had the greatness of mind to with-stand the seductions which Italian nationality necessarily held out to an Italian sovereign of great capacity." After Pius's flight, the *Telegraph* turned on its former Italian champions. "The guilt of the Roman, and generally of the Italian liberals can hardly be exaggerated." The "blood-stained city, in old times the Babylon of the Apostles," was "afflicted with a new Paganism." On 9 December 1848, be-fore editor Father John Roddan of Boston's *Pilot* had learned of the pope's exile, the *Pilot* was still applauding revolution. "Liberty rose again and shouted on the banks of the Po," it cheered when the Lombards launched an offensive against Austria. The *Pilot* encouraged an assault upon "the ferocious despotism of Ferdi-nand [II]" at the very moment when the Bourbon monarch sheltered the pon-tiff from republican ruffians! But when Pius's reversal of fortune became known to Roddan, he condemned the republican democrats who "have been disgracing themselves and horrifying Europe by their bloody doings." Triggering Catholic-liberal polemics with hyperbolic rhetoric, Roddan reported that the democrats "have been laying hands on priests, murdering them, and throwing their bodies in pieces into the Tiber!"[20]

As American bishops learned of Pius's exile, they issued circular letters directing the faithful to receive Holy Communion and practice devotions on behalf of their persecuted pontiff. Their letters, read at all Catholic services, interpreted the Roman events within a biblical idiom. Rome, Archbishop Samuel Eccleston of Baltimore explained, "might yet become for [Pius] another Jerusalem, and the hosannas of the day give way to the shout of the deluded multitude—'Crucify him!—Crucify him!'" But this "apparent triumph of the Powers of Darkness" was "vain and illusory!" God would vindicate Pius as God had glorified the crucified Jesus. Eccleston directed all Catholic sisters to recite the litany of the Blessed Virgin Mary daily and receive a weekly communion for the pope.[21]

The Catholic press sentimentalized and personalized these revolutionary political events, offering an emotional rendition that made an adulatory cult to Pius accessible to women and men, children and adults. In February 1849, both the *Pilot* and *Catholic Magazine* ran an article, "The Private Life of Pope Pius IX," that described his "delicate complexion" and his "simple and natural" gait, revealing "an easiness full of good nature." His "countenance . . . strikes one by its great expression of kindness, intelligence and disinterestedness; his features are eminently sympathetic." The details aroused empathy. How could this holy gentleman with "inexpressible charm" ever merit such barbaric treatment?[22]

In January 1849, Bishop Hughes of New York preached a widely publicized sermon. His neoguelf reading of history condemned the Risorgimento. Although a "wicked world" comprised of "sacrilegious usurpers" had attacked the "Lord's anointed," popes had suffered at the hands of tyrants before, only to civilize their oppressors. "Something providential" was behind "the decline of the Roman Empire," when Italians turned to the pope as a source of unity and protection against the barbarian invaders and established the Papal States. From papal Rome, "Europe was civilized." In response, the *New York Herald* accused Hughes of turning against "the cause of popular liberty and human rights, now in the first throes of parturition in Italy."[23]

American Catholics vilified the Roman Republic and asserted Pius's untainted credentials in the face of criticism that he had betrayed Italy. The *Episcopal Recorder* contended, "the interests of Rome . . . and of Italy are on one side; and the interests of the popedom are on the other side. . . . [Pius's] conscience perverted by his religious views and sympathies, compels him to sacrifice the cause of his country." But the *Catholic Magazine* counterpunched. Pius "fervently desired, and still prays for, the unity and independence of Italy." But he had been "assailed in the rear by license—red-republicanism," whose advocates "are the men who banished the Pope and are now clamoring for his blood." These "envious and blood-thirsty demagogues" were not "champions of the unity and independence of Italy! No! Rome has changed, not the Pope." The *Catholic Magazine* took "the Protestant press" and "our secular journals" to task. They naively "suppose that every popular excitement in European countries must necessarily be a national movement in favor of liberty. Thus, however seditious or mobocratic in their character, the political fanaticism and anarchical raving which have recently disgraced the Roman and Neapolitan territories, are actually blazoned forth by a portion of the press alluded to, as acts of 'the people.'"[24]

Catholics surely had Margaret Fuller in mind. Her twenty-four dispatches depicting the dramatic Roman democratic experiment for Greeley's *Daily Tribune* of New York appalled Catholics. A participant-observer in the Republic, Fuller served as the director of the Hospital of the Fate Bene Fratelli, tending republican wounds while her Italian husband battled French troops intent upon restoring Pius to his throne. Her abiding faith in the Roman people inspired desperate calls for American solidarity with the fledgling Republic. After Pius's April allocution, she scorned his "final dereliction . . . to the cause of Freedom, Progress, and of War." Now the fate of Rome "lies wholly with the People and that wave of Thought which has begun to pervade them." Fuller fulminated, "the only dignified course for the Pope to pursue was to resign his temporal power. . . . No more of him! His day is over." Pius had been "most cowardly" when he made "promises he never meant to keep, stealing away by night," and then denouncing his foes.[25]

Fuller's epic dispatches described how the Romans grew into republican greatness, only to confront the cold indifference of England and the United States and the betrayal of pseudo-republican France. The battle between the Romans and France was a "struggle . . . between the principle of Democracy and the old powers. . . . That struggle may last fifty years, and the earth be watered with the blood and tears of more than one generation, but the result is sure. All Europe . . . is to be under Republican Government in the next century." After the French conquest of Rome, Fuller sniped, "How the Jesuits smile, with thin lips and eyes down-dropped, and think how much better Ignatius knew the world than Jesus of Nazareth." She prophesied, "the next revolution, here and elsewhere, will be radical. Not only Jesuitism must go, but the Roman Catholic religion must go. The Pope cannot retain even his spiritual power. The influence of the clergy is too perverting, too foreign to every hope of advancement and health."[26]

Catholics were aghast at liberal and Protestant suggestions that the pope-king was an outdated institution in the progressive nineteenth century. Bishop Hughes insisted barbarism had overcome Roman insurgents who ventured outside the canopy of civilization when they attacked papal Rome. "They wield the stiletto, and sacrifice by assassination the human victims who are to propitiate the goddess of Young Liberty in Italy." Under Mazzini and Garibaldi the Repub-

lic had established a "reign of terror over the Roman people." However fanciful
these Catholic inventions of violence may have been, Hughes did have a point
when he indicated that "no ambassador from foreign countries has recognised"
the Roman Republic, "except it be the female plenipotentiary who furnishes
the [Daily] Tribune with diplomatic correspondence." Although Americans applauded revolt against despotism, they also feared revolutionaries. Notwithstanding Fuller's literary skills, most Americans favored Risorgimento moderates to
democrats, and the U.S. government never recognized the Roman Republic.[27]

Consul Nicholas Brown in Rome had welcomed the Republic. "So deeply
rooted in every American heart is the love of liberty," he assured the new government on 11 February, "that the [American] nation will at once hail with joy the
independence of the Roman Republic." Secretary of State Buchanan, however, instructed the U.S. chargé d'affaires, Lewis Cass Jr., not to present his credentials
to the Republic. Buchanan "considered the speedy restoration of the Pope highly
probable." Cass concurred. On 9 April he wrote, "the chances for Italian freedom
are but few; and the possibility of that most beautiful of all dreams—the independence of a united country—as far from realisation as ever." When the Republic
fell, Brown could do little more than offer passports to republicans whose lives
were in danger.[28]

Liberal-Catholic sparring intensified over the initiation of a Peter's Pence collection to support the pope in exile. The American Church collected $25,978.24.
Greeley insinuated that the collection was for "Pius IX, in his present struggle
against the Roman Republic." The New York Herald feared the Peter's Pence might
"be expended in paying Russian, Austrian, or French soldiers for slaughtering
the people of Rome and forcing upon them a sovereign and a form of government which they had repudiated." On 27 July 1849, the Daily Tribune published a
long dedication to "the martyrs of human liberty who fell during the siege . . . as
defenders of Rome against the machinations of despotism." America's flirtation
with the liberal pope had come to a definitive and bitter end.[29]

Catholic Intransigence and Revival in the 1850s

After his return to Rome in April 1850, Pius IX projected his condemnations of
the Roman Republic onto the broad canvas of liberalism and "modern" civilization. He restored absolutism, denied his subjects a constitution, strengthened the
Roman Inquisition, forced Jews into the ghetto, and punished revolutionaries.
Alert to the value of international public opinion, Pius convinced the general of
the Society of Jesus to permit a collegio of Jesuits to devote themselves to journalism on behalf of the papacy. They founded Civiltà Cattolica, a formidable arsenal of words and ideas in the Holy See's war against liberalism, pluralism, and
democracy. Civiltà Cattolica taught that the only true civilization was Catholicism

grounded in the authority of papal Rome. The temporal power, at this dangerous moment in history, was an absolute necessity to protect the Church and civilization itself from secularization and degeneration. "It is today an indisputable fact that the world has no other civilization than European, and in Europe civilization has been Christian, Catholic, Roman. . . . Where Roman influence ends, there civilization meets an unsurpassable dam" beyond which lies barbarism.[30]

Civiltà Cattolica flourished during the Catholic revival of the 1850s, while Austrian and French arms bolstered the pope-king. The Austrian concordat of 1855 granted the Church unprecedented privileges. Its terms outraged Protestants and liberals. In December 1852, President Louis Napoleon became Emperor Napoleon III. Pius smiled upon him, aware that Napoleon's power rested upon Catholic support and thus upon France's defense of papal Rome. Liberals and Protestants looked on in horror. Laden with privileges, the Church in Austria and France revived. Ultramontane devotionalism flourished throughout Europe and North America, and the Catholic world rallied around papal Rome. On 8 December 1854, in "Ineffabilis Deus," Pius proclaimed Mary's Immaculate Conception, a popular concession to a worldwide cult to the Virgin. Pius became a global icon of priestly piety, while Protestants and liberals cringed or laughed. When he reestablished the Catholic hierarchies in Holland and England, critics cried "No Popery!" louder than before. Nativism intensified in the United States as Know-Nothings shuddered at the sight of Celtic arrivals with rosary beads overrunning the Protestant Israel.[31]

Archbishop Hughes's sermon on the occasion of Pius's return to Rome captured the sense of redemptive suffering so central to ultramontane devotionalism, even as it provoked angry responses from liberals and Protestants. Hughes likened Pius's exile to Jesus's Passion. The analogy resonated with impoverished Irish Catholics fleeing famine, only to find themselves in a hostile Anglo-Protestant Boston or New York. With unprecedented zeal they offered their affections to the crucified Jesus and their tormented Holy Father. The cosmic victory of both Jesus and Pius assured their spiritual children that pain and deprivation were meaningful. Hughes taught his flock that it participated in "the aspirations and the joyful feelings of two hundred million hearts" from "all round the globe." Catholics everywhere were part of the mystical body of the Church that "accompanied [Pius] with her tears and with her prayers." Catholics everywhere suffered vicariously with Pius, "the illustrious victim," through his wretched exile and humiliation. "For if it be a duty of the members of the Church, that when one member suffers, all the members shall sympathize, how much more, when the visible head of the Church himself is selected, as it were by a general conspiracy of this world, as a victim of suffering for the whole body?"[32]

Hughes emphasized the sacred character the Holy Father endowed the Eternal City, a home to all his children. Catholics "from the uttermost boundaries of this earth, had been accustomed to converge upon one spot, to behold the visible head of the Church; that spot being Rome—sacred, and in spite of recent atrocities, holy and 'Eternal City.'" The Papal States "belong . . . to all Catholics. . . . They have belonged to [the Catholic world] right from the beginning. . . . They were set apart expressly that there might be one spot on the earth from which the vicar of Jesus Christ could give out the supreme voice of the Church of God with freedom, without restraint." Indeed, "there is no Rome without the Pope." And upon papal Rome, civilization depended. "If Rome had a Pope no more, civilized Europe would perceive missing from the headship of safe guidance one who had guided her up through darkness and barbarism."[33]

Rome and Italy meant something quite different to other Americans. William Lloyd Garrison and Lyman Beecher, for instance, identified Mazzini as Italy's true symbol. Beecher went to London to meet the exiled legend in 1846, plotting to disseminate Protestant Bibles in Italy as a prelude to the conversion and liberation of the nation. Samuel Morse and Theodore Dwight, who formed the American Philo-Italian Society in New York in 1842, also linked evangelical fervor to faith in the Risorgimento. Dwight's *The Roman Republic of 1849* (1851) warned, "the evils and atrocities of the papal system are too great to be easily believed." In 1855 Dwight celebrated the sixth anniversary of the Roman Republic at the Broadway Tabernacle, where Italian exiles, Protestant ministers, and Gotham notables insisted, "the Constituent Assembly of the Roman Republic . . . is the only legitimate authority in that State." In 1861 Dwight translated into English the autobiography of Garibaldi, whom Dwight called "Italy's Washington."[34]

Two events in particular during the 1850s brought the 1848 Italian revolution to the United States. In 1853 and 1854, the North American sojourns of Father Alessandro Gavazzi and Archbishop Gaetano Bedini generated civil unrest and crystallized Catholic loyalties to the symbols of papal Rome. Then, in 1858, the Roman Inquisition kidnapped six-year-old Edgardo Mortara, an Italian Jewish boy whom Pius refused to return to his parents. The ensuing international debates strengthened boundaries separating Catholics from their American neighbors.

Gavazzi, a Barnabite priest, took up the revolutionary cause in 1848 and preached to enormous crowds on behalf of war against Austria. Arrested by pontifical police, he escaped to assist the faltering Roman Republic. Under the aegis of the U.S. consul in Ancona, Gavazzi fled to England, where he contacted dissenting Protestants and earned his living on the lecture circuit speaking against the pope. After "not a few ministers and committees from various [Protestant] denominations [in England] . . . had recommended their transatlantic friends to support my missionary visit," Gavazzi arrived in New York City in February 1853. His antipapal tirade delighted Philadelphia's nativists, who awarded him a gold ring. In New York he mingled with Italian exiles who relished his assaults on popedom at the Broadway Tabernacle and the Stuyvesant Institute. Gavazzi's diary recounts violent clashes with "Irish papists," the "ignorant fanaticism of [Irish] women," and his frequent harangues against Bedini, a diplomat in Pius's secretariat of state, who also arrived in the United States in 1853.[35]

Bedini likewise inflamed passions. The Vatican had assigned him to Bologna in 1849 to bring order to the second city of the Papal States as Austrian arms crushed the liberal revolution. Named papal nuncio (ambassador) to Brazil in 1852, Bedini was directed to visit England, Ireland, and the United States before departing for points south. His association with the papal restoration tarnished his reputation among lovers of liberty who assailed "the Bloody Butcher of Bologna" during his American sojourn. Nativists and German and Italian exiles assaulted the symbol of papal Rome verbally and physically. The discovery of an assassination plot targeting Bedini so frightened Archbishop Francis Kenrick of Baltimore that he urged the nuncio to depart. "Members of secret societies are found everywhere," Kenrick shivered. Hughes, on the other hand, deterred an early departure. "For God's sake, for sake of the Holy Father, for sake of the Catholic portion of the people in these United States," the irascible Irishman wrote, "do not allow the object of your mission to be thwarted, defeated, crushed, and turned into ridicule by the machinations even against your life of a few miscreant and outcast Italians in the vile and dark recesses of New York." Wheeling's bishop encouraged Bedini to focus upon "the joy with which Catholics have every where welcomed your approach. . . . Instances of persecution attach Catholics more strongly to their Church."[36]

The Catholic laity embraced the persecuted symbol of the pope, as their letters reveal. William Read of Baltimore consoled Bedini. "At the moment when you are exposed to daily neglect and insult, the hearts of Catholics are only more united in attachment to the Holy Father whom you represent." Adeline Whelan assured the weary traveler that her prayers to the Virgin "shall be often upon my lips and in my daily remembrance of the Holy Father in these days of trouble and of trial." She concurred that "the unjust accusations of the enemies of the Church but serve to render you more dear to the children of faith." Another Catholic wrote Bedini how "the remembrance of your kindness and beneficence will live always in the heart of your devoted children." He comforted the nuncio. "Our prayers will be daily offered for your safe arrival in Rome, then they will not cease, but during the whole of our lives we will pray for blessings, health and happiness for our beloved Nuncio." Anticipating Bedini's visit to Pittsburgh, John Mitchell implored the dignitary to save a "portion of your valuable time to share with us in our own little family circle." William Oram, a school teacher in Detroit, confessed, "there was a time . . . when my feet were out of the true church, when my soul was blackened with heresy; but, thank God, that time is changed and that now I am in the ark of safety." Oram had "chosen an asylum with my God" and asked Bedini to "present my name to our common Father" for a papal benediction.[37]

Bedini issued a positive report on the American Church to his superiors. He stressed the importance for American Catholics to see firsthand "the esteem and veneration which the first Envoy of the Holy See had for their Pastors. . . . Thus, they appreciated my mission as a manifestation of the special benevolence of the Holy Father." He noted the "festive receptions and the joys of every Catholic heart" at the presence of a papal representative and recorded the "desperate persecution by revolutionary refugees from Europe and by an apostate [Gavazzi] who led and inflamed them." Bedini affirmed, "the person of the Nuncio became more endeared to the Catholics" as he suffered, "and so the true fruit of the persecution was not wanting." Like Gavazzi, Bedini was struck by the "most ardent devotion" of Irish clergy for the Holy Father and the respect and power they commanded over their people. The Irish "see in their priests not a simple minister of Religion, but their father, their magistrate, their judge, their king, their 'Papa,' their idol."[38]

The kidnapping of Edgardo Mortara also widened the gulf separating Catholics from other Americans. Even as the event inflamed liberal, Jewish, and Protestant passions against the temporal power, Catholics defended their Holy Father. In June 1858, the Inquisition in Bologna seized young Edgardo from his home amid the wails of parents and siblings. The Mortaras later learned that their Catholic servant claimed to have baptized Edgardo in 1852 when he was an infant. The Inquisition, backed by Church law and the pope, scuttled Edgardo off to the House of the Catechumens in Rome. Jews throughout Europe and America petitioned their governments to exert pressure upon Pius to have the boy returned to his family. European statesmen clamored against the inhumane act. Sir Moses Montefiore, a wealthy British Jew, with backing from France and England, went to Rome on an unsuccessful mission to restore Edgardo to the Mortaras. Pius's intransigence in the Mortara case became a symbol of the anachronistic character of papal Rome when Pius's international prestige ebbed and friends were in short supply.[39]

Catholics faced off against their American neighbors. On 17 December 1858, Archbishop Kenrick wrote the rector of the North American College in Rome, "the country has been convulsed with the Mortara excitement, the press encouraging the Jews, who held several meetings, and called on the President to remonstrate." Jews and Protestants held rallies in New York, Boston, and San Francisco. Rabbi Isaac Mayer Wise thundered in Cincinnati's *Israelite* against "the Pope and his numerous, soul-less lackeys." The servant who performed the ostensible baptism, Wise insisted, was "the hired tool of some priest, who is himself the tool of his superior and who again may be the blind tool of a Jesuit, who in his turn is the instrument of the inquisition, which sacred office is the handmaid of the Pope, who again is the subject of the Jesuits." New York's *Jewish Messenger* excoriated "those Roman Catholic soul-snatchers, the priests." Leaders of two St. Louis Jewish congregations warned, "if the Pope gives sanction to such acts of fanaticism—the Roman Catholic clergy here, obeying his laws as supreme, will be guided by the same principle, and similar acts will occur." *B'nai B'rith Magazine* decried the "remnant of medieval barbarism, which still clings to our own age."[40]

Catholics portrayed Edgardo as a pious Catholic boy transformed by divine grace, infused through the surreptitious sacrament. His stubborn parents, who refused to follow him into the Church, saddened their child. "It is with great joy that this child entered the institution of the Catechumens," contended Baltimore's *Catholic Mirror*. Edgardo was delighted to learn of his father's visit. "He imagined he should be able to convert his father. . . . But when he found [his father] deaf to all his prayers, he began to weep bitterly. . . . And they want a child of such quick faith to be delivered up to the Jews! That would be a cruelty without a name, and the most open violation of that principle of liberty of conscience which the Liberals have ever in their mouths." The *Catholic Mirror* reminded "readers of foreign journals" to "recollect that an immense proportion of them in France and Germany belong to Jews. Hebrews and Protestants will hunt in couples when Popery is on foot." The Catholic *Freeman's Journal* of New York, responding to the *Jewish Messenger*, insisted that Edgardo, age six, was "a lad of eleven years," whose father, "after an interview with the Pope, and long conversations with his son, acquiesced . . . in the arrangement." A Catholic pamphlet published November 1858 claimed it was repulsive that a Christian government should be expected to "leave a Christian child to be brought up a Jew." The pamphlet boasted, "the Holy Father's protection of the child, in the face of all the ferocious fanaticism of infidelity and bigotry, is the grandest moral spectacle which the world has seen for ages."[41]

The Catholic press chose this moment to narrate morbid tales about Protestant kidnappings of Catholic children. The *Catholic Mirror* predicted, "evangelical perverters will have the pious audacity to deny" this practice, "ready as such persons always are with excuses for the abduction and enslavement of Catholic children in this free country." The "kidnapping evangelizers" received instructions from the American and Foreign Christian Union in New York, and their labors extended across the continent. German Catholics concurred. Cincinnati's *Der Wahrheits-Freund*, after lambasting "the anti-Catholic American press" for using Edgardo "as one more pretext to attack 'Catholic bigotry and papal tyranny,'" wondered "how many [Catholic] children here in this country have been taken to the House of Refuge," an American orphanage for impoverished youth. "And isn't it true that at many of these Houses of Refuge Catholic children receive a

Protestant education and become Protestant. . . . This is going on in a country with the slogan 'Equality of all religions' written on its banner."[42]

Shrewd observers discerned how liberals employed the Mortara case as a weapon against the temporal power of the pope. *Brownson's Quarterly Review* reckoned Piedmont, England, and France were holding "the temporal government of the Pope up to public execration, as a pretext either for interfering with its internal administration, or for divesting the Pontiff of his temporal sovereignty." But most Catholic writers lost sight of the political snare the Mortara case created. The *Pilot* degenerated into anti-Semitism. "From that dark hour when the Jewish mob pronounced a malediction upon their misguided race . . . the Jews appear to have been the subjects of a spell from which their own efforts and the kindness of those who have taken pity upon them, have been unable to effect their deliverance. . . . To the enmity excited against them as the descendants of those who crucified our Lord, they have been hated by all classes of people as usurers are always hated."[43]

London Oratorian Frederick William Faber, who sold 45,000 ultramontane devotional books in the United States by 1869, likened Pius under attack during the Mortara case to Jesus. Faber's widely circulated *Devotion to the Pope* (1860) discussed "the instinct of [Jesus's] Church for the interests of little children. For their souls [the Church] fights with the governments of the world; she lays herself open to attacks; she perils her peace; she forfeits the patronage of the great; . . . she is contented to look unintelligibly fanatical or pretentiously false, to those who cannot believe in the sincerity of such a purely supernatural zeal." Defending the pope's refusal to return Edgardo to his family, Faber drew an analogy between Pius's suffering and the crucified Jesus. "Men may load him down with indignities, as they spat into his Master's Face. . . . In every successive generation Jesus, in the person of his Vicar, is before fresh Pilates and new Herods. The Vatican is for the most part a Calvary. Who can behold all the pathetic grandeur of this helplessness, and understand it as a Christian understands it, and not be moved to tears?"[44]

The Kingdom of Italy in the 1860s

In the 1850s, the Kingdom of Piedmont emerged as the hope of Italian liberals. It alone among Italian states had preserved a constitution after the revolutions failed. When King Charles Albert abdicated, his son, King Vittorio Emanuele II, took an oath to honor the 1848 constitution. Piedmont permitted thousands of exiles from throughout the peninsula to reside within its borders, where a free press and liberal political culture thrived. In the 1850s, property owners and moderates, joined by democratic converts to the Piedmontese monarchy, forged the

Destra, the Historic Right, a conservative faction of liberals who governed Piedmont and later the Kingdom of Italy until 1876. Although the overwhelming majority of Destra leaders were Catholic liberals, the ideology of the Roman Question became a weapon of resistance against Piedmont's political elite and later
against Liberal Italy after 1861.[45]

In 1852 Camillo Benso di Cavour became the prime minister and leader of
the Destra. A brilliant student of government, he modernized Piedmont, liber-
alized trade, and urged state support for railroads and irrigation projects. With
liberal institutions and an image of reform intact, Piedmont won the admiration
of England, the United States, and France. Horace Greeley believed Piedmont to
be "a chief point of interest in continental Europe for lovers of liberty." George
Perkins Marsh claimed Piedmont was "waging a noble struggle, and I have been
surprised to find how deep a root the true principles of human freedom have
struck in the breasts of her people." By contrast, the pope and American Catholics condemned Piedmont for anticlerical, that is, liberal, ecclesiastical legislation. In 1850 Piedmont suppressed Church courts and prohibited Church organizations from acquiring property without government consent. In 1855 Cavour
gained supporters from the Sinistra, the Left, when Piedmont suppressed religious congregations not engaged in teaching, preaching, or hospital work and
sold their property to secure stipends for secular clergy and to enrich state coffers.[46]

Cavour's ambitions were modest compared to the outcome of the events he set
in motion. With no faith that Italians could "make Italy" alone through revolution and no desire to unify the entire peninsula into a single state, Cavour plotted
Piedmont's annexation of Lombardy. Toward this goal, he sought French support
against Austria. In July 1858, he met Napoleon III in Plombières to plan a future
northern Italian kingdom under Vittorio Emanuele II. They also envisioned Tuscany uniting central Italy and the proclamation of Pius IX as honorary president
of a confederation of Italian kingdoms. For Napoleon's support, Cavour offered
France Piedmont's province of Savoy. After Cavour instigated an Austrian declaration of war, a massive French army entered northern Italy and defeated the Austrians at Magenta and Solferino in June 1859. But then, without notifying Cavour,
Napoleon abandoned the plans of Plombières and reached an accord with Austria
at Villafranca. However, Piedmontese supporters had already nurtured uprisings
in the northern Papal States. After holding plebiscites, Piedmont annexed Lombardy and the Romagna (which was in the Papal States) and ceded Nice and Savoy
to France. By 1860 King Vittorio ruled all of northern Italy except Venetia. For his
robbery of the Romagna, he earned Pius's excommunication.[47]

Americans organized to back their Italian champions. Encouraged by Cavour,
New York Italians raised $10,623 for Piedmont's army. Hungarians and Poles held
rallies to support the Risorgimento as the press castigated Austrian despotism in

favor of Italian liberty. President Buchanan wrote Lord Clarendon, "the sympathy for poor down-trodden Italy is very strong in this country and our people would hail her deliverer with enthusiastic applause." Catholics, in contrast, held anti-Risorgimento rallies and processions and collected money for the papal army. English-, German-, and French-speaking laymen organized "monster meetings" of thousands in St. Louis, Cincinnati, Chicago, Louisville, New York, Buffalo, Savannah, Boston, and Pittsburgh to communicate their solidarity with the pope. On three occasions in January, six Southern bishops preached in English, French, and German at open-air sessions in New Orleans. Catholics marched with their fraternal societies throughout the Crescent City as the laity gathered 10,000 signatures for a resolution of "veneration for the persecuted Father of the Faithful."[48]

The ideology of the Roman Question took its classic form in a letter to Pius published by nine bishops in the Northeast in January 1860. The American neo-guelfs described the conversion of Constantine in the fourth century and his translation of imperial headquarters to Constantinople (Istanbul). "The people of Italy," left without leadership and protection, "raised their hands to the Sovereign Pontiff calling upon him to be their temporal savior." Central Italy "was not usurped by the Holy Father. It was rather forced upon him by the wishes and clamor of a neglected and ungoverned people." Pepin and Charlemagne in the eighth century "made him a donation of this same territory." Thus, the pope was a popular ruler, "democratically" chosen by the "Italian people." A legitimate sovereign who did not "usurp" another's land, he humbly accepted God's will—the burden of temporal sovereignty hoisted upon him by neglected Italians. Thereafter, these Papal States belonged to all Catholics. "We [American Catholics] are an integral portion of 200,000,000 Catholics, whose eyes are constantly turned to the See of Peter. . . . There is a territory in which we have a supreme interest. It is called the States of the Church. . . . The moment we tread its soil we feel that we have entered on ground which is and ought to be common to the same two hundred millions of our fellow Catholics." When "in the States of the Church," Catholics are "not on a foreign soil."[49]

The bishops put forth a conspiracy theory, one also prevalent throughout the Catholic world and central to the ideology of the Roman Question. Hidden forces had deceived the Italian nation to overthrow papal authority. In an immediate sense, this claim challenged the legitimacy of the plebiscites in the Romagna. But the bishops anchored this claim to a full-blown theory of history. Secret forces conspired to assault God, the pope, and the Church. These powers were behind the Protestant Reformation, the European Enlightenment, and the nineteenth-century liberal revolutions, which would ultimately culminate in socialism, communism, anarchy, and the Antichrist. Luther's appeal to conscience, Voltaire's invocation of reason, and Mazzini's hymns to nationality were mere pretexts in a revolt against God. When pressed, Catholics identified the clandestine agents with Jews or Masons, who enlisted Protestants or liberals to do their bidding. The bishops explained:

> It is well known that, for a period of forty years or more, there have been two governments in the States of the Church. One, the open, mild, paternal government of the Holy See. . . . The other was a subterranean government, organized and supported by arch-conspirators. Its decrees were never published, but its secret enactments were carried into execution . . . by the prompt use of deadly weapons. . . . The free sentiment of the people in the [Papal] States has been . . . stifled and repressed. . . . Take away the fear inspired by the subterranean government . . . and the people of the Romagna will be perfectly contented under the mild government of the Sovereign Pontiff.[50]

In his March 1860 lecture "Italy, Past and Present," Bishop Martin John Spalding of Louisville elaborated upon the ideology of the Roman Question. Italy, he explained, with Rome at its center, had been a beacon of civilization. "Europe owed, and still owes, its Christianity and its civilization to Italy. From Italy went forth the Cross." Claiming Rome "is the capital of Italy, and also the capital of Christendom," Spalding explained that "along with Christianity, we owe our civilization to Italy. . . . The first great law school was established at Bologna; the first great school of medicine at Salerno." From Italy came the telescope, the microscope, the convex and concave lenses, and "the mariner's compass." Rome was still the "centre of civilization," but the "great bane of Italy has been foreign intervention." Pius IX "is an Italian — his people are all homogenous." But "these very men who cry out so much about nationality, are themselves foreigners. . . . [Napoleon III] is a foreigner. . . . Victor Emanuel is a foreigner — a Savoyard."[51]

The ideology of the Roman Question vilified four individuals as the personification of modern evils. King Vittorio, the transalpine usurper in rebellion against God, won excommunication through his "malignant bigotry against the everlasting Catholic faith." His only American friends were Protestants who "would make a god of him" if he were "a scion of the egotistical Anglo-Saxon race."[52] Garibaldi, "foremost among the bloodiest hounds of the Roman Republic," gave Catholic children nightmares. His "robberies, cruelties, and debauchery" and his hatred of "Christ and His Church" had made this "modern Attila" a "by-word of infamy." His band of bloody followers were "more ferocious than Hottentots."[53] Mazzini "taught Europe that secret assassination is the law of humanity." "A murderer in principle and a bandit by choice," he "calculated to defy God, betray man, overturn humanity itself. . . . In lieu of civilization, Mazzini would have thrust Europe back into barbarism."[54] Although "Protestant opinion" ranked Cavour "amongst the most conscientious living Christians," Catholics knew he "had no more religion or conscience than a Turk." This "cunning unscrupulous Calvinist" possessed a "vandalistic determination to destroy the temporal power of the Holy See." His designs on Rome as the capital of Liberal Italy conjured up Catholic invective. "The ferocity of Alaric, of Attila, Totilla . . . did not do more to the Eternal City than the Calvinist Cavour would, if he had the power, in order to strip the Papacy naked."[55]

Notwithstanding their common evil credentials, all was not well among these liberal demons. Garibaldi, much to Cavour's horror, directed his revolutionary fervor to Sicily in May 1860 to exploit an uprising in Palermo. Leading a poorly armed volunteer force, he defeated the Neapolitan army and launched an assault on the mainland. In October he crushed the Bourbons at Volturno and held plebiscites that led to the Piedmontese annexation of the Kingdom of the Two Sicilies. King Vittorio's army was now compelled to march further into the heart of the Papal States in order to prevent Garibaldi's conquest of papal Rome, an exploit that might lead to war with France and Austria. Without so much as a pretext, Piedmont conquered and annexed Umbria and the Marches. Garibaldi greeted King Vittorio near Teano on the Neapolitan border, left Rome to the pope for the time being, and acknowledged the king's authority over Italy. Only Austrian Venetia and papal Rome remained unredeemed.[56]

Americans cheered Garibaldi as he overturned Bourbon despotism. They proudly recalled how the great general had lived for a time as a candlemaker on Staten Island after the 1848 Italian revolution. The *New York World* boasted of "the gratifying consciousness that our country had the honor of giving to such a noble-hearted man a refuge from persecution, and an asylum which their insatiable enemies dared not to invade." In September 1860, Charles Eliot Norton, the eminent liberal Dante scholar, wrote, "the progress of Garibaldi is just now even of greater interest to us than that of our own [presidential] campaign. It is a fine thing to be living in times which can produce such a man. . . . The new birth of Italy is already the grandest event of the modern period."[57]

While the United States government recognized the northern Italian kingdom and Americans held mass meetings to applaud Italian unity, Catholics echoed the pope's insistence that Italy's new subjects were victims of force. During Garibaldi's campaign the *Pilot* described marauding Red Shirts in Catholic Sicily as unwelcome foreigners who violated Sicilian patriotism and offended their Catholicism. The plebiscites orchestrated to legitimate Piedmontese annexations were a hoax. "The polls have not been free, . . . the soldiers of Victor Emmanuel, aliens, incompetent persons, were allowed or forced to vote." The unification of Italy was "a train of lawless inhuman, tyrannical acts, . . . a scourge upon the good Italians, a trial of their faith." Peter's Pence collections soared to aid the Holy

Father—$4,300 from the diocese of Buffalo, $1,597 from Savannah, $2,500 from New York, $300 from St. Mary's Total Abstinence Society of New York. The bishop of Philadelphia sent Pius a list of donors eighty pages long.[58]

The day following the proclamation of the Kingdom of Italy on 17 March 1861, Pius delivered an allocution starkly contrasting "modern civilization" to "true [Catholic] civilization." In this dry run of his "Syllabus of Errors" of 1864, Pius pummeled "progress and Liberalism." Modern civilization stood opposed to "the rights of justice and of Our holy religion" and favored "non-Catholic religions, while it opens access to public offices even to infidels." In short, "this [modern] civilization plunders the Catholic Church" while the "Holy See . . . has been in all times the protector and the initiator of true civilization" and the defender of the true, that is, Catholic, Italy. "How could [the Holy Father] ever abandon [the principles of Eternal justice] so as to imperil our Holy Faith, and bring Italy into imminent danger of losing that brilliant distinction—that glory which for nineteen centuries has made it shine as the centre and principal seat of Catholic Truth?" Italians were loyal to the Church, but they had been hoodwinked "by crafty men." Indeed, "We have received from [the peoples of Italy] many hundreds of thousands of affectionate letters . . . to lament over Our cares, Our troubles, and Our anguish, to assure Us of their love." Three years later in the "Syllabus of Errors," Pius would issue his weighty condemnation of the proposition that "the Roman Pontiff can and ought to reconcile himself to, and come to terms with progress, liberalism, and modern civilization."[59]

Although American Catholics universally condemned Liberal Italy, Italian Catholics were divided. Italian "intransigents" called for a restoration of the Papal States and eagerly awaited the downfall of Liberal Italy. Intransigent editor Giacomo Margotti launched his famous formula on 8 January 1861, nè eletti, nè elettori. "In the next elections we want to be neither the elected, nor electors." His call for abstention from national politics as both voters and candidates galvanized intransigents against "legal Italy," prison warden of "real [Catholic] Italy." The Vatican backed abstention. In 1874 the Sacred Apostolic Penitenary declared participation in national elections non expedit; in 1886, the Holy Office condemned it as non licit. The Vatican only eased this prohibition in 1905 and did not eliminate it until 1919. Catholic power in Liberal Italy was thus limited to municipal politics.[60] Italian "conciliationists," by contrast, sought to reconcile the Church with Liberal Italy. A minority frequently attacked in the intransigent press, conciliationists worked on the municipal level against anticlericalism and Masonry. Although some American Catholics shared the conciliationist position that the Church ought to adapt to modern civilization, American Catholics in the nineteenth century universally supported the intransigent position on the Roman Question.[61]

Violence within Liberal Italy in the 1860s made it vulnerable to Catholic charges that the state had in fact imprisoned the nation. Piedmontese officials sent to the *mezzogiorno*—the Italian south—to represent the authority of the new state depended upon an army of 100,000 men to establish order in the face of local uprisings and brigandage. The invocation of martial law, suspension of civil liberties, and summary executions led to more Italian deaths than all the wars for national unification. Rashly imposed, highly centralized state administration alienated southern Italians who considered the state a colonial power that taxed and conscripted them unjustly and that undermined their local traditions. Although American Protestants and liberals enjoyed an image of the Risorgimento as a popular national revolution against autocracy, in reality shrewd Piedmontese diplomacy and the support of foreign arms had made Italy. Italian elites exploited local resentments and rebellions to create a nation-state. This *rivoluzione mancata*, a passive or failed revolution, in Antonio Gramsci's terms, neither overturned a hierarchical social order nor popularized a national consciousness. Consequently, Catholics and liberals (and later socialists) struggled for cultural hegemony over a divided nation within the centralized state whose oppressive policies often deviated from liberal ideals.[62]

The intransigent condemnation of Liberal Italy, however, should not blind us to the fact that the Destra—the conservative and moderate liberals who governed the Kingdom of Italy until 1876—included Catholic liberals who hoped to see the Church reformed and revitalized. On 11 October 1860, when Cavour insisted Rome must eventually become the capital of Italy, he argued that true religion could only flourish in a liberal environment. The Destra rallied around his shibboleth, "a free church in a free state," and admired American style church-state separation. In this spirit, Cavour negotiated with Pius IX. He offered the pontiff the external signs of sovereignty and Church property for bishops, seminaries, and clergy engaged in pastoral work. The state would withdraw from ecclesiastical matters and leave the Church in freedom. In turn, the pope must renounce the temporal power. In response, Pius unleashed condemnations. Cavour died several months later.[63]

In December 1864, Pius IX shocked the world with "Quanta Cura," supplemented by the "Syllabus of Errors," marking what historian Owen Chadwick calls "a turning point in the history of the Church." Although the Syllabus was drafted before 1864, the September Convention of 1864 provoked its promulgation. In the September Convention, Napoleon agreed to withdraw his troops from papal Rome, and King Vittorio promised to move the capital of Italy from Turin to Florence and not to occupy Rome, a promise he later broke. The Syllabus condemned eighty propositions, including the separation of church and state, freedom of worship, freedom of the press, denial of the temporal power, and, most famously, reconciliation with liberalism, progress, and modern civilization. The staggering document made life difficult for American Catholics.[64]

As Protestants decried papal arrogance, Archbishop Martin John Spalding of

Baltimore defended the Syllabus with a Catholic argument for American exceptionalism. Spalding contended that the errors the Syllabus condemned applied to
the "self-styled" liberals of Europe, who were "really infidels," and not to American advocates of liberalism. "To stretch the words of the Pontiff, evidently intended for the stand-point of European radicals and infidels, so as to make them
include the state of things established in [America], by our noble Constitution, in
regard to the liberty of conscience, of worship, and of the press, were manifestly
unfair and unjust." While King Vittorio, Cavour, Garibaldi, and Mazzini were infidels, the American founding fathers "acted most prudently and wisely" when they
endorsed religious freedom. They "certainly did not intend, like the European
radicals, disciples of Tom Paine and of the French Revolution, to pronounce all
religions, whether true or false, equal before God." The American founders were
"neither Latitudinarians nor infidels; they were earnest, honest men; and however much some of them may have been personally lukewarm in matters of Religion, or may have differed in religious opinions, they still professed to believe in
Christ and in His Revelation." The Holy Father surely could not have meant to
condemn them or the U.S. Constitution.[65]

Spalding's American exceptionalism comprised two dubious claims. The first
related directly to the ideology of the Roman Question. Like Pius, Spalding (and
Catholic intellectuals right up through John Courtney Murray, SJ, in the 1960s)
insisted European moderates were in fact violent revolutionaries and perfidious
infidels bent upon destroying the Church. In fact, Italian moderates were generally Catholic liberals or conservative monarchists eager to preserve social hierarchies and some Catholic privileges. What really made them treacherous to Catholics was their willingness to question the wisdom of the temporal power as it
existed under Pius IX. Spalding's second claim, that America's Founding Fathers
were orthodox Christians, was erroneous. Primarily deists and rationalists, their
understanding of scripture and revelation was heterodox, and they had no soft
spot in their hearts for Roman Catholicism.[66]

This Catholic argument for American exceptionalism became a distinctly
American appendage to the ideology of the Roman Question that functioned to
protect American Catholics. When Protestants or liberals claimed Catholics were
against liberalism and thus anti-American, American Catholics contended they
were only against Europe's "false" liberalism or Protestant distortions of liberalism. When the Vatican suspected American Catholics of deviation from its blunt
antiliberal pronouncements, Catholics insisted that Vatican officials just could
not understand that the American political tradition and environment was totally
different from European liberalism. This explains why American Catholics relentlessly lambasted Liberal Italy, viciously ridiculed liberal values operative in Italian
society (including religious liberty), and cultivated avid ultramontane loyalties to

the Holy Father as a temporal ruler, while they simultaneously extolled the wisdom of the First Amendment of the U.S. Constitution.

The 20th of September 1870

In 1866 the Italian government applied Piedmont's ecclesiastical legislation to all of Liberal Italy. The Vatican and American Catholics cried foul as religious congregations were suppressed, their lands auctioned, their personnel pensioned off. The government abolished chairs of theology in state universities, provided religious instruction in public schools only when parents requested it, and required civil matrimony. Thanks to an alliance with Prussia in a war against Austria, Italy annexed Venetia. Only papal Rome remained outside of King Vittorio's dominions. When French troops left Rome to honor the September Convention, Garibaldi seized the moment, but papal troops defeated him, and the French rushed back to repel him again at Mentana in 1867. Although Napoleon left forces to protect the pope, France abandoned Rome for good when the Franco-Prussian war erupted in 1870.[67]

Garibaldi's failed conquest of papal Rome inspired the *Freeman's Journal* and St. Louis's *Guardian* to urge American Catholics to join the papal Zouaves. Volunteers stepped forward, but Archbishops Spalding, John Purcell, and John McCloskey explained to the Vatican the dubious legality of such a venture and the danger it posed for the American Church. They also confided their fear that the publicity would provoke an even larger force of American volunteers to join Garibaldi. The Vatican agreed that American Catholic money, rather than men, would satisfy Pius.[68]

American Catholic press coverage of the First Vatican Council (1869–70) dramatized the ideology of the Roman Question in the months before the conquest of papal Rome. While bishops debated the council's proclamation of papal infallibility, the press highlighted how papal Rome, the center of civilization, was no mere provincial city. "A Coptic Deacon is vainly attempting . . . to learn from a Roman prelate . . . what route he must take to the College of Propaganda; . . . a Vicar Apostolic from China is embracing a missionary to the Indians on Lake Erie. . . . It is only in Rome that such incidents are possible." The council brought together an "assemblage of dwellers in *all* lands, of strangers from *every* shore. . . . Here in this City of Rome is held the new Pentecost, the assembly of people from the farthest ends of the earth." Rome hosted "the piety of the world." When Pius appeared in public, "a gentle murmur of expectation, . . . swells like the sound of the sea until it reaches the enthusiastic cry of *Viva il Papa Re! Vive toujour Pie Neuf!* Long live the Pope King! . . . Romans, Neapolitans and gay Frenchmen and sedate Germans, Irishmen and Spaniards, are all unanimous in the one great expression of affection for the Holy Father, and in love for the Papal power." Predictably, Protestants ridiculed the spectacle.[69]

After unsuccessful efforts to reach a settlement with Pius IX and after negotiations with European powers to assure their noninterference, the Italian government ordered its troops to conquer papal Rome. The council ended abruptly as forces under General Raffaele Cadorna broke through the ancient Roman wall near the Porta Pia on the 20th of September 1870, and the temporal power came to an end. While the army protected the neighborhood around the Vatican from riotous Romans, Pius proclaimed himself a "prisoner in the Vatican." Not until 1929 did a pope venture outside Vatican grounds. Five popes reiterated Pius's dramatic ascription, claiming they too were prisoners, like the rest of Catholic Italy, of the Savoy monarchy that had usurped the temporal power. The image of imprisonment had a profound impact on the Catholic imagination. Pius, like Jesus and like St. Peter, was now in chains.[70]

Catholics communicated solidarity with their Holy Father. Archbishop John Williams of Boston wrote: "How many trials and sorrows have pressed on your paternal heart during the course of your long pontificate, which may be truly said to have been rendered glorious, no less by the sufferings which you have heroically endured . . . for God's holy church! . . . The overthrow of the temporal power" that made "[you] a prisoner in your own Capital" has "shocked the hearts of your faithful children throughout the world, and fills them even now with grief and indignation." Bishop Patrick Lynch of Charleston lectured in New York City and reiterated the ideology of the Roman Question. "It is necessary for [the pope] to possess [the temporal sovereignty], both for the liberty and interest of the Church, and for the interest of the world. . . . [He] may be a prisoner, and his limbs fettered by chains, yet that authority of his . . . is loved and received with joy and devotion." Spalding returned from Rome to Baltimore to meet 30,000 demonstrators in favor of Pius. On Thanksgiving Day, 50,000 marched in Washington. Grand protests followed in New York, Boston, Philadelphia, and Buffalo. Ellen Ewing, Catholic antisuffragist and wife of General William Tecumseh Sherman, piqued the Italian minister when she flew the papal flag from her Washington home.[71]

Future "liberal" episcopal leaders rallied to Pius and established their intransigent credentials in the 1870s. Father John Ireland, the outspoken "Americanist" archbishop of St. Paul, led a procession of 7,000 through a Minnesota snowstorm in January 1871 to protest the seizure of the temporal power. He called the "spoliation of the Holy See, the most glaring of modern international crimes" and insisted that the pope must not be "under the sway of an earthly power." James Gibbons, vicar apostolic of North Carolina and future cardinal-archbishop of Baltimore, issued a pamphlet justifying the temporal sovereignty through a neoguelf reading of the history of civilization. At Pius's funeral mass in February

1878, Father John J. Keane, future rector of the Catholic University of America, bishop of Richmond, and archbishop of Dubuque, pillaged the Roman republicans of 1848 who "turned Rome into a pandemonium of blood and worse than heathen orgies." Pius, "a father more than a sovereign," had possessed "wisdom and an influence more than human."[72]

German-speaking Catholics were not to be outdone. "We have a great and holy duty, during these days of persecution, to defend our Holy Church . . . [and] to fight bravely for . . . the visible head of our Church on earth, the suffering Pius IX." Louisville's *Katholischer Glaubersbote* prophesied, "the Church will emerge victorious from this struggle." Ridiculing King Vittorio's conquest, the *Glaubersbote* asserted, "If Victor Emanuel has the right to conquer the Papal States . . . then Napoleon had the right to take over Germany!" *Der Wahrheits-Freund* listed seventeen times papal Rome had been sacked since the fifth century. Still, "Rome has been under the control of the pope" for fifteen hundred years, and Pius "does not have to worry about . . . our devotion to him."[73]

Protestants predictably applauded King Vittorio and welcomed the end of the temporal power. Chicago's *Northwest Christian Advocate* sighed, "it is indeed time that the old popedom (as an element of the civil system of Europe) were swept away. It has long been simply a mischief and a disgrace in European civilization — an obsolete, medieval anachronism; a monstrous detraction from Christianity." The confident Methodists conjured up God's wrath. "The Pope, boasting at Rome of his infallibility . . . [is] to-day humbled to the dust, confounded before all the world. . . . How are the mighty fallen!" New York's *Christian Advocate* identified the liberal idea of progress with God's will against the papacy. "The civil sovereignty of the Pope has been annihilated, and thereby the greatest drawback on European progress for a thousand years has been cast off. . . . The trustful faith of the friends of liberty has not been fallacious."[74]

Rev. William Pratt Breed and Rev. J. M. Macdon thought likewise. Preaching on Luke 14:11 — "For whosoever exalteth himself shall be abased" — at the West Spruce Street Presbyterian Church in Philadelphia, Breed charged that the dogma of papal infallibility had exalted "an erring, sinful man into a moral and spiritual dictatorship over the Christian world!" But "the Pope was brushed from his throne as a fly is brushed from the brow of a giant!" Papal Rome nurtured "beggary, robbery, licentiousness, and murder," but now Jews have their rights restored, "Protestant worship is enjoyed and God's holy word is sold even in Rome!" Macdon, expounding in the Presbyterian *Princeton Theological Review*, cited the Book of Daniel and the Apocalypse to explain why "the definition of the dogma of infallibility, and the lapse of the temporal power . . . have occurred so closely." Surely, this "is not to be viewed in the light of an ordinary concurrence or sequence of events."[75]

American friends of Liberal Italy gathered to counter Catholic protests. Arthur

Coxe waxed concerned to the organizer of a celebration at the Boston Music Hall in February 1871. "American sentiment and sympathy must ever be with any people claiming the right to choose their own rulers and to resist the imposition of a detested Sovereign by foreign bayonets." But "at this moment," Coxe complained, "an organized attempt to produce the very opposite impression in Europe is zealously promoted in all our chief cities, with a view to intimidate Italian patriots and to encourage those who would revive the despotic system of 1815." Josiah Holland "heartily rejoice[d] in the consummation of the wishes of the Italian people." He only wished King Vittorio took a harder line with the pope. "There seems to be no menace to the Unity so happily achieved except in the desire of the king and his government to conciliate the papal interest. . . . If Italy could only know that her safety depends entirely on the universal education of her people outside of priestly prescription and authority." Asa Smith of Dartmouth College alluded with alarm to Catholic publicity. "It would be sad, indeed, if the people of Italy should hear from our shores only such voices as have been strangely lifted up in certain gatherings."[76]

Julia Ward Howe composed a "Hymn for the Celebration of Italian Unity" sung at the Academy of Music in New York on 12 January, where eminent Americans gathered to toast the end of papal Rome. Isaac Hecker, founder of the Paulists and editor of the *Catholic World*, mailed the book of addresses and letters from the New York gathering to fellow Catholic convert Orestes Brownson. Hecker marveled, "Every day my admiration increases at the attitude of the Holy Father in his defense of those principles which underlie the political order and natural morality. . . . He is resisting the destruction of all human society. The only power on earth that has had the courage to stand up against violence and injustice in the political order. Wonderful mission for God's Church!" Brownson found it "sad and discouraging . . . to see a large number of the most distinguished and influential men of a great nation . . . assisting, by their presence, addresses, letters, or comments, to applaud events notoriously brought about by fraud, craft, lying, calumny, and armed force."[77]

On 13 May 1871, the Italian government unilaterally passed the Law of Guarantees to regulate the position of the Holy See and the Church within Liberal Italy. It remained in force until February 1929. The Law of Guarantees deprived the pope of his territorial sovereignty, although it affirmed that his person was "sacred and inviolable." The pope retained possession of the Vatican, the Lateran palaces, and his villa at Castel Gandolfo. It protected papal communication networks so the pope could carry out his international spiritual mission. The law assured passage for cardinals to all papal elections and freedom of association for consistories and councils. The pope was permitted his own telegram system, and the secretariat of state—the papal diplomatic corps—was unobstructed. Italy also promised the pope an annual allowance of 3,225,000 lire to compensate for his loss. Under the law the state no longer required an oath of allegiance from Italian bishops and no longer reserved the right to hinder the promulgation of ecclesiastical laws. The law also abolished the *exequatur* and *placet* required for state recognition of ecclesiastical acts but retained them for the allocation of benefices and episcopal palaces. This gave the kingdom something short of a veto power over episcopal appointments that it was expected to soon relinquish but never did.[78]

The Law of Guarantees approximated Cavour's liberal ideal of "a free church in a free state." It fell short of "disestablishment," or separation of church and state, because it did not revise the first sentence of the constitution, the Kingdom of Piedmont's *Statuto* of 1848, which still read: "The Catholic Apostolic and Roman Religion is the sole religion of the State." Under the Law of Guarantees the Church had more freedom than in the preunification states, but it also lost some of its privileges. The Destra mistakenly hoped the law would stimulate progressive developments within the Church. Some leaders of the Destra, advocates of Rosmini's suggestions for Church reform, wanted the state to impose the elective principle on the Church. Marco Minghetti, for instance, insisted that once the administration of parish property was under lay control, the hierarchy would be obliged to listen to the laity. He urged the state to compel the Holy See to reinstate a system whereby laity and priests elected their bishops. Similarly, Carlo Cadorna insisted the law did not permit the state to adequately protect the laity and lower clergy from authoritarian ecclesiastical superiors. He feared that only intellectually narrow and intransigent clergy would receive promotions and that the patriotic clergy—of which there was no shortage on the front lines in Lombardy in 1848—would disappear.[79]

Pius, in any case, would have none of this. On 15 May, in "Ubi Nos," he rejected the Law of Guarantees, which intolerably relegated the status of the Holy See, an international institution, to a matter internal to Liberal Italy. Notwithstanding its name, it guaranteed neither the safety nor independence of the Holy See. Neither Pius nor his successors ever accepted their annual allowance. As Martina explains, "Ubi Nos" "constituted the basis and the justification for Catholic intransigence during the rest of the nineteenth century."[80]

American Catholics followed Pius's lead. The *Catholic World* insisted, oddly, one might think, for a "liberal" Catholic journal, that by permitting free "discussion of religious questions" the Law of Guarantees "deals the most powerful and insidious blow at the spiritual power of the Pope in spiritual matters, encouraging his people to spiritual defection." Father J. J. Prendergast proclaimed that the Law of Guarantees "guarantee[s] nothing." He employed a metaphor popular among nineteenth-century American Catholics eager to make the pope's temporal power seem reasonable to their Protestant and liberal neighbors. Although he professed to admire Italy and to desire "its happiness and glory," Prendergast insisted, "the existence in the interest of the world of a religious District of Columbia within her borders" would never "be an injury to her."[81]

The ideology of the Roman Question contended that the attack on the pope's temporal power harmed the Church and made civilization itself vulnerable to barbarism. Not surprisingly then, Catholics discerned moral degeneration in Italy and Rome, once authority passed from pope to king. Suddenly "blackguardism, ruffianism, and [a] riotous disposition" infected the Romans. "The wine shops were filled," littering the streets "with the choicest specimens of Italian blasphemy," while "the woman were nearly shameless under the influence of wine and the new liberation." In "picture-shops, . . . portraits of the Pope" were replaced with "the saints of the new worship, the gods of the Italian Kingdom—Garibaldi, Victor Emmanuel, . . . and this class of men." Amid this sordid affair, "in his own City of Rome," an aged Pius IX suffered. "The criminals . . . have returned. . . . The followers of Victor Emmanuel and of Garibaldi are now let loose on Rome, and turned this city into one of the most dangerous cities in Europe, where assassination is the order of the night, and where robbery has become an art."[82]

The unrelenting attack upon Liberal Italy was integral to the ideology of the Roman Question. Participation in this assault allowed Catholics in America to express loyalty to Pius and to criticize liberalism without directly maligning the liberal values of their own society, which they insisted was ontologically different from Liberal Italy. Catholics agreed with Paulist Isaac Hecker: "designing men" had unjustly usurped Rome "under the cloak of Italian unity."[83] The plebiscites in support of unified Italy were a sham,[84] public morality had disappeared from once utopian papal dominions,[85] and Liberal Italy was a criminal entity overseen by murderous pagans who plundered religious houses and in so doing robbed Catholics throughout Christendom.[86] Indeed, "Victor Emmanuel's assault upon Rome" had culminated in "a government of banditti bound together by the desire of plunder, a country where no protection is given to citizens, but where brigands, cutthroats and communists act without fear of punishment; where murder and robbery are legalized; where oppression and persecution are applauded; where beggary and starvation are rampant; where assassination and pergery [sic] are prevelent [sic]; where irreligion and immorality are openly practiced; where everything sacred and venerated are rediculed [sic] and carricatured [sic]."[87]

As Pius's pontificate came to an end, American Catholics proclaimed him a saint. America's preeminent nineteenth-century Catholic historian, John Gilmary Shea, vindicated Pius as a miracle worker tormented by demonic forces. Shea's popular biography, a powerful narrative conveying the ideology of the Roman Question, assured readers, "there is not a Catholic family in which the little ones do not recognize the portrait of our Holy Father, Pope Pius IX, and look upon it with affection and reverence. The war which the world has waged upon him so unrelentingly as Pope and Prince has drawn all faithful hearts to him." Justifying the kidnapping of the Mortara child, insisting the "Syllabus of Errors" drew a "similar distinction" between "true liberty and license" as the "constitutions of the American States," castigating Mazzini as "the chief of the enemies of Christ," and denouncing the Republic of 1849 as an eruption of evil in which "every church showed that the reign of the Antichrist had begun," Shea insisted that "the zeal for a united Italy was rooted mainly in a hatred of the Catholic Church." His biography mirrored others that solidified the normative Catholic understanding of Pius's pontificate in the United States.[88]

Reflecting on "the rising generation in Italy" in 1875, the *Milwaukee Catholic Magazine* summed up this arsenal of invective toward Liberal Italy. The "deterioration of the moral sense produced by irreligion," it explained, "is accompanied by an increase of the perils to which youthful morals are exposed, whereby the depravity of the pupils is largely facilitated." This "degeneracy of the Italian youth" resulted from "the adoption of the modern spirit of Liberalism, and . . . the rejection of the old spirit of Catholicism."[89]

American Catholics knew this "rising generation" was on the move. The ideology of the Roman Question took its classic intransigent form just when a trickle of relatively self-sufficient Ligurian immigrants to the United States was growing into a tidal wave of southern Italian sojourners, all raised in the wicked environment of Liberal Italy. Their "degeneracy" was not a product of racial inferiority, as heretical scientists working from atheistic naturalistic premises claimed. The Catholic nation disembarking in New York or New Orleans was in flight, escaping the prison of Liberal Italy. If the newcomers failed to respect clergy, did not know the catechism, and exhibited a bewildering absence of enthusiasm for their Holy Father, it was because they were victims in need of re-Christianization and civilization. Hopefully, as members of a Catholic nation, their "instinctive" loyalties would reemerge under the influence of the sacraments. For some, however, the damage done under the House of Savoy was irreversible. Ensnared by "secret societies" and radical sects, they had become enemies of the Church, the pope, and God. They were no longer real Italians.

THE IDEOLOGY of the Roman Question emerged out of creative, if reactionary, uses of neoguelf ideas about the papacy, Rome, and Italy. American Catholics clashed with their liberal, Protestant, and Jewish neighbors over the meaning of Rome and Italy. They made the ideology of the Roman Question their own, insisting that all Italian liberals were anti-Catholic, antireligious barbarians, who used nationality as a pretext to attack the pope and the Church. The call to restore the temporal power of the pope was an invitation for Europe to return to civilization, stem barbarism, and recognize the true meaning of liberalism personified by Pius himself. American Catholics employed tortured apologetics to distinguish the American liberal tradition from its degenerate European version and thereby to protect themselves against Protestant accusations of disloyalty to the United States.

Until the Great War broke out in 1914, American Catholics maintained their relentless assault upon Liberal Italy, the state that enslaved their Holy Father and the Italian Catholic nation. The presence of Italian immigrants, missionaries, sisters, and state representatives within the United States after 1861 complicated matters considerably. By the second half of the nineteenth century, the contest for hegemony over the Italian nation unfolded not only in southern Europe but also in vast diasporas within dozens of states on five continents, where millions of Italians settled. This new international battlefield of Catholic warfare with Liberal Italy, in principle, changed nothing. American Catholics continued to clash with their liberal and Protestant neighbors through ritual and debate, over the meaning of Rome, the pope, and Italy. In so doing, they performed and strengthened the ideology of the Roman Question.

CHAPTER TWO

The Transnational Symbolic
Contest for Rome, 1878–1914

After the conquest of papal Rome, Catholics bemoaned the imprisonment of their Holy Father and bewailed the suffering of their Church. A violent paroxysm had ruptured relations between heaven and earth. Civilization had lost the only compass that could point humanity on a progressive path. Paulist Isaac Hecker heralded, "the gates of hell have been opened, and every species of attack, as by general conspiracy, has been let loose at once upon the church." Catholics watched states arm to the teeth, science adopt atheistic premises, the arts degenerate into perversity, and reason revolt against God. "Heresy and schism, false philosophy, false science, and false art, cunning diplomacy, infidelity, and atheism, one and all boldly raise up their heads and attack the church in the face; while secret societies of world-wide organization are stealthily engaged in undermining her strength with the people." Catholic nations had fallen prey to wicked men. "Austria, France, Bavaria, Spain, Italy, . . . have yielded to a handful of active and determined radicals, infidels, Jews, or atheists." Passivity, however, was not an option. The *Catholic Times* of Rochester, New York, kept the faith: "The Catholics of the World Own Every Inch of Ground in Rome."[1]

If Pius IX and his spiritual children created the ideology of the Roman Question, the generation of Pope Leo XIII (1878–1903) reinforced it. Under Leo the Church improved communication networks and methods of socialization. Vatican nuncios (ambassadors to governments) and apostolic delegations (representatives to national churches) tied Catholics to papal Rome. The installation in 1893 of an apostolic delegation in Washington strengthened the link between the Vatican and the American Church. Catholic schools and seminaries inculcated an appreciation of the importance of the Roman Question. Producers of Catholic culture—clergy, sisters, lay congresses, editors, mothers in their homes—conveyed sentiments of protest against Liberal Italy and taught the necessity of the temporal power. The ideology of the Roman Question appeared in sermons, journals, newspapers, pamphlets, prayers, and public rituals, and it reinforced boundaries separating Catholics from other Americans.

Italian migration to the United States complicated matters. Italian "colonies" offered new opportunities for Catholics to perform the rituals of their ideology. A contest over the meaning of Rome and Italy unfolded among Italian Americans themselves—liberal nationalists, Catholics, socialists, monarchists, anarchists, and baffling syncretisms of these alternatives. Americans from a variety of national origins participated in this contest for hegemony over Italian Americans. Priests, sisters, charitable lay women, and bishops, particularly of Irish descent, supported Catholic Italy against Anglo-Saxon liberals, humanitarian settlement house workers, Protestant evangelists, and Italian consuls, who backed Liberal Italy.

The internalist historiography of American Catholics highlights the rise of liberal and conservative factions among American bishops between 1880 and 1900. However, no such intra-Catholic division arose regarding the ideology of the Roman Question.[2] This was not because Americans avoided the issue. On the contrary, diatribes against the evils of Liberal Italy and calls to restore the temporal power rang out frequently.[3] But Catholic ideological deviation was remarkably rare. Diversity among American Catholics appeared only in their *style* of expression—moderate versus bellicose swipes at Liberal Italy or cries for a papal princedom. For example, Cardinal James Gibbons of Baltimore exercised prudent caution not to inflame ecumenical Protestants who appreciated the Church's role as an agent of social order. His pacific style, though, was not the norm. Irish Catholic historian Daniel Binchy's description of intransigent Catholics in Italy during these years could readily be applied to American Catholics: "The modern student is almost terrified by the degree of bitterness shown towards the new Italy and her makers. Even such an ordinary event as the death from natural causes of a prominent Italian politician was distorted into a divine judgement on wrongdoing and proclaimed as such with a ghoulish exultation."[4]

After brief consideration of international and Italian politics of the Roman Question during Leo's pontificate, I analyze symbols of Rome and Italy that separated Catholics from other Americans in this period of intransigence. This transnational contest between Catholics and Liberal Italy kept the ideology of the Roman Question strong and vital. Consequently, Catholics in America approached the Great War in 1914 ready to insist upon the restoration of the temporal power when their Holy Father called upon them to do so.

Pope Leo's Policy in Italy and the World

During Leo's pontificate, the Roman Question factored into the international alliances of both the Holy See and Liberal Italy. Italy's 1882 entrance into the

Triple Alliance with Germany and Austria-Hungary was a case in point. Renewed for a last time in 1912, the Triplice protected Liberal Italy from the possibility that the two conservative empires might work to undermine the Law of Guarantees. Italian statesmen believed the Triplice inoculated their fragile kingdom from the Catholic virus. Domenico Farini, president of the Senate in the 1890s, captured the liberal suspicions: "The Pope cannot recognize and will never accept the Italian state as it is presently constituted." Attuned to the unpredictable implications of the Roman Question, Farini advised King Umberto I: "I believe that the Triple Alliance is indispensable, above all since we are in Rome. The Central Powers represent European conservatism; if we were not with them, the whole Roman Question would surface again for them."[5]

The Holy See, for its part, sought alliances to raise the Roman Question in international forums outside of Liberal Italy's control. Leo initially sought German support. He negotiated with Chancellor Otto von Bismarck, notwithstanding the (Catholic) Center Party's disgust at compromise with Prussia, to reverse the Kulturkampf that had devastated the German Church. In 1886 Leo mediated a dispute between Spain and Germany and thus hoped to win Germany's backing to raise the Roman Question as an international issue. During Kaiser Wilhelm II's visit to Rome in October 1888, Leo urged him to disregard his alliance with Liberal Italy. When the bewildered kaiser declined, the Holy See looked to France.[6]

To win France's friendship, Leo "rallied" French Catholics to support the anticlerical Third Republic. Vatican secretary of state Cardinal Mariano Rampolla del Tindaro nudged the French chargé d'affaires: "The Roman Question—believe me—is a great strength for France—against Italy." After the kaiser's unhappy visit to Rome, Rampolla intensified his French courtship: "An entente is necessary between France and the Holy See. We have a common enemy [i.e., Italy], and we must co-operate to fight him." But Leo's French initiative failed. Most French Catholics remained hostile to their Republic and nostalgic for monarchy. Finally, an 1898 Franco-Italian trade treaty undermined Rampolla's scheme to secure a seat for the Holy See at the Hague Conference in 1899, where he had hoped to raise the Roman Question.[7] Thus, the Roman Question nudged Leo into failed compromises with Protestant Germany and Republican France.

Toward Liberal Italy, notwithstanding a brief period in the 1880s when Leo tested the waters of reconciliation, the pope remained intransigent.[8] Class and regional variables conditioned the social composition of Italian Catholicism and the outcome of Leo's Italian policy. The Church held some loyalty among nobles who resented bourgeois successes. The southern peasantry, tied to local mutual benefit societies and confraternities and resentful of state authority, were also a potential Catholic force. But southern peasants were never unambiguously loyal to clerical institutions and notoriously difficult to mobilize. Leo's greatest resource was the deeply Catholic populations of the Veneto and Lombardy. These regions formed the nucleus of the intransigent Opera dei Congressi e dei Comitati Cattolici. Ideologically speaking, Italian Catholics divided into three camps—intransigents in the Opera dei Congressi, conciliationists organized around *Rassegna Nazionale* in Florence, and Christian Democrats who sparked generational conflict in the Opera in the late 1890s.

Between 1874 and 1904, the Opera was a formidable opponent of Liberal Italy, and the Roman Question dominated its agenda. In parts of northern Italy where the Opera gained a popular base, its organizations provided charitable resources, dominated municipal elections, founded newspapers and publishing houses, and ran rural banks, credit unions, cooperatives, and schools. Young Christian Democrats, such as Fathers Romolo Murri and Luigi Sturzo, struggled to reform the Opera in the late 1890s. They contended that their elders' preoccupation with the Roman Question and political abstention had turned Catholics into political eunuchs. Due to conflict Christian Democrats precipitated, Leo intervened to clarify the meaning of "democracy." In "Graves de communi" (1901) he offered an apolitical and paternalistic definition of Christian democracy as "beneficent Christian action on behalf of the people." Murri, in contrast, argued that genuine democracy required "the direct, effective, and organic participation of the people in the government of their affairs." In 1904 Pope Pius X (1903–14) dissolved the conflict-ridden Opera.[9]

Conciliationists promoted Vatican rapprochement with Liberal Italy. The Risorgimento, they argued, had strayed from its proper path but could be set right through Catholic participation in national politics. An influential minority of bishops, clergy, intellectuals, and politicians, the conciliationists maintained informal links between Leo and the government. In 1885 Leo turned to a known conciliationist, Bishop Giovanni Battista Scalabrini of Piacenza, to publish an anonymous pamphlet, *Transigents and Intransigents* (1885), to monitor attitudes toward reconciliation. "What results have intransigents achieved with their program of immobility and abstention?" the pamphlet wondered. "Does it accord with one's duties as a Catholic and a citizen to let everything go to rack and ruin—religion, morality, country—rather than extend a compassionate hand to prevent the loss of souls, the corruption of many youths, the approval of a law contrary to religion?" Alluding to the positive results of Catholic political participation in Prussia and Belgium, the pamphlet urged the same for Italy.[10]

On Christmas Day 1886, Bishop Geremia Bonomelli of Cremona, another conciliationist, published a letter to Leo: "O Holy Father, . . . there is one blessing that I crave above all others—namely, that You may accomplish . . . the pacification of our *Patria*. . . . Youth . . . is steadily detaching itself from the Church and prepares the inevitable apostasy of the entire nation. What will then become of the Holy See, alone in the midst of an unbelieving and fiercely hostile society?" Leo responded, reconciliation "corresponds perfectly to Our own aspirations."

He hinted in an allocution: "If men were willing and finally able to satisfy our just claims, the first to feel the great benefits of such a course would be that nation which had the good fortune to be chosen as the seat of the Papacy and which is indebted to the Papacy for so much of its greatness and glory."[11]

These overtures, vague on particulars, triggered both intransigent rage against Scalabrini and Bonomelli, and firm resistance in the Chamber of Deputies. The state would sacrifice neither its land nor "its indefectible mission to spread enlightenment, to foster progress, to advance civilization." Interior Minister Francesco Crispi confirmed the Sinistra's satisfaction with the Law of Guarantees: "We do not seek reconciliation . . . for our country is not at war. . . . Italy belongs to herself, to herself alone, and she has but one ruler: the King." Italy-Vatican relations deteriorated over the next three years.[12]

By 1887 Scalabrini and Bonomelli realized liberals and Catholics were not ready for the dialogue formal reconciliation required. Both bishops explored pastoral activity among Italian emigrants as a safer terrain where Church and state might cooperate indirectly. Among Catholics, work on behalf of migrant laborers resonated with Leo's social vision expressed in "Rerum Novarum" (1891). Liberal Italy, for its part, understood the economic importance of its emigrants. Although Bonomelli's work for migrants in Europe met with debilitating resistance from intransigents, Scalabrini encountered less interference. He cultivated cooperative North and South American bishops and worked with Leo and Rampolla. In 1887 Scalabrini established his Pious Society of Missionaries of St. Charles Borromeo (the Scalabrini Fathers) to work with Italians in the Americas, and the following year he drafted Leo's letter to the American bishops to alert them to the problems of Italian labor migrants. For the Italian liberal public he wrote *Italian Emigration to America* (1887), the first of several pamphlets urging legislative reforms to aid migrants.[13]

Lay conciliationist admirers of Bonomelli and Scalabrini urged the Church to engage modern society rather than retreat into a ghetto. In the 1890s, they grew enamored with "liberal" or "Americanist" bishops in the United States, who also spoke in favor of Catholic participation in the currents of modern culture. Italian conciliationists translated and commended the works of Archbishop John Ireland of St. Paul, whose accolades for the First Amendment of the U.S. Constitution resonated with their own hopes. Conciliationists, however, grew disillusioned with the Americanists when none of them ever spoke out in support of Italy-Vatican reconciliation. On the contrary, American Catholics replicated intransigent expressions of the ideology of the Roman Question. As John Ireland's biographer affirms, "the archbishop of St. Paul consistently maintained the need for the pope to enjoy an independent political status." Ireland said as much on several occasions publicly and in an article for the prestigious *North American Review*.[14]

The Italian Nation Abroad

The Roman Question complicated pastoral care for Italians in the United States. For each foreign-language group, the American Church built national parishes that employed national symbols to create solidarity with the Church. In the case of the Italians, these symbols—flags, paintings, statues, architectural designs, language, dialect, songs, holidays—required keen vigilance to prevent deviation from the ideology of the Roman Question. Consequently, pastoral care for Italians increased the likelihood of accusations, anxieties, conflicts, and moral ambiguity.

Because Bishop Scalabrini was known as a conciliationist, his priests were suspect in the United States. For example, Mother Frances Cabrini, founder of the Sisters of the Sacred Heart, arrived in New York City to work with the Scalabrini Fathers. Cabrini, however, found the priests "more attached to the tri-color [Italian] flag rather than to the Pope." Proudly intransigent, she refused to direct a hospital founded by Italian Freemasons whose revenues came from 20th of September celebrations, a holiday glorifying the conquest of papal Rome. "I will say 'No' because I am not in accord with the Garibaldini. Two Vice Consuls and even a personage from the Italian legation came to recommend the proposition to me, but I absolutely will not accept it."[15]

Archbishop Michael Corrigan of New York did not share Cabrini's evaluation of the Scalabrini Fathers. Corrigan acknowledged that Scalabrini provincial Felice Morelli, "like many other [Italians] from northern Italy," supported reconciliation between the Holy See and Liberal Italy. But outside of their house Scalabrinians were discrete. Morelli had "separated ten [Italian mutual benefit] societies from other associations that participate in the celebration of the twentieth of September in New York." In addition, when the municipal secretary of New York City "invited Morelli to take part in the festivity, [Morelli] declined stating that this solemnity is a day of mourning for Catholics." Scalabrini defended his missionaries against Rampolla's charges that his priests were "promoting liberal ideas in the Americas." The circumspect bishop responded: "The accusations of liberalism hurt me deeply. . . . Above every abominable thing I abhor every idea that deviates from genuinely Roman doctrines."[16]

Lay Catholics also accused Scalabrinians of ideological deviance. In December 1897, Federico Astorri, speaking for the St. Anthony Society in New Haven, complained to the Vatican because Scalabrini superior general Francesco Zaboglio had blessed an Italian flag. Astorri further insisted Scalabrinians had participated in "a parade and banquet that Italian Masons held in Boston on the 20th of September." He recounted the "scandal" of seeing the "standards of St. Michael, St. Anthony di Padova, and Santa Maria Addolorata carried in procession through Boston" alongside wicked Garibaldini. Zaboglio defended himself: "The missionary . . . gladly blesses the flag of Italy, the same that pushed our soldiers to their noble enterprises [during the imperial war in Ethiopia], the same that denotes the standard of civilization." He proclaimed, "priests . . . do not hate the *patria*. [I] love my *patria* and I do and will do all for the *patria*."[17]

The Italian Servants of Mary, in contrast to Zaboglio, made clear to their parishioners the distinction between the *patria*, understood as the Italian nation, and the evil liberal state. When Chicago's Italian consul visited a Servite parochial school at Assumption Church in 1913, "he could not hold back the exclamation: This is the only place in Chicago where one breaths true *italianità*." Assumption's parish monthly welcomed the endorsement but quipped: "We are far from pretending that the Royal Consul means the same thing as we do by true *italianità*," since "Italian Catholic schools do not observe certain patriotic holidays . . . and do not glorify certain famous heroes."[18]

The ideology of the Roman Question offered American Catholics an explanation for the "Italian Problem." From 1880 to 1940, Catholics lamented Italian immigrants' unwillingness to finance parishes, their lack of respect for clergy, aberrant devotional styles, vulnerability to Protestant proselytizing and radical politics, and veneration of Mary above Jesus.[19] The ideology of the Roman Question placed the blame for this "Italian Problem" on the doorstep of Liberal Italy. Italy, after all, was a Catholic nation whose churches, religious art, pilgrimage sites, saints, and popes demonstrated potent civilizing powers. Italian migrants carried the gifts of civilization with them on their global peregrinations. Hence, religious disorder among these immigrants necessarily resulted from the degeneracy of Liberal Italy. "A living proof of what kind of blessing the new kingdom showers on Italy's population," wrote Joseph Shroeder, "is the great mass of poverty-stricken Italian emigrants who daily land on our shores." Prisoners like the pope, Italian immigrants had escaped from the Masonic clutches of the barbaric despoilers.[20]

As victims of the pope's enemy, Italian immigrants merited charity and offered Catholics in the United States a unique opportunity to sanctify themselves. In 1903, Chicago's archdiocesan weekly, the *New World*, in a fit of neoguelfism worthy of Gioberti, argued American Catholics owed a debt to the civilizing forces of Catholic Italy that should be paid through charity to neglected immigrants.

> Let us try to make amends for our neglect of the Italians in the United States. We have treated them more like animals than like brother Catholics. . . .
>
> The Italians! What have they not a right to ask of us? . . . Hundreds and hundreds of years before we were born into the world as a race and a nation they had sent out missionaries to civilize and Christianize our [Irish?] ancestors. . . .
>
> What have St. Francis and St. Anthony and St. Thomas Aquaina [*sic*] and

St. Catherine and Rapael [sic] and Michael Angelo and thousands of other Italians not done for us? This is their race that we have been neglecting and even despising. . . .

There are gowns [sic] of saints and philosophers and poets and navigators and astronomers and painters and sculptors in those inhabitants of what we have been calling "Dago dons." . . .

We need them and the civilizing repairing influence that is in their race. . . . Who knows but in the years to be, they will build us another St. Peter's here in Chicago.[21]

The *New World* called upon English-speaking Catholics to overcome their aversion to the poor Italians. After all, "the true faith was first permanently established in Italy and disseminated by the Italians throughout the earth. God thought fit to establish the Head and center of His Church [among Italians] . . . and through this race to disseminate His commandments and dogmas and truths and counsels to the whole human family." But the robust civilizing mission fell prey to "an evil spirit" that "has long controlled the temporal rulers of Italy." Italians now suffered under a regime in which the "voice of the Pope is no longer heeded," and "morality and virtue are no longer taught in the schools of the young." Italians had "become oppressed, debased, discouraged and indifferent to their religion." The duty fell upon Catholics in America to rekindle the faith of "the race of him who discovered America" and "the race of nearly all the Popes."[22]

In July 1903, Archbishop James Quigley of Chicago traveled to Joliet to dedicate St. Anthony's Italian Church. Quigley acknowledged civilization's debt to Italians. "We owe more to them than any other nation for our culture and all the arts." Those assembled sent a cablegram to the pope. The fund-raising campaign and dedication at St. Anthony's reinforced the notion of the Italian nation as a potent source of civilization emanating from the papacy. Italian Catholics were victims, as much as the pope, of the ungodly regime that had violently snatched the Papal States. Charity for these Italian victims was therefore an expression of solidarity with the Holy Father.[23]

Burying the Usurpers

The funerals of Italian monarchs Vittorio Emanuele II in 1878 and Umberto I in 1900 provide another opportunity to evaluate the transnational echoes of the ideology of the Roman Question. Although Pius IX had excommunicated everyone involved in the dastardly spoliation of the Papal States, including King Vittorio, the House of Savoy was Catholic, and his family wanted Vittorio reconciled to the Church. So, before Vittorio's death on 9 January 1878, Pius lifted the interdict over the monarchy's Quirinal Palace. The royal chaplain heard Vittorio's confession, pronounced absolution, and administered the viaticum. Did this mean the king repudiated the Risorgimento? Was he now a symbol of Catholic Italy? How should Catholics mark his passing? Ambiguity reigned.

Vittorio's death inspired mourning. After he lay in state for five days, his body was transferred from the Quirinal to the Pantheon on 17 January, and 200,000 grieving subjects lined the streets to honor their deceased king. The choice of a funeral site for the Savoyard turned king of Italy was difficult. The Piedmontese clamored to take "their" king to the resting site of his ancestors, but Interior Minister Francesco Crispi, the most important architect of Liberal Italy in the last two decades of the century, invented a tradition of burying the monarch in Rome. Because the Vatican refused to permit the use of Rome's cathedrals, St. Peter's or St. John Lateran, Crispi selected the Pantheon, the circular temple to the planetary gods of Marcus Agrippa that Pope Boniface IV had dedicated to St. Mary of the Martyrs in 609. Redolent of imperial rather than papal Rome, the Pantheon was a site suggestive of a civil religion within an Italian *polis* and did not communicate the primacy of papal Rome. The Vatican prohibited the appearance of bishops or cardinals at the funeral mass of 16 February.[24]

Outside of Rome, the Holy See responded slowly to the ambiguity this unprecedented situation created. Initially, Italian bishops were instructed to abstain from participation in any ceremony. Days later, after municipal officials had petitioned for funeral services, the Vatican granted permission for mass to be said in a parish church but not in episcopal cathedrals, unless the civil authorities demanded it, and even then bishops were not to participate. In Piacenza, officials became enraged at these offensive restrictions, and the liberal press lambasted Bishop Scalabrini, who left the city on the day of the service. When a mob attacked his carriage upon his return, Scalabrini threatened to place his cathedral under interdict to prevent his clergy from appeasing the mob and holding the service. Soon after, the Vatican granted Scalabrini permission to personally offer the requiem mass and allowed bishops of northern Italy to hold funeral masses, but not if the bishop feared the service might turn into a political demonstration. When the bishops of Parma and Bologna refused the use of their cathedrals, riots ensued.[25]

King Vittorio's death created ambiguity for American Catholics as well. How were bishops and clergy to respond to Italian immigrants who wished to honor the monarch? Before 1893, with no apostolic delegation representing papal Rome in Washington, communication with the Holy See took weeks. Some Catholics looked to newspapers to see how the Vatican had instructed Italian bishops. But the absence of specific directives generated diverse reactions.

When the intransigent bishop of Pittsburgh refused to permit a funeral mass in his cathedral, Italians took matters into their own hands. According to Father Ferdinand Kittell, "the Italians of Pittsburgh have declared open war with us."

They "are holding a service in a Presbyterian Church with both a Presbyterian and a Lutheran minister speaking." A marshal on horseback flying American and Italian flags led a colorful procession trailed by women in a horse-drawn carriage, defiantly passing in front of the Catholic cathedral. Kittell shrugged off the Italians: "Some respect! Good Catholics indeed."[26]

In Philadelphia, Father Antonio Isoleri of Santa Maria Maddalena de' Pazzi parish held a requiem mass with episcopal approval. Italian societies processed into the church, decorated with a twenty-one-foot catafalque "draped in black velvet" and a "handsome sword and massive Italian crown . . . on the coffin lid." Mayor William Stokley and consular representatives from Italy, Spain, France, and Russia attended the service. An Italian priest referred to Vittorio as "Italy's Washington, the liberator and father of his country." He hoped that in his "cold grave where in silence he rests . . . all present political and religious dissentions of Italy, so pernicious to religion and country . . . may be buried." Isoleri's sermon alluded to the Risorgimento, but he assured the mourners that the king and Pope were reconciled. "The prisoner of the Vatican had as deeply mourned the death of Vittorio Emanuele as any good Italian."[27]

Transnational church-state sparring broke out in Chicago, where 200 Italian men, including the vice consul, resolved to ask Bishop Thomas Foley to offer a requiem mass at Holy Name Cathedral. A commission representing the Italians sought the support of Father Agostino Morini, the Servite pastor of Our Lady of Sorrows Church. Morini refused to hold the service at his parish, which was too far from the city center and a stronghold of ultramontane Irish. He discussed the matter with Foley, who "side-stepped the issue by saying that that poor soul certainly had need of a funeral." Father John McMullen, pastor of the cathedral, refused to permit the mass in that most prestigious site. Father Joseph Roles at St. Mary's Church downtown also balked at the thought of a commemorating the usurper. "My parishioners are Irish," he explained, "and I have to contend with them, and they would stone me if I gave such permission." Morini himself boasted to a friend in Tuscany how he himself was a "papista" who refused to preside over the funeral. He finally wrote the "irksome commission" that the refusals were understandable. After all, "the person to be honored was the one under whose government the temporal domain of the Supreme Pontiff had been taken away and religious orders had been suppressed."[28]

Morini's letter to the commission lit up the liberal switchboard. "The Italian press [in New York] flew into a rage" at his curt response. "There were even threats of revenge." The Italian government lodged a complaint with the Servite prior general in Rome and suspended Morini's state pension. (The Kingdom of Italy provided Morini with an annual pension of $400 because he was a priest in a religious congregation suppressed by the government.) Morini's confreres criticized him for not offering a funeral that would have earned at least $100. His prior general agreed. He commanded Morini to apologize to Chicago's vice consul and tell him "you . . . were not motivated by ill will toward the Italian government," and that Morini's confreres "are good Italian subjects, well disposed toward the *patria*, and preachers of love of religion, good morals, and subordination to constituted [civil] power." Morini's pension was reinstated.[29]

In St. Louis, Father Nazareno Orfei spoke after a requiem mass at St. Bonaventure's Church. He acknowledged, "Vittorio Emanuele was penitent of his numerous sins, and . . . died a Christian." But Orfei urged the mourners not to forget about Vittorio's sinful participation in the Risorgimento. "To believe he died a 'Christian Hero' is a bit too much." Orfei concluded, "if he loved God more than his dear Italy, certainly he did not show it when he was despoiling wholesale the Church of God. We can only wonder how he who was only a short time ago the Plunderer of the Church and the Jailer of the Pope, has been suddenly transformed in death into a 'Christian Hero,' a good King and true Patriot."[30]

The Vatican monitored the American Church for its ideological purity. One report from New York to Rome claimed, "the conduct of the great majority of Italian clergy [in America] . . . was an immense scandal. Italians, both lay and clerical, Carbonari, Franciscans and Jesuits, gathered to offer final honors to the vile [king]." This intransigent snitch complained how "Italian Jesuits and Italian [Franciscan] Conventual Friars let the funeral music ring out for the libertine and sacrilegious Vittorio Emanuele." Notwithstanding his or her indignation, the observer described nothing against Vatican norms, only masses held in parish churches or in the cathedral without the bishop present.[31]

The same diversity within orthodoxy characterized Baltimore, Richmond, and Providence. In Baltimore, an Italian priest offered King Vittorio a mass at St. Vincent de Paul. "The church was sober and in mourning," with the altar, balustrade, and catafalque draped in black crepe. Italian societies, before they arrived at the church, met in a hall with portraits of Vittorio, Columbus, Garibaldi, and "the Italian coat of arms . . . flanked by the American and Italian flags." In Richmond and Providence, non-Italian priests led modest services. In St. Peter's Cathedral in Richmond, a diocesan administrator gave a "speech without any special allusions to the deceased King." At St. John's Church in Providence, Father Christopher Hughes found safety in a Latin eulogy. Hughes explained to an uncomprehending crowd how King Vittorio was best known for "his connection with the sad and painful events of our Holy Father and the Church in general. During his reign many calamities fell upon the Church which History must recall with crying eyes." Unimpressed with the unintelligible, Providence Italians processed through their city "with a funeral carriage covered in Italian national colors."[32]

Archbishop John Purcell of Cincinnati, an important episcopal voice in a significant see, alone stood out for his striking deviation from the ideology of the Roman Question. On 17 January, Italians processed into Cincinnati's cathedral for a mass. This is the only instance in which a bishop was present for a mass and, besides the one in Richmond, the only mass held in a cathedral. To close the service, Purcell offered pastoral remarks to the Italians who harked from Genoa, the capital of Liguria, a region within the former Kingdom of Piedmont. "Our prayers today are for one who believed and hoped in Christ." Although King Vittorio had participated in the conquest of Rome, "Vittorio Emanuele remained firm in the ancient Faith of his ancestors, the princes of the House of Savoy." Even during the Risorgimento, "Vittorio Emanuele never wanted to detach himself from the Catholic Church. He was the king of that beautiful city of Genoa, where Christopher Columbus conceived of the great idea to give a new World not only to the glory of Spain, but to the entire universe. . . . Genoa is also where the great Irish leader Daniel O'Connell died on his way to Rome. These are sacred associations and with pleasure Catholics think today of Genoa and its king in union with Christopher Columbus and Daniel O'Connell."[33]

Purcell floated deeper into treacherous ideological waters when he compared the kings of Israel to the pope. God had scolded King Samuel for not heeding his people. Similarly, although "the 275 popes of Rome governed very well . . . and the people enjoyed more peace and security under them than other government," Purcell admitted that Pius IX's subjects had wanted a new regime. "It is a great consolation to know that King Vittorio took the place of the pope in Rome and became the king. He did not do it out of personal ambition, but, like in the time of Samuel, the people wanted a king and if he had declined the Throne, the evil would have been much worse." If by now he had sprung a leak, Purcell's ship of ideological orthodoxy was about to sink. Purcell narrated how, while visiting Ancona in the former Papal States, he asked a shop owner how Italians felt about their new government. "'We Italians love and venerate the pope, but we want a powerful Nation that is equal to other nations.'" According to Purcell, "this was the desire of almost all the people in Italy." With pastoral sensitivity, he comforted Cincinnati's Italians. "I am happy that they have today held this solemn function and I must say that they executed it with patriotism and devotion. . . . The king . . . lived and died as a good Catholic and I hope that he has already followed those among the Saints in heaven."

Purcell's bold deviation from the ideology of the Roman Question earned him praise in the secular press. Cincinnati's *Commercial* found the speech "remarkable for its liberality. . . . No Catholic of equal rank has ever spoken with such cordial respect about the Kingdom of Italy." The *Chicago Times* marveled at the "remarkable sermon." Purcell "takes a democratic and practical view of the question of Italian unity. . . . The anathema of the pope seems to have passed out of [Purcell's] mind." His words were "certainly very radical sentiments from the pulpit of a Roman archbishop; and if they fail to provoke controversy between Cincinnati and the Vatican, they will be sure to bring upon the venerable prelate's head no small quantity of domestic denunciation."[34]

The Methodist *Western Christian Advocate* of Cincinnati delighted in discovering "a Catholic discrepancy" when it compared Purcell's remarks to Cincinnati's *Catholic Telegraph*. According to the latter, Vittorio was "a tool of others," "a lover of pleasure . . . of the viler sort. . . . To set such a man up as a hero, as a savior of society, as a deliverer and leader of his people, as a type of royalty and true manhood, is an insult to humanity." Predicting "United Italy will not see the century out," the intransigent weekly reckoned Vittorio would be remembered "as the pliant and weak tool, under an assumption of royalty, of an organized conspiracy against God, society, and man."[35]

The Vatican demanded an explanation. Purcell stressed his pastoral concern for "our Italian citizens." Propaganda Fide, the Vatican's congregation with authority over the American Church until 1908, scolded the archbishop, whose speech included "many things . . . that cannot in any way be approved and which do not match the truth of the facts." Propaganda commanded Purcell to publish its own description of King Vittorio's life and death "in your area, so those things which were put forward in the matter at issue be restored to the truth."[36]

The assassination of King Umberto I on 29 July 1900 also required circumspection. Bishops, pastors, and Italian American lay societies inundated the apostolic delegate in Washington, Archbishop Sebastiano Martinelli, OSA, with requests for guidance. Could there be a solemn funeral mass for the slain monarch in Italian churches? Could the mass be celebrated in the cathedral? Could there be public processions? Could Italian devotional and mutual benefit societies march with the tricolor flag? With inquiries mounting, Martinelli ascertained from the Vatican that masses were permissible, and each bishop was empowered to decide upon the details. Vatican directives thus granted episcopal autonomy. Improved Catholic communication networks diminished ambiguity because the apostolic delegation could instruct local authorities in a timely fashion.[37]

Umberto's tragic assassination at the hands of an anarchist and the piety of his wife inspired Catholic sympathy. Pope Leo sent condolences to Umberto's sister, the queen of Portugal. Italian bishops instructed churches to ring bells and offer funeral masses at which municipal and religious authorities mourned and mingled. Luigi Vitali, an outspoken conciliationist, compiled a book to highlight the harmony. The "spectacle offered by the Italian episcopacy and clergy . . . on the occasion of the solemn Masses celebrated for King Umberto. . . . was even more beautiful because in such circumstances we saw together, united in agreement, patriotic with religious sentiments."[38]

The initiative for masses in the United States came from Italian mutual benefit societies whose demands compelled their priests, bishops, and onlookers to confront the ideology of the Roman Question. Bastions of provincial loyalties, the fraternal societies also nurtured proud sentiments of *italianità* and patriotic affections for Italian national symbols. The perennial hope of Italian pastors was to direct toward parish coffers the resources of these societies. Regardless of their feelings about Liberal Italy, pastors welcomed occasions to cultivate solidarity with leaders of lay societies, men not usually inclined to trust clergy. Father Antonio Demo, a pastor in Greenwich Village, explained to Martinelli: "My aim" in holding a solemn mass, "besides religious suffrage [for the soul of King Umberto], would be to bring ever closer to the Church that element of the people who remain distant for reasons of prejudice."[39]

Vicar General William Byrne of Boston, whose archbishop was "away on his vacation," penned a panicky request for guidance to Martinelli. Byrne had "given the Italian priests permission to have solemn Requiem Masses in their churches," and "the Scalabrini Fathers and the Franciscans in the North End, had been jockeying for the privilege." The mutual benefit societies, however, wanted the funeral in the cathedral. They believed the North End churches could not host "the grand crowd that will attend." In addition, the societies "organized a vast procession and wish to go to the Cathedral" and "to invite the Governor of the State and the Mayor of the City and make it a quasi civic display of honor." Since Umberto was "under the ban of the Church," Byrne thought it best to write Martinelli for advice, particularly since the societies planned "to carry the Italian flag into the Cathedral."[40]

Boston's Italian societies, Protestant and Catholic, had already gathered in Fanueil Hall for a memorial meeting and processed with "carriages bearing five or six hundred [Italian] ladies in deep mourning, out of respect for the queen, whom every Italian woman worships." Keen to separate Catholics from Protestants, Byrne permitted services at both St. Leonard's Franciscan Church and the Scalabrini's Sacred Heart but preserved the purity of the cathedral. Likewise, throughout New York and New Jersey, Italian clergy in their parishes offered colorful funeral masses following grand patriotic demonstrations with processing Italian mourners of many ideological persuasions.[41]

When the Italian Augustinians at Our Lady of Good Counsel Church in south Philadelphia looked to Archbishop Patrick Ryan for guidance, he suggested to them that they follow Rome's protocol. But since the societies of Philadelphia and the Italian consulate had already planned a service at Santa Maria Maddalena de' Pazzi, a church not under Augustinian administration, the friars asked Martinelli, a fellow Augustinian, whether they might also hold a solemn mass. Martinelli gave tentative approval but urged his confreres to consult their archbishop first.[42]

Notwithstanding the masses, Philadelphia's *Catholic Standard and Times* took the opportunity to reiterate the ideology of the Roman Question. Reprinting a remark from the *London Globe* linking the Vatican's "anti-national attitude" with "sedition" in Italy, the Catholic editor lambasted the "organs of Tory villainy," the "very same organs that hailed Mazzini, the apostle of the dagger, and Garibaldi, the betrayer of Republicanism." "We say it is the English press which is mostly responsible for the growth of the assassination idea in Italy." The editorial also claimed widespread Italian misery resulted from the conquest of papal Rome, which was responsible for Italian regicide and for murder throughout the world.[43]

The diocese of Providence demonstrated exceptional intransigence. Providence's popular *L'Eco del Rhode Island* lampooned Vicar-General Father Thomas F. Doran, "the true enemy of Italy," after he told the *Providence News*, "The Church will do absolutely nothing and will in no way recognize the death of King Umberto." *L'Eco*'s editor, Federico Curzio, reported on the masses in Italian churches throughout the United States and Italy and wondered why Doran distinguished himself from bishops and priests elsewhere. In a public letter to the apostolic delegate, Curzio explained that "sentiments of respect and veneration toward the king" were "the duty of every honest Italian." Doran never budged. No Catholic funeral masses were celebrated in Rhode Island churches. Providence Italians, U.S. state and local dignitaries, and Italy's consular agent processed and commemorated King Umberto in Infantry Hall.[44]

When their usurping kings died, some Italians in America mixed liberal nationalism and Catholicism. They were neither indifferent nor antagonistic to the liberal symbols of their nation. Their demands for public rituals forced Catholics to confront the implications of the Roman Question and to relearn the ideological catechism regarding papal Rome. In the process, Catholics turned to the Vatican, inviting its authoritative guidance into American affairs and establishing a precedent for further intervention. As the Church's communication and education systems improved, and the Vatican monitored the selection of U.S. bishops, the expectations of the ideology of the Roman Question became internalized, routinized, and reinforced. Deviation diminished among Catholics, at least outside of the unpredictable Italian American community. In 1900, Archbishop Purcell had no Catholic counterpart.

New Symbols of Liberal Italy:
Francesco Crispi and Giordano Bruno

After 1887, no one expected an Italy-Vatican rapprochement any time soon. While many factors contributed to volatile relations, Francesco Crispi played a prominent role. If the generation of Pius IX had Garibaldi and Mazzini as favored punching bags, Crispi provided Leo's spiritual children with a galvanizing nemesis. Catholic portraits of this Sinistra statesman rivaled the crudest anticlerical attacks on priests in their invective and vulgarity.

Crispi came from a Greek Orthodox family that had been part of an Albanian migration to western Sicily in the fifteenth century. Until he was seventeen, Crispi attended the Greek seminary in Palermo, where he developed a conventional hostility toward the intrusiveness of the Latin Church and its vast Sicilian landholdings and wealth. In his twenties, he drifted away from the Greek Church, but he never lost belief in God or respect for religion, and he always cherished the ideal of religious freedom. After years in exile, he aided Garibaldi as his secretary of state in the conquest of Sicily in 1860. Crispi the republican reconciled himself to the monarchy as a symbol of national power after the unification. Prime Minister Crispi (August 1887–February 1891; December 1893–March 1896) enacted far-reaching reforms, oversaw autocratic governments, and promoted imperial expansion. His lust for war as a means to cultivate national consciousness and intensify the political education of Italians found an outlet in ill-fated ventures in East Africa, culminating in Italy's humiliating 1896 defeat in Adua.[45]

Like many Italian liberals, Crispi favored the separation of Church and state as well as religious freedom. He argued against the passage of the Law of Guarantees in 1871 because he believed it gave too many privileges to the Church and the pope, who had proclaimed himself an avowed enemy of the Kingdom of Italy and modern civilization. In contrast to the Destra architects of the law, Crispi did not believe liberalism would permeate and reform the Church, which was an aggressively reactionary and terribly dangerous opponent of Liberal Italy. An atheist, however, he was not. He refused to attend the unveiling of the Giordano Bruno monument in 1889 and the inauguration of the Giordano Bruno Society in 1892 because the society's leaders proclaimed the apostate Dominican an atheist. "I admit there is a need to fight prejudices and superstitions; but I do not accept the need to combat the religious idea. . . . Giordano Bruno was not an atheist. . . . The martyr believed in God." Crispi explained, "all of our great men were deists. Dante, Michelangelo, Galileo believed in God. Mazzini and Garibaldi believed in God."[46]

Crispi gave the Vatican cause for concern. In December 1887, he had King Umberto dismiss Duke Leopoldo Torlonia from his post as the mayor of Rome after Torlonia visited the cardinal vicar of the Eternal City to acknowledge Leo's pontifical jubilee for all Romans. Ecclesiastical legislation that passed under his watch restricted Catholic privileges and liberties. In 1889 and 1890, the state reformed the opere pie, vast traditional networks of public welfare and charity, which were often inefficient, corrupt, and monopolized by the Church. Leo condemned the law as an attack on private charity and the Church. The new penal code punished any priest who "publicly blames or belittles the institutions, the laws of the state, or the acts of authority."[47]

As tensions escalated in 1888, the Holy See invoked solidarity from Catholics throughout the world. Cardinal Gibbons of Baltimore discussed the matter with several bishops who then published a letter to Leo. It attacked the conquest of Rome, criticized the Law of Guarantees, and called for the restoration of the temporal power. All American archbishops approved of the letter except Peter Richard Kenrick of St. Louis, who deviated from the ideology of the Roman Question privately in a letter to Gibbons: He "decline[d] to sign any letter to His Holiness in which the question of the Temporal Power would be introduced. The sooner that it becomes known to the Holy Father that there is a diversity of opinion on that subject among the Bishops, the better will it be for Religion." Kenrick had opposed the proclamation of papal infallibility at Vatican Council I, but he eventually, like every American bishop, accepted the teaching. If a "diversity of opinion" truly existed regarding the temporal power as Kenrick suggested, the bishops hid it well from their ultramontane flock and Vatican superiors.[48]

The American Catholic press backed Leo during these years when the Sinistra escalated tension with an intransigent Vatican. The front page of Baltimore's Catholic Mirror detailed the sad Roman events in a front-page column. It printed Leo's 1888 Christmas allocution in which the pontiff declared, "war is systematically declared against everything Catholic" in Italy. Against the Holy See and the person of the pope "there is complete license, even to the extent of insults and threats from the mob." Catholic editorials insisted Crispi undermined liberal freedoms. The government "chokes the voice of Catholic Italy . . . to prevent . . . all such proof of its readiness to defend the cause of the Papacy." Alongside an address by popular Father Bernard O'Reilly entitled "Restoring the Temporal Power," the Catholic Mirror called upon Catholics to pressure the government to aid the Holy Father. "With our Catholic population of ten or twelve millions our voice should swell to thunder. . . . No government can ignore the voice of any considerable number of the people, especially a government like ours."[49] The Catholic Standard predicted "Crispi's Folly," his "religious persecution" of Catholics, could not undermine Catholic international power that would lead to the restoration of the pope-king. Commenting on Gladstone's claim that the "Pope's temporal power is incompatible with the liberty and unity of Italy," the Catholic Standard insisted the temporal power "would be, were it restored to the Holy Father, the strongest possible support and guarantee of Italian freedom and unity."[50]

After Crispi's death, John O'Shea, a prolific Catholic author, reviewed the career of "the last of the quartette of sinister renown. . . . [Crispi] was a mixture of the statesman Cavour, in his profound dissembling mind; the wily conspirator Mazzini, in his readiness to adapt himself to any and every condition to gain his ends; of the impetuous and sensual Garibaldi, in his proneness to get into a fight for fighting's sake." O'Shea employed racial tropes to disparage the deceased. "Although Palermo was his birthplace, he was of Albanian blood—an evil strain, for the Albanians are the descendants of renegade Christians, who . . . renounced their religion and adopted that of their Moslem conquerors." Crispi's "ferocity" and "Sicilian cunning" signified he had been "a member of the Mafia." O'Shea

pilloried the deceased's religious views that "differed in nothing from an atheist. Long association with men of murder and intrigue had obliterated every trace
of that religious instruction he had imbibed in his childhood." O'Shea closed his
unhappy obituary contrasting the happy rule of the Papal States to vice-infected,
criminal-ridden, poverty-stricken Liberal Italy.[51] But even more than Crispi, the
legacy of Giordano Bruno impassioned Catholics in their symbolic contest for
Rome.

Italy-Vatican relations scraped rock bottom when monuments defacing papal
Rome violated the architectural integrity of the Catholic Jerusalem. On 9 June
1889, Pentecost Sunday, a procession from Piazza Esedra made its way down via
Nazionale toward Piazza Venezia and on to Campo de' Fiori to unveil just such
a monument. The anticlerical *Messagero* boasted the marchers numbered 20,000;
Civiltà Cattolica came to an ultramontane reckoning of 5,000. The procession included gray-haired Garibaldini, university professors, municipal politicians, Masonic lodges, and an assortment of freethinkers and atheists. Both the principal
orator and the monument's sculptor were radical deputies and Masons.[52]

The statue to Giordano Bruno (1550–1600) erected in Campo de' Fiori, where
the Inquisition had burned alive the Dominican for his heretical neoplatonism,
became a venerated pilgrimage site among freethinkers. Keen to laud Bruno as
a precursor to modern science, a University of Rome committee had envisioned
a modest statue within the university. But when the committee attracted formidable patrons—Victor Hugo, Ernest Renan, Herbert Spencer, George Ibsen,
Ernst Haeckel—demonstrators demanded a monument in Campo de' Fiori. After
Rome's liberal city council—elected after Torlonia had been dismissed—approved
the site, a preliminary commemoration held in February 1889 led to riotous cries
for a raid on the Vatican. Afraid the unveiling in June might culminate in just such
an assault, Leo XIII considered fleeing the Eternal City. Instead, he passed the day
fasting, prostrate at the feet of a statue of St. Peter.[53]

Bruno was a provocative symbol, invoked as a precursor of progress, science,
and freedom of thought against clerical obscurantism. Msgr. Pietro Balan of
the Opera dei Congressi denounced Bruno supporters as "foreigners, Jews, atheists, and Masons." *Civiltà Cattolica* discerned divine retribution: "From the day on
which hands were laid upon [Bruno's] monument, disasters of every type, such as
floods, avalanches, hurricanes, and similar phenomena have brought desolation
to the countryside of several provinces." The Jesuit organ dubbed Campo de' Fiori
(the field of flowers) "Campo maledetto" (the cursed field) and considered the
monument a triumph of "the rages of the Synagogue, the archabbot of Masonry
and the faction heads of demagogic liberalism."[54]

Leo's 30 June allocution demonized the Dominican "pantheist and material-
ist." Bruno "was . . . deceitful, mendacious, selfish, intolerant of others, a flat-
terer, of abject mind and evil disposition." His contemporary advocates were like

"the secret societies which are striving to alienate whole peoples from God, and fight with infinite hate and unceasing strife against the church and the Roman Pontificate." Leo mourned how the monument had been built in Rome, the "city of faith in which God has placed his Vicar to dwell." "To this have the times led that we should see the abomination of desolation in the holy place." American Catholics took up cudgels against Bruno for decades.[55]

Baltimore's *Catholic Mirror* anticipated the Bruno unveiling by "infidels of all types" as "an extraordinary exhibition of hatred and intolerance in the name of 'liberty.'" The *Catholic Standard* stuttered in disbelief: "For the first time in a political procession in the streets of Rome were seen women, anticlerical women! walking four abreast and bearing a huge bronze wreath to lay at the feet of the statue. That Roman women, formerly so retiring, so home-keeping that they were rarely seen in the streets, . . . should thus forget themselves is indeed a bad sign." The *Catholic Standard* declared, "no person outside of a lunatic asylum would say that the Pope is free." "Brunomaniacs" promoted "Brunomania" in the Eternal City.[56]

Bishop Winand Wigger of Newark reiterated the ideology of the Roman Question in a visceral letter read in his churches. A monument was unveiled in Rome to "honor the memory of a certain apostate monk, infamous for his pantheism . . . and his grossly immoral life." After castigating Bruno, Wigger appealed to the affections of his flock. "What must have been the feelings of the aged and venerable Pontiff on that Pentecost Sunday, so impiously desecrated by such sacrilege! What must have been his grief and sorrow to know that so great an outrage was publicly committed in his own city—none the less *his own* because robbed from him by a usurping government!" Wigger wondered, "What security is there for even the life of the Holy Father, when the government itself aids and abets his most inveterate enemies in carrying out impious and nefarious schemes. . . ? Events like this show clearly how important, nay how *necessary* it is that the Pope be free, that his temporal dominions be restored to him."[57]

Brunomania endured into the twentieth century, when Brunomaniacs took Chicago's West Side by storm. In October 1903, the archdiocesan *New World* pondered, "Was Giordano Bruno a saint? Did the entry of Victor Emmanuel into Rome, by which the Pope was robbed of his possessions, result in liberty of thought? If not so, is it well that sincere Catholics should take part in a demonstration which is intended to celebrate the robbery of the Holy Father, the glory of Bruno, . . . and to exalt Christless freethinkers generally?"[58] These mild inquiries degenerated into a journalistic street fight when Father Edmund Dunne and Alessandro Mastrovalerio, the anticlerical editor of *La Tribuna Italiana Transatlantica*, faced off. Dunne had organized West Side Italians into Holy Guardian Angel parish in 1899, before he became chancellor of the archdiocese in 1904 and Peoria's bishop in 1909. His polemic with Mastrovalerio preceded his 1908 clash with Jane Addams and Hull-House. But the earlier conflict also involved Addams, because Mastrovalerio lived and taught at Hull-House and championed the Giordano Bruno Society, which Hull-House hosted.[59]

The combatants rattled swords when Mastrovalerio promoted the name "Garibaldi" for a new school in the Italian neighborhood. Garibaldi, according to Dunne, was nothing more than "an ignorant bushwhacker, notorious for desecrating and looting churches and monasteries." Mastrovalerio, in response, identified Catholic ideology with Irish interests that worked to the detriment of Italians. He queried, "in order to please a few fanatical Irishmen must we ignore those who, from Dante down to the present day, have desired the freedom of their native country" and given their "blood to liberate it from foreign, domestic, and above all, from Papal tyranny? . . . If the *New World* imagines it has succeeded in having 'doped' the patriotism of Chicago Italians with societies of Saints and Madonnas . . . we assure it that it is very much mistaken." Father Dunne returned, "the papacy has been the greatest benefactor the Italian people ever had." What "are the blessings resulting from the Italian revolution? National bankruptcy, starvation, the forced emigration of the inhabitants." The movement to name the school "Garibaldi" failed.[60]

When an Italian shot and killed a priest in Denver in 1908, the emboldened Dunne linked the crime to the Giordano Bruno Society that had met at Hull-House and to the same society in Rome, where it "has figured luridly in the recent war on religion in Italy." Dunne claimed the Roman Bruno Society "draws its membership entirely from free masons, republicans, socialists, and anarchists," while its Chicago subsidiary was a menace, "an evil thing that city police would do well to kill." The *New World* also moved against "Mother Jane Addams, the . . . patron saint of anti-Catholic bigotry in this city." Indeed, a 25 April *New World* editorial dismissed all settlement houses as "mere roosting-places for frowsy anarchists, fierce-eyed socialists, professed anti-clericals and a coterie of long-haired sociologists."[61]

Addams's response in the *Chicago Tribune* was a model of calm prose that presented a pointedly liberal ideology as if it were a neutral expression of common sense. Italians in her neighborhood, she explained, "are strong admirers of Garibaldi and adherents to the king." Hull-House's Mazzini Club "is . . . devoted to the study of modern Italian literature and history." "Although viewing modern Italy from the monarchist point of view," the club "always maintained a non-controversial attitude." Its "most successful public meeting . . . was held at Hull house on Sept[ember] 20 for the benefit of the eight Garibaldian veterans still surviving in Chicago. A good sum of money was realized and at the same time the 20th of September, which is the Fourth of July of Italy, was celebrated."[62]

Addams set forth her (mis)understanding of Liberal Italy. "The liberality and tolerance of the Italian has been shown in many ways. A statue to Giordano Bruno has been erected in Rome itself on the spot where he was burned for his scientific views." Interpreting the controversial monument as a sign of growing tolerance, Addams claimed Church-state conflict in Italy "is fast dying out and it seems deplorable that it should be continued in Chicago." The "anti-clerical party in Italy," by which Addams apparently meant the liberal ruling elite, supported "the authority of the church in spiritual matters. Doubtless it has many foes of the church in its ranks, but also many devout Catholics and priests."[63]

Addams's apologia for Hull-House as a neutral space rang hollow. Her settlement hosted a club named for Mazzini, whose bust stood in Hull-House. The club studied Italian history taught by Mastrovalerio from a "monarchist point of view." Hull-House celebrated the 20th of September, housed a vociferous Italian anticlerical, and hosted an anticlerical society named for Giordano Bruno. As Addams wrote in *Twenty Years at Hull-House* (1910), "One of our earliest Italian events was a rousing commemoration of Garibaldi's Birthday, and his imposing bust presented to Hull-House that evening, was long the chief ornament of our front hall." Clearly Hull-House served as a liberal nationalist resource for activists who competed with the Church for hegemony over the Italian diaspora.[64]

Dunne responded to Addams in the *Chicago Tribune*. Addams was "in blissful ignorance of the filthy, obscene, and mendacious diatribes that have been launched periodically against the clergy by Mr. Mastro Valerio, who derives a quasi social standing from the fact that he resided in Hull-House for quite a number of years." Dunne maneuvered to avoid direct confrontation with Addams, who is "neither anarchist nor socialist." But it was nevertheless "natural for people there in the neighborhood to conclude that Hull-House must be anti-Catholic and anticlerical, since the enemies of the clergy make Hull-House their rendezvous." If his letter to the *Tribune* was measured, the *New World*'s version of Dunne's response added a combative passage for Catholic consumption. "When the chief of police declares that social settlements are first cousins to the anarchists, we are not prepared to say whether the relationship is in the first or second degree. Recent developments go to show that the anticlerical infidel Giordano Bruno Club, whose members believe in the overthrow of the Catholic clergy, can legitimately claim the head of at least one social settlement as its patroness and defender."[65]

Brunomania did not end in 1908. In 1910 Vatican secretary of state Cardinal Raffaele Merry del Val felt compelled to instruct the apostolic delegation in Washington to protest to the Italian ambassador in the United States against Bruno celebrations.[66] In Chicago in 1914, a new Bruno Society found refuge in Hull-House, where it produced an anticlerical play, *Galileo Galilei*. Predictably, the *New World* protested. Addams claimed she "had been told by an Italian that [the new Bruno Society] consisted of a very fine body of young Italians." A Hull-House committee had determined that since the settlement "was absolutely nonsectarian and . . . the anticlerical movement was a national issue in Italy there was no reason why [the Bruno Society] should not be represented at Hull-House."

In addition, the Bruno Society held a public discussion at Hull-House entitled "The Philosopher of Nola and the Victim of the Infamy of the Catholic Church." The *New World* summarized, "in Miss Addams the Giordano Bruno Society has an ardent defender." Catholics wondered: "Is it not a gratuitous offense to Catholicity?"[67]

The 20th of September

The 20th of September was another inflammatory anti-Catholic symbol that generated heat between American Catholics and their neighbors. On the 20th of September, liberals recalled their "liberation" from papal tyranny and the completion of the Risorgimento. Catholics, in turn, mourned the vile day as a crucifixion of their Holy Father, when the pernicious transalpine usurper imprisoned Christ's Vicar.

In 1895, Liberal Italy celebrated the twenty-fifth anniversary of the 20th of September with pomp and pageantry and declared it a permanent national holiday. The state solicited a popular national hymn in a contest among poets and musicians. Prime Minister Crispi officiated at a ceremony where 20,000 gathered, including the king and 200 aged Garibaldini, on the Janiculum Hill to witness the unfurling of an enormous equestrian statue of Giuseppe Garibaldi, ten years in the making, serenely overlooking the conquered Vatican. Crispi assured the crowd that the destruction of the temporal power "was the fulfillment of God's will, just as it had been the will of the Almighty that Italy . . . should be restored to unity." He counseled, "material power eludes [the pope], and it would be a virtue if he had the wisdom to forget about it." That afternoon Crispi led 50,000 in a procession to the Porta Pia where another monument—an ancient column with a statue of Victory—was erected. The offensive festivities provided the Holy See with another occasion to launch international protests.[68]

The Holy See directed Catholics to denounce the 20th of September festivities. After Leo maligned the Italian government in a public letter, Secretary of State Rampolla instructed his nuncios and apostolic delegations to present the letter to the governments where they resided and to encourage Catholics to broadcast Leo's dissent so that it might receive "favorable commentary in the newspapers." Apostolic Delegate Francesco Satolli summarized Leo's letter for the U.S. secretary of state, Richard Olney. The Holy See, he explained, was unjustly deprived of its temporal power, with disastrous moral and religious consequences. The architects of Liberal Italy were motivated "not by any sincere desire for the union and prosperity of Italy" but by "a spirit of implacable hostility to the Church, and to that which she represents—the interests and government of the Divine Ruler of the world." The Italian nation did not consent to the violence perpetrated upon the pope. It was the papacy, in fact, that "in the course of centuries had brought to the Italian name and nation" glory and "might still form the true greatness of the [Italian] people."[69] When compared to Catholic protests in other states, American Catholics exceeded their European counterparts in the intensity with which they performed the ideology of the Roman Question.

Catholics in the Netherlands and Belgium reacted weakly to Leo's invitation for support. Amsterdam's *Tyd* published a "violent article against Italy" on 11 September, and the "intransigent party" demonstrated against the approaching holiday. In addition, surviving Dutch Zouaves held a reunion to denounce the celebrations. The Italian ambassador in Brussels detected nothing threatening among Belgian Catholics, whose proclamations of solidarity were sent to Leo after some churches held religious ceremonies. A priest brought together aging papal Zouaves in Brussels, and "a similar reunion took place in Antwerp but it went unobserved by the eyes of most. The Catholic papers that have spoken of it have taken care to keep silent on a number of the interventions, which perhaps, if known, would arouse laughter."[70]

The Italian embassy in Vienna reported a moderate reaction. Austrian leaders, directed by the Vatican, instructed the faithful to restrict their resistance to devotional activity. The *Bulletin of the Archdiocese of Vienna* read: "With most profound sadness for all true Catholics, the Supreme Head of our Holy Church is no longer in possession of the Eternal City and is surrounded by tribulations and dangers of every sort." The *Bulletin* urged all Catholics on Sunday, 22 September, to offer "most fervent prayers to the God of Mercy who wants to take into His holy protection the Supreme Head of our Church and benignly liberate him from every tribulation and danger." Catholics were instructed to adore the Blessed Sacrament and to say three Hail Mary's. Vienna's clerical *Vaterland* published a letter from the Austrian episcopacy to the pope, but the Italian ambassador reckoned, "except for calling the taking of Rome in 1870 a crime," it merited no attention. "Neither Italy nor its King nor its government are named. Compared to other clerical documents in other countries and even in Italy, this address seems relatively moderate."[71]

German Catholics turned up the heat, instigating minor state intervention. The bishop of Münster published a letter in the *National Zeitung* on 17 September urging the faithful to denounce the festival that glorified "the ignominious success of a revolution that had robbed the Holy See of its territory." The Italian ambassador in Berlin discussed the letter with Baron Friederich von Holstein at the Foreign Ministry. Holstein, he said, voiced "displeasure with the conduct of the bishop of Münster, and spoke to me of the difficulties the Catholic clergy create for the Imperial government." Münster's prefect lodged a grievance with church authorities. Speaking to the ambassador, Chancellor Adolf Marschall von Bieberstein described the bishop "as an intellectually weak fanatic who believed other German bishops would follow his crusade, but soon realized that he was alone" in insulting "a government friendly with Germany." In light of the chancellor's explanation, the Italian ambassador did not register a formal complaint.[72]

Bavarian Catholics were also outspoken, triggering informal state intervention. At the forty-second annual German Catholic Congress, members of the upper house of the Bavarian parliament attacked Liberal Italy. Neo-Thomist philosopher Georg Baron von Hertling of the University of Munich, a Center Party expert on economics, asserted that the monuments of Christian martyrs and the sacred atmosphere of papal Rome had been destroyed since 1870. The "Pope is no longer the leader of Rome, but rather a prisoner. . . . The 20th of September did not bring a solution but rather it brought conflict; Catholics will not rest until this conflict is settled." Other speakers referred to Liberal Italy as the "enemy of the papacy" and the 20th of September as "the sacrilegious robbery of the Holy See." The Bavarian hierarchy followed the same papal directives as the Austrians — adoration of the Blessed Sacrament and prayers on 22 September. A Bavarian official explained to the Italian legate in Munich that the Catholic dissent was within the bounds of the law and did not justify intervention. He did, however, register with the Ministry of Cults the concern of the Italian government with inflammatory language the bishop of Regensburg had employed against Liberal Italy.[73]

The Spanish hierarchy supported the pope as it attacked Liberal Italy in a letter of protest published by Cardinal Antolín Monescillo y Viso. It provoked immediately ridicule from El Nacional, an unofficial organ of the government. The Italian ambassador in Madrid dismissed the letter and agreed with Spain's minister of justice that it warranted no official response. A Spanish duke assured the ambassador that Catholic protests had only negative effects on the Spanish people and that the government would distance itself from clerical agitation.[74]

In comparison to Europeans, American Catholics responded most forcefully. Preexisting affections for the Holy Father simplified the organization of mass protests. Italian ambassador Saverio Fava explained how American bishops used the 20th of September as a "pretext to stir up the question of the temporal power and attract the attention of the American public." The agitation gave rise to a Catholic "organization having as its aim the re-establishment of the temporal power," but Fava stressed that these sentiments were not new. Every pilgrimage and episcopal visit to the Eternal City began with Catholic addresses to arouse emotions concerning the Roman Question. Fava did not believe non-Catholics took the "impotent maneuvering of intransigent Catholics" too seriously, but the New York newspapers always covered the Catholic protests.[75]

Following Satolli's directives, American bishops mobilized. In a circular to the American episcopacy, Cardinal Gibbons referred to the 20th of September as the anniversary of an "occupation of what had for centuries been papal dominions." He invoked "the faithful children of the Church throughout the world" to unite in "praying to heaven for the freedom and independence of the Pope." Archbishop John Kain of St. Louis instructed his clergy to organize a day of prayer. His chancellor acknowledged that the instruction was tantamount to a call to restore the temporal power. The bishops of Wisconsin recalled how King Vittorio had "robbed the head of Christendom of the last remnant of his temporal dominion, the city of Rome. While Masonic Italy celebrated the memory of this sacrilegious usurpation, it behooves the children of the Church to loudly proclaim their unabated loyalty and hearty affection toward the Holy Father, their strong lasting protest against his despoliation and captivity."[76]

New York Catholics gathered in mass meetings. Archbishop Corrigan addressed his flock on the 20th of September. "There is one sentiment which inspires our souls this evening, and that is one of affection and devotion to the holy father, and of deepest sympathy for the wrong which the sovereign pontiff has been suffering for the past twenty-five years." Catholics had not forgotten how "an invading army in the time of peace entered the city of Rome." Gotham's German Catholics met to proclaim solidarity with their Holy Father. "No lapse of time will ever make that right which is against the principles of justice and charity, and the deed of twenty-five years ago, when an invading army in the time of peace entered the city of Rome in a sin that cannot be condoned." Their meeting concluded: "three cheers . . . for the 'Pope-King.'"[77]

On 7 October, Bishop Michael Tierney of Hartford sent Satolli a notebook, "Meetings in behalf of the Temp. Power of the Pope," bursting with thirty-two pages of newspapers clippings. "In compliance with your letter," Tierney explained, "meetings were held last month everywhere throughout this diocese in protest against the spoliation of the Papal States."[78] The notebook demonstrated how all across Connecticut Catholics had gathered, reiterated the ideology of the Roman Question, and passed resolutions declaring steadfast loyalty to their Holy Father.

In Hartford, Tierney presided over the gathering while laymen hammered away at Liberal Italy. Cornelius O'Neil outlined a history of the Papal States. "There has never been a time since the conversion of Constantine when the independence of the Pope has been more vitally necessary than now, because in no previous age has the civil authority so openly declared itself unchristian." George Bailey hit harder: "The Pope's temporal power was not questioned until the greed and avarice of a king caused his overthrow." Judge Thomas McManus found it "eminently fitting that amid the blare and the glare of the royal festivities [in Italy], the spirit of the sovereign pontiff should be consoled by messages from his loving children in every land." The papacy alone, McManus insisted, gave Rome stature. "Give to Rome all the existing monuments of her Pagan Emperors and what are they? Crumbling, tottering ruins. Add the glories bestowed by her secular rulers, her dukes, princes, kings—you have only an accumulated ruin. . . . Remove the Vatican and its galleries, its museums, its libraries, and there is no Rome."[79]

In New Britain, Judge Walsh asserted, "Victor Emmanuel, in violation of every law, human and divine, entered the Eternal City and despoiled the Pope of his power. It was robbery as much as is the stealing of a note." Judge Roche linked the status of papal Rome to Catholic liberties throughout the world. "The pope's temporal power is all the more a necessity as he is a subject of the Italian government, and as such, subject to its whims and injustices. It is necessary that the place of our faith should be free from all powers, and that 250,000,000 Catholics should be secure in their personal liberty and right of action." Attorney P. J. Markley linked Liberal Italy's weakness to the Roman Question. He sneered, "the history of the past twenty-five years is the history of an overtaxed and down-trodden people."[80]

In the *Catholic World*, John O'Shea lashed out: "Is the civilized world, in its sober senses, to be asked to countenance the principle that violence and plunder are permissible because the plunderer is strong and the victim weak? This is, indeed, the principle which Italy is asking the world to sanction by its celebration of the events of Porta Pia." O'Shea maintained, "if Italy is to be saved from destruction — from the triumph of blaspheming socialism on the one hand, and the dishonorable grave of national bankruptcy on the other — it must be through a restoration of the freedom of the church and a reconciliation with the foremost of Italian citizens, the illustrious occupant of the Chair of Peter. By such a reconciliation the vast power of Catholic Italy . . . would be liberated and set in motion to stimulate the pulses of the national life." Paulist editor, the "liberal" Catholic, Augustine Hewit appended an endorsement of O'Shea. "I desire and I hope that the wicked party of the invaders and oppressors of Rome may be speedily overthrown, and Leo XIII be seated, in triumph and security, on the throne of his predecessors."[81]

As Catholics mourned, some Italians in New Haven held joyful parades, banquets, concerts, and dances. At a Catholic rally in St. Patrick's Hall, Father Ermenegildo Battaglia insisted "that the class of Italians who intended to celebrate [the 20th of September] were not true Catholics; . . . True Italian Catholics . . . would join heartily in [the protest]." Salvatore Maresca, president of the Society Concordia, feared malevolent Catholic designs to "molest [Italians] in our peaceful enjoyment" of Liberal Italy's national holiday. He explained to New Haven's mayor how the Society Concordia had been "chosen by the Italian colony of this city to arrange the celebration of the twenty-fifth anniversary of the delivery of our country and our consciences from the yoke of the pope." Maresca felt "in duty bound to call the attention of the authorities to the current rumors of violent protest against us on the part of the Catholic element in this city." Maresca insisted that "the 20th of September is our Fourth of July. . . . It is the realization of the . . . dreams of our martyrs from Dante to Mazzini. . . . The Catholics of America not need misinterpret our demonstration; it is not an anti-Christian movement. It is rather a loud recognition and defense of the doctrine of Christ: 'Render therefore unto Caesar the things which are Caesar's; and unto God the things that are God's.'"[82]

In Chicago, the secular press disapproved of Catholic protests and suggested that meddling in Italy's affairs might create diplomatic complications harmful to the United States. Disregarding the warning, the archbishop of Chicago and the bishops of Wisconsin issued circular letters protesting the holiday. However, Italians in Chicago, alongside Italian consul Antonio Ladislao Rozwadowski, reveled in the anniversary of Rome's liberation. After participating in several afternoon banquets, Rozwadowski, a practicing Catholic, joined the Italia Club on the evening of the 20th of September. "Italians of every class and some notable American families of the city that in a special way sympathized with the Italian element" gathered for a concert and dance.[83]

On 22 September, 4,000 Chicago Italians from more than thirty mutual benefit societies in 200 decorated carriages made their way to Haymarket Square, where they launched a massive parade. "A great crowd of spectators thronged the pavement and the streets," and "a dozen bands leading the marching parties alternately played the popular and patriotic airs of Italy and America." As the parade made its way through the city, Rozwadowski, Governor John Peter Altgeld, and Mayor George Swift reviewed the procession. The societies and clubs demonstrated the ideological mixing common among Italians. Clubs named for Garibaldi and King Umberto mingled with parish societies whose patrons were madonnas and saints.[84]

In a 1905 history of the Church in New York, John Talbot Smith confirmed, "nothing more hateful to American Catholics could be named than the 20th of September, which the Italian colony celebrated as the consummation of national glory. . . . For very slight cause the Irish would at any moment have attacked the annual procession, eager to drive the Garibaldians off the face of the earth . . . ; and as for considering them Catholics and aiding them to keep their faith alive, that was out of the question." Clearly, the presence of Italians in the United States, many of whom celebrated the symbols of Liberal Italy, provided frequent occasions to reproduce and intensify Catholic commitments to the ideology of the Roman Question.[85]

The secular press supported Liberal Italy during the 20th of September celebrations. Although an editorial in New York's Daily Tribune acknowledged the problem of Italian political corruption and a "military system" that "weighed cruelly upon the people," it blamed centuries of foreign rule for these weaknesses. "Italian unity is on the whole a blessing to the Italian people." The editor suspected that "only a small minority of the Italian people" stood behind "the prelates of the Roman Church" who "have commanded their flocks to observe [the 20th of September] as a time of humiliation and prayer for Papal restoration."

Pope Leo, the editor concluded, "is no more a prisoner than is the Archbishop of
Canterbury." Similarly, the *New York Sun* praised Liberal Italy and the monument
to Garibaldi, "the great liberator." The *Sun* traced flaws in Liberal Italy to "the neglect of centuries." While "*Roma Capitale* has been no unmixed blessing," Italy is
once again "squaring her shoulders to her burden."[86]

The Methodist *Christian Advocate* of New York took the 20th of September as
an opportunity to endorse Crispi and criticize the Church. "Since Christianity
could conquer the world without arms," why does "the Vatican desire a civil prin-
cipality?" The *Advocate* accused Archbishop Corrigan of hypocrisy. "If [he] really
considered the force of his own words when he said that 'no lapse of time will ever
make that right which is against the principles of justice of charity,' what would
become of a large proportion of the claims of the Roman Catholic Church?" Methodists already knew the answer.[87]

An Italian diplomat in New York, tracking Catholic activities, believed it was "a
radical error among many politicians and liberals in Italy and abroad" to believe
the power of Catholicism was diminishing. Sensitive to the international context
of the Italy-Vatican contest and its unpredictable future, he asserted that Catholic
protests "demonstrated the goals and tendencies of Vatican politics. They aim in
the long run to realize their goals; if not now, they prepare the terrain for a day
when some conflagration permits the Vatican to become a force once again. It will
then enter the game strong and ready with clear objectives." He believed that "the
mission of every royal [state] agent, . . . in every part of the world" was "to keep
an eye on these secret attempts" to strengthen Catholic solidarity. The struggle
against the Church knew no national borders. It was "played out in a vast universe where Vaticanism grows before our eyes . . . to inspire among its neophytes
the primary idea that the pope is a prisoner who ought to be free." This astute
observer emphasized the growth of Catholic power in America and foresaw the
international power of the American Church in the future. His insight was prophetic, as we shall see, when we consider the "conflagration" of the Great War
and the rise of Italian Fascism in the 1920s.[88]

The Vittoriano

Another symbol that inspired an American Catholic assault upon Liberal Italy was
the massive monument to King Vittorio Emanuele II. After the conquest of papal
Rome, the architecture and urban design of the Eternal City became a violent
ideological battlefield. Catholic observers ridiculed the "huge and tasteless structures of the new Rome" that brought a false "aspect of stability . . . to the Italian
sojourn" in the Eternal City. They linked the "sickly self-conscious artificiality of
stucco Rome" and the "great damage" its "appetite for bigness" had inflicted to

the degeneration of Liberal Italy. Vast public building projects in the last three decades of the century had caused "debt and collapse, leaving in its stead ruin."[89]

Liberal Italy had indeed intended to subvert papal Rome. The principal target of liberal innovation was Counter-Reformation urban designer Pope Sixtus V (1585–90). Sixtus repaired ancient aqueducts to enhance the water supply and restore fountains. He constructed bridges across the Tiber and improved roads to dramatize the polycentric character of papal Rome. Under his guidance new streets, such as one radiating from Santa Maria Maggiore to St. John Lateran, linked Rome's basilicas and encouraged new settlements. Sixtus had massive obelisks moved to accent street crossings that pilgrims encountered en route to imposing structures of the Church militant. Sixtus himself alarmed traditionalists as he mercilessly demolished ancient buildings and attempted, without success, to transform the Colosseum into a wool factory.[90]

Liberal Italy, in turn, set out to modernize the sleepy city and improve its unhygienic housing conditions. Public works projects undermined pastoral charms that Catholics remembered with nostalgia. The government appropriated lovely villas, convents, and palaces of the "black" nobility, those who remained loyal to the pope and snubbed the "foreign" House of Savoy. The road from the Porta Pia, where the army had entered papal Rome on the 20th of September 1870, to the Quirinal Palace, the pope's former residence, had its name changed from via Pia to via XX Settembre. After the king took the Quirinal from the pope, via XX Settembre hosted the new ministries of war and finance. On one of its corners, the American Methodist Episcopal Church dug in and began a seventy-year proselytizing campaign that never ceased to outrage popes and American Catholics. The imitation of a Parisian boulevard constructed between the Quirinal and Termini station, completed in 1876, took the name via Nazionale, replacing its predecessor, via de Merode, named after the former Belgian cardinal and papal minister of war. Americans constructed an Episcopal church, St. Paul's Within the Walls, off via Nazionale, another blight on papal Rome. More than any structure, the enormous white marble monument to King Vittorio Emanuele II, the Vittoriano, made architectural purists shudder. Overlooking Piazza Venezia at the end of the Corso, the Vittoriano irked both Catholics and observers of the new Italy who clung to fanciful memories of overdressed *monsignori* scuttling about to avoid ornate carriages of cardinals clopping through the ancient city.[91]

After King Vittorio's death in 1878, municipal and national governments called for a monument to honor the Father of the *Patria*. On 16 May a commission announced an international competition of architectural proposals and selected the Capitol Hill as the site for the monument. Giuseppe Sacconi's ambitious, eclectic design became the basis for the Vittoriano, whose first stone was laid in March 1885. The dense symbolism of the Vittoriano, an object of recurring debate among political factions over the next thirty years, honored classical virtues, Risorgimento heroes, and the many regions of united Italy. Vittorio's bronze statue on horseback sits at the center of the 500-foot-long, 200-foot-high marble mass on the northern slope of the Capitol, behind which the Forum reaches out toward the Colosseum.[92]

America, the Jesuit weekly, attacked the "fearsome sight" and "marble folly" as a fitting monument to Vittorio, the "Sardinian upstart." "Rarely indeed does a national monument tell its own story frankly or portray faithfully the ethos of the event it is designed to commemorate. . . . In this respect the monument of Victor Emmanuel is a masterpiece." The event in question, the Risorgimento, was "a comic opera," cast with "a red-shirted Falstaff" who worked alongside "the choicest collection that the ranks of the Carbonari could furnish" and a chorus "recruited from the streets." Although "Imperial Rome and Papal Rome had their faults, . . . each upheld the dignity and majesty of a world power. They may be hated, but they must be respected." Papal Rome had been "the City of the Soul, the delight and despair of every cultured and discriminating mortal who has ever beheld it." But it was "here, of all places in Italy and the habitable world, a ridiculous, usurping government has chosen with monumental idiocy to build a tasteless memorial to a king who in life never dared to sleep in the stolen Papal palace allotted to him by his fellow-thieves."[93]

Anglo-Americans, like poet Lilian Whiting, did not share this harsh reading of Liberal Italy. In 1907, anticipating the completion of the Vittoriano in 1914, Whiting calculated that the "great monument to Victor Emmanuel will be of the most artistic and beautiful order. . . . All the old buildings in the vicinity will be torn down to give a fine vista for this transcendently noble and sumptuous memorial." Even under its new rulers, she found Rome "a city of spiritual symbolism." Historian of Italy William Roscoe Thayer, commenting in 1907, believed there was "a new spirit in the air, a more hopeful tone, a feeling that an era of true prosperity lies just ahead." Thayer noted the "new broad streets," which "bring light and pure air into what were lately the most unhealthy wards of Rome." Liberal Italy's ability to survive and tolerate "the sleepless, unscrupulous, far-reaching enmity of the Vatican" reflected commendable strength.[94]

ALTHOUGH HISTORIANS have insisted that the Roman Question meant little to American Catholics, the end of the temporal power in fact had far-reaching implications for Catholics and their American neighbors who argued in word and ritual to define the meaning of Rome and Italy. American Catholics preserved and strengthened the ideology of the Roman Question, which became a constituent element of their culture and linked them to Catholics throughout the world. Although a Catholic resolution to the Roman Question appeared unlikely at the turn of the century, astute observers understood that the Vatican was waiting for a more opportune moment when international events might create an opening to restore the pope-king. The theological, journalistic, ritual, and devotional performance of the ideology of the Roman Question, in the meantime, kept Catholics prepared for that day. It also separated them from their American neighbors and reminded them that the pernicious cause of secularization, warfare, injustice, and the degeneration of civilization was a fallen liberal world that had attacked the pope, the Church, and God when it conquered papal Rome.

When the Vittoriano was inaugurated on 4 June 1911, the Italian royal family, aged Garibaldini, and 6,000 Italian mayors listened to the carabinieri play the Garibaldi hymn. Ernesto Nathan, Rome's progressive, anticlerical mayor, spoke to his colleagues. "The imposing vast work imagined by Sacconi for the Capitol Hill as the Altar of the *Patria*, with its broad arcade surmounted by the many Italian regions, is not only a monument to the King: it symbolizes the Third Italy!" Nathan had already earned an international reputation as a provocative living symbol of anti-Catholicism. His clashes with the pope and American Catholics during his sojourn to the United States, the subject of the next chapter, marked the last major episode in the period of intransigence.[95]

CHAPTER THREE

The Mayor of Rome
Is an "Atheist Jew," 1910–1914

On the 20th of September 1910, Ernesto Nathan, the mayor of Rome, delivered an antipapal address at the breach in the ancient Roman wall near the Porta Pia. His speech inaugurated plans for the Rome Exhibition of 17 March 1911 to celebrate the fiftieth anniversary of the proclamation of the Kingdom of Italy. Of course, the 20th of September was the very day Italian forces conquered papal Rome in 1870, and the breach near the Porta Pia marked the very site where the army had broken through the wall defended by the pope's army. Nathan's calculated salvo against the ideology of the Roman Question was a dramatic performance that tapped into powerful associations in the international contest between the Church and Liberal Italy.

Nathan contrasted modern Rome, "the champion of liberty of thought," to papal Rome, "the fortress of dogma where the last despairing effort is being made to keep up the reign of ignorance." The progressive mayor lambasted the 1907 papal condemnation of modernism—"the compendium of all heresies." The Vatican, Nathan cut, "thunders forth a ban against men and associations desirous of reconciling the practices and dictates of their faith with the teachings of the intellect, of practical life, of the moral and social aspirations of the civilized world. Like cosmic matter in dissolution, [the Vatican] . . . is the fragment of a spent sun caught within the orbit of the contemporary world." Nathan dismissed the 1870 proclamation of papal infallibility, which "was the inverse of the Biblical revelation of the Son of God become man—it was the son of man who made himself god upon earth." The proclamation of infallibility had been "the last great affirmation before the world of the Rome of the days before the Breach—it was the last pilgrimage to the Pontiff-King."[1]

Mayor Nathan was an English-born liberal with radical democratic roots and a leading Freemason of Jewish descent. The international Catholic campaign against him became most intense in the United States, where, in 1914 and 1915, he served as Liberal Italy's commissioner general and envoy extraordinary to the Panama Pacific International Exposition in San Francisco. American Catholics rose up to express loyalty to their Holy Father through an attack upon Nathan, an unworthy symbol of papal Rome and Catholic Italy. Their intransigent assertion of the ideology of the Roman Question separated Catholics from other Americans who honored Nathan as a prestigious representative of Liberal Italy. Catholic reactions made explicit a covert anti-Semitism embedded within the ideology of the Roman Question.[2]

The International Protests of 1910 and 1911

Pope Pius X (1903–14) responded to Nathan's speech in a public letter that appeared in *Civiltà Cattolica*. "A public functionary," Pius began, "not satisfied with solemnly commemorating the anniversary of the day on which the sacred rights of the Pontifical Sovereignty were trampled under foot, raised his voice to heap abuse and outrage on the doctrines of the Catholic Faith, on the Vicar of Christ on earth, and on the Church itself." Pius invoked support from his spiritual children. The "mass of impious statements, as blasphemous as they are gratuitous, . . . will certainly not escape the notice of the faithful of the whole world, outraged as they are by it. They will be united with Our beloved children of Rome to raise up fervent prayers to the Almighty that He may rise in defense of His Spouse, the Church, so shamefully made a target for calumnies." In response, Nathan quipped that the pope's letter gave further evidence of the gap between Rome's pontifical past and its progressive present.[3]

Historian Matteo Sanfilippo has described the Vatican's international campaign against Nathan. Vatican secretary of state Cardinal Raffaele Merry del Val directed papal nunciatures and apostolic delegations throughout the world to organize protests. Letters of solidarity poured into the Vatican from Berlin to Madrid and from São Paolo to New York. Protests erupted throughout the Catholic world—25,000 Catholics gathered in Montreal, 10,000 in Vienna, 10,000 in Berlin, 9,000 in Santiago, and thousands more marched in Buenos Aires. The campaign tapped into the abundant repository of affective loyalty Catholics harbored for their Church and Holy Father and demonstrated the Holy See's ability to mount symbolic crusades.[4]

The Italian Foreign Ministry nervously tracked the demonstrations. On 26 October 1910, 1,000 Bavarian Catholics met in Munich to protest against Nathan and communicate solidarity with Pius. The *Bayerische Kürier* insisted every Catholic had a duty to condemn the grave offense against the Holy Father, which was not merely an Italian matter. The *Kürier* attacked the popular *Münchner Neuste Nachrichten* for its silence on the issue. In December, demonstrators in Würzburg's churches denounced Nathan. The gatherings culminated in two vast meetings where a Jesuit and a Dominican cudgeled Nathan and "lamented the unworthy and unacceptable position of the Pope, calling for the full independence and liberty of the pontiff."[5]

Aggressive challenges to Liberal Italy erupted in Vienna. On 6 November, following one month of Catholic protests, the vice-burgermeister, Doctor Porzer of Vienna, called upon Austria to occupy Rome and restore the pope's temporal power. A Socialist deputy mocked Porzer's speech as an "ignominious" and "scandalous stain" and asked the Austrian foreign minister to repudiate the attack upon an ally and friendly nation. The liberal press bitterly criticized Porzer, but the Catholic *Reichspost* demanded an international conference to resolve the Roman Question. The Austrian foreign minister implicitly accepted Liberal Italy's position on the status of papacy when he explained to the Italian ambassador that Austria would not get involved in this Italian domestic affair.[6]

Austrian Catholics, however, continued their offensive. Catholic student groups passed an order of the day to denounce Nathan's address. The Viennese Christian Women condemned "the unworthy and abusive offenses pronounced by the Jew Nathan." Austrian liberal defense of Liberal Italy instigated volatile debates in the diets of Trieste and Tyrol over Nathan's speech. In December, the *Bonifazius Blatt*, a monthly published at the Benedictine Abbey in Prague, entered the fray. The abbey's prior, Father Galen, a leading Austrian clerical close to Archduke Francis Ferdinand, distributed the December issue personally at Vienna's cathedral. Demanding a solution to the Roman Question, the *Bonifazius Blatt* called for "our own government to address this concern of the majority of its subjects." "Our Holy Father's cause is our cause, his struggle, our struggle. We state openly, that if no Emperor and no King wants to be the shield of the Church and the Holy See, the Catholic people will assume this mission: blood and riches for our most delightful Holy Pius X."[7]

Responding to Porzer's call for Catholic unity throughout multinational Austria-Hungary, the *Vaterland* announced a mass gathering in Vienna on 4 December. The demonstration against Jews, Freemasons, and socialists demanded an end to Catholic passivity in the face of anti-Catholicism. The Austrian bishops addressed their faithful: "The unspeakable manner in which the Mayor of Rome has dared to insult the pope demonstrates clearly that the time of disrespect toward ecclesiastical authority has arrived." Insisting the matter concerned all Catholics, the bishops attacked liberal newspapers "in Italy and other countries, . . . full of Masonic fervor and hatred against the Church." Referring favorably to Porzer, the bishops called for the "restoration of a state of things that secures the Pope's full and effective liberty and independence."[8]

American Catholics participated fervently in the international campaign. On 26 September, Merry del Val instructed Apostolic Delegate Diomede Falconio, OFM, to alert the American hierarchy to Nathan's "deeply offensive speech."

Nathan's address had already made a splash in New York's *Evening Post*. The pope felt "deep sorrow" at the "anti-clerical speech delivered by Mayor Nathan." The *Post* reported how Pius had called "the attention of not only the faithful in Rome, but of the faithful throughout the world, to the constant and ever-growing offenses against religion perpetrated even by public authorities in the very seat of the Roman Pontiff." The American Church responded to the cue. *America*, the Jesuit weekly, set the pace: "In the Pope's own dominions a usurper rules, while an atheist Jew is the Mayor of the Eternal City."[9]

Over the following months, *America* expounded upon the degeneration of Italy since 1848 and paraded negative images of Jews to castigate Nathan. The Jesuit weekly recast Catholic Holy Week liturgies of the trial and passion of Jesus with contemporary characters. It described how a "howling and blood-thirsty mob gathered before the Praetorium of Pontius Pilate," clamoring for Jesus's execution and Barabbas's freedom. "That was Good Friday morning. At noon they nailed the Christ to the cross." *America* then transposed the event "from the Holy City of the past to the Holy City of the present; from Jerusalem to Rome; from the Praetorium of Pilate to the neighborhood of the Quirinal." Now the pope, "the hated and helpless Vicar of Christ," stood in for Jesus. "The [Italian] political statesmen of to-day" played the role of the spineless Pontius Pilate. The "misguided multitude" of anticlerical Romans who had voted Nathan into office was cast as the Jewish mob. They called for the freedom of their contemporary Barabbas, "Nathan, the Jew! Nathan, the enemy of Christ. . . . We have already made him Mayor of Rome."[10]

America elaborated a distinctly Catholic anti-Semitism. Nineteenth-century Italian Jewry, like Jews elsewhere, was deeply committed to liberalism and its promise of equality and citizenship. The Napoleonic invasion of the Italian peninsula and later the Risorgimento had brought Jewish emancipation from discrimination under Catholic rulers and had liberated Jews from ghettos. Catholic animosity toward Jews, not merely a medieval remnant, intensified in the nineteenth century as Jews aligned themselves with the liberal order the papacy so violently condemned. Sensitive to the affinity between Italian Jewry and the Risorgimento, *America* made an anti-Semitic interpretive leap. It insisted Liberal Italy had become captive to Jews. "Cavour's closest friends were . . . all Jews," and "the Jew bankers, both Italian and French, were indispensable in financing" the Risorgimento. "If a Jew is Mayor of Rome to-day it is only because Italy is paying a political debt. There never could have been a united Italy without the help of Hebrews." *America* reminded its readers of "the Jew boy Mortara," who had been taken from his family by the Inquisition in 1858 to be raised Catholic. "On that occasion Cavour was conspicuous for his ferocious abuse of Pius IX. It was not done merely for political effect though incidentally it served that purpose, but Cavour was intensely and we suppose sincerely Judaic in his affections." In turn, Jews "repaid him with devotion. So that if the Italians are proud of the unification of their country they ought to be satisfied if the men who brought it about are not only rewarded with the highest honors but control its destiny."[11]

America was not alone. Boston's *Pilot* pummeled Nathan the "parvenue [sic], an Englishborn among Romans, a Jew among Christians unable to speak intelligibly the Italian tongue." It lamented the demagoguery and deceit that reigned in a once just and happy land of Catholic rulers. "It has become a saying in Rome, that gentlemen are not wanted at the polls, where the hooligan element reigns supreme." The *Pilot* lambasted Nathan's progressive urban reforms as "attempts to vandalize historic streets and buildings" and as evidence of his sympathy for "anarchist and revolutionary demonstrations."[12] Boston's weekly editorialized about "the unblushing audacity of this English-born Jew," "this ill-mannered and bombastic Hebrew," "the brazen ill-bred utterance of this Masonic irreligious Jew." Nathan had revealed "once again to the world how insincere and valueless is the Italian Law of Guarantees," and he had "brought again to the forefront the Roman question."[13]

Nathan's speech became but another opportunity to reeducate American Catholics about the Roman Question, the injustice of the Law of Guarantees, and the pernicious evils of Masonry. The *Pilot* reminded Catholics of Liberal Italy's ostensible unwillingness to protect the Holy Father from the "hideous mob" that had tried to hurl Pius IX's "coffin into the Tiber" while en route to his final resting place. It referred once again to "the insane followers of Giordano Bruno" who "publicly insult the Holy Father and maltreat the clergy." Nathan, "who espouses the cause of the Modernists," was in fact a man "bound hand and foot to the iron clad will of those secret associations of which he is nominally a leader. . . . He dares not assert his own independence or free will for fear of the lash of deposition or the dagger of some assassin deputed by his lodge to punish those members who pretend to have a will of their own."[14]

Dziennik Chicagoski, the daily published by the Resurrectionist Fathers who worked among Polish immigrants, and *Naród Polski*, the organ of the powerful Polish Roman Catholic Union, also reported Nathan's outrageous speech. The *Dziennik*, however, denied that Catholic protests came at the urging of the Holy See. Faithful Catholics hardly needed prompting from Cardinal Merry del Val to rise up spontaneously in support of the pope.[15]

American Catholic solidarity with the Holy Father revealed once again how affective bonds cultivated since 1848 could be mobilized. Bishops sped off pledges of filial loyalty to Pius, condemning the "blasphemous speech." At a Catholic Club of New York reception, Archbishop John Farley called upon 1,000 willing members "to send a cable to protest to Rome against Nathan. . . . The announcement was received with great applause."[16] Supreme Knight James Flaherty informed Falconio that the Knights of the Columbus "from far and near have kept sending to the Board of Directors of our Order resolutions and letters couched in burning words of protest against the impious and blasphemous utterances of the Mayor of Rome." French Canadians, Holy Name Societies, the National Conference of Catholic Charities—all communicated loyalty to Pius through animosity toward Nathan.[17]

A marked response emanated from German American Catholics. Typical was the resolution of the German Catholic Central Illinois District Federation. It condemned "the unwarranted and vicious attack on the person of our Holy Father and vigorously protest[ed] against such a nefarious conduct." The resolution closed with expressions of "filial love and unswerving loyalty for our Holy Father Pius X."[18] Nicholas Gonner, editor of several German-language and English-language newspapers, mailed Merry del Val a resolution, "one of hundreds" from branches of the massive German Catholic Central-Verein, "to again prove the loyalty and filial devotion of the German-speaking Catholics . . . in these times of persecution of Christ's Vicar on earth." Gonner linked Nathan, the "Jewish-Freemason Mayor of Rome," to "the oppressed condition of our Holy Father."[19]

As Catholics reenacted the ideology of the Roman Question, Pius took steps to counter the anti-Catholic character Liberal Italy had endowed the Rome Exhibition. Pius instructed Catholic mayors to avoid the congress of mayors to be hosted at the exhibition. For those who attended, Pius suggested they pay homage to the pope by visiting his sisters or St. Peter's Cathedral. The Jesuit's *Civiltà Cattolica*, closely linked to the Vatican, described preparations for the jubilee as "a frenzy of sectarian joy" that echoed the nineteenth-century invitation for "international Freemasonry to see the capital of the Catholic world transformed into the capital of a neo-pagan Italy. . . . No Catholic worthy of the name can but regard this year as a year of religious mourning, nor can he do other than oppose festivities which are an insult to his faith."[20]

American Catholics mourned as well. On 12 February 1911, Archbishop Farley instructed his clergy in New York to read a circular letter at their masses reiterating the ideology of the Roman Question. Liberal Italy's celebration was the work of "open and secret enemies of the Holy See," who seek to "prolong the insult implied" in the jubilee that commemorated "the sacrilegious taking of Rome. . . . The evident and declared intent . . . is to inflict the deepest and most poignant pain on the Vicar of Christ in his own city and under his own eyes." Farley reminded his flock that "the insult thus offered to the Holy See, . . . is directed not less against every member of the Catholic Church." He instructed "devoted clergy and faithful people to enter their most emphatic protest against the vile character of this celebration, wherever and whenever an occasion offers to loyally defend the rights of the Vicar of Jesus Christ on earth." Farley called for prayers for the pope at mass and contributions to the Peter's Pence collection.[21]

Italian immigrant clergy, eager to fund parochial education at their national parishes, found themselves in a difficult position. Msgr. Gherardo Ferrante, a chancery official for the archdiocese of New York, explained the situation to Apostolic Delegate Falconio. The priests had planned to participate in an exposition in Turin—part of the larger national celebrations—to demonstrate the contributions of New York's Italian parochial schools to the dissemination of the Italian language. In 1901 Liberal Italy had begun to subsidize Italian schools abroad, and the immigrant clergy hope to capitalize upon this program. Archbishop Farley, however, believed participation at Turin amounted to "hostility toward the Holy See" and "an offense to the Holy Father." Falconio backed Farley. "It seems to me the opinion of the Monsignor Archbishop is perfectly just and should be followed."[22]

The Vatican discouraged Catholic pilgrimages to the Eternal City in 1911 to avoid any hint of Catholic participation in the Rome Exposition. After learning that Father Urbano Naeleisen, director of the Leo Home for German [American] Catholics, planned a pilgrimage to Rome in April, Falconio dissuaded the entourage.[23] But the allure of papal Rome was not easily thwarted. Falconio discovered that Catholic tour company advertisements promised an audience with the Holy Father as the climax of a pilgrimage. Falconio notified McGrane's Catholic Tours and Daniel Toomey of the Columbus Travel Society that audiences with the pope could not be granted. When the pious businessmen attempted to persuade Falconio to reconsider, the unimpressed delegate once again arrested the pilgrims in their North American tracks.[24]

Chicago's *Extension Magazine* flaunted Catholic political power when it learned that B. J. Rosenthal of Chicago had had audiences with both Pius X and Nathan. Rosenthal, it reported, "takes occasion to 'boost' the coming [Rome] exhibition, and also Mayor Nathan. He thinks the mayor is a wonderful man. He is going to ask that a formal invitation be extended by Chicago to Mayor Nathan to visit our great city." *Extension* wondered, "from whom should this invitation come? . . . While in the past we have had in Chicago our share of queer mayors and queerer specimens of aldermen, yet, so far as we know, we have never elected political idiots to these positions; therefore, an official invitation to the atheistic, socialistic garrulous Mayor of Rome will not be extended by the great city of Chicago. At least, not unless somebody wants about one million respectable voters as a handicap against him."[25]

In moments of conflict, Catholics took great delight in the failures of Liberal Italy. When the March 1911 festivities began and "crowds filled the squares shouting 'Viva Roma!," *America* sneered, "a black pall of impending bankruptcy" loomed over the city. "We have seen the sons of Italy by the thousands landing on our shores, toiling for a pittance and thanking their stars that they have escaped 'United Italy.'" Father Giovanni Bonzano in Rome, soon to become the apostolic delegate in Washington, boasted of the failure of the Rome Exhibition to his friend Auxiliary Bishop George Mundelein in Brooklyn. Referring to the cholera epidemic in several Italian cities, Bonzano exclaimed: "Here are the delights that the apotheosis of Vittorio Emanuele II and the celebration of the unity of Italy bring us!"[26]

Tension within the Ideology of the Roman Question

Before Ernesto Nathan arrived in the United States in 1914 to serve Liberal Italy at the Panama Pacific International Exposition, he was voted out of office in Rome. Indeed, the government would never have offered the mayor of the capital city an appointment as envoy extraordinary. The Church contributed to the political changes that led to Nathan's ouster. A brief summary of Pius X's policy toward Liberal Italy illuminates Nathan's mayoral defeat and subsequent events in the United States.

Seen within an Italian context, one could argue the pontificate of Pius X belongs to part 2 of our story—the transformation of the ideology of the Roman Question. In "Il fermo proposito" (1905), Pius X relaxed the prohibition of Catholic participation in national elections in special cases deemed appropriate by the local bishop. In 1913 Pius gave informal approval to Catholics who voted for conservative liberals against anticlerical candidates. Thus, selectively, tentatively, and under careful scrutiny from the hierarchy, Italian Catholics began to enter national politics.[27]

The American Church also began to ease its intransigence toward Liberal Italy. In 1903 Giovanni Giolitti, the Piedmontese moderate who would dominate Italian politics for the next decade, appointed Tommaso Tittoni, a Catholic conservative, as foreign minister. Tittoni's ambassador in Washington from 1901 to 1910, Edmondo Mayor des Planches, grew to admire Cardinal James Gibbons of Baltimore, the unofficial but uncontested primate of the American hierarchy. Mayor discerned a shift in the attitude of clergy toward Liberal Italy. He attributed this transition to Pius X's "evangelical charity" for Italian immigrants and to the "liberalism" of Gibbons. Catholic clergy, "intransigent and anti-Italian, constituted especially by Irish," had begun to mellow, according to Mayor. In 1909 he described his informal "relations not only correct, but friendly" with Apostolic Delegates Sebastiano Martinelli and Diomede Falconio. In fact, he noted how Falconio "exhibits the most correct Italian sentiments, and I believe him a man of . . . liberal ideas."[28]

According to Mayor, Gibbons privately deviated from the ideology of the Roman Question. In January 1910, the ambassador spoke at a banquet in Washington in honor of Gibbons. Mayor sat beside the cardinal, who "was animated by genuine sentiments of liberalism. He spoke with admiration of the great progress he witnesses in Italy each and every time he goes there and he said, literally, the *unification of Italy had been a blessing*." According to Mayor, Gibbons believed that if Pius X were "free in his actions, he would change the system toward Italy, but he is surrounded by people" who prevented him. Gibbons also spoke highly of the king and queen.[29] Clearly, the personal frost had melted in relations between some Church dignitaries and Italian diplomats. Gibbons, however, never voiced an affirmation of Liberal Italy in public. And on the international stage, papal diplomacy did not anticipate a transformation in the ideology of the Roman Question. Notwithstanding Gibbons's reported remark, when Nathan delivered his address on the 20th of September 1910, American Catholics predictably attacked Nathan and Liberal Italy and reenacted rituals of solidarity with their imprisoned Holy Father.

Ernesto Nathan was born in London in 1845 to a middle-class Italian family. His mother, Sarina Nathan Levi, helped Mazzini during his exile. As a young man, Ernesto embraced republicanism, edited works by Garibaldi and Mazzini, and founded the Dante Alighieri Society to promote liberal patriotism among emigrants. He became "a living symbol of integral Mazzinianism." In 1887 he joined the Freemasons and served as grand master from 1896 to 1904. His Judaism, foreign birth, Freemasonry, and republicanism made him an ideal target of Catholic symbolic warfare. Indignant Catholics wondered, how could a foreign-born bourgeois anticlerical, both a Freemason and Jew, represent papal Rome and speak for Catholic Italy?[30]

The first mayor of Rome not from the nobility and a living symbol of the democratic wing of the Risorgimento, Nathan matured into a pragmatic reformer. His 1907 mayoral victory brought a popular bloc to power with promises to build schools, expand social services, tax manufacturers, and enact municipal modernization. His coalition of reform socialists, radicals, republicans, and democrats was an experiment Nathan hoped to spread to other communes and to national politics. Anticlericalism and dreams of a progressive Italy cemented his bloc.[31]

Although Prime Minister Giolitti supported Nathan's bloc in 1907, religious policies separated them. Adverse to debilitating conflict between Catholics and liberals, Giolitti maintained an ambiguous reticence toward clerical factions that he deployed to his advantage when he needed them in the decade before the Great War. Nathan's infamous 20th of September address was probably motivated to compel the enigmatic Giolitti to clarify his position. Nathan hoped his speech would provoke unseemly Catholic protests against Liberal Italy. Giolitti would then have no choice but to end his silent flirtation with the clericals. If Nathan compelled Giolitti to openly support left-wing forces, Nathan might forge a progressive party free of clerical elements. Giolitti, however, ever cryptic, preserved his options. Nathan lost the mayoral election in 1913 when Giolitti turned to Catholics rather than Nathan's bloc to stem the socialist tide.[32]

In the spring of 1914, just before the Great War began, the government selected ex-mayor Nathan as its commissioner general, minister plenipotentiary, and envoy extraordinary to the 1915 Panama Pacific International Exposition (PPIE) in San Francisco to commemorate the completion of the Panama Canal. The appointment triggered a second round of protests against Nathan as American Catholics floated dubious schemes to have the envoy recalled or to boycott the PPIE. No pontifical prompting instigated the protests of 1914, and the hierarchy did not mobilize a coordinated effort. The schemes failed to achieve their utterly unrealistic goals. Nevertheless, the 1914 protests demonstrated how thoroughly Catholic priests and laity had internalized the ideology of the Roman Question.

American Catholic Protests of 1914

In attacking the PPIE, angry American Catholics launched an offensive against a cultural Leviathan of modern civilization. In 1904 prominent business and civic leaders jockeyed to secure San Francisco as the site for the PPIE. President William Taft officially recognized San Francisco as the host on 15 February 1911. Private citizens, the city, the state of California, foreign governments, and exhibitors raised approximately $50 million as the PPIE brought business and civic leaders together in a massive planning exercise that embodied the administrative values of the Progressive Era. In April 1912, Taft sent a commission to Europe to encourage participation. The PPIE's Propaganda Division overwhelmed the press with advertisements for this grand testament to the progress of modern civilization.[33]

The Catholic assault on Nathan between April and July 1914 coincided with his visit to the United States. But earlier stages of planning for the PPIE had already generated religious tensions that exacerbated the protests against Nathan. The *Menace*, a notorious anti-Catholic publication, tracked PPIE preparations with an eye for Catholic intrigue. Citing a San Francisco informant, the *Menace* accused "pope lovers" and PPIE president Charles Moore of favoring Catholics for work projects. "Unless one has a letter from McQuaide, Crowley or Riordan he cannot obtain a job in connection with the exposition. The dirty scoundrels are running the city and Mayor [James] Rolph is wax in their hands. Our fire, police and park commission are in the hands of Catholics. The police and fire department are more than 90 percent Catholic. There are less than seventy-five Masons in the police department."[34]

The *Menace* provoked a storm of inquiries when it claimed that San Francisco's archdiocesan weekly, the *Monitor*, had reported that "the center of the exposition grounds will be known as the 'vatican,' and will be a replica of the world-famed structure at Rome. . . . The immediate surroundings of the 'vatican' will be entirely Catholic in character, with Brazil on one side and Honduras on the other, while Bolivia, Portugal and the Philippine Islands will face it."[35]

The notion of an imitation Vatican at an American exposition boasting its progressive technological powers to foreign nations set churlish Protestant pens to paper. An exasperated Lutheran pastor in Paterson, New Jersey, wondered "why any recognition should be given to a church among a people who know something of Separation of Church and State, and especially to a church which has always been a bane to free institutions wherever it has had power." Less gracefully, H. W. Moore of Knobnoster, Missouri, promised, "Protestants in these parts are going to boycott the Expo. . . . You Catholic fellows think you are smart but you can't fool us any longer. Every member of the Panama Exposition is a Jesuit." Frank Smith in Cincinnati contended the PPIE would be "a direct and unforgivable insult to the Protestants of this country, for there is no reason why the grasping two-faced Catholic traitors should be so favored" with a Vatican building. Smith predicted, "the Exposition ought to be a flat failure and not patronized by true Protestants." He opined, "the man who suggested such a plan ought to be strung up."[36]

Correspondent N. F. Caufield of Minneapolis kept vigilant tabs on Catholic power, enclosing the irksome *Monitor* article in her epistle of dissent. She could not comprehend "why in a Protestant country containing only 12,000,000 Catholics (by their own figures), in a Protestant city, this distinction [of a Vatican replica] should be accorded to this gigantic political machine which is inimical to free speech, free press, free schools, and separation of church and state." Paraphrasing Archbishops John Ireland and James Gibbons, she insisted Catholics planned "to make America all Catholic (Ireland 1899) when all churches will be united, but as the first requirement the acknowledgement of the Pope as the pontifical head (Gibbons 1913)." Caufield produced statistics touting Catholic power: "89% of the army, 90% of the navy, 75% of the militia, 85% of the firemen, 92% of the police, 85% of the labor, all but 7 navy chaplains and 60% army chaplains Catholic, one battle ship without a Protestant on it, 500,000 Knights of Columbus armed by our Government, 300,000 Sons of Hibernia." She ghoulishly prophesied, "an American St. Bartholomew's Day is only a question of time."[37]

Catholics marched onto this mined battlefield to wage their war against Nathan. German Catholic *vereine* filed complaints with PPIE officials. Typical was the St. Bonifatius Bund von Iowa, representing 5,000 men. "A grievous insult has been offered the Catholics of the United States and of other countries . . . by the appointment of Ernesto Nathan. . . . His recognition by your management would be considered, to put it mildly, most unfortunate by all Catholics everywhere on the Globe, as well as by thousands of non-Catholics who are not in sympathy with Ernesto Nathan's conduct." Branch 74 of the Polish Catholic Mutual Benefit Association in Grand Rapids proffered its resentments, as did the Federation of Catholic Societies in several states. The Arizona Knights of Columbus assured the PPIE, "Ernesto Nathan cannot be and will not be persona grata with fair-minded American people."[38] As Catholics entered the fray, friends Nathan never knew he had surfaced. "I am informed that certain parties affiliated with a certain Religious Denomination are attempting to prevent Ernesto Nathan . . . from being received by the officials at the Exposition," W. P. Oliver chimed in from La Crosse, Wisconsin. "I want to protest against these trouble Makers. . . . If this is to be distinctively a Roman Catholic Exposition I and thousands of others want to know it so that we may govern ourselves accordingly, and arrange to spend our time and money in other directions." Master Bushnell of the Guardians of Liberty in Chicago assured PPIE president Moore that Nathan "is a great statesman and patriot," and that the movement afoot against him "is approved by the Pope."[39]

Nathan's arrival in May 1914 inspired Catholic harangues. One recurring theme rehearsed in the Catholic press was that "official Italy . . . dishonored herself" with the "unhappy choice" of Nathan as her commissioner. The Monitor editorialized, "the civilized world can but marvel and wonder at the great and proud nation of Italy sending such a commissioner to us." Brooklyn's Tablet reasoned that "as a Jew and a Mason and foreign born to Italy, [Nathan] is not representative of a Catholic country, when that nation is the one whose Capital is also the center of Christendom." The Knights of Columbus protested, "a notorious anti-Catholic bigot, a rabid Socialist, [and] . . . an enemy of social order and religious freedom" could not serve as "the representative of Catholic Italy and as the bearer of her fraternal message." Buffalo's Die Aurora und Christliche Woche spoke for a large German Catholic community when it chortled that Nathan's mission was "an insult" to the pope and all Catholics.[40]

Segments of the Catholic press degenerated into anti-Semitism. The Western Catholic of Springfield, Illinois, castigated Nathan, "the little Jew Mayor of Rome," whose ancestors "hounded Jesus Christ to the darksome and bloody heights of Calvary." The Jews themselves "were men of no country who work for or against government for gain — veritable 'Hessians,' whose services are at the beck of the highest bidder." Sigmund Livingston, chairman of the Anti-Defamation League of Chicago, lodged protests with Western Catholic's editor, Father M. J. Foley, and Apostolic Delegate Bonzano. To Foley, Livingston dismissed the "accusations you bring against the Jew" because the "enlightened judgment of mankind requires no refutation of them." Instead, Livingston focused on the mistaken notion that "Signor Nathan, . . . was the representative and spokesman of the Jewish people." Livingston explained, as "Mayor of Rome, [Nathan] did not represent the Jews; in his official utterances in Rome, he did not speak as a Jew for the Jews." Reasoning from the position of a fellow religious minority, Livingston observed how Foley had "had occasion vigorously to condemn attacks" upon Catholics as "un-American, inspired by ignorance, bigotry, intolerance and fanaticism. If such influences and such methods are wrong when applied to Catholics, are they not equally wrong when applied to Jews? If they are un-American with respect to Catholics and Catholicism, are they not equally un-American with respect to Jews and Judaism?"[41]

Bonzano assured Livingston "that the Catholic Church is opposed to provoking race hatred or to attacking people on account of their religious or political tenets. Hence it is needless for me to say that I do not approve of what the Rev. M. J. Foley has written." Bonzano, however, never reigned Foley in, although he did "feel confident" that Livingston "will join [Catholics] in protesting against the attitude of Mr. Nathan," who "because of his vulgar insults to the Pope . . . has offended Catholics of every nationality the world over."[42]

Foley's uninspiring response to the Anti-Defamation League unveiled the covert anti-Semitism implicit in the ideology of the Roman Question and its conspiratorial "anti-Risorgimento" view of history. "What we said about the dirty little Jew, Nathan, and the Jew ring-leaders of the IWW was not intended for or directed against the great body of law-abiding Jews in this country. . . . The [Anti-Defamation] League, if consistent, should have condemned the insulting and blasphemous attitude of Nathan, the Jew, towards the Prisoner in the Vatican. The members of the League must know that the Popes ever have been the traditional friends of the persecuted Jews, therefore they should have gone on record as condemning the hideous tactics of Nathan, the Jew, towards the Holy Father." Foley relentlessly drove home his point. "Nathan, though not your spokesman, is still a Jew—a rabid Jew—a Christian-hating Jew—a Pope-insulting Jew—and it was up to you and your League . . . to voice a protest against the blasphemous conduct of Nathan, the Jew, towards the Venerable Head of the Catholic Church."[43]

While Catholics tendered appeals to compel PPIE officials to renounce Nathan and then to boycott the PPIE altogether, the Jewish-Catholic polemic continued. Chicago's Jewish weekly, the Sentinel, reiterated Livingston's point. "All high-minded and liberal men know that the ex-Mayor of Rome has no authority to speak on behalf of the Jews, nor do his utterances represent the views of the Jews." Sentinel editors wondered, "is it any less in keeping with the traditions of our country, for the Catholic press to attack the Jew than for the Protestant press to assail the Catholic?"[44] After the Anti-Defamation League issued a circular letter to the editors of Catholic newspapers regarding the anti-Semitic attacks on Nathan, Brooklyn's Tablet responded to its Jewish fellow citizens in an unattractively titled editorial, "Nathan 'the Jew.'"

"Catholics in this country," the Tablet complained, "and Irish Catholics in particular have been too persistently the victims of a discrimination" against race and religion "not to be allied with any race or class against which oppression . . . is leveled." The editorial expounded upon the "bond" Catholics and Jews shared. "We Catholics acknowledge the Hebrews to have been the chosen people of God, albeit a people to whose patrimony of divine prerogatives we believe we have succeeded." Furthermore, "the Jew has been most generous in his benefactions to Catholic charitable institutions." After ostensibly seeking common ground, the Tablet sallied ungrammatically forth. "We don't think that the objection to Nathan as Exposition envoy is based upon the fact as such that he is a Jew; nor indeed upon the other fact as such that he is a Mason. But as a Jew and a Mason and foreign born to Italy he is not representative of a Catholic country, when that nation is the one whose Capital is also the center of Christendom and against the spoliation of which as the seat of his necessary temporal dominion Christendom's Head, in the person of our High Priest, still makes his dignified protest as he has protested against the insults of this man, once mayor in the Eternal City and now sent as an envoy to these shores."[45]

American Catholics demanded that PPIE officials reject Nathan as Italy's representative. To compel the PPIE toward this end, Catholic organizations threatened a boycott. Herbert Hadley provided the rationale in *America*. "We can in no way move Italy to change this appointment, but we can force the directors of the Exposition to refuse to receive him." Hadley proposed "an appeal to the pocket. Let every Knight of Columbus; let every member of the Catholic Federation; let every Catholic priest in this country pledge himself not to go to the Exposition if Nathan holds his appointment." A boycott would assure "this 'undesirable' will be excluded from our shores."[46]

At the annual meeting of the Alumni Association of the North American College of Rome, the delegates—111 priests, 2 archbishops, 4 bishops—voiced indignation "in several heated addresses" at Nathan's appointment by "the Free Masons that control the Italian Government." They protested to Mayor Rolph and relocated their 1915 meeting from San Francisco to Chicago. The Laymen's League for Retreats and Social Studies unanimously passed a resolution to join the Alumni Association and boycott the PPIE. "Nathan is an avowed enemy of the Catholic Church and notorious for his insults to the Pope, and through him to all Catholics." Through "his conduct in Italy he has shown himself [to be] an unprincipled enemy of religious liberty and therefore against the spirit of the American Constitution."[47]

The Catholic press, so captive to its ideology, convinced itself non-Catholic support was forthcoming. The *Monitor* asserted, "the people of California will not welcome Nathan, whatever the officials of the Panama-Pacific Exposition may do." Nathan's appointment "is an insult to the whole American nation." Other Americans, however, were unmoved. Brooklyn's *Tablet* reported that the Mercer County Federation of Patriotic Fraternities, a nativist organization in New Jersey, adopted a resolution to "heartily approve" the "most worthy" Nathan. The Patriotic Fraternities, affectively dubbed "Trenton Bigots" in the Catholic press, "condemn[ed] the action of the American Federation of Roman Catholic Societies in protesting against this appointment, their protest being inspired by religious animosity." The Patriotic Fraternities sent its resolutions to President Woodrow Wilson and King Vittorio Emanuele III.[48]

American Catholics had no impact on Italy's government or their own. Thomas

Nelson Page, U.S. ambassador in Rome, considered "Mr. Nathan . . . a man of intelligence and character. He is one of the greatest authorities living on the history of the Italian struggle for union and liberty." When Felice Santini, a conservative Catholic politician, broached the subject of Nathan's appointment, Foreign Minister Antonio di San Giuliano dismissed the "handful of noisy Irish Catholics" in the United States who "on all occasions" pass "motions in favor of the restoration of the Church's temporal power."[49]

Unduly impressed with their ability to stir Italy's foreign minister, some American Catholics mistakenly believed victory was imminent. The protests have "had an enormous effect upon Italian thought," claimed the *Tablet*, "and it is still possible that Nathan may be superseded." The *Tablet* urged Catholics "to make known their state of mind in the matter direct to the government of Italy." Some editors seemed to think that American Catholics had played a role in Nathan's poor performance in the June 1914 municipal elections, which the American Catholic press celebrated as evidence of his nefarious character.[50]

As Catholics insulted him far and near, Nathan received a warm welcome upon his arrival in New York on 25 May. Masonic officials, Ira Nelson Morris for President Wilson, New York's Italian consul general, representatives of the Italian Chamber of Commerce, and Italian Protestant ministers all greeted the envoy. When he was spirited away, Italian Americans cheered their commissioner. The next day, accompanied by Morris and the Italian ambassador, Nathan met Secretary of State William Jennings Bryan and President Wilson. Although nothing in the *New York Times*, *San Francisco Examiner*, or the Italian-language daily *Il Progresso Italo-Americano* hinted there was a problem with a Freemason of Jewish descent representing Italy, *America* insisted his appointment was unpopular in Italy and the United States.[51]

Nathan's arrival in San Francisco on 31 May sparked celebrations among Italians who flew the tricolor flag. The consul general and Italian American leaders welcomed Nathan. During his five-day sojourn, the Ancient and Accepted Scottish Rite of Freemasonry, President Moore, PPIE directors, Mayor Rolph, and San Francisco elite wined and dined their guest. The Italian flag-raising ceremony on 2 June brought out over 1,000 Italian Americans. The *San Francisco Examiner* boasted how Nathan stood at "the forefront of the intellectual forces of Italy." Nathan extolled Liberal Italy as an instrument of progress and was honored with a twenty-one-gun salute and a rendition of the Garibaldi hymn. Each evening Nathan took center stage at a banquet that brought community leaders together to praise the contributions of Liberal Italy to modern civilization. Catholic clergy, however, were absent from the gala events.[52]

The PPIE officials still had their share of letters to answer. The executive committee's minutes on 5 May recorded how "a great many letters . . . from Catholic organizations" objected "to the appointment of Ernesto Nathan as Commissioner to the Exposition." President Moore "had been endeavoring to get prominent Catholics to take some action in regard to this matter and to take same up with Archbishop Riordan [of San Francisco] but thus far he had not met with any success."[53]

The executive committee, which included one Catholic among twelve, was not impervious to Catholic concerns. After it learned that the League of Patriotic Voters was an anti-Catholic organization, the committee studied the league's constitution and by-laws. When the sole Catholic member asserted, "the invitation to this organization . . . if allowed to stand, would be resented by all Catholics," the committee withdrew its invitation in a telegram to the league. "Your official communication . . . that we need relief from a certain crooked grafting political machine posing as a religion, is a direct attack upon a religious faith held by many." The committee, however, never considered steps against Nathan.[54]

On 20 February 1915, Archbishop Edward Hanna of San Francisco gave the invocation and Rabbi Martin Meyer read a psalm to over 300,000 people attending the opening of the PPIE. The festivities lasted 288 days and by all accounts were a grand success. On the same day, Hanna wrote Apostolic Delegate Bonzano: "It makes one burn with shame to think of the Italy so glorious, so Catholic, is represented here by a free-mason, a socialist, a Jew. These are long, hard, waiting days."[55]

IF THE CAMPAIGN to rid the PPIE of Nathan failed, it still provided an opportunity for American Catholics to act out the most intransigent expression of the ideology of the Roman Question. As the rhetoric of Catholic speeches, editorials, private letters, sermons, and prayers revealed, before the Great War American Catholics imagined Italy as a Catholic nation imprisoned with the pope within an illicit and evil liberal state. A powerful and growing component of an international Church, American Catholics responded as did their European brothers and sisters to papal cues for Catholic solidarity.

Hanna's remark to Bonzano — "these are long, hard, waiting days" — revealed a uniquely Catholic sense of history. The pope, the Church, and Catholics everywhere suffered as they waited for vindication in a fallen, repaganized world. Suffering, however, was both redemptive and temporary. After death comes resurrection, when Christ takes his seat on his throne. The Great War, a tragic and brutal end to the idolatrous liberal fantasy of human autonomy, was a death that anticipated resurrection. The transformation of Catholic ideology accelerated as the Great War reopened the Roman Question in unexpected, providential ways.

PART II

Transformation,
1914–1929

CHAPTER FOUR

The Great War

"Keep the Roman Question Alive," 1914–1920

In the nineteenth century, Catholics heaped abuse upon Liberal Italy, the prison warden of the pope and the incarnation of modern evils. Inseparably linked to that intransigent condemnation was the Catholic cry to restore the temporal power. In the twentieth century, these two sides of the same nineteenth-century coin became disengaged from one another. Part 2 analyzes this transformation of the ideology of the Roman Question from 1914 to 1929, when the Holy See's quest for a territorial sovereignty no longer implied an intransigent condemnation of Liberal or (after 1922) Fascist Italy. The seeds of this change, planted during the pontificate of Pius X (1903–14), broke earth under Benedict XV (1914–22) and flowered under Pius XI (1922–39). Although both Benedict and Pius XI protested the conquest of papal Rome, neither unequivocally denounced Liberal (or Fascist) Italy. This ideological transformation culminated in February 1929, when the Holy See formally recognized the Kingdom of Italy, and the pope became temporal sovereign over the State of the Vatican City.

Social theorists have emphasized how moral ambiguity generates ideological change.[1] Two factors created moral ambiguity for the ideology of the Roman Question before the rise of Fascism. First, the growth of Italian socialism inspired Catholic-liberal cooperation to contain the radical threat. Second, the Great War rocked the very foundation of world order and opened up the possibility for restructuring on terms favorable to the Church. Next to the specter of red revolution and the monstrous cataclysm of total war, Liberal Italy no longer appeared to be the irredeemable sin that embodied the horrors of modern civilization. From the papal perspective, Liberal Italy became like other states — France, the United States, or the Netherlands. Secular and Protestant ideologies within these states troubled the Vatican, but they were not adequate cause to deny the formal legitimacy of these states. The battle for true civilization — a Catholic social order — was now to be fought within these states, including Italy.

Sifting through the monumental scheming of European realpolitik between 1914 and 1920, we can discern the Vatican's bid to resolve the Roman Question through international diplomacy as the Holy See tentatively tendered legitimacy to Liberal Italy. Vatican secretary of state Cardinal Pietro Gasparri dangled the threat of mass international Catholic protests — manipulating liberal paranoia of a subversive Catholic monolith loyal to papal Rome — to governments preoccupied with their internal unity. A world power with nearly sixteen million Catholics in 1916, the United States was important, at times central, to this strategy. Vatican diplomacy during the Great War instigated intense public debates in the United States that strengthened the boundaries separating Catholics from other Americans, in spite of the patriotic support American Catholics displayed for the U.S. war effort.

Scholarship about the Vatican and American Catholics during the Great War is confusing. Catholic historiography restates the rhetoric of its subjects: The Vatican under Benedict was neutral, and its diplomacy was impartial. American Catholic historiography has further claimed that Catholic patriotism and participation in the war effort was tantamount to an endorsement of President Woodrow Wilson's international vision. Thus, the war brought Catholics closer to other Americans. Indeed, some Church historians insist that Wilson's Fourteen Points merely restated Benedict's peace Note of August 1917.[2] Diplomatic and Wilsonian historians, on the other hand, repeat an accusation of the liberal press and Allied statesmen: the Vatican favored the Central Powers. They never explore the impact Vatican diplomacy had upon American Catholics or their relations with other U.S. citizens.[3] I proceed differently. I neither evaluate American Catholic patriotism, the authenticity of Vatican neutrality, nor the veracity of accusations made against Catholics and their Holy Father. Instead, I highlight how accusations against the Church and defensive Catholic responses strengthened boundaries separating Catholics from other Americans.

Inhabiting different ideological universes, Benedict and Wilson held contrary views of the proper role of the pope in international affairs and opposing visions for the postwar order. Benedict sought to resolve the Roman Question. Toward this end, he wished to lead the peace movement, occupy a seat at the peace conference, prevent the dismemberment of Austria-Hungary, and sit at the center of a league of nations — not the League of Nations. The distraught pope witnessed his children massacre one another and believed their sacrifice earned the Holy See the moral authority to participate in the peace conference, where the Roman Question might be resolved. Wilson, in contrast, considered Benedict a "spiritual" leader who should not "interfere" in politics. The liberal ideology embodied in the international nation-state system had no place for the Church, a strange international institution that Wilson, good liberal that he was, insisted ought to attend to purely spiritual affairs.

Relaxing the Condemnation of Liberal Italy

During the pontificate of Pius X, the ideology of the Roman Question tottered toward transformation. Pius X desired Catholic unity in Italy. Toward that end, he condemned modernism in 1907 and instituted an antimodernist oath to root out theological pluralism. He curtailed intra-Catholic fighting between Christian Democrats and intransigents when he suppressed the Opera dei Congressi in 1904. He reorganized Catholic Action, the vast institutional networks of Italian Catholicism, into the Unione Popolare and the Unione Elettorale, which operated to promote the Church's ends in public life under strict control of the hierarchy. Pius then cautiously deployed this unified body to protect the Church in Italy. As the Partito Socialista Italiana (PSI), organized in 1892, won over much of the working class, Catholic alliances with conservative liberals became informally permissible. However, there were no serious negotiations regarding the Roman Question. The restructuring of Europe brought about by the Great War gave Benedict XV leverage to bring new life to the Roman Question.[4]

Before he became pope, Giacomo Della Chiesa, a seasoned diplomat, had been intransigent on the Roman Question. But the Great War accelerated the accommodation of Catholics to Liberal Italy, and Benedict did not try to obstruct them. In March 1915, he granted greater autonomy to the Unione Popolare, whose leaders lent patriotic support to the war effort. Catholic chaplains served valiantly in the Italian military, with Benedict's endorsement. A cohort of Catholic deputies in the Chamber of Deputies, some with ministerial posts, participated actively in the war mobilization. Benedict did not impede the establishment of the Partito Popolare Italiano (PPI), a nonconfessional but Catholic party founded in 1919, when Benedict abolished all remaining restrictions on participation in national politics. His 1920 encyclical "Pacem, Dei munus" ended the prohibition placed upon Catholic heads of state from visiting the monarchy's Quirinal Palace. In short, under Benedict the ideology of the Roman Question underwent a noteworthy transformation as the Vatican implicitly acknowledged Liberal Italy was a legitimate polis in which Catholics could work to realize a Christian social order.[5]

Vatican Neutrality and Allied Anxiety

Benedict expressed disgust for the Great War. Between his election on 3 September 1914 and his famous peace Note of August 1917, he described the war as a "monstrous spectacle," "dreadful scourge," "appalling carnage," "suicide of civilized Europe," "tragedy of human madness," and most famously, as a "useless slaughter." He expended vast resources and intervened frequently to offer humanitarian relief to the suffering. American Catholics boasted of his generosity to liberals and Protestants suspicious of Benedict's wartime commitments.[6]

Why were the Allies and United States so suspicious of the pope? Not long after the war began, the Allies surmised that Benedict would use the war to resolve the Roman Question. They noted that the Central Powers initially had better diplomatic channels to the Holy See, and that the pope hosted mysterious informal diplomatic missions, turning the Vatican into a buzzing hive of intrigue.[7] Furthermore, throughout the conflict Benedict emphasized the manner in which the war violated international and natural law. But he neither stressed, nor frequently elaborated upon, particular transgressions of international treaties or accusations of barbarous actions. This infuriated the Allies, who believed German aggression merited unequivocal condemnation.

The activities of Msgr. Rudolf Gerlach, Benedict's chamberlain, also troubled the Allies. Gerlach worked with Matthias Erzberger, the leading (Catholic) Center Party deputy in the Reichstag, who collected money from German Catholics, German Protestants, and the German Foreign Ministry for the Vatican. The flow of funds began in August 1914 and continued at least until 1917. Erzberger bribed Italian deputies to maintain Italy's neutrality just when the Vatican intervened in Italian negotiations with Austria-Hungary to keep Italy out of the war. Gerlach funneled money to Italian clerical journals to weaken Italian unity. Eventually, the Italian government claimed to have evidence that Gerlach was linked to an espionage ring that had sabotaged Italian warships and condemned him to life imprisonment in absentia, after it had escorted him to Switzerland. Gerlach received military decorations from Prussia, Bavaria, Austria, and Turkey.[8]

Finally, the Vatican's war goals disturbed the Allies and American Protestants and liberals. Benedict desired to preserve the Austro-Hungarian Empire and harbored apprehensions of Russian Orthodoxy. In the later stages of war, when Wilson clamored for the self-determination of national groups within Austria-Hungary, the Vatican vied to prevent the dissolution of its historic friend. Austria-Hungary had been a Catholic bulwark against the democratic and liberal values professed by the Allies. Furthermore, Germany served as a rampart against the expansion of Orthodoxy into regions inhabited by Catholic Poles. The loss of Prussian military power would open the floodgates to Russian barbarism. With these factors in mind, the Allies assumed the Holy See was in league with their enemies. This made Catholic populations within Allied states suspect and insecure.[9]

After war broke out, German intrigue reopened the Roman Question, much to the horror of Liberal Italy. Erzberger circulated an alarming proposal in October 1914. In order to maintain Italian neutrality, he suggested, Austria should cede Trentino, an Italian-speaking region on Italy's border, to the pope. Benedict, in turn, would give this territory to Italy and receive a temporal sovereignty around Rome. Then, in November Prime Minister Antonio Salandra learned of a letter from the former German chancellor, Prince Bernhard von Bülow, to the director

Map 3. Modern Italy

of the Italian Banca Commerciale, in which he threatened to restore the temporal power if Italy intervened against Germany. Bülow arrived in Rome on 17 December to work with Erzberger, bribing and cajoling Italian deputies to remain neutral.[10]

Benedict's first encyclical, issued on 1 November, further heightened Italian anxieties. "Ad beatissimi apostolorum" condemned the war as a consequence of the secularization of the modern state. In the absence of "the precepts and practices of Christian wisdom," it declared, class antagonisms, exaggerated nationalism, disregard for constituted authority, and war had ensued. Benedict coupled this analysis with a reminder: "for a long time past the Church has not enjoyed that full freedom which it needs." He linked the absence of European peace to the Roman Question. "And so while earnestly desiring that peace should soon be concluded amongst the nations, it is also Our desire that there should be an end to the abnormal position of the Head of the Church, a position in many ways very harmful to the very peace of nations." Predictably, the liberal press thundered against "Ad beatissimi apostolorum" as an adumbration of a papal strategy to isolate Liberal Italy, secure a place for the Holy See at the peace conference, and raise the Roman Question.[11]

The Italian government responded quickly. Sidney Sonnino, the foreign minister throughout the war, informed his ambassadors that Italy "will be absolutely intransigent in its opposition to any concession of any kind that could signify an internationalization of the Roman Question." England, France, and Russia concurred with Sonnino's opposition to papal representation at a peace conference. At this point, the Italian government had two paths of action before it. It could seek a commitment from the Allies to exclude the Holy See from any peace conference where the Vatican might bring up the Roman Question. In addition, it could physically isolate the Vatican and block its diplomatic activities, in violation of the Law of Guarantees. Advocates of this second choice in the Foreign Ministry circulated a memorandum on 14 December that urged the suspension of those articles of the Law of Guarantees relative to the Holy See's diplomatic and postal freedoms and advocated the transfer of Benedict from Rome. But Sonnino chose only the first path. Through diplomacy he secured the exclusion of the Holy See from postwar peace negotiations.[12]

Sonnino's choice shaped Italy-Vatican dynamics until 1918. Over the status of Rome they remained at loggerheads, and both sought support beyond the Alps and across the Atlantic. Liberal Italy found aid in England, France, Russia, and the United States, where President Wilson and his State Department had no patience with the meddling of a spiritual sovereign in political affairs. The Holy See flirted with the Central Powers because they broadcast their interest in a reappraisal of the Roman Question. Crucial for our story, the Holy See also drew upon the loyalty of Catholics within all states to support a peace brokered by the pope.

Sonnino's decision also set the stage for Italy-Vatican cooperation. Sonnino and the Italian war governments were committed to contain anticlericals who wished to suspend the Law of Guarantees and who criticized the Holy See as a subversive foreign body within Liberal Italy. Conversely, because the Vatican lived in perpetual fear of red revolution in Italy, the Holy See appeased and nurtured forces of order to protect the Church. The U.S. ambassador in Rome, Thomas Nelson Page, recalled how Italian troops protected the Vatican "to prevent any 'accident'" during the period of Italian neutrality. Page noted, "the feeling between the Vatican and the political elements composing the order of Free Masons was such as to render advisable the forestalling of any 'regrettable incident.'"[13]

While the Vatican tried to keep Liberal Italy out of war, Sonnino negotiated with both the Allied and Central Powers for the best deal. Aware of the Vatican's initiative with Austria-Hungary to promote Erzberger's plan to resolve the Roman Question, Italy intensified its discussions with the Allies. These conversations culminated in the secret Treaty of London, signed on 26 April 1915. Article XV of the treaty read: "France, Great Britain, and Russia shall support such opposition as Italy may make to any proposal in the direction of introducing a representative of the Holy See in any peace negotiations or negotiations for the settlement of questions raised by the present war." Barring the Holy See from any postwar peace conference, article XV diminished the likelihood the Roman Question would be discussed in an international forum. In addition, the Allies promised Italy Trent, Trieste, their hinterlands, portions of the Adriatic coast, and Slav Dalmatia, all part of Austria-Hungary, as spoils of war. The Treaty of London did not secure the future Italian annexation of the Adriatic city of Fiume, whose fate became a crucial focal point of disorder after the war. Thus, Salandra, Sonnino, and King Vittorio committed Italy to a war without informing the army, the Chamber of Deputies, or the Italian people, a majority of whom were against intervention. On 4 May, Salandra privately denounced the Triple Alliance in a note to Germany and Austria-Hungary. On 23 May 1915, Liberal Italy declared war on Austria.[14]

Benedict's reaction had two parts, which reflected the transformation in the ideology of the Roman Question. He continued to try to resolve the Roman Question on Catholic terms. Nevertheless, although critical of Italian intervention, he supported the establishment of military chaplains who provided Catholic services to the armed forces and consecrated the national cause.[15]

On 21 June 1915, Benedict gave an interview to Paris's La Liberté. A salvo against the Law of Guarantees, the interview also appeared to some observers to suggest the pope would call on Austrian military intervention to resolve the Roman Question. "We have faith in the present government, but we fear our exposure to the uncertainty of Italian public life. Rome is a furnace in perpetual ferment. You will say that it is absurd to fear revolution these days. But what will happen tomorrow? . . . The future is obscure." The interview was so disruptive that

L'Osservatore Romano denied its accuracy. The Allies and the United States interpreted it as evidence that the Vatican favored the Central Powers and would call upon them to resolve the Roman Question. Ambassador Page informed Secretary of State Robert Lansing that the interview demonstrated Benedict would "align the Vatican against the Allies." Wilson agreed.[16]

To quell the charge of pro-Germanism and calm suspicions, Vatican secretary of state Gasparri repudiated the interview in *La Liberté*, which "in no point reproduced exactly the thought of the Holy Father." The abnormal situation of the Holy See under the Law of Guarantees would be corrected "not through foreign arms, but by the triumph of the sentiment of justice, which I hope increasingly spreads itself among the Italian people in conformity with their true interests."[17] In a 4 August circular to his nuncios, Gasparri launched an international journalistic campaign. It is noteworthy that he sent the circular to Apostolic Delegate Giovanni Bonzano in Washington, neither a nuncio nor a formal diplomatic representative of the Holy See to the United States. American Catholics and the United States, it was clear, were to play a role in papal diplomacy during and after the Great War.

Gasparri's circular had two parts. It highlighted the urgency of the Roman Question when it claimed that Italian intervention undermined free communication between the Holy See and Catholics in belligerent states. Although Gasparri acknowledged the "good will" of Salandra, he wondered "what would happen in the future if [Prime] Minister Salandra were succeeded in the event of a crisis by a radical Minister? . . . Clearly the present situation of the Holy See set in place by the facts of 1870 is essentially precarious and uncertain since it relies upon the changing condition of men and events."[18]

Gasparri also put forth an international strategy to resolve the Roman Question. He urged his nuncios (and Bonzano) to promote "authoritative publications useful to illuminate public opinion" about the Roman Question. Gasparri urged Bonzano to exert pressure upon the U.S. government to favor a resolution of the Roman Question.

> Just because the Holy Father . . . does not call foreign armies to reestablish his temporal throne, this does not mean that the governments of Catholic states or the governments of those states that include Catholics among their subjects [such as the United States], do not have the right to occupy themselves with the abnormal situation of the Holy See. In fact they have such a duty. If the states are Catholic, they must in some way be urged to consider all that concerns the independence, authority and divine mission of the Papacy. If the states are not Catholic, they must still defend the interests, including the religious interests, of their Catholic populations. The Holy See, therefore, trusts that governments will never forget this right and

this duty on every favorable occasion . . . to keep the unresolved Roman Question alive.

Finally, Gasparri instructed Bonzano to pressure the secretary of state to discuss the Roman Question "with Italian diplomats accredited to" Washington and to urge the U.S. State Department to "order its representatives in Rome" to discuss the Roman Question "with the Italian foreign ministry."[19]

Although historians acknowledge that Liberal Italy generally respected the Law of Guarantees, the Holy See had cause for concern. After the Italian declaration of war against Austria on 23 May 1915, the diplomatic representatives from Austria, Prussia, and Bavaria to the Holy See moved to Lugano, Switzerland, insisting Italian authorities obstructed their work. Italy denied the accusations. But in a blatant violation of the Law of Guarantees, after Austria bombed Venice, the Italian government confiscated the historic residence of the Austrian embassy to the Holy See on 25 September 1916.[20]

U.S. Neutrality and American Catholics

Historian Thomas Knock has demonstrated how President Wilson synthesized ideas from English and American liberals, progressives, and radicals into a "progressive internationalism." Rather than seek a traditional balance of power, Wilson hoped to use the war to establish collective security grounded in democratic ideals of self-determination. Less directly, Wilson's vision had roots in covenantal Reformed theology.[21] Although the United States remained neutral until April 1917, it clashed with Benedict on practically every issue.

The Holy See's ambition to maintain intact Germany and Austria-Hungary— bulwarks of conservatism—did not endear the Church to the U.S. State Department. Wilson judged papal diplomacy to be inappropriate interference by a spiritual leader in worldly affairs. He opposed the inclusion of a papal representative at an eventual peace conference, deflected Benedict's efforts to arbitrate among belligerents, and ignored Vatican pleas to keep America neutral. The Holy See, for its part, opposed official U.S. positions regarding arms sales, German submarine warfare, and the English embargo. American Catholic newspapers generally supported the pope's positions and claimed Wilson deviated from his professed neutrality.[22]

Wilson consistently deflected Vatican "interference." When German submarines sank the *Lusitania* on 7 May 1915, the *Arabic* on 19 August, and the *Sussex* on 24 March 1916, the Vatican acted to prevent U.S. intervention in the war. In August 1915, hoping to stem the impending U.S.-German diplomatic rupture, Gasparri informed Wilson that the Holy See was negotiating with Germany to resolve U.S.-German differences. The American press saw in the papal initiative evidence of pro-Germanism. After the *Sussex* was sunk, the Vatican intervened again. Although Wilson drafted a polite reply to Benedict, he considered the papal initiative, undertaken during the American preparedness campaign, as an intrusion.[23]

On 12 December 1916, Germany launched a peace proposal backed by the Vatican. Wilson, in turn, on 18 December deflected German efforts and himself called all belligerents to propose terms for peace. Ambassador Page explained to Lansing that the Holy See wanted to arbitrate the peace in order "to be recognized and have a seat in that conference." Page reckoned, "it shows very clearly that the Vatican is working with all its power for Austria." After further investigation, Page insisted that the Vatican's "prime wish" was "the internationalization of the law of guarantees which at present is the work of Italy alone, and as a first step towards this a seat in the peace congress when it shall assemble." The American Catholic press fumed when Wilson rejected the German peace initiative. Ultimately, the deterioration of U.S.-German relations culminated in Wilson's war address on 2 April 1917.[24]

Because statesmen in England, Italy, and the United States believed the Holy See favored the Central Powers, they feared the disruptive potential of the American Catholic population. Before America entered the fray, the Allies worried that American Catholics might keep Wilson out of the war, and they monitored the American Catholic press carefully. In April 1916, Italian ambassador Vincenzo Macchi di Cellere ominously warned Sonnino of "the progressive increase of the number of Catholics in the United States." Their "great importance" could "tip the balance" in U.S. domestic and foreign policy. The Church's power in city politics "must not escape our attention in view of the possible future repercussions in the relations between the United States and Italy that could be influenced by the mistrust and adversity against our country from that nucleus of Irish fanatics who are the principal nucleus of Catholics here."[25]

The fear of an American Catholic power bloc was real, but scholarship on this period of U.S. neutrality ignores the Church. While diplomatic historians say nothing at all about the papacy and the American Catholic population (as opposed to Irish Americans or German Americans), scholars of the Church have not updated their classic historiographical argument forged before 1965, when the Catholic population was burdened with a minority mentality. That argument asserted that American Catholics were patriotic citizens who never posed problems for their government in moments of national trial, and who never were lackeys of a "foreign" power. In this defensive scholarship, criticism of Wilson had to result from Irish and German ethnicity and not Catholicism. This school of thinking turned Catholic publications such as the Jesuits' *America*, the Paulists' *Catholic World*, the Extension Society's *Extension Magazine*, and countless diocesan papers into mouthpieces for Irish and German ethnic anxieties during wars or crises but treated them as voices of Catholic America at all other times.[26]

National or ethnic sensibilities were, of course, important. But the American Catholic press, while not homogeneous, clearly supported Benedict on all his major diplomatic initiatives. It backed his right to arbitrate world affairs, his desire to maintain U.S. neutrality, his wish to participate at the peace conference, and his call to resolve the Roman Question. Although the American Catholic press in some instances supported Irish independence or expressed solidarity with the people of Germany, it also lashed out at France and Italy for their ostensibly Masonic and anticlerical governments and at Russia for its heretical Orthodoxy. It evaluated states based upon how they treated the Church and to what extent they supported papal initiatives. The liberal and Protestant press, in contrast, attacked the Church and the Holy Father. Allied embassies in the United States carefully tracked these debates, reasonably assumed the Catholic arguments represented popular Catholic opinion, and acted accordingly. Furthermore, as we shall see, American Catholic leaders and the Vatican strategically manipulated Protestant and liberal fears of a Catholic monolith working in league with the pope.

In line with Gasparri's instructions, the apostolic delegation, dubbed "Rome on the Potomac" in the Protestant press, did in fact direct and discipline Catholic editors. Soon after his arrival in 1912, Apostolic Delegate Bonzano received an overture from Nicholas Gonner, who wished "to place my experience and knowledge . . . under the direction and guidance and at the disposal of Your Excellency [Bonzano] as personal representative of the Holy Father." Former and honorary president of the German Catholic Central-Verein, executive board member of the American Federation of Catholic Societies, active participant in the Catholic Press Association, and polemical editor of the *Katholischer Westen, Luxemburger Gazette*, and *Catholic Tribune*, Gonner was a force to be reckoned with. Bonzano urged Gonner, "on every favorable occasion, [to] deeply inculcate in our readers the duties of loyalty and devotion to the Holy Father. Endeavor to make His needs better known to them, and insist upon His necessity of being free and independent for the government of the universal church."[27]

Gonner proudly displayed his journalistic effusions on the Roman Question to Bonzano. On 7 May 1913, he attacked secret societies on the front page of the *Catholic Tribune*, which he enclosed in a letter to the delegate. "I have not omitted to emphasize that secret societies have been the chief instrument in robbing the Pope of his temporal possessions and this was done with the distinct intention of obeying Your Excellency's wishes to make known to American Catholics one of the causes that has made the position of the Holy Father and the Holy See so deplorably disagreeable in Rome."[28]

In the period of U.S. neutrality, the Catholic press assailed article XV of the no-longer-secret Treaty of London. In January 1916, Gasparri informed Bonzano of the general contexts of "this odious act of the Italian government" to exclude "the highest moral authority in the world" from the peace conference. Bonzano encouraged the Catholic press to protest article XV and the vulnerability of the Holy See under the Law of Guarantees. Gonner wondered if he and his colleagues "may become over-zealous and perhaps overstep the boundary line of a cautious and effective defense by too much impetuosity" regarding his "treatments of the question of the Independence of the Holy See." But Bonzano assured Gonner he "heartily approved" of the polemics. As in all cases when the Vatican directed American Catholic affairs, Bonzano reminded the zealous editor, "the encourage-ment that I give you must . . . be kept entirely secret and confidential." In January and February 1916, Gonner's papers critiqued the "odious" article at a fever pitch. "It is a pity and a shame that Mr. Wilson, the president of the United States, the greatest of neutral nations, appears to be *so unfair* in his dealings with the Catho-lic Church. . . . There is hardly any hope that he will recognize the Holy Father and the Holy See as factors for real neutrality and real peace for the world."[29]

Gonner became Bonzano's watchdog. "Some Catholic papers appear to be-lieve that a strong and persistent defense of the Independence of the Holy See is not agreeable to the Roman authorities," he slyly noted as he mailed Bonzano copies of other papers. Bonzano, in response, called upon Bishop Joseph Glass of Salt Lake City to discipline the editor of Los Angeles's *Tidings*. "Its number of December 24," Bonzano reproved, "would seem to blame anybody that would at-tempt to keep alive the so-called Roman question by insisting on the rights and privileges of the Holy See." The delegate enforced Catholic unity. "I must say that the position taken by this paper is not at all worthy of praise, and in fact, other Catholic editors have resented it." Bonzano suggested, "the enclosed clipping, taken from [Gonner's] 'Catholic Tribune' of Dubuque, seems to me to outline the proper stand to take in this question." "Not acquainted with anybody in Los Angeles," Bonzano directed Glass to contact the editor of *Tidings* to let "him know that his point of view is not in favor with the authorities." The delegate added, "any other action that you may see fit to take, for instance in your local paper, towards keeping the question of the rights and privileges of the Holy See before the people will be appreciated. My name must not be mentioned in either case, as this is entirely in confidence to you."[30]

Richard H. Tierney, SJ, the vociferous editor of *America*, was another combative Vatican mouthpiece. On 21 January 1916, Bonzano sent Tierney the same *Catholic Tribune* article sent to Bishop Glass on the Roman Question and peace negotia-tions. He instructed Tierney to prepare "as strong an article as possible develop-ing ideas expressed in the enclosed few lines regarding the position of the Holy Father." In addition to *America*, "get it, or at least extracts from it, published in some representative daily papers." The delegate reminded the Jesuit, "of course my writing to you is in strictest confidence and no hint as the source of your in-formation must appear." Tierney promised to do his best but feared resistance from "the secular press . . . because the Jew is all but omnipotent here." He urged

Bonzano to "enlist Dr. [Peter] Guilday, Professor of History at the Catholic University [of America]," who was writing a series for the *New York Sun*. Guilday might "suggest to the editor that the final article be on 'The Pope and The War.' This will give occasion to introduce the idea you suggest."[31]

The American episcopacy, in no uncertain terms, broadcast Catholic loyalties to the United States when Wilson led the nation into war. The bishops reminded their people that obedience to civil authorities was a duty, and the National Catholic War Conference, created to mobilize Catholics, became an effective organization in the U.S. war effort. However, Catholic expressions of patriotism were not evidence of Catholic self-confidence in wartime America, and the exaggerated nationalism of American Catholics was not an endorsement of Wilson's progressive international vision. American Catholic nationalism grew in response to the insecurity Catholics felt as their fellow citizens attacked the Holy See and questioned Catholic loyalty.

Benedict did not only call upon his Catholic spiritual children to aid his quest to sit at the peace conference. Oddly, he also sought the support of Jews. Historian David Kertzer explains how the pope agreed to condemn anti-Jewish violence in Russia perpetrated among retreating troops on defenseless victims, if Jews within England, France, and the United States would try to convince their governments to offer the Holy See a place at the postwar peace conference. The Jewish communities in France and England, however, did not take the bait. Leaders of English Jewish organizations wrote the president of the American Jewish Committee in New York that the conditions of a papal humanitarian intervention would offend liberals among the Allied powers and perhaps endanger Jews throughout the world.[32]

The Peace Note of August 1917, Caporetto, and the American Church at War

On 15 August 1917, four months after the United States entered the war, Benedict floated his famous peace Note to belligerents. It called for a return to the status quo ante bellum—the restitution of occupied lands and proposed reduction of armaments, the substitution of arbitration for warfare, the renunciation of reparations, and the return to freedom of the seas. Benedict urged border negotiations between Italy and Austria and between Germany and France. He hoped peace would inspire among them "a conciliatory spirit, giving due weight, within the limits of justice and feasibility, . . . to the aspirations of the populations, . . . bringing their particular interests into harmony with the general welfare of the great community of mankind." He also wanted "the same spirit of equity and justice" to inform negotiations for Armenia, the Balkans, and Poland.[33]

Wilson and Lansing dismissed Benedict's enterprise. Lansing told Wilson that the Note "emanates from Austria-Hungary and is probably sanctioned by the German Government." The pope "practically goes no further than the German peace proposal of last December." Lansing reproved the absence of reparations for Belgium, Montenegro, Serbia, and France. He reasoned, "the Pope, probably unwittingly or out of compassion for Austria-Hungary, has become in this matter the agent of Germany." In his diary, Lansing added that the Note had been shaped by "an earnest wish to preserve the Dual Empire," which "has been the main support of the Vatican for half a century, and has been always faithful to the doctrine of temporal power."[34]

In Wilson's response to Benedict on 29 August, the president explained, "the object of the war was to deliver the free peoples of the world from the menace and the actual power of a vast military establishment controlled by an irresponsible government." The pope's Note, however, was a call for a truce, not a means to mobilize the democratic sentiments of Europeans to combat despotism. In fact, Wilson disapproved a priori of papal mediation because it violated his liberal understanding of the proper place of a spiritual leader in international affairs. Fifteen years later, French ambassador Jules Jusserand recalled how Wilson "plainly showed me his ill-humor at Benedict's wanting to 'butt in' (his own words)."[35]

The Note, which received negative front-page and editorial coverage during the second half of August, reinforced boundaries between Catholics and other Americans. The *New York Times* claimed that among the Allies "the proposal of the Pope is looked upon as emanating from the Government of Austria-Hungary." In London the Note generated "much discussion, which is not altogether devoid of anxiety when the question is narrowed down to its influence upon Catholic opinion in America." Editorials stressed, as did Wilson, that "his Holiness leaves quite untouched the really fundamental problems of war, the all-important conditions of peace. . . . Unmistakably it is a peace overture, and it comes from the Teutonic Powers." The pope had proposed an armistice, not a genuine peace that would bring democracy to autocratic Europe; the Note, hatched in Berlin, placed all belligerents on the same level of moral culpability.[36]

The Note made the delicate position of the American hierarchy even more difficult. During the war, the bishops tried to protect their people from accusations of disloyalty and to defend their Holy Father. They hoped Benedict might take the lead in peace negotiations, but they also knew that in order to protect him from defamation, they must not antagonize government officials or inflame public opinion against the Church. Thus, although the bishops agreed the pope should exercise leadership on the international stage, they varied in the degree to which they spoke out for the peace Note and other papal initiatives. These differences were matters of temperament and strategy and should not be mistaken for divergent ideological factions within the U.S. hierarchy.

For instance, in a speech before the Federation of Catholic Societies days after the Note became public, Archbishop Edward Hanna of San Francisco called upon "the men who sway the destinies of nations" to listen to Benedict, "who, in the ways of Providence represents Christ upon earth." The pope, "by his very place in the world's economy, is by divine appointment mediator of peace."[37] This rather direct endorsement can be contrasted to Cardinal James Gibbons's vague blurb in the *New York Times.* "The Pope is actuated by lofty, humane, and disinterested motives." Gibbons explained to Bonzano, "the present moment is a most delicate one . . . [and] unfortunately unfriendly critics are not few." Still, he was "determined to use to the utmost whatever power I may possess to influence the people and the Government of the United States toward favorable consideration of the proposals made by our Holy Father." In fact, Gibbons took no aggressive steps to promote the Note.[38] His caution did not reflect deviation from the Catholic position that the pope ought to lead the peace process but rather a realistic assessment of the possibilities for papal support from the U.S. State Department, the president, and American society. Gibbons, on two or three occasions over the course of five or six years of loyal papal diplomacy, practiced a thoughtful inactivity to protect both the pope and the American Catholic population from unnecessary defamation.

Notwithstanding Gibbons's caution, the Catholic press promoted the Note with steadfast consistency in uncompromising language. New York's archdiocesan *Catholic News* insisted "the secular press" that rejected Benedict's Note was the moral equivalent "of an inventor of explosives. . . . [A] cold-blooded mortal knows an end of the war will hurt his business, and he favors going on with the slaughter." *America* blustered, "the nation that refuses to harken to [Benedict's Note] writes itself down not as a vindicator of justice but as a monster lustful of men's blood." But after Wilson issued his firm rejection, *America* salvaged what it could: "In certain fundamentals these exalted authorities [Wilson and Benedict] are in complete harmony."[39]

As October and November brought further suspicions of Vatican motives, *America* lashed out at "the enemies of the Papacy" who found "some cryptic and sinister meaning" in the papal initiative. When the *Atlantic Monthly* suggested Benedict hoped to gain "a larger temporal power" that would make the pope "the final arbiter between kings," *America* fought back. When Herbert Croly in the *New Republic* equated the Note with "a stubborn attempt made by Catholicism to recover some of its lost prestige," the Paulists' *Catholic World* questioned Croly's honesty. Invoking "the patriotic activity and unselfish service" of Catholics, the *Catholic World* explained that the work of the Holy Father "is of this world: yet it is above the world." Those "alleging that he pleads the cause of one nation rather than another, simply do not see the larger, the higher mission." Sparring over the motives of the Holy See continued throughout the war, separating Catholics from their neighbors.[40]

The papal Note kicked up a whirlwind in Italy, where the liberal press alleged it undermined the war effort. In a speech to the Chamber of Deputies on 25 October 1917, Sonnino sounded like Wilson. "We all want peace" but "a peace that is not only a treaty." He expressed concern for the injustices perpetrated upon Belgium, Russia, and France and insinuated that the Note favored the Central Powers. Privately, Sonnino feared the Note might lead the Allies to negotiate a separate peace with Austria-Hungary, undermine the Treaty of London, and open the door to a papal representative at the peace conference. To complicate matters, Sonnino's speech coincided with Italy's crushing military defeat at Caporetto. Liberals accused socialists and Catholics, under the pernicious influence of Vatican propaganda and Benedict's peace initiative, for the humiliating loss.[41]

Accusations of papal complicity in the defeat at Caporetto intensified American Catholic isolation from fellow citizens. Ambassador Page wrote Wilson to credit "partly Socialistic and partly Clericalistic or Vaticanistic [propaganda] in favor of bringing the war to a close" for the defeat. According to London's *Morning Post*, the "Vatican is implicated in a conspiracy largely responsible for the recent Italian disasters." The *New York Tribune* editorialized, "Austrian and German kaisers have promised the Pope that the restoration of the temporal power of the Papacy shall be one of the first fruits of their triumph. Every clerical influence has been exerted to break down the morale of the Italian soldiers." The *Catholic News* ridiculed such "outrageous misrepresentation," as the Catholic press, predictably, defended Benedict's authentic neutrality. *America* reminded readers how Italy's government had "given unreserved praise to the clergy and Hierarchy of Italy." Harsh debates about the causes behind the collapse of the Italian army at Caporetto persisted even after the war.[42]

Even as they served in the armed forces, American Catholics clashed with wartime state agencies. In April 1917, to direct domestic and international propaganda, Wilson established the Committee on Public Information (CPI) under George Creel, the progressive publicity director of the president's 1916 reelection campaign. The CPI, a bastion of progressives, liberal reformers, and muckrakers, mobilized to shape public opinion. It monitored the press and supplied patriotic copy to foreign-language papers. In April 1918, an Italian bureau—the Roman Legion—was organized within the CPI to work with Italian American associations. Catholics considered the Roman Legion's president, Dr. Antonio Stella, and its executive director, Dr. Albert C. Bonaschi, suspicious liberals.[43]

The Roman Legion comprised an uncomfortable mix of liberal nationalists and Catholics. Msgr. Alfonso Arcese of Brooklyn, one of the legion's vice presidents, wrote Bonzano, "Dr. Stella has taken special care to see that the Legion and its work be acceptable to the official representatives of the Italian Government. Its national office is made up of 'liberali' but up to this [moment] they have always shown marked respect for the Catholic Italian clergy." The legion, however, appointed a Protestant minister as a delegate and promoted a celebration on the 20th of September. Although assured by legion colleagues that "there is no intention to offend the Catholics," Arcese felt "it is hard to see how . . . this could be prevented. At least our enemies would so interpret it and it would also be so interpreted in Italy. I told them so. It is hardly proper that the Committee on Public Information and the United States Government should be a party and pay at least in part, the expenses of the celebration."[44]

But little could be done. On 9 September 1918, Archbishop Dennis Dougherty of Philadelphia, approached by his Italian clergy, requested guidance from Bonzano. "If Catholics participate they will seem to approve of the spoliation of the Holy See; if they refrain from sharing in it, they will be stigmatized as unpatriotic." Dougherty had informed his priests that "Catholics, especially priests, should not participate. Some other date should be chosen for a merely patriotic demonstration." He wondered "whether some one like Card. Gibbons should secretly induce our Government to stop [this celebration] in a prudent manner." Bonzano reasoned that it would be impossible to prevent the celebration but agreed that clergy ought not participate "in these festivities that unfortunately have an antipapal significance."[45]

The work of the CPI in Italy was even more troubling to Catholics. In February 1918, the CPI opened a news bureau within the U.S. embassy in Rome. Its director, Charles Merriam, a University of Chicago political scientist and progressive reformer, brought suspect liberals such as Fiorello La Guardia, Rudolph Altrocchi, another Chicago professor, and speakers affiliated with the YMCA to lecture throughout Liberal Italy. Merriam also organized trips to America for Italian liberal journalists, including Paolo Cappa of *Avvenire d'Italia* and Antonio Agresti of *Tribuna di Roma*. Both had accused the Vatican of pro-Germanism.[46]

Father Tierney of *America* objected that Creel permitted "Italian journalists as guests in the United States to calumny with impunity the Head of many million American Catholics." He claimed Creel gave the YMCA too much control over the CPI. Just for good measure, the Jesuit editor insinuated that Creel was Jewish. Bewildered, Creel wrote Father Peter Guilday, a professor at the Catholic University, about Tierney's editorial. "While very cheap in its sarcasm, [it] nevertheless contained many untruths that I would not like to see circulated. In the first place, while I admire the Jews greatly, I happen to be intensely Irish." Creel also explained that Tierney had mistaken CPI literature for YMCA pamphlets that called for Protestant workers.[47]

Guilday sought clarification. He sent Tierney Creel's letter and commented how Tierney's editorial "pained me very much, for from my own relations with the Committee on Public Information I can honestly say its personnel is made up of high class men without the slightest trace of bias." Tierney was unmoved. "The burden of our complaint is not that, contrary to the American spirit, the YWCA, or any other organization of its kind, demands Evangelical cooks, athletes, cafeteria managers and social workers, but that a pamphlet making such requisitions was printed on the Government printing press." For clarity's sake, Tierney added, "'America' did not say Mr. Creel is a Jew, but quoted a statement to that effect without affirming or denying the truth thereof."[48]

1918: The Catholic Campaign against Article XV

On 15 November 1917, one month after the Bolshevik Revolution knocked Russia out of the war, the Soviets published an inaccurate version of the Treaty of London. It confirmed that the Allies had conspired against Benedict's cherished hope to participate in the peace conference, but it erroneously added that article XV prohibited the Holy See from taking "any diplomatic steps for the conclusion of peace." Outraged but undeterred, Catholics escalated their campaign against article XV until the peace conference in Paris began on 18 January 1919.[49]

On 9 January 1918, Wilson put forward his Fourteen Points. On the same day, Father John Wynne, SJ, instructed all Catholic papers east of Pittsburgh to argue Benedict's Note and Wilson's Fourteen Points were identical. "It seems to me eminently desirable just now that the similarity of these two messages should be emphasized in order to offset the manifest propaganda in our [non-Catholic] Press to construe the Pope's attitude as pro-German and to blame him for the collapse of the Italian armies." Wynne confided to Bonzano, "it is a pity [Benedict's] message was not more strongly urged on the attention of the country." Although some details of Wilson's Fourteen Points resembled the papal Note, the ideological framework of the president's New Diplomacy and his vision for postwar Europe make narrow comparisons with Benedict misleading. Wilson's polite dismissal of the papal initiative reflected his a priori rejection of a spiritual sovereign meddling in politics. Wilson's liberal position differed from the Catholic assumption that the Holy See was a neutral moral force that ought to mediate conflict in international affairs.[50]

The Catholic campaign against article XV roused the ire of Americans preconditioned to shudder at papal designs for global domination. In May 1918, John Cowles, a high-ranking Freemason, sparred with a sacerdotal critic on the pages of *America.* "Our criticism is of the Roman Hierarchy, and you know, Reverend sir, that your Church is after temporal power, that it mixes up greatly in politics, not only in this, but in every country in which it exists." Cowles vented the frustrations of many Americans who believed the Holy See was a medieval despotism that backed the kaiser. "Prussia is about two-thirds Protestant, and yet I believe it is generally conceded that the Vatican has been, and still is, pro-German. The Pope's private chamberlain, Gerlach, a German, conducted his nefarious traitorism right in the Vatican and only managed to escape before he was condemned to death." Bombarded with a barrage of Wilsonian messianism denigrating autocratic governments, many Americans shared Cowles's hopes. "Prussia, an autocracy, and the Roman Catholic autocracy, are the only two great autocracies left in the world today, and they will go in time."[51]

In 1918 several components of the Holy See's strategy required cooperation from the U.S. episcopacy and deployed American Catholic public opinion as a diplomatic weapon. First, the Vatican appealed to Wilson's distaste for secret treaties and the "old diplomacy" of European imperialism. The Holy See maintained that America's allies were selfish schemers motivated by greed for spoils and not democratic ideals. It presented itself as a moral force sympathetic to the Fourteen Points. In this way, the Vatican planned to persuade Wilson to pressure Italy to renounce the Treaty of London. To enact this goal, Gasparri urged Gibbons to meet with Wilson. The American cardinal, however, did not comply, because he correctly assumed that the president would resist the plan. Predictably, U.S. officials suspected Benedict's motives, never made a public statement about article XV, and did not speak to the Allies on the Vatican's behalf.[52]

Second, the Vatican threatened a Catholic campaign against England if it did not urge Italy to renounce article XV. The British ambassador in Washington, after reading the American Catholic press thunder against article XV, feared that the Treaty of London "has done the Allies a good deal of harm." The Catholic hierarchies in England, New Zealand, Canada, and Australia all pressured England. Cardinal Gibbons visited the British embassy to warn, or rather threaten, that protest from the U.S. hierarchy could be averted only if article XV was stricken.[53]

It is not by chance that Gibbons took this very moment to publish "The War Policy of the Pope" in *America* on 23 February 1918. Praised by both Bonzano and Benedict, it tapped into the affective bonds linking Catholics to their Holy Father, poignantly portraying the Holy Father as a suffering servant crucified for humanity. "One lone and majestic figure calls for all my sympathy and love. More perhaps than any other single individual our Holy Father, Pope Benedict XV, has suffered in this tragedy. Others have but their own individual sorrow. He bears the sorrows of all. . . . He cannot but mourn over the slaughter of his spiritual children." Gibbons implored: "He is a co-sufferer with all the nations in the conflict." Persecuted by calumnies, "the Holy Father has faced a terrible ordeal. . . . On all sides he is surrounded by pitfalls. Every act of his is watched, scrutinized by jealous, critical, hostile eyes, only too ready to find fault and to register blame. More than ever he needs the support of his loyal children. . . . We are not going to fail our Holy Father." This reference to loyal children rising up to back their Holy Father in his suffering generated no little anxiety at the British embassy, especially when Gibbons arrived for a visit on 24 February to discuss article XV. In fact, "The

War Policy of the Pope," reprinted in the Catholic and secular press, inspired such a fear of American Catholic protest that the English urged Liberal Italy to support the abolition or revision of article XV. Sonnino, however, stood firm.[54]

The third component of the Holy See's strategy was direct negotiation with Italy. On 16 February 1918, Sonnino, in a speech to the Chamber of Deputies, re-affirmed that the Holy See could not attend the peace conference and that the Law of Guarantees would remain unchanged. However, Prime Minister Vittorio Emanuele Orlando, who had come to power in October 1917, and Treasury Minister Francesco Saverio Nitti did not support Sonnino's uncompromising stance. Orlando believed the Vatican could be useful in Italy's bid to acquire her *terra irre-denta*, her "unredeemed land," namely, Italian-speaking regions within Austria-Hungary. On 19 February, Orlando sent a report to the Holy See. He explained that article XV required "states allied with Italy to support any objection Italy might make to the possible admission of the Holy See to the Peace Congress." But article XV "does not exclude that circumstances can render possible the inter-vention of the Holy See at the Peace Congress." The phrasing emphasized how the decision was in Italy's hands, and therefore Italy could permit the Holy See to participate. Encouraged by Orlando's overture, Gasparri continued his campaign against article XV.[55]

If the Allies could not be compelled to drop article XV, perhaps they might alter its wording. The alternative Gasparri proposed replaced the phrase that singled out the Holy See with one that included all nonbelligerents. This, he suggested, would eliminate the discriminatory nature of the exclusion. However, a care-ful reading of Gasparri's modification reveals his attempt to undermine Liberal Italy's exclusive veto power and thereby introduce ambiguity into article XV that could work to the Holy See's advantage if its campaign bore fruit. The modified version read: "No non-belligerent will be admitted to the possible peace confer-ence if there is not consent of the undersigned," that is, without the consent of France, England, and Italy.[56]

Sonnino, however, was alert to Gasparri's machinations. On 3 August 1918, Sonnino notified his ambassadors in Washington, London, and Paris to commu-nicate that Italy would consent to neither the alteration nor abolition of article XV. Britain, France, and the United States backed Sonnino. Macchi di Cellere cabled Sonnino: "We should not have any fears about this since the convictions, direc-tives, and program of [the United States] government are and will remain in com-plete disagreement with the . . . aspirations of the Vatican."[57]

In the meantime, Catholic protests mounted. Cardinal Désiré Mercier, the Bel-gian primate, was eager to urge bishops and the faithful throughout the world to clamor for papal representation at the peace conference and for a temporal sov-ereignty for the pope. He wrote Gasparri: "If Italy wants to avoid the antipathy and contempt of all Catholic peoples, if it wants to contribute to the goal of universal pacification of those who meet at the peace conference, it must recognize a territorial sovereignty for the Head of the Catholic Church." Gasparri and Benedict approved Mercier's plan and plotted, unsuccessfully, to have Mercier named to Belgium's peace delegation. Gibbons, in contrast, deflected Gasparri's request to speak to Wilson and to mount protests from the U.S. hierarchy, although other American bishops, more aggressive than the octogenarian cardinal, were eager to launch a campaign on behalf of their Holy Father.[58]

By May 1918, Wilson and Lansing had made it clear that they favored the dissolution of Austria-Hungary and the recognition of the national aspirations of peoples within the faltering dual monarchy. To prevent this outcome, the Vatican urged Wilson to make a separate peace with Austria-Hungary, and it encouraged Austria-Hungary to enact internal reforms to appease the rising tide of national sentiments. On 15 June 1918, "The Just Aspirations of Peoples" appeared in *Civiltà Cattolica*. It stressed the dangers inherent in the modern idea of nationalism—that each nationality ought to attain its own state. This effort to counter the excitement generated by the 29 May Congress of the Oppressed Nationalities held in Rome did not, however, deter Wilson. He ignored Benedict's plea to consider the dual monarch's request for an armistice.[59]

Wilson's visit to Italy, scheduled for January 1919, presented the Holy See with another opportunity to pressure the president to revise article XV or to discuss the Roman Question. Bonzano directed several American Catholics in November 1918 to encourage Wilson to meet with the pope upon his visit. Bishop Patrick Hayes, bishop for Catholic chaplains, soon to become the archbishop of New York, tapped his New York connections toward this end. On 29 November, he "had a conference with [Associate] Justice [Victor] Dowling [of the Supreme Court, Appellate Division], Mr. Morgan J. O'Brien, Mr. Nicholas Brady and Congressman Thomas F. Smith. Judge Dowling also had a word with Mr. John D. Ryan, who recently resigned as Second Assistant Secretary of War. All felt the importance of the matter. Proper representation will be made in the right place." Dowling prepared a letter for Colonel Edward House, Wilson's foreign affairs operative, delivered to Paris by Chairman William J. Mulligan of the Knights of Columbus Committee on War Activities. Hayes received assurances from Governor-elect Al Smith "that he will make known how important the matter is politically." Senator David I. Walsh of Massachusetts assured Bonzano, "I shall at once use my influence to see that your suggestion is carried out. . . . It would be very unfortunate if the President should visit Rome without visiting the Holy Father." The visit, however, never came about.[60]

As the Paris peace conference approached, Catholic Americans rose up to call for papal representation and a solution to the Roman Question. Anthony Matre, secretary of the Federation of Catholic Societies, feared "that unless some dignified request is now made by the Catholics of this country and by Catholics of the Allied nations, the Father of Christendom may not be invited." Matre asked Bonzano for permission to act. Cardinal William Henry O'Connell of Boston received Bonzano's praise and front-page coverage in the *Boston Sunday Post* for an address he delivered to the League of Catholic Women in which he called for papal representation in Paris. O'Connell complained to Bonzano, "the Associated Press seems far more intent upon reporting what distinguished prelates have to say in superlative adulation of the President than in anything concerning the Holy See." Probably referring to Gibbons's cautious style of intervention, O'Connell remarked, "no cause takes care of itself."[61]

As the peace conference approached, the American Catholic press pleaded for papal representation. The *Catholic World* argued that peace and prosperity could only be built upon a religious foundation "strong enough to outweigh self-interest, . . . powerful enough to make us look beyond material welfare, . . . independent of the nations." This "final arbiter, when the nations themselves disagree, . . . is the Papacy." "The spiritual power and the spiritual influence which [Benedict] can contribute is necessary for the success of permanent peace of an enduring league of nations. We have fought for the spiritual rights of man. The historic protagonist of those rights should sit at a peace table where the future of the world is to be determined."[62] *America* was unrelenting. The Holy See's absence from Paris would be a "calamity." As "the only depository of information concerning all the great events of the conflict," as the "greatest moral force in the world," as the only reliable bulwark against "the new-found emotions" among liberated Czechs, Slovaks, Poles, and Lithuanians, the world needed the Holy Father.[63]

Letters to editor Tierney at *America* demonstrate how debates about the Roman Question strengthened boundaries separating Catholics from others. "It makes my blood boil," stammered one frustrated "Loyal American" to Tierney,

> when I read the false pretenses, professing to be true and loyal Americans when all your articles are reeking with intentions to disrupt and destroy the Liberty of our Grand Republic, and turn it over to the power and glory seeking pope and the cunning and treacherous jesuits. . . . It is getting too evident that the Roman Catholic hydra headed monster is trying to rule again like it did in the days of the Inquisition. . . . You are trying to muzzle the press or in other words strangle that what our forefathers fought for, *Freedom.* . . . Neither can you wipe out the History of your popes or blood thirsty jesuits who were nothing more but a bunch of whores, pimpos and cutthroats, torturing, murdering and turning into exile millions of people, and getting in possession of their property.

Another correspondent peppered Tierney with questions after reading that Benedict was praying for Wilson. "Who ever before heard of a Pope pinning his faith on the President of a Republic? The Pope praying for the success of our President in this war. No, no! That is really too good to be true. Pray tell us when he stopped praying for the Kaiser? Pray tell us when he stopped doing all he could to help the Kaiser?"[64]

The Postwar Quest to Resolve the Roman Question

Although the Paris peace conference began without papal representation, the Holy See, with American Catholic backing, demanded a resolution of the Roman Question. On 13 January 1919, Gasparri instructed Cardinal O'Connell to elaborate upon his speech in favor of papal representation in Paris. O'Connell was disappointed he had not been notified earlier. "I had very powerful machinery all in readiness to bring strong pressure to bear on the President and others to bring about some sort of representation, if not direct at least indirect, of the Holy Father's voice at the Peace Conference." On 17 January, Gasparri directed Gibbons and O'Connell to empower Cardinal Mercier "to ask the Peace conference in the name of the Cardinals, Episcopacy and Catholics of America for the territorial sovereignty of the Pope." The Americans complied. Gibbons's letter read: "Against the present state of affairs"—the pope's position under the Law of Guarantees—"the conscience of the whole Catholic world protests and will not be satisfied until full independence be given to" the Holy Father. O'Connell agreed that "every occasion to advertise the abnormal position of the Holy See should be taken advantage of."[65]

By March 1919, the Catholic press was crying out for a resolution to the Roman Question. John C. Reville, SJ, published a four-part series in *America* on the history of the Papal States, their "destruction" during the Risorgimento, the injustice of excluding the Holy See from the conference, and the restoration of the temporal power. Reasserting the ideology of the Roman Question in colorful language, Reville explained how marauding pagans led the unjust spoliation of the Papal States. Reville claimed he understood why Liberal Italy "feared that the Roman question would be opened at the Conference," but he insisted, "the Holy See did not intend to create embarrassment for the Italian Government" at Paris. "Sadly needed there," Benedict was "ignominiously thrust aside." He was a victim of a perverse liberal idea, "that unnatural and dangerous theory of separation, the complete divorce of religion from the realm of politics and international law." Had the Holy Father been in Paris, "the atmosphere of religion would have penetrated into the assembly," and "the Pope would have been Italy's best adviser, best friend." But "the representatives of the Italian Government, heirs of the unscrupulous statesmen who unjustly seized Rome, would have been ill at ease before the victim of that cruel spoliation."[66]

The Great Powers at Paris remained unmoved by Mercier's intervention and

Catholic public opinion. They had no interest in the Roman Question, did not want the pope at the conference, and resisted his admittance into the League of Nations. The *Catholic World* lamented, "the Peace Conference falls short and the plans for a League of Nations is insufficient because our Holy Father the Pope has not been asked to sit with the one, nor consulted, . . . with regard to the other."[67]

As Catholics broadcast their indignation about the Roman Question, the sensitive radar of Protestants beeped. The *Herald and Presbyter* asserted that the Vatican had unjustified designs for power. It accused the Church of "political preferment" in America and voiced suspicions of Catholic connections to Wilson through his personal secretary, Joseph Tumulty. Senator Lawrence Sherman of Illinois, eager to undermine ratification of the Covenant of the League of Nations in Congress, reckoned the league's high composition of Catholic nations would give the pope dominion over the world, and he said so on the Senate floor. *America* attacked Sherman. Another polemic ensued.[68]

Although Catholics failed to bring papal Rome to Paris, the combination of Prime Minister Orlando's territorial ambitions and civil unrest in Italy opened a new door to papal aspirations. While inflamed Italian nationalists clamored for Adriatic lands beyond the boundaries set by the Treaty of London, Gabriele D'Annunzio, the swashbuckling one-eyed warrior-poet, called for a seizure of Fiume, Dalmatia, and Rome itself, to liberate the capital from weak politicians. A National Council within Fiume proclaimed its annexation to Italy on 30 October 1918, but the Italian government refused to recognize the unlawful act. After Italian delegates at Paris clashed with Wilson over the status of Fiume, they theatrically stormed out of the conference on 4 April, only to return one month later. Wilson remained firm and refused to relinquish the coastal city to Italy.[69]

Orlando then made an overture that placed the Holy See in a position it had sought throughout the war. He asked the Vatican to help Liberal Italy acquire Fiume. The reward: a resolution of the Roman Question on Catholic terms. During the war the Holy See had tried to mediate between Italy and Austria-Hungary. Now, in the postwar world, Wilson and the United States became the target of Vatican mediation on behalf of Italy. Woodrow Wilson, Presbyterian moralist and progressive internationalist, now held the key to the Eternal City.

Msgr. Francis Kelly, a Chicago priest attending the Paris conference as an unofficial observer, had published a critique of Wilson's Mexico policy. This perhaps explains why the Italian government sought him out at Paris. After Wilson reproached Kelly's effort to speak to the U.S. delegation about the Roman Question, a member of the Italian delegation arranged a meeting between Kelly and Orlando. Both parties understood that if the Roman Question and Fiume became linked, Catholic opinion could be mobilized against Wilson to remove obstacles to an Adriatic settlement favorable to Italy. Gasparri sent Archbishop Bonaventura Cerretti to Paris to meet Orlando on 1 June to continue the negotiations. They agreed on general terms for a territorial Vatican state. Gasparri's instructions to Cerretti were quite explicit. A territorial state would not only realize the demands of the ideology of the Roman Question but also permit the Holy See to become a member of the League of Nations. Orlando, in turn, assured Cerretti that when the pope became a temporal sovereign Italy would request a place for him in the league.[70]

Orlando, however, never had an opportunity to present this scheme to his ministers. King Vittorio Emanuele III, the jealous sovereign of Liberal Italy, squashed the plan. King Vittorio believed that any revision of the Law of Guarantees would endanger both Italy and the Holy See. When Orlando's faltering government fell on 19 June, however, all was not lost. After King Vittorio asked Nitti to form a government, the new prime minister continued negotiations with Gasparri about the Roman Question. These ongoing negotiations were important in light of Gasparri's directives to Bonzano in February 1920 concerning the status of Fiume.[71]

The Fiume Mission of the American Episcopacy

In the months preceding the peace conference, Wilson acquired the status of a messiah among Italians. They anticipated the arrival of their heroic liberator who would redeem the nations of the Old World from their despotic rulers. The CPI assured Wilson that the Italian nation, in contrast to its autocratic politicians, "by conscious preference and natural attitude . . . come within the . . . definition of liberal." The war had prepared Italians for a grand progressive reform. The CPI Wilsonians directing propaganda from Rome worked to forge an Italian left-center party of reform socialists, labor, and radical liberals. The CPI funded Italian journalists smitten with wilsonismo. For a time the CPI was even convinced it had found the man to lead Italian Wilsonians—Benito Mussolini, a charismatic revolutionary socialist who broke ranks with his comrades when he backed intervention in the war. The CPI subsidized a Roman edition of Mussolini's Il Popolo d'Italia. In January 1919, during Wilson's visit to Italy, Mussolini proclaimed, "I kneel before the duce of the peoples." Il Popolo d'Italia heralded Wilson as the "knight of Humanity, Mazzini's intellectual heir." Wilsonismo, however, did not survive the president's "betrayal" of Italy's territorial ambitions at Paris. Many Italians later embraced the myth of the "mutilated victory" that fueled the budding Fascist movement when they became convinced that the Allies and their own liberal statesmen had forsaken them at Paris.[72]

After the Treaty of Versailles was signed on 28 June 1919, the Adriatic still smoldered, and the flames of civil unrest spread down the Italian peninsula. In 1919 and 1920, demilitarized veterans and unemployed workers instigated strikes, riots, and agrarian violence. Peasants seized latifondi, vast agricultural estates, in Sicily; socialists fomented class agitation; paramilitary Fascist Blackshirt squads

targeted socialists for violence. On the morning of 12 September 1919, D'Annunzio led a private force of mutineers and demobilized soldiers in a triumphal seizure of Fiume. He hoped his theatrical gesture would force Italian politicians and
foreign diplomats to recognize Italy's claims to the port city. D'Annunzio proclaimed his Regency of Carnaro, whose short sixteen-month life belied its importance as a harbinger of the violence, rituals, and politics of Fascism. In the midst
of this postwar unrest that seemed linked to the status of Fiume, the vulnerable
Vatican shuddered at the specter of revolution.[73]

In February 1920, Gasparri directed Bonzano to pressure Wilson to "take an
attitude more favorable toward Italy." Perhaps, Gasparri reasoned, the legitimate annexation of Fiume might quell the violence that haunted Liberal Italy and
threatened the safety of the Church. If Wilson did not change his position, "the
internal peace of Italy would be seriously compromised with grave repercussions
in all of Europe." Gasparri suggested Bonzano seek out Senator Walsh of Massachusetts and Msgr. John A. Ryan, professor at the Catholic University, as liaisons
to Wilson. But Gasparri entrusted Bonzano to use his own "prudent judgement"
on the particulars. On 24 February, Bonzano asked Archbishops George Mundelein of Chicago, Dougherty of Philadelphia, and Hayes of New York, through
their connections in the Democratic Party, to perform "a favor in a delicate and
not simple affair." He directed these three Roman-trained, rising stars in the U.S.
hierarchy, residents of cities with large Catholic populations where the Church
had strong ties to the Democrats, to work to change Wilson's position toward
Fiume. In his letter to Mundelein, Bonzano suggested the Chicago archbishop
write to Wilson's son-in-law and former secretary of the treasury, William G.
McAdoo. "Furthermore perhaps you could suggest to [William Randolph] Hearst
a journalistic campaign."[74]

The Holy See's objective was not merely to calm Italian unrest. In light of the
fact that Nitti and Gasparri were engaged at that very moment in negotiations
over the Roman Question, Gasparri's directives were part of a larger strategy.
If Catholics in America could pressure Wilson to "redeem" Fiume to Italy, Italy
would settle the Roman Question on Catholic terms.

The archbishops responded with alacrity. Dougherty reported to Bonzano,
"Mr. Mitchell Palmer, Attorney-General, has more influence than any man with
President Wilson," adding, "I have already spoken to one intimate friend of Mr.
Palmer, and tomorrow I shall reach another of his intimate friends. . . . Through
these two friends, I trust that Mr. Palmer will call the President's attention to the
proper course in the matter." Dougherty assured Bonzano, "no mention has been
made, nor will be made, of Your Excellency or of the Apostolic Delegation." On
the same day, 25 February, Hayes informed Bonzano, "the big men of the [Demo-
cratic] party are just assembling here" in New York. "By this evening press, I will
see the new appointment of Secretary of State, [Bainbridge Colby]. I know him;

and I know others who know him well. You may rely on me to do everything in my power and prudently."[75]

It was not an ideal time to try to reach Wilson. On 2 October 1919, after an exhausting tour to promote the League of Nations and Treaty of Versailles to the American people, Wilson suffered a debilitating stroke. His recovery was slow and partial. His wife and his private secretary, Joseph Tumulty, regulated the president's contact with the outside world. In November 1919 and again in March 1920, the Senate voted against ratification of the covenant of the league and the treaty. Wilson had reason neither to compromise his position on the Adriatic nor to cater to Vatican aspirations. Furthermore, he lacked the political capital.[76]

On 27 February 1920, Dougherty informed Bonzano, "nobody at present has access to Mr. Wilson, except Mrs. Wilson and Mr. Tumulty." Although Dougherty's "Washington friend . . . intends to reach Mr. Tumulty," the archbishop was "convinced that [Wilson] will pertinaciously stick to his Fiume policy. However, we shall do our best to dissuade him from it." Mundelein's news was no better. "Two parties, well-informed," had assured him that nothing could be done. "Nobody can even see [Wilson]." Mundelein rejected the utility of contacting McAdoo. And "Hearst would act like a red rag to a bull, for his very name is distasteful to Wilson." Mundelein had learned that "Wilson is practically powerless, and the others, namely England, France and Italy, know it just as well as we do." The president's inner circle was divided: "You see for yourself what a mixed-up condition of government we are living in, so that no one knows what to do and no one has the courage to take any steps." Consequently, Mundelein advised Bonzano to "remain inactive," although the young archbishop still promised "to take any steps [Bonzano] would think for the best interest of the Church."[77]

Bonzano also called upon his own connections, namely, Admiral William Benson, chief of Naval Operations, "whose influence, prudence and devotion to the Holy See are well known." The admiral, who had discussed the Adriatic question with Wilson at Paris, believed the president was determined to stay his course. But Benson agreed to take up the matter with Senator Thomas Walsh of Montana, a Democratic force in Congress. Senator Walsh of Massachusetts, Benson observed, "is no longer in [Wilson's] graces." After he had spoken with Walsh of Montana, Benson met with Bonzano again and confirmed that Wilson would not budge. Benson advised Bonzano not to seek out Tumulty because Wilson would not be pleased to learn that the Vatican was pushing the issue.[78]

Bonzano also met twice with the Italian ambassador, Baron Camillo Romano di Avezzana, who urged the delegate to use his "American friends in regard to the Adriatic question." Romano di Avezzana suggested to his superiors that the Chamber of Deputies, in its ratification of any international treaty, ought to reserve judgment on the question of Fiume and insist that it was an internal affair of the Italian state. Romano di Avezzana asked the delegate to inform Gasparri of this ploy in the hope, according to Bonzano, that Gasparri would influence "the deputies of the [Catholic] Popular Party" in the Chamber of Deputies to support the measure. By now, however, Bonzano believed there was little that could be done in regard to Fiume, due to the unstable and isolated context in which Wilson operated.[79]

Ever eager to please the Vatican, the archbishops had not yet given up. Reflecting upon Wilson's weak position, Hayes suspected that "sentiment might easily be created favorable to Italy" in the U.S. Senate. Hayes knew "big men" who "would be glad to do everything possible." Hayes was still in contact with Colby and Romano di Avezzana. "The former is very friendly to us." Romano di Avezzana had invited Hayes to a private dinner, but the archbishop had "thought it better not to go." Nevertheless they would meet soon. Dougherty referred to "one of . . . Tumulty's most intimate friends," who discussed Fiume with Wilson's secretary. The contact claimed Tumulty would do "whatever was in his power. He would bring the subject before President Wilson as soon as an opportunity was presented." But Wilson's present condition made that impossible.[80]

The failed Fiume mission marked the rise of a new cohort of American episcopal leaders who would negotiate the Church's relationship with Fascism and the New Deal. These Roman-trained bishops governing large urban sees were confident overseers of growing Catholic power and steadfastly loyal to the Holy See. In the 1920s, tensions eased between the Holy See and Fascist Italy. Cardinal-archbishops O'Connell, Dougherty, Mundelein, and Hayes led the episcopal endorsements and celebrations of Benito Mussolini as a great man who brought order and God back to Italy. They also struck up excellent relations with the Italian embassy and its consulates, whose cultural and political activities expanded within the United States.[81]

THE GREAT WAR marked a transformation in the ideology of the Roman Question. Notwithstanding the Italy-Vatican duel over the Law of Guarantees and the Roman Question, a contest once again international in scope, the Holy See implicitly recognized Liberal Italy in an unprecedented manner. Indeed, during the postwar ferment the Vatican worked to secure Italian territorial aspirations. One wonders what Pius IX would make of his favored American sons pressuring their government to take steps to stabilize the Kingdom of Italy and aggrandize its borders!

The United States was clearly an important player in papal diplomacy during and after the Great War. Wilson's liberal resistance to papal aspirations blocked Benedict from arbitrating the peace, participating in the peace conference, and presenting the Roman Question in an international forum. The new generation of American Catholic leaders who emerged after the Great War understood that Catholic power made a difference in America and that Wilson and the Allies had feared the disruptive potential of that power. The war, notwithstanding patriotic participation by American Catholics, strengthened the boundaries dividing Catholics from other Americans and ushered in the "tribal twenties," when Catholic sparring with Protestants and liberals escalated. Before I consider the interwar years, however, I explore in greater detail the nature and implications of this transformation of the ideology of the Roman Question for the United States' largest foreign-born group and their ethnic and religious leaders.

CHAPTER FIVE

The Church Encounters the Order
Sons of Italy in America, 1913–1921

In October 1920, the Vatican sent Apostolic Delegate Giovanni Bonzano in Washington a detailed report on the Order Sons of Italy in America (OSIA). Barnabite priest Giovanni Semeria, author of the report, had been the chaplain to the Italian Supreme Command during the early years of the Great War. After he organized an apostolate to aid refugees and orphans, Semeria came to America in search of resources in the Italian diaspora, where he encountered the OSIA. By 1920 Bonzano knew the OSIA well. He received Semeria's report at the tail end of an encounter between the Church and the OSIA, the outcome of which conditioned the Church's relationship to Italian ethnic organizations for the next two decades.[1]

Three competing Catholic ideologies emerged in response to the meteoric rise of the OSIA in the decade before the Great War: (1) to unconditionally consecrate the OSIA; (2) to condemn the OSIA outright; and (3) to coax, cajole, and coerce the OSIA to reform itself into an organization less offensive to the Church. Competition among these three Catholic responses to the OSIA culminated in the victory of the third alternative, what I call a Catholic mediating ideology toward Italian ethnic nationalism. Just as Pope Benedict XV eased the intransigent condemnation of Liberal Italy, so too did the Vatican conditionally legitimize the ethnic nationalism that structured the OSIA. The mediating ideology, in other words, reproduced in a local context the deeper and broader transformation of the ideology of the Roman Question described in the previous chapter. In order to illuminate this intra-Catholic ideological competition and the subsequent victory of the mediating ideology, I review the history and character of the OSIA and the resources available to each of the three ideological alternatives.

Social theorists have demonstrated how the outcome of ideological competition depends in large part upon the allocation of resources within social structures.[2] To speak intelligibly about resources in this case, we must make sense of the murky and unexplored world of Italian clerical migration. Italian sacerdotal migration was a search for work and wealth not entirely unlike the vaster labor sojourns of millions of Italian workers. Hundreds of priests who left dozens of dioceses from Sicily to Piedmont or who belonged to heterogeneous religious congregations (Franciscans, Scalabrinians, Salesians, Augustinians, etc.) met one another for the first time on American soil. The upshot was never pan-Italian clerical solidarity. Italian immigrant clergy never created an institution, a coalition of organizations, or a newspaper that could even pretend to represent Italian American Catholics at the national level. They remained deeply divided and maintained enduring transnational commitments to regional traditions, religious congregations, and family economies, always conscious of their responsibility as sons and brothers in nuclear families. Unlike their parishioners, they did not assimilate into the American Church. Furthermore, their new commitments to American parishes and bishops further undermined Italian American Catholic unity. Their lack of social solidarity and institutional unity helps explain the utter absence of an "Italian voice" in the American Church, while the German Catholic Central-Verein or the Polish Roman Catholic Union wielded significant power within Catholic America. It also explains the success of the Catholic mediating ideology toward the OSIA.

Masonic Juggernaut or Italian Knights of Columbus?

Not long after its creation, the OSIA sparked the curiosity of priests and bishops. What was the OSIA? How should Catholic authorities evaluate it? Was it an Italian American version of Masonry, the Odd Fellows, or the Knights of Columbus? Could it be converted into a Catholic dynamo, or would it degenerate into an underworld syndicate? How should priests respond to the OSIA when their parishioners joined or when entire parish societies entered as a lodge? Enormous resources and thousands of souls hung in the balance.

In 1897 Vincenzo Sellaro, a Sicilian physician, arrived in New York City, where he established the first lodge of the OSIA in 1905. The founder of Columbus Hospital and a school for midwives under the city health board, Sellaro understood that the resources of immigrant Italians resided within their village-based mutual benefit societies. These societies, not the Catholic parish, labor union, or local political club, were spontaneously transplanted institutions that provided a forum for immigrants to socialize among Old World neighbors, speak in their dialects, celebrate patronal holidays, and receive modest insurance benefits. Any successful parish, labor union, or neighborhood club would have to tap into the resources of these jealous, status-conscious societies in order to succeed. Sellaro hoped the OSIA would unite the societies for common goals. An active Mason who borrowed Masonic structures and symbols for his new organization, Sellaro organized the OSIA hierarchically into a supreme (national) lodge, grand (state) lodges, and local lodges. The OSIA followed a constitution with general laws and a ritual book, which replicated Masonic vocabulary. Highly ritualized behavior characterized OSIA proceedings, including oaths of secrecy imposed upon members.[3]

By the end of 1918, the OSIA had mushroomed into a national organization of 125,000 members in twenty-four states and two Canadian provinces. Its power, however, rested in the New York metropolitan area, Philadelphia, and New England. Because expansion came primarily through the absorption of preexisting mutual benefit societies, the OSIA did not substitute a national-ethnic consciousness for a provincial or village-based one as much as harmonize them and ease their regional antagonisms. Within the OSIA, a mutual benefit society that became an OSIA lodge could maintain considerable autonomy and yet still put its resources at the service of the OSIA. The OSIA and parish priests had similar goals. Priests wished to integrate mutual benefit societies into the parish, harmonize an Italian Catholic national-ethnic identity with a village-based identity, and tap into the enormous resources of the societies (which led to constant conflicts over money collected during *feste* (feasts) sponsored by the societies but consecrated by priests). By the time of the Great War, the OSIA had became a powerful force in Italian American life, but its affiliation with, and even integration into, Liberal Italy alarmed Catholic authorities, while parish priests grew jealous of what they perceived to be OSIA poaching.

Father Semeria's report to Bonzano described the OSIA after it had ridden the wave of nationalist sentiments sparked by the war and Gabriele D'Annunzio's escapade in Fiume. Semeria noted the rapid growth and financial power of the OSIA, which offered a generous $400 to the family of a deceased member. Its "pompous and somewhat mysterious external forms" appealed to "the tastes of our Southern Italians." Semeria lamented how Italy's government had linked itself to the OSIA. For example, when General Emilio Guglielmotti was sent to America to coordinate propaganda activities during the war, he permitted the OSIA to host his arrival, and he became an honorary member. "His bad example was followed by Ambassador Baron Camillo Romano di Avezzana, who was not only solemnly received [by the OSIA], but permitted his wife to be hosted by a female lodge in Philadelphia." Banquets honoring dignitaries were the most important ritual activity linking ethnic organizations to one another and to state personnel. They often culminated in honorary membership.[4]

The OSIA tried to co-opt Semeria's considerable prestige. When Semeria met with the OSIA leaders to gain support for war orphans, "they made me understand that if I wanted" help, "I must be initiated [like] General Guglielmotti and Baron Romano," as an honorary member. After Semeria refused, "except for rare local exceptions, I found the Sons of Italy cold or contrary. . . . This resulted not from my lack of patriotism, but from their anticlericalism." Indeed, Semeria invoked the specter of "the long hand of masonry," which had imprisoned the Holy Father during the Risorgimento. The leaders of the OSIA "are Masons or Masonic," although this character "is not obvious" because "in public its leaders claim neutrality toward religion." Although OSIA leaders refused to participate in "patriotic functions when they are Catholic, such as funerals for victims of the war," Italian immigrants, who "are poorly instructed in religion even if they are religious, have difficulty understanding the latent anticlericalism" of the OSIA.[5]

Three Catholic responses emerged to this ostensibly Masonic organization whose anticlerical leadership had developed links to Liberal Italy. Each response can be correlated to the resources — the wealth and status — of Italian immigrant clergy in America. A profile of Italian sacerdotal migration and settlement is therefore in order.

The Underside of Italian Clerical Migration

In 1917 and 1918, the apostolic delegation compiled data on Italian diocesan priests in the United States. (Diocesan priests were those who did not belong to a religious congregation such as the Franciscans or the Jesuits.) A remarkable 80 percent of the priests, approximately 330, had not been "incardinated" (made a full member) into an American diocese. For example, a priest ordained in Piacenza but working in Cleveland, if he were not incardinated, remained a member of the diocese of Piacenza and under the authority of the bishop of Piacenza. He was only on loan, so to speak, to the bishop of Cleveland, who could expel the vulnerable clerical labor migrant at will. Many unincardinated clergy had worked for decades in the United States. They frequently requested incardination to attain job security, local prestige, possibility for promotion, and support in retirement, but American bishops often refused to accept Italian migrant clergy. This situation persisted into the 1940s, as long as Italian clerical migration continued, and it generated ethnic animosities because American bishops were often of Irish or German descent.[6]

Bonzano summarized the situation: "Unfortunately, these immigrant priests give a rather unedifying spectacle, with their facility to change dioceses, sometimes forced, often spontaneously, to find a more lucrative post. They give an impression of being mercenaries always in search of a higher salary. The fault is not entirely their own, but rather lies in their precarious condition."[7]

Father George Mundelein, as the chancellor of the diocese of Brooklyn before he became the archbishop and cardinal of Chicago, had an opportunity to track this transnational clerical economy. He wrote the apostolic delegation in 1907:

> within the last year or two . . . the number of priests from southern parts of Italy arriving in this country has become alarmingly large. The greater

number of them settle in New York and Brooklyn, and though their [Italian] Bishops furnish them with but six months' leave of absence, yet they have no intention of returning home at the expiration of that time, but hope in some way and by some means to obtain a means of support and remain here. Following the positive instructions of the Holy See in this matter, we endeavor to discourage them from remaining here by notifying them in advance that their permission to celebrate Mass will not be renewed when their present leave of absence expires. As they almost invariably settle in some particular street or district, where their relatives and other emigrants from their own town are gathered in a small colony, very often when the church is a few blocks distant, an agitation will be begun for the erection of a church in their midst, in which the priest is either actively or silently interested, hoping to gain for himself thereby some position here. And naturally, when they are discouraged by the diocesan authorities, they will be advised to write to the Holy See or to the Apostolic Delegation.[8]

This rich description merits unpacking because it illuminates the difficult quest for resources migrant clergy pursued in America.[9] Bishops in Italy often permitted their priests to visit relatives abroad or to seek resources in America to help support their needy families. (A priest was, after all, an Italian son as well as a priest.) In some instances, Italian bishops were eager to rid themselves of abusive priests or those involved in unchaste relationships. By the twentieth century, the Vatican required a migrant priest to acquire two documents — one from his Italian bishop and the second from the Vatican. The migrant priest had to present these papers to an American bishop before the receiving bishop could give the priest permission to say mass for the faithful and thus to earn money. (The receiving bishop retained the right, which he often exercised, to refuse permission to a migrant priest with proper papers.) Furthermore, those papers had to be renewed every six months or one year or two years by all parties involved. Father Mundelein made reference to these documents in his letter. These restrictive measures, put in place after centuries of relatively unregulated clerical migration from Europe, aimed to limit the notorious abuses of sacerdotal wanderers that had plagued U.S. bishops since the American Revolution. But the measures did not always work. As Mundelein explained, many Italian priests without permission to work simply lived with their families or fellow villagers.

American bishops, unable to evaluate the quality of the Italian priest who came knocking at their door, often refused him permission to work whether he had proper papers or not. Bishops often favored Irish American priests who spoke Italian and were known to the bishop over foreign clergymen who arrived from dioceses with strange names, spoke no English, and presented recommendations from unrecognizable patrons. Without means of support, a migrant priest had several options, which were not mutually exclusive. As Mundelein mentioned, the priest might instigate the laity to agitate for a new church or parish where he could work. He might seek charity from fellow villagers who resented American bishops for dishonoring "their" priest. He might track down clerical friends who could recommend him to their American bishop. He might beg the apostolic delegation to help him find work. He might wander from diocese to diocese begging bishops for employment. He might try to undermine other clergy with a secure post in order to take their jobs. He might take paid ministerial positions in Protestant denominations. Finally, he might enter the lay work force. Vatican Archives reveal dozens of instances of priests selecting these options or of one priest exercising many of these options during an unstable career. Pervasive unemployment among migrant clergy and mobility in and out of the priesthood created intense competition for salaried positions, generating mutual recriminations, accusations of immorality and corruption, and disorder in Italian American communities.[10]

Father Luigi Pozzi, a well-established pastor in Trenton, New Jersey, found the situation so perilous he requested permission from the Vatican to open a Catholic hospice for unemployed Italian priests! His goal was to "open the door of salvation next to the door of perdition that the Protestants hold perpetually ajar" to migrant priests. Pozzi described the sacerdotal wanderers:

Some . . . left Italy for proper mission work [or to escape problems with their bishops] . . . others to better their position and make money, others inspired by a mania to travel and see the world, others because they have their relatives here in [America]. . . . The fact is that while there are some bad and perverse ones, there are more who are good and could do well. . . . The [American] bishops in general are not inclined to admit these priests in their dioceses [because some are corrupt]. This reason, combined with a type of racial antipathy, leaves almost all Italian priests enslaved and completely abandoned. Even those who have appropriate documents from both their Italian bishops and from [the Vatican], are not able to obtain a post to exercise their ministry, nor even [permission] to celebrate [mass and thus collect their livelihood for] more than a few days. It then happens that the destitute priests, not able to earn their own food, live off the charity of friends from their village or their families and relatives. But these become annoyed after a while and the poor priest is left deprived of every means of support and thus finds himself in a terrible situation; he either goes to work [in a secular profession], or he abandons himself to the Protestants, who are always close by to offer support and a post, especially for Italian priests.[11]

In 1918 Msgr. Gherardo Ferrante of the archdiocese of New York could list fifty-one apostate priests who lived in or near New York City. Thirty-five of them were active Protestant ministers, twenty were married, and four were fleeing the law in Italy. An Italian-born Episcopalian minister who had completed three years of theological training in New York City, Enrico C. Sartorio, estimated in 1918 that in the approximately 400 Italian Protestant churches and missions in the United States, "more than half of the Italian ministers are ex-Roman Catholic priests."[12]

Second-generation Italian Americans did not bring order to this clerical chaos, which continued well into the 1940s, because Italian American children rarely went to the American seminaries that historians have deemed crucial to the creation of "American Catholicism." Of the 1,164 secular priests ordained for the archdiocese of Chicago between 1903 and 1939, only 10 were of Italian descent and only 2 were ordained before 1926. Although 2,023 diocesan priests worked in Queens, Brooklyn, and on Long Island (the diocese of Brooklyn) between 1820 and 1944, only 34 men of Italian descent graduated from Brooklyn's seminary. The diocesan seminary of the archdiocese of Boston graduated only 20 men of Italian descent among the 1,519 priests ordained there between 1884 and 1945. Before 1940, Italian American priests rarely, if ever, held positions of influence in the bureaucracies of American dioceses, and between 1875 and 1946 there was no Italian or Italian American bishop in the American hierarchy, unless one includes the pope and the apostolic delegate.[13]

Three Catholic Responses to the Order Sons of Italy

The nature of the competitive clerical labor market is germane to our analysis of intra-Catholic ideological competition because clerical status determined the resources available to each of the three Catholic responses to the OSIA. The first response was to unconditionally baptize the OSIA. The Italian clergy who capitulated to the OSIA became lodge members and brought their own parish societies into the OSIA as lodges. These priests never challenged the OSIA's structure or values. Some were apostates in search of power or wealth, but most held unstable positions in U.S. dioceses as unincardinated hired hands. They eagerly accepted the benefits an alliance with the OSIA provided. Their capitulation to middle-class ethnic liberal nationalists or Liberal Italy's consular initiatives enhanced their status in the ethnic community and brought resources into their parishes. Power in their ethnic community compensated for their ecclesial marginality and became a weapon they used to leverage American bishops to regularize their position within the Church. Formally, Bonzano and U.S. bishops, who followed Bonzano's directives entirely in matters concerning Italians, prohibited this unconditional baptism of the OSIA.

A second Catholic response was to unconditionally condemn the OSIA, prohibit membership, and organize a Catholic alternative. Semeria articulated this response when he equated the OSIA with Masonry and proposed pandiocesan action under the U.S. episcopacy and the Bishop of Italian Emigration, a new office in the Vatican, to slay the unredeemable OSIA. According to Semeria, the Catholic alternative should provide similar insurance benefits as the OSIA, but it should implement Italian symbols in accordance with Catholic ideology. "I do not believe that it can be an Italian section of the Knights of Columbus, a highly praiseworthy association, but one in which our Italians will always be second in line." Semeria's proposal actually described the Italian Clergy Union and Lay Union, organizations already created to replace the OSIA. Unfortunately, they were nearly lifeless by 1920. Semeria and an influential minority of immigrant priests like him were concerned with the Roman Question and the status of the Holy See and not with the integration of Italians into American Catholic institutions. Impressed by Italian American subscriptions for Liberty Bonds, Semeria predicted Italian American wealth "will exercise a great influence on the *Patria*. . . . These Italians will help the Catholic Popular Party [Partito Popolare Italiano], and they will increase . . . the number of those who surround the pope with affection and veneration."[14]

If professionally unstable priests baptized the OSIA, those who called for a blanket condemnation of the OSIA were securely employed, often in American bureaucracies and apostolates of a panparochial nature. Their prestige was linked to their status in the Church and less dependent upon their connections in the ethnic community. In order to construct a Catholic alternative to the OSIA at the national level, they required the solidarity and resources—material and moral—of Italian priests throughout America. Such resources were not forthcoming from men whose professional instability, familial economic obligations, or institutional commitments to their particular religious congregations made Italian American Catholic mobilization on a national scale fanciful.

Two other factors undermined any chance for a formal Catholic condemnation of the OSIA; one related to the regional Catholic cultures of Italy; the other grew from the American context. The call to condemn the OSIA came from priests who harked from those regions of northern Italy where an intransigent, papal, social Catholicism took institutional form during the nineteenth century in the Opera dei Congressi. In the early twentieth century, those regions cultivated clergy active in the Christian Democratic struggle to forge an alternative subculture within Liberal Italy. This Catholic subculture, however, never evolved out of the antiquated ecclesiastical and civil structures in the poorer regions of southern and central-southern Italy.

The nineteenth-century Church in the *mezzogiorno*, notwithstanding noteworthy exceptions, had expressed little intransigent or organized opposition to Liberal Italy. Southern clergy were only rarely engaged in Catholic activism. Although the *fasci siciliani*, Sicilian worker uprisings in the early 1890s, created a receptive Catholic audience for the social message of Leo's encyclical "Rerum

Novarum" (1891), particularly among elite in Palermo and Naples where neo-Thomistic ecclesiastical schools thrived, the dissemination of the Leonine social vision was strictly circumscribed. From the unification until the Fascist era, the southern clergy remained inert in the face of political transformations, careful not to offend those upon whom they were economically dependent.[15]

Father Luigi Sturzo, the Sicilian Christian Democratic founder of the Partito Popolare Italiano (PPI), vividly described the "great moral and material inferiority" of the clergy in southern Italy. Their dependence upon municipal administrators and local nobles for benefices — positions and salaries — compelled them into uncomfortable but unavoidable alliance with lay confraternities and commissions, "often in the hands of liberals and Masons" who controlled religious *feste*. As Sturzo explained in 1906, southern clergy "depend upon rich and powerful families who provide for the many expenses needed to administer the cult, but hold the priests captive as administrators, butlers, and private teachers. This state of true and real dependence is aggravated by the fact that the priest lives a family life; he cares for his family's material and moral interests as the head of a household." The priest's engagement in secular economic activity undercut the respect he required if he were to lead his people.[16]

As clients to uncooperative patrons, southern priests were never able to mobilize Catholics the way their northern counterparts in the Veneto or Friuli-Venezia did. According to Sturzo, the situation in the *mezzogiorno* "renders the formation of a serious and true Catholic diocesan organization, either economic or electoral, not only difficult, but impossible." Sturzo ultimately believed that only a vast transformation of the *mezzogiorno* could liberate the clergy. His solution was to enter the political realm. Hence, in 1919 he founded the PPI.[17]

Southern Italian perceptions of the clergy also undermined their potential for leadership. Sicilian religious practices, according to Sturzo, "consist in an exterior form of homage to a saint, in a form too profane and little religious. You find few people who confess, or who receive the Eucharist; one searches, instead, for the protection of a saint invoked" against misfortune. Consequently, peasants believed the clergy's proper function was to perform superstitious or magical rites, not to mobilize Catholics into a political or economic bloc.[18]

In the United States, southern Italian clergy found themselves, once again, financially dependent, this time upon liberal ethnic nationalists. Once again they led parishioners beholden to rituals in honor of saints rather than sacramental regularity. The economic foundation of these patronal feasts was not the parish but lay societies, whose leaders did not always trust priests and who were not interested in the ideological challenges of the Church in a liberal society. Thus, most immigrant priests had neither the knowledge, nor interest, nor resources to wage war against the OSIA or to construct a Catholic alternative.

The final factor that weakened the possibility of a successful Catholic challenge to the OSIA related to the American environment. The prohibition of the OSIA as a Masonic or secret society was untenable during the Great War. While the rhetoric of its official texts was redolent of Masonry to educated Catholics, the OSIA appeared to most Americans to be a typical ethnic association that provided life insurance. The preamble in its Fundamental Statute invoked "a sacred and solid tie of fraternity," and its emblem proclaimed "Liberty, Equality, Fraternity." These liberal shibboleths, with affinities to U.S. revolutionary mythology, communicated to most Americans none of the ominous connotations they held for Latin Catholics. Finally, OSIA support for the war effort and its mission to Americanize immigrants made a blanket condemnation unwise when the Vatican was being accused of pro-Germanism.[19]

The third Catholic response, articulated most forcefully by Bonzano, emerged between the two extremes of baptism and condemnation. This third response, a mediating ideology, assumed (correctly) that the OSIA was malleable. Its anticlerical leadership and the Masonic phrasing of its official documents could be reformed, and its local lodges could be directed toward a neutral ideological foundation. Bonzano shrewdly deployed advocates of a Catholic condemnation to exert pressure upon the OSIA in order to bring it to the bargaining table, where he could compel reform. Bonzano's response was best suited for most immigrant clergy who were engaged in local parish work. They needed guidance to understand the new organization. They wanted neither to join nor to combat the OSIA, and as parish priests they had no inclination and no support from their bishops to share their parochial resources on ambitious, unrealistic projects to construct a Catholic alternative to the OSIA.

The Catholic mediating ideology reproduced the transformation of the ideology of the Roman Question within a local context. It rejected an intransigent condemnation of the liberal nationalist diaspora organization. At the same time, the mediating ideology sought to purge the OSIA of dangerous Masonic symbols and to strengthen elements in the OSIA favorable or neutral toward the Church.

First Contact with the Order Sons of Italy

As the apostolic delegate, Bonzano stood at the pinnacle of an international Italian clerical network that monitored clerical migration, apostasy, separatist movements, and morality. He had informants. He received reports on dozens of clerical wanderers and apostates from Leonardo Marretta, a Sicilian ex-religious living in Brooklyn. On 19 April 1913, Marretta informed Bonzano that the goal of the OSIA "is to draw Italians away from the Holy Mother Church, [and] to sow hatred against the Roman Pontiff and the Catholic clergy." The informant reminded Bonzano that the grand venerable of the New York lodge was "the famous Crescenzo Pitocchi," a priest who had fled Italy for America, where he apostatized. Marretta reported that Father Adolfo Gabbani, the pastor of St. Anthony's Church in Elmira, New York, had joined the OSIA and participated in lodge meetings. Gabbani, who left the diocese of Pescia in 1908, was not yet incardinated into the diocese of Rochester. Marretta feared Gabbani's activities had inspired lay Catholics to enter the OSIA.[20]

After Marretta informed Bishop Thomas Hickey of Rochester about Gabbani's activities, Hickey questioned Bonzano: "What attitude if any should I take in regard to the . . . Sons of Italy, . . . also what direction if any should be given to a priest joining this society?" Bonzano directed Hickey to supply the delegation with the General Laws of the OSIA and added, "from general information that has reached me concerning the [OSIA] it would seem that the spirit is anti-Catholic." Bishop James McFaul of Trenton, after his Italian priests "asked me what course they should take in advising their [parishioners] regarding" the OSIA, also sought Bonzano's "authoritative decision." McFaul had heard that "the officers of the [OSIA] are for the most part Freemasons."[21]

The initial step toward Italian American Catholic unity came from Father Edoardo Marcuzzi, who had all the qualities of an intransigent warrior. In his home diocese of Udine (in Friuli-Venezia), he had been a seminary professor and boasted thirteen years experience as a journalist combating pagan liberalism. By 1915 Marcuzzi was a member of the archdiocese of New York's Italian Apostolate. An important institution in the American pastoral strategy for Italians, the Italian Apostolate gave parish missions in New England and Middle Atlantic states. Marcuzzi also took over a languishing Catholic newspaper, *L'Italiano in America*, hoping to transform it into a national publication. He sought Bonzano's support through a friend and fellow Friuliano, Msgr. Luigi Cossio, an official at the apostolic delegation. Marcuzzi deplored "the great apathy of the [Italian] clergy [in America], who know how to complain about vices, but who do not understand how the press can be one of the principal remedies."[22]

In February 1916, although he commanded a circulation of 8,500, Marcuzzi reiterated his frustration. He contrasted the languid Catholic press to the vitality of the radical press. "L'Era Nuova, la Cronaca Sovversiva, il Proletario, la Voce del Proletario, l'Avvenire, la Lotta di Classe—to mention to you only the most strikingly anti-religious. In pamphlets such as these: God does not exist, Jesus Christ never existed. . . . What stands in opposition to this infernal propaganda? Nothing. The so-called [Italian] Catholic weeklies—two or three good-for-nothings, because they do not deal with the vital questions, they are not organs of battle. And they cannot be because they are edited by incompetents." Marcuzzi conveyed his urgency: "80% of Italian adults do not go to church; they do not have contact with the clergy; they are abandoned to the propaganda of Protestants and subversives." Initiatives failed because Italian clergy had neither a bishop nor support from American bishops. "The American bishops . . . recommend to their priests the diffusion of their [English-language] weeklies: the Catholic News, the Sunday Visitor, etc. Indeed, they have said, 'This newspaper will be the official organ of the [diocese].' . . . And thus these weeklies have reached 30–50–80 thousand copies. The Bishops in Italy do the same. Now we [Italian clergy in America], hominem non habemus; namely, we do not have an Italian bishop; and American bishops, at least generally, do not know our situation. . . . For us there is only one authority: the Apostolic Delegate."[23]

Bonzano acknowledged the sad religious state of Italians and "the necessity to act immediately . . . not only to save souls, but also for the prestige of the good Italian name." Bonzano tendered Marcuzzi a blurb: "*L'Italiano in America* will be, without a doubt, an efficacious means . . . to combat the ominous anti-religious and anti-social propaganda that slaughters souls through the anti-Catholic and subversive press. Every priest has a duty, not only to subscribe to it, but even to procure numerous subscriptions."[24]

One year later, however, Marcuzzi floundered in the face of divisions that undermined his ambitions. For example, he had procured only ninety subscriptions among the 300,000 Italians of Brooklyn. "The difficulty," Marcuzzi suspected, was the Brooklyn "Bulletin that is published there for Italian churches." Local diocesan papers were not aggressive enough for Marcuzzi's taste and reinforced debilitating divisions. "New York works for itself; Brooklyn for itself; Newark for itself and so on. And what do we have? . . . Misery and useless efforts, while the Colony" falls deeper into the snares of "Protestants, subversives, and Masons."[25] For Marcuzzi, the rise of the OSIA provided a potent symbol of all the old and new enemies of the Church and an ideal target to stimulate clerical unity and to mobilize Italian American resources.

By April 1917, Marcuzzi's polemic with the OSIA was in full swing. He argued that the OSIA could not be harmonized with a Catholic conscience. The pugnacious *L'Italiano* posed three questions to its nemesis. "1. Is it true that the OSIA is an occult [secret] association? 2. In the case of an affirmative, does the secrecy imposed by the Order bind the member even when it may contrast with the principles of his religious conscience? 3. What exactly is meant by the phrase 'prejudice and superstition' from which the Order wants to emancipate the masses?"[26]

Marcuzzi cited the OSIA's official documents with an argument that made sense to any Italian-language reader familiar with the basics of Masonry. The first article of the *Costituzione fondamentale e leggi generali* (fundamental constitution and general laws) read: "It is a secret fraternal institution." Each member, according to the *Rituale* (ritual book), was required to "vow and promise to reveal to no one what I learned and saw in this room and all of the secrets of the Order revealed to me." Marcuzzi insisted such a vow violated "the principles of the religious conscience" and that the language in the documents was Masonic and amounted to an attack upon the Church. The constitution called for "the emancipation of the masses from every superstition and prejudice." The ritual book referred to "free-dom of thought and liberty of conscience" and acknowledged the OSIA's aim to "demolish prejudice and obscurantism." Marcuzzi explained: "'Obscurantism' means the teachings of the Church; 'prejudice' means faith in Her truths or dog-mas; 'freedom of thought' or 'liberty of conscience' means emancipation from all religion." Although the constitution claimed to respect "any religious or political opinion," in reality, Marcuzzi concluded, the OSIA was "contrary to religion."[27]

The following week, Marcuzzi again took the offensive when he aired an OSIA conflict with the Italian consul general of New York. The OSIA's *Bollettino Ufficiale* lambasted the consul when he had neglected to include the OSIA on a committee related to the Italian war effort. Marcuzzi aired the dirty laundry when he cited the *Bollettino*, which described the consul's "foolish ambition to be the guardian angel of this colony" and asserted his "accomplices" were "slave-drivers, exploit-ers, pimps, losers, [and] survivors of the homeland's prisons." Without praising Liberal Italy's representative, Marcuzzi scorned the OSIA's expectation to repre-sent the Italian diaspora. The OSIA's officers were nothing more than a "dozen peasant overseers that work hand over foot to impose on the Colony the czarism that Russia has thrown into the sea."[28] Upon receiving copies of this polemic, Bonzano praised Marcuzzi, who had attracted the OSIA's attention.

On 14 April 1917, the OSIA responded to Marcuzzi, asserting it was neither antireligious nor connected to the Masons. But in a private meeting with Mar-cuzzi, Grand Venerable Stefano Miele of New York agreed to remove phrases of-fensive to Catholics from the OSIA's official documents. Because Marcuzzi be-lieved he lacked the authority to negotiate on behalf of the Church, he called upon the apostolic delegation. Cossio knew that "a modification" of official texts "does not signify a change in spirit," but he hoped the concessions would "render access to the good elements [within the OSIA] easier, and that in time they will be able to improve the [OSIA]." Cossio's faith that the OSIA harbored "good elements" receptive to improvement revealed a crucial disparity between Marcuzzi and the apostolic delegation.[29]

In the archdiocese of New York, a commission composed of Msgr. Michael Lavelle, Msgr. Gherardo Ferrante, and Father Antonio Demo convened to nego-tiate with the OSIA. All three priests were members of the archdiocesan Italian Bureau formed in 1913 to improve Italian pastoral care. Demo was the Eastern regional superior of the Scalabrini Fathers. Lavelle, not of Italian descent, was vicar-general of the Italian Bureau. Ferrante, born in 1853 in Frosinone (Lazio), a provincial town southeast of Rome, was the bureau's secretary. He arrived in New York in 1891 to coordinate Italian clerical migration with the Vatican. In 1915 he became vicar-general of the archdiocese, the highest ranking Italian priest in America. Ferrante was the consummate insider to the veiled world of sacerdotal migration. He served as a type of clerical employment broker, rehabilitating and placing priests. His power to regularize the status of wandering priests without proper papers and thus to open the door to employment gave him enormous influence. Significant to our story, Ferrante also served as the superior of Italian women religious congregations in the metropolitan area of New York. This position gave him power to oversee the progress of emigrant sisters.[30]

Ferrante's secure position of bureaucratic authority within the archdiocese would suggest he shared an affinity with the combative ideology of Marcuzzi. However, Ferrante equivocated in his attitude toward the OSIA and tried to avoid conflict. There are two possible explanations for Ferrante's ambiguous behavior. First, Ferrante harked from a central-south Italian diocese from which he emigrated before Pope Leo XIII endorsed social Catholicism in "Rerum Novarum." He probably had no exposure to the social apostolate that drove men like Marcuzzi to develop rural banks, newspapers, discussion circles, youth organizations, peasant leagues, and labor unions under Catholic auspices. Another explanation, however, merits consideration: perhaps Ferrante was blackmailed.

When he informed the delegation of his meeting with Grand Venerable Miele in April 1917, Marcuzzi explained: "I cannot trust Msgr. Ferrante; he is a sphinx. No one can understand him."[31] Marcuzzi met with Miele again in June. At this session, Miele claimed Ferrante "had told [Miele] not to respond to [me] regarding questions I had raised in [*L'Italiano*]." When Marcuzzi sought out information on the progress of the commission negotiating with the OSIA, Ferrante told him that there was no reason for the OSIA to modify its documents. According to the stunned Marcuzzi, Ferrante stated, "'The Order wants to emancipate the masses from superstition; and so do we. The Order combats obscurantism; and so do we. The Order wants liberty of thought and conscience; and so do we. We are in complete agreement. . . . The Commission disapproves of the journalistic polemic.'" In recounting this strange encounter, Marcuzzi told the apostolic delegation that he had learned the possible motives for Ferrante's "fear" that he would "agitate" the OSIA, "but such matters are so serious they cannot be written."[32]

Bonzano took Ferrante to task. The delegate reaffirmed his support for "the polemic conducted with so much clarity and ability by the first-rate newspaper, *L'Italiano in America*." Bonzano hoped to exploit the leverage *L'Italiano* had earned to purify the OSIA of its anti-Catholic elements. Hence, the delegate was dumbfounded with Ferrante's capitulation to the unredeemed OSIA.

Among the most influential leaders of this Order, one finds not only Catholics in name alone, but anti-Catholics; and even apostate priests and religious. The majority of the names of the lodges are themselves insults to the Catholic Church; more than once the Sons of Italy have refused to participate in demonstrations that in some way favor religion and ecclesiastical authorities. All of this is more than sufficient to put ecclesiastical authority and the faithful on its guard against this association. The obscurantism and superstition that the Order claims to combat, and the liberty of conscience and thought that it wants to sponsor, are very equivocal expressions in the mouths of certain people and in this case could not be explained other than as expressions of opposition to the Catholic Church. Even the oath that is imposed on its members, without any restriction, is at least very suspect. It seems to me that the Commission could avail itself of this opportunity to at least demand that the Constitution and Ritual be explained . . . [and] that a limit be put on the secrecy imposed on members, and that no lodge be denominated with names notoriously hostile to the Catholic Church. . . . Such steps could benefit the faithful and ease the anxiety already expressed to me by some bishops regarding the Order Sons of Italy.[33]

Ferrante's response to Bonzano differed from Marcuzzi's description of his conversation with Ferrante. To the delegate, Ferrante explained that the most opportune moment for OSIA reform was when the Order met specifically for that purpose. In the meantime, the commission believed "it was better to treat the representatives of the OSIA in a friendly manner rather than initiate a journalistic polemic with uncertain results that possibly could provoke opposition . . . difficult to overcome." Ferrante agreed to unleash Marcuzzi's pen, however, if Bonzano wished. Ultimately, the OSIA did meet in Washington in November 1917, at which time it altered its constitution to accommodate the Church. It did not, however, change its ritual book, which remained a point of contention.[34]

The specter of scandal hung over Ferrante in 1917. Accusations of immorality or corruption were not unknown tools of self-promotion among migrant clergy. Hence, they need to be interpreted carefully. But the accusations against Ferrante relate too directly to the OSIA to be ignored. As the superior of Italian women religious in the New York metropolitan area, Ferrante controlled, with no supervision, enormous resources. On 8 September 1917, Bonzano directed Auxiliary Bishop Patrick Hayes of New York to investigate charges against Ferrante that dated back to the 1890s. Ferrante had been accused of engaging in sexual relations with several of the Italian Pallottine Sisters of Charity at their houses in New York and New Jersey and of taking tens of thousands of dollars of their money. To cover his tracks, the accusation charged, Ferrante had sent, or threatened to send, sisters back to Italy if they spoke of his wrongdoings. Other New York priests, including Marcuzzi, learned of Ferrante's ostensible exploitation of the sisters. In fact, Marcuzzi wrote a letter (in Friulian dialect) to Cossio claiming the sisters would not speak openly to an investigator because Ferrante had threatened to send them back to Italy. Bonzano believed the sources of the accusations were reputable.[35]

Bishop Hayes found the Pallottine Sisters in shambles. He did not interrogate the sisters at their house on Charlton Street in New York because it was "under surveillance of the civil authorities and the police." The Charlton Street house was connected to the St. Raphael Society, an apostolate for immigrants. The Scalabrini priest who directed St. Raphael's from 1905 to 1921, Father Gaspare Moretto, had helped "the self-confessed murderer of the young Cruger girl" at the house in June 1917 to escape to Italy. It was later discovered that Moretto had embezzled funds from the St. Raphael Society originally collected by the Pallottine Sisters. Hayes was afraid to make an appearance at Charlton Street because he did not want the sisters during testimony in court at a future date to mention they had conferred with ecclesiastical superiors about matters there.[36]

Hayes's investigation of the Pallottine community in West Hoboken, New Jersey, however, was revealing. In the "past few years," Hayes reported, "some twenty sisters have left the community, [and] it would appear that they have taken with them the evidence of mis-conduct, if such ever existed." Hayes could state with certainty that Ferrante had been "careless" in financial matters. He "failed to hold regular business meetings, . . . failed to give an annual accounting to the sisters for the moneys he have [sic] received from them, . . . failed to govern the community as the ecclesiastical superior," and committed administrative neglect of this sort for quite some time. Most important for our story was the testimony Hayes received that a Sister Edvige, the biological sister of OSIA grand venerable Stefano Miele, had been in the West Hoboken house and had been threatened many years before with deportation to Italy by Ferrante. In response, she had left the convent and moved in with her brother Stefano. Later she married.[37] Did Miele learn of Ferrante's abuses from his sister? Did Miele use this information to blackmail Ferrante to ease the Church's attack upon the OSIA? If so, Ferrante's odd behavior would make sense. Afraid Miele might make public his abuses, Ferrante may have done what he could to make the commission organized to negotiate with the OSIA back off.

Toward a Catholic Alternative to the OSIA

In September 1917, Marcuzzi visited Bonzano to discuss a plan for a congress of Italian priests. Marcuzzi hoped to lay foundations for "a Society similar to the OSIA." Bonzano supported the congress, noting the success of "great American congresses of other nationalities." Marcuzzi advertised the congress as a means to fight the "indifference . . . that reigns among our countrymen in regard to religion." His model was clearly the social Catholicism that had developed in northern Italy and Germany. Religious "indifference was overcome or at least opposed in European countries with a diligent and wise social apostolate developed by the clergy among the people; action that gives life to Committees, Mutual Benefit Societies, Rural houses, Youth Groups, etc. The old confraternities of a purely religious character [which had no political component] are no longer enough." Clergy must demonstrate respect and love for working people through social action outside of the Church. A Catholic organization would make the OSIA obsolete. Marcuzzi had no desire to redeem the fallen OSIA.[38]

On 5 December 1917, 260 Italian priests from Eastern dioceses gathered in the Knickerbocker Hotel after a mass celebrated at St. Patrick's Cathedral by Cardinal John Farley of New York. Bonzano delivered a speech, and a banquet followed at which Enrico Caruso sang for his sacerdotal countrymen. In their enthusiasm the priests sent telegrams to President Woodrow Wilson, Pope Benedict XV, King Vittorio Emanuele III, and Bishop Angelo Bartolomasi, superior of Italian military chaplains. While affirming to Benedict their "unshakable attachment to the Cathedral of St. Peter," the priests sent wishes "for the coming complete triumph of the fighting *Patria*" to the king, the "August Head of the valorous army." At end of the congress, $333.25 was collected for Italian war refugees.[39]

The priests drafted plans for a Clergy Union, a Lay Union, and a Catholic newspaper. The Clergy Union would combat "the indifference of the masses" and promote a "democracy that will be Christian rather than pagan." Priests would lead "the masses" away from the "corrupt principles of revived Paganism" that characterized liberalism. The Clergy Union would put out a bulletin, funded by contributions from each priest, to encourage work among immigrants. The Lay Union would overcome the suspicion Italians held of priests who did not engage in a social apostolate on behalf of workers. Organized to undermine antireligious or non-Catholic associations, the Lay Union would provide assistance for workers and their families in cases of injury, sickness, and death. Each priest was expected to join the Clergy Union and recruit at least twenty people to join the Lay Union. Finally, the congress laid the foundation for a Catholic press to battle the Italian Protestant, liberal, and radical newspapers. Priests were expected to procure subscriptions and refuse support to alternative papers.[40]

The congress was a unique event in Italian American Catholic history, an unprecedented gathering, although modest in comparison to Polish, German, or Negro Catholic congresses. It was the first and only pandiocesan meeting among Italian clergy in the United States. But it included neither laity (besides Caruso) nor women religious. In spite of a few priests from elsewhere in attendance, it was a New York metropolitan affair. Remarkably, this meeting of 260 priests and the apostolic delegate passed unmentioned in the New York archdiocesan paper, the *Catholic News*. Equally strange was the lack of coverage in New York's Italian-language *Il Progresso Italo-Americano*.

Initially, Bonzano was reluctant to attend the congress. The delegation's policy was never to endorse embryonic organizations that had an uncertain future, which was surely the case with the Clergy and Lay Unions. Furthermore, Bonzano did not want to be identified as an Italian ethnic leader within the American Church—a perception that would undermine his claim as a Vatican representative to symbolize the universality of Catholicism. Much to his dismay, Bonzano's speech at the congress became the focal point for future conflict.[41]

The *Acts of the Congress* were not published until April 1918 because Marcuzzi and Msgr. Alfonso Arcese, the chairman of the congress and president of the Lay Union, had a difficult time convincing Bonzano to permit them to publish a version of his extemporaneous speech. Bonzano had disapproved of the telegrams the congress sent without his permission, particularly to President Wilson and King Vittorio.[42] The telegram to King Vittorio, still viewed as an illegitimate sovereign, had been sent, Arcese explained, to belie the anti-Catholic propaganda that blamed the Church for the Italian defeat at Caporetto in October 1917. All reference to the telegrams, Arcese promised, would be eliminated from the published *Acts*. After Arcese sent Bonzano a reconstruction of the delegate's speech at the congress, Bonzano acquiesced but sent his own version of his speech in which he endorsed the Clergy Union, the Lay Union, and the new newspaper.[43]

In contrast to Arcese's reconstruction, Bonzano's version of his speech welcomed modifications of the OSIA's official documents. Bonzano described the OSIA as one of many "more or less secret" societies, "if not openly hostile, . . . at least indifferent . . . to religion." While not condemned, the OSIA was held suspect by the Church. He criticized its "many lodges whose titles named notorious enemies of the Church," its rhetoric about "ignorance, prejudice, and superstition," and its oaths of secrecy. Bonzano stated clearly that no priest should dare join the OSIA or encourage the faithful to do so. The speech emphasized that love of the *patria* for Italians meant love of one's village, the mountains, and the monuments. Most importantly, it meant love of the Catholic faith and the pope, the true symbols of Italy. Although Bonzano permitted the inclusion of his own version of the speech in the *Acts of the Congress*, Arcese was directed to remove Bonzano's name as the general president of the Clergy Union. The prestige of the Vatican could not be used so directly for this untested experiment.[44]

The goals of the congress were extraordinarily ambitious. By 1917 the OSIA's leadership overlapped with most Italian ethnic institutions on the East Coast. Notwithstanding important radical, labor, and Catholic figures, most Italian American leaders were small business owners or professionals presiding over minor ethnic associations that may have had a nominal affiliation with an Italian parish and that worked cautiously with local consulates when a need arose. The relatively high level of conflict and competition among this emerging middle-class leadership should not blind us to their ideological similarities and their role as mediators integrating families into local political life. The OSIA had integrated these leaders into a national organization. When priests such as Marcuzzi chose to wage battle with the OSIA, they were calling the Italian priesthood and parishes into an aggressive countercultural stance toward the very ethnic culture that nurtured them.

The congress also hoped priests within the Clergy Union would exert authority over transplanted Old World mutual benefit societies that cultivated devotional loyalties within southern Italian families. These "old confraternities of a purely religious character," which Marcuzzi deemed "no longer enough," controlled vast resources that all parish priests struggled to co-opt. In 1920 these societies were not yet beholden to clerical authority. Thus, the Catholic alternative to the OSIA would require rather grand, or better, grandiose, transformations in both the ethnic and religious culture of Italian Americans.[45]

Antonio Bove of Providence

One conflict between a parish priest in Providence, Rhode Island, and the OSIA had significant consequences. Father Antonio Bove's polemic with the OSIA illuminates the victory of a Catholic mediating ideology. Born in Albano di Lucania (Basilicata), an underdeveloped *mezzogiorno* province, Bove arrived in Providence in February 1901 after his ordination to the diocese of Tricarico. After years of vying for a post, Bove became pastor of St. Ann's parish, was incardinated into Providence in July 1918, and became a force in Providence's Italian community until his death in 1931. In October 1918, Bove published a controversial pamphlet that challenged the OSIA's claim to represent the Italian nation. Invoking Bonzano's speech at the congress of December 1917, Bove insisted that "to remain a Catholic in good conscience, one must not take part in the Order Sons of Italy as long as its [documents] remain as they are now." Bove, following Bonzano's lead, was open to a reformed OSIA.[46]

The OSIA hit Rhode Island like a tidal wave. Among the 5,000 members it attracted between 1914 and 1918 were the Ocean State's most visible Italian Americans. Furthermore, the Scalabrini Fathers, who administered five parishes in the diocese of Providence, openly baptized the OSIA. Grand Venerable Luigi Cipolla represented Rhode Island's Italian organizations on its Liberty Loan Committee during the Great War. Federico Curzio, editor of *L'Eco del Rhode Island*, was a lodge member and gave the OSIA upbeat copy. When the Catholic Club at the Scalabrini Holy Ghost parish hosted Columbus Day celebrations in 1917, Cipolla, Curzio, and the Scalabrini priest celebrated the virtues of Columbus, the Italian royal army, and its chaplains. When Father Vittorio Cangiano, Scalabrini pastor of St. Bartholomew's Church, gave a funeral mass for fallen Italian soldiers, Cipolla, also the president of the Society Marinai di Tripoli, led his members at the service. As the OSIA grand orator, Paolo Ambrifi exuberantly boasted: "Our Order is a cry, a roar, a volcano that will bury into oblivion the past prejudices, village factionalism, exploitation and bossism, that until now have profited with impunity from the good faith of the Italian people." Bove's polemic against the ethnic juggernaut may very well have confused Italian American Catholics who saw priests and OSIA leaders, prestigious members of their community, working in harmony to support the U.S. and Italian war effort.[47]

Bove and the Scalabrini Fathers occupied different positions within the Church and ethnic community, which explains their divergent attitudes toward the OSIA. The Scalabrini Missionary Society, unlike proper religious congregations, did not have perpetual vows (until 1934) that bound priests in a lifelong commitment to the organization. It functioned from 1887 until 1924, when the Vatican took direct control over its faltering administration, more or less as an employment agency for migrant clergy in search of a regular position in the United States. Many of its priests left (or entered) the society. They never experienced seminary training together in Italy, and often they did not know one another. Thus, most Scalabrini Fathers exhibited an affinity with the first Catholic response to the OSIA—they baptized it without hesitation. They sought status and wealth through the ethnic community, not within the American Church.[48]

Bove himself had used the Scalabrini Fathers as a protective canopy to help him regularize his status in the American Church. After he become the pastor at St. Ann's Church, he separated from the Scalabrini Society and sought incardination into the diocese of Providence. His rise to prominence at St. Ann's was indebted to his ecclesiastical connections rather than influence in the ethnic community. To his bishop's delight, he led the successful construction of a parish convent school plant, and he cultivated support in the Vatican. In 1916 the Vatican considered making Bove a domestic prelate (a monsignor) after he gave $500, in the name of Bishop Matthew Harkins of Providence, to support a pet project of Cardinal Antonio Vico. The unappreciative Harkins deterred the Vatican. "At least twenty pastors have rendered far more service to religion," he explained. Besides, "it would occasion unfavorable comment if a *stranger* like Father Bove is especially honored by Our Holy Father for a few years['] work, which all have been doing for many years" (emphasis added). By this time Bove, a successful pastor, had resided in Providence for sixteen years, built a church, a parochial school, a nursery school, a rectory, and a convent for a community of sisters. Harkins, nevertheless, still deemed Bove a "stranger" and had not incardinated him into the diocese. The Vatican withheld the honor.[49]

Evidence suggests that Bishop Harkins directed Bove to take on the OSIA. Harkins had been impressed by Bonzano's speech at the December 1917 congress and was eager to please the Vatican. In July 1918, he incardinated Bove and in November tried to withdraw his reservation to Bove's award. Why? Cardinal Vico had brought news of Bove's generosity to Pope Benedict XV, who in turn presented Bove with a medal for his work. It is likely that Bove's incardination was

Harkins's reward to him when Bove agreed to follow Bonzano's line and push the OSIA to reform. Only three months after Harkins granted Bove a permanent home in the diocese of Providence, Bove's pamphlet appeared in print.[50]

On 15 September 1918, Father Giuseppe Silipigni, an outspoken priest working within the OSIA, came from New York to speak at St. Bartholomew's Church in Providence. Born in 1877 in Gioia Tauro (Calabria) and ordained to the diocese of Mileto, Silipigni arrived in New York in August 1912. A popular wartime speaker, Silipigni rode the wave of nationalism along with the OSIA to generate wealth within the ethnic community. He worked with the highest-ranking officials in the OSIA and was rewarded for it. By February 1918, through speaking engagements, Silipigni had collected $2,500 for an "Altar of Victory" to be constructed in a New York parish to gain supernatural favors for Italian soldiers. Silipigni's prestige in the ethnic community served as leverage within ecclesial structures. In 1919 the archdiocese of New York named him pastor of Our Lady of Loretto Church in Manhattan. By the early 1920s, Silipigni had become a vocal supporter of Fascist Italy and New York Blackshirts, speaking at their functions and opening his church to their activities.[51]

Silipigni's Providence visit and his blatant baptism of the OSIA disrupted Bove's parish. Until then none of Bove's twenty-two parish societies had affiliated with the OSIA. But after Silipigni's speech, two of St. Ann's societies enlisted. Bove explained to Bonzano, "in response to my strong protests to the presidents of the two societies I was told that they intended nothing contrary or offensive toward the Church or pastor who represented it. But that they felt sufficiently justified [in their actions] by the presence of a priest in the [OSIA]."[52]

Bove's pamphlet elaborated upon Bonzano's speech at the December 1917 congress. Bove attacked the Masonic character of the OSIA that embodied the "cult of Nature and Reason" and linked Masonry to nineteenth-century attacks on the papacy. The OSIA ritual book suggested that the smaller states that comprised the Italian peninsula before the Risorgimento, including the Papal States, had damaged and oppressed the Italian nation. "Was the Pope a petty tyrant who oppressed and damaged Italy?" Bove indignantly inquired.[53]

Bove also addressed the local scene. He attacked the Warren, Rhode Island, lodge named for Giordano Bruno as evidence of the OSIA's Masonic character. He challenged the morality of the OSIA leadership through an allusion to a notorious apostate priest, familiar to Providence Italians, who had married and divorced the daughter of a Federal Hill tailor and had served as the grand venerable of the OSIA in Rhode Island. Bove, however, was relatively gentle with the two societies from his parish that had become OSIA lodges, the Fratelli Bandiera and the Prata Sannita. They had supported the parish and school, he admitted, and the individuals in them were patriotic Italians who held the Church in high regard.[54]

Bove's pamphlet contended that the Italian nation was Catholic and that priests embodied Catholic authority, and therefore pastors inherited moral leadership over the Italian diaspora. The OSIA was merely an immoral usurper of Catholic authority. "We must not forget that the existing societies in the parishes . . . always contain Italian members; and Italians can be considered Catholics without discussion; non-Catholic Italians are like white flies; thus, when a pastor addresses such [societies], implicitly he speaks to people already under his jurisdiction." Therefore, the OSIA absorption of mutual benefit societies was tantamount to "interference" and "vandalism, an autocratic act more savage than African cannibalism."[55]

Notwithstanding the polemical rhetoric, Bove cultivated the Catholic mediating ideology toward the OSIA. He invited the OSIA to reform and surely did not envision a national alternative to it. When the "small ignorant minds that scorn and mock the Church" are eliminated from the OSIA, it will "have removed the stumbling blocks." It could then welcome "the true sons of the ancient Italy, great in her incomparably pre-Christian past, but many thousand times greater because of [Saint] Peter, from whom the most vital energy, the most profound wisdom, and the most genuine progress of the entire world emanates." Bove had neither the journalistic skill nor intellectual powers of Marcuzzi. The religious culture and seminary training of nineteenth-century Basilicata had not made Bove familiar with the social Catholicism and Christian democracy that drove Marcuzzi. Not surprisingly, Father Roberto Biasotti, Marcuzzi's Friulian friend and leader of New York's Italian Apostolate, felt Bove's pamphlet did not go far enough in implicating the Masonic leadership of the OSIA.[56]

Bove's salvo may have pleased Harkins, but it landed Bove in the ethnic doghouse. The new editor of *L'Eco del Rhode Island*, another OSIA brother, lambasted Bove's "monument to bad faith that . . . tried to confuse Masonry with the Order Sons of Italy." *L'Eco* contrasted Bove to the Scalabrini Fathers, whose service in honor of ninety-one parishioners in the military brought local societies, OSIA lodges and state delegates, Providence's Italian consular agent, and Assistant District Attorney A. A. Capotosto together in harmony.[57] *L'Eco's* offensive against Bove continued on 16 November 1918, when it insisted that Bove's goal in publishing the pamphlet had been "to raise money . . . while, the Order Sons of Italy in America is motivated by the cult of the *patria*." Bove had "vilified the most beautiful, outstanding, and worthy Italian institution that the emigrants of our race have organized in the United States." *L'Eco* also contended that Bove's pamphlet had cited OSIA texts "relegated to the attic." Bove had ignored documentary revisions made at the OSIA meeting held on 12 November 1917 in Washington.[58]

Bove responded to *L'Eco*. "I did not intend to condemn the Order Sons of Italy as a vast Society of Mutual Aid that aims to reunite in one family all Italian emigrants, . . . nourishing in them the cult of the *patria* of origin and of the adopted country. But, I was compelled to call [the] attention of Catholics belonging to the

Order Sons of Italy to the fact that one cannot reconcile subjection to the Roman Catholic Apostolic Church with subjection to an Order which praises the religion of [Giordano] Bruno."[59]

The Giordano Bruno Lodge of Warren, the Rhode Island Grand Lodge, and Supreme Orator Michele Albano in New York all joined the fray. The Bruno Lodge distributed gratis a pamphlet, which L'Eco described as "a praiseworthy work of literary and philosophical criticism," to vindicate the lodge's patron. To refute Bove's claims, the pamphlet listed the many priests who were OSIA members. The Grand Lodge issued a statement: "[We] deplore that a minister of the Roman Catholic Church should make false and malicious assertions against an organization which is absolutely and entirely secular." Furthermore, it accused Bove of launching erroneous insinuations about the OSIA's constitution.[60] Albano insisted, "the Order Sons of Italy, in declaring one of its objects to be to combat ignorance, prejudice and superstition, did not mean to make the slightest reference or allusion to the Catholic church." In fact, Albano noted, several lodges had religious names, and no religious views were excluded from the OSIA. In December 1918, two more societies from Bove's parish became OSIA lodges. By now, the English-language press had picked up the controversy.[61]

The OSIA welcomed publicity. Although OSIA rhetoric looked Masonic within an Italian linguistic context, the same rhetoric resonated positively among Americans. English words such as "liberty" and "fraternity" gave the OSIA an assimilationist and thus patriotic connotation. Nevertheless, the OSIA was careful to tread lightly to avoid conflict with the Vatican. Besides reminding Italian Americans that priests were members of the OSIA, the organization emphasized that it had already revised its official documents on 12 November 1917 to eliminate anti-Catholic language. It was true that the OSIA had revised parts its constitution, but it had refused to change its ritual book, and thus it maintained phrases offensive to the Church.[62]

The Demise of Intransigence and the Victory of a Mediating Ideology

Bove, even under attack, had reason to be pleased. Just as Marcuzzi's polemic of April 1917 brought Grand Venerable Miele to the bargaining table, so too did Bove's pamphlet initiate negotiations. On 3 December 1918, Supreme Orator Albano sent the apostolic delegation a copy of the OSIA Bollettino Ufficiale to "refute each false interpretation" Bove had made "of the program and attitude of the Order in regard to the Roman Catholic Church."[63]

Both Silipigni and Marcuzzi attempted to shape Bonzano's interpretation of the OSIA at this critical juncture. Silipigni sent the delegate copies of the Bollettino, which he insisted were "explicit enough . . . to remove . . . any ambiguity" regarding the OSIA's attitude toward the Church. "Any polemic" against the OSIA, "especially now," would be disastrous. Silipigni included a summary of minutes from an OSIA Supreme Executive Council meeting held on 15 October 1918, which gave the Rhode Island Grand Council permission to "select the name to give to their lodges, admitting even the names of [Catholic] saints."[64]

Marcuzzi in turn insisted Albano was a Mason and reminded the delegation that, although the constitution had been revised, the ritual book remained "Masonic from top to bottom." Marcuzzi was preoccupied with the fate of the Clergy and Lay Unions founded at the congress. "The [OSIA], and I mean its leaders, is moving to impede the [Lay] Union," he wrote with alarm. The bishop of Brooklyn, Marcuzzi elaborated, had recently read to his clergy a secret letter from the head of the American Masons that called for all Masons to "prepare themselves for intense propaganda activity against the clericalism which the war had occasion to awaken. Just imagine," Marcuzzi harped, "what the Sons of Italy, whose leaders are Masons, will do!"[65]

Bonzano maintained his mediating position. He wrote Albano that he "had verified with pleasure that the equivocal expressions [in the constitution] that had lent themselves to hostile interpretations of the Church were modified." But the ritual book still required vows that "could disturb the conscience of Catholics." Their elimination "will render possible the enrollment of Catholics in the Order so that it can gather all of the energies of Italians in this country for the mutual good and honor of the *patria*."[66] Upon reading a copy of this relatively conciliatory letter to Albano, the combative leaders of the Lay and Clergy Unions were stunned. They penned a curt letter to Bonzano, dismayed by his claim that the OSIA could "'gather all of the energies of Italians in this country.'" They griped that they no longer had "any motive to continue to develop" the Lay and Clergy Unions or the Catholic newspaper, which were "Catholic Action projects for Italian immigrants voted upon by 300 Italian priests at the Congress of 5 December 1917."[67]

Bonzano responded: "[You] give to my letter to the Supreme Orator . . . far greater significance than I intended. . . . The wishes I express for the Order are not unconditional, but subordinate to the modifications of the Ritual [book]; and I believe that when the Ritual is modified and no longer offends Catholic sentiments," there will no longer be reason "to impede the Faithful from entering the Sons. Permitting Catholics to enter does not mean impeding other similar Associations; since it is known that Catholics, like Protestants, want to belong to more than one Association." Bonzano's mediating position, a path between Marcuzzi and Silipigni, could not be stated more clearly. He thanked *L'Italiano in America* for its campaign that had led to modifications in the constitution, and he acknowledged that both the ritual book and "the spirit of some lodges [were] openly contrary to the Church." But that "spirit will not change if we take a hostile attitude toward the Order and remain far from it."[68]

Bonzano justified his position through a comparative assessment of the resources available to the OSIA and Italian American Catholics. "It is undeniable that the Order Sons of Italy has become an influential organization among our countrymen in terms of the number of its members and finances. It is therefore difficult to oppose it with an organization of equal importance and you gentlemen know from experience the difficulty involved, in view of the fact that after more than one year since deliberations were taken to found the . . . Union, it is still in the preliminary stages." Bonzano had no faith in a Catholic substitute for the OSIA. "It seems to me that it is the duty of the Catholic clergy to save, whenever possible, [the OSIA] entirely or in part, which I am told counts approximately 100,000 members." By February 1919, after salaries and expenses were paid, the Clergy Union had received only $905.95 from 207 members and had failed to reach priests outside of New England, metropolitan New York, and Pennsylvania. Although Archbishop Hayes gave $1,000 to Marcuzzi to support the Lay Union, nothing came of any of the initiatives planned at the congress. By 1920 the Lay and Clergy Unions had all but disappeared without a trace.[69]

In 1919 Bonzano withdrew from the controversy and relaxed his opposition to the OSIA. He maintained that the OSIA ought to modify its ritual book and that priests should not join it, but regarding the laity he equivocated. Some local lodges "are named after Saints and are sometimes composed of good elements not hostile to the Church," even if other local lodges remained anticlerical. "While in the first case one could permit the Faithful to belong to a local lodge, one should dissuade them in the second case, and not because the Order is condemned, but for the danger it poses for souls." The local bishop in consultation with his priests, according to Bonzano, should determine the "spirit" of each local lodge. Henceforth, Catholic resistance to the OSIA had no sanction from the Vatican. A crucial obstacle to OSIA expansion was gone.[70]

Priests in the OSIA reaped substantial rewards. Marcuzzi, commenting on Silipigni's rise from obscurity, claimed "three or four yours ago [Silipigni] was unknown; now, thanks to the Order Sons of Italy he has purchased a 'farm' with a house on Staten Island. I have never heard him preach but I'm told it is an event more suited to the stage than the church." By August 1919, Silipigni informed Ferrante a movement was afoot to elect Silipigni to an office in the New York Grand Lodge. Although the apostolic delegation scolded Ferrante for even suggesting the idea, by 1921 Silipigni had become the OSIA's supreme curator.[71]

By October 1922, when Benito Mussolini took the reins of government in Italy, OSIA lodges and parish societies overlapped without tension. The transformation of the ideology of the Roman Question had permitted the Church to tentatively baptize the OSIA as a legitimate association within the nation's diaspora, notwithstanding the OSIA's increasingly close ties to Fascist Italy. The OSIA, in turn, earned this Catholic support. Just as Fascist Italy shed liberal anticlericalism and attacked Masonry as an anti-Italian enemy, the OSIA discarded its explicit anticlericalism and celebrated Italian American Catholic parishes as a force for *italianità*.

This transformed relationship between the Church and the OSIA can be generalized to other ethnic nationalist institutions. The Italian-language press, excepting radical and anti-Fascist newspapers, also benefited from this transformation. For example, before the Great War, Alessandro Mastrovalerio, cofounder and editor of Chicago's *La Tribuna Italiana Transatlantica*, had deeply troubled Catholics. A typical nineteenth-century anticlerical liberal, Mastrovalerio had disapproved of a *festa* in 1905, claiming it was "a disgrace to our [Italian] name. The sponsors, priests and racketeers, have always promoted festivals with which the real religious spirit has nothing to do." Father Edmund Dunne, as we noted in chapter 2, engaged in an extended polemic with *La Tribuna*. In 1908 the Chicago archdiocesan *New World* summed up the Catholic view of the Italian paper when it proclaimed, "every intelligent man who looks upon [*La Tribuna*] is sick for a month."[72]

By the 1920s and 1930s, these hostilities had largely disappeared as a result of the transformation of the ideology of the Roman Question. For instance, Maurice Marchello coedited *La Tribuna* before the paper closed in 1935. Marchello, a graduate from the University of Chicago Law School and a Democratic politician, was president of the Venetian Union, the secretary of the Tito Schipa Lodge of the Italo-American National Union, and a member of the highbrow Dante Alighieri Society. Mastrovalerio would have been comfortable in these organizations in 1910. But Marchello was also a trustee at St. Anthony's parish, a contributor to its parish bulletin, and a charter member of the (Catholic) Newman Club at the University of Chicago. Father Giacomo Gambera, in a memoir from the 1920s, discerned the transformation when he quipped, "it is comforting to certify that the principle Italian newspapers have shed their old and foolish anticlericalism, and become more moderate and reasonable."[73]

But we are getting ahead of our story. In the 1920s, the Roman Question remained unresolved, the pope was still imprisoned in the Vatican, and the Italian nation was still living within a state not formally recognized by the Holy See. After the Great War, the Holy See, supported by American Catholics, worked feverishly to resolve the Roman Question. But the instability of Liberal Italy, its weak, short-lived governments, and an uncooperative monarch undermined the Church's best efforts. The collapse of Liberal Italy, however, created new opportunities to place the Holy Father back upon his temporal throne.

CHAPTER SIX

Catholics Meet Mussolini

"The Chosen Instrument in the Hands
of Divine Providence," 1919–1929

In February 1929, the Vatican and the Kingdom of Italy signed the Lateran Pacts. The pacts resolved the Roman Question and brought Fascist Italy (1922–45) and the Holy See into formal diplomatic relations. The pope became (and remains) the temporal sovereign over the State of the Vatican City. The tiny size of that theocratic state should not mislead us into thinking that the Vatican in any sense acquiesced to liberal ascriptions of the pope as merely a "spiritual" leader. A mere ten years after the Great Powers blocked papal participation in the Paris peace conference, the pope-king reigned once again. How did this shocking transformation come to pass? What role did the United States and the American Church play in this outcome?

Fascist, not Liberal, Italy was the Holy See's partner in the reconciliation, a fact that gives pause. Catholic apologists have insisted that the nature of Italy's government in 1929 was unimportant; after all, Pope Benedict XV had been quite ready to reconcile with Liberal Italy in 1919. Liberal critics have contended that only with a dictatorial regime could an authoritarian Church have found common ground. More generally, a vast historiography on the relationship between the Vatican and European authoritarian regimes, some of them fascist, still inspires indictments and apologias, particularly when the Holocaust takes center stage in the discussion. Considering the dominant role of the United States in the postwar European economic reconstruction, a curious myopia has excluded America and its Catholics from analyses of the reconciliation between the Vatican and Fascist Italy. The United States and the American Church did more than witness "European" events from afar. American Catholics *participated* in the transformation of the ideology of the Roman Question that placed Pope Pius XI (1922–39) on his temporal throne.

Once again, heated debates about the status of the pope in Italy and the character of the Italian nation generated boundaries that separated Catholics from their American neighbors. At first glance, this might appear unexpected. During the 1920s, Catholics, Protestants, Jews, liberals, journalists, politicians, and Wall Street bankers all discerned admirable qualities in Fascism, an unknown newcomer on the world stage that inspired excitement and speculation. So enthused did some Americans become with the new regime that everyday folk from all walks of life took pen to paper and wrote "His Excellency" Benito Mussolini letters. They applauded his leadership style, boasted that some of their best friends were Italians, congratulated the Duce for outwitting assassins, requested employment, shared military inventions, promoted personal schemes for international peace, shared experiences of Italian tourism, and hawked religious paths to spiritual well-being. The Duce's remarkably protean image inspired admiration simultaneously from Protestants for whipping lazy Italian Catholics into shape and from Catholics for his crackdown on conspiratorial Masons. But if arguments about Fascism *in general* did not structure polemics that distinguished Catholics from their American neighbors, *religious questions* about the relationship between the Vatican and Fascist Italy, and what that relationship meant for the Italian nation, clearly separated American Catholics from Protestants, Jews, and liberals.

Ideology Trumps Utilitarianism and Theology

Students of religion in the United States have ignored Fascist Italy. Studies of the interwar years rarely mention the Italy-Vatican rapprochement of the 1920s or the Lateran Pacts of 1929. Historians John McGreevy and Philip Gleason have analyzed mid-twentieth-century American liberal critiques of Catholicism as an antidemocratic, authoritarian culture with affinities to "fascism" or "totalitarianism." In their work, "fascism" (not *Fascism*) is a generic term for authoritarianism, and the "rise of fascism" happened in the 1930s, as if Fascist Italy did not exist in the 1920s. They tend to conflate informed anti-Fascists struggling for a democratic Italy with the bigotry of Paul Blanshard, indiscriminately classifying all of their writings "anti-Catholic." Ultimately, they sidestep the issue liberals raised: the substantial links between the American Church and Fascist Italy for two decades.[1]

Historian John Diggins, not a specialist in religious history, makes the best attempt to address the particular relationship between the American Church and Fascism. Diggins errs, however, when he suggests that among Catholics two warring camps of pro-Fascists and anti-Fascists collided for two decades. He acknowledges that "the Church's pro-fascist image had been cast even before the Spanish [Civil War] by the seemingly countless clergymen who waxed eloquent about Mussolini." But he also asserts that every Catholic sympathizer with Fascism had a Catholic anti-Fascist counterpart.[2] I have found only two consistent American Catholic anti-Fascists—Fathers Giuseppe Ciarrocchi and James Gillis.

The Vatican, at the prompting of Fascist Italy, intervened to silence both of them. Neither led a movement, and they worked in isolation from one another. In short, there was no American Catholic anti-*Fascism*.

On occasion American Catholics did criticize Fascism. It does not follow, however, that "what appeared to Italian exiles and American liberals to be a monolithic pro-Mussolini Catholic chorus were in reality the voices of individual churchmen."[3] This claim ignores hierarchical structures of power and community vigilance that belie the notion that the Church was a group of atomized individuals free to articulate broadly divergent views on matters relating to the Roman Question. Attention to the timing and content of American Catholic criticism of Fascism during the Italy-Vatican rapprochement of the 1920s reveals the collaboration of a transnational church. When the Vatican praised Fascism for outlawing Masonry, American Catholics voiced similar praise. When the Vatican protested Fascist interference in the moral development of Italian youth, so did American Catholics. When the Vatican instigated the dissolution of the Partito Popolare Italiano (PPI), American Catholics agreed it was a wise policy. When the Vatican withheld commentary on the beating, imprisonment, or murder of an anti-Fascist, American Catholics also remained silent.

American Catholic collaboration with the Holy See was an important form of *participation* in the transformation of the ideology of the Roman Question and not merely insignificant cheerleading from across the Atlantic. Both Fascist Italy and the Holy See believed—and knew the other believed—that American Catholics were a variable in the political life of the United States. Mussolini, a journalist par excellence, was keenly, even obsessively, conscious of U.S. public opinion. He understood that it was imperative to secure financial support from the United States to consolidate his dictatorship. The Italian embassy and consulates in the United States worked to shape U.S. public opinion. They thrilled at the sight of Italy's historic American nemesis, Catholics, particularly those of Irish descent, embracing Fascist Italy. Diligent Fascist observers noted how Fascist clashes with the Church in Italy led those same American Catholics to withhold praise. Thus, the Holy See's diplomatic hand in its negotiations with Fascist Italy was strengthened when the American Catholics reiterated at appropriate moments papal signs of approval or disapproval of Fascism.

Diggins contends American "Catholic thinkers responded to Fascism . . . as a historical movement whose usefulness should be measured in light of *the interests of the Church*" (emphasis added). He argues that Catholics subordinated their natural law teachings about the individual and the state to a crude utilitarianism, a "secularized approach."[4] Thus, Diggins repeats a liberal indictment of the Church during the interwar years. But what were "the interests of the Church"? Would American Catholics have concluded that the dismemberment of a mass Catholic political party, one of the last forces of democracy in Fascist Italy, was in "the interests of the Church" if the Vatican had not deemed it so? Would every Catholic spokesperson and newspaper have publicly concluded that the resolution of the Roman Question with a violent dictatorship was in "the interests of the Church"? Absent a preexisting ideology of the Roman Question and ongoing Vatican communication specifying the "interests of the Church," Americans Catholics by 1929, in my judgment, would not have shared the public consensus they expressed regarding the Lateran Pacts. Diggins ignores what Catholics had said in solidarity with their Holy Father for three generations: Italy was a Catholic nation, the Italian state should honor that divinely ordained fact, and the Holy See's independence required a temporal sovereignty. In short, ideology, not utilitarianism, structured American Catholic responses to Fascism.

If ideology trumped utilitarianism, ideology also trumped theology. In this sense Diggins is correct. The Catholic apologia that Catholics evaluated Fascism based upon neo-Thomistic natural law theology, an eternal tradition of universal values opposed to the flabby relativism of pragmatic liberals who could not take a definitive stand against totalitarian evil, contradicts the historical record.[5] The aesthetic, symbolic, and mythic power of papal Rome and Catholic Italy led Catholics to ignore or rationalize Fascist violations of natural law. American Catholics limited their natural law critiques of Fascist Italy in the 1920s to those moments when the Holy See appeared to invite diplomatic leverage in its strategy to resolve the Roman Question.

American Catholics participated in the Italy-Vatican rapprochement of the 1920s in three ways. First, the American Church supported measures to diminish the debilitating debts that saddled Fascist Italy after the Great War. Second, the American Church supported Vatican policies that helped to undermine Liberal Italy and strengthen the Fascist consolidation of power. Finally, American Catholics participated in a startling array of public rituals legitimizing Fascist Italy.

The Financial Dimension

The failure to resolve the Roman Question after the Great War had resulted from the resistance of King Vittorio Emanuele III and from the political instability of Liberal Italy, where governments fell before negotiations could reach fruition. In Mussolini, the Holy See found a negotiating partner who dominated the monarchy. But in order for Mussolini to stabilize his government, he needed generous terms on Italy's war debt and a vast infusion of capital. U.S. Republican administrations in league with Wall Street capital complied. The Holy See encouraged the U.S. government and the American Church to support these developments.

The Vatican, American Catholics, and U.S. Republican administrations of the 1920s shared perceptions of, and goals for, Fascist Italy. They harbored excessive fears of Bolshevism, demonized Italian liberalism and liberal statesmen, and saw

Fascism as the sole bulwark against revolution. Mussolini cultivated an image of responsible statesmanship. Although he orchestrated the "revolutionary" March on Rome in October 1922, he made certain King Vittorio followed protocol and invited him to form a government. Once in power, Mussolini appointed only four Fascists to ministerial posts and named respected diplomats to lead the embassies in Paris, Berlin, London, and Washington. He convinced U.S. policy makers and press agents that Italy was a secure environment for investments.

Much to the Vatican's relief, Republicans did not bandy about dangerous Wilsonian ideas about European social reform, self-determination, and civil liberties. The State Department in the 1920s looked upon Italy as a Latin nation unprepared for democracy. By the 1920s, many Anglo-Saxon elite had abandoned their fathers' and grandfathers' liberal faith in the Risorgimento. Popular representations of violent Italian American criminals reinforced racialized understandings of Italians as a people in need of an authoritarian leader. Mussolini appeared as a welcome antidote to weak liberal leaders and to Al Capone.

Did the Holy See and the U.S. government discuss Fascist Italy? The victory of President Warren G. Harding in 1920 ushered in a strikingly open relationship between the apostolic delegation and the White House. (Unfortunately, we can only track this development until January 1922, after which the Vatican archives remain closed.) When Harding took office, the press speculated upon rumors of U.S.-Vatican diplomatic relations. Although the Vatican welcomed the possibility, Apostolic Delegate Giovanni Bonzano feared "strong opposition from intransigent and fanatical Protestants who would immediately cry out against the danger of a union between Church and state and the invasion of the Vatican." To calm "intolerant Protestants," Harding drafted a public letter. Remarkably, he invited Bonzano to the White House on 29 April 1921 to proofread the draft for "expressions that might offend Catholics." After Bonzano corrected two prejudicial remarks and gave the hapless Harding a polite catechism on the fundamentals of Catholic ideology, the president and delegate rewrote the letter together. "It was truly providential that President Harding took the courtesy to consult me," Bonzano reflected, "since the letter he prepared, if published, would have been seriously offensive regarding the Roman Question."[6]

This was neither their first nor their last private conversation. On 11 March 1921, Bonzano informed Harding that the Holy Father trusted the United States to bring stability to postwar Europe. Harding could become "the father and savior of Europe and the world," Bonzano flattered. To Bonzano's delight, the president revealed he was working for European stability on different terms than Wilson, a reference to the economic diplomacy that characterized U.S. policy in the 1920s. On 9 May, Harding invited Bonzano to the White House again. The president from Ohio asked the delegate to promote a certain Father Joseph Smith to the vacant episcopal see of Cleveland. Bonzano apologized. The Holy Father had already ap-

pointed Joseph Schrembs to that post three days earlier. Bonzano then received
a presidential invitation to attend a service honoring South American diplomats.
He marveled to Vatican secretary of state Cardinal Pietro Gasparri, "[during] the
[Wilson] Administration [it was] almost impossible to obtain an audience with
Mr. Wilson. Now it is the President of the United States himself who, even though
for his own ends, calls me!"[7]

Not impressed with Harding, Bonzano expressed respect for Secretary of Commerce Herbert Hoover and Secretary of State Charles Evans Hughes, who both
loomed large over U.S.-Italy relations in the 1920s.[8] U.S. foreign policy in the
1920s brought government officials, bankers, and business people together in
negotiations with European states and their central banks to stabilize the international order. Policy makers sought to promote American economic interests
without political entanglements. The key American figures were Hoover, Hughes,
J. P. Morgan banker Thomas Lamont, and Richard Washburn Child, U.S. ambassador in Rome from May 1921 to February 1924. They differed markedly from Wilson, who had sought to mobilize the Italian people from below, accepted social
conflict as a necessary step on the path toward democracy, and never saw a danger of revolution in postwar Italian unrest. The Republicans, in contrast, saw Italy
in bipolar terms: conservative autocracy or Bolshevism. They leaned on the side
of order and stability and painted all anti-Fascists, even liberals who had worked
against socialism for decades, with a red brush.[9]

The State Department embraced Mussolini. Before the Fascists came to power,
Ambassador Child intimated an impending Bolshevik revolution, and the American business community withheld financial support for Liberal Italy. Child portrayed Fascism as a popular force for order. "People like the Italians . . . hun-
ger for strong leadership and enjoy . . . being dramatically governed." Mussolini
visited Child to feel out how the United States would react to the March on Rome
in October 1922. After the fact, Child took credit for the "fine young Revolution"
and boasted how his encouragement had fortified a hesitant Mussolini.[10] A Harvard College and Law School graduate and the Massachusetts state chair of the
Progressive Party, Child had worked in Wilson's Treasury Department before he
became the editor of Collier's Weekly in 1919. As ambassador he became an enthusiastic adviser to Mussolini and, after he resigned, a propagandist for the Fascist
regime. In 1928 he and Luigi Barzini Jr. ghostwrote Mussolini's popular autobiography. After Child's conversion to Catholicism days before his death of pneumonia at age fifty-three in 1935, Italian American churches honored the Duce's friend
with a funeral mass.[11]

The U.S. government invited investors to reap financial rewards as they bolstered Fascist Italy. Hoover's Commerce Department distributed a circular in
January 1923, three months after Mussolini took power, to announce that the
new government, "turning back to private ownership all government owned utili-

ties," offered "an opportunity for the profitable investment of American capital." Treasury Secretary Andrew Mellon assured American capital that Fascist Italy would "emerge from the chaos of war, straighten out her industrial troubles, cut her expenditures and put her budget into equilibrium, all under the direction of one strong man with sound ideas." In November 1924, Secretary of State Hughes "rejoiced in the new manifestations of Italy's energy and resourcefulness, as she has girded herself with extraordinary unity, vigor and determination to meet the economic difficulties which followed the war." Ambassador Child's successor, Henry P. Fletcher, worked with Lamont to promote investment in Fascist Italy. In 1926 William Castle, the State Department's Western European Division chief, endorsed the dictator whose "methods which would certainly not appeal to [Americans] might easily appeal to a people so differently constituted as are the Italians."[12]

The press found it profitable and expedient to celebrate Fascism. Journalists friendly to the regime received free telegram services, discounts for travel, and admission to newsworthy events. In contrast, Fascist Italy censored and expelled critics such as George Seldes of the *Chicago Tribune*. According to historians Philip Cannistraro and Brian Sullivan, of the twenty-five journalists in Rome writing for U.S. newspapers from 1922 to 1935, the most important, Thomas Morgan of the United Press, Salvatore Cortesi of the Associated Press, and Arnaldo Cortesi of the *New York Times*, "were also agents of the regime." Morgan dined with Mussolini and Margherita Sarfatti, the Duce's Jewish mistress, who provided generous copy for the UP. In return the couple earned thousands of dollars and gained unprecedented access to hundreds of American papers in which they justified Fascist policies, called for reduction in Italy's war debts, and pleaded for low tariffs. William Randolph Hearst, an admirer of the Duce, paid the UP for permission to print Mussolini's articles in the Hearst papers, whose circulation reached 5.7 million. After Mussolini took Hearst's wife on a drive in his Alfa Romeo to the ruins of Ostia in 1930, she signed on her tour guide to write directly for Hearst at $1,500 per article. Sarfatti ghostwrote the pieces.[13]

The most important business spokesman for Fascist Italy was Thomas Lamont of J. P. Morgan and Company, treasurer of the Italy America Society from its founding in March 1918 until 1925, when he became its president. Italy America reported upon Italian economic developments to U.S. business and financial communities and worked closely with the State Department and the Fascist government. Its officers and trustees included Hughes, Child, Paul Cravath (an attorney for J. P. Morgan), Hamilton Holt, Otto Kahn (a senior partner at Kuhn, Loeb, and Company), Marshall Field, Henry Burchell, and other moderate progressives and conservatives, who feted Fascist officials and facilitated Italy's economic reconstruction. Italy America's officers were aware of the Italy-Vatican rapprochement of the 1920s. Their guests included Italian ambassador Giacomo De

Martino in March 1925 and Finance Minister Giuseppe Volpi di Misurata, leader of the Italian War Debt Commission, in November 1925. Lamont invited Cardinal Patrick Hayes of New York to join Gotham's financial doers and shakers to banquets in honor of the Fascist dignitaries. Hayes sent chancery official Msgr. Michael J. Lavelle to the dinner lauding Volpi.[14]

In concert with U.S. statesmen, the Holy See intervened to ease Fascist Italy's financial burden. Before U.S.-Italy war-debt negotiations began, Apostolic Delegate Pietro Fumasoni-Biondi informed Cardinal William Henry Φ'Connell of Boston, "the conclusion of an agreement between the United States and Italy on the question of the debt which the latter owes to the United States would redound indirectly to the good of ecclesiastical institutions which have been impoverished by the late war." The delegate instructed O'Connell "to speak a word toward this end." Fumasoni-Biondi probably singled out O'Connell for this task because the Boston archbishop "had used all his authority in the last presidential elections in favor of Coolidge's candidacy." Furthermore, O'Connell's nephew, the chancellor of the archdiocese of Boston, had been Coolidge's guest at the White House. While economic stimulation might indirectly fortify ecclesiastical institutions, war-debt reduction would boost Mussolini's prestige, facilitate the consolidation of his regime, and thus keep the Italy-Vatican rapprochement on track.[15]

At this sensitive time, Fascist officials needed all the prestige they could muster. After meeting Mussolini for the first time in May 1923, Lamont described the ex-revolutionary as a "very upstanding chap" who had "done a great job in Italy." He left Rome "impressed with the innate strength of the present government and sound ideas which govern it."[16] But Italy's occupation of Corfu that summer complicated Lamont's task of selling Fascist Italy. Worse still, the June 1924 murder of Giacomo Matteotti, the reform socialist leader of the anti-Fascist opposition in the Chamber of Deputies, threw Mussolini's government into crisis and implicated U.S. financial interests.

In 1923 Sinclair Oil began negotiations for rights to exploit Italian oil and natural gas. Fierce Italian protest met the announcement of these transactions in May 1924. In Matteotti's 30 May speech to the Chamber of Deputies, he ominously suggested he would expose high-ranking Fascists engaged in illegal activities. Secretly visiting England in April, Matteotti had acquired evidence that Mussolini's government had solicited bribes from Sinclair and other businesses eager to invest in Italy. This sordid chapter in U.S. business history culminated in the assassination of Matteotti by a Blackshirt squad led by the director of Mussolini's press office. The murderers implicated Mussolini in the crime and provoked a crisis that nearly brought down the government. After a period of vacillation, Mussolini entered the Chamber on 3 January 1925, declared a dictatorship, and began construction of a totalitarian regime.[17]

Lamont, to the Vatican's delight, worked to ease his client's burden at this difficult time. During a 1925 visit to Italy, Lamont dismissed "exaggerated" reports of a crisis. He wrote Ambassador Fletcher that the political situation was "much sounder than most Americans appreciate," adding, "you have turned me into something like a missionary for a little quiet preaching on my return to New York." Indeed, back on Wall Street a signed photo of the Duce appeared in Lamont's office. Business historian Ron Chernow explains, "in 1925 [Lamont] made a moral leap and cast his lot with Mussolini." Lamont was eager to float a $100 million Morgan loan to Italy, but the State Department prohibited transactions until Rome settled terms for its $2 billion war debt. At this crucial juncture, Lamont employed his considerable skills as a public relations specialist to sell Fascist Italy. He supported Italy's argument that "ability to pay" ought to determine war-debt payments. Emphasizing Italy's economic difficulties, Lamont prepared data for the Italian Commission in its negotiations. He assured Ambassador De Martino, "I am planning to see a good many of my friends in the public press within the next few days. I shall discuss this situation with them."[18]

Lamont's efforts paid off. During the Great War, the Allies had received U.S. loans at 5 percent interest. Although Lamont, the State Department, and Catholic commentators preferred deep cuts or cancellation of the principal, such radical revisions were not politically viable. Still, the U.S. Debt Commission reported that Italy's $1,647,869,197 principal plus interest would be paid off over sixty-two years, reaching a total of $2,042,000,000. This corresponded to an interest rate of approximately 0.4 percent, considerably lower than the original 5 percent. Interest rates on the loans to England and France were negotiated to 3.3 and 1.6 percent, respectively. Immediately after the negotiations, Lamont announced Morgan's $100 million loan to Fascist Italy. Coolidge, Hoover, and Mellon twisted many congressional arms before the treaty was ratified in April 1926. By 1930, U.S. direct investment in Fascist Italy reached $121 million, and portfolio investments topped $401 million. By then, the regime was secure and the Matteotti crisis long past.[19]

The most important American Catholic social thinker, Father John A. Ryan, professor at the Catholic University of America, came out forcefully in favor of war-debt and reparations cancellation just before Italy began negotiations with the U.S. War Debt Commission. Cancellation, Ryan argued in the *Annals of the American Academy of Political and Social Science*, was sound economic policy and in harmony with the moral law. After the favorable agreement, he wrote, "European ill-feeling toward the United States . . . has happily been somewhat softened in consequence of the settlement with Italy." Ryan's argument for Italy's generous settlement, identical to those of the Coolidge administration, put him at odds with congressional Democrats who opposed stabilizing an oppressive regime.[20]

The Crisis of Italian Liberalism and the Rise of Fascism

In order to understand how the American Church supported Vatican policies that helped to undermine Liberal Italy, consider three developments familiar to students of modern Italy. First, the PPI, a nonconfessional Catholic party that sought to reform Italian society within the Liberal state, weakened the reigning liberal governments. This left a political vacuum that Fascism filled. Second, Pius XI, unwilling to countenance Catholic political independence from the Vatican, undermined the PPI and its resistance to the Fascist government. Finally, the consolidation of the Fascist regime that was willing to formally recognize a sphere of Catholic autonomy, notwithstanding its totalitarian aspirations, paved the way for a settlement of the Roman Question.[21]

As Liberal Italy's political base eroded after the Great War, Catholics and socialists gained unprecedented opportunities. When a Sicilian Christian Democrat, Father Luigi Sturzo, founded the PPI in January 1919, Catholic unions, peasant leagues, and parish clergy flocked to its support. Internal tensions, however, racked the new party. At the first party congress in June 1919, Fathers Agostino Gemelli and Francesco Olgiati advocated a true confessional party and deplored the PPI's half-hearted commitment to the Roman Question. To such conservatives, left-wing *popolari* (party member) activists resembled socialists. Sturzo, who understood that the PPI could never directly attack the Law of Guarantees in Liberal Italy, won the struggle to maintain PPI independence from the Vatican, but he could not always control his deputies in the Chamber.

The PPI fared well in its first election. In November 1919, it won 100 seats in the Chamber; the Partito Socialista Italiana (PSI) took 156. The weakened liberal parties fell from 380 to 252 seats. The PPI refused to play the docile role of prewar Catholics who backed liberals in order to secure socialist impotence. Sturzo resisted compromise with liberals at both the second (April 1920) and third (January 1922) PPI congresses. He called for female suffrage, the election of senators (then royal appointments), and decentralized bureaucracies to enhance local autonomy and to weaken liberal control over the apparatus of government. In the election of May 1921, liberal stalwart Giovanni Giolitti, vexed by the success of the PPI and PSI, bargained for Fascist support. Draped in respectability, Blackshirts won 35 seats, but Giolitti's liberal center still collapsed. The PPI representation increased to 107 seats, the PSI attained 123 seats, its reformist wing won 29, the new Communist Party captured 15 seats, and radical democrats secured 68 seats. The liberal center, with barely 100 seats, failed to gain a majority.

American Catholics applauded the PPI's meteoric rise. *America* stamped Sturzo's program with a Jesuit imprimatur. The Paulists' *Catholic World* contended that "the strength of the Popular Party is due to the attitude which the Italian press . . . has adopted in favor of a permanent reconciliation between the Holy

See and Italy." In January 1922, a Jesuit author for the *Catholic World* predicted the PPI "may look toward the future with full confidence, since it derives its strength from the Cross which shines on its shield and is an unfailing sign of victory." The Catholic press also condemned Fascist violence in Liberal Italy. Chicago's *New World* attacked "unruly Fascisti bands" for "adopting practices much akin to those of the Ku Klux Klan." Catholic assertions that Mussolini saved Italy from Bolshevism became commonplace only after 1924.[22]

But the PPI had inadvertently created a dynamic that served Fascist ends. As PPI power grew, Mussolini communicated to the Holy See his willingness to discuss the Roman Question, if only the PPI were reigned in. This required Mussolini to set aside his vociferous anticlericalism. A youthful Benito had described clergy as "black microbes as fatal to mankind as tuberculosis germs," and his anticlericalism had known few bounds when he edited the PSI newspaper *Avanti!* The first Fascist program, promoted after the rally at Piazza San Sepolcro in Milan on 23 March 1919, had called for "the seizure of all goods belonging to religious congregations and the abolition of episcopal revenues." The earliest Fascists comprised an anticlerical band of ex-socialists, futurists, syndicalists, war veterans, and youth. After the elections of November 1919, Mussolini's *Il Popolo d'Italia* had reasoned, "there is only one possible revision to the Law of Guarantees and that is its abolition, followed by a firm invitation to his Holiness to clear out of Rome." Thus, Mussolini's overture to the Holy See signaled a stark break from his past.[23]

The "Occupation of the Factories" in September 1920 separated the revolutionary from the reactionary phases of Liberal Italy's postwar unrest. With tacit state approval, Fascist squads unleashed a wanton wave of violence against the Left, and Mussolini's public attitude toward Catholicism suddenly changed. The atheist announced, "I believe that Catholicism can be used as one of the greatest forces for the expansion of Italy in the world." Elected to the Chamber in May 1921, he declared, "Fascism neither preaches nor practices anticlericalism." He enraged syndicalists and Masons within his Fascist movement when he affirmed "that the Latin and Imperial tradition of Rome today is represented by Catholicism. . . . The only universal idea which today exists at Rome is that which radiates from the Vatican. . . . Should the Vatican definitively renounce its temporal dreams, Italy . . . would be well-advised to furnish it material aid . . . for schools, churches, hospitals . . . because the development of Catholicism throughout the world . . . is a matter of interest and pride to us Italians." Nationalists, right-wing *popolari*, and the Vatican liked what they heard. In November 1921, the ostensibly antiparty Fascist movement became the Partito Nazionale Fascista (PNF), and Mussolini reigned in violent Blackshirt squads whose centers in Cremona, under Roberto Farinacci, and in Ferrara, under Italo Balbo, threatened Mussolini's bid for respectability in Rome.[24]

With Mussolini's star rising, Archbishop Achille Ratti of Milan became Pope

Pius XI on 6 February 1922. In a gesture that signaled his desire for reconciliation with the Kingdom of Italy, Ratti blessed the crowds from the outer balcony of St. Peter's. The authoritarian pontiff, who shared Mussolini's disgust for liberalism, socialism, and democracy, defined Catholic Action in "Ubi arcano Dei" (December 1922) as "the participation of the laity in the Apostolate of the Hierarchy." Under strict episcopal control, Catholic Action would dedicate itself to the moral and spiritual education of youth, students, and workers. A Catholic party compromising values within liberal pluralistic political structures did not fit into Pius's plan for restoration. The autonomy of the PPI from the Vatican and its indifference to the Roman Question unsettled the pope. The PPI's growing influence over Catholic Action challenged hierarchical control, and activist labor unions and peasant leagues disrupted social order. The formidable political power of the PPI, however, was a sacrificial lamb Pius could offer on the Fascist altar to win temporal sovereignty from Fascist Italy.

By 1922 liberal governments had lost the will to control Blackshirt violence. Right-wing PPI senators, tied with the Vatican to the interests of the Banco di Roma, undermined Sturzo's bid for an alliance with reform socialist Giacomo Matteotti to stem the paramilitary Fascist onslaught. King Vittorio chose not to direct his army to halt the Blackshirt March on Rome. Instead, he invited Mussolini to form a government. Waiting nervously in Milan, ready to flee beyond the Alps if the march were repulsed, Mussolini arrived in Rome on 30 October to take the reins of government. Under pressure from the Vatican and against Sturzo's wishes, the PPI filled two ministries in Mussolini's first government.

Once in power, Mussolini orchestrated striking symbolic overtures to the Vatican. His first ministerial speech invoked God to "bring my heavy and difficult task to a successful conclusion."[25] For the first time, a Catholic mass honored the Unknown Soldier. The cross in the Coliseum, erected in 675 but removed in 1874, was restored. The crucifix appeared in law courts and schools; blasphemy was made a penal offense. L'Osservatore Romano welcomed new legislation against drugs, pornography, contraceptive devices, and gambling. Mussolini deterred the construction of a mosque in Rome. He had his children baptized and confirmed in April 1923, sanctified his civil union with Rachele Guidi in a religious marriage in December 1925, increased the number of military chaplains, and raised clerical salaries. He gave a collection from the Chigi Palace library on the history of the papacy to the pope, the former prefect of the Vatican library who had failed to obtain the collection years before.

On 20 January 1923, Mussolini had a secret meeting with Secretary of State Gasparri at the home of Carlo Santucci, a right-wing PPI senator and president of Banco di Roma. Mussolini agreed to bail out the collapsing bank, which held significant Vatican investments. In turn, a Catholic Fascist loyal to Mussolini, Prince Francesco Boncompagni-Ludovisi, replaced Santucci as bank president, and Gasparri assured Mussolini that the PPI would be more supportive of his government. Historians have hypothesized that the principals agreed to work toward a settlement of the Roman Question.

In February 1923, the Fascist Grand Council (created 15 December 1922) encouraged the Nationalists to merge with the PNF. A political force since 1910, the Nationalists called for Italian expansion and an authoritarian state. Like the Vatican, they were staunch opponents of Masonry, liberalism, and democracy. Although their monarchism and elitism alienated Fascists of syndicalist and republican origins, their ties to industrial interests and their intellectual stature brought the PNF advantages. To attract their support, Mussolini expelled Masons from the PNF.

While the Vatican and American Catholics welcomed the purge, Scottish Rite lodges and Protestants in America grew alarmed. Ambassador Gelasio Caetani di Sermoneta in Washington, himself a Nationalist, informed Mussolini on 17 February 1923 that the expulsion had upset Americans who feared "a possible restoration, even if partial, of the temporal power and thus the supremacy of the Catholic Church." Mussolini instructed Caetani to assure anxious Americans that Fascism "can never lead to a partial let alone a total restoration of the pope's temporal power dissolved permanently on 20 September 1870." To inquiring Masons, Caetani emphasized "the difference existing between the two organizations of Freemasonry in the United States and Italy." The former, "essentially a religious and phylosophical [sic] movement," pursued "humanitarian and uplifting purposes, perfectly undisguised, without plotting or scheming." By contrast, Italian Masons were "a secret organization with political aims and exercises, activities which have tended to become prevalently demagogic."[26]

Delighted with Mussolini's swipe at Masonry, American Catholics hoped he would quell Protestant proselytizing in the Eternal City. English Wesleyan Methodists had arrived in Italy in 1859, English Baptists in 1861, and American Baptists in 1870, and most significantly, the American Methodist Episcopal Church began its Italian work in 1873. It established a school and house of worship in 1894 near the Quirinal Palace and then purchased land in 1914 on Monte Mario overlooking the Vatican. In 1921 New York's *Christian Advocate* scorned the "subtle ways" the Vatican was trying to undermine Methodist hopes to build its International College on Monte Mario. Deputies of the PPI and Nationalists, who feared Protestantism as a cloak for Anglo-American colonization, also raged against Methodist ambitions.[27]

The Knights of Columbus mobilized to defend papal Rome. In August 1921, Benedict XV urged an entourage of visiting Knights to combat the menace. Protestants, he said, threatened "to rob our children nearest to us of the most precious heritage left them by their forefathers, the Catholic faith." The Knights established a $1 million fund against their enemies, whose "vast program" was "anti-

Catholic, anti-Latin, and has for its end American imperialism." On the front line of the Methodist-Catholic polemics, the *New World* hissed: "If you take the Catholic Faith away from an Italian you leave a void. Nothing can replace it. You cannot make him a good Protestant. You leave him without any faith at all. It is a queer sort of Christianity that de-Christianizes people."[28]

In Rome in early 1922, Cardinal O'Connell slammed the Methodists for setting heretical sights on the Eternal City. A Methodist minister, the Reverend Mr. Bayley, dubbed O'Connell's speech "an echo of papal thunder." Bayley complained of the "growing political influence of Catholics in Italy which has brought to the fore two old questions, . . . namely, the temporal power of the Pope and the school question." Bayley's evangelical defense of the Methodist presence in Rome sounded strangely similar to Catholic responses to U.S. nativists: "They say we are a foreign church, aiming at political penetration. We may dismiss the last part. If our government is backing us we have never heard of it." Methodist operations "[are] and will be Italian. The large majority of the students and professors are and will be Italians. . . . We have not created an American Church but an Italian Church." Denying Catholic claims that the Italian nation was necessarily Catholic, Bayley insisted the "Italian nation has always been international in its thought and service."[29]

Bertrand Tipple, president of the Methodist International College, insisted Italy was his adopted fatherland. Awarded the title of Commander of the Crown by King Vittorio for making Americans aware of Italy's sacrifice during the Great War, Tipple insisted his college would neither Americanize Italians nor deface Monte Mario. Tipple attributed the campaign against the college to clerical forces subservient to the Vatican, and he inspired Methodist bishops to denounce Cardinal O'Connell and "to aid in every possible way the Monte Mario Board of Directors." But Tipple's dream of a Wesleyan City never came to pass after the Fascist government stalled the extensive Methodist building plans.[30]

American Protestant-Catholic polemics coincided with Fascist overtures calculated to make the PPI appear redundant. What could the PPI do for the Vatican that Mussolini could not? Fascism's 1923 educational reforms made such significant concessions to Catholics that the *L'Osservatore Romano* suggested the PPI no longer had reason to exist. The government suppressed Primo Maggio (1 May), the socialist labor day, and established as a substitute 21 April, the classical birthday of Rome. Mussolini declared what no liberal leader had dared: "We are a Catholic nation, not only because the vast majority of our people is Catholic, but because Catholicism is inseparable from our history."[31] Aware of the Vatican's tacit support, he dismissed his PPI ministers. In 1924 he formally recognized Milan's Sacred Heart University, founded by Fathers Gemelli and Olgiati, Sturzo's right-wing PPI critics. Sacred Heart, the intellectual center of Pius's Catholic renewal, had close links to the finances of "clerico-Fascists," a term coined by

Sturzo and used by scholars to describe ex-*popolari*, conservative Catholics, and Catholic nationalists who pledged their loyalty to the Fascist regime.

By 1923 the American Catholic press had shifted its allegiance from the PPI to the PNF. In March the *Catholic World* editorialized, "the Fascist party is committed to peace." It noted approvingly that the Fascist "Grand Council has decreed that Masons can no longer belong to the Fascist Party." One year later, the *Catholic World* analogized, "Mussolini has been fighting political degeneracy and Communist destructive efforts, just as the Papacy fought Modernism and [Ernesto] Nathan" before the Great War. Now, "both Mussolini and the Papacy are triumphant" and could resolve the Roman Question without resistance. *America* celebrated Fascist opposition to Masonry and reasoned that the PPI's demise might not be tragic, if Fascism continued on its path toward Catholic restoration. The San Francisco archdiocesan *Monitor* praised the March on Rome as "one of the most marvelous political phenomena that have marked the history of any country for many years." Chicago's *New World* also breathed a sigh of relief after the March on Rome. "[Mussolini] himself has announced that he is a Catholic, and recognizes the authority of the Church in moral affairs." Applauding his friendly gestures, the *New World* boasted in February 1924 that Mussolini has "reconstruct[ed] the new Italy on the spiritual lines of the Catholic Church," leading to "a rebirth, greater and more beautiful than the Renaissance of the Middle Ages."[32]

In June 1923, the Vatican pulled the plug on Sturzo's battle to save democracy. As he campaigned against the Acerbo bill, which would give two-thirds of the seats in the Chamber of Deputies to any party with a relative majority, Blackshirt violence against the Church escalated. The pope intervened. On 23 June, the conservative Catholic *Corriere d'Italia* of Rome published an interview with Msgr. Enrico Pucci, a Vatican journalist and intermediary between the government and the Holy See. Considered a papal mouthpiece, Pucci suggested Sturzo was an embarrassment to the Vatican. The following week, forty-three Roman nobles loyal to Pius proclaimed their solidarity with the Fascist government. At the request of the Vatican, Sturzo resigned as PPI secretary on 10 July. Nine right-wing *popolari* broke party ranks and voted for the Acerbo bill. When it became law on 25 July, Fascist domination of the Chamber was assured. As for Sturzo, in August 1924 Gasparri provided him with a Vatican passport and ordered him into exile. The strongest voice for Christian Democracy in Italy took up residence in London to write against the regime and await a better day. He arrived in New York in October 1940 for the duration of World War II and did not return to Italy until September 1946.[33]

Mussolini's regime faced a serious test in 1924 during the Matteotti crisis, but the forces of reaction came to his rescue. King Vittorio, who could at any time dismiss the prime minister, ignored evidence implicating Mussolini in the murder. The Vatican signaled its desire for order rather than change. Jesuit Enrico Rosa, editor of *Civiltà Cattolica*, described Matteotti as a victim of the political delinquency that, as a socialist, he had helped to create. Two days after Matteotti's murder, the opposition left the Chamber in a gesture of protest known as the Aventine Succession. Rosa dismissed those in opposition as delinquents and defended the Fascist government that had suppressed socialist tyranny, rejected Masonry, and brought order out of revolutionary chaos. On 9 September, the pope devastated the Aventine Succession when he repudiated the PPI for testing the waters of an anti-Fascist coalition with moderate socialists. Pius finally rang the PPI's death knell when he denounced the very idea of an autonomous Catholic party in Italy. Dependent upon Mussolini to achieve his ends, Pius claimed that divine intervention had spared the prime minister's life after a failed assassination attempt.

Although Pius emasculated the PPI and supported the Fascist consolidation of power, he also rebuked the clerico-Fascists' unconditional praise of Mussolini. His goal was to carve out a unified bloc of Catholics under his authority, disengaged from political activities and not subservient to the regime. Armed with a unified Catholic bloc, Pius could deploy Catholics in his negotiations to settle the Roman Question and establish a concordat to protect the Italian Church in its bid to restore Christian values to society.

American Catholics followed the lead of their Holy Father and rushed to Mussolini's aid during the Matteotti crisis. L. J. S. Wood and Harvey Wickham, both living in Italy, were the most prolific Catholic journalists covering Fascism in the 1920s. They turned *Commonweal*, the lay Catholic weekly, into a mouthpiece of Fascist apologetics. Mussolini, according to Wood, was a good-willed moderate who had saved Italy from anarchy. He was beleaguered by "extremists" on the right, "the ultra violent on the Fascist side," and on the left, "the extreme Socialists and Communists among the opposition." Wood equated these factions, as if, in 1924, both "sides" were equally opposed to Mussolini's wise centrist leadership. He barely acknowledged the existence of liberal, Catholic, and socialist anti-Fascism. According to Wood, both extremes resisted "Mussolini and the best of his men," who "are sincerely desirous of regularizing, normalizing, constitutionalizing things." Matteotti's murder was the work of Fascist extremists, who, like communists, were entirely out of the prime minister's control. Given the opportunity, according to Wood, Mussolini would rein in all extremists, as he had saved Italy from "Communism and chaos" after the Great War.[34]

Not to be outdone, *America* dismissed any possibility of Mussolini's involvement in Matteotti's murder and insisted the prime minister stood "for progress which is coupled with law and order." Unshaken by the governmental crisis, the Jesuit magazine predicted, "Fascism will continue its wonderful work for the reconstruction of Italy," which had "only just begun."[35]

Among English-language Catholics, Paulist priest James Gillis alone growled at Mussolini. In 1925 the irascible *Catholic World* editor charged, "it is frequently asserted that Mussolini saved not only Italy but Europe, and not only Europe but the world, from Bolshevism. He may have saved it from Bolshevism, but he did not save it for democracy. He considers democracy absurd. . . . He is, therefore, not a democrat but a demagogue."[36]

American Catholic Rituals of Reconciliation with Fascist Italy

On 3 January 1925, Mussolini awoke from his political torpor, took responsibility for Blackshirt violence, and proclaimed his dictatorship. Over the next four years, as he constructed his authoritarian state, he sought reconciliation with the Holy See. American Catholics, through their press and ritual behavior, participated in the transformation of the ideology of the Roman Question. They consecrated the symbols of Fascist Italy in frequent public rituals with representatives of the Fascist state.

After 1925 the regime cracked down on the independent press, ended civil liberties, and repressed all opposition. Mussolini also struck out against revolutionary, anticlerical elements within the PNF—violent agrarian Blackshirts and syndicalists—to secure support from industrialists, landowners, the Church, the monarchy, and foreign states. State apparatus dominated the domesticated PNF as Blackshirt radicals lost power or joined opportunistic careerists in entrenched bureaucracies. True believers in Fascism as a continuous revolutionary struggle suffered demotions. The regime's historian wrote in 1925, "We are readier than the generation that came after 1848 and 1860 to recognize the greatness of the papacy, of Catholicism, of the religious life in general."[37]

Notwithstanding its totalitarian boasts, the regime awarded the Church an apolitical sphere of autonomy relating to moral and religious education. When the state encroached upon that sphere, Pius cried foul and, in some instances, halted negotiations on the Roman Question. But Pius watched passively as Catholic unions perished and the regime forced Catholic workers into collaboration. On 2 October 1925, the Pact of Palazzo Vidoni gave Fascist unions exclusive rights to bargain with employers. In April 1926, the state denied Fascist unions the right to strike and made them agents of the state. This legislation, accompanied by the establishment of a Ministry of Corporations, laid the foundation for the corporate state. In August, Balbo's squads murdered Father Giovanni Minzoni, an activist among youth near Ferrara. For their protection, Pius forbade priests from belonging to political parties. Mussolini quelled Catholic criticism when he erected a cross on the Campidoglio.[38]

In 1925 the regime took up the Roman Question in earnest. On 6 January 1925, Minister of Justice Alfredo Rocco, an ex-Nationalist and harsh critic of the agnosticism of the Liberal state, appointed a commission to report on ecclesiastical legislation. Although the Italian episcopacy welcomed the report, Pius protested the absence of Vatican representation on the commission. One year later, Mussolini formed another commission presided over by clerico-Fascist Paolo Mattei-Gentili. Although it included three canons of the Roman Patriarchal Basilicas, Pius disparaged the absence of Vatican representation. These Fascist overtures alerted the world to a coming reconciliation.[39] To further grease the wheel, Mussolini substituted Augusto Turati, a supporter of the Duce's religious policy, for anticlerical Fascist radical Roberto Farinacci as PNF secretary in August 1926. Secret negotiations with the Holy See began that autumn.[40]

On 12 January 1925, Rocco introduced a bill to suppress Masonic lodges and criminalize membership of government officials in secret organizations. This sweeping measure evoked Catholic applause and aroused American concern. Joseph Tibe, an Italian-born Freemason in Columbus, Ohio, explained to Mussolini, "His Excellency is held in high esteem by the American people for various and sundry reasons, chief among which is the most extraordinary methods employed and the success attained by him against the Bolsheviks." However, repression against the Masons has been "looked upon with extreme disfavor by not only the Masons, who are strong in themselves, but by the American people generally." The anti-Masonic policy will "cause the esteem in which you are held to wane considerably." He assured "both the Government of Italy and His Excellency that they have absolutely nothing to fear from the order, and that they shall find [Freemasonry] ready and anxious to give its most staunch support."[41]

American Masons launched into action. The *New Age*, organ of the Scottish Rite, insisted the Church and Fascist Italy had joined hands to oppress Masonry. John H. Cowles, grand commander of the Supreme Council, urged every member of Congress to reject the Italian war-debt settlement. Ambassador De Martino sought out Democratic congressman Sol Bloom, a Mason known personally to Mussolini, to gather information. Bloom, according to De Martino, said that the Masons were "particularly agitated by the events last summer in Florence and in Rome," when Blackshirts attacked their brothers. Bloom urged the Italian government to demonstrate it had taken steps against the perpetrators, and he proposed that an American commission of Masons visit Italy, an idea rejected by De Martino. In February 1926, Bloom gave a speech among his brothers defending Fascism. Mussolini urged De Martino to stress to the American public the distinction between Scottish Rite and secretive Italian Freemasonry.[42]

Wood made the Fascist assault on Masonry palpable to Catholics. "Continental Freemasonry," he explained in *Commonweal*, was "an association of definite political views and practice, the most definite of which is a fanatical hostility to the Catholic religion. Signor Mussolini is the only European statesman who has had the pluck to oppose Freemasonry openly." He assured American Catholics that Masons "hidden in the Fascist ranks" were criminals. "The connection with the Craft of many of the Fascists now under accusation in the Matteotti case, has been proved." Mouthing Fascist propaganda, Wood avowed Freemasonry was responsible for the anti-Italian results of the peace negotiations after the Great War and was still working against Italy.[43]

Stephen Grayson, a journalist in Italy writing for *America*, also celebrated the crackdown on Masonry. Fascism "began as a determined and successful attempt to save the country from the Bolshevist peril, which I for one can testify was a very real peril." After ridding Italy of reds, Fascists "addressed themselves to what was no less a menace, the professional politician[s]," who had "all but ruined Italy," "were Freemasons, and took their orders from the Lodges." Grayson claimed that the Fascist legislation was "practically the same law as that passed in various [American] States . . . against the Ku Klux Klan." Although Masonry promoted democratic values, "Mussolini has never concealed his contempt for 'democracy,' and it must be admitted that what passed for democracy in Italy never gave him much reason for admiring it." Several weeks later, *America* excused the Blackshirt "mobbing" of liberal anti-Fascist Giovanni Amendola. In its account of a beating that proved to be fatal, *America* speculated that Amendola's wounds were not serious, and the Jesuit weekly actually complimented Fascists for allaying violence.[44]

By the mid-1920s, the most visible U.S. prelates had visited Mussolini, touted his Catholic credentials and providential mission, and accepted awards from the regime. In 1924 Cardinal O'Connell boasted, "Italy was in a process of undergoing a transformation since Premier Mussolini has been in power. . . . I have never seen such a change. There is order, industry and cleanliness everywhere." On 4 July 1926, Mussolini wrote O'Connell to award the cardinal the Order of the Crown of Italy. O'Connell affirmed, "Mussolini is a genius in the field of government, given to Italy by God to help the nation continue her rapid ascent towards the most glorious destiny."[45] In 1925 Cardinal Mundelein became the first American awarded the Grand Officer of the Royal Italian Order of the Crown. He praised the Duce: "Mussolini is a great big man—the man of the time." Cardinal Hayes received awards from Fascist Italy on four occasions. Upon his return to New York after a trip to Rome in 1926, he observed, "Mussolini shows himself unusually favorably disposed to the Catholic Church and felt that it was vitally necessary to the progress of the Italian nation. . . . Rome is becoming a great city under the Mussolini regime. . . . The open religious processions which occurred last year would not have been possible fifty years ago." In 1926 Cardinal Dennis Dougherty "exalt[ed] religion and Fascist Italy" at the inauguration of a parochial school. The following year, he too became a Grand Officer of the Italian Crown. Less known but no less enthusiastic, Augustinian assistant general Joseph A. Hickey assured the *New York Times* that Mussolini was "a superman who has solved order out of chaos, a man who brought peace and prosperity to Italy."[46]

By 1925 King Vittorio Emanuele III had positioned himself as a symbol of Fascist Italy. Rather than direct his willing and able army in 1922 to repulse lawless paramilitary squads terrorizing royal subjects and marching on Rome, he asked Mussolini to form a government. Thereafter the monarch frequently violated the constitution that he had pledged to protect. He cleared the path for Mussolini, temporary prime minister during a political crisis, to become the Duce of a two-decade dictatorship. King Vittorio permitted the creation of the Fascist Grand Council that weakened his cabinet of ministers. By royal decree he founded a Fascist militia exempt from a royal oath of loyalty. In a May 1924 speech to the Chamber of Deputies, King Vittorio praised the new era Fascism had initiated. During the Matteotti crisis, the king issued a decree to limit the freedom of the press. He ignored evidence demonstrating Mussolini's complicity when he could have simply asked for the weakened prime minister's resignation. By royal decree he eliminated the seats of the anti-Fascist Aventine deputies. After the declaration of the dictatorship, King Vittorio signed off on laws terminating constitutional civil liberties.

As a symbol of Fascist Italy, the monarchy, previously usurper of the Papal States, became worthy of American Catholic consecration. Following Mussolini's directives, consulates spearheaded festivities among Italian Americans to honor the twenty-fifth anniversary of King Vittorio's reign on 7 June 1925. Italian Americans rose to the occasion. A committee in Chicago raised funds for a cancer institute in Milan, while Denver's Italians dedicated a library to the sovereign. The Church backed these initiatives. Father Nicolo De Carlo of Holy Rosary Church in Washington held a solemn mass honoring King Vittorio for the Italian embassy staff. In Boston, consuls general of several states, U.S. military officers, and the Knights of Columbus gathered with representatives of the governor, mayor, and archdiocese, and Boston consul general Agostino Ferrante di Ruffano for a solemn mass at St. Leonard's Church. As they waited for the service to begin, a procession of men, women, and children, "each bearing a miniature Italian flag," marched into St. Leonard's. "Black-shirted members of the Fascisti" flanked the procession into the church.[47]

The American Church's ritual participation in the transformation of the ideology of the Roman Question was visible everywhere the symbols of Fascist Italy had a public presence. The Twenty-Eighth International Eucharistic Congress in Chicago, 20–24 June 1926, as well as the inauguration of a new cathedral in St. Louis, Missouri, days later, communicated that the Italian state, regenerated under Fascism, legitimately represented the Catholic nation. The Foreign Ministry instructed Chicago consul general Leopoldo Zunini to accept all invitations to the congress and to participate in ceremonies honoring Italian prelates. Zunini alone among diplomats in Chicago was invited to greet the cardinals, who arrived in a train painted red in their honor. He was also the only consular official who received an invitation to attend religious ceremonies at Chicago's Holy Name

Cathedral. He took a seat of honor with Mayor William Dever, just behind Cardinal Giovanni Bonzano, the papal legate to the congress, and Cardinal Mundelein, who had been awarded by Fascist Italy the previous year at Zunini's request.[48]

The Eucharistic Congress, organized into seventeen national sections, held its Italian section at Municipal Pier on 20 June for an audience of 20,000. Representatives of the Vatican, the Italian Church, the American Church, and Fascist Italy, including Bonzano, Mundelein, and Zunini, shared the platform. The speakers intoned upon the marriage of the Church and Fascist Italy. Archbishop Pietro Pisani and Zunini celebrated "the return of brothers after a long unfortunate separation. Religion and *patria* are no longer enemies, but now reappear as the essence of our mentality and spirituality, as the hinge of our history, as the most brilliant gem of our *patria*." They sent a telegram to Pius XI and King Vittorio.[49] Zunini elaborated upon the Italian character of the papacy, the Eternal City, and the Catholic Church. "The papacy is a universal institution not limited to one nationality; it has, however, a reflection of *italianità* and is certainly a great glory for Italy. . . . We Italians are delighted to draw upon the advantage that directly and indirectly the [Eucharistic Congress] reflects upon *italianità* here in America. Americans can verify that from Rome and from Italy the religious light that illuminates the entire world emanates."[50]

In the evening, Giuseppe Rossi, Chicago correspondent for *Il Progresso Italo-Americano*, held a banquet for Italian American leaders and ecclesiastical and Fascist officials. Absent only Bonzano, the entourage from the platform at Municipal Pier mingled with the officers from the Italo-American National Union, the Order Sons of Italy in America, the Italian Chamber of Commerce of Chicago, and Italian American politicians and clergy. They repeated the afternoon toasts to Fascist Italy, Mussolini, King Vittorio, and Pius XI. On 22 June, Bonzano received Zunini and his staff for a private audience to thank them for the splendid celebration at the Italian section. Although Bonzano received no other foreign representatives, he did grant a special audience to the Illinois delegate of the Fascist League of North America, Mario Lauro. A symposium in honor of the Italian pilgrims held on 23 June culminated in cries of "Viva il Re, Viva Mussolini, Viva il Papa," after Lauro and Zunini read telegrams from Count Thaon di Revel, president of the Fascist League, and King Vittorio.[51]

On 28 June, the pilgrims performing the transformation in the ideology of the Roman Question trekked from Chicago to St. Louis to celebrate the centennial of the diocese and to consecrate the new cathedral. Archbishop John Glennon, Mayor Victor J. Miller, Consul Paolo Emilio Giusti, and members of Italian American societies waving the tricolor greeted the travelers as bands played the "Marcia Reale." A religious ceremony at the cathedral and a banquet for 1,800 followed. Giusti took a seat of honor at the table with Bonzano. The following day, Bonzano, Giusti, Glennon, Archbishop Giuseppe Palica, an official from the archdiocese of Rome, Bishop Luigi Cossio of Loreto, and Msgr. Lucius Leccisi of the Vatican's Sacred Consistorial Congregation visited Dago Hill, the Italian American district. Met by the Knights of Columbus and Italian societies, they consecrated a new St. Ambrose church building. The papal, Italian, and American flags flew side by side as bands trumpeted the "Marcia Reale." Bonzano never left the archdiocesan residence, cathedral, and seminary, except to visit St. Ambrose.[52]

Protestants took note of these extravagant displays of reconciliation between Fascist Italy and the Church. James Gill, a Methodist immigrant from Northern Ireland, tendered his concerns in a letter to Mussolini. "You seem to be raised up by GOD for a herculean task, . . . and if you are given a free hand, you will place Italy alongside, if not in front of the Nations of the World." Gill continued, "there is no bitter feeling in the heart of any intelligent Protestant toward the Roman Catholic Church, so long as they recognize the fact of a division between Church and State." Repulsed by French Catholics who sought control of the state, Gill complained how the governor and mayor of New York "bowed and kissed the hand" of Cardinal Bonzano during his stay in Gotham en route to the Eucharistic Congress in Chicago.[53]

American Protestants urged the Duce to fulfill his providential mission, left incomplete by Mazzini, Cavour, and Garibaldi, to free Italy from the shackles of Roman Catholicism. As T. S. Horry of Greensboro, North Carolina, explained in 1926: "On September 20th, 1870, Victor Emmanuel, King of Italy, entered Rome and it was thought that Italy would be emancipated from this yoke and curse to the country, but the Pope retained the Vatican." While "it has been your dream . . . to try to establish again the passed [sic] greatness of Rome," thus far "[you have] failed to take into consideration" how Catholicism caused "the dark ages to last over a thousand years." "Italy would have been again today the greatest power in the world, if on September 20th, 1870 the Government of Italy had driven the Pope not only out of Rome, but out of the Kingdom of Italy as well, expelled all the Hell Hounds represented by the Priest of the Roman Catholic Church, if they had taken the lids off of the convents and stopped the prostitution of the best blood in Italy, the life blood I should more properly say of the Italian Nation." Horry recounted how his father witnessed the draining of a lake situated beside a convent in Florence in 1860. The bottom of the lake contained "10 to 12 inches of decomposed bones of infants drowned in the lake like puppies. . . . Picture a beautiful young girl thinking she is giving herself to God, enters a convent to be debauched by the Priest. Her offspring is torn from her breast and drowned like a dog. . . . These Fiends of Hell would murder the infant to suit their purpose." Horry pleaded for the Duce to drive the Church out of Italy.[54]

Eugene Holgius of Brooklyn concurred. "Roman Catholicism has produced illiteracy in Austria, Italy, Poland, Spain, Mexico—and wherever the Papal Clergy has dominated. . . . Wherever the Priesthood Reigns there one may expect to find poverty and Ignorance. It is so in your beautiful country." The "Farce, Cere-mony and ostentatious displays" of Catholicism are "purely material and princi-pally superstitious. Why hold races of people in such bondage? Break these iron shackles, Mr. Premier, and destroy the pretensions of mere men. . . . Free your people from Popery . . . and the hardy Sons of Italy will soon be second to none."[55]

The celebrations of the seventh centenary of the death of St. Francis of Assisi on 4 October 1926 further communicated the ideological transformation to joy-ous Catholics and anxious Protestants. Festivities began after Pius issued "Rite expiatis," dedicated to St. Francis, on 30 April. Although Liberal Italy had not ac-knowledged saint days and religious pilgrimages, Mussolini declared 4 October a national holiday and put a train at the disposal of papal legate Cardinal Merry del Val. Bands played national hymns to Merry del Val at stops from Rome to Assisi, where he received a twenty-one-gun salute. The papal flag waved beside the tri-color when Merry del Val referred to Mussolini as "the man who has raised Italy's reputation in the world, and is visibly protected by God."[56]

Mussolini flaunted the medieval friar's Italian credentials. He wrote an intro-duction to a new edition of St. Bonaventure's *Life of St. Francis,* edited by Guido Battelli, a clerico-Fascist scornful of Liberal Italy. Battelli dedicated the book to the Duce, who "broke the shameful tradition of timid and inept governments." Mussolini's introduction had already circulated among consuls with instructions directing the diaspora "to exalt" this most Italian saint in "meetings, sanctuaries, schools, [and] associations." Just as Italy had the greatest poet in Dante, naviga-tor in Columbus, and artist and scientist in Leonardo da Vinci, it now claimed the most holy saint of the Church. The "saint of Assisi" with the "soul of an Italian" initiated the Italian Renaissance, revitalized the religion of Christ, and antici-pated the language of Dante. "Unsatisfied with the confines of his own land," St. Francis left for the East, where his "disciples . . . were both missionaries of Christ and missionaries of *italianità.*" Fascist Italy, "with a new soul," was again "ready to hear him."[57]

In America, Franciscan celebrations brought Fascist officials together with bishops and immigrant clergy to toast Fascist Italy. Italian Franciscans and Capu-chins (a branch of the Franciscans) invited Ambassador De Martino and the "most distinguished personalities of New York [City]" to honor the saint. De Martino acknowledged, "I am an old admirer of the Italian Franciscan Fathers, whom I saw work with wisdom and passion for religion and for Italy during my stay in the Orient." Italian and American flags flew side by side in a procession that entered St. Anthony's Church to the "Marcia Reale." The Franciscan provincial "exalted the renewed Italian religious spirit and love of the *patria*"; the ambassador af-firmed the "indivisible links of religion and the *patria*"; and Capuchin provincial Leopoldo Adreani closed the service applauding "the work of Italy fulfilled by Fas-cism, the King, and Mussolini."[58]

American bishops also performed these rituals of reconciliation that anticipated the Lateran Pacts. On 7 November, Bishop Joseph Schrembs of Cleveland celebrated a pontifical mass in his cathedral to commemorate St. Francis. That evening, before an audience of 1,000, Consul Valerio Valeriani and Schrembs offered a conference on the medieval friar. Valeriani noted how "the bishop, a Bavarian, sincere friend of Italy, and fervent admirer of Fascism, proclaimed enthusiastic words for Italy and Mussolini, words of great political importance considering the prestige Msgr. Schrembs enjoys in Catholic, cultural, and journalistic circles." Italian American parochial schools received the proceeds from the ceremonies.[59]

Boston consul general Ferrante coordinated his efforts for the Franciscan observance of 1 May 1927 with Cardinal O'Connell. Italian American religious societies came out in force to hear O'Connell celebrate a pontifical mass and "speak enthusiastically of [Italy] and of the Government of Your Excellency Mussolini." The mass was followed by a procession, vespers at the Cathedral, and a "magnificent musical, vocal, and cinematographic concert (with salient episodes from the life of Saint Francis) at Symphony Hall." The concert, "packed with Americans and Italians of every class, made an unforgettable demonstration of italianità." Companions over many years in their consecrations of King Vittorio, St. Francis, and Italy-Vatican reconciliation, O'Connell recommended Ferrante to the apostolic delegate for "some Papal decoration or honor. I know him to be a very good Catholic and agreeable person."[60]

Franciscan revelry in Baltimore broadcast the transformation of the ideology of the Roman Question. The Maryland Grand Lodge of the Order Sons of Italy rented out Alcazar Hall, the Knights of Columbus temple, to commemorate St. Francis at its fourth annual convention. The glossy program for the gala event of 28 November 1926 quoted Mussolini on its cover. Festivities began with renditions of the "Marcia Reale" and the "Star-Spangled Banner." Grand Venerable Placido Milio welcomed his guests, and Archbishop Michael Curley of Baltimore offered a prayer. Bishop Thomas Shahan, rector of the Catholic University of America, lectured upon the medieval friar. Mayor Howard Jackson praised the hard work and intelligence of Italian Americans. De Martino sent a colleague to read his address before the audience enjoyed a Fascist propaganda film, The New Italy, and a lecture by philo-Fascist professor Bruno Rosselli. De Martino's address emphasized how "Italy is following today in the footprints of Saint Francis. In the fervor of civil struggles with ravaged cities, St. Francis preached a message of peace and work. And Italy now enjoys civil peace and the triumph of work." Just as St. Francis brought rebirth culminating in the Renaissance, today there is "a rebirth of the Italian genius which we see made flesh and symbolized in the Man whom the world calls 'The Man of Destiny' and 'of the charmed life,' in Benito Mussolini."[61]

Italian consuls worked to cultivate good relations with Catholic leaders. Throughout the 1920s, Consul Carlo Tornielli of Baltimore nurtured the support of Archbishop Curley. When Curley launched a salvo against the anti-Catholic Mexican government during a Knights of Columbus convention, Tornielli complimented the archbishop and mailed him a flattering article from *Il Progresso Italo-Americano*. However, Tornielli considered it unfortunate that Curley, who harbored "profound and personal sympathy for Italians" and Fascist Italy, exhibited a "total absence of tact and diplomacy." The "rawness of his words and acts" undermined his chance to become a cardinal. Indeed, friends and critics called Curley "Iron Mike" for his authoritarian style of leadership and combative dealings with non-Catholics. To compensate, De Martino, upon Tornielli's recommendation, urged the Foreign Ministry to award Curley the Grand Officer of the Crown in 1927.[62]

The consuls merely followed their ambassador's lead. De Martino exploited Cardinal Dougherty's appreciation for Mussolini, King Vittorio, and Fascist Italy. On 24 January 1928, De Martino arrived in Philadelphia, where Dougherty paid his personal respects. At a celebration for Madonna House, a Catholic settlement, De Martino, Dougherty, Mayor Harold Mackey, and other Italian American and clerical leaders lauded one another. The mayor bragged of his recent trip to Italy, where he found everyone brimming with happiness. According to De Martino, "Dougherty both in private with me and in public offered high words of admiration" for Mussolini and for Italy. "At the Sons of Italy banquet, when the name of Your Excellency [Mussolini] was pronounced, Dougherty rose to his feet. He did the same for the name of His Majesty the King." One month later, De Martino wrote the Duce that he had "had a long conversation" with Dougherty "during which I spoke to him again about the teaching of Italian. He promised me that he would do whatever I wanted" in that regard. Even before the Lateran Pacts of 1929 initiated Italy-Vatican diplomatic relations, De Martino laid the groundwork with this cooperative cardinal to promote Fascist propaganda in parochial schools.[63]

These ostentatious performances of Fascist-Catholic affinities diluted Protestant enthusiasm for Mussolini. In 1927 an American identified only as "Sincere Observer" reminded the Duce that "none can serve two masters." The correspondent wondered: "Which is your love, and to whom do you devote your help and the benefit of your powerful influence? To United Italy, for the first time in centuries made a Nation by Mazzini, Cavour, Garibaldi and Victor Emmanuel of Savoy? Or, the political papal institution which for centuries . . . kept the territories of the kingdom of Naples, Calabria and Sicily in a poverty and filthy condition, in ignorance and Superstition almost incredible, raised among them generations upon generations of low mental stratum and for years never lifted a finger to instruct them, but allowed, if not encouraged brigandage, Camorra, Mafia, Blackhand." Signs of a Catholic resurgence in Mussolini's Italy disturbed the Sincere Observer. "You persecute, not as much malefactors and Russian reds as Masons, the YMCA and Protestants. The Masons of Italy to merit your treatment must be very different from our Masons who are very highly esteemed in this country!" Eternal punishment awaited the Duce if he continued to falter. "Will not the God above hold you and punish you as a murderer and why does not your friend Pius XI tell you that. No murderer can enter the kingdom of Heaven!" The correspondent queried, "what is Italy's danger from the YMCA? Can they, if it were their purpose, corrupt the youth of Italy as much as the Papacy? . . . And why persecute Protestants? Have not the Holy Fathers killed hundreds of thousands of them? Do you do that work for Italy . . . or is it for Pius XI whose soul is bound in attempts to regain his provinces, be a monarch again, and then get rid of all the 'tools' he used for his purpose! Mussolini will not be an exception, but a choice victim!!"[64]

Clerico-Fascism in the United States

The principal source of Roman news for American Catholic newspapers after the Great War was the National Catholic Welfare Conference (NCWC) news service. Who was Msgr. Enrico Pucci, the NCWC's press agent in Rome from 1919 until World War II? In 1946 Italy's postwar High Commission for Sanctions against Fascism published a list of informants who had spied for OVRA, the Fascist secret police. Pucci appeared on the incriminating list but was acquitted after Vatican intervention. Pucci's OVRA file reveals a shadowy figure who, through multifarious intrigues, mediated messages among the regime, the Vatican, foreign press agencies, Italian newspapers, and foreign embassies.[65]

A graduate of the Capranica College in Rome, Pucci pursued a journalistic career for the conservative Catholic *Corriere d'Italia* and served several foreign press agencies after the Great War, including the NCWC. A right-wing PPI member, Pucci was close to Chamber deputy and *Corriere d'Italia* editor Paolo Mattei-Gentili. Both became clerico-Fascists after Mussolini came to power. As we have seen, Pucci delivered the Vatican's deathblow to Sturzo's political career in the *Corriere d'Italia*. Pucci's prominence within the Vatican was derived from the status of his patrons, Undersecretary of State Giuseppe Pizzardo and Secretary of State Gasparri. Expelled from the PPI for voting in favor of the Acerbo bill, Mattei-Gentili became the Fascist undersecretary of justice (1924–29). He conveniently had Pucci released from prison after various speculation schemes had landed the monsignor in the tank. The author of a clerico-Fascist study of the Lateran Pacts in 1929, Pucci baptized the infant of Lando Ferretti, head of Mussolini's press office, and maintained "very tight relations" with the Interior Ministry.[66]

It is difficult to disentangle Pucci's roles as Fascist informant and press agent. His OVRA file refers to the "notorious monsignor" as an "international spy" employed by both the government and the Vatican. Historian Carlo Fiorentino hypothesizes that the ubiquitous prelate may have been "an informant for [Fascist police chief Arturo] Bocchini with Vatican approval in exchange for confidential news of interest to the Holy See." Indeed, Pucci's OVRA file is full of recriminations against him as a double agent. He apparently played as many angles as possible to finance the "many relatives that live with him."[67]

Police Chief Bocchini hired Pucci in October 1927 for a monthly fee of 3,000 lire. His OVRA file indicates he sold texts of the Lateran Pacts before they were signed. In May 1929, Pucci furnished Mussolini with recollections of Cardinal Bonaventura Cerretti's 1919 negotiations with Prime Minister Vittorio Orlando over the Roman Question. During the 1931 crisis between the papacy and the regime, many in the Vatican believed that Pucci exacerbated tensions through the irresponsible manner in which he disseminated information.[68] The Fascist Ministry of Propaganda paid Pucci from 1936 to 1938 to write articles for foreign newspapers with such titles as "The Thought of the Pope in the Italo-Ethiopian War" and "Religious Instruction of the Italian People in the Fascist Regime." His 1938 piece "The Threat of Communism against the Family" attacked the United States, which, Pucci explained, was corrupted by communist propaganda.[69]

A busy press agent and author, Pucci voiced papal positions in the *Corriere d'Italia* and interpreted Italy-Vatican relations to American Catholics. He monopolized a Vatican news bulletin that he edited and hawked it to foreign embassies and press agencies. French, American, Polish, and Czechoslovakian news services lamented their dependence upon Pucci but paid for his information just the same.[70] Although Pucci's ambitions found their best outlet in Fascist Italy, World War II found him, never one to avoid a volte-face, supporting the Holy See and the United States. Wartime Fascists were dismayed to learn that he mediated information from Vatican undersecretary of state Giovanni Battista Montini, the future Paul VI, to Pucci's contacts in the Associated Press, the United Press, and the International News Service.[71]

This sometime Fascist spy in the Vatican, papal collaborator in the disembowelment of Italian democracy, and clerico-Fascist intriguer with connections at the highest levels of the regime supplied the NCWC with its Roman news from 1919 until World War II. By 1920 there were fifty-two subscribers to the NCWC *News Sheet* and twenty-three subscribers to its cable service. These were principally diocesan weeklies in the East and Midwest. By 1934, fifty-two Catholic papers subscribed to the service (thirty-six diocesan owned, sixteen privately owned), as well as five magazines and five papers published by lay religious societies. According to the NCWC, "the strongest papers and papers with the largest circulation are the papers that are using the service most extensively." Moreover, periodic inquiries about the Church directed to the NCWC by nonsubscribers, as well as Pucci's sale of information to secular news services, lent his clerico-Fascist perspective vast importance in the United States.[72]

Justin McGrath, NCWC news service director until 1931, vented frustrations with Pucci's performance and tried unsuccessfully to replace him. Pucci, however, protected his position. He kept McGrath informed of efforts among U.S. bishops to undermine the NCWC. Pucci saw the need for "some one . . . here to inform and explain viva voce the work of the NCWC. I endeavor to do that as best as I can whenever occasion arises." Ultimately, directives from Archbishop Edward Hanna of San Francisco prevented McGrath from dismissing Pucci. "There is no mystery here," Hanna shrugged, "Card. Gasparri and Msgr. Pizzardo make the request that we give [Pucci] another chance."[73]

McGrath harbored concern about Pucci's relationship with the Fascist regime because the monsignor had a "personal arrangement" with the government to cable "1500 words a month, free of charge." Pucci "says that he is not obligated to send propaganda for the government." But McGrath wondered, "How will we know when propaganda of a very insidious kind is slipped into the service? And would it not be a shocking revelation if it was ever discovered that the National Catholic Welfare Conference News Service was sending out Italian propaganda?" After consulting with several bishops, McGrath instructed Pucci to discontinue his arrangement with the Italian government.[74]

McGrath's fear of Pucci's proximity to Fascism, however, was coupled with racist presumptions about Italians and a bewildering ignorance of Catholics, liberals, radicals, and socialists struggling to preserve democracy in Italy. "You have read the pronouncements of Mussolini. You know that he is an unbeliever in democracy. . . . The Italian mind, therefore, I think, would not be able to define the relation of the spiritual authority of the Church with democracy in a way that would be satisfactory to believers in democracy." In 1924 McGrath hoped to replace Pucci with Wood, whose effusions in *Commonweal* in favor of Fascism were far less restrained than those of Pucci. Thus, it does not seem likely that greater Anglo-Saxon or Celtic efficiency would have in any way diminished the enthusiasm of American Catholic papers for Fascist Italy. In any case, the clerico-Fascist tenor of the NCWC's Roman correspondent helps explains the clerico-Fascist orientation of American Catholic papers.[75]

American Catholics Respond to Papal Signals

Between 1926 and 1929, Mussolini's dictatorship periodically challenged Pius's favored spheres of Catholic autonomy. Although Pius welcomed the dismemberment of the PPI, he jealously guarded Catholic Action, particularly its youth and student organizations. When the regime created parallel youth and student organizations to replace Catholic ones, or when Blackshirts attacked Catholic youth, Pius dissented and suspended negotiations to resolve the Roman Question. These fits and starts in Italy-Vatican relations generated two American Catholic responses. Some Catholics, like clerico-Fascists in Italy, ignored or minimized Vatican critiques of Fascism and celebrated Fascist Italy as the unproblematic home of the Catholic nation. Other authors voiced anti-Fascist protests in conjunction with their Holy Father. Both claimed to represent the pope, although in my judgment, only the later cohort understood Pius. Once the Vatican and the regime sorted out their difficulties, however, American Catholic criticism of the regime disappeared altogether.

Fascists hoped to substitute the Opera Nazionale Balilla, the Fascist youth organization, for the Exploratori Cattolici, the Catholic Scouts; and the Gioventù Universitaria Fascista for the Federazione Universitaria Cattolica Italiana (FUCI). Pius would have none of it, and violence ensued. At the 1926 FUCI National Congress, police remained idle as Fascists assaulted Catholic students. Mussolini blamed the violence on Catholic "agitators." In January 1927, he instructed prefects to dissolve the Catholic Scouts in all communes with fewer than 20,000 residents. Soon after, the regime banned all Catholic youth organizations from athletic activities. Pius responded with a pointed allocution in December 1926 and a public letter on 24 January 1927. He attacked any state—but not Fascist Italy directly—that would arrogate prerogatives belonging to the Church. From early January to late February 1927, he suspended negotiations with the regime.[76]

Violence against Catholics continued. Historian John Pollard explains how the suppression of Catholic sports clubs came as a "blow to the Pope's confidence in the good faith of the men with whom he was negotiating, and from June 1927 until January 1928," Pius "effectively suspended" negotiations. Tensions intensified. In March, Pius praised the FUCI. "Everyone knows by now that to touch them is to touch the Holy Father himself, and that the father is not willing to remain insensitive to the pains of his sons." After the regime outlawed all non-Fascist youth organizations, Pius cut off negotiations in April and May. Even when the parties worked out a compromise that protected strictly religious organizations, Pius decided to suppress the Scouts himself rather than permit the government to usurp that right.[77]

Some American Protestants cheered any news that the Duce had "emancipated" Italy from the Church. One New Yorker, after reading a 1928 newspaper article entitled "Italy Suppresses Catholic Societies for Training Youth," congratulated Mussolini for "giving Italian youths education *free from Priestly domination. You have placed Italy in the front rank of free nations, and History will so record it. . . .* You are an instrument of God to free and advance your nation."[78] A Mrs. Le Moyne from Denver suggested Mussolini extend his assault on the Church beyond Catholic youth. "Rob the Vatican and take the millions the Pope has stored up there, and use it for the good of all the people of Italy," she insisted. "Make a rade [sic] on the Vatican at midnight and get that fortune for your people."[79]

Like the Holy Father, more discerning American Catholics played the carrot and stick game. When the regime aroused Pius's wrath, they criticized Fascism with normative Catholic theories of the state. The most forceful critique of Fascism came from Father John A. Ryan in two articles for *Commonweal*. In November 1926, Ryan dissected Alfredo Rocco's effort to define Fascism as a political doctrine. Shrewdly equating Rocco's static definition with a regime that in fact contained an eclectic, unstable array of intellectual currents, Ryan stilled an erratic enemy for Thomistic target practice and philosophical execution.[80]

Ryan challenged both the pervasive American Catholic boast of an affinity between Catholicism and Fascism and the attacks upon liberalism found in *Civiltà Cattolica* and *L'Osservatore Romano*. These Vatican organs stressed how liberalism inexorably led to socialism and how both atomized society, undermined authority, and ushered in an anarchic individualism and democratic decadence. Rocco issued the same condemnation of liberalism and socialism and promoted a Hegelian state, an omnipotent entity that absorbed individual and nation. Ryan attacked Rocco's statist pretensions. He argued Catholicism shared an affinity with liberalism and socialism, because all three taught "the welfare of individuals is . . . the end of the state." To Catholic "doctrine the principles of Fascism are as fundamentally opposed as they are to liberalism and socialism." Ryan thus turned Rocco's attack upon liberalism and socialism into one upon Catholicism as well (although Rocco never mentioned Catholicism in his text).[81]

The following week, Ryan assaulted Fascism in practice. The Duce, the ethicist wrote, had undermined democratic elections, eliminated any semblance of a legislature, and abolished local autonomy in cities and provinces. Ryan acknowledged that in Catholic theology "these restrictions upon political liberty" were not "contrary to the moral law," if the Italian people consented. But Ryan questioned the premise of Italian consent. He ridiculed the claim heard frequently in the 1920s that "the Italian people . . . are not capable of maintaining genuine democratic and representative political institutions." Ryan insisted "that the charge of political incapacity against the Italians is nothing short of a cruel libel upon a nation which is the equal in native intelligence of any other people in the world." Ryan believed Italians merited the right of all political communities to "learn the art of government" through "the slow process of education in self-government."[82]

In response, clerico-Fascist Harvey Wickham attacked Ryan and endorsed Fascism without qualification. Wickham had already established himself as a Fascist apologist on the pages of *Commonweal* when he ridiculed Italian liberal freedoms. American editors eager for negative copy had given Mussolini good reason "to suppress newspapers and to deport newspaper men." Reasoned Wickham: "The suppressed newspapers of Italy . . . [were] not so much newspapers as party organs — mouthpieces of those petty factions . . . that brought parliamentary government to a standstill and the Italian nation face to face with a dilemma — one horn being anarchy and the other Moscow." According to Wickham, the Duce "has faced . . . the fact that Italy is a Catholic country" and merited unqualified Catholic support.[83]

In December 1926, Wickham turned on Ryan for ignoring the privileges the Fascist regime had granted the Church. The Duce had moved "in the direction of hearty cooperation with that vast program implied by the proclamation of Christ the King." Wickham found it "amazing when a Catholic scholar of the prominence of Dr. John A. Ryan attempts to prove . . . that the principles of Fascism in regard to the ends of government are as fundamentally opposed to Catholicism as they are to liberalism, Socialism, and Bolshevism. Here is a perfect example of a preconceived opinion working in the unconscious depths of a subtile [sic] mind, and bringing forth its fruit very much out of season." The "season" was the Fascist era, superseding liberalism and the Law of Guarantees; the "fruit" was the resolution of the Roman Question.[84]

Others backed Wickham. "Business man" William E. Kerrish reminded Ryan that Mussolini's regime achieved results. If the Duce's methods "do not fall in line with [American] ideals of democratic government, it might well be remembered that Premier Mussolini is dealing with the Italian nation and not the American republic. Certainly he has not violated fundamental human rights to the extent that certain communistic legislation does in our country. . . . Mussolini's work has been constructive. That strict discipline was needed in Italy there can be no doubt."[85] After Ryan took issue with his critics, one of them countered with an undeniable claim: "highly-placed churchmen in Italy itself" supported Mussolini. In response, Ryan cited Pius's December 1926 allocution, which condemned "a conception of the state making headway, which is not a Catholic conception because it makes the state an end unto itself and citizens mere means to that end."[86]

Commonweal also opened its pages in January 1927 to Sturzo, who put forward a neoguelf anti-Fascist vision. The exiled priest living in London claimed Italy had a historic mission. "She stands for labor by her emigration; for culture, by her trimillenary civilization; for religion, as the centre of Catholicism and the seat of the Papacy." The "immense moral value in the influence radiating from Italy through the many civilizations she has known" has made "Italy, more than any other country, a sort of ideal centre." In contrast to Ryan, Sturzo's anti-Fascism was not a synchronic exercise in moral theology. Appealing to history, Sturzo imagined a Risorgimento that harmonized the pope and modern Italy. The Risorgimento's goal had been to renew Italy's "mission of peace," a complement to the "moral and pacific function" of the Vatican. The "international mission of the Papacy obliges Italy to follow a delicate and exceptionally skilful [sic] policy, and gives her a mission of indirect mediation among the peoples of the world." In short, "Italy is and must be a pacific nation."[87]

"The problem of Italy," then, was "the irremediable contradiction between the

character and aims of Fascism, and the natural and historical mission of the kingdom of Italy." Fascism, "an abnormal phenomenon," "owes its success to the
attitude of the wealthy and conservative classes." Their effort to control the state
after the Great War created an overcentralized government that turned the state
into a "leviathan, assimilating every other force, the embodiment of an oppressive political pantheism." Unlike any American Catholic, Sturzo insisted that "it
will be necessary to face in its entirety the unsolved problem left by the Risorgimento." The legacy of an incomplete democracy haunted Italy. This problem "of
the complete participation of the people in political life" had been "raised, each in
his own way, by Mazzini, by Cattaneo, and then successively by the Radicals, the
Socialists, and the Christian Democrats." Invoking the radical democratic energies of the Vatican's many Italian enemies, Sturzo never won American disciples
and exercised no demonstrable influence over the content of American Catholic
thought regarding Fascism.[88]

Ryan was not alone in his pungent if altogether brief critique of Fascist Italy
during these moments of tension between the pope and Mussolini. At the height
of the Italy-Vatican rupture in negotiations, Father Francis P. Duffy, a popular war
chaplain, told the *New York World*, "Less Benito Mussolini and more Thomas Jefferson would be a mighty good dose for Italy at the present time." Msgr. John L.
Bedford of Brooklyn quipped, "I think Mussolini has overreached himself. . . . Apparently he is drunk with power." The *New York Times* quoted the Catholic Writers'
Guild's spiritual director, Father John B. Kelly: "[Mussolini's] theory is that the
will of the State is supreme and that no elements of human life are exempt from
the authority of the rulers." Jesuit editor Wilfrid Parsons of *America* explained that
Catholic theory "has stood for the right of the parent over the education of his
children against undue encroachment of the State." In April 1928, both *Commonweal* and *America* critiqued Mussolini's policies toward youth and education.[89]

But this was not the beginning of an American Catholic anti-Fascist movement. These one-time critics raised their voices against Fascism to support their
Holy Father during a rough spot in Italy-Vatican negotiations, not to undermine
Fascism. Ryan, for example, never criticized Fascism again until 1937, and he tendered a spirited defense of the Lateran Pacts in 1929.[90] After the pope and Mussolini resolved their differences in the summer of 1928, dissent among American
Catholics conspicuously disappeared.

Catholics and Other Americans, 1927–1929

Historians of American anti-Catholicism in the 1920s have highlighted the re-
vitalization of the Ku Klux Klan, conflicts about the Church in Mexico, and the Al
Smith presidential campaign. Oddly, they ignore the transformation of the ideology of the Roman Question. But the anticipation of an Italy-Vatican rapproche-

ment intensified polemics with Catholics. Alert to rumors of reconciliation, non-Catholics worried about religious liberties in Italy and feared for the Duce's well-being. Ambassador De Martino warned Mussolini, "each time the news highlights the improved relations between the Italian Government and the Holy See, favorable repercussions in the Catholic milieu accompany unfavorable ones among Protestants." To accompany his warning, De Martino sent Mussolini an article from the 28 January 1928 *Independent* of Boston entitled "Il Duce Visions a Pope King." De Martino had received the article from one of his vigilant consuls, who explained that the *Independent* "represented the sectarian Protestant spirit" that permeated New England.[91]

John Hearley, the author, was a formidable polemicist. A cradle Catholic educated at a Jesuit college, Hearley flirted with Anglicanism, Christian Science, and agnosticism while he awaited a reformed Catholicism. His observations of the Church in Rome when he worked for the Roman news bureau of the Committee on Public Information during the Great War turned him definitively away from his ancestral faith. In the *Independent*, Hearley contrasted Italy in 1870, which "enthusiastically keened: 'The Pope King is dead!'" to Mussolini's "chorus, . . . 'Viva il Papa Re!'" Reconciliation boded ill. "Out of the old temporal power and states of the Church grew the theological bigotry and materialism which went far toward producing the unchristian Inquisition, widespread ecclesiastical corruption, a divided and hostile Christendom, and foreign wars. What possible batlike calamities for the future lurk in the Pandora's box of modern Italy's salute to the Pope as king! Surely, liberal Catholics must be embarrassed . . . ; thoughtful non-Catholics, resentful; international diplomacy, bewildered and terrified."[92]

Not content with his warnings in the *Independent*, Hearley introduced a series of four articles in the *Atlantic Monthly* between January and May 1928 that exacerbated tensions between Catholics and their neighbors. Hearley described his encounter with a sensitive American priest in Canterbury, England, after the Great War. Ten years later, that priest, a college professor and closet modernist, had sent Hearley some manuscripts and requested their publication. Deeply critical of modern Catholicism, the series linked the Roman Question to the authoritarian, antidemocratic nature of the Church. The third article, "The Incubus of the Temporal Power," sounded remarkably like Hearley when its author contended that "the history of papal temporal power . . . might well bring the blush of shame to the enlightened Catholic mind." Its story was one of "the political intrigue, the tyrannous oppression, and the militaristic greed practised by this long line of men who claimed to represent the teachings and the spirit of Him who was styled the Prince of Peace." The article lambasted U.S. bishops for "methods of feudalism" and authoritarian domination over their clergy to raise money to buy power in Rome.[93]

American anxieties at the approaching resolution of the Roman Question appeared frequently in Mussolini's mail. For example, Nicolas Norris wrote the Duce that "Christian people" were "fed up" with Italy. "Church and State should be kept separate." Norris felt dejected that "the Nation of Italy is to concede more territory . . . to the Vatican." He pondered with disgust whether "the Pope and Vatican property" was "exempt from Taxation." Another correspondent cited scriptural warrants for the separation of Church and state. The anonymous writer added, "the Church has an Army behind her today in the Knights of Columbus with headquarters in Rome, which is held in obedience to the Pope—at his command. They are a Secret Society, known only to the Church by passwords and signs." The writer lamented how the pope also had links to Tammany Hall, whose "corrupt political organization [secures] public office by stuffing Ballot Boxes and getting the inmates of Lodging houses . . . and the Sisters of Convents" to vote. One ex-Catholic explained, "the Holy Father . . . is none other than the master mind of a religious criminal organization." Catholics "are supremacy seekers with an eye upon ruling the world." The correspondent warned, "Roman influence has taken control of our country," including "the papers in my city, Pittsburgh," which "are affected by the evil influence of the Vatican. . . . God alone can say what will happen, for the enemy of Christianity and all nations with headquarters in your Country" will punish "those who rebel."[94]

Some of the Duce's correspondents believed he was in danger. One self-identified "100% American," who "admires you immensely and would greatly deplore any harm that might come to you," warned, "your greatest danger of injury is from the Roman Catholic Church." This writer assured Mussolini that reforms to modernize Italy and liberate her from papal intrigue put the Duce "in constant danger. Protect yourself physically and mentally from assassination. You are vitally necessary at the present time for the good of Italy." Another author claimed to have traced threats upon Mussolini's life to the Vatican and reminded the Duce, "in Mexico priests and church workers were caught in the act of attempted bombing on the next President." A harried Philadelphian cautioned of the ominous threat St. Ignatius's followers posed. "You are the greatest man that Italy has seen since Cavour, Mazzini, Garibaldi and Victor Emmanuel. . . . Your accession to your present power is the greatest blessing that imperial land has received since it was freed from papal domination and spoliation. But—a friendly hand is holding this pen—*Beware of the Jesuits!* . . . They will put an end to your life. 'Rule or Ruin' is the law of their Order. . . . Ave Caesar!"[95]

Italian immigrants simultaneously praised Mussolini as a liberator of their nation and raised the red flag of papal intrigue. Alfredo Camerano, "an old Garibaldino of eighty-three years," wrote "the Holy Savior, Honorable Benito Mussolini," from New York City. He shared memories of how Garibaldi, General Cardorna at Porta Pia on the 20th of September 1870, and the House of Savoy "liberated the holy *patria* from papal slavery." Camerano praised the Duce for "exterminating all of the gangsters, all of the societies, all of the parties, that are dangerous to the *patria*." But the elderly Garibaldino feared "entanglements with the pope, . . . who is nothing more than a president of fanatics called Roman Catholics." Michele Speciale, veteran of the Great War, praised the Duce's "work of resurrection and progress" that he executed "with a spirit of justice and love for the *patria*." Speciale scorned the pope's "resentful protests against the will of Your Excellency with respect to the education of the young Italian generation, not to mention his insistent pretensions to the temporal power. The Vatican was never patriotic, but rather always adverse to Italy." Speciale warned, "the Jesuitism of the Vatican will always be what it was and is with respect to Italy." He dreamed of that "one fine day," when "the supreme head of the Catholic Church will be a worthy Fascist, . . . free of fanaticism, superstition, prejudices."[96]

If Protestants and liberals understood Mussolini as Italy's liberator from the papal yoke, Catholics cheered the premier for setting the pope free. Months before the signing of the Lateran Pacts, Msgr. M. J. Foley, editor of the *Western Catholic* in Springfield, Illinois, tendered "sentiments of profound respect" to the Duce and enclosed a favorable editorial on Fascism. Foley added: "My admiration for you and your marvelous record leads me to believe that your Excellency is the chosen instrument in the hands of Divine Providence to right the wrong of 1870 by settling the 'Roman Question.'" David Hickey, who eagerly followed the steps toward reconciliation, expressed concern about a newspaper report of a possible breach between Fascist Italy and the Vatican at the end of 1928. "As one of the rank and file I can assure you that [talk of a breach] gives great Joy to the enemies of our Italy, Father Pius XI and the Catholic Church. . . . I do hope and pray that you will use your great influence towards unity between your High Office and our Holy Mother Church."[97]

THE AMERICAN CHURCH emerged from the Great War more outspoken in defense of papal Rome than ever before. It demanded the resolution of the Roman Question on Catholic terms in 1919 and 1920. Because the Vatican and Harding's White House shared common goals for Italy, the apostolic delegation gained greater access to the U.S. government than before. As Republican administrations and Wall Street wealth brought stability to Mussolini's government, so too did the Vatican buttress Fascist Italy in order to secure an enduring negotiating partner. Pius XI sacrificed the PPI, and with it Italian democracy, to resolve the Roman Question. As Fascist Italy carefully monitored U.S. public opinion, American Catholics supported their Holy Father. When he backed the Fascists, so did the American Catholic press; when he critiqued the regime, some American Catholics joined him. In unprecedented public rituals for Protestants and liberals as well as Catholics to see, Catholic authorities consecrated the symbols of Fascist Italy, ridiculed Liberal Italy and its struggles for democracy, and took seats of honor next to the official representatives of the Fascist state in public ceremonies.

Although American historians have ignored the Roman Question and the Lateran Pacts, debates about the proper role of the papacy and the Church in Fascist Italy strengthened the boundaries separating Catholics from their neighbors during the 1920s. American letters to the Duce in the 1920s and 1930s reveal Catholic, Protestant, and liberal preoccupations with Rome. Their correspondence indicates how citizens in barbershops, bars, schools, and living rooms read the newspapers, debated foreign policy, and reacted to the transformation of the ideology of the Roman Question. The Lateran Pacts of February 1929, the realization of the ideology of the Roman Question, ended the long incarceration of the Holy Father. The pope ruled the Vatican City. The far-reaching implications for the United States of the restoration of the temporal power are the subject of Part III.

PART III

Realization,

1929–1940

CHAPTER SEVEN

The Lateran Pacts of 1929
and the Crisis of 1931
Defending "The Holy Island"

On 11 February 1929, Prime Minister Benito Mussolini and Vatican secretary of state Cardinal Pietro Gasparri signed the Lateran Pacts, a three-part agreement. First, a treaty abrogated the 1871 Law of Guarantees and established the State of the Vatican City, a territory of approximately 109 acres over which the Holy Father reigned absolutely. Second, a financial convention, formally part of the treaty, compensated the Holy See for the lost Papal States. Finally, a concordat regulated Church-state relations within the Kingdom of Italy.

Predictably, many American liberals, Protestants, and Jews cried foul. Territorial sovereignty for a "spiritual" leader offended their theological and political sensibilities. The concordat imposed medieval canon law upon a modern nation, destroyed civil liberties, and oppressed religious minorities. American Catholics rose up to defend the pacts. They insisted that the pope required territorial sovereignty to assure his independence and that Italy was a Catholic nation best served within a confessional state. The Roman Question, even after its resolution, separated Catholics from other Americans.

Part 3 analyzes the realization of the ideology of the Roman Question; that is, it explores the implications of the Lateran Pacts for American society in the 1930s. Later chapters examine how the reconciliation facilitated cooperation between Catholics and the Italian embassy and consulates in the United States. This cooperation had important implications for inter-religious relations, the integration of Italian Americans into the Church, and the travail of American Catholic anti-Fascists. This chapter considers debates about the Lateran Pacts among Americans. Surprised by the intensity of animosity the 1928 Al Smith presidential campaign had stirred up, Catholics received news of the Lateran Pacts battered, shell-shocked, and perhaps resentful that their sacrifices in the Great War had not taught their fellow citizens that a Catholic could be trusted in the White House. Still, they celebrated the reconciliation and defended their Holy Father.

Even before the Italian Chamber of Deputies and Senate ratified the Lateran Pacts, Pope Pius XI and Mussolini clashed over their meaning. Their conflict peaked in the summer of 1931 and culminated in the anti-Fascist papal encyclical "Non abbiamo bisogno," which appeared to put the pacts themselves at risk. The resolution of the crisis, however, ushered in relatively harmonious relations between the Holy See and Fascist Italy and between the Italian Church and the Fascist state. While no American Catholics spoke out publicly against the pacts, ideological variations emerged in the way Catholic intellectuals scrambled to justify the terms of the treaty and concordat. Different Catholic paths to support the realization of the ideology of the Roman Question became permissible after February 1929.

The Lateran Pacts and the *Culti Ammessi* Debate

The day after the Lateran Pacts were signed, the *L'Osservatore Romano* proclaimed on its front page, "Italy has been given back to God and God to Italy." The Duce's brother Arnaldo rejoiced in *Il Popolo d'Italia*: "We Fascists, as Italian Catholics who were born and educated according to Christian principles, baptised in our churches, which are full of national memories, are transported with joy by the resolution of the 'Roman Question.'" Similar official expressions of jubilation erupted throughout the Catholic world.[1]

The financial convention comprised a cash payment of 750 million lire and Italian government stock worth 1 billion lire, approximately $88 million. The cash payment was invested in Italian government stock, as well as in French and Hungarian railways. In practice this meant that a vast financial investment tied the Vatican to Fascist Italy's economic stability, a situation that invited suspicion. Ambassador Henry Fletcher in Rome wrote the State Department that the Holy See now had an interest in keeping Fascism in power.[2]

The treaty was an international agreement reached bilaterally. It recognized the international status of the Vatican City and the territorial sovereignty of the pope. The Holy See agreed to remain neutral in war but reserved the right to exercise moral force in temporal matters. Italy and the Holy See recognized one another and established formal diplomatic relations. According to article 1, "Italy recognizes and re-affirms the principle contained in the first article of the Constitution of the Kingdom of Italy, March 4th 1848, by which the Holy Catholic Apostolic and Roman Religion is the only State religion." Oddly, this affirmation of Catholic privileges within the Italian state appeared in the international treaty, not the concordat. This arrangement suggests the pope's strong desire to secure and protect Catholic privileges in Italy. In a sense, it placed Catholic Italy at the center of world Catholicism. Would other states be expected to hold the Italian state accountable if it failed to properly privilege the Roman Catholic Church? In stark contrast to the constitution of 1848, neither the treaty nor the concordat guaranteed liberty or toleration of religious minorities.[3]

By the terms of the concordat, the Italian state acknowledged "the sacred character of the Eternal City" and pledged "to prevent in Rome anything that might clash with that character" (article 1). In addition to affirming the liberty of the Church, the concordat compelled the state to enforce aspects of canon law and clerical discipline. Priests could not work for a public body of the state without episcopal permission; "no apostate or censored clergy can be appointed or kept in any teaching position, office or employment in which they would be in direct contact with the public" (article 5). The state observed "all holidays of obligation prescribed by the Church" (article 11) and, "considering the Catholic tradition of the nation, recognizes the civil effects of the sacrament of marriage as laid down by Canon Law" (article 34). The state honored "the teaching of Christian doctrine in accordance with the Catholic tradition, as both the basis and the crown of public education." This Catholic education was "extended [from primary] to secondary schools," and its teachers required Church approval (article 36). Crucial to the pope, the state recognized "the organizations forming part of the Italian Catholic Action." They were required to "maintain their activity wholly apart from every political party and under the immediate control of the hierarchy." The concordat restated the papal prohibition on clergy "to be members of, or take part in, any political party" (article 43).[4]

Some articles in the concordat appeared to subordinate the Italian hierarchy and clergy to the state. "Leaving unaltered all fiscal privileges already granted by Italian laws to ecclesiastical institutions," article 29 declared the bishops were expected to "take an oath of fealty to the Head of State." The oath included a promise "not to take part in any agreement, nor to be present at any meeting, which may injure the Italian State and public order." Moreover, "desirous of promoting the welfare and the interests of the Italian State [the bishop] will seek to avoid any course that may injure it" (article 20). The state could veto the appointment of parish clergy and appeal for their removal whenever civil authorities detected resistance to the regime. As a contemporary Irish Catholic observer remarked, "it is unnecessary to stress the effect which this formidable power vested in the totalitarian State must have on the average ecclesiastic's outward attitude toward the regime."[5]

To implement the concordat, a committee of Vatican and state representatives devised new ecclesiastical legislation regarding marriage and the status of ecclesiastical corporations (religious congregations and missionary societies), in accordance with article 45. On 21 April, King Vittorio, speaking before the Chamber of Deputies, called for this new legislation, but he also asked for legislation to regulate the *culti ammessi*, non-Catholic religious bodies. Nothing in the Lateran Pacts suggested legal recognition or tolerance of religious minorities, and the

Vatican expected the regime to end the menace of Protestant proselytizing in Italy. Mussolini, however, sensitive to American and British public opinion and eager to assure Fascists that he had not capitulated to the Vatican, ignored Catholic protests. Ironically, thanks to Fascist legislation protecting religious minorities passed on 24 June 1929 against Vatican wishes, Mussolini made the difficult American Catholic task of defending the Lateran Pacts easier.[6] Catholic apologists could now assure their fellow citizens that no harm would come to Jews or Protestants. Remarkably, the Fascist ecclesiastical legislation on the heels of the pacts turned Mussolini into both the American Catholic hero who resolved the Roman Question and enhanced the privileges of the Catholic Church as well as the American Protestant and Jewish hero who protected religious minorities from Catholic repression and bigotry.

The new ecclesiastical legislation of 24 June reinstituted article 2 from the defunct Law of Guarantees: "There is complete freedom of discussion as far as religious matters are concerned." The legislation permitted freedom of worship and exempted non-Catholic students from Catholic religious education. The Holy See strenuously objected to these freedoms granted to the culti ammessi. Pius asserted, "It is clearly and honestly understood that the Catholic religion and it alone is, according to the Constitution as well as the [Lateran] agreements, the religion of the State, with all the logical and juridical consequence of this Constitutional principle, especially in regard to propaganda [evangelism]." According to historian John Pollard, "despite this defeat, the Church continued to pursue its crusade against the Protestants." In 1930 the Vatican created the Opera per la Preservazione delle Fede to battle heretics in Rome. In the provinces, Catholics exploited the regime's xenophobia. They asserted that foreign governments funded the culti ammessi. Although in some instances prefects or police shared and acted upon Catholic prejudices, no national policy of hostility toward Protestantism followed. The regime did, however, withdraw legal recognition of Pentecostalism in 1935.[7]

While the Vatican and the Fascist government debated ecclesiastical legislation, the Duce delivered his famous speech to the Chamber of Deputies on 13 May in support of ratification of the Lateran Pacts. While a favorable outcome was never in question, his harangue, nearly four hours long, communicated to both anticlerical Fascists and the Church that the regime had not capitulated to the Vatican.

Although he squirmed to justify the financial convention and the state's concessions regarding marriage and education, Mussolini painted the pacts with a Blackshirt brush. "Education must belong to us: these children must, of course, be educated in our religious faith, but we need to integrate this education, we need to give to youth the sense of virility, of power, of conquest." He ominously swore to monitor Catholic political tendencies. "The regime is vigilant, nothing escapes it. Let nobody believe that the smallest parochial bulletin of the small-est parish is unknown to Mussolini." He claimed that the "sacred character of the Eternal City" mentioned in the concordat referred to the Tomb of the Unknown Soldier, the monument to King Vittorio Emanuele II (the Vittoriano), and the Altar to Fascist Martyrs on the Capitol, not to the Vatican. He assured his Cham-ber deputies that the statues to Giordano Bruno in Campo de' Fiori and to Gari-baldi menacingly overlooking the Vatican from the Janiculum would remain un-touched. Moreover, there would be no respite on construction of the monument to Anita, Garibaldi's anticlerical wife. The Duce endorsed a summary of modern-ist theological scholarship condemned by the Church: "We should be proud of the fact that Italy is the only European nation which contains the headquarters of a world religion. This religion was born in Palestine but became Catholic in Rome. If it had stayed in Palestine, then in all probability it would have shared the fate of the many sects, like the Essenes or the Therapeutae, which vanished without a trace." Dismissing Cavour's call for a free church in a free state, Mus-solini countered: "Inside the State the Church is not only not sovereign, it is not even free. It is not sovereign because that would be a contradiction of the con-cept of the State, and it is not free because it is subject to the institutions and the laws of the State." On the Roman Question, Mussolini insisted, "We have not resurrected the Temporal Power of the Popes, we have buried it."[8]

On 24 May, during the ratification debate in the Senate, liberal philosopher Benedetto Croce courageously asserted that the concordat repudiated the heri-tage of the secular state forged in the Risorgimento. Not hostile to the idea of rec-onciliation, Croce nevertheless objected to "the way in which it is being effected." Reconciliation should, as Cavour had hoped, give the Church complete liberty, "the only gift that modern thought can make to the Church." Croce admired Mus-solini's "political skill, but over and above the men who think Paris well worth a Mass, there are others for whom hearing or not hearing a Mass is infinitely more important than Paris, because it is an affair of conscience."[9]

The Vatican responded to Mussolini's provocation. Enrico Rosa, the Jesuit edi-tor of *Civiltà Cattolica*, swiped that Napoleon's fate also awaited the Duce. After the police sequestered the paper and summoned Rosa for a trial, the pope offered *Civiltà Cattolica*'s staff a special blessing. On 6 June in *L'Osservatore Romano*, Pius con-demned the Duce's remarks on the origin of Christianity as "heretical and worse than heretical." He reasserted the terms of the concordat: The Church had au-thority over education and marriage, and it was the state's duty to curtail Protes-tant evangelism. Pius insisted that the treaty and the concordat were inexorably linked—violations of the concordat put the treaty and the prestige it brought to the regime at risk. When tensions over education and youth continued, Pius issued "Rappresentanti in terra" on 31 December. It stressed the rights of the family and Church over education and opposed the Opera Nazionale Balilla's pro-

motion of militarism among children. This conflict notwithstanding, the Holy
See never broke diplomatic relations with Fascist Italy. <u>Indeed, on 25 July 1929,
Pius XI became the first prisoner pope to leave the confines of the Vatican, and
on 5 December, he hosted a visit from King Vittorio and Queen Elena.</u>[10]

Anti-Fascist exiles, known as the *fuorusciti*, attacked the Lateran Pacts. Historian and radical democrat Gaetano Salvemini opined, "Mussolini's Concordat
with the Vatican is a purely individualistic and political manoeuvre. It is a piece of
presumptuous and high-handed arrogance, which sweeps away the whole Italian
inheritance of the democratic Risorgimento of Mazzini, Garibaldi and Cavour.
On her side the Papacy has definitely chosen reaction rather than progress. The
choice is certain to prove a boomerang." Salvemini denied that any single "religion of Italians" existed. His view echoed exiled *popolaro* Francesco Luigi Ferrari,
who argued that if the creation of an Italian national identity was still incomplete,
"even more arrested is the unitary [national] formation in the religious sphere."[11]

The Catholic chorus, however, drowned out the voices of democratic exiles.
Catholics cheered in 1930 when Mussolini struck the 20th of September from the
state calendar and replaced it with 11 February, the day the Lateran Pacts were
signed. The Rome correspondent for the National Catholic Welfare Conference
(NCWC), Msgr. Enrico Pucci, recalled for American Catholics how "the enemies
of the Church [had] found [the 20th of September] their favorite time to renew
their insults and attacks against her." He reminded Americans that "the highest
offense and insult on this holiday" was "when the Capital was in the hands of the
most extreme anti-clerical elements and the Mayor of Rome was Ernest Nathan,
a Jew and an ex-Grand Master of Freemasonry." Now Fascist Italy had discarded
that tradition and acknowledged that "on February 11, 1929, the moral unity of
the Italian Nation had been achieved."[12]

Good News from Rome

Even before the details of the Lateran Pacts became known, American Catholics
celebrated the "Good News from Rome!" which, according to *America*, "must have
made every Catholic heart throb a prayer of gratitude to God." The pope was "no
longer the Prisoner of the Vatican but its august Sovereign." Rejoicing "in the
day of deliverance," the Jesuit weekly proclaimed, "the Father of Our Lord Jesus
Christ . . . has made the Successor of Peter to prevail mightily!" The NCWC *Bulletin* claimed the pacts had "ended an almost unbearable situation of fifty-eight
years standing and ushered in a period of happiness that was welcomed by joyous
acclamations from all parts of the globe." Jesuit professor Moorhouse Millar at
Fordham University, after he attacked Protestant theological understandings of
the Church and the weakness of liberal thought in "Latin countries," trumpeted,
"At last the Roman question is settled and the Pope is again free!"[13]

The *Sign*, the monthly publication of the Passionist Fathers, could not contain itself. "Undoubtedly, the greatest event of this century so far as the Catholic Church is immediately concerned is the settling of the Roman Question." In the same breath, the *Sign* attacked "that parlor Bolshevik, the *Nation*," which had forecast "a lessening of the moral force of the Church for political aggrandizement." The Passionists also castigated the *New Republic* for its "show of shallow learning" in covering the pacts. Revealing Catholic cultural insecurities after the Al Smith presidential campaign, the *Sign* article celebrating the reconciliation ended in an attack on "other Americans" who see in the pacts "confirmation of the fact that the Papacy is still greedy for territory and political prestige. They are people who believe that the Pope has nefarious designs on the White House and that he shall hardly have left the Vatican before he is in Washington. It is almost impossible to undeceive them. They seem impervious to argument. Their obsession can be cast out only by prayer and fasting."[14]

The diocesan press celebrated enthusiastically. *Our Sunday Visitor* of Fort Wayne, Indiana, reported, "the Eternal City took on a new aspect and for the first time in 59 years papal and Italian flags are floating side by side." Chicago's *New World* editorialized how "Mussolini was too much of a historian not to know that Italy divorced from Catholicity was a thing unintelligible, both to the Italian and to the foreigner." When other Americans questioned the wisdom of the pacts, the *New World* staked out its position. "The solution of the biggest problems of European reconstruction [since World War I] has no more ardent promoter" than Mussolini. "The ultimate verdict of history will show Benito Mussolini not as a dictator but as a pacifier."[15]

The German Catholic *Nord-Amerika* of Philadelphia highlighted the symbolic details of reconciliation, dwelling upon the gold pen used to sign the pacts and Pius's gestures as he blessed the throng outside St. Peter's. It recalled the sad Passion Sunday in 1885 when "the cornerstone in Rome was laid for the monument to glorify the memory of King Vittorio Emanuele [II]," the transalpine usurper. The pacts had reversed the fortunes of the "kings of the new Italy, [and] of the Mazzinis, Garibaldis and Cavours" of anticlerical Liberal Italy. *Dziennik Chicagoski*, the Resurrectionist priests' daily for Polish Americans, reported the resolution of the Roman Question on its front page.[16]

Father James Gillis, the anti-Fascist editor of the *Catholic World*, bit his tongue in the midst of this journalistic exuberance. He only allowed himself to quip that the pope proved he was no politician because he had criticized Mussolini's Chamber of Deputies speech before the ratification of the pacts. The writers for the *Catholic World*, on the other hand, joined the jubilation. Bishop Thomas Shahan, rector of the Catholic University of America, painted a dark picture of Liberal Italy, when only the Church held "modern society . . . back from total apostasy." "The new lord of the world, Democracy," had brought on an epoch of "the iron man, cold, hard, and pitiless." Only "the Rock of Peter shone out in all these years as the divine refuge of mankind amid the intellectual anarchy of the times." The Duce, according to Shahan, saved Italy from "collapse in the direction of pure democracy or communism" and brought "reconciliation with the great moral power of the nation." Listing Mussolini's deeds in favor of the Church, Shahan invoked the happy restoration of "the temporal endowment conferred upon the Pope by Constantine sixteen centuries ago, when [he] . . . bowed his imperial head before the Cross of Jesus Christ." Charlemagne, "gazing to-day on the Vatican over the Alpine barriers," Dante, "that faithful son of the Roman Church," the "old historic [Roman noble] 'famiglie,' Colonna and Orsini, Massimo and Borghese and Barberini, . . . and Father Tiber himself," all had found peace in the realization of the ideology of the Roman Question.[17]

The U.S. hierarchy extolled the reconciliation in word and ritual. Ambassador Giacomo De Martino lauded Cardinal William Henry O'Connell's "magnificent speech" in praise of the pacts. In May 1929, Boston consul general Agostino Ferrante di Ruffano gleefully described enormous crowds greeting New England pilgrims upon their return from the Eternal City. O'Connell, who had led the pilgrims, lavished praise upon the beauty and order of Fascist Rome. "Alluding to the pact of reconciliation between Church and State," Ferrante reported, O'Connell said that only "the force of character and of moral courage of two truly great men," "'the Holy Father and the Duce,'" had made the resolution possible. "'God bless the great statesman who rules the destiny of Italy—Mussolini.'"[18]

Cardinal Patrick Hayes of New York issued a pastoral letter read in his churches. He proclaimed the "unfeigned and unprecedented joy" with which "the Catholic World rejoices over the happy and peaceful reconciliation that Divine Providence has vouchsafed as a blessing to the Holy Church in the recognition by the Italian Government of the God-given right to independence of the Holy See." The reconciliation "enhances the dignity of Italy and presents a noble example to all civilized powers."[19]

Bishop Joseph Schrembs of Cleveland reckoned "the accord between the Vatican and Italy" as "perhaps the most important and far-reaching event since the end of the great World War." He continued defensively, "The 'Pope's temporal power' . . . has been a perfect bugaboo to millions of people, and has constantly been used for the purpose of vilifying the Church." The concordat's provisions on canon law, Schrembs predicted, "will, no doubt, be much misunderstood and abused by anti-Catholic writers." Schrembs tendered a common American apologia for the pacts. Bishops and pastors will be freely appointed "just as we have it here in the United States." Religious marriages will be recognized, "just as is done in this country." Religious training in public schools, "even here in our own country . . . has been in increasing demand." With respect to ownership of property, the Church in Italy is now "just as the Church in the United States." Schrembs wrote Cleveland's Italian consul, "I rejoice with you in the happy settlement of the Roman Question." He predicted "the names of Pope Pius XI and Prime Minister Benito Mussolini will be linked in the history of Italy for all time."[20]

Catholic author and speaker James J. Walsh wrote a series on the Roman Question and the Lateran Pacts for the diocesan press in the spring of 1929. He also dedicated his 1930 edition of *What Civilization Owes to Italy* to "Benito Mussolini, Il Duce, Leader of Italy from politics to higher things." In a letter to Father Peter Guilday, professor of church history at the Catholic University, Walsh confided that the Duce "certainly worked some miracles in transforming the country, and he has done it exactly by suppressing politics and giving Italians a chance to think about other things." Those "other things" were the arts and sciences, not democracy.[21]

American Catholics appreciatively wrote the Duce to thank him personally for liberating their Holy Father. "You have done the grandest and greatest deed that was accomplished by any human being in history giving the Pope all what he lost and almighty God will reward you for it," wrote one woman. "This [concordat] is the greatest Victory the Catholics ever got and you are a hero for it." A Catholic man in Bethlehem, Pennsylvania, hoped the pacts were just the first step. "So my dear Benito you having accomplished so many great things, especially the settlement of the Roman question. I suggest that you do at least one thing more for the Church and add greatness to Italy by setting an example to the rest of the world by withdrawing your recognition of the tyrannical Mexican government." Catholic students in Detroit told the Duce "how very happy you made millions of Catholics in this country and in Canada when you completed the Roman settlement. Bishop [Michael] Gallagher reports upon his return to Detroit that Rome is better pleased even than we supposed. So much greater the glory for your honored self." The students complimented Mussolini on his "magazine articles and believe you to be a man of Destiny." They speculated that the Duce "may in the providence of God be fated to bring" about the restoration of "the outlines of Rome in Her glory. If by means of his Eminence Cardinal Gasparri the Catholic Countries of Italy, France, Spain and Belgium would rally it would no doubt sway England. If she refused to cooperate in the noble movement, means are at hand to force her as you know." With the Great Powers united, "Greece, Romania, Egypt, Turkey would no doubt co-operate and the lesser group of Jugo-Slavia or the Southern Slavs would likely be co-operative."[22]

John Griffin, "an old soldier of Irish birth," begged a "tremendous favor" from Premier Mussolini, "one of the noblest humans." The favor was for "Ireland — Erin, . . . a faithful daughter to Rome through all the storms that the 'Gates of hell' have ever sent against her." In 1932 Ireland would host a Eucharistic Congress. "The Pope has promised to visit Ireland; and he would have kept his word if you Italians had not made him Pope. . . . Do anything in your power to get him there—even if you have to imprison him for a week or two. It would not be the first time that a Roman imprisoned a pope, but I know yours would be bonds of love." Griffin closed his plea with a reminder: "Ireland is still suffering from many shackles and may God grant that the Brilliant, the Beautiful Italy, under your leadership may remove them."[23]

American Protestants and Jews looked upon the pacts through their own lenses. Most attacked the pope, the temporal power, and the confessional Catholic state. The Lateran Pacts gave rise to anxiety that their coreligionists might suffer persecution under the new Italian order of things. But once Fascist legislation on the heels of the pacts protected religious minorities from the full impact of canon law, these Protestants and Jews thanked Mussolini, the strongman who preserved religious toleration against Catholic discrimination. Outside of the cultural orbit of the dominant modernist, liberal, and conservative Protestants within "mainline" denominations who comprised a faltering American "establishment," noteworthy numbers of fundamentalists with premillennial leanings and biblical folk attuned to prophesy belief tendered their own understandings of the pope, Mussolini, and a revived Roman Empire.

Mainline Protestants: "More Prince" and "Less Priest"

At the request of the Italian Foreign Ministry, the Italy America Society analyzed the reaction of the American press to the Lateran Pacts. The report, a study of Associated Press and United Press news stories and 150 editorials, discerned an exaggerated fear of lost Italian religious liberties. In particular, "Southern and some mid-western papers were really violent." They spoke about a "reversal to the middle ages, persecution of non-Catholics, abolition of religious freedom, [and] compulsory church education." They dug up "the old 'know nothing' accusations of [Catholics] being dependent on a foreign sovereign, of not being loyal to American institutions."[24] Indeed, the report accurately identified mainline Protestant preoccupations.

The ecumenical voice of liberal and modernist Protestantism, the *Christian Century*, began its 21 February 1929 editorial sarcastically: "Hail to King Pius XI." The pacts were really about the Church's worldly ambition, not spiritual sovereignty. The new papal state was "no guarantee of unbroken communications or of an uninterrupted spiritual ministry" free from "judgment or interference by any earthly power. Absolute and worldwide sovereignty is the only thing that would meet that condition." The pacts merely "consolidate the gains in prestige and influence which the Catholic church has made since the war, and establish a new line of trenches from which [the Church] may proceed to the realization of its further ambitions." After all, "there has never been a time or a place in the modern world in which the Catholic church did not seek more prominence and dominance than it had."[25]

The Northern Baptist Convention's *Baptist* reckoned that the pope "has lost a certain moral prestige" and "seems to have committed himself to an unqualified endorsement of fascism and the Catholic primacy of Italy." *Baptist* editorials followed. As one headline put it, Pius was now "The More Prince the Less Priest." The question of diplomatic representation emerged once again. "Shall the United States be diplomatically represented at the pope's new—whatever it is?" the *Baptist* wondered. Absolutely not, for the pope's "double role of monarch and hierarch does not fit the modern world." Citing *Commonweal*'s contention that critics of the pacts did not understand the idea of spiritual sovereignty, the *Baptist* queried, "Are we to understand that for the last seventy years the Italian government has kept the pope in jail? . . . Has not the Catholic church been, in every part of the world, just as free as the Baptists have been to teach and to carry on all forms of church and missionary work?"[26]

The Methodist *Christian Advocate* also saw only a medieval mentality striving for worldly power. The "advantage of the recognition of the papal claim to be a member of the family of nations is invaluable to the ambitious Vatican group which looks forward to membership in the League of Nations and the World Court." The provisions concerning canon law were "the culmination of a thousand-year effort of the papal power to make its decrees supreme wherever they come in conflict with the civil authority." The *Advocate* quoted U.S. Congressional debates. "'This will bring up again the question of double allegiance. Can an individual bear allegiance to the heads of two different sovereign states at the same time. . . ? It occurs to me that the Pope, in pressing his claim to temporal authority, has done the Roman Catholic citizens of this country a disservice.'" The *Advocate* imagined "our naturalization laws," which require "an applicant . . . [to] 'renounce and abjure all allegiance and fidelity to any foreign prince, potentate, state or *sovereignty*,'" might now require rethinking.[27]

Zion's Herald, the voice of Boston Methodism, waxed biblical. "What did Jesus say to the Tempter, who offered Him temporal power? 'Get thee hence, Satan. . . .' Though the Roman Catholic Church will gain a new prestige for the time being as a result of [the pope's] decision, in the end it will pay the price in a sad loss of spiritual power." Professing belief "in the democratic principle," *Zion's Herald* took heart. "In this hour when the mouth of the Roman Church is once more watering in anticipation of the flesh-pots of Egypt, we thank God for Protestantism, facing all the pains and privations of the wilderness, but also all the glory of the promised land and the assurance of spiritual freedom."[28]

The Presbyterian *Christian Observer* saw in the pacts "an event of world-wide significance, which confirms statements often made by non-papists and as assiduously denied by loyal papists." The *Observer* reiterated ominous speculations of *Christian Century* editor Winfred Garrison, a University of Chicago divinity school professor and author of *Catholicism and the American Mind* (1928). Garrison had predicted reconciliation would lead to the Holy See's membership in the League of Nations. Moreover, "'it requires little imagination to picture the Pope being put forward as the permanent president of the Council' [of the League of Nations]." The *Observer* considered these musings "so large and so far-reaching that one is almost stunned by the possibilities involved in it." The Presbyterian editor wondered with disgust "whether the United States government will restore representation at the Vatican."[29]

Once American Protestants learned about Fascist legislation that protected religious minorities, they thanked Mussolini, the savior of vulnerable Protestants trembling at the yoke of papal serfdom. John Alfred Faulkner's hope, voiced in the *Princeton Theological Review*, that Mussolini would protect "the freedom of Protestant work on the [Italian] peninsula" from "the treaty of 1929" and its "dark possibilities to Protestant minorities" was realized. The *Christian Advocate* reproduced a letter from the governor of Rome affirming the freedom of the Methodist International College on Monte Mario. "The new laws, instead of suppressing Protestant liberties, provide new and stronger guarantees for the protection of individuals and societies in freedom of conscience and worship." The chairman of the Italian district of the Methodist Church explained how the Duce pushed through a policy of liberty. "One must admire the courage and force of Fascism, which has never hesitated to look its enemies in the face, and in this momentous crisis has opposed itself to the embattled forces of bigotry and fanaticism." The *Advocate* sniped, "this news . . . should tend to quiet the apprehensions raised by the extravagant and ill-founded assertions of the Catholic press as regards the new status of Papal authority."[30]

In November 1929, Rev. Alfredo Taglialatela of the Italian Methodist Conference argued in the *Christian Advocate* that Mussolini had preserved the heritage of the Risorgimento. "The Italian religious minorities have obtained fuller rights; consequently the young kingdom of Italy has taken a fresh and irrevocable step on the road opened by the Risorgimento." Like other mainline Protestants, he took this opportunity to attack Roman Catholicism. History teaches "that liberty and civil rights of 'the heretic' have been curtailed almost every time some reconciliation occurred between states and the Roman Catholic Church." But Fascism saved Italian Protestants from the concordat. Ignoring the illiberal premises of all ecclesiastical politics in Fascist Italy, Taglialatela asserted, "Mussolini made the desire of Cavour [for reconciliation] his own, in sincerity and truth."[31]

"Is the Antichrist at Hand?":
Mussolini and the Pope in Bible Prophecy

A sizable subculture of American Protestants turned directly to scripture in their assessment of the Duce. Many premillennialists, committed to a biblical philosophy of history based upon discrete dispensations or ages that marked God's relationship to his people, considered Mussolini either the Antichrist or his forerunner. Their reckoning of dispensations and scenarios for the end of times, derived from apocalyptic texts such as the Book of Daniel and Revelation, hinged upon the revival of the Roman Empire as a federation of ten nations under a Gentile nation led by the seventh emperor. The litany of newspaper articles quoting the Duce's intentions to restore ancient Rome triggered premillennial prophesy among those who argued that the Lateran Pacts heralded an alliance between the revived empire and the ecclesiastical beast or Babylon of Revelation.[32]

After the Lateran Pacts, the *Moody Bible Institute Monthly* of Chicago printed Rev. L. Sale-Harrison's "Mussolini and the Resurrection of the Roman Empire." More familiar than European foreign desks with the Book of Daniel, Sale-Harrison boldly asserted, "those who deny that the Bible prophesies of the resurrection of the Roman Empire cannot understand present day happenings in Italy." The Duce, after all, "has made treaties with Roumania, Albania, Greece, Hungary, Spain. . . . Now comes the startling news that Mussolini has signed a treaty with Turkey. This is an act of deepest significance in connection with the resurrection of the old Roman Empire." The settlement "between the Vatican and the Italian government . . . is a remarkable advance towards the furtherance of Mussolini's ambition to become the Roman leader. Though he cannot be Anti-christ, he is certainly preparing for the manifestation of the Roman prince."[33]

The Australian Sale-Harrison had no monopoly on Duce prophecy. Oswald Smith captivated thousands in Toronto's Alliance Tabernacle with his 1927 address, *Is the Antichrist at Hand? What of Mussolini.* Smith prophesied, "the next great event in the world's history is to be the revival of the Roman Empire; the Bible is unmistakably clear about this." He reckoned "the Great Tribulation, the revival of the Roman Empire, the reign of the Antichrist and the Battle of Armageddon, must take place before the year 1933." At the head of the ten nations federated into the revived empire will be "a great Gentile nation," whose emperor might be Mussolini. "This Roman Emperor will be assassinated [and] . . . before his body is cold, the spirit of the Antichrist will enter into him and he will suddenly be resurrected, but in his resurrected life he will combine both Emperor and Antichrist." Smith then, it seems, predicted the Lateran Pacts. "After becoming established over the ten nations forming the revived Roman Empire, [the Antichrist] will make an alliance with the Roman Catholic Church."[34]

Gerald Winrod, anti-Semite, Kansas senatorial candidate, rabble-rouser, and

Nazi sympathizer, penned his *Mussolini's Place in Prophecy* in 1933. Winrod explained how two world leaders from northern and southern Europe had emerged at the end of World War I: Lenin and Mussolini. "This is an exact prophetic development" from "the prophecies of Ezekiel and Daniel" who described two rulers, the Kings of the North and of the South. From these leaders "two leagues of nations will be formed" under the northern monarch Gog and the "Southern Dictator, known to students of Bible prophecy as the *Antichrist*," Mussolini. The northern and southern armies will fight in Palestine where the Southern Dictator, the Antichrist, will reign until Christ defeats him in the battle of Armageddon. "Mussolini," Winrod wrote, "has frequently given expression to the fact that his government desires to take over the mandate of Palestine" from England. Winrod cited British military leaders, Nietzsche, anti-Fascist Francesco Nitti, journalist Marcus Duffield, and the Duce's biographer and mistress, Margherita Sarfatti, to establish the imminence of war in Palestine and to garner biographical details from Mussolini's life that likened him to the Antichrist.[35]

Paul H. Holsinger brought his exegetical talents to bear upon the fate of Ethiopia as Mussolini stood poised for his invasion in 1935. Holsinger's *Ethiopia and Mussolini in Light of Prophecy* speculated how "the pressure that Mussolini may soon put upon this nation may be the means of bringing them back to the Lord." Although it possessed a rich Christian history, "Ethiopia means darkness." Its name, he explained, is derived from the descendants of Ham who sinned against Noah. Holsinger argued, "the negro races," descendants of Ham, "have a right to exist and to enjoy life, liberty and the pursuit of happiness, but they cannot be in a position of DOMINANCE over the white races." Holsinger believed the coming conquest of Ethiopia fulfilled the Lord's judgment against Ethiopia described in Zephaniah 2:11–12: "'Ye Ethiopians also, ye shall be slain by my sword.'" This "special judgement" for Ethiopia "during the end time" suggested that "Mussolini could be the instrument to bring Ethiopia back to God." Indeed, Holsinger speculated that "Mussolini could well be the 'John the Baptist' preparing the way for the coming Super Man, the Anti-Christ."[36]

Political developments after Mussolini's Ethiopian conquest in 1936, such as the Berlin-Rome Axis, complicated matters considerably for the likes of Holsinger. Germany, never in the Roman Empire, was not supposed to enter an alliance with the new Roman emperor. Louis S. Bauman of the Los Angeles Bible Institute, however, kept the faith. His *Light from Bible Prophecy: As Related to the Present Crisis* (1940) quotes Mussolini's speeches and sets them beside apocalyptic biblical texts to make his argument that "the Rome-Berlin Axis is foredoomed." Bauman insisted "THE RESURRECTION OF THE EMPIRE" was at hand. Mussolini was shrewdly waiting for the Soviet Union and Germany to extinguish one another. Then he, the seventh emperor, the Antichrist, would reign before Christ reappeared in glory.[37]

A variety of American evangelicals wrote the Duce. For instance, one "Mother in America" threw down the biblical gauntlet in 1930. "I think it is about time you sit down and reasoned with God. Don't you think you have caused enough suffering in the world among your people? Do you know you are called the 'Anti Christ'? Isn't this an awful thing? How dare you and this Pope, and you Anti Christians do the awful things you do to your people?" Indignant at the journalistic exposés of Fascist activities in the United States, the voice of evangelical motherhood glared: "How dare you send Agents here in our Wonderful God loving God fearing and trusting country?" She nudged the Duce. "Why don't you talk with the Pope and try to reason together and read Gods holy book and forget this Romanist Catholic [stuff?]."[38]

Not all evangelicals and premillennialists saw in Mussolini the Antichrist or his forerunner. An Adventist in Kewanie, Illinois, after he expounded upon the biblical basis for a Saturday Sabbath, urged Mussolini to "use [his] influence to bring this about." William Reitmann, a "Missionary in the Lord's Vineyard," directed his plans for world peace and disarmament to the Duce. "You have known courage and done great good, by the mercy of the Lord, to crush the Mafia (black hand devilish gang), now show that you are not afraid to face, as a 'whole man', the superstitions of the ages, and if the Vatican opposes the harmonious truth of the holy interior sense of Sacred Scriptures . . . then stand up with your faithful ones and de-liberate Italy and the world!"[39]

"In Italy the Jew Is Free": American Jews and Fascist Italy

American Jewish interest in Fascist Italy revolved around the fate of Italian Jewry and Mussolini's role in the politics of Zionism. Mussolini protected Italian Jews from the Church, gave greater authority to their leaders over the structure of their communities, and checked his own anti-Semitism before the mid-1930s. But he never came to terms with the rise of Jewish consciousness evinced in the Zionist movement.

After the Risorgimento, Jewish communities and corporate fraternities had autonomous legal relationships to Liberal Italy. Although a consortium of communities was established in 1914, the communities were not obliged to join, and funding within them remained voluntary. Rabbinical and lay leadership lacked authority, and the precise function of community organizations was ambiguous. In 1927 the consortium submitted reform proposals to the government. Justice Minister Alfredo Rocco named a commission to prepare legislation, which passed in 1930 and 1931 and earned praise from Italian Jews. The new legislation integrated the communities and gave their leaders greater authority and the ability to tax. Although exiled anti-Fascists condemned the betrayal of liberal principles, the legislation protected Jews in Fascist Italy from the harsher implications of the concordat. Municipal schools made Jewish religious education available, with textbooks modified to eliminate inappropriate references to Catholicism. Plans to demolish the dome of the synagogue in Rome were abandoned. School atten- . dance, however, remained mandatory on Saturday, the Sabbath.[40]

It was not until 1938 that the Fascist regime passed anti-Semitic legislation. Five Jews belonged to the original Fasci di Combattimento, the first Blackshirt bands, that met in Milan on 23 March 1919. In 1923, when the rabbi of Rome met Mussolini to discuss European anti-Semitism, the premier assured his guest that Fascism had no anti-Semitic policy. In fact, the government exempted foreign students, mostly Jews, from school taxes and granted military leave for Jewish holidays. In April 1926, Foreign Ministry Undersecretary Dino Grandi assured the Jewish Telegraph Agency (JTA) that there was no Jewish question in Italy. The following year, Mussolini met with David Prato and lauded his appointment as chief rabbi of Alexandria, Egypt, as a sign of Italian prestige. In a highly publicized meeting on 19 October 1927, the Duce received President Nahum Sokolov of the World Zionist executive committee, who applauded the absence of Fascist anti-Semitism. The Duce's classic essay on Fascist doctrine published in June 1932 defined the Italian nation in nonracial terms. During his famous 1932 interviews with Emil Ludwig, the Duce condemned racism as "a stupid mistake." "Nothing will ever make me believe that biologically pure races can be shown to exist today." He reiterated, "anti-Semitism doesn't exist in Italy. . . . Italian Jews always behaved as good citizens, and as soldiers they fought bravely. They occupy leading positions in the universities, in the army, in the banks. Quite a few of them are generals."[41]

Although Mussolini did not publicly embrace racial anti-Semitism until 1938, he criticized Zionism as an unacceptable form of separatism and internationalism that favored British imperialism. Two months after he formed his first government, Mussolini met with an international Zionist delegation and explained Italian Jewish participation would provoke a conflict of interests. On 3 January 1923, Mussolini discussed Palestine with Chaim Weizmann, president of the World Zionist Organization, who later claimed that Mussolini's anti-Zionism resulted from anti-British sentiment rather than anti-Semitism. Nevertheless, when he grew annoyed by publicity for a Zionist congress in Milan, Mussolini published a cutting article, "Religion or Nation?" in Il Popolo di Roma in November 1928. "Jews of Italy were Italians who believed in Moses and expected the Messiah," but now "Christian Italians will perhaps be a bit surprised and disturbed to find that there exists in Italy another people, which [not only] declares itself completely foreign to our religious faith but also to our nation, our people, our history, our ideals. . . . We then ask the Italian Jews: are you a religion or are you a nation?" In the uproar that ensued, anti-Zionist Jews declared their patriotism while Zionists insisted their destiny was linked to Italy. But Mussolini repudiated the Zionists. If an autonomous Jewish state were created, the Duce insisted, the problem of dual loyalties would be inevitable.[42]

Although Italian Jews were divided, the American Jewish press generally praised Mussolini. In 1927, Chicago's Jewish weekly, the *Sentinel*, celebrated the "powerful movement towards the revival of Jewishness . . . in Italy." The *Sentinel* attributed the revival to "the Fascist movement," whose "accentuation of nationalism in Italian life has had the inevitable effect of rousing the Jewish youth of Italy to the realization of their own Jewishness." The *Sentinel* reported the vast difference between the first congress of Jewish youth held after the Great War and the 1924 congress, which marked "a bold proclamation of Jewish distinctiveness" and "created the basis of Jewish national and cultural revival in Italy."[43]

An American Jewish monthly, the *Reflex*, voiced similar sentiments when it claimed in 1927 that Italian Jews under Fascism were as well off as ever. It cited Mussolini's 1923 conversation with Rabbi Angelo Sacerdoti of Rome at which the Duce announced, "'The Italian government is not anti-Semitic, nor does it practice anti-Semitism. . . . I refused to receive Hitler (the Bavarian Jew-baiter) and the Bavarian papers printed that I had sold myself to the Jews. When they will know what I am telling you now, they will say that I have become a Jew altogether.'" One observer writing in the *Sentinel* commented, "I do not like Dictators. . . . However, I am glad to read an encouraging article on the Jewish situation in Italy."[44]

When the Lateran Pacts provoked Jewish anxiety, the Duce put their fears to rest. The JTA nervously pressed the apostolic delegate to explain how the concordat would affect Italian Jewry. Alfonso Pacifici also wondered in *Israel*, an Italian publication, about the concordat. But Mussolini calmed Italian and American Jews in his 13 May speech to the Chamber of Deputies: "It is ridiculous to think, as it has been said, that it will be necessary to close the synagogues. The Jews have been in Rome since the times of the kings; perhaps they provided the clothes after the rape of the Sabines. They were fifty thousand at the time of Augustus and they asked to weep over the dead body of Julius Caesar. They shall not be disturbed." The speech brought *B'nai B'rith Magazine* comfort. Mussolini "has declared for freedom of conscience in religion and the equal rights of all religious groups in Italy." Happy with "the religious tolerance of a dictator," *B'nai B'rith* gleefully paraphrased Mussolini, ignoring the anti-liberal premises of Fascist legislation: "'In Italy the Jew is free. He is an equal citizen. He is an Italian. The Jewish community in Italy is 2,000 years old. . . . The Jew wept on Caesar's grave and has throughout a period of more than 20 centuries participated in the history of the country during all of its trials and tribulations.'"[45]

In 1933 a survey of forty-three editors of Jewish publications voted the Duce one of twelve Christians who "most vigorously supported Jewish political and civil rights and who have been the most outstanding in their opposition to anti-Semitism." Mussolini had taken "pains to demonstrate that Italian Fascism does not tolerate racial or religious persecution." The Duce, B'nai B'rith assured readers in its 1934 overview of European dictators, tolerated no anti-Semitism. In June 1936, when JTA director Jacob Landau planned a family trip to Rome, Italian ambassador Augusto Rosso described his "cordial personal relations" with influential Jews in New York like Landau. "On more than one occasion Landau has disseminated news demonstrating the equity and the generosity of the Italian Government in its treatment of Jews." In fact, "for this impartial attitude toward us Mr. Landau has attracted the criticisms of some of his anti-Fascist co-religionists who have accused him of philo-Fascism."[46]

Although American Jews praised religious liberties under Fascism, they feared the Lateran Pacts might impede the development of a Jewish homeland in Palestine. The *Sentinel* insisted, "with the Vatican as a sovereign state, working hand in hand with the Fascist government, Italy's foreign policy in the Near East will be strongly influenced by the traditional policies of the Vatican." The mandate of the League of Nations had entrusted to Great Britain the development of a Jewish home in Palestine. Zionists feared the Holy See, now a sovereign state, would seek membership in the league to work against a Jewish homeland. The Lateran Pacts might mean that "the Zionist movement in Italy may be declared illegal, and those engaged in work in its behalf may be subjected to arrest and prosecution."[47]

In October 1932, the pro-Zionist *Israel* participated in celebrations of the tenth anniversary of the March on Rome. It bragged, "after ten years of the Fascist regime, the spiritual life of the Jews in Italy is . . . much more intense than before." Moreover, *Israel* highlighted the "radical difference between true and authentic Fascism—Italian Fascism, that is—and the pseudo-Fascist movements in other countries which . . . are often using the most reactionary phobias, and the especially blind, unbridled hatred of the Jews, as a means of diverting the masses from their real problems." Indeed, historian Meir Michaelis has concluded, "after a decade of Fascist rule, Italy was still a model of tolerance as far as treatment of her Jewish minority was concerned."[48] American Jews, like mainline Protestants, at least until the late 1930s applauded the Duce for his tolerance of religious minorities, whose leaders feared the Vatican and the Church more than the state in Fascist Italy.

Intellectuals Debate the Lateran Pacts

Not surprisingly, American Catholics welcomed the Lateran Pacts. The three most important Catholic intellectuals to rush to support the realization of the ideology of the Roman Question were Columbia University historian Carlton J. H. Hayes, Father John Ryan at the Catholic University, and Wilfred Parsons, the Jesuit editor of *America*. However, their arguments, which in all three instances placed their commitment to ideology above their allegiance to natural law theology, were not identical. Hayes, who must have raised the eyebrows of his Columbia colleagues, contended the Lateran Pacts were "liberal" and realized Cavour's dream of a free Church in a free state. He insisted that the pacts created an Italian church-state relationship similar to that in the United States. In contrast, Parsons recognized the limitations of such an insupportable argument. He claimed that Italy, a Catholic nation with an inauthentic liberal tradition, should not be compared to religiously pluralist America and its genuine liberalism. Ryan stood between these two apologists. Like Hayes, Ryan suggested the pacts approximated the American model, but like Parsons, Ryan spoke about "Italians" not as individuals with rights but as a Catholic collective or nation. All three met stern opposition from liberals and Protestants in public debates that divided Catholics from their American neighbors.

A Catholic convert and original contributing editor to *Commonweal*, Hayes published two articles on the Lateran Pacts before the Fascist regime passed laws to protect the *culti ammessi*. Hayes refrained from the usual Catholic bashing of Liberal Italy and acknowledged the weaknesses of the pope-king. "At times [the papacy] was so absorbed in Italian politics as to neglect or deal unwisely with broader concerns. At other times it sought success in distant places so zealously as to imperil or even to sacrifice local Italian interests." Hinting at flaws in the policy of Pius IX, Hayes dispensed exonerations. "The objective historian cannot blame Italy for undergoing, like other countries, a nationalist transformation" that sought unification. "Nor can the dispassionate historian blame the Papacy for feeling that it had been despoiled by force." Moreover, no one could "wonder at the attitude of Catholics outside of Italy after 1870. They sympathized with the Pope." Although "the law [of Guarantees of 1871] was surprisingly liberal," Pius IX could not accept his status as a "subject to the Italian Parliament," so he "jailed himself in the Vatican. A stubborn form of internationalism had encountered an equally stubborn form of nationalism."[49]

This manicured detachment from the violence of the contest between Liberal Italy and the Vatican served Hayes well when he tried to harmonize the concordat with American church-state relations. Preoccupied on the international front, the papacy neglected Liberal Italy, where "Cavour's formula of 'a free church within a free state'" degenerated into "a despised and enslaved church within an anticlerical middle-class state." Mussolini arrived and "put the house in order," restoring Cavour's Risorgimento dream. Hayes attacked the press for asserting "the startling and sensational information that Italy was about to substitute for its own civil law the entire canon law of the Church! . . . The veriest nonsense."[50]

Hayes's point was that "the Catholic Church in Italy has secured by the concordat only such rights as any church in the United States enjoys under ordinary American law. Only in its interesting prescriptions about religious education does the concordat go farther [in the rights it grants the Church] than our American experience. In its requirements about the appointment of bishops [who must take an oath to the king] the concordat actually falls short of our American practice of religious liberty." Trivializing "its interesting prescriptions about religious education" and ignoring the pacts' implications for religious minorities and Catholic defection from Catholicism, Hayes concluded, "the concordat regulates the relations between Church and state on the basis of a free church within a free state." Pius XI and Mussolini, unbeknownst to them and to their common horror, had arrived at Cavour's liberal ideological formula! In light of his startling conclusion that "liberal principles . . . underlie the" concordat, Hayes believed that "Italy has shown that nationalism can make terms with internationalism, and thereby has given a hopeful and helpful omen for the future peace of the world."[51]

Ryan must have experienced déjà vu during his debate with Count Carlo Sforza and Charles C. Marshall on 16 March 1929 at the Foreign Policy Association luncheon in New York. Their discussion took place before the passage of Fascist legislation protecting religious minorities from the full weight of the concordat. It continued the Marshall-Ryan polemic that had broken out during the Al Smith presidential campaign. Marshall, a New York lawyer, had published an open letter questioning the Catholic candidate's loyalty in the *Atlantic Monthly* in April 1927. The press took up the issue and brought to the surface animosities that shook many Catholics, exacerbating their insecurities as a minority. Both Smith and Ryan responded to Marshall, who elaborated upon his views in a book published less than a year before the 1929 luncheon.[52]

Sforza spoke first, offering a Catholic liberal's critique of the Lateran Pacts. A former Italian foreign minister and anti-Fascist senator in the Aventine Succession, Sforza had fled Fascist Italy in 1927 for Brussels. In 1940 he would take refuge in the United States, and after World War II, he would serve again as Italy's foreign minister for the Christian Democratic Party. A favorite among postwar U.S. statesmen, Sforza would advocate Italian participation in the Marshall Plan and sign the North Atlantic Treaty to mark Italy's entrance into NATO in April 1949. A Catholic liberal with moderate conservative politics, Sforza could not simply be dismissed as an anticlerical or dangerous radical in the way American Catholics had smeared Italian Catholic moderates for two generations before the Lateran Pacts.[53]

Sforza staked out a liberal neoguelf position that deviated from Catholic ideology. He emphasized how Dante and Manzoni, both Catholics, had supported the end of the temporal power in order to purify the Church. Sforza doubted "the Church has gained at all" as a result of the Lateran Pacts. Instead, the Church has "awakened new suspicions in the world" and demonstrated that it will "ask full liberty of you, democracies, in the name of your principles, but" once it gets "stronger, deny you all liberty in the name of [its] principles." The Church in Italy before the unification had been "the slave and servant of regimes of violence." Only "liberal Italy, the Italy of Cavour, . . . made it possible for the Holy See to gain a prestige in the world." Loyal to the settlement embodied in the Law of Guarantees, Sforza believed the Roman Question had been solved in 1871. "What has happened in the past days is not the solution of a problem, which was already solved, but the creation of a new and, morally, much more serious problem."[54]

Marshall's observations raised difficult questions. "The international world has long desired to know just what might be expected in a State developed in accordance with the demands of the Pope, supported by a Roman Catholic majority. In this treaty such a State is disclosed. The Pope has spoken, and religious liberty is destroyed in Italy." The combative liberal wondered if the Italian people and American Catholics approved of the pacts. "If so, how do you account for the disappearance from their minds of the noble sentiments expressed by [Al Smith] when he said: 'I believe in equality of all churches, all sects, and all beliefs before the law as a matter of right and not as a matter of favor.' Did the American statesman and his applauding co-religionists mean this only for the United States with a Roman Catholic minority, and not mean it for Italy with a Roman Catholic majority? Would they preserve religious liberty in America and stab it to death in Italy?"[55]

Ryan's awkward defense of the pacts had two parts. First, he insisted the new Italian situation approximated the American situation. "As regards marriage there is one provision of the concordat which merely establishes what we have in the United States; that is, the provision which makes legally valid [the] marriages performed by Catholic priests." Then he acknowledged, "the concordat goes further" than the American arrangement when it compelled the state to recognize "marriage as a sacrament." To justify this difference, Ryan insisted Italy was a Catholic nation whose members did not require their state to protect individual rights of conscience when it came to religion. "Well, after all, Italy is a Catholic country. . . . I don't see anything remarkable in the proposition that the State should recognize marriage to be what the vast majority of the people believe it to be." Ryan thus absorbed the Italian individual into a homogeneous nation of perfectly orthodox Catholics.[56]

Ryan employed the same defense for the articles on education. On the one hand, the concordat "restores to Italy what we Catholics in the United States enjoy," the opportunity for religious education. But because the concordat stipulated "that the Catholic religion must be taught in the public schools," Ryan quipped, "Yes! Again I call your attention to the fact that the vast majority of people in Italy are Catholics, and if they want religious teaching in the schools, why shouldn't they have it?" Regarding the "privileges of the clergy," once again Ryan first stressed similarities to the United States, where clergy were also exempt from military service. But to explain their state salaries under the Italian concordat, the ethicist (incorrectly) insisted that their stipend "is paid them by the government out of [the Church's] property which the government seized and . . . [is] considerably less . . . than a fair interest on the total amount of confiscated property." Ryan closed with an odd assertion for a defender of universal norms of justice: "There is just as much religious liberty in Italy for those who aren't Catholics as there is in England for Catholics."[57]

The luncheon's question-and-answer session obliged Ryan to discuss the status of non-Catholics in Italy. Because the concordat said nothing about them, Ryan was at a loss. Ironically, he had faith that the Fascist government would protect religious minorities from Catholic intolerance. His colleague at the Catholic University, Filippo Bernardini, the nephew of Cardinal Gasparri, had assured Ryan that the religious liberties of minorities would be guaranteed, but Ryan never made clear that such guarantees would come from the regime, not the Church. One questioner probed Ryan about his 1922 book, *The State and the Church*, in which he declared that if Catholics comprised a civic majority they had a duty to establish the Catholic Church as the state religion. Frustrated, he explained, "the Catholic Church in this country has a great many troubles of its own which more nearly occupy its attention than any project" to establish the Church "in the dim, remote and exceedingly hypothetical future." But he reaffirmed that the Church in America "most certainly" accepted "the Papal teaching on the general subject of union of Church and State."[58]

Sforza also fielded questions. He distinguished the "great formula of Cavour, 'Free Church in a Free State,' which . . . is the very embodiment of your [American] constitution," from the concordat that "contradicts completely the position taken by Cavour and followed by the Italian liberals." Sforza added, "Cavour was far from being an anti-Catholic." Sforza advocated the liberal position, heralded by Cavour, that had been pummeled into silence within Catholic discourse since 1848. "I am deeply convinced that the greatest Catholic spirits in the world— those . . . like Montalambert in France, . . . think that Cavour will some day be considered as one of the men who has most beneficently worked not only for human freedom, but also for the greatness of religion." Sforza finally directed a remark at Ryan's Catholic collectivist formula. "In Italy there are many who are born Catholic but who are not church-goers. . . . The situation of millions of individuals who theoretically are Catholics but practically are not, is certainly made extremely difficult under the new laws."[59]

Wilfred Parsons, in *The Pope and Italy* (1929), offered the most detailed American defense of the Lateran Pacts. Parsons identified "a twofold impulse" in the Risorgimento. "There was a Masonic, so-called democratic, agitation, which was republican in aim and had the Carbonari [secret societies] and Garibaldi as its instruments; and there were the dynastic ambitions of the House of Savoy." American liberal supporters of the Risorgimento had been duped. Unlike Pius IX, who had discerned Masonic menace and royal greed behind liberal rhetoric, American liberals were "drawn to the insurgents, who called things by the same names which we [Americans] use" but whose "ideas were, and have always been, poles apart" from Americans. After the conquest of Rome in 1870, "sectarian prejudice and hatred kept Italy from making peace with the Pope. Freemasonry was in the saddle, and to Freemasonry, Catholicism was l'*infâme*, to be crushed out of existence." Parsons served up the traditional Catholic conspiracy theory adopted by many Fascists. "Italian Masonry practically did the bidding even in internal affairs of a foreign ministry, that of France, and it was never the policy of France to allow Italy to grow strong." But the Duce liberated Italy. "Mussolini and his Fascists" broke "the grip of a Masonic clique." The Great War had made Italy "truly conscious of [its] unity," and "Fascism was foreordained to rule Italy from then on."[60]

After his Catholic rendering of modern Italian history, Parsons took up the Lateran Pacts. In contrast to Ryan, the Jesuit insisted that Italy should not be understood "in terms of conditions in the United States." Americans were "accustomed to a variety of religions. . . . All sorts and conditions of people and religions exist here side by side. We are used to that, and let them live." Italy, however, whose "people are ninety-nine per cent Catholic," was "totally different. . . . Their religious and civic relations are so inextricably commingled, and have been so for centuries, that for the State and the Church to be at loggerheads is like war in the family." The status of religion in Liberal Italy had been "an anomaly" that was "removed by the Treaty and the Concordat. . . . Italy has resumed a normal existence." The Lateran Pacts signaled "the dawn of a new day for Italy."[61]

Against these Catholic defenders, pugnacious journalist John Hearley led the liberal charge against the Lateran Pacts in his *Pope or Mussolini* (1929). Blending overheated rhetoric with insightful polemic, Hearley tendered his thesis: "to show that the recent moves of Pope and Duce on the strange checker-board of religion and politics are out of line with the twentieth century and its revelations, scientific, educational and spiritual." Hearley quoted an anonymous modernist priest, whose articles had already generated heat when he introduced them in the *Atlantic Monthly* in 1928. "For the citizens of this country the Concordat will doubtless have a twofold effect: 1—The bigots it has filled with joy and fanatical madness; 2—The thoughtful are amazed at this brazen piece of medievalism that has been put forth in these modern times."[62]

Hearley rushed to educate the public because he believed others had failed to do so. "Our secular press approached the settlement of the Roman question with a conspicuous show of nervousness. . . . The traditional terror of offending Catholic sensitiveness hung like a death's head in the editor's sanctum." No such terror inhibited Hearley. He attacked the "naive and enthusiastic frankness in Father Parson's outburst" in *America*, which reported that canon law would be imposed on Italy. Hearley cut: "Canon Law has been the antechamber of the medieval inquisition, the deathknell of scientific research and the mockery of American democracy." He lashed out at New York's *Catholic News*, whose "impulsive and extravagant praise" included a call for an American diplomatic representative to the new papal state. "Did the November voters" who elected Herbert Hoover over Al Smith "register the hope that it never would have such representation? Should we be represented there, moreover, the Papacy would return a papal nuncio to Washington, who at the worst might be the victim or the master of the Italian ambassador, and at the least his collaborator."[63]

Hearley left no liberal anxiety latent. On religious minorities: "Neither Italian Protestantism nor Italian Judaism is given legal status in either [treaty or concordat]. . . . Logically, should not all non-Catholics be excluded from the realm?" On the pacts' international implications: "Does this mean that the Papacy will follow Fascism in its Balkan and Hungarian adventures and anti-French and anti-Jugo-Slav intrigues?" Hearley fulminated: "Will the modern world see a species of Catholic League of Nations?"[64]

Hearley took this occasion to belittle American Catholic intellectual life. In contrast to Europe, where "the pro and con of religious polemic are common, . . . American Catholics for the most part are religious sentimentalists, going about with chips on their shoulders. . . . They can tolerate only one side of a question and that is their own side. Any Protestant debater is a bigot. At the same time, these Catholics reserve the right to say and do whatever they please about Protestants and Protestantism." Hearley favored "the brilliant English Catholic" polemicist, Hillaire Belloc, who "has the public courage of his orthodox faith and his religious convictions. No forensic pussy-footing for him."[65] Needless to say, the Lateran Pacts provided Hearley and others another opportunity for an unsparing assault that sharpened boundaries between Catholics and other Americans.

If defensiveness marked the comments of Hayes, Ryan, and Parsons, all of whom tangled with the nasty likes of Marshall and Hearley, a serene sacramental sensibility infused Gilbert Keith Chesterton's musings in *The Resurrection of Rome* (1930). The larger-than-life English master of paradox, a towering figure in the transatlantic Catholic Revival from 1920 to 1950, touched English-speaking Catholics through fiction and journalism, even before his conversion to the Church in 1922 and after his death in 1936. Residing in Rome for three months in 1929, when he met Pius and Mussolini, Chesterton published his impressions of the Eternal City the following year.

Like other heroes of the Catholic Revival, Chesterton maligned the materialism, naturalism, and sectarian liberalism that had undermined true religion in the modern world and left pestilent communism and pseudoreligious Nazism to fill the spiritual void. Jesuit promoters of the Catholic Revival, such as Francis X. Talbot and Daniel A. Lord, supported Fascism as a bulwark against communism, liberalism, and the corroding acids of capitalism. John La Farge, SJ, who served with Talbot on *America's* editorial board, was conventional among Jesuits. He favored dictatorships in Portugal and Italy, supported Fascist Italy's "Catholic" conquest of Ethiopia in 1936, and "praised Mussolini's respect for religion and his 'humane labor laws.'" If American Jesuits demonstrated theoretical fuzziness regarding the many European fascisms and corporatisms of the 1930s, no confusion appeared in their laudatory coverage of Fascist Italy. Indeed, Revival authors like Chesterton distinguished sharply between "Catholic" Fascism and atheistic Nazism, and the Lateran Pacts appealed to their neoguelf sense of history.[66]

Transfixed by the view atop the Spanish Steps overlooking the valley that led his eye to St. Peter's dome, Chesterton discovered his theme. "Rome looked to me like the City of the Seven Valleys," not of the seven hills. "Truth is not at the top of a tower but really at the bottom of a well." From the "Rome of the Fountains . . . secret things thrust upwards from below." This "sense of something continually rising from below" did not make Rome a lifeless museum of antiquities. Typical Chesterton: "It is not a place where life is dull or dead or deadly; it is a place where the dead are alive. . . . I do not mean that it is a place where the mind can dreamily return to the past. I mean it is a place where the past can actually return to the present." Rome "has a sort of access to its own origins, and a power upon its own vanished youth, which is what is really meant by calling it The Eternal City." Hence, *The Resurrection of Rome* described the city's "unique capacity for renewal or the return of forgotten things."[67]

The last two sections of *The Resurrection of Rome* took up contemporary Rome. "The Return of the Romans" he devoted to Fascism "and especially that aspect of Fascism that is really symbolized by the Fasces. I mean . . . the old Roman ideas of dignity and authority and the re-erection of the far-off imperial ensigns and salutes." The book's finale, "The Holy Island," examined "the reappearance in Europe of a Papal State, of the Pope as a secular prince in the council of kings; a typical example of something which forty years ago men would have been certain could return no more."[68]

Fascism, according to Chesterton, was a resurrection of ancient Romans brought forth to correct "modern madness and treason and anarchy." Northern European racial conceits, "the legend of the dirty and dingy Dago," were "inhuman unhistorical nonsense. For fully a thousand years . . . all the nations of the North lived cheerfully by a culture that had come from . . . the old international realm of Rome." The nineteenth-century "notion of the New Nations" was a superficial mental map of Europe that the Great War demolished. The real meaning of that war was found in "something . . . lying to the south in the old centres of our civilization. . . . It was . . . simply Rome shaking off the barbarians." During the nineteenth century, Rome lost the respect of Europe. "The Latins were a sort of luxurious and yet impecunious remnant left over from a lazier age and incapable of effort or efficiency; capable only of gesticulating over organs and ice-cream carts." But Fascism heralded the resurrection of Romans, the rise of "the people of the old civilization which for centuries had been mocked for its divisions and its decay; but of which the subconscious had never forgotten that it was once not only the master but the maker of the world."[69]

Chesterton's Italians were moved by "unconscious symbols."

> At the moment I am . . . bearing testimony to a miracle. I have seen men climbing the steep stones of the Capitol carrying the eagles and the *labellum* that were carried before Marius and Pompey, and it did not look like a fancy-dress ball. I have seen a forest of human hands lifted in a salute that is three thousand years older than all the military salutes of modern armies; and it seemed a natural gesture and not a masquerade. I have seen a great and glorious people, torn through ten centuries with too many splendid passions, . . . now plainly possessed . . . by an ancient human passion forgotten for many centuries; the passion for order.

Indeed, "the very faces of the crowd carrying the eagles or the Fasces are not the shifty obliterated faces of a modern mob, but those faces of the old Roman busts which we have tried in vain to trace or remember when we saw them in beggars in Naples or waiters in Soho." The Roman had returned as the Fascist.[70]

Chesterton left his visit with the Duce impressed. "There is a great deal more fun in him than masks of bronze are supposed to indulge in." Mussolini disarmed the Englishman. "The very first thing he did was to dump me down in a chair and ask me about the Disestablishment of the Church of England." Unable to get the upper hand, Chesterton found himself being charmed in French. "I should hardly have thought he had ever heard of . . . the debate on the Revised Prayer-Book." The visitor departed struck by the Duce's "most polished courtesy," a quality which "belongs to all Italians; to men of a much humbler station than Mussolini, though he also is a man of the people."[71]

The Resurrection of Rome employed Fascism to critique the plutocracy and decadence of liberalism. "There has come back in Italy a thing sometimes known in the ancient world, but very nearly unknown in the whole of the modern world. This thing is a Government, which is not merely a Governing Class." Condemning the despotic rule of capital in England and America, Chesterton described Fascism as a force able to discipline both the powerful and the weak. In England, "small and secret brotherhoods" of Masons held power, and "professional politics has got itself mixed up with a plutocratic orgy." "Ours has not been an age of popular self-government; but of very unpopular secret government." In contrast, Mussolini "has reacted violently against those two modern Republican vices," secrecy and luxury, "in the name of the two ancient Republican virtues." Hence, "many a modern young man on the make would probably laugh at him, but [Thomas] Jefferson would have understood him perfectly." Chesterton acknowledged the Duce was a dictator and tyrant, but "Liberalism has unfortunately lost the right to attack [Fascism]." "By every instinct of my being, by every tradition of my blood, I should prefer English liberty to Latin discipline. But there is the Latin discipline; and where is the English liberty?"[72]

The new papal state, "the Holy Island," overwhelmed Chesterton. "There is something that I find enormously moving to my own imagination in the idea of that sacred island far inland, so small in its size, so absolute in its boundary, so strange and awful in its significance; the Holy Land of Europe; the minute microcosm of Christendom." St. Peter's new home triggered paroxysms of paradox. "For though the Magnificat magnifies the Lord, it is only just after the Lord has minimized Himself. And there is here a mansion within a mansion, a new Bethlehem or House of Bread, and in the smallest of the tabernacles something yet little more than a child." The Lateran Pacts incarnated an eternal reality. "The Papacy is as much a thing of the Future as a thing of the Past; it is very sharply and plainly a thing of the Present."[73]

The Crisis of 1931

Although the Lateran Pacts demonstrated that both the pope and the Duce wanted to end the division that had defined Vatican-Italy relations since 1870, conflict nevertheless persisted. Struggles over Catholic Action and the work of the Church with Italian youth intensified in 1929 and 1930. When the crisis peaked in 1931, Pius XI issued his 29 June anti-Fascist encyclical, "Non abbiamo bisogno," which then set the stage for the negotiation of the September Accords. During the conflict, American Protestants tended to side with Mussolini, while Catholics rose up to support their Holy Father. Once again, the status of the Vatican and the Church in Italy divided Catholics from their American neighbors. From the September Accords of 1931 until the Fascist anti-Semitic decrees of 1938, Fascist Italy and the Vatican shared "idyllic years," in the somewhat exaggerated estimation of historian Richard Webster. Predictably, once the 1931 conflict was resolved, American Catholic anti-Fascist arguments grounded in Catholic natural law theory of the state evaporated, and the Lateran Pacts were never again called into question until during and after World War II.[74]

In early 1931, Partito Nazionale Fascista (PNF) secretary Giovanni Giuriati led an inflammatory press campaign in which he accused Catholic Action of anti-Fascist activities and plots to rehatch the PPI. The Fascist state, he boasted, was totalitarian, and autonomous Catholic organizations had no right to exist. Violence against Catholics escalated. In a letter to Cardinal Ildefonso Schuster of Milan published in *L'Osservatore Romano* on 26 April, Pius dismissed accusations that Catholic Action interfered in politics. The state, he added, might claim a "subjective totalitarianism . . . in the sense that the totality of the citizens shall be obedient to and dependent on the State for all things which are within the competence of the State." But an "objective totalitarianism" that subordinated citizens to the state "is a manifest absurdity in the theoretical order and would be a monstrosity were its realization to be attempted in practice." Pulling no punches, Pius insisted: "Fascism declares itself to be Catholic. Well, there is one way and one way only to be Catholic, Catholics in fact and not merely in name, true Catholics and not sham Catholics . . . and that is to obey the Church and its head."[75]

The crisis intensified. Catholics held an international rally in Rome on 15–17 May to celebrate the fortieth anniversary of "Rerum Novarum" and the publication of Pius XI's "Quadragesimo Anno." Its critique of a single state-controlled labor system implicitly challenged the regime. On 30 May, Mussolini ordered his prefects to dissolve Catholic Action youth groups and shut down their offices. In turn, the papal legate canceled his mission to celebrate the 700th anniversary of the death of St. Anthony of Padua, and the Vatican suspended open-air processions on the Feast of Corpus Christi. Mussolini called upon all Fascists to defend their revolution. Catholic Action was anti-Fascist, and the totalitarian state could not tolerate, in the words of an Italian radio broadcast, "the absurd spectacle of a powerful organization taking its orders from a foreign power, the Vatican." Throughout June, *L'Osservatore Romano* printed letters from Catholics all over the world, especially the United States, proclaiming their solidarity with the Holy Father.[76]

The Knights of Columbus felt the regime's wrath when the Fascist police targeted their five Roman playgrounds for confiscation. Ambassador John Garrett urged Edward Hearn, the Knights' Rome administrator, to cooperate with the regime, but Hearn believed submission would be "a gesture inimical to the Holy See." Msgr. Francesco Borgongini-Duca, papal nuncio to Italy and Vatican liaison to the Knights, urged Hearn to deploy the fields as a bargaining chip for the Holy See in its tense negotiations with the regime. Charged to protect the Knights' investments, Hearn felt unauthorized to comply. Hearn's effort to distance himself from the conflict was met with displeasure in high places. On 1 June, the Paris edition of the *New York Herald* quoted Hearn: "[The Knights of Columbus] have no connection whatever with the Azione Cattolica [Catholic Action]. . . . We are in no way interested in domestic troubles between the Government and the Vatican. It is none of our business." Secretary of State Cardinal Eugenio Pacelli, disappointed with such an open display of detachment from the Holy Father, demanded Hearn's recall. His "presence in Rome is very embarrassing and dangerous both to the Holy See and to the work of the Knights of Columbus." The Vatican demanded a successor "capable of justly appreciating 'Azione Cattolica' in all its aspects."[77]

Thereafter, the fate of the playgrounds the Knights had purchased and maintained for the Vatican in its battle for the soul of Italy's youth, was linked to the pope's struggle to save Catholic Action. After the resolution of the crisis in September, the playgrounds were reopened for recreational activities only but not for athletic training. That is, the playgrounds fell under government provisions for Catholic Action and no longer maintained an independent character. But before the resolution of the crisis, during the tense days of June and July, Msgr. Francis Spellman of Boston, under orders from the pope, smuggled "Non abbiamo bisogno" out of Rome to be published abroad.[78]

American Catholics rose up to support their Holy Father. Archbishop Edward Hanna of San Francisco proclaimed, "The Holy Father . . . is standing fearlessly for the Christian rights of every individual and of the peoples of every nation. . . . The Whole world is again indebted to the Father of Christendom." *Commonweal*'s lead editorial on 10 June, "Caesar Challenges Peter," predicted papal victory. "Emperors, kings, conquerors, statesmen, parties, have challenged Peter during nearly twenty centuries. . . . But Peter, in the person of the Pope, remains undefeated." *Commonweal* urged Catholics to obey "the one super-national organization in the world, the one universal leader of moral and spiritual action among all races and all nations—the Vatican, the Catholic Church, the Holy Father of humanity." The Holy Cross Fathers at the University of Notre Dame in turn attacked both the Duce and his American supporters. "Absolute overlordship of the state is un-American," *Ave Maria* exhorted. Fascist Italy "out-spartans Sparta" when it attempts to "own and seize and train and standardize and wholly absorb the child." Notwithstanding Mussolini's immorality, "certain Americans will . . . stand with Il Duce because the Church stands against him."[79]

Dziennik Chicagoski narrated the drama of Catholic Action and Fascist violence for Polish Americans on its front page throughout June 1931. The 4 June headline screamed, "'Death to the Enemies!'—Mussolini," emphasizing the Duce's fanatical belligerence toward "the enemies of the [Fascist] revolution." Not content to merely highlight the regime's violation of the Lateran Pacts, *Dziennik* informed its anti-Soviet readership that Mussolini's attack upon the pope had triggered celebrations throughout the Soviet Union and inspired Russians to write the Duce letters of congratulation for his revitalized anticlericalism.[80]

James Gillis, the pugnacious Paulist, swiped at both the Duce and fellow Americans outside the Catholic fold. In July, Gillis insisted, "one cannot espouse the Fascist side in this controversy without holding the implausible theory that the Pope is arrogant, ignorant, aggressive and mendacious." By August, Gillis admitted that the "implausible theory" had won converts. "It must be confessed that a rather considerable number of the American people are disposed to believe *a priori* that whenever Church and State come into conflict, the Church must be to blame." Listing state violence against the Church in Italy, Spain, Mexico, and the Soviet Union, Gillis contended that Rousseau, Jefferson, and the pope shared a belief in the rights of man over the state, "whether for a supernatural reason or for a natural reason." Each American "ought to take off his hat and fling it into the air with a good loud hurrah for the Pope. But how many American hurrahs have you heard?"[81]

Gillis had a point. In the midst of this titanic struggle between the Church and a state asserting totalitarian claims, American Protestants still suspected papal absolutism. The *Christian Century* admitted, "the pope is on safe ground when he declares that the Church has a right to 'look after the good of the workingmen to safeguard and enhance the good of souls.'" After all, "Protestant churches also believe that they must work for the welfare of labor." But "the difference is that [the Protestant] method is that of investigation, publicity and persuasion. The pope," on the other hand, "assumes the right to command the state."[82]

The *Christian Advocate* had less sympathy. Fascist Italy permitted Protestants "to make converts in Rome. Such toleration [Pius XI] seems to find intolerable!" As the conflict heated up, the *Advocate* reprinted a letter from a Methodist minister, a "convinced democrat" who "had a rare experience of an audience" with Mussolini. Fascism, the minister reported, "has at least disciplined—some say dragooned—an undisciplined people." And "while Mussolini rules Italy, religious freedom has a chance; . . . At least while he stands, I believe we Methodists may worship in Italy without fear." When the crisis peaked, the *Advocate* bought the Fascist contention that Catholic Action was a political Trojan horse. Fascism "is not hostile to religion. . . . But it views with intense and probably well-founded suspicion anything which looks like a conspiracy on the part of the Roman Church as a political engine to set up an organization which parallels and which might eventually attack the system which Il Duce has so carefully built up."[83]

"Non abbiamo bisogno" denied such accusations. Pius asserted that Catholic Action had refrained "absolutely from any and every kind of party-political activity." Fascist "inventions, falsehoods and real calumnies" notwithstanding, the regime unjustly persecuted Catholics. When it tried to "tear away from the Church the young," the regime violated "sacred and inviolable rights of souls and of the Church." Pius condemned the Fascist "resolve . . . to monopolize completely the young . . . for the exclusive advantage of a party and of a regime based on an ideology which clearly resolves itself into a true, a real pagan worship of the State— the 'Statolatry' which is no less in contrast with the natural rights of the family than it is in contradiction with the supernatural rights of the Church."[84]

Pius portrayed the Church as an intimate family united around its Holy Father to mourn the violence unleashed upon his "little ones." Bland descriptions of the abstract principles embedded in allocutions and encyclicals have ignored how modern papal documents tapped into emotions with familial imagery. Affective associations, nurtured in frequently practiced devotions, tied Catholics to the sacred geography of Rome and to their Holy Father. The "generous and affectionate intervention which does not cease, . . . the fraternal and filial devotion, . . . that sentiment of high supernatural solidarity, that intimate union of thoughts and of feelings, of intellects and wills, which your loving messages breathe forth, have filled Our soul with inexpressible consolations." The Vatican could never be a "foreign power" in Rome as Mussolini suggested. "Thanks to this apostolic power which is now, unworthy though We be, entrusted by God to Us, the good Catholics of all the world consider Rome as the second country of each and every one of them."[85]

"Non abbiamo bisogno" not only taught ethical principles about the dangers of the state, it spoke of loyalty and betrayal, trust and dishonesty, and the patience of a Holy Father looking out for the good of souls. "The clergy, the Bishops, and this Holy See have never failed to acknowledge everything that has been done during all these years for the benefit and advantage of religion" in Fascist Italy. Anti-Catholic actions or words, the pope had hoped, were only expressions of "individual authors" and not "of a programme." But recent events undermined "this fondly held supposition." Mussolini had betrayed an international trust. Faithful Catholics "cannot be grateful to him who, after putting out of existence Socialism and anti-religious organizations . . . has permitted them to be so largely re-introduced that the whole world sees and deplores them." Still, Pius did not condemn the PNF or the Fascist state specifically but only "those things in the programme and in the activities of the party which have been found to be contrary to Catholic doctrine and Catholic practice."[86]

The encyclical further divided Catholics from their American neighbors. *Commonweal* portrayed "Non abbiamo bisogno" as part of a "world-wide battle with the new paganism of the State" in Italy, Russia, Mexico, Spain, and Lithuania. It dubbed the situation "a war for the liberty of the human soul." The *Christian Century*, in contrast, implied the pope and the Fascist regime stood on the same moral turf. "The encyclical constitutes, in fact, a direct and frontal attack upon both the personnel and the principles of the fascist state. In view of that fact, the pope's solemn assertion that the leaders of Catholic Action have scrupulously abstained from political activities cannot be wholly convincing. Undoubtedly he might assert with equal sincerity that he himself, in writing this encyclical, is abstaining from every form of political activity."[87]

The *Christian Advocate* concurred. It attacked *Commonweal* for speculating upon the steps President Herbert Hoover might take if the pope were to seek refuge from Fascist violence. Hoover, according to the *Advocate*, "would remind the Holy Father that a country that had been hospitable to Brigham Young and Mary Baker Eddy would not be likely to exclude anybody on religious grounds." But the *Advocate* also hoped Hoover "would find a courteous way of indicating that the pontiff's baggage would be subjected to rigid inspection, and if he proposed to set up a papal court or a Vatican City state . . . in the New World he would find the conditions better on the Tiber than on the Potomac, the Hudson, or the Father of Waters."[88]

Negotiations between the Vatican and Fascist Italy culminated on 2 September 1931. In the September Accords, the regime reaffirmed its legal recognition of Catholic Action. In December, as an olive branch to the Vatican, Mussolini removed Giuriati from his PNF post. The accords required Catholic Action to reorganize strictly under diocesan authority. (This never came to pass. The lay-dominated board in Rome remained intact.) More important to Mussolini, the accords forbade ex-*popolari* from leadership positions. (Many dioceses ignored this ban with impunity.) Finally, the accords reiterated the earlier ban on Catholic youth organizations for sports and athletics, restricting them to religious and educational activities.[89]

If the crisis of 1931 portended that Pius XI might reenact the intransigence of Pius IX and deny the legitimacy of the Italian Kingdom, the omen evaporated quickly. In January 1932, Pius XI awarded the Duce the prestigious Papal Order of the Golden Spur, and the following month, on the third anniversary of the pacts, Mussolini made his first and only papal visit. Chicago's *New World* described the Roman crowds "applauding and waving flags and handkerchiefs in a fervent demonstration of approval," "proof that the Italian people ardently desire amity between the Holy See and their national government." King Vittorio received the collar of the Supreme Order of Christ. Conversely, Fascist Italy awarded the Order of the Annunziata to Francesco Pacelli, Gasparri, and Pietro Tacchi Venturi, SJ, the Vatican negotiators of the Lateran Pacts. King Vittorio conferred the Supreme Order of Santissima Annunziata upon Cardinal Eugenio Pacelli, the new Vatican secretary of state. Thereafter, the regime, the Vatican, and the Italian Church enjoyed relatively harmonious relations until 1938.[90]

THE LATERAN PACTS realized the demands of the ideology of the Roman Question that had shaped the Church as an international institution since the loss of the Papal States. The controversial status of the Eternal City dramatically symbolized the international contest between Catholicism and liberalism. Never merely an Italian city, Rome was a fount of civilization, the sacred center of the Catholic world, the home of the Holy Father and his children. Consequently, it served American Protestants and liberals well as the primary target for their attacks upon the Church, a "medieval" institution out of place in the modern world.

The resolution of the Roman Question generated conflict between American Catholics and their neighbors. Intense debates extending animosities that surfaced during the Al Smith presidential campaign persisted into the 1930s. Catholic apologias in support of the Lateran Pacts—both the temporal power and a confessional state for the Italian nation—revealed an abiding commitment to

Catholic ideology and a disregard for neo-Thomistic natural law theology. Catholics tendered diverse, often contradictory, arguments to defend the Lateran Pacts. They rose up to support their Holy Father, even when it meant trivializing the natural rights of Italians that they cherished as an American minority. American Protestants and Jews, in their praise of the Duce, also disregarded the illiberal premises of Fascist ecclesiastical legislation.

How did the realization of the ideology of the Roman Question affect the United States in the 1930s? What were the implications of the Lateran Pacts for Americans in the decade before World War II? These questions are the subject of the remainder of the book. Catholics did not merely laud the restored freedom of their Holy Father and applaud the privileged status of the Italian Church from across the Atlantic. They forged working relationships with representatives of Fascist Italy within the United States. These relationships, important for Italian Americans, also permitted English-speaking Catholics to participate in glorious, Latinate, expressions of a resurgent Rome in the modern world. Frequent, dramatic, public gestures signaling the acculturation of English-speaking Catholics into the revitalized and militant Church of Rome had lasting consequences on the imagination of American Protestants and liberals.

CHAPTER EIGHT

Preaching Fascism
and American Religious Politics

In his thoughtful study *The Pope and the Duce* (1981), historian Peter C. Kent explores the implications of the Lateran Pacts for international relations. But neither Kent nor historians of religion in America have considered what formal diplomatic ties between Fascist Italy and the Holy See meant for the United States. Generally, American Catholics cheered Fascist Italy from afar in the 1930s. Before bishops and editors rose up to defend Franco's insurgents in the Spanish Civil War, many had already applauded Benito Mussolini's defiance of the League of Nations and his Catholic civilizing mission among Africans in the Ethiopian War (1935–36). In addition to celebrating the Duce from across the Atlantic, American Catholics enjoyed excellent relationships with representatives of Fascist Italy within the United States.

In churches, schools, offices, and clubs, Catholics received reassurance from the Italian ambassador and his consuls that the Holy Father was free and that the Italian nation worshipped God with dignity under Fascism. These consuls, itinerant preachers of Fascism, had to negotiate the complexities of the American religious landscape, dominated as it was by Protestants, as well as volcanic rivalries among Italian Americans. The consuls have left a rich paper trail that reveals how the Lateran Pacts offered Fascist Italy new opportunities to influence Catholics in the United States. American Catholics, both English and Italian speaking, performed public rituals with Italian consuls consecrating Fascist Italy and relishing the realization of the ideology of the Roman Question. Suspicious Protestants and liberals took notice as democracies collapsed in Europe and war loomed on the horizon.

Fasci all'estero and Consuls in the 1920s

While this chapter analyzes the activities of the Fascist state within American society in the 1930s, it is helpful to ask how the consuls came to represent Fascism in the United States. When Mussolini came to power in 1922, diplomatic personnel had forged their careers in the service of Liberal Italy. The 1920s, consequently, were a volatile period of transition both in Italy and among Italian consuls abroad.

One month after Benito Mussolini came to power in October 1922, he appointed Gelasio Caetani di Sermoneta, a Nationalist, to the embassy in Washington. Caetani hoped to foster Italian American participation in public life, but his staff tendered a dour report on the weak Italian American performance in the 1922 elections. Outside of New York, they "do not yet take an active part in the political life of the country and, due to defective organization and the individualistic tendencies of our race, Italians . . . do not exercise . . . an influence proportionate to their numbers." After an extensive tour of his "colonies," Caetani returned to Washington impressed with Italian American resources but dismayed at their divisions. "Discord, dissension, and criminality" plagued Detroit. Chicago was in a "deplorable situation." He bemoaned pervasive regional conflicts "onto which are added political struggles among naturalized Italians which the ringleaders of the Black Hand . . . exploit to obtain their goals." Provincial banquets, parades, balls, and processions "not only cost striking sums, but, due to the undignified form in which they are carried out, . . . discredit us in the eyes of Americans."[1]

To remedy the situation, Caetani recommended consular expansion and activism. The consuls should urge immigrants to naturalize and form a voting bloc to support Italian interests. Furthermore, the consuls should implement programs to promote the study of Italian language and culture in order to strengthen the "spiritual" bonds linking Italian Americans to the patria. Significantly, Caetani visited Catholic churches and parochial schools and discovered they brought unity to Italy's diaspora. "The two most influential elements that unite our countrymen are the inborn love of the patria and the Catholic Church, which through its perfect organization successfully permeates our colonies much more than any other political or social institution."[2]

Caetani highlighted the utility of Catholicism as a force of national order and solidarity. Like many Nationalists, he believed Catholicism was a historic force of Latin expansion that imbued Latin peoples with communal values of discipline and faith. But notwithstanding his acknowledgment of the patriotism and social mission of immigrant priests and sisters, Caetani wanted to empower consuls, not clergy. The Church was a means toward an end. In nineteenth-century Liberal Italy, Catholic solidarity had posed an alarming specter. But Caetani welcomed the national solidarity that Catholicism, respectful of tradition, hierarchy, and authority, inculcated in people of Italian descent. Nationalists such as Caetani and Alfredo Rocco, an architect of the Fascist state, merged with the Partito Nazionale Fascista (PNF) in 1923 and shaped Fascism's policy toward the Church and its understanding of Catholicism as a force of discipline and social order.

Catholic cooperation with Fascist Italy in the 1920s was not uncritical. American Catholics, like the pope, supported conservative forces that struggled for hegemony over revolutionaries and their cult of violence within the Fascist movement. When American Catholics sprinkled their holy water, it consecrated the conservative, authoritarian, Catholic dictatorship, eager to resolve the Roman Question, not the antiparty Fascist movement, anticlerical in thought and deed; not marauding Blackshirt squads, whose intransigent leaders sought to use the PNF to dominate the state in the 1920s.

Although the embassy and its consulates were official representatives of the state, they encountered challenges from the PNF to their claim to represent authentic Fascism. The most vocal challenge came from *fasci all'estero* (bands of Blackshirts abroad). The first *fascio* in the United States had been organized in New York City eighteen months before the March on Rome. Mussolini, pleased with the initiative, described the purpose of the *fasci* abroad in his *Il Popolo d'Italia*: "To arouse, conserve, and exalt *Italianità* among the millions of fellow Italians dispersed throughout the world; . . . to bind together and intensify the links of all kinds between the colonies and the mother country; to establish tried and true 'fascist consulates' for the legal and extra-legal protection of all Italians." The *fasci*, however, often became a thorn in Mussolini's side after the Blackshirt leader became a prime minister in search of respectability. *Fasci* extremists boisterously dismissed diplomats like Ambassador Caetani as anti-Fascist, insisting Foreign Ministry personnel lacked Fascist credentials. As historian Alan Cassels describes, "the smoldering hostility between a cautious bureaucratic class and the exuberant party zealots burst into the open in a dozen places in the United States."[3]

The struggle between the *fasci* and the consuls was a diaspora variation on the conflict between PNF intransigents who wanted to export Fascism and cautious Foreign Ministry diplomats with professional roots in Liberal Italy. Both the *fasci* and the consuls claimed to represent the nation, authentic Fascism, and the will of the Duce. Their conflicts grew so poisonous that they rivaled dramatic clashes between Fascists and anti-Fascists that triggered sensational newspaper accounts of Italian American violence and instigated public indignation against Fascism and Mussolini.[4]

After taking the reins of government, Mussolini appointed the young, intransigent PNF political secretary Giuseppe Bastianini as general secretary of the Fasci Italiani all'estero, a position Bastianini held until December 1926. Although

Mussolini required the *fasci* to work under the authority of the Foreign Ministry, Bastianini considered Italian diplomats anti-Fascist and fought ruthlessly to undermine their authority. The embassy, working against legislation for U.S. immigration restriction and for war-debt reduction, found itself having to answer uncomfortable questions from an aroused American public reading colorful accounts of immigrant political violence and starry-eyed predictions about the Fascist penetration of American institutions.[5]

Although Mussolini's Janus-like mediation between the *fasci* and the consuls confused both, the regime moved unsuccessfully to discipline the *fasci*. After a Fascist Central Council (1923) failed to douse the flames of extremism, the government established the Fascist League of North America (FLNA) in July 1925. By this time, the United States harbored seventy *fasci* with 7,000 members and two newspapers. Governed by four party stalwarts in Rome, the FLNA incorporated in New York State to veil its ties to the PNF. The FLNA president, Ignazio Thaon di Revel, a scion from a noble Piedmontese family, was a decorated war veteran who worked for a brokerage company that handled the J. P. Morgan loans to Italy. A member of the powerful Italian Chamber of Commerce in New York and a friend of the Duce, di Revel did not reign in his FLNA charges. Before 1929, *fasci* brawled repeatedly with anti-Fascists, disrupted consular initiatives, engaged in unproductive polemics with the Italy America Society, and displayed Blackshirt bravado to an unappreciative U.S. public.

As the FLNA and the consuls clashed, the Foreign Ministry absorbed PNF members. Work within a careerist bureaucratic class tamed many zealous Fascists. But this also "fascistized"—the term employed by historians of Italy—the Foreign Ministry. In May 1925, Mussolini named trusted lieutenant and *squadrista* Dino Grandi the Foreign Ministry undersecretary. In 1929 Grandi became the foreign minister. His loyalty to the state apparatus superseded his violent, revolutionary past commitments as he worked with liberal and Nationalist converts to Fascism and brought the troublesome FLNA to heel. In 1928 and 1929, the Foreign Ministry opened seventy new consulates and appointed 120 new Fascist career consuls. These consuls, younger and more aggressive then their liberal predecessors, spearheaded a new community activism as they sought to integrate Italian American cultural institutions and mutual benefit societies into Fascist transnational networks. Consuls assumed broad discretionary powers over the allocation of employment contracts, visas, and government subsidies for emigration assistance.[6]

Mussolini's emigration policy evolved with his foreign policy. In 1927 he suppressed the Commissariat of Emigration of 1901 and replaced it with the Direzione Generale degli Italiani all'estero (General Bureau of Italians Abroad), an arm of the Foreign Ministry. This restructuring paralleled Mussolini's new demographic policy, announced in his 1927 Speech of the Ascension, that Italy must acquire a population of 60 million by the 1950s to achieve its rightful place in Europe. Within Fascist ideology, emigration became a form of demographic expansion, and the word "citizen" replaced "emigrant" in the Fascist lexicon.[7]

FLNA violence provoked members of the U.S. Congress to raise the problem of Blackshirt violence during sensitive debates over the Italian war-debt settlement. When FLNA disorder continued, Ambassador Giacomo De Martino explained to Mussolini that the majority of Americans admired the Duce "and the marvelous rebirth of Italy sustained by the new spirit that pervades it." But the ambassador warned that those same Americans "view the action of Fascism *in the United States* without sympathy and with mistrust." De Martino offered Mussolini an alternative to *fasci* trying to export Fascism to the United States.[8]

In a long letter to Mussolini in May 1926, De Martino asserted, "it is an error to believe the strength of Italians in this country is diminishing." De Martino urged the regime to take advantage of the improved economic status of a new class of Italian American professionals. Although they spoke little or no Italian and had only a superficial knowledge of Italian history and culture, they followed developments in Italy with great interest and pride. Their "pride in belonging to the Italian race" resulted from the "growing . . . strength and prestige" of Italy after the "Fascist Revolution." Once naturalized, Italian Americans had "concrete political value." "It is typically these American citizens, who have left Italy many years ago," or their children "who are always ready and disposed for any initiative . . . that can be to the advantage of our country." De Martino encouraged naturalization, "a juridical act" that "does not influence the spiritual ties Italians in America feel for their *patria* of origin, [but] gives Italians an opportunity to penetrate the heart of American political life and bring to it the defense of Italian interests."[9]

Like Caetani, De Martino emphasized the role of consulates as focal points for cultural reform and political mobilization. However, because Americans feared foreign interference in local ethnic associations, consular influence must be exerted "under conditions of utmost prudence without assuming an attitude that contrasts with the American program." A remark made by Labor Secretary James Davis, a Welsh immigrant, at an Order Sons of Italy in America (OSIA) convention, struck De Martino. Davis had claimed that one could not be a good American if he forgot his homeland. This was "the line that the diplomatic and consular authorities in America must follow." A preliminary affirmation of "loyalty to America, . . . renders possible the most fervid exhortations to the cult of the *patria* of origin." De Martino underscored the utmost necessity of reigning in the *fasci*, whose strident rhetoric and foolish performances of Blackshirt bravado instigated American anxieties and accusations of foreign interference. De Martino's program of consular activism and aggressive penetration of Italian American culture won the day, but only after 1929.[10]

Anti-Fascists challenged both the FLNA and the consuls at every turn. The United States, however, was not a popular destination for anti-Fascist exiles. France was the favored meeting ground among *fuorusciti*, and Belgium and Switzerland "each drew more [Italian] anti-fascist labor leaders than the United States, Argentina, and Brazil combined." In her comparative study of Italian diasporas, Donna Gabaccia claims that outside of Italy, Fascism had its greatest success in the United States. Still, the Anti-Fascist Alliance of North America (AFANA), "a discordant coalition" of socialists, syndicalists, anarchists, communists, and unionist organized in 1923 from both exiles and immigrants, kept Fascist activities in the public eye. Newspapers frequently reported Blackshirt clashes with anti-Fascists and triggered American xenophobia of immigrant rabble-rousing. The State Department asked De Martino to identity anti-Fascists who had entered the United States illegally and offered to deport the subversives. Although appreciative, De Martino tried to alter FLNA activities to end the bad press.[11]

Sensational exposés by liberal journalists led the Fascist regime to dissolve the FLNA in 1929. Ray Tucker's "Tools of Mussolini in America" in the *New Republic* in 1927, as well as Marcus Duffield's 1929 *Harper's Magazine* piece, "Mussolini's American Empire: The Fascist Invasion of the United States," provoked public outrage. De Martino warned his consuls to moderate their activity because the FLNA's "tactical errors" had compelled the State Department to probe "the interference of some Italian consuls into the schools of this country." After Mussolini dissolved the FLNA, the AFANA quipped: "Fascism has encountered here its Caporetto."[12]

In fact, Fascist consuls became integral parts of Italian American political and cultural life in the 1930s. They worked tirelessly to improve the image of Italy and Italians in the United States and to coordinate activities among Italian Americans to raise funds, create an effective political lobby, and forge a voting bloc, or at least the fear of one. Consular agents spearheaded language and culture classes and distributed propagandistic texts to schools and libraries. Fellow travelers celebrated the role of Italian explorers, missionaries, and scientists in the creation of American civilization through filiopietistic scholarship and public lectures. Consuls orchestrated the invention of an ethnic civil religion, replete with an annual cycle of Fascist holidays, and under their auspices busts, statues, and cultural centers appeared in public spaces throughout America. Consuls also cultivated connections with doers and shakers outside the Italian American community, such as bishops, educators, editors, politicians, business elite, and civic boosters. By the 1930s, shortwave radio and film propaganda orchestrated by the Fascist Ministry of Popular Culture permeated America and consuls had become constituent elements of ethnic and Catholic life at the diocesan and parish levels. Indeed, the extraordinary cooperation between the consuls and the Catholic Church was both a sign and a result of the Italy-Vatican reconciliation formalized in the Lateran Pacts.

What was the Church's relationship to *fasci* in the 1920s? In Italy the Vatican called for political peace, order, and stability. It favored conservative state institutions to radical Fascist insurgents who condemned state concessions to the Church. The American Catholic press, like the Vatican, distinguished Mussolini's "responsible" Fascism from Blackshirt violence. We should, therefore, expect to find the American Church interacting with the consuls rather than the *fasci*, and for the most part this was true. I have not been able to learn much about the Popular Fascist University at the Jesuits' Loyola University of Chicago in 1926. Set up by Mario Lauro, state deputy of the FLNA in Illinois and political secretary of a Chicago *fascio* established in 1923, the Popular Fascist University hosted lectures on the merits of Fascism. Generally, it was only when *fasci* marched in black shirts, sang Fascist anthems, and offered Roman salutes in the same public or religious ceremonies as consuls that the Church was present to legitimize the event. For example, when the first congress of the FLNA met in Philadelphia in October 1925 to mark the third anniversary of the March on Rome, Cardinal Dennis Dougherty sent a telegram of support. But the congress was not exclusively a Blackshirt affair, since the president of the Elks club as well as Italian and American government representatives were also in attendance.[13]

Fascist Consuls and Protestantism

Ambiguities plagued the relationship between Fascist Italy and Protestants. The consuls, like officials in Italy, uncomfortable with evangelical proselytizing, harbored anti-Protestant prejudices but wanted to avoid offending American public opinion. The embassy urged pragmatism and welcomed Protestant supporters, but it defended the Lateran Pacts, the state religion, and the Vatican City in the face of Protestant criticism. The career of Consul General Giuseppe Castruccio (1928–35) of Chicago, one of the new Fascist consuls after the "fascistization" of the Foreign Ministry, illuminates consular dealings with American Protestants. A decorated veteran, he directed a New York City *fascio* in 1924, presided over the Federation of the Italian War Veterans in America in 1925, and served on the original executive council of the FLNA. A PNF faithful, Castruccio became vice consul in Pittsburgh in 1926 before he was promoted to Chicago, where his tenure exemplified the new brand of Fascist diplomat.[14]

Castruccio considered Fascism the culmination of Italian history, and he thought Roman Catholicism was a significant dimension of Italian identity. Although this was not the same as the claim that Italy was first and foremost a Catholic nation, Castruccio shared the Catholic attitudes toward the *culti ammessi*, religious minorities in Italy. He considered Waldensians and Protestants to be deviant Italians, inherently anti-Fascist.

In 1929 Castruccio ominously described the American fund-raising visit of Rev. Paolo Bosio, representing Rome's Waldensian congregation. Castruccio argued that the campaign to strengthen Waldensians with American money demonstrated their "profoundly anti-Fascist mentality." He feared Bosio's visit had inspired a 17 April editorial in the *Christian Century*, "Protestant Strategy in Italy," which forecast "the introduction of Protestantism to Italy on a vast scale." Feigning patriotism, Waldensians were funded by "foreign money . . . and actually controlled by foreign elements, neither more nor less than Masonry, which Fascism had to suppress precisely because, under the guise of a hypocritical patriotism, it was a FOREIGN emanation." Castruccio reasoned, "the Catholic Church has always been Italian, while the Protestant Church has always been clearly anti-Latin and anti-Italian." It posed "the gravest danger of de-nationalization to the Italian soul." He argued, "even among the Slavs the Church has profoundly influenced their mentality and attitudes toward Italy. For example the Poles, precisely because they received Latin influence, are greater friends of Italy than the other Slavic races; the Serbs, on the other hand, who received Eastern influence from Constantinople rather than Rome, are hostile to Italy."[15]

Although Castruccio dismissed Protestantism as "foreign," Italian Protestants in America tried to harmonize their religious heritage with their national identity. In 1923, Rev. Carlo Fama of the Italian Evangelical Minister's Association of Greater New York called for a free church in a sovereign state—a Cavourian shibboleth for the modification of the first article of the Italian Constitution that privileged the Catholic Church. Fama contended Protestantism was "not an esoteric import [to Italy]" but a tradition with Italian origins, "its cradle in the Waldensian valleys; like all great things, it originates from the Land of Dante." Protestantism also had Roman roots. Rome's "Christian martyrs belonged to the Church of Christ, that, through human events is divided into groups, but that recognizes in the Redeemer, the Lord and Savior." In short, Fama offered a Protestant understanding of the Italian nation. According to him, Rome was the home of primitive, authentic Christianity, uncontaminated by the Church's fourth-century Constantinian compromise with the state. Reacting to Fama's reading of history, Ambassador Caetani confided to Mussolini, "I have always viewed with manifest displeasure the ruthless campaign of evangelical ministers to attract our countrymen from the Catholic Church into their sects." They "do serious damage to our country," because "the Catholic religion is a powerful force in the integration of the social conscience of our people." Fama soon became a formidable anti-Fascist.[16]

Castruccio had no patience whatsoever for the Protestant co-optation of the history and symbols of Italy. His animosity surfaced in an indignant report about Rev. Pasquale Riccardo de Carlo, the "pastor of a filthy shack that is pompously called the Presbyterian Church of St. John. . . . Annexed to the church is another dirty building called the 'Garibaldi Institute.' . . . The activity of De Carlo . . . is principally to sow hatred against the Catholic Church and to attract Italian families to the Protestant religion, transforming simple and pure people into rebellious and corrupted souls. . . . These rodents of the Italian conscience, these most dangerous enemies of Italy, . . . give themselves a patriotic air and EXPLOIT THE NAME OF GIUSEPPE GARIBALDI."[17]

Ambassador De Martino did not share his subordinate's fervor. He reminded Castruccio that consular strategy put a premium on pacific relations with all Americans. He warned the zealous consul general not to "provoke an anti-Italian movement among the Protestant masses of this country" and stressed Mussolini's effort to preach toleration of religious minorities.[18] Dismissing Castruccio's Latin nightmare of a Protestant invasion of Italy, De Martino countered, "among Italian Protestants in the United States it is possible to pursue a useful reconciliation with the Fascist Regime. After all, many of them are aligned against Fascism because they assume Fascism could initiate a persecution against Protestants in Italy. The new law on religious liberty [immediately following the Lateran Pacts] has calmed their apprehensions and diminished their hostility." As evidence, De Martino described his plotting with Ariele Bellondi, a Protestant minister "animated by the most high sentiments of *italianità*," to combat the anti-Fascism of Carlo Fama.[19]

Italian American Protestants were in fact generally supportive of Fascism. Immediately after the ink dried on the signatures of the Lateran Pacts, the Fascist government passed legislation, over Vatican protests, to protect the religious minorities. In turn, Italian American Protestant ministers informed their congregations and celebrated the prestige thus gained for their Fascist homeland. For instance, the July 1929 edition of De Carlo's *Vita Nuova* magazine celebrated the origins of Fascist symbols such as the lictor. "The DUCE," it proclaimed, was "the man of Providence, who each day renders our *patria* stronger and more respected abroad. . . . Viva il Duce! Viva il Fascismo!" At an Italian American Protestant 4th of July celebration held in conjunction with a commemoration of Garibaldi's birthday, the words of Protestant hymns were put to the tune of "Giovinezza," the Fascist anthem.[20]

Castruccio's anti-Protestantism had roots in unpleasant encounters with suburban congregations. A frequent speaker for curious Americans in their clubs and churches, Castruccio could barely contain his anger at Anglo-Protestant condescension toward the Italian nation. His lecture at the First Presbyterian Church in River Forest, Illinois, earned enthusiastic applause. Listeners "assured me, 'now I have a more clear opinion about Italy.'" However, the missionary who followed with a description of arduous evangelical labor and a film demonstrating apostolic trials and tribulations infuriated the proud consul. "I expected the work of the Mission to be in India or Africa or China; instead it was in Chicago, precisely in the Italian quarter." The missionary referred to Italian neighborhoods as "true centers of vice," whose residents "became criminals; hence the necessity to offer money to give them a true civic and American education, which naturally is the education of the Presbyterian Church." The film captured a Catholic religious procession with a band, "saints, and children dressed in white like angels. The speaker tried to impress upon [the congregation] how in this way future criminals were prepared." A collection was gathered for De Carlo's Garibaldi Institute. Castruccio lashed out at the "prejudice and ignorance against [Italians]" that dismissed "our contributions to civilization." He resolved to intensify his activism "within Italian communities to improve conditions there and to end the disgraceful misery, brutishness, and presence of the underworld. Although it only involved a tiny minority of residents, it somehow justifies the diffusion of prejudice on the front page of the newspaper, and the establishment of evangelical missions among proud and honest Italians."[21]

But Castruccio learned to bite his lip and could charm Protestants when they stayed clear of his people. When Rev. Clark Wallin Cumming of the First Christian Church of Springfield, Illinois, requested a stone from the Coliseum "as a memorial to the devoted men and women who suffered martyrdom in the earliest days of church history," Castruccio dutifully endorsed the request. Within a year, the Fascist regime accommodated Cumming.[22]

Although the Foreign Ministry instructed consuls to refrain from antagonizing Protestants, it also prohibited displays of unity with any but the state religion. On 12 December 1930, at the invitation of a wealthy widow, Castruccio attended a reception at the Blackstone Hotel to raise money for the Episcopal cathedral in Washington. The consul took the opportunity to boast about the Duce to the Episcopal bishops of Washington and Chicago, ex-Senator George Wharton Pepper of Pennsylvania, Princess Alexandra Victoria of Schleswig-Holstein, and the German and French consuls. Castruccio left with "the impression that they want to create a type of Episcopal Protestant Vatican" in the capital. To his dismay, his superiors scolded him. "It is opportune for Royal Agents abroad to make and maintain those contacts that they can effectively use to learn about the conditions of the countries in which they reside, or make known our country." But "it is nevertheless forbidden for them to participate in meetings or to associate at initiatives that have as their aim . . . direct or indirect propaganda in favor of a religion other than that of the Italian state." In defense, Castruccio meekly chirped that he had merely been an unofficial guest, and his "presence went completely unobserved by the public."[23]

The Lateran Pacts made Castruccio's mission to promote the regime more difficult outside of Catholic circles. At the annual Chicago's Women's Club commemoration of Abraham Lincoln on 12 February 1931, a rabbi confronted the consul with questions concerning the conditions of Jews in Fascist Italy. "From the conversation," Castruccio confided to De Martino, "I was able to understand how a vast, insidious propaganda hostile to Italy had permeated the Protestant, Masonic, and Jewish masses." But Castruccio did not relent. He made "another small but not negligible contribution to the diffusion of Fascist ideas and the truth" at the Garrett Bible Institute at Northwestern University in Evanston, Illinois, when he spoke to over one hundred students and earned "interminable" applause.[24]

Methodist Bishop Francis McConnell, oddly, invited the obliging consul to speak at the World Fellowship of Faiths convention linked to Chicago's Century of Progress Exposition in 1933. In his speech at the Morrison Hotel, Castruccio promoted the civilizing power of Fascist Rome. There was no reason "for the exponents of civilization among white men to go in search of inspiration in faraway countries . . . when Rome offers to our minds and hearts all that we could desire." He denounced "the Goddess REASON the Jacobins had erected on the altars of the French Revolution." Enlightenment liberalism had separated "the emotions, the sentiments, the feelings, the religious atmosphere in which our spirit finds its natural nourishment from our intelligence." The rise of Fascism indicated civilization had been "led back to Rome where we find the foundation of our ethics." Roman values—simplicity, fear of the gods, respect for law and education—were the source of the human spirit and morality. Rome was also the "cradle of the Christian Church." Castruccio insisted that Mussolini made the rejuvenation of Roman values possible. He replaced the 1st of May, a labor feast, with the 21st of April, the classical birthday of Rome, "the mother of all Western civilization" and the source of "eternal youth. . . . This modern reaction against the materialistic and anarchistic tendencies that strive for supremacy all over the world" marked "the right path," "the return to Rome—our Alma Mater."[25]

English-Speaking American Catholics and Fascist Italy

Among American Catholics, the Lateran Pacts brought the consuls prestige. The Glenola Club, affiliated with Loyola University of Chicago, made this clear to Castruccio after Duffield's *Harper's Magazine* exposé proclaiming a Fascist invasion of the United States upon the heels of the pacts. Eager to hear the real story, the Glenola Club, "approximately 600 Catholic men and women (almost exclusively Irish)," invited Castruccio to defend his government. On 26 November 1929 at the Rogers Park Hotel, Castruccio addressed the club. "This was an atmosphere extremely sympathetic to Italy, especially after the concordat." Castruccio sensed that "everyone *wanted* me to defend Italy against the awful accusations of Marcus Duffield." Castruccio assailed Duffield's claim that Mussolini controlled a fifth column of Italian Americans. The consul reminded the Glenola Club of the thousands of Italians who had died or suffered wounds in the U.S. armed forces during the Great War. "Here is the Italian invasion: the invasion of loyalty, courage, heroism and devotion! The applause were majestic." Insisting Duffield worked for "subversives," Castruccio "spoke of Italy, Fascism and Mussolini, concluding, 'Every time you strike at the Italy of Mussolini, you strike at the best part of America, you prepare the work of the Bolshevik disintegration of America that lies in waiting everywhere.'" Boasting about the applause he inspired, Castruccio concluded his report: "The evening was simply splendid."[26]

Castruccio made many Catholic friends on his itinerant Fascist ministry. One ally was Bishop James Griffin of Springfield, Illinois. Speaking on 22 February 1931 at the Chicago Palmer House to 1,500 Knights of Columbus, Griffin gave "a magnificent speech." His "enthusiastic and admirable exaltation of His Excellency Mussolini and of Fascism" rose "to such as extent that at the end of his speech in the delirium of the enthusiasm, the bishop gave those present the Roman salute." Castruccio cultivated Griffin on downstate excursions. Attending a Springfield commemoration of Abraham Lincoln with other Fascist officials preparing for the 1933 Century of Progress exposition, Castruccio was a personal lunch guest at Griffin's home. The consul urged his superiors to confer an honor upon the bishop, who "speaks Italian and is certainly a great friend of Italians" and "who is known as an enthusiastic and authoritative admirer of His Excellency Mussolini."[27]

Castruccio's popularity among Chicago Catholics never wavered. Before his departure in 1935, he was invited to speak at St. Ita's Church. "Encouraged by an atmosphere more than favorable," he recited for two hours his Fascist stump-speech to an appreciative audience of 200 men in the Holy Name Society. The media acknowledged Castruccio's consulate as a link between Fascism and the Church when a *Herald Examiner* reporter asked Castruccio to organize a "solemn funeral to honor the memory" of Fascist Italy's friend, Richard Washburn Child. The ex-ambassador to Italy and ghostwriter of the Duce's autobiography died of pneumonia in 1935, just days after he had converted to Catholicism. Castruccio nudged prominent Italian Americans to honor Child and secured the cooperation of the pastor at Holy Guardian Angel Church. The funeral mass for Mussolini's friend doubled as a Fascist celebration. Msgr. Philip Mahoney, rector of the Quigley seminary, "offered a splendid sermon."[28]

Castruccio took advantage of the formal relations he, as a representative of the state, now shared with the Church. He did not hesitate to meddle in ecclesiastical appointments. In reports to superiors, he evaluated Italian immigrant clergy and endorsed Irish American clergy who spoke out in favor of the regime. In 1932 he petitioned Ambassador Augusto Rosso to have Bishop Bernard Mahoney of Sioux Falls transferred to Albany, New York, where Italians lived in great numbers.

Mahoney had spent eighteen years at the North American College in Rome before he was consecrated to Sioux Falls in 1922. He was "a sincere friend of Italy, of the Italians, and is a fervent admirer of [Mussolini] with whom he corresponded during the concordat." Undersecretary of Foreign Affairs Fulvio Suvich promoted Mahoney to Count Cesare Maria De Vecchi di Val Cismon, Italian ambassador to the Holy See. "I have discerned in [Mahoney], with satisfaction, a certain combative spirit . . . he would willingly adopt for the benefit of our [Italian] community and for the diffusion of the teaching of our language in the parochial schools." (The language and culture textbooks used in the schools were Fascist propaganda published in Rome.) Mahoney met Mussolini in 1932 and assured the Duce that "Americans likened his attitude to that of George Washington." De Vecchi also supported Mahoney's transfer, and it is likely he took up the matter at the Vatican. Mahoney, however, was never transferred.[29]

Castruccio earned praised from Cardinal George Mundelein of Chicago, who had positive relations with Chicago's consulate general after the Lateran Pacts. Mundelein's monument to the American Church, St. Mary of the Lake Seminary, impressed Castruccio. "I am told that from such a seminary excellent priests exit." He also noted, "I do not believe there are Italian students," a fact that probably worked to Fascist Italy's advantage. Chicago, like the rest of the United States, had Italian parishes manned by immigrant clergy whose direct juridical ties to the Italian Church made them vulnerable to pressure from the Fascist state. Mundelein's clerical Americanization policy, therefore, never collided with Fascist consular policy. Mundelein learned, "with a great deal of personal regret," that Castruccio was leaving Chicago in 1935. "You have been the best Consul Italy has had here in Chicago, always watchful for the best interests of the Government you represent and its people in this country."[30]

Castruccio, however, was not the most popular Fascist in Chicago. That honor belonged to Blackshirt daredevil Italo Balbo, the violent *squadrista* turned charming minister of aviation, who led his fliers to Chicago's Century of Progress in 1933. After receiving a hero's welcome, Balbo became a doctor of law. The Jesuit president of Loyola University of Chicago, Robert Kelly, SJ, conferred the degree on Balbo, whose fliers joined the dashing Blackshirt at a solemn mass in Holy Name Cathedral. Kelly explained, "the university, . . . in honoring [Balbo] honors the dynamic 'Duce' who has done so much in ten years to give Italy the stability, the enterprise and the prestige which are deservedly hers. . . . I see a special fitness . . . that General Balbo has this honor from a Catholic university. He, literally, has flown from a land which was the nursery and later the heart and the center of the Catholic religion for nineteen centuries; the official messenger of a government one of whose distinctions it is to have closed the breach of long-standing between Church and State."[31]

Chicago feted Balbo at a gala banquet at the Stevens Hotel. The musical program included the "Marcia Reale," "Giovinezza," and "Star-Spangled Banner." Chicago bishop Bernard Sheil offered the invocation, and Richard Washburn Child toasted the guest of honor in front of Mayor Edward Kelly, Governor Henry Horner, Ambassador Augusto Rosso, Father Kelly, and Castruccio. During their stay, Balbo's squadron visited Columbus Hospital, where "[the Cabrini] sisters presented each aviator with a medal specially blessed" and greeted "Balbo with an exquisite bunch of roses." Although anti-Fascists had ostensibly made known Balbo's complicity in the murder of Father Giovanni Minzoni in 1926, all apparently was forgiven. Balbo's success, the New World assured readers, meant "we will hear less about the decaying Catholic nations in the future." The archdiocesan paper emphasized how "the aviators had received the Holy Eucharist on their departure, arrival, and during their stay in Chicago."[32]

Bishop Griffin's admiration for the Duce and Fascism outlived Castruccio's tenure. After the Italian conquest of Ethiopia in 1936, Chicago consul general Mario Carosi attended the dedication of a stone from the ancient wall of Servius Tullius at the remodeled Lincoln Tomb in Springfield. Griffin gave the invocation for the ceremonies, and greetings were read from President Franklin Roosevelt, Governor Giuseppe Bottai of Rome, and Cardinal Dougherty of Philadelphia. Governor Horner praised Italian contributions to America before Carosi offered Lincoln the Emancipator a Fascist embrace. Carosi recounted how the king of Rome in 578 BCE, Servius Tullius, had granted citizenship to Rome's residents, and how in 1865 the liberty-loving people of Rome had given Lincoln the stone now at his tomb. "The Italy of today, inspired and imbued with the spirit of Rome, feels particularly close to the ideas and achievements of Lincoln as she, too, has been completely united in the last fifteen years through the Fascist Regime." Just as Lincoln "abolished slavery and molded together the United States," so too has "the Fascist regime . . . accomplished a great mission of civilization by emancipating the people [of Ethiopia], the last stronghold of slavery." Carosi stood next to Griffin at the end of the ceremonies when he noticed the bishop had joined the Italian societies in their vocal rendition of "Giovinezza."[33]

Struck by the gesture, Carosi reflected, "it was not the first time that I have had the opportunity to notice gestures of open sympathy [for Fascism] on the part of Catholic authorities [in America]." He recalled, "at the laying of the first stone of the seminary for the Scalabrini [Fathers] in Melrose Park, [Illinois], Bishop [William] O'Brien, at the playing of Giovinezza, notwithstanding the sacred vestments he wore, gave the Roman salute." Bishop O'Brien's Fascist sympathies delighted Foreign Ministry officials, who observed how a long list of Irish American Catholics, the most vociferous enemies of Liberal Italy, had become Fascist admirers. O'Brien, one of Cardinal Mundelein's Chicago auxiliary bishops, was the president of the Catholic Church Extension Society and a generous benefactor of Italian religious congregations working in the United States during the 1930s.

O'Brien's *italianità* extended beyond financial support. In 1937, Chicago consul general Franco Fontana, at the inauguration of the Scalabrini seminary before a crowd of thousands, noted that "during the execution of the Fascist hymn, . . . O'Brien raised his arm in a Roman salute and held it in the same position for the duration of the hymn." The Fascist Empire awarded O'Brien the Commander of the Order of the Crown in 1940.[34]

American bishops and priests, in fact, accepted many awards from Fascist Italy. Under Castruccio's watch in Chicago, Bishop Edward Hoban of Rockford, Illinois, was awarded the Commander of the Order of the Crown of Italy in 1931. Bishop Bernard Sheil received the same award the following year. Between 1931 and 1934, Fathers Luigi Giambastiani, Carlo Fani, Luigi Valetto, Michael Cavallo, and Stanislaus Giambastiani, pastors in Italian American churches, were made Knights of the Crown. Castruccio also had honorary titles awarded to Mary Agnes Amberg, director of the Madonna Center settlement house, John Lavecchi, Mundelein's official photographer, and President Charles O'Donnell, CSC, of the University of Notre Dame. Giovanni Peona, pastor of St. Maria Incoronata, received the prestigious Cross of St. Maurice and St. Lazarus in 1932.[35]

Although the prestige of Fascist Italy in the United States fell precipitously after the Ethiopian invasion, most American Catholics supported the conquest. Jesuit Mark Gross, a professor at Marquette University, congratulated the consular agent in Milwaukee for his "admirable letter" to the editor of a local newspaper "defending the rejoicing of Milwaukee's Italo-American citizens over the end of the [Ethiopian] war. Owing to British propaganda in this country—a perennial plague from which we Americans suffer—the Italian side of the recent war was obscured and even entirely smothered up. But to informed persons . . . who are acquainted with the utter barbarism of Ethiopia, Italy was entirely justified in taking over that land by force of arms." Gross continued, "I myself am intensely interested in both the old and the new Italy, and it seems to me that now at last that that glorious people is entering on an epoch extremely beneficial both to civilization and Christianity." Gross requested "picture magazines . . . illustrating the various improvements made in Ethiopia—the roads, the bridges, the new farms, the settlements of Italian colonists, churches. . . . I should be deeply grateful to you if you could procure for me regular subscriptions to one or two of such publications. I think, as I am a professor in the University here and therefore of some influence, the Italian government could well charge it up to advertising and count it a gain."[36]

The Jesuits at Fordham University outdid their Marquette confreres when they awarded Ambassador Fulvio Suvich an honorary doctorate in the wake of the Fascist conquest of Ethiopia. Suvich explained to his superiors that Fordham's president, Robert I. Gannon, SJ, "has always had a very sympathetic attitude regarding us." The degree-awarding ceremony coincided with the inauguration of an Italian studies program at Fordham. Suvich proudly noted that both Fathers Gannon and Lawrence Walsh, the head of the program, gave speeches rich "in feelings of very explicit sympathy for Italy and for the [Fascist] regime." The ambassador left convinced that "it is the Catholic world in which we can find our best support."[37]

Many American Catholics shared Gross's appreciation for Fascism and authoritarian regimes throughout Europe. After the Ethiopian conquest, Catholic layman Francis Murphy wrote his "dear Friend" [Mussolini] "very much disturbed" by the situation in Spain. He urged the Premier to "send arms to [Franco's] rebels" who fought "for a religious cause." Murphy predicted, "some day you will have to take Spain and also Portugal. These Countries like Italy are Roman Catholic and if you are a devout Catholic they need your protection." He implored the Duce, once "you get hold of any Loyalists or Communists or their like," "execute them without any mercy as they did the priests and nuns. Make the ones that started this trouble also the ones who burned these beautiful churches rebuild them bigger and better, as I think you are a good Catholic go ahead in God's name and bring succor to these Spaniards."[38]

Even while Fascist bellicosity monopolized headlines, the embassy, the apostolic delegation, and the American episcopacy collaborated. In 1935 Ambassador Augusto Rosso was "preoccupied to maintain cordial relations with Apostolic Delegate [Amleto Giovanni Cicognani] . . . with the possibility of obtaining collaboration in many questions concerning Italian-American communities and in which the action of the clergy can effectively support those of the consuls." Rosso described Cicognani as "a man of broad vision, vast culture, and great comprehension of the problems that interest us." He added, "recently I have had the opportunity to procure from him some data concerning the distribution of the Italian population in New York according to the location of the parish churches."[39]

Bishop John Noll of Fort Wayne, Indiana, shared an affinity with Fascism and feared the same enemies—international Jewry, Masonry, and communism. Noll wrote Mussolini in 1936 "to congratulate Your Excellency on the stand which you have taken against Communism which has even made inroads into the United States." Noll explained, "since the Catholic Church is unalterably opposed to all forces of disorder which attack orderly governments, as well as religion, it seems to me that the cooperation of Christianity generally, and of the Catholic Church in particular, would bring success to your aims." After he complimented the Duce's "great respect for religion," Noll inquired "whether Free Masonry and the Jews have been enemies to the stability of your government."[40]

American Catholics appeared frequently with Fascist diplomats after the Lateran Pacts, communicating their solidarity with the regime, even as the Duce's popularity sank among other Americans. However, Archbishop John McNicolas of Cincinnati created a moment of ambiguity when he preached at the American Eucharistic Congress in Cleveland on 24 September 1935. McNicolas ripped "proud leaders, insane in their own conceits, strutting up and down the nations, speaking as if not answerable to any higher authority, disregarding the dignity of human nature and the eternal destiny of man." Spoken at the early stage of the Italian offensive against Ethiopia, McNicolas alarmed the Foreign Ministry about a crack in its American Catholic support.[41]

However, McNicolas was not referring to Italy but rather to Nazi Germany, the Soviet Union, Spain, and Mexico; namely, to states attacking the Church. Cincinnati's consular agent reported in detail upon the incident. McNicolas, a former student and professor at the Minerva in Rome, fluent in Italian and influential in Vatican circles, "has a reputation for interfering a bit too much in politics, especially in regard to the civil administration of the city and the state." The agent knew priests close to McNicolas who spoke of the archbishop's "great ambition to become a cardinal." They assured the agent that McNicolas admired Mussolini and had directed his criticisms only at anti-Catholic states. The agent's report reached the Italian ambassador to the Holy See, who took up the matter at the Vatican.[42]

Cleveland consul Romeo Montecchi reported in May 1936, after the Ethiopian campaign, that "in Cincinnati the impression remains that a phrase in the archbishop's speech . . . was directed against [Mussolini]." But when Montecchi visited McNicolas, the archbishop "was exceptionally kind and expressed in the most emphatic ways his regard for Italy and the Fascist Regime. Regarding our victory, he said, literally, 'England has received the rebuke she deserves.'" Montecchi consulted McNicolas's friends, who vouched for the archbishop's enduring respect for Fascist Italy. "Msgr. Ermenegildo Allais, an Italian priest resident for many years in Cincinnati teaches in the seminary here. He has known the Archbishop for sixteen years and is considered a personal friend of the Archbishop himself. Allais has assured me formally that McNicolas has never expressed any criticism of the Fascist Regime. Indeed, in an interview given some years ago to the newspapers, when he had returned from Rome, McNicolas expressed a lively admiration for the Head of the Government." After Allais researched the matter further for Montecchi, he described a conversation with McNicolas in which the archbishop claimed that the phrase "'speaking as if not answerable to any higher authority' excluded any allusion to the Duce because everyone knows that he believes in God."[43]

Bishop Ralph Hayes, rector of the North American College in Rome, was another ardent episcopal fan of Fascist Italy. On 26 October 1936, Father Ercole Dominicis, an Italian pastor, wrote Mussolini "to fulfill a duty of justice and as an act of patriotism." Dominicis described an address Hayes delivered to the Knights of Columbus on 18 October in Crafton, Pennsylvania. "A true Italian patriot could have done neither more nor better." In that address Hayes insisted that "no Ameri-

can newspaper I read had spoken the truth about Italy and Benito Mussolini."
Boasting of land reclamation projects, the health of Italian youth, the tranquility
of the Italian people who "work happily without threats of dangerous strikes
and are satisfied and proud of their government," Dominicis reported how Hayes
proclaimed, "in no Nation is the Catholic Church respected as in Italy." Hayes
contrasted Fascist Italy to "the unhappy years when he was a young student in
Rome and knew the Italy dominated by Masonry." Dominicis commented, "It is
impossible to explain to you the impression Bishop Hayes's speech produced.
Many commented how America also needed to be blessed with a Government like
the one Italy has." Its curiosity piqued by Dominicis's letter, the Foreign Ministry requested information from the Philadelphia consul general, who confirmed
"Hayes, during the period of our Ethiopian war, had on many occasions expressed
himself in public in favor of our Country." Hayes received a Commander of the
Order of the Crown.[44]

In October and November 1936, Cardinal Eugenio Pacelli, Vatican secretary
of state and the future Pope Pius XII, visited the United States. Historians have
neglected to consider how Pacelli's visit communicated to observers that the
Holy See and Fascist Italy shared a special relationship. Pacelli's mission sparked
speculation. The Italian embassy tapped its contacts at the State Department and
at the apostolic delegation and came up with a variety of hypotheses. The embassy
speculated upon possibilities. Pacelli was in the United States: (1) to end Father
Charles Coughlin's campaign against President Roosevelt with the 1936 election
only weeks away; Roosevelt, in turn, would explore the possibility of diplomatic
relations with the Holy See; (2) to strengthen the American bishops' anticommunist front; (3) to collect funds for the Church in Spain. The embassy discovered that neither U.S. officials nor Apostolic Delegate Cicognani knew for certain
the purpose of the extraordinary visit. The new ambassador, Fulvio Suvich, sailed
from Europe to New York with Pacelli and "had the opportunity to get to know the
cardinal well." Upon their arrival, Pacelli met Suvich's wife and "even suggested,"
according to Suvich, "that [Pacelli] attend the Italy America Society lunch honoring [the ambassador]."[45]

Foreign Minister Galeazzo Ciano instructed his consuls general in cities with
American cardinals (Philadelphia, Chicago, Boston, and New York) to offer "some
act of deference" during Pacelli's sojourn. In fact, an Italian consular official was
invited to dine with Pacelli and each American cardinal in Philadelphia, Chicago,
and Boston. (I have not found a report from New York). In Philadelphia, after
Dougherty invited a consular representative to dine with Pacelli, the representative reported that the only other guests were "dignitaries of the Church within
the diocese" and Enrico Galeazzo, Pacelli's companion. In Chicago, "Pacelli cordially received" Consul General Carosi at Mundelein's home. Carosi "brought to
[Pacelli] the reverent homage of all the Italian communities in my jurisdiction."

The Boston consul general also paid Pacelli respects. "[I] carried to him my devoted personal homage and the reverent salutations from the Italian communities in my jurisdiction." After Roosevelt won reelection, Pacelli met the president. Upon his departure, Pacelli assured Suvich "of the interest he held in the maintenance of the spirit of *italianità* in the Italian colonies and among Italian Americans. . . . He assured me again that he was well pleased each time he had the opportunity to do something in favor of 'our Italy.'"[46]

The Ethiopian conquest, the declaration of the Italian Empire, and Mussolini's support for Generalissimo Francisco Franco in Spain diminished the Duce's popularity in the United States. But Pacelli's visit made clear to American Catholic authorities that Fascist Italy remained the favored home of the Catholic nation. What else were they to make of the cardinal–secretary of state receiving and dining with Fascist Italy's consuls on his American sojourn right after Italy's conquest of Ethiopia? Count Bonifacio Pignatti Morano di Custoza, the Italian ambassador to the Holy See, made it his mission to learn the motives and outcome of Pacelli's visit. He discovered that, in order to circumvent Protestant and congressional resistance, Roosevelt and Pacelli had agreed that an American spokesperson to the Holy See "will not be . . . a true and proper diplomatic representative" but a person "accredited to the pope . . . for the treatment of special questions." This ambiguous status describes exactly Roosevelt's 1940 appointment of a "personal representative" to the Holy See, Myron Taylor. Pignatti also learned that Pacelli had solicited the views of the American cardinals on the establishment of U.S.-Vatican diplomatic relations. "The four Princes of the Church, in agreement, were against the idea."[47]

In Chicago, Mundelein reigned over a vast archdiocese both loyal to the Vatican and favored by the Roosevelt administration. Consequently, his cooperation with the Fascist government was significant. After a meeting of the National Conference of Catholic Bishops in Washington in November 1936, the Italian ambassador reported how the hierarchy addressed the problems of communism, Nazism, and the persecution of the Church in Mexico. "It is noteworthy that the meeting was presided over by Cardinal Mundelein . . . whose favorable sentiments toward Italy are well-known. During the Italo-Ethiopian conflict they had a new confirmation through the official periodical of the archdiocese of Chicago, 'The New World.'"[48]

Mundelein reassured Consul General Fontana in 1937 of his admiration for the Duce and Fascist Italy, where the Church held a privileged place. The cardinal added, "the anti-Italian campaign in the American press" since the Ethiopian war reflected "the influence of British public opinion." Mundelein gave an address in May 1937 in which he called Adolf Hitler "an Austrian paperhanger and a poor one at that." His remark, triggered by the Nazi persecution of the Church, was surely no indication of reservations about Fascist Italy. Mundelein, like most

American Catholics, was anti-Nazi, not anti-Fascist. His support for Fascist Italy, harmonized with the Roosevelt State Department's hope to use the Duce to pacify Hitler. A journalist for the *Chicago Daily News* informed Fontana that upon Mundelein's return from Mother Frances Cabrini's beatification in Rome in 1938, the cardinal told Mayor Edward Kelly, "he had found Italy serene and tranquil. . . . He added that the priests were treated well and enjoyed the fullness of liberty in the exercise of their religious mission. He said in closing that the Government of Mussolini was not treated with equity in the [American] press."[49]

In November 1937, Ambassador Suvich reported to the Foreign Ministry, "the clergy and American Catholics in general represent one of the most formidable anti-communist forces in this country and at the same time are among those that demonstrate the greatest comprehension and sympathy for Fascist Italy." American Catholics clearly distinguished Catholic Fascism from atheistic Nazism before the passage of Italy's "racial laws" of 1938, unlike many liberals who predicted a titanic struggle between democracy and fascism. For instance, at the end of 1937, Secretary of the Interior Harold Ickes recorded in his diary: "The whole international situation is desperately serious. . . . There are two irreconcilable systems of government in the world today and they are fighting for supremacy. On the one side is fascism and on the other is democracy." This interpretation of world affairs in the late 1930s in dualistic terms — fascism against democracy — was common among liberals such as Freda Kirchway at the *Nation* or I. F. Stone.[50]

Even into the late 1930s, Fascist Italy supplied American Catholic institutions with propaganda materials that arguably shaped their understanding of Rome and contemporary politics. In 1938 Father James Connolly, spiritual director of the seminary and director of the Historical Commission in St. Paul, Minnesota, requested and received the catalog for the exposition on the ancient Roman Empire. St. Paul's consular agent explained, "Rev. Connolly is very interested in everything related to the history of Rome. He is our friend and it is wise to assist him if possible in his activities." Claretian Brother James at the National Shrine of St. Jude in Chicago wrote the Italian foreign minister, "I am very pleased with what you are doing for the Italian and Spanish Nations. I would be very grateful if you could send me propaganda material on Fascism." Within six weeks, Brother James received twenty-five books on such topics as the Duce, the corporate state, theories of maternity and infancy, and the PNF. In March 1938, the archdiocese of St. Louis held a clergy conference on religion under the corporate state. According to the Italian vice consul, Father John Kane, the principal speaker, was "very favorably known for his sentiments of admiration for Fascism." The vice consul supplied Kane with relevant speeches by the Duce and clerico-Fascist Father Agostino Gemelli and with a recent address by Pius XI "to members of the Italian clergy awarded by Mussolini for their contribution to the battle for economic autarky."[51]

Nevertheless, by 1936, as Mussolini's alignment with Hitler began to take shape, the Catholic chorus of support for Fascist Italy could no longer drown out emerging dissonance. One New York Catholic, "a Sincere Friend of Italy," had visited Italy when Mussolini was "first taking control of the affairs of the country. I also spent the entire two months vacation there in 1932 and 1933. What a transformation! We found a great people made conscious of their rich heritage, and still retaining that gracious courtesy to strangers which has always made the Italian people beloved by travelers." The Sincere Friend admitted, "every Christian country . . . has to acknowledge Rome as the source of its civilization, its jurisprudence, its literature, its art in all forms, its religion." But by December 1936, this Catholic felt compelled to explain America's growing disillusionment with Fascist Italy. "We Americans who have only the fondest and friendliest thoughts for Italy have, perforce, had our sentiments tinged with the feelings we entertain for Nazism, about which, perhaps, the least said by me the better. Even you, Sir, will admit that our Holy Father, . . . in his references to Nazism, re-echoed the sentiments of the hearts of the American people. . . . We have had the utmost respect for Fascism because Fascism has respected Democracy. But now we see Fascism lined up with Nazism." After listing the Italian monasteries and churches his friends had supported financially, the Sincere Friend appealed to Mussolini to distance himself from Hitler and "the arrogance" and "cold aloofness of the German people." An October 1938 embassy report confirmed the letter writer's sentiment. American Catholics "had never feared . . . to exhibit philofascist sympathies," but the "not-too-subtle eyes of the [wider American] public" had begun to conflate Nazism and Fascism.[52]

The appearance of boisterous Italian anti-Semitism in 1936 and the passage of Fascist anti-Semitic racial laws in 1938 undermined the Duce's popularity and consular prestige. Consuls general in New York and Chicago, caught unaware by the legislation, were "perplexed . . . by the latest developments in our racial politics." The director of the Bank of Naples in Chicago visited Consul General Fontana to report that Jewish clients had become disillusioned with Italy and were withdrawing their deposits.[53] An Italian American in New York informed the Duce that his business suffered as a result of Fascist molestation of Jews. An anonymous New Yorker similarly castigated the Duce. "Jews since the Medici's time have always thought well of your Italy all over the world so it is too bad of your hatred after all these years, but what could have been expected of a friend and associate of Hitler. . . . At first it was hard to believe you coming up from the oppressed should join the oppressors now. Thank God there are still many other beautiful places to visit." Max Guggenheim, a German Jewish immigrant in Middletown, Ohio, was "very much astonished a Gentleman like yourself should want to become aligned with a cruel, brutal man like Adolf Hitler. Why the acts of atrocities which already he has committed on innocent people of my nationality also of Catholic, must and shall be dealt with severely when the time of reckoning arrives." Guggenheim warned Mussolini that "Germany now is worse off then ever, as with the persecution of Jew and Catholic, it has lost its prestige with every other nation."[54]

Italian American Catholics and Fascist Italy

The Lateran Pacts of 1929 brought Fascist Italy into the parishes, rectories, convents, and schools of Italian American Catholics. It is difficult to appreciate this dimension of Italian American Catholicism without an analysis of ethnic community life more generally—not the topic of this study. But this was not merely an "ethnic" matter. The contours of this phenomenon are identical to the English-speaking Catholic context. Italian American Catholic institutions reproduced the same stages of the ideology of the Roman Question as their English-speaking counterparts. Italian American Catholic publications, like any American Catholic magazines that reported on Fascist Italy, expressed concern for the pope, the Church, and the resolution of the Roman Question. They boasted about Mussolini's authentic Catholicism and his defeat of atheistic Bolshevism. In this sense, Italian American Catholic literature mirrored *America*, *Catholic World*, and *Sign* and not the philo-Fascism of the (non-Catholic) Italian American press. Put another way, Italian American Catholicism was not a ghetto religion hermetically sealed within an ethnic community. It was a porous part of the Catholic Church in America and an extension of the Church in Italy.

Consider the monthly *Calendario della Parrocchia dell'Assunta*, edited by Father Federico Angelucci, a Servite pastor of Assumption parish in Chicago. Shortly after Mussolini's March on Rome in 1922, *Calendario* reported, "the churches in Rome gave thanks to the Lord for the salvation of Italy from revolution." Mussolini, a brave Catholic, "presented himself to the Chamber . . . [and] closed his speech by invoking God's aid to help him fulfill his duties, something never done before by any other Italian minister." *Calendario* boasted how Mussolini ordered a mass to commemorate the Italian victory of 5 November at the close of the Great War and went to midnight mass on Christmas. He returned the crucifix to schools and dismissed their "liberal, Masonic, and socialist administrators." He planned to have catechism taught in schools, fund religious congregations abroad such as the Servites, and work for the "reconciliation between the Church and the State, the Pope and the King. If he succeeds, then he will truly be, as he is already called, a man of providence." Like *America*, *Calendario* justified social conflict under Mussolini. "Fascism without a doubt will make mistakes as a result of irresponsible individuals who commit unprovoked acts of violence." But this was a necessary price "to put socialists, communists, and anarchists in their place" and to prevent Italy from becoming "a second bolshevik Russia, without a King, without a

Pope, and without God." *Calendario* hoped God would help Mussolini make Italy "the teacher of truth to all the nations."[55]

Angelucci explained the transformation of the ideology of the Roman Question to his parishioners in 1927:

> After having noticed more than a dozen ecclesiastics at the banquet offered to Ambassador Giacomo De Martino; . . . after having heard Rev. [Luigi] Giambastiani, OSM, invoke the benediction of God over one thousand and five hundred in attendance; and, better still, after having read in *ITALIA* [the Italian-language newspaper] that at the demonstration given to the ambassador . . . *"The children from the parochial school, under the guidance of Rev. Angelucci and the [Cabrini] Sisters, have sung . . . the fascist hymn 'Giovinezza'"*: not a few ask themselves: How is it that at one time the priests never took part in patriotic demonstrations and now they are in the front row?
>
> We respond Romanly: *"Tempora mutantur, et nos mutar cum illis,"* namely, the times change and we change with them! . . . When patriotism consisted . . . in shouting: "Down with the Pope!," naturally the priests preferred being called enemies of the *patria.* . . .
>
> Now that the Government respects and makes respected the Catholic Church in Italy; now that the representatives of the Italian Government declare publicly in America the true and only deserving ones of the *patria* are priests, friars, and nuns, because they found churches, open schools, and maintain hospitals for Italians; now we—priests, friars, and nuns—are able, and if we are able, we must also want to shout: VIVA L'ITALIA![56]

Unprecedented cooperation between consuls and Italian immigrant clergy followed upon the heels of the Lateran Pacts of 1929. Father Luigi Giambastiani, the Servite pastor at Chicago's Sicilian parish, St. Philip Benizi, earned high praise from Consul General Castruccio. In July 1929, Giambastiani gave the solemn invocation to an audience of 2,000 assembled to initiate Lodge 41 of the Italo-American National Union (IANU). The IANU had changed its name from the Unione Siciliana in 1925 in an attempt to recruit non-Sicilians and improve its public image. A mutual benefit society organized in 1895, the Unione Siciliana had been infiltrated by criminal elements. By 1928, it was the largest Italian ethnic organization in the Midwest, numbering over 4,000 adult members and 1,000 children. The assembly gave the Fascist salute after it heard speeches from Castruccio and Lauro, the Illinois deputy of the FLNA. Castruccio described Giambastiani to his superiors as a "true saint." "Previously called the chaplain of the black hand," he had taken great steps to polish the tarnished "Sicilian name." Castruccio followed suit when he "accepted the honorary presidency of the [IANU] precisely in order to defend [the Sicilian name] from calumny." The following year, Castruccio participated in a meeting at St. Philip's organized to stem Sicilian out-migration from, and African American in-migration to, the near North Side neighborhood.[57]

After the Lateran Pacts, the Italian government collected data on its religious orders and missionary societies in and outside of Italy before it formally recognized them as juridical personalities, as the concordat required. The consuls participated in these evaluations. They offered their highest praise for the Scalabrini Fathers, who ran a disproportionately high percentage of Italian parishes in Chicago, Providence, Syracuse, and Boston. De Vecchi, the Italian ambassador to the Holy See, lauded the memory of the conciliationist founder, Bishop Giovanni Scalabrini, the Scalabrini houses in Italy that "continued . . . the great spirit of italianità of the founder," and the Scalabrini missionaries in the Americas. The Scalabrini Fathers were "one of our most deserving missionary organizations, to be singled out as exemplary in the national field." Indeed, they were at the center of Castruccio's cultural activities among Chicago Italians.[58]

For example, when Castruccio, Mayor William Thompson of Chicago, and officers from the United States Army and Navy met at the Grand Banquet Hall of the Palmer House to welcome Italo Balbo, Scalabrini Giovanni Peona offered the prayer. On 27 January 1929, when the Italian government promoted General Luigi Cadorna to the rank of marshal, Scalabrini Carlo Fani led the religious service. After the Lateran Pacts, Fani celebrated the commemoration mass attended by Castruccio. When Order Sons of Italy supreme venerable Giovanni Di Silvestro, Illinois grand venerable George Spatuzza, and Consul General Fontana gathered at an installation of a new lodge in April 1937, Scalabrini Riccardo Secchia consecrated the flags at the ceremony.[59]

The consular reception at the inauguration of the Scalabrini Sacred Heart seminary in 1937, where Bishop O'Brien offered the Fascist salute, brought Scalabrini authorities from Italy to mingle with Fontana. One Scalabrini provincial was pleased to report that the consul general took an active part in the ceremony, "not only remaining with us all day, but also offering us and those present noble words of admiration and encouragement for Scalabrini missionaries and their work." For his part, Fontana reported how Scalabrini authorities referred to the anniversary of the Fascist Empire and evoked applause for Italian soldiers, the king, and the Duce.[60]

One of the principal consular directives after the Lateran Pacts was to promote Italian language and culture in public, private, and parochial schools abroad. Before Castruccio arrived in Chicago in 1928, two Servite parish schools offered Italian classes, neither subsidized by the Italian government. By 1939 the consulate boasted that Italian could be studied at twenty-four centers for children and thirteen for adults, as well as Crane College, Loyola University, Providence High School, and Sacred Heart College in Lake Forest. Besides parochial schools, these centers included night schools or doposcuola (after-school) programs implemented at Italian American parishes and the popular Doposcuola della Madonna della Grazia run by the Cabrini Sisters at Mother Cabrini Hospital. Fascist Italy paid language teachers, provided textbooks, outlined curricula, and offered free trips to Italy as an incentive to students and pastors.[61]

The Cabrini Sisters ran the school at Assumption parish. At St. Philip's, Giambastiani had a Servite sister teach Italian, although the American Sinsinawa Dominicans administered his school. Italian was taught at the other parochial schools, secular centers, and colleges through the initiative of Castruccio and consular attaché Piero Pomante. Pomante, a fervent Catholic PNF member, had experience in Balilla youth programs in Italy and as an officer of the Fascist Militia in Salonica, Greece, and Cairo, Egypt. Pomante arrived in Chicago in 1934. By 1936 he had become the secretary of Chicago's branch of the highbrow Dante Alighieri Society. He spearheaded the consular infiltration of the parochial schools.[62]

Textbooks supplied from Rome for use in Italian schools abroad, the Foreign Ministry's designation for American parochial schools, were attractive and colorful tools of Fascist propaganda. The elementary reader taught Italian through simple lessons about God the Creator, the "great beautiful house" along the sea called Italy, the handsome royal family, and the Duce, whom God sent to guide Italy. In their second reader, Italian American children learned that they were part of the providential emigration of youth, destined by God to carry civilization all over the earth, and how a good Blackshirt gives the Roman salute. In their third reader, children prayed, "Help me, O God, to become a good Italian," and soon after memorized the Decalogue of the Balilla. Upper-level readers taught a doctrinaire history that emphasized the imperial grandeur of Roman civilization, Rome as the cradle of Catholicism, the accomplishments of the Renaissance, the splendor of the Risorgimento, and the historical inevitability of the Fascist Empire. The texts juxtaposed pictures, photos, and lessons about classical art with scenes from Fascist Italy, illustrating to youthful eyes the revival of ancient Roman glory. The "program" that accompanied the texts included lists titled "Historical Dates to Remember for Children," such as the March on Rome, which inaugurated the Fascist Era, and the birthday of the king. Each lesson in the program started with religious reading and Italian hymns. All in all, the texts and the program were organized to cultivate a consciousness of being an emigrant child from a great land chosen by God for rebirth under the Duce.[63]

In 1930 consular agent Antonio Ferme began to supply these texts to Scalabrini pastor Riccardo Secchia for use at the Holy Guardian Angel parish school. Castruccio received data from Italian pastors about the size and nationalities of the student body and the sisters teaching at their schools. By 1933 Secchia reported a "noteworthy reawakening and great interest on the part of the children of our emigrants to learn the Italian language." By the 1933–34 academic year, Italian was taught at Holy Guardian Angel by three women other than the sisters in the school; one was paid a "modest wage" and the other two worked for free. The classes totaled six hours weekly and included 200 students in grades five through eight.[64]

In 1934 Castruccio and Piero Parini, director of the Foreign Ministry's General Bureau of Italians Abroad, had a "cordial meeting" at La Rosetta Restaurant with Italian pastors from the archdiocese of Chicago. They discussed how best to disseminate Italian culture through language study. In a follow-up letter, Castruccio reminded the pastors: "It is only with the knowledge of our language that [Italians born abroad] will be able to conserve [the Italian language], our magnificent spiritual and religious patrimony, that otherwise would be lost." He reassured the pastors that Fascist Italy wanted to help them. It would provide textbooks and facilitate the emigration of Italian teaching sisters. By this time, many of the pastors already had Italian instruction in their schools, so Castruccio offered another incentive. "To the pastors who have exhibited the greatest concern in this work of utmost cultural and spiritual interest, and whose schools have given the best results, they will be conceded a first-prize title . . . to go to Italy," along with their best students. The latter would participate in summer Balilla programs alongside Fascist youth.[65]

The 1934–35 academic year was the first one in which parochial schools employed Italian teachers, who were paid $15 per month and were supplied textbooks from Fascist Italy. When the year ended, Pomante congratulated pastors and language teachers on their success in "this new apostolate." "I am perfectly sure that in the new year the Italian parishes, with renewed ardor, will take up once again the work already admirably initiated and that they will further perfect these courses in Italian culture . . . with the aim of inculcating in the small Italo-Americans the knowledge of our sweet language and the consciousness of the . . . civilization of our people." The following week, Pomante dined with the pastors at the Vesuvio Restaurant on East Wacker to distribute free tickets to Italy to three prize-winning priests. In the spring of 1935, the consulate held an Italian language contest among seventh and eighth grade children from each parish. Five winners were sent to Italy for thirty days.[66]

Parochial school graduations became grand celebrations of Fascism. Typical were the June 1935 festivities at St. Anthony's. Pomante and Consul General Carosi joined Scalabrini pastor Giuseppe Chiminello, IANU president Philip D'Andrea, IANU treasurer and vice president of the Chicago Italian Chamber of Commerce Vincent Ferrara, and prominent ethnic leaders. By 1935, parochial schools offered adult evening courses. The consulate chose their teachers and supplied free propagandistic texts for those in attendance. Pomante offered talks on Fascism for these night classes. These programs funded by Fascist Italy continued until World War II. Each spring, Fascist representatives appeared at graduations, and each summer, children visited the *patria* as guests of the government.

Consuls, priests, and ethnic leaders established an annual "Evening of Italian Language" at which money was raised to finance the expanding educational programs in Chicago and its suburbs. In 1938, the event raised $4,634; in 1939, $3,246.[67]

The Cabrini Sisters boastfully designated their Doposcuola della Madonna della Grazia at Cabrini Hospital as a "solid and true forge of italianità . . . tempered in Fascist ardor." Their monthly, Le Mammole della Madre Cabrini, left little doubt about their "great affection for Italy" and described their saintly founder as the "Ambassador of Italianità throughout the world."[68] In their zeal, the Cabrini Sisters clashed with the American sisters who ran Our Lady of Pompeii school across the street from Cabrini Hospital. In 1932 the general chapter of these Franciscans of the Immaculate Conception recorded that Italian was not taught at Our Lady of Pompeii. In 1938, however, the sisters noted: "One outstanding problem that confronts us at present is the competition evinced by the Sacred Heart Sisters (Mother Cabrini). During the past they have made strenuous efforts to gain admittance into our school to teach Italian. Through the untiring efforts of our Sisters, they did not obtain their object and are carrying on their assumed work in their own institution. Recently our [Scalabrini] Pastor brought up the subject again, and by the way he spoke he seems in favor of them coming into the school in September after 3:00 P.M. if the Bishop will agree. . . . The important point on hand now is how to handle this matter."[69]

This episode of territoriality suggests the limits of consular effectiveness in the use of parochial schools as centers for Fascist propaganda. In the archdiocese of Chicago, American sisters ran all Italian parochial schools except two. Because the archdiocese had standardized the curriculum of the schools, Italian was only a special class, never the primary language of instruction. The Italian language teachers, in most cases, were not sisters in the congregation that ran the school and therefore had to be paid directly by the consulate. In addition, in 1930 only 3,746 children were enrolled in Chicago's Italian parochial schools, compared to the 11,307 in German schools and 49,517 in Polish schools.[70] This suggests that doposcuola programs and cultural institutes outside the cultural orbit of the Church were more important outlets for Fascist propaganda.

THE REALIZATION of the ideology of the Roman Question explains the cooperation between Fascist Italy and American Catholics, both English and Italian speaking. Fascist consuls negotiated American religious pluralism carefully after the Lateran Pacts increased their prestige among Catholics. The consuls appeared frequently in public ceremonies with Catholic authorities and offered Catholic organizations their authoritative interpretation of Fascist Italy. As far as Catholics were concerned, the Lateran Pacts had settled the issue of the temporal power and the status of Catholicism in Italy. Even when Catholics grew nervous about a Fascist-Nazi alignment or the anti-Semitic decrees of 1938, no Catholic ever questioned that the Lateran Pacts had definitively settled the Roman Question and the proper and privileged place of the Church in the Kingdom of Italy. Unlike many liberals in the 1930s, Catholics distinguished Fascism from Nazism. Indeed, Catholics feared that a Fascist alignment with Nazi Germany, in the event of a war, would put the Lateran Pacts at risk.

In light of the behavior of English-speaking American Catholics, it does not make sense to consider the Italian American Catholic consecration of Fascism exclusively an ethnic issue. Italian American Catholics were, to state the obvious, Catholics, and their praise for Fascism had different roots than the conservative nationalism of their non-Catholic Italian American neighbors. The interaction between consuls and immigrant clergy was admittedly more direct and frequent than cooperation between U.S. bishops and consuls. But we must not forget that American bishops had two generations of precedent for forbidding celebrations of Italian *feste*, ethnic holidays, public rituals on Church property, and the teaching of unfavorable curriculum in parish schools. There is no evidence that the bishops sought to restrict masses at which Italian American women sacrificed wedding bands on the altar of Fascist imperialism, masses to celebrate the proclamation of the Fascist Empire, or any other rituals or activities that fortified the Italian Church-state union within the United States. In fact, it seems that the Lateran Pacts had, for the first time, turned this problematic Latin nation into a people worthy of praise from other American Catholics.

Just as it had in the nineteenth century, the Vatican enforced proper boundaries of loyalty to Catholic ideology in the 1930s. As a result, two outspoken American Catholic critics of Benito Mussolini and Fascist Italy earned the wrath of the Vatican when they challenged Catholic ideology. Although they did not attack the Lateran Pacts themselves, the intensity of their hostility to Fascist Italy triggered Vatican intervention to silence these lonely and stubborn Catholic anti-Fascists, who are the subject of the next chapter.

CHAPTER NINE

Stubborn and Lonely
American Catholic Anti-Fascists

Between September of 1931 and 1938, very few American Catholics criticized Fascist Italy or Benito Mussolini. The pope and the Duce had forged the Lateran Pacts, and no Catholics publicly doubted their justice and wisdom. The pope, restored to his divinely ordained freedom, ruled happily over his "civil princedom," thanks in large measure to the Duce. Italy, a Catholic nation tied through history to the Holy See, was free to worship God in the church Christ had founded. The Vicar of Christ reigned in the Eternal City, unmolested by cultic Freemasons, sectarian liberals, or marauding revolutionaries. To many observers, criticism of Fascist Italy seemed tantamount to insulting the pope.

Fathers James Gillis and Giuseppe Ciarrocchi thought otherwise. As priest-editors whose papers boasted 10,000 and 12,000 subscriptions, respectively, neither could be ignored. Consuls tracked these troublesome anti-Fascists and gathered their subversive writings for Foreign Ministry superiors. Sadly for Gillis and Ciarrocchi, powerful forces in Fascist and papal Rome worked together against them. The Foreign Ministry alerted Secretary of State Cardinal Eugenio Pacelli, the future Pius XII (1939–58), to the activities of these sacerdotal subversives. The outcome revealed the power and limits of Italy-Vatican cooperation after the Lateran Pacts.[1]

What did Fascist and Vatican diplomats discuss behind closed doors in the Eternal City? What was the political climate in the secretariat of state under Pacelli's leadership when authorities moved to curb Gillis and Ciarrocchi? In 1936, Count Bonifacio Pignatti Morano di Custoza, Italian ambassador to the Holy See, discussed with Pacelli appointments to apostolic delegations in Iran and Syria and the Italian influence in the Near East. Pignatti also contended that the clergy among Italians in Europe and the Americas should be under stricter Fascist oversight, and he recommended the establishment of an office toward that end. Foreign Affairs Undersecretary Fulvio Suvich, soon to become the ambassador in Washington, agreed: "Missionary work abroad can be of great utility for us. We can more easily take advantage of it as a result of the climate created by the Lateran Pacts." Referring to the Church's support for the Ethiopian War, Suvich emphasized how the new "climate has had tangible results even recently."[2]

After conversations with Pacelli and the superiors of major religious congregations, Pignatti concurred. A dualistic worldview permeated the Vatican's rarified atmosphere. "The Italian episcopacy and clergy during the Ethiopian conflict" were "without a doubt [and] . . . almost without exception, praiseworthy." During "the Italo-Ethiopian conflict, the papacy found itself facing a Jewish-Masonic-Bolshevik coalition, strongly supported . . . by Anglican clergy and by Protestantism." Pignatti stressed this division—Catholics backed Fascist Italy, while Protestants joined an international, subversive, "Jewish-Masonic-Bolshevik" coalition. Only this, Pignatti insisted, "explains the favorable attitude toward Italy of Irish Catholics in North America and in many other parts of the world." Two battles, "Italians against Ethiopia, [and] Catholics against the enemies of the Roman Apostolic Church," had created international alliances. "This is the language I employ in the Holy See without anyone contradicting it," Pignatti assured Suvich. His analysis of the secretariat of state in 1936, when democracies were collapsing and dictatorships arising, suggests the lines were clearly drawn when Gillis and Ciarrocchi attacked the stalwart Latin Catholic enemy of Protestants, Jews, Masons, and Bolsheviks.[3]

James Gillis: A Pugnacious Paulist Howls in the Wilderness

Paulist priest James M. Gillis, editor of the *Catholic World*, was a vociferous critic of the Duce and Fascism in the 1930s. A social and political conservative deeply suspicious of state power, Gillis idealized a nineteenth-century America in which nature and liberty ostensibly reigned and government did not. Mussolini, however, was never a privileged target when so much was wrong with the world. Gillis's avid attacks upon secularization, birth control, academic freedom, Masonry, and materialism all competed for attention. He thundered against William Randolph Hearst, President Franklin D. Roosevelt, and most any non-Catholic author he had occasion to read. The Paulist was such an extreme voice of isolationism that Msgr. John A. Ryan urged the U.S. government to suspend the *Catholic World*'s mailing privileges. Historian David Southern comments that, in spite of Gillis's criticism of Jim Crow, "his utility for racial reform was limited" because he "was so extreme on a range of issues." Consequently, it is difficult to gauge the weight his opinion carried when it came to Fascism and Mussolini in light of the frequency of his diatribes against so broad an array of enemies. Nevertheless,

Gillis reached a significant audience. Sponsored by the National Conference of Catholic Men in 1928, Gillis authored a syndicated column in the diocesan press. In 1930, his *Catholic Hour* hit the airwaves, extending his influence to radio.[4]

Gillis's superficial, moralistic analysis took the form of caustic broadsides, sardonic observations, and intolerant outbursts. Neither his confreres nor the NCWC press service always appreciated his combative style. His Paulist superior was compelled to appoint censors for Gillis's editorials, and the NCWC intervened to mute his rancor. Justin McGrath, director of the NCWC news service, held up publication of a column in which Gillis wondered, "what becomes of boy evangelists. Perhaps they grow up to be bootleggers." McGrath reckoned, "we should [not] run the article with that objectionable statement about Protestants in it." Another column implied the Hearst newspapers had motivated President William McKinley's bloodthirsty assassin. In the 1950s, a relentlessly anticommunist Gillis embraced Senator Joseph McCarthy.[5]

Gillis's vehement critique of Italy's invasion of Ethiopia instigated Vatican intervention at the request of the Fascist government. Gillis launched his first salvo against Italian militarism at the Seventh National Eucharistic Congress in Cleveland in September 1935. The congress hosted a section devoted to journalism, where Gillis delivered an address, "The Press as an Instrument of Catholic Action." He insisted that Catholic ethical judgments must be universally applicable. "A true Catholic is not opposed to German tyranny or Italian tyranny: a true Catholic is opposed to tyranny." Gillis broadsided his journalist colleagues. "If we wait until Mussolini threatens the peace of the world with his truculent declaration, 'Geneva or no Geneva; League or no League, we are going into Ethiopia,' and only then profess to be shocked and scandalized, may not the intelligent subscriber ask 'Couldn't you see from 1922 that this man was a menace? Has he not for 13 years been violating Catholic principles of right and justice? Where was your Catholic moral theology, and your Catholic ethics all these years?'" Gillis anticipated Catholic apologias for Fascism: "And are there—can there be—in the present crisis some Catholic editors who look with equanimity or even with delight upon the Italo-Abyssinian conflict because it promises to make trouble for England?" A Catholic rebuttal to Gillis in the *Cleveland News* did not deter the cantankerous Paulist.[6]

In the October 1935 *Catholic World*, Gillis lashed out again. First, he dutifully consulted his Paulist censors and his superior, Father John Harney, who "expressed himself even more strongly than I concerning the injustice of an Italian war against Abyssinia and the high-handed attitude of Mussolini." Harney had concern "for the feelings of Father [Thomas] O'Neill [at the Paulist house in Rome], but said 'I would not care even if we were put out of Rome' on account of our advocacy for what we think to be a just cause." The editorial, "The Ambition of Mussolini," diagnosed that "Europe is reeking with infection" and "all western civilization is the sick man." Gillis foresaw that "the fate of all Europe may be determined by the outcome of a 'punitive expedition' against a tribe of fuzzy-wuzzies," the Ethiopians, who comprised "a tiny State of half-savages in a corner of Africa." He prophesied ruin for those engaged in the "folly of empire-building" and wondered why "theologians in Italy do not condemn the threatened war with Ethiopia . . . as not in accordance with the Gospels or the [Church] Fathers. If our Catholic ethics is colored by nationalism, can it still be Catholic?" Gillis predicted, "if Italy persists in disturbing the none-too-firm equilibrium of western civilization, Italy, instead of recapturing the ancient glories of the [Roman] empire, may destroy herself and all the rest of us."[7]

The pugnacious Paulist did not desist. In November he ridiculed Arthur Brisbane, a Hearst reporter, Colonel George B. McClellan, the former mayor of New York, business leaders, Italian Americans, Luigi Pirandello, Major Leon A. Fox of the United States Army Medical Corps, and Mussolini himself, all who spoke in favor of the invasion. War, Gillis argued, undermined reason. "We Catholic Americans should have the intellectual honesty to face the real issue and the courage to say what is right and what is wrong in the light of moral theology." Outlining the African events, Gillis forthrightly concluded, "the prerequisites to a just war were not observed" so "the invasion of Ethiopia is unjust." He acknowledged faults with the British Empire but insisted "England's cupidity is not an excuse for Italy's rapacity." In January 1936, the director of the NCWC news service asked Gillis to "shift to something less controversial" because his column had generated reader protests.[8]

Consequential actions against Gillis were taken in Cleveland, the site of his anti-Fascist speech at the Eucharistic Congress. His syndicated column appeared in Cleveland's *Catholic Universe Bulletin*. But in January 1936, Msgr. Joseph N. Trivisonno, the pastor of Holy Rosary Church, who was born and trained in America, protested to both the NCWC and Cleveland auxiliary bishop James McFadden. Trivisonno insisted that Gillis's "articles protesting against Fascism and Mussolini are not doing us any good as Catholics, and to Italians in general they are a stumbling block. It makes our ministry among them so much more difficult." Gillis was out of step with both the "Holy Father, [who] has never definitely expressed himself concerning the present conflict in Africa," and "the Italian hierarchy," which "has shown unanimous approval of Il Duce by contributing their pectoral crosses and episcopal rings to the cause." Trivisonno claimed Catholicism and Fascism shared an affinity. "Mussolini's enemies are the enemies of the Church. The two Roman Monsignors here during the recent Eucharistic Congress confidentially told me that English Masonry and Sovietism were attempting to even up scores against Mussolini." Trivisonno wondered, "how can a Catholic journalist attack one who has done more than any other person since the days of Charlemagne to give to the Church and the Supreme Pontiff the liberty of action so necessary for the well-being of our Catholic Faith? . . . How different from Hitler is Mussolini in recognizing the rights of the Church!" Trivisonno made his request: "I ask you then, dear Bishop, to exercise your office as head of the Editorial Board of the diocesan weekly, to exclude these articles of Father Gillis which manifest a bias and hatred of Fascism and Mussolini." McFadden complied the following day, assuring Trivisonno that "censorship will be exercised in the future on Father Gillis articles," which disappeared from the *Catholic Universe Bulletin*.[9]

Gillis was unmoved. His May 1936 editorial in the *Catholic World*, "The Shame of Italy," accused the Italian army of "Christian murder." The Fascist invasion gave "glaring evidence . . . of the cold-blooded, ruthless and incredibly cruel slaughter of the Ethiopians by the Italians. On the one side was an army equipped with a superabundance of modern instruments of mass-murder, high-powered rifles of the most recent make, tanks, planes, mines, poison gases. On the other side was a higgledy piggledy, hobble-de-hoy mob of bareheaded barefooted black men, whose military training was largely of the age of the Queen of Sheba." The carnage outraged Gillis. "If I were an Italian I should blush for my country, my *Duce* and my army."[10] Gillis vented outrage again in an 8 May radio address. Equally enraged, on 27 May, Trivisonno protested to Gillis's superior, Father Harney.

Trivisonno's blistering letter recounted Gillis's anti-Fascist activities. The Eucharistic Congress speech had been "an uncalled-for attack on Italy and Mussolini." Trivisonno proudly identified himself as the author of the effective protests to both the NCWC and Bishop McFadden. Trivisonno wondered, "is it in keeping with priestly dignity, not to say Christian charity to attack a nation, a people, a man to whom the Church owes so much? In the May issue of 'the Catholic World,' . . . [Gillis] gave expression to one of the most virulent and unjust attacks on a Catholic country that I have ever had the misfortune to read. This editorial comment has caused great dissatisfaction, distress, and anguish among Italians high and low, lay and clerical. You would be surprised to know how many letters and requests I have received from people, asking me to take up cudgels against Fr. Gillis." The incensed monsignor listed the ways "the Catholic Church is indebted to Mussolini," including "the hospitality that you and your Order [the Paulists] enjoy in Rome. Imagine the base ingratitude of which you are guilty when you attack a country that has been host, friend and protector to you during all these years that you have had the church of Santa Susanna in Rome." Trivisonno queried, "Does the reverend Father forget that the Holy Father is also an Italian, albeit a sovereign in his own right?" Finally, Trivisonno concluded with a threat. "What we want is a cessation of these insidious attacks by a Catholic priest, the only one in the United States so far as I am able to ascertain. You as the Superior of the Paulist Order ought to know what to do to redress the wrong that has been done to a noble, Catholic people. Otherwise, I intend to carry this protest as far as Rome and the Vatican, if necessary. I have friends there to whom this issue of 'The Catholic World' will be a revelation to say the least."[11]

Harney never blinked. He protected his confrere and challenged Trivisonno to take on Gillis in public rather than through mysterious Vatican connections. Harney regretted "that you and other sympathizers with Italy and the present rulers of its national life take Father Gillis's caustic comments on Mussolini's policies and dealings with Ethiopia as an attack on the Italian people and a display of hatred for them. Your inference is overdrawn. . . . It seems to me he has simply expected something better, nobler, and more magnanimous from them than from other nations in dealing with a backward, undeveloped, half-barbaric people, and is grievously disappointed to find their leaders apparently animated by the spirit of this world rather than by the principles of Catholicity." Harney urged Trivisonno to "take up the cudgels against Father Gillis" in the *Catholic World*. "To me that is not only our American way of dealing with an opponent, but more important still, it is the right way and the Catholic way. . . . We Americans, you of Italian ancestry as well as we of other national antecedents, are not subject to Mussolini. We owe him nothing more than we owe Julius Caesar or Hitler or Stalin. . . . Though we have a right, I think, to expect of him and of Italy something higher and nobler than of other countries, something more in accord with the teachings and spirit of our holy religion."[12]

Trivisonno bypassed the cudgels and instead acted upon his threat.[13] On 19 June, Father Thomas O'Neill at the Paulist house in Rome informed Harney that Cardinal Giuseppe Pizzardo, secretary of the Vatican's Sacred Congregation of Extraordinary Ecclesiastical Affairs, had dispatched an attaché of Cardinal Pacelli. The agitated attaché arrived at the Paulist house with a marked copy of the May 1936 *Catholic World*. He "protest[ed] against the immoderate language used in the magazine," specifying Gillis's editorial, and raised objections "against certain expressions in [Gillis's] speech on the radio of May 8."[14]

Unlike many clerical authorities who fawned obsequiously or apologized feverishly when Roman winds blew, Harney stood firm. He informed Gillis that the response to the Vatican would "be of the same tone and temper as my letter to Monsignor Trivisonno. I will probably tell Archbishop Pizzardo that the cause of religion will suffer more everywhere in the world from truckling to some Italian sensibilities than from open and just, though possibly severe, criticism of Italy's political leaders." Although "not anxious to antagonize ecclesiastical authorities in Rome, . . . I am ready and determined to stand up for freedom of thought and speech in all political questions, and to hold out against even ecclesiastical pressure to the contrary."[15]

American Catholic principled resistance to the Vatican was not new. But ideological deviance in regard to relations between the papacy and the Italian kingdom was extraordinary indeed. Harney's decision to defend Gillis's right to assert that the Italian nation deserved better than the Fascist state, and Harney's persistence in this stance in the face of strong disapproval from Vatican dignitaries, was exceptional. This ideological deviation, however, was not the fulcrum of an organized Catholic anti-Fascism.

Gillis may have inspired the "militant" lay managing editor of Baltimore's *Catholic Review*, Vincent de Paul Fitzpatrick, to take a strong stand against the Fascist conquest of Ethiopia. As pugnacious as the Paulist, Fitzpatrick wrote the *Baltimore Sun* on 14 August 1936 that Catholic hierarchies all over the world, including the United States, disapproved of the Ethiopian War. His anti-Fascist stance inspired a heated response from Italian Americans. Reiterating the many privileges Fascism granted the Church and the absence of any papal condemnations of the African invasion, the unidentified Italian American authors accused the "Irish-American Editor" of "racial prejudice," saying it was nothing "new to us Italo-Americans. Ever since flocks of our forefathers came to this country as immigrants, we have encountered and been made to feel such a prejudicial attitude, often involving patent neglects and violations of, nay, open opposition to, our spiritual and civil rights as members of the Catholic fold and citizens of the American community." The remainder of the long letter enumerated the evils of Ethiopian slavery and the cruelties perpetrated against Africans as well as Italians for decades preceding the war. It closed with an unlikely theory that "European Freemasonry and Nordic Catholics of America" were working "arm in arm in a campaign of unscrupulous denigration and dishonest opposition to a Catholic nation." But notwithstanding Fitzpatrick's boasts about the American hierarchy, his anti-Fascism in fact put him in a tiny minority. A brief exploration of the situation in Cleveland, where Gillis first launched his public assault, demonstrates the impotence of Catholic anti-Fascists.[16]

Bishop Joseph Schrembs of Cleveland, a known supporter of Fascist Italy, was on good terms with the Cleveland consulate in the 1930s. After Schrembs learned Fascist Italy had awarded him the Commander of the Order of the Crown in 1931, Schrembs wrote Consul Cesare Gradenigo, "it has been my constant aim to be a real father to [the Italian People], and to aid them in every way to live up to the glorious traditions of their home country." Schrembs had "a lurking suspicion" that the award was "due to [Gradenigo's] very kind initiative, and I want to express to you my sincere appreciation of this new proof of your good will."[17] In September 1935, Consul Romeo Montecchi arrived in Cleveland, where he too developed a cordial relationship, if not a friendship, with Schrembs. Montecchi arrived to spearhead the mobilization of Italian Americans during the Ethiopian War and to promote press coverage favorable to Italy's civilizing mission in Africa. Cleveland's Church cooperated.

Montecchi introduced himself to Ohio's Italians in a radio address charged with the principal themes in the propaganda campaign. "Civilization has radiated from Italy for more than two millennia." A "glorious and great nation" that has not received good press, "Italy is no longer the Italy of years ago." Italy leads civilization once again "thanks to the Fascist revolution." Montecchi boasted recent accomplishments—land reclamation projects, "the victorious battle of the grain that has given to Italians their own bread, . . . public works projects, . . . protection of mothers and children, the moral and physical education of youth, . . . insurance against tuberculosis, unemployment, and the disabled." Broadcasting these attractive images to a working-class population in the midst of the Depression, Montecchi promised, "Italy's corporate system . . . has completely resolved the old struggle between capital and labor." In a transparent reference to Italy's justification for war, the new consul insisted, "one cannot possibly think of suffocating in a restricted territory a large, growing population. Italy cannot be denied her place in the sun for her peaceful workers and children." He offered assurances. Italian Americans could be both "faithful American citizens and at the same time honor and love" Italy. Finally, "whoever comes to my office will be welcomed cordially and will receive every possible assistance. In any case, you should address your consul as a father, as an advisor interested in your welfare, your peace, and your well-being."[18]

Before his arrival in Cleveland, Montecchi had surely seen a Foreign Ministry circular that instructed consulates to impose greater discipline over their jurisdiction. Consuls henceforth tracked the activities of all ethnic organizations and reported upon their progress monthly. Montecchi's nine consular agents in Ohio and Kentucky dutifully provided lists of every Italian American patriotic, cultural, social, welfare, and religious organization. Shortly after his arrival, Montecchi visited every Italian parish or hosted their pastors in his office.[19]

During the war, Montecchi and his agents worked up a frenzy of activity, coordinating, instigating, nudging, or simply recording with delight Ohio's bacchanalia of *italianità*. Criticism of Fascist Italy triggered Mussolini supporters to bombard newspapers and politicians with counterclaims. Montecchi directed his jurisdiction's participation in a successful national campaign to pressure Congress and the Roosevelt administration to maintain U.S. neutrality. That neutrality prevented arms sales to belligerents at a time when Italy did not need them but Ethiopia did. The legislation did not prohibit companies who ignored Roosevelt's plea for a moral embargo from selling essential war items such as oil, cotton, copper, and scrap iron to Italy. In January 1936, when Roosevelt tried to modify the law so he could limit the sale of these items, Italian Americans, directed by the embassy and the consulates, flexed their political muscle. A letter-writing campaign inundated Washington with threats of electoral retaliation. Prominent Italian Americans such as Generoso Pope, the powerful Democratic owner of *Il Progresso Italo-Americano*, Justice Salvatore A. Cotillo of the New York

Supreme Court, and the Order Sons of Italy descended upon Washington to cajole administration officials and the president. The status quo was preserved and crucial goods continued to find their way to Fascist Italy.[20]

Banquets, dances, bazaars, spaghetti dinners, conferences, reunions, and religious rituals generated Italian American solidarity. Subscriptions and precious metals for the Italian Red Cross mounted. Montecchi highlighted the role of clergy and churches in the campaign. By the end of April 1936, he collected $37,490.99 and 2,160 gold wedding rings. (I have found no records of the collections made after April.) Other gold and silver articles made their way to Fascist Italy outside consular channels. For instance, a veterans association raised $2,092.83, which was sent directly to the embassy. Montecchi boasted to his superiors of Italian Americans who made pilgrimages to his office from residences distant from urban centers to sacrifice wedding bands or war medals. Priests blessed steel rings sent from Italy engraved with "Benito Mussolini" for remarriage ceremonies among couples who had sacrificed their gold bands to the *patria*. A Cincinnati monthly claimed that that city had raised $10,393.36 between 28 October 1935 and 12 June 1936. Ohio was not unique. Consular collections in New York City amounted to $741,862; the Rhode Island committee of the Italian Red Cross raised $37,132 for Fascist Italy. Philadelphia's consul general reported that the OSIA Grand Lodge collected $33,272.32 for Italy during the course of the war. In Chicago, one remarriage ceremony included 3,000 couples.[21]

On 31 March 1936, Ambassador Augusto Rosso distributed a "Prayer for the Patria" to his consulates. "The Prayer," he explained, "is now being recited throughout Italy and I am sure that the Italians in America, who demonstrate such sympathetic devotion to the *patria*, will want to unite with serene joy their prayers to those of their brothers across the Ocean who struggle in Europe and in Africa for the cause of Christian civilization." Montecchi circulated the prayer to his agents, the editor of Cleveland's *La Voce del Popolo*, and Italian pastors in his jurisdiction. Soon the prayer appeared in Italian-language papers, parish bulletins, and leaflets of benefit societies and organizations. In Cincinnati, the Scalabrini pastor of Sacred Heart Church printed and distributed thousands of copies. Msgr. Ermenegildo Allais, a professor of music and Italian at St. Gregory Seminary and a friend of Archbishop John McNicolas of Cincinnati, recited the prayer at the Solemn Easter Mass at Sacred Heart. Italian pastors throughout the jurisdiction recited the prayer at masses and parochial schools. The prayer petitioned the Lord to "bless Italy" and the king and to "sanctify the exhausting toils and generous heroism of our soldiers who combat, in the name of Rome, to fulfill their duties to spread Christian civilization."[22]

After the conquest of Ethiopia, Montecchi awarded honors to priests in his jurisdiction. On 26 May, he petitioned the Foreign Ministry to award Trivisonno the Knight of the Order of the Crown. Trivisonno, Montecchi explained, had started a parish school, became the first "Italian" monsignor in the diocese, worked with the consulate to have Italian taught in the public schools, disseminated propaganda during the Ethiopian War, and collected funds as the vice president of the Italian Red Cross in Ohio. Trivisonno also "effectively contributed to halting the anti-Italian campaign that Father James M. Gillis had initiated in the Catholic Universe Bulletin." Schrembs stood at Trivisonno's side when Montecchi decorated the popular priest before a crowd of 2,000, which included diocesan officials, Alexander De Maioribus, president of the city council, and Mayor Harold Burton. The May 1937 gala affair ended with but another rendition of "Giovinezza." By this time, most Italian parochial schools in Ohio were teaching Italian classes with textbooks, replete with propaganda, supplied from Fascist Italy. Until World War II, Montecchi was a popular speaker at churches, colleges, civic associations, settlement houses, and social clubs throughout Ohio, where he boasted the glories of Fascist Italy.[23]

Father Gillis disapproved the Catholic consecration of Fascist Italy, but no one in Bishop Schrembs's flock was listening. Schrembs, in fact, even expressed his personal desire to make a contribution to the Italian Red Cross during the Ethiopian invasion! Montecchi made certain that Schrembs received a discounted fare on a summer trip to Rome in 1936, and he instructed the captain of the vessel to show every possible courtesy to "Commander of the Crown Schrembs." During the bishop's stay in Rome, the *Cleveland Press* printed a story in which Schrembs claimed Italian workers were paid a living wage—that is, that the regime fulfilled Catholic social teachings. On 11 August, Schrembs was attacked for his remark, but "Mr. Farley," a Catholic layman, defended the bishop in a letter to the editor: "Just because he said he approved Mussolini's policy of paying Italian workers a living wage, does that make him a Fascist? . . . Isn't it just possible for even a man like Mussolini to do one right thing?" Montecchi took this opportunity to send Bishop McFadden a publication from the "National Fascist Institute of Social Insurance, . . . for whatever use you judge to make of it." McFadden believed the text was "one more impressive proof of what has won the praise of Bishop Schrembs on many occasions." Upon his return in September, Schrembs assured the press, "Italy is the only safe country in continental Europe. They enjoy a unity they never had before and the Italian people are happy." That December, Commander of the Crown Schrembs sent King Vittorio, grandson of the original transalpine usurper, a telegram: "Merry Christmas and Happy New Year."[24]

Giuseppe Ciarrocchi: On Christian and American Democracy

Historian Philip Cannistraro has reconstructed the fascinating story of the diplomatic crisis surrounding Vice Consul Giacomo Ungarelli and Italian Americans in Detroit from 1933 to 1935. Msgr. Giuseppe Ciarrocchi, pastor of Santa Maria parish, was the key figure in the anti-Fascist struggle against Ungarelli, a Black-shirt intransigent from Ferrara. Shortly after his arrival, Ungarelli "had become the subject of national debate and had caused a divisive split within the Italian-American community in Detroit." When the vice consul met opposition to his strong-arm tactics, he purged uncooperative members of the Order Sons of Italy and the Dante Alighieri Society. As President Homer Martin of the United Auto-mobile Workers testified before the U.S. House of Representatives Un-American Activities Committee (HUAC): "Prominent Detroiters, American citizens of Italian ancestry, were called in by Ungarelli to fall into line in support of the Fas-cist Government. . . . When these requests met with refusal threats of physical violence were made, and when this did not succeed, Ungarelli set into motion an economic boycott against these persons. . . . Attempts were made to compel Detroiters, American citizens, to contribute financially to organizations and ac-tivities sponsored by the Italian Government. Threats of injury to relatives and friends in Italy if resistance was offered constituted one means of persuasion em-ployed by Mussolini's puppet."[25]

An anti-Fascist coalition coalesced around Ciarrocchi. In coordination with the Detroit Labor Conference against Fascism, Methodist Rev. Vincent Castel-lucci, and Adia Battilocchi of the women's division of the Order Sons of Italy, Ciarrocchi filed complaints with the State Department. He also briefed anti-Fascists in New York City who testified before HUAC. After the U.S. government protested, Mussolini acknowledged Ungarelli's "lack of discretion" and trans-ferred the defiant vice consul to North Africa. But Ciarrocchi's anti-Fascist activi-ties did not end with this victory. Another vice consul arrived, and the struggle continued.[26]

The most thorough biographical information on Ciarrocchi comes from a re-port Ungarelli prepared and an extensive police file the Italian government kept on the outspoken monsignor.[27] Born on 6 August 1879 in Montegiorgio, Ciar-rocchi grew up in Campofilone, province of Ascoli Piceno (The Marches), and was ordained for the archdiocese of Fermo in 1902. After initial studies in Fermo, he pursued theology at the Capranica College in Rome and earned a doctorate at the Gregorian University before completing a postgraduate degree in canon law at the Appolinare University in 1905. Equipped with the best education Catho-lic Rome had to offer, Ciarrocchi was sent in 1906 to teach philosophy and the-ology at the Saints Cyril and Methodius Seminary in the diocese of Detroit. Unga-relli's report claimed Ciarrocchi clashed with the seminary director. In retrospect, the conflict is not surprising. In Italy, during his studies in Rome, Ciarrocchi had been influenced by Father Romolo Murri, a leader of Christian Democracy. Murri was also a Fermo priest and had heard socialist Antonio Labriola lecture at Rome's Sapienza University. Thereafter, Murri had sought to integrate economic and political analysis into his Christian worldview and, like Ciarrocchi after him, found it difficult to separate religious calling from political action. Murri was suspended from his priestly duties in 1907 and excommunicated two years later for his modernist leanings. Ciarrocchi shared Murri's commitments and, like Murri, found his Christian Democratic ideas a source of trouble during the modernist crisis.

Dismissed from his teaching post in Detroit, Ciarrocchi, a young immigrant priest, found himself like many other qualified Italian clergy in the United States: without post and income, vulnerable to expulsion, marked as a potentially untrustworthy clerical wanderer. In addition, he was theologically suspect. Luckily, Father Francesco Beccherini of St. Francis Church in Detroit took him in. To make his way, Ciarrocchi freelanced, so to speak, at a variety of German, Polish, and Irish congregations before he organized Italians into Santa Maria parish in 1919 and directed the construction of both a church and a parochial school. In 1921, Liberal Italy awarded Ciarrocchi the Knight of the Crown for his support of the Italian Red Cross during the Great War. In 1924, at the recommendation of Bishop Michael Gallagher of Detroit, Pius XI made Ciarrocchi a domestic prelate.

Ciarrocchi had become a U.S. citizen and was incardinated into the Detroit diocese. Consequently, when Fascist Italy sought to undermine him, it could not simply coerce or direct his Fermo bishop to recall him. Instead, to reach Ciarrocchi, the Fascist government had to work through Detroit's bishop and the Vatican. Ungarelli described Ciarrocchi as "ambitious, intelligent, cultured, and egotistical." An intellectual forced into demanding pastoral work, Ciarrocchi published his Detroit weekly *La Voce del Popolo* (not to be confused with the Cleveland newspaper of the same name) from 1910 until his death in 1954. In comparison to other Italian American Catholic publications, the longevity and quality of *La Voce* was a remarkable accomplishment. According to Ungarelli, "during the period of Don [Luigi] Sturzo [(1919–24), Ciarrocchi] was one of the most ruthless extremists . . . taking a demagogic attitude against the regime." This indicates Ciarrocchi made his anti-Fascism known during the early years of the regime. In 1931, the Ministry of the Interior banned *La Voce* from Italy, and in 1935, the regime stripped Ciarrocchi of his knighthood. Postwar American Catholic references to Ciarrocchi's anti-Fascism self-servingly applaud his activism and ignore the determination of American and Vatican ecclesiastical superiors to stifle him.[28]

Ciarrocchi's this-worldly, politically engaged spirituality was grounded in an abiding faith that American democracy was a worthwhile approximation of a normative Catholic order. Extant versions of *La Voce* indicate a deep commitment to a democracy that, in contrast to papal formulations of "Christian Democracy," not only invited participation in movements with clerical leaders but gave lay people and workers power. *La Voce* vigilantly tracked and commented upon Detroit's civil and political affairs. There is no evidence that *La Voce* ever fell under ecclesiastical censorship until its editor's outspoken anti-Fascism during the Ungarelli affair brought complaints from Fascist Italy to Catholic authorities, although it had been banned from Italy in 1931. Ciarrocchi informed Bishop Gallagher, "I have been always in good terms personally, with all [Ungarelli's] predecessors, and when the last one left, I praised his ways of a gentleman, although I did not agree with his worship of Mussolini." Ciarrocchi's anti-Fascism of the 1920s, it seems, never had serious repercussions.[29]

Ungarelli's effort to coerce Italian American voluntary associations met resistance and alerted Ciarrocchi to the danger the vice consul posed. Ungarelli met with Methodist minister Castellucci in April 1934. Cannistraro recounts how Ungarelli offered Castellucci funds to publish a pro-Fascist newspaper and urged Castellucci to boycott the Italian Publishing Company, which owned *La Voce*. Ungarelli forced the dismissal of anti-Fascist language teachers at Castellucci's Italian school at the public library and supplied the school's new texts with Fascist propaganda from Rome. These tactics were not unique to Detroit by any means and rarely met active resistance from clergy, Protestant or Catholic. But in Detroit, while Father Beccherini of the Scalabrinians and the Italian Sylvestrians cooperated with Ungarelli, Castellucci and Ciarrocchi resisted. Castellucci wrote Ciarrocchi a supportive letter of "admiration and praise." "Although working in different camps but for the same ideals," Castellucci applauded "the sane qualities of a man of great character and an apostle of the good who 'fights the good fight'" against the "enemies of democracy and religion." This unique Italian Protestant-Catholic friendship, forged with representatives of organized labor and aligned against the Italian Catholic priests in the diocese, may very well have struck Ciarrocchi's superiors in Detroit and Rome as inappropriate.[30]

Ciarrocchi launched a typical attack on Ungarelli in *La Voce* in September 1934. "Watch vigilantly if you wish to conserve your liberties," he cautioned. "Civil, social, political liberty which we enjoy in America is a gift of God that the heroes of this land conquered for us with their blood. But it is a gift that can be snatched from our hands when we least expect it." Ciarrocchi specified the danger. "Those who know us well know we are alluding to neither the NRA [National Recovery Act] nor to President Roosevelt. For us the politics of the President are not only not an attack on the rights of liberty, but rather they constitute the most strenuous defense against the danger and the invasion of destructive elements." His warning went out to the "Italian colonies in America [that] are becoming enslaved."[31]

Ungarelli protested to Bishop Gallagher that "Mons. Ciarrocchi is taking advantage of his position of influence." The self-righteous monsignor obstructed "the uplifting and unity of the Italian people" and "efforts to give to the Italian Community Pride and Self-conscience [sic]."[32] Gallagher sent Ungarelli's protest to Ciarrocchi and sought clarification. In response, Ciarrocchi welcomed the opportunity to educate his bishop about Italian affairs.

Ciarrocchi contended that Ungarelli "has tried to put his nose into my school and church." "When I had my usual Festa last summer, [Ungarelli] got together with Fr. Beccherini and the Sylvestrian Fathers to try to scatter away the Italian people as much as they could. He had a picnic of his own Fascist organization (The [Italian War] Veterans), and Fr. Beccherini had a picnic for his church, and the Sylvestrian Fathers had a picnic at the Holy Family parish—all the same day! A blind person could see the common purpose." Ciarrocchi insisted that Ungarelli had promoted a boycott of La Voce and its printing office. The vice consul paid businesses to seek other forums in which to advertise and encouraged Ciarrocchi's employees to quit by tendering offers of other jobs. The indignant monsignor provided Gallagher with articles from L'Avvenire Italiano, another Detroit newspaper that attacked Ungarelli. L'Avvenire had exposed a "secret agreement binding together a few Italian societies and institutions of Detroit (including the Sylvestrian Fathers), for a common action toward enforcing Mussolini's ideas in the Italian colony." Ungarelli's claim "that he works here in Detroit to uplift the Italian colony, is a lie. He is here to make everything and everybody fascist, and nothing else." Ciarrocchi insisted, "the Italian colony is in a turmoil, just on account of [Ungarelli's] crazy ways. . . . The Columbus Day celebration which in the past years brought together fifty or sixty Italian Societies, this year had only 15 of them." Ungarelli aggressively promoted "the fantastic idea of [the construction of] a royal 'Casa Italiana,'" which would undermine the payment of parish debts throughout the city. Ciarrocchi got personal. Ungarelli "does not show any faith and does not practice any religion." He was "known for his drinking and his women companions . . . [and there have been] many scandalous stories . . . about his private life."[33]

Gallagher's cautious response to Ungarelli was curious. The bishop informed the vice consul, "the whole affair is a fight in the Italian Colony of Detroit which consists of different factions, and it behooves us to steer clear of the trouble." In fact, this was not merely an isolated ethnic affair. Italian ambassador Augusto Rosso had already visited Apostolic Delegate Amleto Giovanni Cicognani in February 1934 to discuss the "anti-Italian and anti-Fascist character of" La Voce. In Ciarrocchi's "violent" opposition to Fascist Italy, La Voce "very often echoes the invented or intentionally distorted news of those notoriously subversive anti-Fascist newspapers of Paris." Rosso informed his superiors that Cicognani, "sharing fully my judgement and my observations toward the attitude of Ciarrocchi, assured me that he would do everything in his power to bring this Italian priest to a better sense of moderation." Cicognani had called Ciarrocchi to Washington, but the stubborn priest continued "his nefarious campaign of malice and partisanship." Cicognani's intervention with Gallagher had brought no satisfaction. Rosso lamented that the immigrant priest had incardinated into the diocese of Detroit and thus made direct Vatican or Fascist intervention difficult. In addition,

Ciarrocchi had shrewdly linked his anti-Fascism to a "defense of 'Americanism'" and portrayed himself as a "champion of freedom of the Church against foreign interference." This made it difficult for Cicognani "to pronounce an open condemnation" of La Voce.[34]

But Rosso had a plan, one that took for granted Cardinal Pacelli's support for Fascist Italy against Ciarrocchi once the secretary of state had a pretext to intervene. Rosso's scheme was to provoke Ciarrocchi into an aggressive polemic with Detroit's pro-Fascist La Tribuna Italiana d'America. Rosso noticed that when La Voce had sparred with this rival before, Ciarrocchi "became most bitter and completely flew off the handle." If it happened again, his "profession of anti-Fascism" and "attitude of rebellion . . . could then work to our advantage." Rosso reasoned that since Ciarrocchi was a domestic prelate—awarded papal honors—Pacelli could be instigated to suppress La Voce if it became too divisive. To alert the Vatican to the regime's displeasure, Rosso urged his superiors to revoke Ciarrocchi's Knight of the Crown, awarded in 1921.[35]

Ciarrocchi's Vision

Ciarrocchi's abiding commitment to Christian Democracy shaped his critique of Fascism and his understanding of Italian Americans. Extant fragments of La Voce are not an ideal source from which to construct an intellectual biography, but in them an Italian priest and American citizen articulated his Catholic vision in the heat of a battle with an integral Fascist cultural program. Although unknown to historians of religion, Ciarrocchi was the most consistent voice of a religiously grounded American anti-Fascism.

Ciarrocchi endowed Italy and Italians with a higher mission. "We appeal to centuries of Latin civilization as our contribution to American civilization; centuries of brilliant ancient and modern history, beginning with the Rome of Romolo and Remo down to the Risorgimento and ending with the Italy of Vittorio Veneto; enviable traditions of purely Italian literature, art, and science that are luminous beacons throughout the history of human progress." An ardent neo-guelf, Ciarrocchi did not end here. "Last but not least, we carry twenty centuries of Christian history; of Christianity that had its origin and its martyrs in Rome, and in Rome established a Church that sent the spiritual light to every corner of the known world, and because of this is called the Roman Catholic Church." Ciarrocchi insisted that Fascist Italy was an illegitimate home for the Catholic nation and that Fascism obstructed Italian Americans from their ethical duty to contribute the gifts of Latin culture to America. "It is the duty of Italian colonies here settled to make the best traditions of our patria of origin known. But to accomplish this we neither need nor want to appeal to Italy today under the Fascist regime." As a Latin people, Italian Americans had a mission to inculcate

Catholicism "as our contribution to the edifice of the American social system." Ciarrocchi answered his Fascist critiques. Are we, he asked, "Renegades of our *patria*? Never. Are we renegades of the medieval government that today dominates Italy? Yes."[36]

Ciarrocchi's use of "medieval" as a metaphor for authoritarianism indicates how his neoguelfism deviated from Catholic ideology after the Lateran Pacts. Furthermore, it demonstrates that his understanding of Christian Democracy was not a form of restorationism, which was common among Catholics who idealized medieval guilds and social hierarchies. According to Ciarrocchi, the Italian nation progressed providentially within the liberal state, which culminated in the military and spiritual victory of Vittorio Veneto in November 1918. Then Fascism appeared, "a black parenthesis in the history of Italian progress," a "transitory period of Italian political decadence." Students of modern Italy recognize in Ciarrocchi's reading of Fascism, as a "parenthesis" in Italian progress, an anticipation of the philosopher Benedetto Croce's liberal argument. But Ciarrocchi's affinities rested closer to Luigi Sturzo, the most famous voice of Christian Democracy, whose *Italy and Fascismo* (1926) described "the irremediable contradiction between the character and aims of Fascism and the natural and historical mission of the Kingdom of Italy." For Sturzo, as for Ciarrocchi, Fascism was "an abnormal phenomenon."[37]

Ciarrocchi acknowledged his solidarity with Sturzo. His reconstruction of Italian history replicated the exile's reading of the postwar years. The Italian "democratic political movement with authentic spiritual origins," embodied in the Partito Popolare Italiano (PPI) under Sturzo, was "an application of the principles of social justice taught by the Gospel and inculcated by modern Popes." The PPI, not the Partito Nazionale Fascista (PNF), waged the decisive battle against socialism, because it operated within the law. But "the Popular Party was not a party to illegal private violence. Thus, when it became the target of combat with the cudgel, only two camps remained: that of the reds and that of the blacks." At this crucial moment, the Italian government failed to use its authority to protect the constitution.[38]

Ciarrocchi's interpretation of the ascension of Fascism ignored the role of the Holy See in the dissolution of the PPI. His apologia rang hollow when he explained how Pius XI never called Mussolini a "man of Providence." "The Pope simply said that in order to complete the concordat it HAD BEEN PROVIDENTIAL that he had had to deal with a man who was not a slave to the vices and exaggerated concepts of liberty." When he discussed the papacy, Ciarrocchi highlighted "Non abbiamo bisogno," an unequivocal expression of anti-Fascism.[39]

"Our creed," Ciarrocchi proposed, included "a democratic form of government, . . . elected by the people for the benefit of all the people"; freedom of thought, speech, the press, and association; personal security; and "the equality of citizens before the law." Fascism, however, was a "dictatorial government, elected arbitrarily against the will of the majority." In "Italy today there is no freedom of speech, the press, association or vote. There is, though, we must admit, still the freedom to shout 'long live Fascism.' In Fascist Italy personal security is a myth. Citizens are arrested with no knowledge of the accusations, and sent into *confino*. The rights of citizens belong only to those who are members of the Fascist Party."[40]

To Catholic and Fascist authorities, Ciarrocchi sounded too much like the radical democratic and socialist exiles whom he cited in *La Voce*. In 1934 Ciarrocchi quoted Mussolini in the early months of 1922, before the March on Rome, when the future Duce wrote that the Bolsheviks no longer posed a threat of revolution. This, of course, undermined Fascist propaganda claims that the Blackshirts had saved Italy from communism. "Whoever does not believe this citation," Ciarrocchi asserted, "may find it with pleasure in *The Origins of Fascism* by Saudino." Domenico Saudino of the National Council of the Italian Socialist Federation in the United States was an anti-Fascist activist and anticlerical.[41]

Ciarrocchi reiterated arguments formulated by other anti-Fascist authors. During the height of Mussolini's American popularity in 1934, Ciarrocchi interpreted the Duce's bellicose rhetoric as a means to distract attention away from the regime's "disastrous financial conditions." War would then provide an excuse for the Duce to confiscate private property and for the state to absorb all industry. Ciarrocchi's claim that the Duce employed foreign policy statements to distract attention from domestic weakness came right out of Gaetano Salvemini's *Mussolini Diplomatico* (1932). Salvemini, an Italian historian, radical democrat, and *fuoruscito*, had just begun his tenure as a professor at Harvard University. Like other anti-Fascists, Ciarrocchi interpreted the regime's condemnation of Cesare Rossi as further evidence of Mussolini's complicity in the murder of socialist deputy Giacomo Matteotti in 1924. Ciarrocchi, however, distinguished himself from the anti-Fascist left when he scorned class conflict in favor of "the principles of the Gospel of social justice" that taught "the duties of one class to another."[42]

La Voce forcefully contended Fascism was an exaggerated, noxious, party nationalism, not authentic patriotism, and consequently it disrupted Italian American communities. Detroit Italians, he claimed, had attained true civic unity during the second decade of the twentieth century under his leadership. He recalled the 1910 establishment of *La Voce* and the coalition of Italian American societies culminating in the inauguration of a monument to Christopher Columbus. *La Voce* supported the *patria* during the Libyan War (1912) and the Great War and fought against Black Hand violence. But Fascism intruded and undermined this unity. In Ciarrocchi's view, Liberal Italy had honored worthy men like Fiorello La Guardia and Ciarrocchi himself with the Knight of the Crown. In contrast, Fascist Italy honored criminals, gangsters, and "a bankrupt swindler and bloodsucker of

Italian workers from Pennsylvania," a thinly disguised allusion to Giovanni Di Silvestro, the powerful philo-Fascist supreme venerable of the Order Sons of Italy in America.[43]

Ciarrocchi argued that Ungarelli, in his effort "to make everything and everyone Fascist," brought discord to the Sons of Italy, the Dante Alighieri Society, Italian-language schools, and the Columbus festivals in Detroit. Fascism dangerously isolated Italians from the larger society. "The 'Little Italies' may have been a necessity to gather together our co-nationals, but they certainly did not constitute an ideal." Glory would come with contributions to "the adopted *patria*." Italian American unity had to be grounded in common American experiences.[44]

His polemic with *La Tribuna Italiana d'America* compelled Ciarrocchi to defend himself. In so doing, *La Voce* exaggerated the unity among Detroit Italians before the rise of Fascism. In the heat of battle, he opened *La Voce* to readers whose letters to the editor disparaged the patriotism of Fascism. He also attacked his enemy's social base when he reprinted anti-Fascist letters from Italian war veterans. "We did not fight for Fascism but for our *patria* Italy, namely the Italy of Garibaldi and Mazzini." These anonymous authors spoke of their fears that the Fascist regime would harm their families in Italy if they revealed their names.[45]

Vatican Intervention

The polemic between *La Voce* and *La Tribuna* had two noteworthy results. It publicized Fascist activities, which compelled HUAC to expedite its investigation that led to Ungarelli's transfer. But it also played into Ambassador Rosso's plan to trigger Vatican intervention. The Foreign Ministry alerted Cesare Maria De Vecchi di Val Cismon, Italy's ambassador to the Holy See, to Ciarrocchi's anti-Fascist campaign. De Vecchi made the Detroit situation known to Cardinal Pacelli. In addition, the Foreign Ministry called for the revocation of the monsignor's Knight of the Crown "in a way that will most effectively call the attention of Secretary of State [Pacelli] to the activities of Ciarrocchi." Ten days later, Apostolic Delegate Cicognani penned an incensed letter to Bishop Gallagher explaining that Ciarrocchi's activities had "been called to the attention of the Holy See."[46]

Cicognani did not hide his anger. "What was begun as a political debate, in which a priest should never have taken part, has developed into a vulgar controversy." He found it "most unbecoming for any priest, not to say a pastor, one honored by the Holy See, . . . to engage in a controversy which cannot but bring discredit upon the priesthood." Cicognani commanded Gallagher to silence Ciarrocchi without implicating the Vatican in the matter. "It is now Your Excellency's duty, *acting entirely on your own authority*, to put an end to this controversy. . . . He should be ordered to end the present controversy immediately and absolutely, and he should be forbidden to engage in any further debate or controversy." Cicognani voiced frustration that Gallagher had not admonished Ciarrocchi sooner. Now, with Pacelli looming ominously, Cicognani threatened Gallagher. "Inquiries about the activities of Monsignor Ciarrocchi . . . may prove embarrassing not only to Monsignor Ciarrocchi, but to Your Excellency as well."[47]

Ciarrocchi equivocated in his response to Gallagher's request to cease with the polemic. While the priest considered it "a great sacrifice" to desist, he agreed to communicate through *La Voce* on 18 January "that any personal controversy is ended." He explained to his bishop that *La Tribuna* and its supporters "were just waiting for an interference of the Ecclesiastical Authority, which would come to their rescue." But the battle was not over. "Anyhow," a stubborn Ciarrocchi closed his letter, "I thank Your Lordship that your order refers only to the personal controversy, and does not affect the general policy of my newspaper, according to which, besides teaching Religion, I have always tried to teach the true American spirit to my people, as it is my duty as a citizen of the U.S."[48]

The controversy took a new turn when Ungarelli visited Gallagher with a copy of *Stampa Libera,* "a subversive newspaper, published in New York." Its headline screamed: "In Detroit Fascism Appeals to Ecclesiastical Authorities to Gag Rev. Ciarrocchi." *Stampa Libera* described how Fascist authorities in Rome had pressured Cicognani and Gallagher to muzzle the monsignor. In a letter to Gallagher, Ungarelli insisted that *Stampa Libera* "could not have been published without some direct information from some one who could have known of this, and the source could have been none other than Mons. Ciarrocchi himself." On the same day, 6 February 1935, Gallagher wrote Cicognani to explain that his intervention with Ciarrocchi had "succeeded to a great extent." "Ciarrocchi has promised to keep personalities out of his paper." But Gallagher admitted, "as far as the issues are concerned, that is another question. The deep-rooted antagonism between the Catholic 'Voce' and the non-Catholic 'Tribuna' dates back almost thirty years. Therefore, it is quite impossible to bring about perfect peace between these two papers." Gallagher asked permission to visit in order to explain "all the different ramifications fully."[49]

Cicognani instructed the bishop to remain in Detroit and to "put an end to the political controversies of Monsignor Ciarrocchi." Cicognani could not contain his anger. "The main purpose of my letter was to ask Your Excellency to instruct Monsignor Ciarrocchi, on your own authority, as his Ordinary [bishop], to abstain from further political controversy. . . . It is regrettable that a priest should misuse talents that might be employed to advantage in the service of God." Cicognani informed Gallagher that he had summoned Ciarrocchi to the delegation a year ago to point out "the inadvisability of his present course. I thought that a desire expressed by the representative of the Holy Father would be regarded as a command by any priest who has the proper attitude toward ecclesiastical authority. I was sadly mistaken."[50]

In the next issue of *La Voce*, Ciarrocchi hammered away at the Duce. He analyzed the mobilization of Fascist military forces for the coming conflict between Italy and Ethiopia, reported on HUAC's progress, and refuted Ambassador Rosso's claim that Fascist propaganda in the United States was merely educational.[51]

The Ethiopian War brought Ciarrocchi into closer contact with radical anti-Fascists and led him to criticize the hierarchy. Throughout the war Ciarrocchi insisted nationalism was an affront to Christian morality. Bravely, particularly in light of the fact that he derived his sustenance from Italian Americans, Ciarrocchi proclaimed that Fascist Italy was a bellicose aggressor in Africa and that the League of Nations sanctions against Italy were entirely just. He permitted anti-Fascists, such as Giuseppe Borgese, to publish in *La Voce*, and claimed that the archbishop of Milan, Cardinal Ildefonso Schuster, "had given a bad impression to the Catholic world" when he spoke out in favor of the war. Ciarrocchi speculated that "the good Card. Schuster is anxious to demonstrate that he is more Italian then the Italians in spite of his origins and German name."[52]

Finally, Ciarrocchi indirectly attacked Gallagher. After a two-hour conversation with Vice Consul Belcredi, Gallagher tried to impose a silence upon Ciarrocchi regarding the Ethiopian War. After the Italian conquest of Ethiopia, Gallagher gave, in the words of Detroit's vice consul, "a magnificent speech at the Italian church" at a service in May 1936 commemorating the Fascist military victory. In the speech Gallagher criticized the magazine *At Home and Abroad* for attacking Italy's African enterprise. In an editorial following the commemoration Ciarrocchi made an indirect reference to his bishop's speech when the monsignor asked, "What kind of propaganda is the one which makes people believe such a ridiculous hoax like the one that Selassie [the Ethiopian ruler] had 6,000 children and women slain because their husbands went over to the Italians?"[53]

After the Ethiopian War, the Ministry of the Interior began to compile information from its prefects on Ciarrocchi's four siblings in Italy, but it found nothing that could be used against the stubborn priest. In July 1936 Fascist Italy by royal decree stripped Ciarrocchi of his knighthood. "It does not concern me," he explained. "I am an American citizen. . . [My] activities, based on the principles of Christianity and American democracy, . . . shall continue in the future to the best of my ability." Detroit anti-Fascist Michele Valente, on the occasion of the revocation of the title from Ciarrocchi, published a letter congratulating the lone anti-Fascist priest.[54]

On 9 June 1937, *fuorusciti* Carlo and Nello Rosselli were murdered in France. *La Voce*'s coverage of the event, as the Fascist government hoped, finally triggered Cardinal Pacelli's intervention. The Rosselli brothers had been dangerous enemies of the regime. Carlo had been an active anti-Fascist within Italy before he escaped from a Fascist prison to Paris, where he organized *fuorusciti* around the

Giustizia e Libertà movement, plotted to assassinate the Duce, and commanded Italian radicals who battled Fascist forces in the Spanish Civil War. Ciarrocchi's 18 June editorial, "Another Historic Political Crime," linked the murders to Mussolini, a claim later proven true. Upon its publication, Rosso addressed superiors in Rome who, on 13 August, urged the Italian ambassador to the Holy See to discuss the matter with Pacelli. On 6 September 1937, Pacelli wrote Cicognani a pointed letter threatening Ciarrocchi.[55]

Pacelli outlined "serious complaints surrounding [Ciarrocchi's] persistent and pungent anti-Fascist campaign." He insisted, "it no longer seems possible to postpone an energetic intervention of ecclesiastical authority. It is, in fact, unbecoming for a priest, decorated moreover with pontifical honors, to occupy himself almost exclusively with politics in a way, both passionate and spiteful, that makes one doubt his good faith; that he, destined for a vocation as a minister of peace, foments with his journalistic campaign divisions and hatreds." *La Voce* lacked "that self-restraint that is right and proper for a Catholic newspaper." Pacelli was troubled that *La Voce* was "too well-disposed toward Masonry" and did not exhibit "that serene spiritual inspiration that one would expect in a Catholic newspaper"—an odd comment in light of the violent rhetoric of *Civiltà Cattolica*, *L'Osservatore Romano*, and U.S. Catholic papers on behalf of the Vatican for three generations. Pacelli commanded Cicognani to act "with that tact and prudence that distinguishes you, but also with serene firmness, in a manner that you believe most opportune, to make the said Monsignor understand that his persistence in an attitude thus blameworthy is no longer tolerable, and therefore it must not surprise him if, in case he relapses, he will see his name canceled from the *Annuario Pontificio*."[56] This last reference was a threat to withdraw Ciarrocchi's papal honors.

On 21 September 1937, Cicognani sent Pacelli's letter to Archbishop Edward Mooney of Detroit, Gallagher's successor. Mooney had already spoken to the editor-priest in August and employed a censor for *La Voce*. Mooney believed that "following this interview, there was a notable improvement in [*La Voce*]." The archbishop, however, spoke with Ciarrocchi again, "to impress upon him the seriousness of the situation. I do not flatter myself with the thought that I deeply influenced his personal conviction about the world and the Church, but I am inclined to think that I inspired him with a salutary sense of fear. . . . He clearly understands that . . . he is on trial. . . . I shoudl [sic] perhaps add the expression of my own conviction that, if failure comes, it will be due to lack of judgment rather than to lack of good will." Cicognani informed Pacelli, who, in turn, summarized the correspondence for the Italian ambassador to the Holy See.[57]

Although I have not discovered evidence of further Vatican intervention, Ciarrocchi's principles led him into new battles that instigated ecclesiastical censure from the archdiocese of Detroit. On 28 January 1939, Chicago's *Daily Record* ran

"'Lift Embargo'—Catholic Priest." It cited *La Voce*'s condemnation of the U.S. embargo on Spain: "It is a fact that the whole world admires the heroic resistance of the Republicans of Catalonia, [who] are opposing this triple fascism [of Italy, Germany, and Portugal], determined to die rather than surrender. It is an example of heroism that will remain in history." Against U.S. policy makers who insisted the embargo evinced neutrality, Ciarrocchi argued the embargo favored Franco against the legitimate republican government. The stalwart priest-editor also took European democracies to task. "No one . . . openly hazards to make . . . purchases on a large scale for Republican Spain, because the democratic nations are afraid to disturb the 'European peace,' at least as long as their own skins are not touched."[58]

Archdiocesan chancellor Father Edward Hickey lashed out at Ciarrocchi. Praise from "the pro-communist Daily Record in Chicago" was tantamount to betrayal of the Church. "At a critical time when pro-communist rallies were staged in Washington to influence Congress and the President to lift the embargo, when the National Council of Catholic Men organized a movement to petition Congress to keep the Spanish embargo and to maintain neutrality, when the Chancellor of the Archdiocese, . . . organized the gathering of petitions to keep the Spanish embargo, it seems to me a very imprudent thing for the editor of La Voce del Popolo to give aid and comfort to the enemy. It is no wonder the Daily Record flaunts your article." Stubborn and lonely, Ciarrocchi replied, "I am sorry for having caused trouble. But I am sorry too that I can not retract what I have said in the matter, as I would be a hypocrite and betray principles of Justice as I see them."[59]

On 14 October 1940, just eleven days after anti-Fascist priest Luigi Sturzo arrived in New York, he wrote Ciarrocchi. "It would be my pleasure to enter into correspondence with you and to learn about your newspaper." With little money and in poor health, Sturzo had reluctantly abandoned his apartment in a London quarter that had been bombed by the Germans. He received an immediate reply from Ciarrocchi. "You have well earned the respect and admiration of those who still believe still in truth and in justice, if not in Christianity." Sturzo corresponded frequently over the next six years with the ideologically heterogeneous leaders of the Italian anti-Fascist community in New York. But in Ciarrocchi Sturzo found a kindred spirit.[60]

Sturzo offered Ciarrocchi an outlet for his reflections. "I am inspired by the nobility of [your] feelings and faith. It is so rare to find priests who understand," Ciarrocchi wrote. "We find ourselves [today] at the same point as the Jewish church in the time of Christ. I respect the Pope who certainly is no Caiaphas [the high priest at the time of the trial of Jesus]; but I do not believe that the others in general are any better than the priests of the old law." Sturzo's love of American political liberty sat uncomfortably next to his deep disillusionment with the Fascist leanings of the American Church, and in particular with the Italian American clergy. Ciarrocchi helped interpret America to Sturzo. "Caro Don Luigi, you ask me how our [Italian] priests who live in this earthly paradise of liberty can participate in Fascism." Ciarrocchi explained how priests from Italy catered to the worst elements of their community. In addition, their only model of success was the Irish priest who hates England. After comparing "the generosity and regularity of Irish Catholics with the . . . inconsistency of our Italians, [the Italian priest] comes to the conclusion that our people must be governed" by a dictator. Sadly, Ciarrocchi continued, "I have found no Italian priest who has a clear concept or a sincere love of democracy and liberty. Not equality, but privilege is what they want."[61]

Upon his arrival, Sturzo received a letter from George La Piana, another Sicilian priest who left Italy in 1913 during the modernist crisis. Now a church historian at Harvard University who moved in liberal and radical anti-Fascist circles, La Piana sent Sturzo fifty dollars and acknowledged his deep respect for the famous exiled leader of the PPI. Sturzo struggled during his American sojourn with the fact that he often shared common goals for Italian reconstruction with men like La Piana and Gaetano Salvemini, who were stern critics of the Church. Conversely, Sturzo saw American Catholic leaders, supporters of Fascism for two decades, backing Fascist collaborators, particularly the monarchy, during the reconstruction. Ciarrocchi understood this dilemma. "Dear Don Luigi, how should we carry ourselves in the face of these antifascist movements that today are taking shape in America? I am always in agreement with the ideas expounded in 'Parola' of New York, or in 'Mondo' [two secular, left-wing anti-Fascist papers]. But on the other hand I see that there is an anticlericalism that seems anti-Catholic." Ultimately, the Vatican prevented Sturzo's return to Italy from America for one full year in 1945 in order to weaken his influence on Italians who prepared for a plebiscite to chose whether to live under a monarchy or in a republic. Notwithstanding Vatican machinations, Italy became a republic after the war.[62]

AS THE REACTIONS to Fathers Gillis and Ciarrocchi demonstrated, the Holy See and the Kingdom of Italy, once mortal enemies, worked together in the 1930s. Fascist Italy and the Vatican City were friendly states whose diplomatic relationship enhanced their communication networks and their capacity to monitor deviance. After the realization of the ideology of the Roman Question in the Lateran Pacts, the Vatican simply did not tolerate Catholic frontal assaults on Fascist Italy. Surely Father Charles Coughlin generated more publicity, upset (and inspired) more Americans, and displayed, to put it generously, less charity, than Father Ciarrocchi. But neither Cardinal Pacelli nor Detroit's bishops ever cracked down on Coughlin—even after he viciously attacked Jews and President Roosevelt—in the manner that the cardinal–secretary of state disciplined Ciarrocchi. This tells us a great deal about priorities within the Vatican and within the American Church during the 1930s.[63]

Although admired by an Italian Methodist minister, Ciarrocchi appeared to have no Catholic friends among the clergy and hierarchy. It is difficult to know how deep his following ran among Italian American Catholics. Gillis received noteworthy support from his superior. Father Harney realized the pugnacious editor's mode of expression was not delicate, but he still backed Gillis's right to speak out and supported Gillis's position. But a Catholic anti-Fascist coalition never crystallized around Gillis. Among liberal Catholics, such as Father John A. Ryan, who tentatively began to express their reservations about Mussolini during and immediately after the Ethiopian War, Gillis was a problem, not a comrade. His isolationism and anti–New Deal rancor earned him few collaborators among anti-Fascists.

The image of discipline and solidarity was important to Fascist Italy and the Holy See. Consequently, the Italian diaspora merited close attention. If stubborn anti-Fascists damaged the image of Catholic solidarity, Italian American parish conflicts embarrassed bishops and consuls in charge of maintaining order in their dominions. In the next chapter, we take up two parish conflicts. The dynamics of Italian American Catholic life had always been transnational, engaging institutions and interests in both the United States and Italy. After the realization of the ideology of the Roman Question in the Lateran Pacts of 1929, however, cooperation between the Church and Fascist Italy to bring discipline and order to these troublesome American Catholics reached new heights.

CHAPTER TEN

Parish Conflicts

The Church and Fascist Italy Manage
"All Spirit of Rebellion"

In September 1936, in defiance of the police and Bishop Francis Patrick Keough of Providence, angry Italian Americans seized Sacred Heart Church in Natick, Rhode Island. They bolted the doors and windows from the inside, threatened their new pastor with bodily harm if he attempted to enter, and demanded the immediate return of their previous pastor, an Italian Sacred Heart missionary. On 18 February 1940, recalcitrant parishioners at Holy Redeemer Church in Cleveland clashed with diocesan authorities and the police in their second successful effort to forestall the installation of a new pastor chosen from the Fathers of Our Lady of Mercy. They, too, stormed the church and took it by force. Beleaguered and scandalized by the embarrassing display of disobedience, Archbishop Joseph Schrembs of Cleveland placed Holy Redeemer under personal and local interdict.[1]

The resolution of these two explosive episodes of mass protest reveal how Fascist Italy, the Vatican, and American bishops cooperated to create and preserve an image of unity, order, and discipline within the Italian diaspora. This was no small task. In the 1920s and 1930s, the American public associated Italians Americans with violence, criminality, and irreligion or superstitious fanaticism. The Fascist regime in league with Italian American organizations mounted antidefamation campaigns against Hollywood producers of films with pernicious representations of Italians or Italian Americans, such as *Scarface* and *A Farewell to Arms*. Although the consulates, the apostolic delegation, and the U.S. hierarchy had always wanted, for their own reasons, positive images of Italians, the Church and the Italian state had never worked in concert before the realization of the ideology of the Roman Question in the Lateran Pacts of 1929.

Fascist Italy and American bishops had their own images to consider as well. Consuls labored under directives from the Foreign Ministry to present themselves as responsible agents of moral order who brought harmony to Italians abroad, just as Fascism unified Italy. American bishops presented themselves as benevolent shepherds who graciously earned the loyalty of their flock and commanded respect for their divinely ordained authority. When consuls provided damage control to an embarrassed or humiliated bishop whose authority had been flouted, they helped the bishop salvage his image. In so doing, consuls won respect from the Vatican and the American episcopacy as agents of order and discipline.

The "Italian Church" Overlaps with the "American Church"

Italian American Catholic institutions had a distinctive sociology that we must consider before we can appreciate the impact of the Lateran Pacts. Sociologists and historians have ignored this distinctive sociology because they have approached the study of Catholic parishes with a congregational model. They assume that parishes are autonomous units that reflect purely local social dynamics. One historian claims, "each parish was a small planet whirling through its orbit, oblivious to the rest of the ecclesiastical solar system." This assumption of a "de facto congregationalism" has blinded observers of parishes to transnational dynamics built into the very structure of Roman Catholicism. In the Italian American Catholic case, matters were even more complicated.[2]

Italian American parishes in the 1930s were responsive to international ideological currents. Because both American and Italian institutions comprised the parishes, it is difficult to draw boundaries between the American and the Italian Churches. The conflicts in Natick and Cleveland were not strictly congregational, diocesan, or even American affairs. In both instances, protagonists included not only American bishops and Italian Americans but also Fascist Italy (consulates and the embassy), the Vatican (the apostolic delegation), and the Italian Church (immigrant priests who were members of Italian provinces of their religious congregations).

When we mapped out (in chapter 5) the transnational clerical economy of Italian *diocesan* priests with data from 1917 and 1918, we discovered hundreds of priests, more or less permanently affiliated with bishops in Italy, residing in the United States. In the 1920s and 1930s, more of these "unincardinated" priests arrived from a new Pontifical College for Italian Emigration in Rome, under the direction of the Bishop for Italian Emigration. For these reasons, and because only a minuscule number of Italian American boys entered the diocesan priesthood, American-born Catholics of Italian descent found themselves in national parishes run by immigrant clergy with close juridical and cultural ties to Fascist Italy and with weak ties to American dioceses. This increased the likelihood that parish conflicts would become international events.[3]

The structure of *religious congregations* (religious orders and missionary societies) whose clergy worked in Italian American parishes further exacerbated this problem of "dual jurisdiction." Religious congregations generally include "religious" priests who take special vows (as opposed to "diocesan" priests) from many regions or nations. For administrative purposes, religious congregations divide themselves into geographical "provinces." This is significant to our story because many Italian religious priests who were members of provinces in Italy worked in parishes in the United States. In other instances, Italian priests in an American province led separatist movements to affiliate themselves and their Italian American parishes with Italian provinces, even though they remained pastors in the United States. Fascist Italy encouraged this separatism, or dual jurisdiction, because it put these "missionaries" under authorities that the Fascist regime could control, cajole, or threaten.

For instance, Italian priests in the Servants of Mary, who had worked with many ethnic groups as part of an American province since 1909, segregated themselves from their American province in 1927 and became part of their Roman province. Italian Augustinians in the United States initiated a similar separatist movement. In 1925, they decided that they did not want to work under the jurisdiction of their American province. So, they formed their own Italian vice-province segregated from all other national groups of Augustinians in the United States. Italian Missionaries of the Most Precious Blood formed an Italo-American Delegation in 1928 and remained outside of the jurisdiction of their large American province. The Italian Fathers of Our Lady of Mercy, who are discussed in this chapter, worked in America directly under their Roman province. The Italian Fathers of the Most Holy Trinity formed their own Italian vicariate in the United States in 1920. The Society of the Catholic Apostolate (the Pallottine Fathers) formed an Italian American province in 1909, separate from their confreres of all other nationalities who had an American province. Italian Capuchins formed an Italian American Custodia, which was recognized in 1918. Italian Franciscans (Minor) had their own Italian American province after 1901, autonomous from Franciscans of other nationalities. The Salesians' and Scalabrinians' provinces in America also worked as diaspora extensions of Italy. In other words, while American provinces of religious congregations were a melting pot of priests of many nationalities (including Americans themselves), Italians immigrant priests segregated themselves (or were segregated) from this American melting pot.[4]

The Vatican approved of these institutional alignments, which, by the 1920s, resonated with Fascist demographic and foreign policy. As a result of the distinctive segregation of Italian clergy—religious and diocesan—from the American Church and their close juridical, social, and political ties to the Italian Church, enormous sums of money collected from Italian Americans were diverted to Italy. (Historians have underestimated Italian American Catholic offerings because they have ignored this distinctive sociology.) Moreover, after the Lateran Pacts, the Fascist regime had coercive powers over religious congregations and bishops in Italy. Therefore, the government had easy access to the immediate superiors of Italian clergy in the United States when those clergy did not cooperate with consular initiatives.

The conflicts in Natick and Cleveland became entangled in international systems of communication and authority. Both conflicts might have remained contained within American ecclesiastical structures—here we can only speculate—if diocesan authorities had had connections in the ethnic community and a better understanding of Italian American life. But the dioceses of Providence and Cleveland, like most others, had no Italian clergy in positions of authority. No one was available to interpret events to the bishops and advise them judiciously.[5] As a result, Fascist consuls became episcopal informants, advisers, negotiators, diplomats, and even fund-raisers. Consulates, and by extension Fascist Italy, won the praise of American bishops and the Vatican for their efforts to diffuse explosive situations where the bishops had neither the trust nor the knowledge of their flock.

The Missionaries of the Sacred Heart and Italians in Rhode Island

By the 1930s, a vital Italian subculture flourished in Rhode Island. Italian immigrants and their children, 70,665 strong in 1920, constituted one-ninth of the population and exercised political clout at the city and state levels. Their most powerful institutions supported the Duce, and the popular weekly *L'Eco del Rhode Island* galvanized others. By July 1936, the Rhode Island committee of the Italian Red Cross had raised $37,132 for Mussolini's Italy. That autumn, Italians flexed their political muscle when 6,000 gathered at the Providence State House for Columbus Day. Master of ceremonies Lt. Erminio Migliori, Italian consul general Guido Segrè of Boston, and Providence vice consul Vincenzo Verderosa prodded the governor. "Although we Italo-Americans appreciate your Excellency's courtesy in granting us an Italian Day, may we remind you that full legalization of Columbus Day is what we want and will achieve with time. We can draw a crowd of more than 1,000 Italo-Americans any day just by calling it Benito Mussolini Day!" In April 1937, 1,500 turned out at Providence's Uptown Theater to honor the 2,690th anniversary of the birth of Rome. Pietro Carbonelli, correspondent of the Milan-based *Corriere della Sera*, lauded the corporate state. As always, Vice Consul Verderosa and a host of ethnic leaders from the Order Sons of Italy and the Dante Alighieri Society sang Fascist hymns and the "Star-Spangled Banner."[6]

Fascist Italy funded Italian-language programs and schools and awarded honors to students and teachers for their accomplishments. In May 1937, at the Providence Dante Alighieri School, headmaster Domenico Lombardi, Verderosa, state ethnic leaders, and Italian American youth gathered for a gala assembly. Principal T. Franklin Walsh of Central High School, himself a Knight of the Crown of

Italy, praised Headmaster Lombardi. Central High's orchestra and chorus performed the "Marcia Reale," "Giovinezza," "Leggenda del Piave," and "Faccetta Nera." Students heard poetry recitations and speeches celebrating Mussolini's "New Italy." In June, fourteen pupils from two parochial schools and the Dante Alighieri School received scholarships for summer trips to Fascist Italy.[7]

It was within this context of nationalist euphoria after the Ethiopian War that conflict erupted at the Sacred Heart Church. In 1899, the Missionaries of the Sacred Heart arrived in Rhode Island, where they established St. Joseph's parish for French Canadians. Father Pierre L'Espérance (born in Putnam, Connecticut), was the head of the American Province of the Missionaries of the Sacred Heart, a province composed primarily of French Canadian priests. He responded to Italian pastoral needs and supported the construction of Sacred Heart Church in Natick in 1929 as a mission of St. Joseph's. For its first six years, Sacred Heart Church had no problems. The Roman Province of the Missionaries of the Sacred Heart sent Father Achille Tirocchi to administer the church. He was a popular leader among the Italians and lived happily with his confreres at St. Joseph's rectory. When Tirocchi died in March 1935, the Roman province sent Father Francesco Russo to replace him. Russo insisted upon building a rectory at Sacred Heart rather than live with his confreres at St. Joseph's. Russo's recall to Rome in September 1936 coincided with a conflict between the American and Roman provinces. The conflict compelled Bishop Keough of Providence to take Sacred Heart Church from the Missionaries of the Sacred Heart and placed it under the administration of the diocese. Keough then appointed Father Eugenio Cormuto to be administrator of the church. In response, outraged Italians stormed the church, occupied it by force, and demanded Russo's return.[8]

At a mass meeting on 7 September 1936, Italians of the Pawtuxet Valley "unanimously voted to oppose through all means the departure of Father Russo." The following day, to appease the Italians, Keough petitioned the Vatican to make Sacred Heart Church into a national parish independent of St. Joseph's.[9] But the Italians wanted Russo back. They organized a Citizens Committee, threatened to boycott Sacred Heart Church and school, and protested in letter and in person to Apostolic Delegate Amleto Cicognani. The delegate instructed the insurgents to submit to the will of their bishop, but they refused. The Citizens Committee claimed the French-Canadian priests at St. Joseph's, and American provincial L'Espérance in particular, had always discriminated against Italians. The committee also noted that Italian Americans, "the majority of whom were unemployed and on relief," had collected more than one-third of the required $5,000 to build a rectory at Sacred Heart Church.[10]

L'Eco del Rhode Island mobilized the resistance. According to *L'Eco*, L'Espérance had maltreated Russo and then had him recalled for attempting "to liberate the

Italian church from slavery . . . and put it under the direct dependence of Rome."
L'Eco recounted how on 9 September Russo was leaving Rhode Island as ordered,
but someone rang the church bell and "within moments hundreds and hundreds
of people, men, women and children, surrounded him . . . imploring him not to
leave." Russo left in tears. Infuriated at the loss of their priest, the Italians closed
the church by force. *L'Eco* claimed that Italians had invested $200,000 in the prop-
erty, but L'Espérance had "washed his hands of the situation like a Pontius Pilate"
and gave the property to the bishop.[11]

Vincenzo De Orchis, director of *L'Eco*, rallied 600 protesters in the basement
of Sacred Heart Church on 14 September. Apparently, they had grown enamored
with Russo for his ardent nationalism during the Ethiopian War. Russo "was the
first priest in Rhode Island who offered, with spontaneous enthusiasm and with
patriotic fervor, his work for the collection of precious metals" for Fascist Italy
during the Ethiopian campaign. De Orchis and Pasquale Parente, a leader of the
Citizens Committee, encouraged resistance to Cormuto's installation and tele-
grammed the Roman provincial to demand Russo's return.[12] Notwithstanding
L'Eco's insistence that "Canadian" or "French" racial prejudice incited the conflict,
Keough and Cicognani suspected Russo of fueling vain hopes that he might return. Keough informed Cicognani, "Father Russo, the [Citizens] committee and
others report, urged [the Italians] to continue their resistance."[13]

Cicognani backed Keough. He wrote Roman provincial Pietro Pillarella to respond to Keough's account of the conflict. Keough, "a worthy Prelate of good
faith, above all partisanship, tells me that without a doubt Father Russo is in large
part responsible for the serious situation that now exists among the Italians of
Natick." Keough had worked to reconcile L'Espérance and Russo, but Russo incited Italian Americans to resist. According to Keough, when Russo left he transferred funds collected for the rectory to two laymen who deposited the money in
a bank account under their own names. Cicognani instructed Pillarella to have
the superior general of the Missionaries of the Sacred Heart assure Keough that
neither Russo nor any other Sacred Heart missionary would be sent to Sacred
Heart Church. Cicognani also commanded Pillarella to have Russo write Keough.
In the letter, Russo was to acknowledge that he "would encourage Natick Italians to respectfully welcome the new pastor in the spirit of obedience." Finally,
Cicognani reminded Pillarella of the fragile status of Italian clergy in America:
"You must understand how episodes of this type damage the good name of Italian
priests and religious here in America. . . . The Bishop made the best decision"
when he affiliated Sacred Heart Church "with an Italian priest [Cormuto]. In this
way, Msgr. Keough has respected the just aspirations of the Italians of Natick."[14]

The most interesting turn of events in this story was when Keough turned to
Vice Consul Verderosa of Providence for help. Before the Lateran Pacts of 1929,

such a step would have been unthinkable. However, once the Holy See and Fascist Italy made their reconciliation public and formal, the consulates became available as resources for American bishops troubled by their Italian American Catholics.

Keough sent his secretary, Father Charles Mahoney, to see the vice consul. The visit was made "out of courtesy" to inform the vice consul that Keough had appealed to the local police to reopen Sacred Heart Church by force. Concerned that Keough would damage the image of order and discipline so important to Fascist propaganda, Verderosa warned Mahoney that such confrontational methods would only instigate "uncontrollable and serious rioting." With the threat of violence imminent, Verderosa rushed to Sacred Heart Church. Upon his arrival, he encountered a crowd on the steps of the church faced off against both state and local police, who were "ready to use force to open the church." He acted swiftly. He secured a respite from the police assault and assembled his "countrymen" in a room within the church. He spoke "for over an hour using persuasive arguments and appealing to our national dignity." But his arguments failed to pacify the angry insurgents, who remained disposed "to fall as martyrs on the steps of the church, intending to oppose force with force." Verderosa convinced Keough, uninformed of the local situation, to rescind the police assault.[15]

Boston consul general Guido Segrè and Ambassador Augusto Rosso directed Verderosa's activities throughout the conflict. They instructed Verderosa to promote Italian interests through institutions and channels respected by the American public. Ideally, the vice consul should make the Fascist government a useful, indeed, an indispensable part of the ethnic and ecclesiastical apparatus within the United States. His superiors also urged Verderosa to make Italian autonomy appear to harmonize with American interests. Rosso saw in the events an opportunity to have Sacred Heart Church elevated to an Italian national parish, a step already initiated by Keough. Therefore, Rosso encouraged Verderosa to continue his work "of moderation and pacification" to find a "solution to the unpleasant situation with the ecclesiastical authorities so that . . . they will not cease to hold in high regard the italianità of Sacred Heart Church."[16]

Frustrated by his own impotence, Keough wholeheartedly endorsed Verderosa's work. On 17 October, Keough reported to Cicognani, "the situation undoubtedly is improving. However, the church has not been reopened as yet as I think it would be better to wait until it can be done peacefully. This moreover is the opinion of the Italian Consul at Providence who has been extremely helpful in the present circumstance. He has contributed wonderfully to creating a better mentality at Natick and has done an excellent piece of work by forcefully stressing strong Catholic principles with certain individuals among the opposition. His efforts are gradually but surely bringing them to a more reasonable state of mind." To simplify matters, Keough paid L'Espérance $1,000 to release any claim the American provincial might make on Sacred Heart Church.[17]

Following Cicognani's instructions, Roman provincial Pillarella wrote Keough. He acknowledged the "pain which without doubt you have suffered as the pastor of the diocese" and the "imprudent acts" committed by Russo. Pillarella's letter, however, amounted to an attack upon American provincial L'Espérance. "When Russo arrived in America, he found the Italian colony on the brink of war with the Canadian fathers." Pillarella had asked L'Espérance to move Sacred Heart Church from the jurisdiction of the American to the Roman province, but L'Espérance refused. With his flock "on the brink of war," Russo met with Keough, but "L'Espérance had already made all arrangements alone. . . . Believing himself deceived by back-handed maneuvering and seeing himself impotent to calm the coming fury [of his congregation, Russo] requested by telegram to return [to Rome]." According to Pillarella, Russo did not correspond from Rome with Italians in Natick. Furthermore, Pillarella insisted that before Russo left, he had urged the Citizens Committee "to deposit the money [for the rectory] in the bank in the name of the Bishop." Parente of the Citizens Committee "compelled [Russo] to give his signature so that the money could be withdrawn." Pillarella added, "I cannot forget that the parish of the Sacred Heart was initiated by an Italian missionary of the Sacred Heart . . . and that Father Tirocchi gave his best energies, his devotion and his life" to the church.[18]

With both Keough and the two provinces of the Sacred Heart missionaries embroiled in accusations, Verderosa emerged as the moral arbiter. Verderosa explained, "the favorable result of the conflict was entirely the result of the work of persuasion and calm accomplished by me." Keough, "after the well-known incident" in which the police and community clashed on the church steps, "gave me complete liberty to settle the conflict with dignity." Verderosa detailed his negotiations with the Citizens Committee, whose leaders understood the "uselessness of resistance" and the benefit of a national parish. On 31 October 1936, Sacred Heart was elevated to a national parish and reopened.[19]

Absent diocesan personnel trusted within the embittered community, Keough relied entirely upon the Fascist vice consul. When Verderosa met with the leaders of the Citizens Committee to negotiate, his "countrymen" demanded that "the keys of the church be consigned to [Verderosa]." Keough accepted the arrangement. The Citizens Committee demanded "the restitution of the individual offerings already collected by our countrymen of Natick for the erection of a rectory, amounting to approximately $3,000." Keough complied again. The bishop gave Verderosa "complete authority" to withdraw the diocese's money from the bank, to administer its restitution to appropriate parties, and to begin a new campaign to raise funds for the rectory. Keough explained to Verderosa, "I shall authorize you to make withdrawals from the said fund in such amounts and at such times and in such manner as you in your discretion may deem necessary and proper. You may disburse this fund to those individuals and societies directly when you have satisfied yourself that they have really contributed and that they have requested that their money be returned."[20]

Verderosa earned the admiration of the American Church, the Vatican, his superiors, and most of the Italian leaders in the Pawtuxet Valley. Keough wrote Cicognani to praise the "untiring efforts and splendid cooperation of Dr. Vincenzo Verderosa [who] has been the contributing factor of great importance in bringing about a peaceful settlement."[21] Ambassador Rosso congratulated Verderosa for his "activity performed with energy and prudence" and urged the vice consul to "come to an agreement as soon as possible for the construction of the rectory for the new Italian parish of the Sacred Heart."[22] L'Eco celebrated the discipline and order Verderosa brought to the diaspora under Fascist authority.

> As an admirable act of deference toward the representative of our homeland's government, the Natick community wanted to give the keys of the church to Doctor Verderosa, expressing to him their heartfelt gratitude for the dignified resolution of the unpleasant but justified agitation. [The event] demonstrated how generously disposed is the heart of Italians toward pure and honest priests and how equally admirable is their attitude, shaped by discipline and duty, toward a representative of the Italy of Mussolini. . . . We are the sons of the Wolf of Rome . . . Good blood does not lie and the descendants of the ancient stock of Rome know how to tackle with pride and boldness all sacrifices and all duties.[23]

There were limits, however, to Verderosa's accomplishment. Militant Italian American Fascists resisted the settlement. Although Verderosa "was able to convince in some sense the Citizens Committee" to cease its resistance, there remained "some unruly elements of our community." He explained how "these obstinate and boisterous individuals . . . threatened to destroy the church with violence." The vice consul met with them to deter any "rash acts," but he could not convince them to disband. These hard-core protesters formed the Società Benito Mussolini for men and the Società Rachele Mussolini for women. Notwithstanding Pillarella's claims to the contrary, Russo corresponded with these militants. Cicognani, who had acquired a letter from Russo that insisted Sacred Heart Church was faltering without him, concluded that the Roman province was still maneuvering to gain control of Sacred Heart Church.[24]

Keough assured the apostolic delegation, "except for a few agitators who never did go to church much anyway," Sacred Heart was a vital parish.[25] The Ladies of St. Ann, a parish society, had "developed a membership of eighty mothers of families all of whom frequent the Church regularly. The Children of Mary Society has likewise been recently reorganized and now consists of about forty regular members who go to Church." Parish societies for youth thrived. Their members "attend Church and about thirty-five of them are workers for the Church. They have already put on a play that netted a gain of $225.00 which is extraordinary for a village like Natick." Keough boasted seventy-six confirmations in December, a recent Passion Play "showing a great deal of active interest in parish affairs," and a "large banquet" for Father Cormuto planned for the month after Easter. "As regards Father Russo's claim that the people generally do not attend Church, I would remark in all fairness that 50% of them never did, not even when Father Tirocchi was pastor." Keough once again singled out Verderosa for praise. "The Italian Vice Consul at Providence is still giving us his wholehearted support and cooperation. He is aiding in the collecting of funds for the new rectory and is a great source of consolation not only to me but to the Pastor and Assistant in Natick."[26]

Keough shed light on "the opposition." "Parish and Catholic Societies have not been supplanted by the Rachele Mussolini and Benito Mussolini Societies . . . as Father Russo falsely contends." The bishop estimated a membership of 175 in the Rachele Mussolini Society but added, "Father Cormuto has every confidence that these women will come back to Church since they now know that Father Russo cannot return to Natick. . . . As regards the Benito Society thirty of the men now go regularly to Church and if the others do not see Father Russo by Easter, Father Cormuto regards it as certain that they will resume the practice of going regularly to Church." Keough, perhaps defensively, contended that most members of these societies were never good Catholics anyway or were "not motivated by the real faith." He could not, however, dismiss their importance. "During the recent Mission at Natick . . . the pastor was obliged to have a policeman on duty outside the church because some of those who did not attend the services were attempting to intimidate those who were making the Mission." Keough supplied Cicognani with a copy of a letter from Russo to a parishioner, who had surrendered the letter to Cormuto and who provided the names of several of Russo's correspondents in Natick.[27]

Keough was surprised that "the leaders in the agitation . . . have even gone so far as to publicly criticize . . . Dr. Verderosa. Dr. Verderosa has shown the greatest respect for the ecclesiastical authorities in this affair, and has even planned a campaign to be conducted under his personal supervision in order to obtain funds for the erection of a new rectory." The bishop, briefed on Italian matters by Verderosa, contended, "the respectable business and professional men in the other Italian colonies in the State, particularly in the City of Providence, have let their fellow countrymen in Natick know in plain terms that they think the unruly element in Natick is acting in such a way as to throw discredit and bring disgrace upon the Italian name." Keough encouraged Cicognani to discuss the situation with the Italian ambassador. According to Keough, "the Vice Consul holds to the judgment that but five families are the agitators." They are "inflamed by letters from Father Russo, in turn [they] intimidate and threaten other members of the community who are thus made fearful of practicing their religion."[28]

The enduring opposition protested to the Duce. Giovanni Petrarca of the Benito Mussolini Society never mentioned the matters of greatest importance to Fascist Italy in his letter. Petrarca ignored the elevation of Sacred Heart to the status of a national parish, the appointment of Father Cormuto—an Italian ex-army officer—as pastor, and the trust and respect the vice consul had earned from a bishop and the apostolic delegation. Petrarca wrote:

> The Italian colony of Natick, R.I., had an Italian priest sent directly from Rome. Through plots of the Canadian provincial, Father Russo was compelled to return to Italy and the church and money contributed by the Italians were put under the direct control of Canada. We Fascists, belonging to the Benito Mussolini and Rachele Mussolini Societies, inspired by the idea of emancipation from foreign slavery, addressed Vice Consul Verderosa of Providence R.I. who from the beginning refused to intervene on behalf of his countrymen, reconciling with French priests from Canada, and treating us as ignorant and lost people, incapable of defending ourselves, obliging us to remain under foreign control. And the church, built through the fruit of our money and sweat, was to remain governed by the French and not Italians.
>
> Why did this government representative of your Excellency continue to remain neutral in this controversy between us and the Canadian church?
>
> We were sold out by your representative, and we protest to Your Excellency in order that justice be done for us, who at any time are ready to contribute with all of our moral and material resources to our beloved homeland afar. Among the 500 Italian families resident in Natick and Pontiac who contributed, we gave $3000 and gold and silver to our beloved homeland afar during the Ethiopian War."

Petrarca closed his letter with a Roman salute.[29]

Fascist Italy, the Vatican, the American Church, L'Eco and its editors, and the majority of Italians in the Pawtuxet Valley forged a powerful consensus, notwithstanding the resistance. Cicognani and Keough had welcomed cooperation from Verderosa, who proved himself a force for order and obedience to civil and ecclesiastical authority. L'Eco similarly elaborated upon how "authentic" Fascism united Italian Americans under the authority of the Church and Fascist Italy. On 11 December 1936, L'Eco criticized those unwilling to contribute to the new rectory as deviant Italians. "Is it an expression of national dignity to appeal to wretched spite—a weakness of the old mentality surpassed by Fascism—in order to impose childish wishes upon high ecclesiastical authorities? Was the religious consciousness of 100,000 Italians of [Rhode Island] not wounded enough by the audacious collective rebellion against the high authority of the church?" *L'Eco* insisted that the rectory must be built with Italian money rather than diocesan funds so that "one associates the Italian name with discipline, with order, with work, with respect toward the authorities and toward the laws, with devotion toward religion and toward the homeland." *L'Eco* attacked the opposition. "We advise against the formation of societies, feigning patriotism, whose programs could be in open conflict with religion. We take this opportunity to remind our good countrymen of Natick that the Fascist Revolution has placed once again the Crucifix upon the altars and has reopened the churches to the faithful."[30]

The implications of the Lateran Pacts were vividly evident at the extravagant banquet in honor of Father Cormuto on 25 April 1937. The 700 guests included an array of prestigious speakers: Governor Robert Quinn of Rhode Island, Mayor Albert P. Ruerat of Warwick, Auxiliary Bishop Charles Mahoney of Providence, Verderosa, Justice Antonio Capotosto of the state supreme court, Capt. Angelo Martella, president of the Federation of Italian War Veterans of Providence, and thirteen Rhode Island Italian priests. The banquet did not lack for Fascist hymns, invocations of blessings for the Italian Empire, frequent tributes to Mussolini, and a hymn to the Duce and the pope, "who succeeded in reconciling the church and the state, forming a feast of patriotic union."[31]

In his last reports, Verderosa expressed pleasure with the outcome, although he acknowledged that the resistance persisted. "The religious aspect of the question can be considered closed. The church was opened to the faithful; our community has acquired a parish perfectly Italian; the priests are carrying out their religious mission with great feelings of *italianità*. The moral situation could be considered excellent if it had not been for a few agitators who, motivated by the lowest feelings of personal revenge against the bishop, have established a society aiming to incite resistance, boycott religious functions and cause continuous disturbances for the local priests and civic authorities." Verderosa could not reign in the agitators. "At various times I have summoned the organizers to the consular office and made them understand that their goals . . . are in contrast to the patriotic and religious feelings of their countrymen in Natick, and in open conflict with the directives of the local Catholic and civic authorities." They refused, however, to dissolve their societies.[32]

Verderosa, serving as the bishop's informant, notified Keough that the resistance threatened to lead at least fifteen parishioners from the Sacred Heart to an Italian Protestant church if two Roman province missionaries of the Sacred Heart were not called to Natick. But the vice consul assured Keough that the resistance was weakening. In fact, Verderosa pronounced the issue closed in July 1937 when he mailed to Keough the financial reports regarding his successful fund-raising activities for the rectory.[33]

In the summer of 1937, Cormuto found dynamite in the basement of Sacred Heart Church. Much to the consternation of the Federation of Italian War Veterans, an organization aligned with the consulate, members of the Benito Mussolini and Rachele Mussolini Societies held a Fascist march in West Warwick, clad in black shirts. The parish history of Sacred Heart also explains that "when Italy formally declared war on the United States, the FBI rushed in to investigate the leaders and other members [of the Fascist Societies], an event destined to hasten their demise."[34]

The Fathers of Our Lady of Mercy
and the Italians in Cleveland

The events at Holy Redeemer parish in Cleveland in 1940 also illuminate the implications of the Lateran Pacts when the Church recognized Fascist Italy as the legitimate home of the Catholic nation. In Cleveland, as in the diocese of Providence, tensions emerged with a religious order working directly under Italian rather than American religious authority. Unable to deal effectively with the conflict, the bishop of Cleveland, like his counterpart in Providence, turned for help to Fascist Italy and the Vatican. Once again, the Vatican intervened while the consul employed his knowledge of the Italian American community and his negotiating leverage. The outcome, once more, increased the prestige of Fascist Italy as a force of discipline and order in the eyes of the American Church and the Vatican. However, in contrast to the conflict in Natick, at Holy Redeemer the parishioners wished to end their relationship with an Italian religious congregation, not maintain it, in order to integrate themselves more fully into diocesan institutions. So long as the parish remained under an Italian pastor, neither the Vatican, nor the consulate, nor the bishop opposed that integration.

In 1914 Italian immigrants in Cleveland began to celebrate the feast of St. Rocco. By 1917 St. Rocco devotees had built a chapel to shelter a statue of their patron. Bishop Joseph Schrembs recognized the congregation when he established St. Rocco's parish in 1924, administered by the Fathers of Our Lady of Mercy (the Mercedarians). Father Sante Gattuso, the first pastor, was a Sicilian who served in the Italian army during the Great War before he established the Roman province of the Mercedarians in the United States in 1921 at a monastery in Hudson, Ohio. By 1926 a mission from St. Rocco's Church for 800 families in the Collinwood area of Cleveland grew into Holy Redeemer parish under the administration of Mercedarian priests. By 1928 Holy Redeemer had its own church, rectory, school, and a substantial debt of $88,000.[35]

Cleveland Italians exercised influence in local and state politics. The Order Sons of Italy in America (OSIA) had effectively federated provincial societies throughout Ohio. Its mortuary fund had 5,098 subscribers and was worth

$20,736 in 1924. By 1934, the OSIA Grand (Ohio) Lodge boasted 9,000 members and successfully petitioned Cleveland's public schools to teach the Italian language. In 1935, the OSIA built a Temple that included a restaurant, classrooms, offices, a lounge, and a 1,200-seat auditorium. In May 1936, Cleveland's Italians, ardent supporters of Fascist Italy, gave $12,404.21 for the Italian Red Cross to aid in the Ethiopian struggle. In addition, 1,000 Italian women in Cleveland sent gold wedding rings to the *patria*, and 4,000 Italians gathered in Murray Hill to celebrate the first anniversary of the Fascist Empire the following year. Since the Great War, OSIA membership had overlapped with Catholic parishioners. The Ohio Lodge celebrated masses, and the diocesan newspaper, the *Catholic Universe Bulletin*, reported on OSIA activities.[36]

The Mercedarians administered a mission and two of the six national parishes among Italians, who comprised 10 percent of the diocese of Cleveland in 1930. Consul Cesare Pier Alberto Buzzi Gradenigo praised the Mercedarians' "precious apostolate of faith and *patria* among Italians and Italo-Americans." But they struggled with large debts on their properties. On 16 December 1925, the Mercedarians had purchased a farm for $35,000, paid for with a $27,000 loan at 6 percent interest from the diocese. In September 1938, when the Mercedarians still owed the diocese $19,750, Father Gattuso requested "some relief in the balance of the mortgage." Gattuso explained that only great sacrifice had allowed the Mercedarians to pay the mortgage with "meager income both [from St. Rocco's] and . . . Holy Redeemer." He claimed that his confreres had never accepted full salary at either parish, and that he was only able to give $100 to the Mercedarian Roman province in June 1938. Holy Redeemer, a vital parish, rich in parish societies, still carried a $25,000 debt in 1939.[37]

Until the summer of 1938, Consul Romeo Montecchi of Cleveland (1935–41) had had a productive association with the Mercedarians. He described his relationship with Gattuso as "not only one of deference between consul and pastor, but even a certain friendship. Fruitful cooperation existed between my office and the parish, and patriotic ceremonies always had good results. I had noticed in Father Gattuso a tendency to place his parish above everyone and everything, and an excessive sense of authority, and I had received some complaints about his difficult search for money. But this . . . was part of the normal conduct of every religious." Cordial relations between pastor and consul deteriorated, however, before the conflict at Holy Redeemer. "In an amateur theatrical competition of the Italian Cultural League, Father Gattuso's group finished in a dead heat with the Order Sons of Italy in America. I thought that the quarrel, based on the rivalry between the two groups, was settled, and Father Gattuso had accepted a solution that would resolve the incident in which I intervened only to calm the animosities. . . . Instead, Father Gattuso . . . declined the award and had me withdrawn from the Italian Cultural League. Before then, his parish . . . had joined in the initiatives of the entire community. But from that day forward he began openly and without restraint, a true and proper boycott."[38]

When Holy Redeemer's pastor, Martino Compagno, died on 6 October 1939, Gattuso transferred his young assistant at St. Rocco's, Vincent Caruso, to lead Holy Redeemer. But the parishioners resisted. They feared Caruso would invite Gattuso's authoritarian control into the parish and thereby inhibit the development of Holy Redeemer. Nevertheless, on 10 January 1940, Schrembs confirmed Caruso's appointment.[39] In response, the parishioners blocked Caruso's installation by force on both 11 and 18 February. In turn, Schrembs had Msgr. Floyd Begin place Holy Redeemer under personal and local interdict. Under local interdict, the parish property—church, school, rectory—was closed. Under personal interdict, every parishioner except children under fourteen was excluded from the sacraments. They could only receive the sacraments at neighboring parishes when they submitted to civil and ecclesiastical authorities.

To Schrembs's dismay, Cleveland's newspapers gave the "riot" at Holy Redeemer front-page coverage on 19 February. The *Cleveland News* screamed, "Prelate Brands Riot at Church 'A Mortal Sin,'" over a photo of Begin surrounded by a mob of angry parishioners. Not to be outdone, the *Cleveland Plain Dealer* captured the climactic moment when the rebellious crowd and police officers circled Begin as he lifted his arm to place the interdict. The articles narrated the arrival of Begin, Caruso, and 100 "uniformed Knights of St. John and members of the Fourth Degree, Knights of Columbus, in full regalia." Italian American children pelted the procession with snowballs as parishioners, alerted to the arrival of the entourage, stormed the church to prevent the installation.[40] "A shrieking milling crowd of 1,500 men, women and children," who "kept up an unceasing babble" and shouted "imprecations and threats," defied Begin's authority. Sixty police officers in seventeen cruisers were unable to force their way through the crowd. Seven men were arrested, and Police Sergeant Percy Ball sustained injuries from a tear gas bomb. Schrembs expressed remorse. "I have been exceedingly kind to all nationality groups, particularly the Italians. I have tried to be a real father to them. . . . I do hope that they will come to their senses and stop giving public scandal to the whole city. For it makes a holy show of these people themselves."[41]

This pastoral and public relations disaster for the diocese imploded at the tail end of unsuccessful negotiations. Caruso had gone to Holy Redeemer by himself on 16 January 1940, but he met threats of violence. His two trips with Begin that followed on 11 and 18 February triggered predictable results. The notes of Vice Chancellor Father Vincent Balmat, taken 11 January, indicate that Helen Sanzo spoke to him as Holy Redeemer's representative. She explained that parishioners preferred Father Louis Loi-Zedda, the Mercedarian assistant pastor at Holy Redeemer, to Father Caruso. But Sanzo even more forcefully called for the removal of the Mercedarians altogether. The parishioners objected "to the foreign influence in the parish and to the foreign priests they often get." Gattuso, who had refused to answer letters from Holy Redeemer parish societies, wanted to interfere in Holy Redeemer affairs through the installation of his assistant. "'Father Gattuso wants to be a dictator,'" Sanzo quipped. She warned Balmat that parishioners would obstruct Caruso's installation and withdraw their children from the parish school.[42]

On 19 January, Sanzo and John Trivisonno, a Holy Redeemer councilman, visited Balmat once again, after they had been denied an audience with Schrembs. Sanzo and Trivisonno warned of impending violence and reminded Balmat that "the parish resents the interference of Father Gattuso in the affairs of Holy Redeemer." Although parish leaders had nothing against Assistant Pastor Loi-Zedda, they now demanded diocesan priests to replace the Mercedarians. Armed with a petition, Sanzo and Trivisonno warned "there will be serious trouble if Father Caruso comes. . . . There will be violence . . . that . . . will cause untold harm to the parish and to the cause of religion." Unmoved, Balmat informed the Holy Redeemer representatives that their request could not be accommodated.[43]

Negotiations took a new twist when Sanzo and Trivisonno telephoned the diocese, hinted at a financial scandal, and requested a meeting with Schrembs. Diocesan notes taken 30 January explain the substance of their claim. "Some checks had been found by the [parish] councilmen which had been made out to a person of the parish for services rendered. The checks had been cashed, but the person to whom they were made out says that the endorsement is a forgery, and that no checks from the parish were given to her . . . [The councilmen] threatened to bring this out in the open, but most of all they want an interview with the Archbishop. John Trivisonno said that he is going to write to the Apostolic Delegate."[44]

Archbishop Schrembs finally met with a committee from Holy Redeemer on 31 January 1940. His overriding concern was their unconditional submission to his authority. He began the meeting flatly stating that "if the people of Holy Redeemer Parish did not accept the pastor whom he had appointed, he would excommunicate them. As Archbishop, he would not allow anyone to dictate to him. That Father Caruso was a splendid young man . . . That the Mercedarian Fathers had done good work in the Diocese of Cleveland, that he was well satisfied with their work . . . and had no cause to be dissatisfied with their administration of the parish. . . . The law of the Church was the same today as when Our Divine Lord founded the Church and malcontents could not dictate to the Archbishop."[45]

Trivisonno presented his case. An audit had revealed discrepancies in checks to the organist, Angelica Marcini. Marcini had requested that Compagno pay her in cash for her services so that she could work for the Works Progress Administration, which forbade a worker to earn two salaries. Compagno had agreed, but a check was still made out to Marcini that Compagno asked her to endorse. Marcini, however, never received any money from the check. Furthermore, Compagno made out other checks to her, which she had not endorsed but which had been cashed just the same. Trivisonno produced an affidavit from Marcini testifying to the veracity of these claims. Representatives from Holy Redeemer had gone to see Gattuso several times to air their complaints, but he had ignored or insulted the visitors.[46]

Further testimony at the 31 January meeting described how Father Compagno had prevented Holy Redeemer women from affiliating their societies with the National Council of Catholic Women (NCCW) and from organizing a parent-teacher association. Holy Redeemer women "were never allowed to participate in any diocesan work with the exception of the Eucharistic Congress" held when Compagno was away. When the women of the parish "wanted to pay the $10 to the NCCW for affiliation, they were told, 'Why should we let money go out of the [Mercedarian] Order?'" But when Compagno "came to [the parishioners] to raise money for the Red Cross during the Ethiopian War . . . they had raised $1,000. . . . When it came to affairs of the city and diocese, [Compagno] would always shrug his shoulders—the money had to stay in the Order."[47]

Notwithstanding Mercedarian mismanagement, enforced segregation of parish societies from the diocese, and ebbing weekly collections, Schrembs insisted "he would excommunicate [those who] persisted in their rebellion." He conceded, however, that after a proper submission he would investigate.[48] Although Loi-Zedda informed Schrembs that Caruso would not be welcome at Holy Redeemer, the archbishop directed Begin to proceed with the installation on 11 February anyway. When this first attempt failed, Schrembs accused Loi-Zedda of instigating the disturbance and threatened to "send him back to Italy."[49] Gattuso, in turn, directed Italian superiors to recall Loi-Zedda. But the second attempt to install Caruso failed just the same and culminated in the interdict.

Schrembs's mail reveals diverse views of the interdict. One "Committee of Fifty People" from Holy Redeemer complained that, although the newspapers stated the archbishop welcomed anyone to his office, "our parishioners have come to your office" only to be "told to leave." The indignant letter continued, "after seeing the dirty crooked ways of [the Mercedarians], we refuse to stay under [them] any longer. They used the people's money to buy their farm—a merry $40,000 for it. This of course was payed [sic] for by the money of the poor people. The people who worked hard giving card parties, dances, bazaars, and festivals. . . . Is it a shock now to find instead of using this money for the purpose they had in mind, the money was used to be given to Rev. Fr. Sante Gattuso for the farm." The Committee of Fifty People threatened Schrembs. "You know about the forged checks. The press of course does not know this, because we did not want the whole city of Cleveland to know how crooked the Catholic religion is getting in Cleveland. And believe us we could tell the press plenty." The letter unpleasantly concluded, "You certainly are showing the other faiths that you are a 'dictator.'"[50]

Schrembs also received letters of encouragement. Theresa Piscioneri lamented, "we are ashamed even to call ourselves Italians since such a wide spreading scandal slapped our nationality down lower than beasts." She unveiled provincial rivalries that divided parish factions. The "scandlers" were "those from 'Campo Basso' city in Italy. . . . The other fourth of the parish are 'Calabreses' and 'Sicilians' which did not meddle with the church affairs. Two of these 'Campo Basso' ladies came around and went house to house forging signatures to put in pastorate [sic] the Reverend Louis Loi Zedda ODM, but we refused and so did many others. So every one that refused they said will be revenged." Another parishioner assured Schrembs that the parish leaders "are a group of dictators." Captain Grotenrath complimented Schrembs for taking a hard line. "Your decisions and appointments should not be questioned and disobeyed." Such disobedience amounted to "outright Communism and must be stamped out. . . . This same element [of rebels] . . . has closed many factories, caused deaths, [they] have overthrown governments, and now they attempt to overthrow the House of God." Schrembs, exhilarated by support, answered Grotenrath's "splendid letter," which gave the Archbishop "a consolation" amid his sufferings.[51] Nevertheless, only a small minority of parishioners submitted to Schrembs.

With the "good Italian name" on display, and at the request of Holy Redeemer parishioners, Consul Montecchi sought a meeting with Schrembs. According to Montecchi, Gattuso's "excessively overbearing manner toward parishioners, . . . incontestable and unquestionable absolutism, . . . [and conduct] worthy of the Middle Ages" was the source of the difficulty. From "informants," Montecchi learned that "St. Rocco's parishioners live in a kind of terror under the system established by Father Gattuso. It is astonishing that the religious sentiments of this group of our countrymen is so strong that they tolerate the vexations to which they are subjected." Holy Redeemer parishioners were "more than a little afraid to see the super-authoritarian system of St. Rocco's installed in their parish."[52]

Montecchi described his meeting with Schrembs to superiors. Schrembs would receive a commission of parishioners but would require their submission before any investigation of the Mercedarians. If the Mercedarians had, in fact, taken parish funds for their religious congregation, Schrembs pledged to remove them from the diocese. Montecchi warned, "if this happened, two parishes and their respective schools, constructed through the sacrifice of the Italians, would pass into the hands of American priests." Therefore, Montecchi suggested the Foreign Ministry "intervene with the General of the Order [of Our Lady of Mercy] and direct his attention to what is happening to the detriment of this community and the good Italian name due to Father Gattuso. The General of the Order

is an Italian, a certain Father Scotti I believe, and thus he should easily understand and take to heart the question that, in my opinion, could easily be resolved
with Gattuso's recall. . . . [Gattuso's] stubbornness justifies the . . . [diocesan]
measures to de-nationalize the Italian parishes that are among the best centers
of our patriotic activity." As sensitive as Schrembs to negative images of Italians,
Montecchi sent his superiors copies of the sensational newspaper coverage of the
clash between parishioners and police.[53]

In his investigation, Monsignor Begin concluded that "the opposition came
from a small minority . . . of some of the better educated people of the parish."
He asserted the "definite conclusion that Father Luigi [Loi-Zedda] was the cause
of it all." Begin backed Schrembs. He dismissed Helen Sanzo: nothing "could be
gained from further discussion." He urged her to "submit to Ecclesiastical authority and return to the Sacraments." But Begin assured her, if the Mercedarians "have violated the trust by maladministration of the parish, an adjustment
will be made." On 4 March, the diocesan tribunal took a statement from organist
Angelica Marcini, who testified that she had seen ten or twelve $30 checks made
out to her that she had never received. The checks were dated 1939, although she
had seen "them for the first time a month ago. . . . The checks were endorsed by
someone else. I think some were endorsed by Father Compagno; it looked like his
writing. There were at least 3 different handwritings on the endorsed checks."[54]

In March, two events changed the dynamics of the conflict. Cleveland's chancellor and auxiliary bishop, James McFadden, returned after a three-month absence to replace Begin as the diocesan negotiator. Second, the Vatican intervened.
According to Montecchi, Begin had an overbearing style, not suited for negotiations. He had once been the diocesan chancellor, but due to Vatican intervention
at the recommendation of the apostolic delegate, Begin had been removed from
the post. Begin had dismissed warnings from Italian professionals in Cleveland
not to proceed with the installation of Caruso. Instead, Begin went forward "in
great style with a grand following of the Knights of Columbus and of St. John in
uniform, without knowledge of the situation he was walking into, and without
making necessary preparation."[55]

Montecchi met with Schrembs a second time on 15 March. The consul emphasized how parishioners at Holy Redeemer were in rebellion against the Mercedarians, not the archbishop. Nevertheless, Schrembs remained preoccupied with his
own authority and public image and still required Holy Redeemer's unconditional
submission. Schrembs planned "to convince some of the faithful" to submit by
offering to celebrate a Palm Sunday Mass at Holy Redeemer. Montecchi dissuaded
the archbishop, explaining the plan would backfire.[56]

The following morning, after a long meeting with Montecchi, Chancellor
McFadden drafted a report for Schrembs. The report stressed that "the situation, far more grave than it had been depicted by Begin, could be resolved only

through a settlement and not with force." McFadden planned to ask Gattuso to withdraw the Mercedarians from Holy Redeemer. McFadden reckoned only 200 of 1,200 families had submitted, and they "are being treated roughly and scornfully by those who still stand out against the authority of the Church." McFadden referred to Montecchi as Schrembs's "investigator," who "maintains that [the recalcitrant parishioners] will not accept any member of the Mercedarian Order as pastor." McFadden conceded, "what little investigation has been made seems to indicate certain grounds for" Holy Redeemer's grievances against the Mercedarians. McFadden pointed to a juridical way out of the dilemma. "It is well to recall that the Canon Law asks the removal of a pastor who has incurred the hatred of the people whether this be justly or unjustly. . . . How then can a pastor be imposed upon this congregation whose presence is absolutely opposed?" McFadden acknowledged, however, that "everything must be done to safeguard the authority of the Archbishop. . . . There must be no confusion about this in the minds of the public."[57]

On the previous day, 15 March, Apostolic Delegate Cicognani had urged Schrembs to resolve the conflict by Easter "so that the church could be again officiated and the parishioners would be able to receive the Sacraments and make their Easter duty." Cicognani instructed Schrembs "to find some way of using clemency with [Holy Redeemer]" whose disturbances "first came to my attention in the newspapers." Cicognani suggested, "under the guise of a temporary appointment, some acceptable priest, who of course would have to be an Italian, could be sent there." He added a note of disapproval for episcopal stubbornness, invoking the same passage of canon law as McFadden. "The 'odium plebis' against the priest who was designated for this parish was quite notorious, and I am sure that much of the difficulty would have been avoided if the Diocesan Curia had pointed out this factor—which is indeed a canonical motive for removal—to the superiors of his religious community."[58]

Cicognani had already discussed Holy Redeemer with the Italian ambassador. The ambassador informed Montecchi that Cicognani "was in full agreement with the Embassy that the substitution of [non-Italian] pastors for Italian pastors must be avoided. [Cicognani had] expressed his hope . . . to resolve the question in a permanent way to the satisfaction of the Italian community, without recourse for the time being to ecclesiastical superiors [of the Mercedarians] in Rome." On 18 March, McFadden reported to Schrembs, "the only available Italian American priest with the proper requisites" required by Cicognani was Father Achilles Ferreri. McFadden also mentioned "the Reverend Stephen Towell, ordained in 1933 in Rome," as a possible pastor. Ultimately, Ferreri was named pastor and Towell his assistant.[59]

Sensing the Vatican's displeasure, Schrembs tried to salvage his standing with Cicognani with a recounting of events at odds with the notes taken by diocesan officials. "The imposition of the interdict was not a rash measure. It was imposed only after long deliberation and an unfortunate public scandalous riot." Schrembs placed the blame upon Father Loi-Zedda, who "stirred up the people" and urged them "to resist to the dead end." In stark contrast to diocesan notes, Schrembs recounted his "infinite patience and kindness for almost three hours" in his meeting with Holy Redeemer representatives. The parishioners, according to Schrembs, "insisted" on the appointment of Loi-Zedda "and said unanimously: 'Give us Luigi [Loi-Zedda] . . . or diocesan priests or excommunicate us.'" The installations had been prevented because the people were "stirred up by a communistic crowd." Schrembs claimed he had communicated "again and again in the kindliest and most positive manner" with "the so-called parochial committee." He assured Cicognani that the installation of diocesan clergy and the removal of the Mercedarians would bring "this entire trouble . . . to a happy end and . . . at the same time be a salutary lesson to those who would attempt mob violence against the Church."[60]

Although the ambassador and Cicognani chose not take Montecchi's advice to pressure Mercedarian superiors in Rome to recall Gattuso, they entered the fray just the same. Gattuso urged his Roman provincial, Francesco Contorni, to protest the imminent loss of Holy Redeemer. Contorni promised Schrembs "that in the future we will take every precaution." He "would gladly appoint another" Mercedarian instead of Caruso and pleaded with Schrembs to reconsider. "It is too sorrowful a duty to abandon in an instant our oldest field of labor in Cleveland." To compensate for their loss, Schrembs gave the Mercedarians St. Rocco's *in perpetuum.*[61]

Schrembs heeded Cicognani's instructions. On 19 March, he lifted the interdict in a service calculated to present an image of episcopal compassion and wisdom. The *Cleveland Press* described Schrembs's arrival at Holy Redeemer "amidst jubilant applause and cheering from about 1000 parishioners." Schrembs required that each parishioner "sever yourself from all spirit of rebellion" and cite a pledge of submission: "[I] humbly beg pardon for any offense I might have given by word, deed, intention or omission in connection with the resistance of Holy Redeemer Parish to ecclesiastical authority and to civil authority. . . . I hereby pledge unqualified submission to lawful ecclesiastical authority. . . . And I further pledge unqualified submission to lawful civil authority." Schrembs introduced Ferreri as pastor and Towell as assistant pastor. No mention was made of Caruso or the Mercedarians. The diocesan *Catholic Universe Bulletin* observed how "thousands were on hand to greet the Archbishop," as opposed to the "small group of parishioners" who had resisted Caruso's installment the previous month. The *Bulletin* dryly commented: "The Fathers of the Order of Mercy, who have had charge of the parish since its establishment in 1924 notified the Archbishop that they were withdrawing."[62]

Only the Lateran Pacts of 1929 made such extensive cooperation possible among American bishops, the Vatican, and Fascist Italy. In moments of conflict, consuls operated as constituent elements of the American Church—negotiators, investigators, episcopal confidants, fund-raisers, and public relations specialists. Performing these tasks, consuls filled a power vacuum. There were no Italian clergy knowledgeable about local conditions and trusted by American bishops. Thus, even as World War II unfolded, American bishops found themselves dependent upon Fascist Italy to maintain their episcopal authority and their image of pastoral decency. Just as bishops and consuls worked together within the United States, the Vatican and the Fascist state cooperated in Washington, D.C., and Rome.

Epilogue

Although the Italian invasion of Ethiopia in 1935 and 1936 strained relations between Italy and America, U.S. policy makers did not rethink their assumptions about Benito Mussolini and Fascism. President Franklin D. Roosevelt and his State Department held to the view that Mussolini, a moderate Fascist, could restrain Adolf Hitler and help maintain peace in Europe. The Roosevelt administration considered the Ethiopian conquest a colonial war, troubling only insofar as it might spark a European conflagration. Harsh sanctions against Mussolini, besides alienating Italian Americans from the Democratic Party, might just push the Duce into Hilter's arms. The administration wanted to avoid this risk.[1]

Ambassador William Phillips in Rome, an advocate of appeasement, stood in a long line of Mussolini admirers. "Through his dynamic personality and great human qualities [the Duce] has created a new and vigorous race throughout Italy. He is essentially interested in bettering conditions of the masses and his accomplishments in this direction are astounding and are a source of constant amazement to me." Historian David Schmitz has argued that Mussolini was central to Roosevelt's effort to appease Germany from 1936 to 1938, through international trade and economic interdependence. The president's October 1937 quarantine speech did not mark a departure from the policy of appeasement toward one of collective security. After the speech, Phillips wrote in his diary, the "Italian people were so accustomed to an authoritarian form of government that any [government] along the lines of democracy would be a complete failure. . . . I sought to impress upon the President the mistake of condemning [the] dictator form of government as such."[2]

Even after U.S. policy makers abandoned appeasement in 1938, they clung to the hope that Mussolini would moderate Hitler. In June 1938, Phillips reckoned, "the Italians can be counted upon to counsel moderation in both Berlin and Prague." After the May 1939 Pact of Steel aligned Fascist Italy with Nazi Germany, Phillips wrote Roosevelt, "I believe that Mussolini is so anxious to avoid war that we may hope for his calming influence upon Hitler." As German armies swept across Europe, Roosevelt tried to keep Mussolini out of the conflict. The president sent Italy America Society officer Myron Taylor as a personal representative to Pope Pius XII (1939–58) to work with the Vatican to keep Italy out of the war, but to no avail. Fascist Italy attacked France on 10 June. Angry and betrayed, Roosevelt delivered a bitter speech at the University of Virginia. "The hand that held the dagger has struck it into the back of its neighbor." The speech, whose imagery made Italian Americans cringe, intensified American Catholic repudiations of Fascist Italy, which had begun only slowly in 1938.[3]

The Vatican felt the wounds inflicted upon Catholic Italy during World War II. When Pius sent a letter of support to the Archbishop of Palermo after Sicily experienced the heat of war, American Jesuit Vincent McCormick wrote in his diary: "Holy See seems to manifest very keen interest in sufferings of civilian population when this population is Italian. They are fully aware of what cruel sufferings have been inflicted on civil population in Slovenia, Croatia and Greece, and this by Italians—burning of whole towns, murder of innocent hostages in revenge, and no letter of sympathy has been published as sent to Bishops of those parts. I am finding it more and more difficult, really impossible to defend the neutrality of the present-day Vatican."[4]

In World War II, as in the Great War, the status of papal Rome shaped relations among the Holy Father, the American Church, and the U.S. government. Pius persistently tried to prevent Allied bombers from striking the Eternal City. In May 1943, he pleaded with Roosevelt to recognize the sacred character of Rome. In July, after the Allies struck the basilica of San Lorenzo and killed 1,500 civilians, Pius XII wrote the president: "Since divine Providence has placed Us head over the Catholic Church and Bishop of this city so rich in sacred shrines and hallowed, immortal memories, We feel it Our duty to voice a particular prayer and hope that all may recognize that a city, whose every district, in some districts every street has its irreplaceable monuments of faith or art and Christian culture, cannot be attacked without inflicting an incomparable loss on the patrimony of Religion and Civilization."[5]

Pius urged the U.S. hierarchy on numerous occasions to save Rome from ruin. In September 1943, Archbishops Samuel Stritch of Chicago, Francis Spellman of New York, and Edward Mooney of Detroit drafted a memorial to remind Roosevelt of "the moral risks our Country assumed in bombing Rome." "The City of the Popes" was under the "control of forces that hate Christianity and its outstanding spokesman in the world today." Those forces "would welcome any pretext for wreaking destruction there." The archbishops threatened Roosevelt. "More than twenty million American Catholics" hope "their government will not have to share further responsibility for even more disastrous developments that threaten the Holy See."[6] Notwithstanding these efforts, the bombing continued until the Allies liberated the Eternal City in 1944.

On the evening of 24 July 1943, the Fascist Grand Council voted nineteen to seven to compel Mussolini to return to King Vittorio Emanuele III sovereign power over the army. When Mussolini visited the monarch the following day, King

Vittorio dismissed the Duce, had him arrested, and named Marshal Pietro Bado-
glio head of government. Sadly, the status of Italy remained unclear until Bado-
glio finally surrendered on 8 September, when he and the king abandoned Rome.
During the interim, the so-called Forty-Five Days, Germany reinforced its position in Italy and occupied Rome. The Nazis engineered Mussolini's escape from
his Allied prison and installed the aging Duce at the head of a Nazi puppet state,
the Fascist Social Republic (1943–45), in northern Italy. While partisans struggled
against Fascists and Nazis in the north, the Allies invaded Sicily, thrust north-
ward, and got bogged down 100 miles south of Rome.[7]

As these events unfolded, fierce debates ensued over the fate of postwar Italy.
U.S. liberals and conservatives clashed, anti-Fascist exiles and Italian American leaders locked horns, and factions within Roosevelt's government, the Vatican, and Great Britain also struggled to define Italy's future. American Catholics
clashed with liberals over the legitimacy of the monarchy and the role the Vatican
had played in Fascist Italy. In September 1943, anti-Fascists held a conference at
Carnegie Hall entitled "After Fascism What?" Gaetano Salvemini and George La
Piana answered in their 1943 book, What to Do with Italy. A fuorucito and eminent
historian driven from his post at the University of Florence in 1925, Salvemini had
filled the Lauro De Bosis lectureship in Italian culture at Harvard University since
1933. La Piana, a Harvard divinity school church historian, was a Sicilian modernist priest who had left Italy before the Great War. Both U.S. citizens, they sought
to reshape the terms of the debate about Italian reconstruction.[8]

The Harvard historians wrote with urgency against British and American
schemes for postwar Italy and to counteract the influence they believed the Vatican and the U.S. hierarchy had on Roosevelt. Against Allied plans to preserve an
authoritarian system cleansed only of Mussolini, the anti-Fascist historians contended that the monarchy, the Vatican, and the Italian Church had collaborated
with the regime and did not merit postwar support. What to Do with Italy produced
statements from American bishops who had lauded Fascism and Mussolini for
two decades, while it castigated racist myths that Latin people could not govern
themselves and that Italians were unprepared for liberty. The authors cited Vatican radio broadcasts that condemned the atheistic United States and reprinted
anti-Semitic passages from Civiltà Cattolica that mirrored Fascist legislation.

Salvemini and La Piana took to task the Catholic reading of Italian history
that "the unification of Italy, having been the work of anticlericals bent upon destroying the Church, could not but produce criminal statesmen using criminal
means. Hence Garibaldi was . . . a highway robber, Cavour an immoral cheat,
and Mazzini a leader of a gang of assassins and a mad dreamer. But finally Mussolini arrived and he saved the Church from the Italian gangsters. This was the
picture of Italy and of her pre-Fascist history that the average American Catholic
had, and perhaps still has, in his mind." The Harvard historians criticized "the

constant and unscrupulous [clerical] propaganda . . . [that] tries to mislead the American public into believing that the Italian republicans are only a few desperadoes, revolutionary socialists, and what not." They cited Father John Tracy Ellis, historian at the Catholic University of America, who wrote in 1942 that those advocating an Italian republic to replace the monarchy were "socialist revolutionaries under the cloak of republicans," who wanted to instigate "an international socialist revolution." Salvemini and La Piana contrasted Ellis to Luigi Sturzo. A priest and founder of the PPI in 1919, Sturzo had fled Fascist Italy in 1926 for London and arrived in New York in October 1940. Unlike the pope, Ellis, and other American Catholics, Sturzo called for a republic and political democracy in Italy.[9]

Salvemini and La Piana envisioned a republic that embodied a pure liberalism. Liberal Italy had outgrown its monarchy, a transitional institution hobbling awkwardly between absolutism and republicanism. The monarch had stunted the evolution of democracy and become "a parasitic survival" and a "menace to democratic institutions." So, too, the "hybrid" liberalism embodied in Liberal Italy's Church-state union had to go. While Vatican City should be left untouched, Salvemini and La Piana called for the separation of the Church and the state and an end to state enforcement of ecclesiastical law. The concordat, they insisted, imposed measures "taken at the expense of the people's rights to freedom of religion, freedom of association, and equality before the law—the cornerstone of democracy." Promoting an "American system" for Italy, as liberals had for a century, Salvemini and La Piana predicted howls of protest from Ellis and Wilfred Parsons, the Jesuit author of *The Pope and Italy*. They also suspected that the Vatican "will do again what it did in 1870," namely, take "the attitude that it is the innocent victim of Italian anti-religious groups bent on destroying the Church."[10]

The Sturzo-Salvemini exchange that followed the publication of *What to Do with Italy* put Sturzo in a difficult position. Although he meekly suggested that La Piana and Salvemini had not understood the "psychology" of Pius XI, the Christian Democrat did not even try to deny Salvemini's claim that American Catholics had supported Fascism and Mussolini. "There have been Catholic journalists in this country who have refuted [Salvemini's] accusation with the affirmation of principle: the Church is the antithesis of totalitarianism. They are right, but they leave Catholics and their adversaries unconvinced, because the facts are there to attest [to] the collaboration of the Church with [Italian] fascism, and the enthusiasm toward fascist gestures in favor of the Church on the part of many Catholics, laymen, priests and bishops—a thing that has disturbed many consciences."[11]

After Italy had been knocked out of the war, interim governments under the king and ex-Fascists did little to remove collaborators from power, and Great Britain and the Vatican in particular were averse to liberal or Social Democratic anti-Fascist calls for reform. The purge of Fascist police, prefects, state bureaucracies, and the judiciary generally failed. The liberation of Rome in the summer of 1944 brought unstable coalitions of anti-Fascist parties to power, but they lacked adequate Allied backing and were weakened by internal divisions.[12]

In June 1946, Italians voted to replace the monarchy with a republic and to elect a Constituent Assembly to write a new constitution. The assembly debated the concordat of 1929 until Palmiro Togliatti, the leader of the Partito Comunista Italiana (PCI), who had recently returned from Moscow, shocked his followers and called upon them to vote to preserve the concordat. Incorporated into the new constitution, the concordat contradicted other constitutional assurances of equality before the law for all citizens regardless of religion. (Anti-Protestant discrimination continued, or perhaps intensified, in Republican Italy.) Although Prime Minister Alcide De Gasperi, the leader of Democrazia Cristiana (DC), temporarily included communists and socialists in his governments before 1948, the papacy mobilized Catholic Action to back the DC, reconciled to the fact that an authoritarian Catholic regime along the lines of Franco's Spain was not possible in postwar Italy. In the elections of 1948, 1953, and 1958, the American Church and the U.S. government worked to undermine the PCI in favor of the DC, the dominant political force in postwar Italy for five decades. One century after Pius IX fled papal Rome into exile in 1848 and launched unequivocal condemnations of the Risorgimento, a Catholic party with ties to the Vatican took the mantle of the Italian republic.[13]

The birth of the republic coincided with a wave of anti-Catholicism in the United States. Historians Philip Gleason and John McGreevy have outlined the mid-twentieth-century U.S. liberal critique of Catholicism as an authoritarian culture with affinities to generic "fascism" or "totalitarianism." What explains this outbreak of anti-Catholicism? America, of course, had a long history of bigotry toward Catholics. Furthermore, by midcentury, thoroughly naturalistic strands of liberal thought were deeply critical of Catholic belief in the supernatural. Debates over whether the United States ought to establish formal diplomatic relations with the Holy See generated tensions as well. I would suggest, however, that the Catholic Church's relationship to Fascism since 1922 and the near absence of any self-critical Catholic evaluation of those two decades contributed in part to these postwar criticisms of the Church.[14]

Words such as "anti-Catholicism" and "anticlericalism" can mislead if they homogenize informed (even if angry) critics with those imprisoned within the pathologies of prejudice. Several liberal critics of Catholicism, such as George Seldes, Salvemini, and La Piana, were quite knowledgeable about the relationship between Fascism and the Church. Seldes, whose book The Catholic Crisis (1939) Gleason and McGreevy cite as an exemplar of anti-Catholicism, was the Chicago Tribune's Rome correspondent until Mussolini had him expelled in 1926 for his efforts at honest journalism. In The Vatican: Yesterday, Today, Tomorrow (1934), Seldes penned an informed discussion of the relationship between Catholicism and Fascism, and his hostile biography of the Duce, *Sawdust Caesar* (1935), accurately reported Mussolini's attack on civil liberties.[15] In *What to Do with Italy*, Salvemini and La Piana assailed all supporters of Mussolini. Their polemic was aimed not only at Catholics but at British and U.S. statesmen, journalists, social scientists, humanists, Wall Street bankers, and fellow liberals. It would be misleading, however, to conflate these critics with Paul Blanshard.

Catholics were not the only Americans to "forget" their relationship to Fascism, but they rose up most aggressively to insist that the Church had always been anti-Fascist. *America*, the Jesuit weekly that had so warmly praised the Duce between the wars, blissfully contended in 1945 that Mussolini had precipitated his own downfall when he violated the concordat! Fascism, *America* had rather suddenly learned, was a "poison" that "struck at the very roots of human dignity." Historians have highlighted the swift, opportunistic volte-face among Italian American leaders away from Fascist Italy at the end of the 1930s.[16] Catholic historiography, in contrast, has explored neither the American Catholic association with Fascism nor how that relationship shaped perceptions of the Church during and after World War II.

During the Cold War, Catholic intellectuals boasted how their neo-Thomistic natural law tradition and its eternal, unchanging truths shielded Catholics from the lures of totalitarianism. In the hands of Hannah Arendt and other Cold War intellectuals, totalitarianism came to signify Nazism and communism. Italian Fascism fell off the radar screen. Hence, Catholics could contend that the flabby relativism of liberals left intellectuals unarmed against the radical evil of totalitarianism, which Catholics opposed.[17] While no one can challenge American Catholic anticommunist credentials, that Cold War crusade cannot stand in for a nonexistent anti-Fascism during the 1920s and 1930s. Ideology, not a commitment to natural law theology, shaped Catholic responses to Fascism. Exuberant participation in the realization of the ideology of the Roman Question, not theology, reigned among Catholics when Father John A. Ryan, Carlton Hayes, and Father Wilfred Parsons defended the Lateran Pacts and a confessional state in Italy. Ideological commitments, not theology, motivated U.S. bishops to consecrate Mussolini's diplomats and the symbols of Fascism with the Roman salute or to call upon Fascist consuls to solve their administrative problems with ethnic minorities.

Remembering the Catholic Past:
Reflections on American Catholic Exceptionalism

Salvemini and La Piana wrote with informed urgency in 1943 for constructive purposes. Paul Blanshard, on the other hand, notwithstanding his claims to be defending democracy, appeared to have less wholesome motives. He unflinchingly likened the Vatican, a "totalitarian church," to the Kremlin, a "totalitarian state." In 1951 he warned, "Catholicism is not merely a religion; it is also a foreign government with a diplomatic corps." He elaborated: "The Pope's sovereignty is a special limited imperialism, operating within each nation as a government outside the government. . . . The Catholic colony in each country is . . . an imperial segment obedient to the Vatican in a strictly limited sphere."[18] Less acerbic arbiters of the boundaries of loyal Americanism believed Blanshard lacked civility, and they began to talk and listen to Catholic neighbors in a new way.

Father John Tracy Ellis earned the respectful attention of the new pluralists. In 1955 he delivered four addresses on the American Church at the University of Chicago under the auspices of the Charles R. Walgreen Foundation for the Study of American Institutions. Civility reigned supreme. The foundation also sponsored lectures on American Protestantism and Judaism. Ellis's lectures were published as *American Catholicism* (1956) in the Chicago History of American Civilization series edited by Daniel J. Boorstin. Predictably, Ellis stressed how Catholics in seventeenth-century colonial Maryland and New York granted forms of religious toleration that anticipated the First Amendment of the U.S. Constitution. Although he never mentioned the Roman Question, the installation of an apostolic delegation, the Lateran Pacts, or Mussolini and Fascism, Ellis stressed Catholic anticommunism. "If Americans wish to oppose communism, it is scarcely the part of wisdom to continue attacks upon" the Church. He quoted Tocqueville: "I think that the Catholic religion has erroneously been regarded as the natural enemy of democracy."[19]

The anti-Catholicism of Blanshard and his intellectual ancestors shaped the structure and content of *American Catholicism*. Reflecting on this period, historian Alan Brinkley explains, "the task of intellectuals was the defense of the pluralistic assumptions of American democracy and the delegitimation of the dangerous ideologies that challenged them from both the left and the right." Ellis sought to convince the arbiters of legitimacy that the Church was not dangerous; that it dwelt within the boundaries of normative Americanism. Dismissing Blanshard's cutting assertions, midcentury pluralists such as Boorstin, Martin E. Marty, and Will Herberg welcomed Ellis's assurances. Hence, alongside its Protestant and Jewish counterparts in Boorstin's series, the Catholic Church was an "American Institution," a constituent element of "American Civilization." The legacy of this victory of civility endured when John F. Kennedy became the first Catholic president.[20]

Before the Vatican Council II (1962–65), Church historians like Ellis invented an "American Catholicism" to offer evidence that the Catholic minority was comprised of loyal and valuable citizens. The Church educated patriotic citizens, Americanized immigrants, and contributed to the social welfare. It was not divisive, and it took care of its own. With measured civility, midcentury pluralists welcomed Ellis's assurances that Roman Catholicism in the United States was "American Catholicism," one form of Americanism in the pluralist trinity: Protestant, Catholic, Jew. Catholics were not ready in 1960 to explore what I have called the ideology of the Roman Question.[21]

For more than a century before Vatican Council II, American Catholics had been making two claims central to the invention of "American Catholicism." First, like Pius IX, they demonized a vast spectrum of European liberalisms as evil, Masonic, and linked to secret and criminal forces bent on attacking the Holy Father and destroying the Church. I have demonstrated that American Catholics joined wholeheartedly in this international onslaught against Italian liberals and Italian liberalism. Second, American Catholics insisted that the liberal premises of the U.S. political order were profoundly different from the false, degenerate liberalism of Europe. Normative American liberalism was warm and welcoming, and it granted true liberty to the Catholic Church. In fact, Catholics argued, the natural law principles behind American liberalism and the U.S. Constitution were derived from medieval Catholicism. Both claims shaped Father John Courtney Murray's classic essays brought together in *We Hold These Truths* (1960).[22]

A new generation of Catholics who lived through, or vicariously participated in, the enthusiasms of Vatican Council II have reinvented "American Catholicism." From Murray's Catholic argument for an *American* exceptionalism, the new generation made a theological and historical leap to an environmental argument for an American *Catholic* exceptionalism. The unique American environment of liberty, this new generation of historians and theologians claimed, gave birth to a unique Catholicism in the history of the Church. This American Catholicism was part and parcel of the American landscape, a mainstream denomination, and not, as Murray or Ellis had assumed, a loyal minority religion operating under distinctive premises within the United States. This American Catholicism was a denomination like any Christian denomination, not "the Church." For Ellis and Murray, it had been self-evident that the Church was a hierarchical, clerical, patriarchal, and international institution (although they might not have used those terms). Their concern had been to demonstrate that the one, holy, apostolic Church founded by Christ thrived legally and loyally within a properly ordered republic. The new generation, in contrast, claimed *normative* American Catholicism was democratic in impulse, congregational in polity, collegial in leadership; a Catholic version of the *novus ordo seclorum*.

Examples of this shift abound in Catholic scholarship since 1960, but I can only point to a few instances here. Historian Jay Dolan, in his influential 1985 synthesis, contended that small outposts of colonial Catholics in the 1770s "began to articulate an understanding of Roman Catholicism that was unique in Western Christendom." When parish studies came into vogue as the way to do "people's history" in the 1970s, historians discerned an American Catholic democracy in unexpected places. Historian Leslie Woodcock Tentler, for instance, described how angry Polish peasants in Detroit in the 1880s revolted against their pastor. She acknowledged that the immigrant rebels appealed for justice to their bishop, the apostolic delegation, and the Vatican and thus they affirmed traditional hierarchical structures of Church authority. But writing amidst postconciliar exuberance, Tentler asserted that the redemptive American environment, in this case in Detroit in the 1880s, had turned angry Polish peasants into democratic American Catholics who anticipated the reforms of Vatican Council II. She concluded that the insurgents had developed "an alternative vision of Church authority, one that is obviously more democratic" than a "clerical vision."[23]

One salient characteristic of this "Americanist" historiography was to use a monolithic "Europe" as a foil. For example, historian James Hennesey, sj, began one essay asserting his "underlying thesis" in these bipolar terms: "The Roman Catholic Church in the United States developed in a political and social climate radically different from the European, and . . . its unique development affected its theological thinking in ways that can scarcely be understood if we attempt to fit them into categories conditioned by the European experience." The essay, however, made no analysis whatsoever of "the European experience," its "climate," or its "categories." Hennesey's was a comparative argument without comparison.[24]

Americanist historiography glaringly ignored how some European Catholics struggled to develop liberal and democratic traditions. In the case of Italy, as we have seen, American Catholics ferociously condemned advocates of liberal Catholicism after 1848, particularly the representatives of the Historic Right (the Destra), the statesmen who established the Kingdom of Italy and hoped its liberal environment might trigger Catholic reform. Americanist historiography unquestioningly accepted the claims of their American Catholic subjects (and Pius IX) regarding the significance of the Risorgimento.

In this historiographical tradition of heroes and villains, "European Catholicism" and "the Vatican" were static, ahistorical forces of reaction. Dolan's survey narrates how European immigration brought regressive "European Catholicism" into the United States and undermined the evolution of "American Catholicism." Unenlightened Vatican "interference"—a phenomenon rarely studied in any systematic manner but always invoked—undermined the intellectual development and collegial leadership of American Catholicism. Consequently, before 1965 true American Catholicism subsisted as a stillborn vision or an unused blueprint hidden beneath the institutions, devotions, ideas, and social life of the enormous Catholic ghetto. Then, Vatican Council II awakened this dormant American Catholic tradition, which taught the Catholic world about liberty, pluralism, and democracy. While this historiography inspired valuable studies of laity, women, and ethnic groups and was therefore welcomed by the historical profession, it was still a Catholic internalist tradition, shaped by intra-Catholic debates about contemporary reforms in parishes, dioceses, and educational institutions.[25] And although recent studies of Catholic devotionalism and intergroup relations have moved beyond these intra-Catholic political concerns,[26] Americanist historiography still persists and inhibits the integration of Catholic history into the larger narratives of U.S. history.

This internalist historiography has parallels to other fields of history that struggle with the issue of American exceptionalism. In search of a unique American Catholic past, postconciliar (post–Vatican Council II) historians and theologians ignored the profound connectedness of European and American Catholic peoples, ideas, practices, and institutions. They imagined into existence "Europe" as a foil and thus set up a falsely autonomous "American Catholicism" when one never existed. My point is not that national traditions do not shape modern Catholicism. It is, rather, that Catholicism (or better, the Catholicisms) in the United States were never independent, autonomous, and unconnected to Europe, which itself was dynamic and profoundly heterogenous. As historian Daniel Rodgers has stated, "the antithesis at the core of exceptionalist history was never that between difference and sameness but between autonomy and connection." In this study, I have tried to demonstrate, as Rodgers says, that the "abandonment of dichotomous for connected development" reveals a transnational story in which the papacy, Rome, and the Kingdom of Italy had a central place in the development of the American Church and social relations between Catholics and their non-Catholic American neighbors.[27]

Vatican officials had good reason to be wary of arguments for American exceptionalism. If Old World liberalism was merely a pretext for assaults on the Church, New World liberalism appeared to be a disguise for Protestant hegemony. What did the Holy Father learn about America from the letters his faithful children sent him? Americans assaulted Archbishop Bedini in 1854 and devoured fiction that portrayed priests as nun violators and infant murderers. Americans tried to exclude immigrants because they were Catholic and invented paranoiac stories of a global Catholic conspiracy to conquer North America. Americans read illicit Bibles in state schools, shrieked in horror at the success of Catholic politicians, and classified Italians from Liguria, Tuscany, or Umbria as "South Italians" whose misshapen foreheads made them unlikely material for citizenship. Americans refused to establish diplomatic relations with the Holy See when other non-Catholic and non-Christian states had done so. The Vatican observed how the American Catholic elite lived a type of double life. They patriotically praised America in the public culture but carried out seemingly harmless and perfectly legal activities on behalf of their Church in secret in order not to trigger irrational condemnations or insults.

In 1953 Msgr. Giovanni Battista Montini of the Vatican Secretariat of State, the future Pope Paul VI (1963–78), with understandable frustration, wrote Cardinal

Francis Spellman of New York that "the Holy See cannot remain indifferent to the unreasonable and unreasoning attitude of non-Catholics in the United States. In connection with this matter of diplomatic representation and on other occasions in the recent past, there have been repeated, vulgar, bitter and entirely unjustified attacks against the Holy See, with unwarranted deductions and unmerited conclusions that are scarcely compatible with the 'freedom' of which the United States claims to be the champion and the custodian."[28]

The two foundational claims of American Catholic exceptionalism need to be historicized and relativized, because their unquestioned persistence in Catholic scholarship inhibits comparative analysis that might bring insight into what was "American" about the Church in the United States. First, there was no shortage of anti-Catholicism in the eighteenth-century embryonic American nation. The founders, both deists and a broad spectrum of English-speaking Protestants, did not have to seriously contend with Catholicism and surely did not have to protect the new state from the intransigent likes of Pius IX. If they had, anti-Catholic fangs would surely have shown themselves more frequently. Whether or not the American Revolution was a transatlantic religious war between dissenting Protestants and Anglicans (the English approximation of "papists"), it surely drew upon cultural forces that were deeply anti-Catholic. Anti-Catholicism was a constituent element of the identity of colonial Britons who created the republic. Only the timidity of a tiny colonial Catholic population permitted the architects of the federal government to grant religious liberty. (Not all state governments were so generous.)[29]

Second, many European liberals were also liberal Catholics. The moderate advocates of the Risorgimento, those men who ruled the Kingdom of Piedmont and then the Kingdom of Italy until 1876, were overwhelmingly Catholic. After they defeated their republican opponents and protected the Church in Italy from a Kulturkampf, they granted privileges to the Church and secured the safety and independence of the pope. Had the papacy cooperated with the Catholic constitutional monarchy and taken the opportunity to reform the Church's more antiquated structures, forces that were genuinely anti-Catholic might never have won the influence they gained in the later decades of the nineteenth century. Even Daniel Binchy, the Irish Catholic author of the 1941 classic *Church and State in Fascist Italy*, referring to "the responsible leaders of the national movement" in Liberal Italy, claimed, "none of them can be fairly described as anti-Catholic, and most of them were believing Catholics." King Vittorio Emanuele II "certainly was a Catholic, and if his religion was not of a very high quality it was at least sincere." Binchy remarked with irony, "The Roman Question was created by a Government of Catholics and settled by a Government largely composed of agnostics." He added, "the power of Masonry in the past has been grossly exaggerated by Catholic publicists."[30]

Once scholars subject these two normative claims to historical analysis and thus qualify their significance, testable hypotheses about what may be distinctive to the Church in America may emerge, and the isolation of the study of American Catholics from that of Europe may end. This would require, however, studies of transnational institutions such as religious congregations of men and women, missionary societies, diocesan immigrant priests, popular devotions to saints and madonnas, Catholic families, and the Vatican's delegations and nuncios. Presently, studies of these institutions are usually arbitrarily divorced from their European matrix. While historians of U.S. immigration explore homelands abroad, Catholic historians stay home.[31] In 1968, historian David O'Brien suggested, "church historians might utilize the insights of historians who insist on a comparative dimension for the study of American history and attempt to evaluate the character of the social and religious background from which the immigrants came in order to determine what was uniquely American in Catholic life in the United States." O'Brien's proposal fell on deaf ears. Furthermore, the integration of American and European Catholic history would also require Americanists to acknowledge that English-speaking Catholics are not the whole story of the Church in the United States.[32]

This study has employed ideological analysis to map out a transnational story that reveals the dynamics of the international Church and its impact within American society. Keen to preserve civilization as they understood it, Catholics united to the Holy See worked within, around, through, and across modern states to promote distinctive values. A common culture, however diffuse and uneven, shaped Catholic understandings of politics and international relations. Catholic immigrants surely assimilated into American society, but this did not end American Catholic participation in an international Catholic community. Indeed, American Catholic spokespeople and cultural producers acculturated into an international Roman Catholic order, a culture of juridical guidelines, common myths, texts, rituals, and symbols. This process of Catholic acculturation generated tension with liberal and national ideologies everywhere. The unfortunate intellectual habit of reducing the actions, writings, and beliefs of Euro-American Catholics to a function of their ethnicity has made Catholicism disappear as a historical variable in U.S. history, much to the detriment of our understanding of the United States within the wider world.

Notes

ABBREVIATIONS

AAB	Archive of the Archdiocese of Boston
AAC	Cardinal Joseph Bernardin Archive and Record Center, Archdiocese of Chicago
ACQR	*American Catholic Quarterly Review*
ACS	Archivio Centrale dello Stato, Rome
CPC	Casellario Politico Centrale
DPP	Direzione Generale di Pubblica Sicurezza, Divisione Polizia Politica, Ministero dell'Interno
MCP	Ministero della Cultura popolare
Nupie	Nuclei Propaganda Italiana all'Estero, Ministero della Cultura popolare
ACUA	Archive of the Catholic University of America
NCWC	National Catholic Welfare Conference
ADC	Archive of the Diocese of Cleveland
HR	Holy Redeemer Parish Papers
SP	Joseph Schrembs Papers
ADP	Archive of the Diocese of Providence
APCMR	Archivio del Pontificio Consiglio per la Pastorale dei Migranti e Itineranti, Rome
APF	Archivio della Congregazione "De Propaganda Fide," Rome
SOCG	Scritture Originali riferite nelle Congregazione Generali, America Centrale
APIE	Archivio del Prelato per l'Emigrazione Italiana, Rome
ASMAE	Archivio Storico Diplomatico, Ministero degli Affari Esteri, Rome
LSRD	I Fondi Archivistici della Legazione Sarda e delle Rappresentanze Diplomatiche Italiani negli Stati Uniti d'America, 1848–1901
AMB II	Fondo Ambasciata a Washington, 1920s
AP1	Affari Politici verso gli Stati Uniti d'America, 1915–30
AP2	Affari Politici verso gli Stati Uniti d'America, 1931–45
AP2SS	Affari Politici verso la santa sede, 1931–45
CLE	I Fondi Archivistici dei Consolati in Cleveland
GAB	Archivio Politico Ordinario e di Gabinetto, 1915–18
SP	Serie P. Politici, 1891–1915

ASV	Archivio Segreto Vaticano, Rome
DAUS	Delegazione Apostolica negli Stati Uniti
SS	Segreteria di Stato
Spogli	Spogli di Cardinali e Officiali di Curia
b.	busta or Pacco
BLUCB	The Bancroft Library, University of California, Berkeley
PPIE	Panama Pacific International Exposition Records
c.	Cassetta (from Morini to Carraresi)
CA	*Christian Advocate*
CM	*Catholic Mirror*
Com	*Commonweal*
CP	Giuseppe Ciarrocchi Papers, Archive of the Archdiocese of Detroit
CPA	*Calendario della Parrocchia dell'Assunta*
CST	*Catholic Standard and Times*
CT	*Catholic Telegraph*
CW	*Catholic World*
ERI	*L'Eco del Rhode Island*
f.	foglio
fasc.	fascicolo
FLNF	Foreign Language Newspaper Files, Special Collections, Regenstein Library, University of Chicago
FLS	Fondo Luigi Sturzo, Archivio Luigi Sturzo, Istituto Luigi Sturzo
GUA	The America Magazine Papers, Archives, Special Collections Division, Georgetown University Library
NW	*New World*
NYT	*New York Times*
OLP	Records of Our Lady of Pompeii, Center for Migration Studies, New York
PFA	Paulist Fathers Archive, St. Paul's College, Washington, D.C.
SGP	Superior General Papers
PIA	*Il Progresso Italo-Americano*
rubr.	rubrica
TWLP	Thomas W. Lamont Papers, Harvard Business School, Baker Library Archives
USCM	*United States Catholic Magazine and Monthly Review*
VP	*La Voce del Popolo* (Detroit)
WC	*Western Catholic*

PREFACE

1. For the text of the speech, see the Vatican office's Web site at <http://www.vatican
.va/holy_father/john_paul_ii/speeches/2002/november/documents>.

INTRODUCTION

1. Martina, "La fine del potere temporale."
2. Camaiani, "Motivi e riflessi religiosi," 65–128.

3. See Steinfels, "Failed Encounter"; Gleason, "American Catholics and Liberalism"; and McGreevy, "Thinking on One's Own." These rich essays on liberalism and Catholicism more or less ignore the Italy-Vatican contest.

4. There has been no systematic study of the topic, which is usually ignored. M. O'Connell, in *John Ireland*, 276, and Hennesey, in "Papacy and Episcopacy," 184, dismiss the topic as irrelevant.

5. See Marty, *Righteous Empire*; Herberg, *Protestant-Catholic-Jew*; Wuthnow, *Restructuring of American Religion*; and Hunter, *Culture Wars*, 67–106.

6. Moore, *Religious Outsiders*, 48–71 (quote on 71). On presentist uses of Catholic history, see Appleby, "Triumph of Americanism"; and Gleason, "New Americanism in Catholic Historiography."

7. Dolan, "Catholicism and American Culture," 63 (quotations). See Byrne, "American Ultramontanism."

8. See Warner, "Place of the Congregation," 54 (on parishes); Dolan, *Catholic Revivalism* (on parish missions); T. Smith, "Religion and Ethnicity in America" (on the Exodus paradigm); Appleby, "*Church and Age Unite!*" (on the Catholic modernist impulse); Hutchison, *Modernist Impulse in American Protestantism*; Kim, "Roman Catholic Organization since Vatican II" (on Catholicism as a denomination); and K. Briggs, *Holy Siege*.

9. For recent works that capture Catholic distinctiveness, see Tweed, *Our Lady of the Exile*; Orsi, *Thank You, St. Jude*; and McGreevy, *Parish Boundaries*. Tweed as well as D. Molony, in *American Catholic Lay Groups*, and Allitt, in *Catholic Converts*, also deal with transnational Catholic issues.

10. See Bender, *Rethinking American History in a Global Age*; and Iriye, "Internationalization of History." For exemplary works, see Kloppenberg, *Uncertain Victory*; and Rodgers, *Atlantic Crossings*.

11. The literature is vast, although it rarely deals with religion. See Bezza, *Gli italiani fuori d'Italia*; Franzina, *Italiani al nuovo mondo*; Gabaccia, *Italy's Many Diasporas*; and Bosworth, *Italy and the Wider World*.

12. See the special issue of the *Journal of American History* 86 (Dec. 1999) titled "The Nation and Beyond: Transnational Perspectives on United States History." "Imagined community" is from Anderson, *Imagined Communities*. See also Iriye, *Cultural Internationalism and World Order*.

13. Heilbronner, "From Ghetto to Ghetto."

14. I draw upon Giddens, *Central Problems in Social Theory*, and *Constitution of Society*; Sewell, "Theory of Structure"; Thompson, *Studies in the Theory of Ideology*, 148–72, and *Ideology and Modern Culture*; Held and Thompson, *Social Theory of Modern Societies*; Wuthnow, *Meaning and Moral Order*, *Restructuring of American Religion*, and *Communities of Discourse*; Burns, *Frontiers of Catholicism*; and Therborn, *Ideology of Power*.

15. Giddens, *New Rules of Sociological Method*, 121; Sewell, "Theory of Structure," 6.

16. Burns, *Frontiers of Catholicism*, 9; Wuthnow, *Meaning and Moral Order*, 145.

17. Cassels, *Ideology and International Relations*, 1–8; Thompson, *Ideology and Modern Culture*.

18. Thompson, *Ideology and Modern Culture*, 59–67, 163–271. On the importance of repetition in Catholic ideology, see Dillon, *Catholic Identity*, 74; and Anderson, *Imagined Communities*.

19. Wuthnow, *Meaning and Moral Order*, 97–109 (quote on 109).

20. On ideological competition, see Wuthnow, *Meaning and Moral Order*, 148–49, 159–61.

21. On "negative autonomy," see Burns, *Frontiers of Catholicism*, 8–12.

22. Scholars have incorrectly assumed that Catholics, because they supported the First Amendment of the U.S. Constitution or liberal political parties, did not support the pope's temporal power. See, e.g., Burns, *Frontiers of Catholicism*, 79–80; and von Arx, "Cardinal Henry Edward Manning," 8, 92, 96.

23. See Chesterton, *Resurrection of Rome*, 263.

CHAPTER ONE

1. Marraro, *American Opinion*, 5 (Brady), 6 (van Buren and Dallas), 7 (Buchanan and Greeley), 315–17 (reprints the entire address to Pius IX).

2. Lyttelton, "Creating a National Past"; Traniello, *Da Gioberti a Moro*, 1–24; M. Clark, *Italian Risorgimento*, 7–15.

3. Chadwick, *History of the Popes*, 1–60; M. Clark, *Italian Risorgimento*, 16–35.

4. Lyttelton, "Creating a National Past"; Salvatorelli, *Risorgimento*, 1–109; Traniello, "Religione, nazione e sovranità," 322–26, and *Da Gioberti a Moro*, 43–62; Formigoni, *L'Italia dei cattolici*, 13–19; Giovagnoli, "Il neoguelfismo."

5. Traniello, "Religione, nazione e sovranità," 327 and 330 (quotations); Lyttelton, "Creating a National Past," 45–46; Giovagnoli, "Il neoguelfismo," 42–47.

6. Traniello, *Da Gioberti a Moro*, 25–42; Leetham, *Rosmini*, 337–71; Giovagnoli, "Il neoguelfismo," 48–50.

7. Scoppola, *Dal neoguelfismo alla democrazia cristiana*, 14 ("Levites"); Giovagnoli, "Il neoguelfismo," 46 ("human kind"); Traniello, "Religione, nazione e sovranità," 334 ("Italian genius" and "a nation of priests"). For a brief intellectual biography, see Rumi, *Gioberti*.

8. I borrow "anti-Risorgimento" from Salvatorelli, *Risorgimento*.

9. "Italian Nationality," USCM 6 (Sept. 1847): 457, 458, 459, 462, 466; "Italian Nationality," USCM 6 (Oct. 1847): 515–16. Both articles reviewed Gioberti's *Moral and Civil Primacy*.

10. "Italian Nationality," USCM 6 (Oct. 1847): 518, 522.

11. Hunt, *Ideology and U.S. Foreign Policy*, 102–6.

12. Coppa, *Pope Pius IX*; M. Clark, *Italian Risorgimento*, 47–49.

13. Fuller, "*These Sad but Glorious Days*," 136; Marraro, *American Opinion*, 10–27 (quotes Polk, 18); Vance, *Catholic and Contemporary Rome*, 111 (quotes Lester); Light, *Rome and the New Republic*, 308–16.

14. "Foreign Intelligence," CT, 17 Feb. 1848, 53 ("illiberal ecclesiastics"); "Pope Pius IX," CT, 23 Mar. 1848, 91 ("noble efforts"); CT, 27 Apr. 1848, 135 ("some even imagine"); "Foreign Intelligence," CT, 30 Mar. 1848, 100 ("a great blessing").

15. M. Clark, *Italian Risorgimento*, 51; Lovett, *Democratic Movement in Italy*, 114–15; Binchy, *Church and State in Fascist Italy*, 354–56.

16. Scoppola, *Dal neoguelfismo alla democrazia cristiana*, 18–19 (quotes Durando); M. Clark, *Italian Risorgimento*, 53.

17. Martina, *Pio IX*, 1:226, 245 (quotes Pius).

18. Coppa, *Cardinal Giacomo Antonelli*, 47–72; M. Clark, *Italian Risorgimento*, 51–58.

19. Lovett, *Democratic Movement in Italy*, 130–44.

20. "Position of Pius IX," CT, 22 June 1848, 194; "The Roman Outrages," CT, 28 Dec.

1848, 409; "Europe in Revolutionary Movement," *Pilot*, 9 Dec. 1848, 1 ("Liberty rose again" and "ferocious despotism"); "The Roman Crisis," *Pilot*, 9 June 1849, 7 ("disgracing themselves" and "laying hands on priests"); and Merwick, *Boston Priests*, 20–40.

21. "Prayers for the Pope," *Pilot*, 30 Dec. 1848, 3 (prints Eccleston's pastor letter).

22. "Private Life of Pope Pius IX," *Pilot*, 10 Feb. 1849, 5, reprinted in "Private Life of Pope Pius IX," *USCM*, 17 Feb. 1849, 97–99.

23. John Hughes, "The Present Position of Pius IX," in *Complete Works*, 2:13, 12, 13, 16, 17; Marraro, *American Opinion*, 54–55 (quotes the 12 Jan. 1849 *New York Herald*). For more on Hughes, see Mize, "Defending Roman Loyalties."

24. "Pius IX," *USCM*, 20 Jan. 1849, 33–34 (cites *Episcopal Recorder* and "fervently desired"); "Who Are the People?" *USCM*, 3 Mar. 1849, 131–32 ("Protestant press").

25. Reynolds, *European Revolutions*, 54–78; Giorcelli, "La Repubblica romana," 53–88; Douglas, *Feminization of American Culture*, 313–48; Fuller, *"These Sad but Glorious Days,"* 225, 229, 243–44, 249 (quotations).

26. Fuller, *"These Sad but Glorious Days,"* 277–78, 318, 321.

27. John Hughes, "Letter from Bishop Hughes in Reply to Hon. Horace Greeley," in *Complete Works*, 2:23; D. Fiorentino, "Il governo degli Stati Uniti," 89–130; Hunt, *Ideology and U.S. Foreign Policy*, 102–6.

28. Marraro, *American Opinion*, 70 (quotes Brown); Stock, *United States Ministers*, 18 ("speedy restoration"), 19 ("chances"), 59 (on passports); D. Fiorentino, "Il governo degli Stati Uniti," 89–130.

29. On diocesan contributions, see "Peter's Pence," *USCM*, 10 Nov. 1849, 712; Marraro, *American Opinion*, 58 (quotes Greeley), 61 (quotes *New York Herald*), 82 (quotes *Daily Tribune* dedication).

30. Martina, *Pio IX*, 1:377–422; Kertzer, *Popes against the Jews*, 113–17; Dante, *Storia della "Civiltà Cattolica,"* 57–77; Scoppola, *Dal neoguelfismo all democrazia cristiana*, 34 (quotes "Il giornalismo moderno e il nostro programma," *Civiltà Cattolica* 1 [1850]).

31. Martina, *Pio IX*, 2:153–286; Chadwick, *History of the Popes*, 95–131; Spalding, *Premier See*, 172–73; Billington, *Protestant Crusade*, 262–436; Taves, *Household of Faith*.

32. John Hughes, "Sermon on Pius's Return to Rome," in *Complete Works*, 2:35, 30–31.

33. Ibid., 31, 33, 34.

34. Monsagrati, "Gli intellettuali americani," 25–30; D. Fiorentino, "Il governo degli Stati Uniti," 95–96; Vance, *Catholic and Contemporary Rome*, 135–39 (quotes Dwight); Marraro, *American Opinion*, 92–93 ("Constituent Assembly").

35. On Gavazzi's sojourn, see Sanfilippo, "Tra antipapismo e cattolicesimo"; Marraro, *American Opinion*, 269–74; Gavazzi, "Diario autobiografico," 091273–091685, 091772 ("not a few ministers"), 091793 ("papists"), and 091771 ("ignorant fanaticism"), Biblioteca dell'Archivio di Stato di Roma.

36. Francis Kenrick to Gaetano Bedini, 13 Jan. 1854 ("secret societies"), John Hughes to Bedini, 1 Oct. 1853, and Bishop Richard Vincent to Bedini, 11 Jan. 1854, ASV, SS, Spogli, Bedini, b. 5A, fasc. c, "Corrispondenza dei Vescovi Americani."

37. William Read to Gaetano Bedini, 16 Jan. 1854, Adeline Whelan to Bedini, 26 Jan. 1854, Frank to Bedini, 9 Jan. 1854, John Mitchell to Bedini, 10 Nov. 1853, and William Oram to Bedini, 28 Jan. 1854, ASV, SS, Spogli, Bedini, b. 5A, fasc. c, "Corrispondenza dei Vescovi Americani."

38. Connelly, *Visit of Archbishop Gaetano Bedini*, 190–287 (quotes on 194, 195, 241, 240).

39. See Kertzer, *Kidnapping*.

40. Francis Kenrick to Francis Chatard, 17 Dec. 1858, Francis Silas Chatard Microfilms, University of Notre Dame Archives; Korn, *American Reaction to the Mortara Case*, 24, 25, 37, 45.

41. "The Mortara Case," *CM*, 20 Nov. 1858, 2 ("great joy" and "he imagined"); *CM*, 4 Dec. 1858, 2 ("Popery is on foot"); "The Alleged Kidnapping of a Jew Boy," *CM*, 20 Nov. 1858, 5 (cites *Freeman's Journal*); Kertzer, *Kidnapping*, 128 (quotes the pamphlet).

42. "Kidnapping Catholic Children," *CM*, 4 Dec. 1858, 5 ("evangelical perverters"); "Die Mortara Affaire," *Der Wahrheits-Freund*, 25 Nov. 1858, 162.

43. Korn, *American Reaction to the Mortara Case*, 143 (quotes *Brownson's Quarterly Review* [Apr. 1859]: 238–39), 145 (quotes *Pilot*, 18 Dec. 1858, 4).

44. Faber, *Devotion to the Pope*, 17, 27–28.

45. See Chabod, *Italian Foreign Policy*.

46. Hearder, *Cavour*; M. Clark, *Italian Risorgimento*, 62–74; Marraro, *American Opinion*, 187 (quotes Marsh).

47. M. Clark, *Italian Risorgimento*, 70–80.

48. Marraro, *American Opinion*, 238–43, 232 (quotes Buchanan); "The Bishops of the Province of New Orleans in Council," *Pilot*, 25 Feb. 1860, 6 ("veneration"). For descriptions of rallies and circular letters, see APF, Congressi America Centrale, vol. 18 (1859–60), f. 1104–339. See also Marraro, *American Opinion*, 269–71; "Grand Demonstration of Sympathy with the Pope," *Pilot*, 28 Jan. 1860, 4; "Sympathy with the Pope," *CM*, 3 Mar. 1860, 3; "American Sympathy for the Pope," *Pilot*, 17 Mar. 1860, 5; and "Sympathy with the Pope," *Pilot*, 26 May 1860, 5.

49. "Interesting Manifesto," *Pilot*, 4 Feb. 1860, 5.

50. Ibid. On the conspiratorial worldview, see Chabod, *Italian Foreign Policy*, 334–37; De Felice, *Jews in Fascist Italy*, 25–40; and Kertzer, *Popes against the Jews*.

51. "Lecture," *CM*, 17 Mar. 1860, 4–5.

52. "Protestant Editors and the Excommunication of Victor Emanuel," *Pilot*, 19 May 1860, 4.

53. "Garibaldi," *Pilot*, 16 June 1860, 4; "Garibaldi," *Pilot*, 14 July 1860, 4; "The Pope," *Pilot*, 30 Mar. 1861, 4.

54. *WC*, 16 Mar. 1872, n.p.

55. "Cavour's Speech in Turin," *Pilot*, 27 Apr. 1861, 4.

56. M. Clark, *Italian Risorgimento*, 80–85.

57. Marraro, *American Opinion*, 277–78 (quotes *New York World*, 6 Aug. 1860, and Charles Eliot Norton to A. H. Clough). For American views, see "Giuseppe Garibaldi," *North American Review* 92 (Jan. 1861): 15–56.

58. Marraro, *American Opinion*, 285–300; Lowenthal, *George Perkins Marsh*, 220–66; "Italy," *Pilot*, 22 Dec. 1860, 4 ("polls" and "train"). American steamers transported men and weapons between Genoa and Sicily for Garibaldi; and some of their men enrolled in his army. See "Facts about Sicily," *Pilot*, 16 June 1860, 4. Donations to the pope were ongoing; my numbers come from "The Church: United States," *Pilot*, 14 July 1860, 2; "Sympathy for the Pope," *Pilot*, 14 July 1860, 6; "Real Sympathy for the Holy Father," *Pilot*, 21 July 1860, 5; "Real Sympathy for the Pope," *Pilot*, 28 July 1860, 2; and *Names of Contributors*, 13–93.

59. "Allocution of Our Holy Father Pope Pius the Ninth," *Pilot*, 20 Apr. 1861, 1; Chadwick, *History of the Popes*, 176.

60. Scoppola, *Dal neoguelfismo alla democrazia cristiana*, 39 (quotes "Nè eletti, nè elettori,"

in *L'armonia della religione con la civiltà*); Formigoni, *L'Italia dei cattolici*, 33–56; Spadolini, *L'opposizione cattolica*, 41–211; G. De Rosa, *Il movimento cattolico in Italia*, 7–252.

61. Confessore, *I cattolici e la "Fede nella Libertà"*; Jemolo, *Chiesa e stato in Italia*, 241–482.

62. On the *mezzogiorno*, see Lumley and Morris, *New History of the Italian South*; Schneider, *Italy's "Southern Question"*; Riall, *Sicily and the Unification of Italy*; and Salvadori, *Il mito del buongoverno*. On the efforts to create an Italian national identity, see Levra, *Fare gli italiani*; Porciani, *La festa della nazione*; and Gentile, *La grande Italia*.

63. Jemolo, *Chiesa e stato in Italia*, 137–70; Halperin, *Separation of Church and State*, 1–39.

64. Chadwick, *History of the Popes*, 165–81 (quotation, 169); Martina, *Pio IX*, 2:287–356.

65. Spalding, *Martin John Spalding*, 240–45 (quotation, 241–42).

66. On the Founders, see Gaustad, *Neither King nor Prelate*, and *Sworn on the Altar of God*.

67. Martina, "La situazione degli istituti religiosi"; Binchy, *Church and State in Fascist Italy*, 380–81; M. Clark, *Italian Risorgimento*, 86–94.

68. Madden, "American Catholic Support"; Spalding, *Martin John Spalding*, 255–60.

69. "Ecumenical Council," *Pilot*, 1 Jan. 1870, 1 ("Coptic Deacon"); "The First General Council of the Vatican," *Pilot*, 8 Jan. 1870, 1 ("assemblage of dwellers"); "The Council," *Pilot*, 8 Jan. 1870, 1 ("Viva il Papa Re!"); Hennesey, *First Council of the Vatican*. One-half of the U.S. bishops deemed it inopportune to declare infallibility. But as historian Eric Yonke states regarding German Catholics, "the vote on papal infallibility at the Vatican Council" is "a poor indicator" as a "litmus test of ultramontanism" (Yonke, "Cardinal Johannes von Geissel," 37).

70. Martina, *Pio IX*, 3:233–54.

71. John Williams to Holy Father, 7 Nov. 1870, AAB, Archbishop John Williams Papers, box 4, folder 27; "Bishop Lynch on the Italian Occupation of Rome," *Pilot*, 8 Oct. 1870, 5; Spalding, *Martin John Spalding*, 326; Kenneally, "Question of Equality," 127.

72. M. O'Connell, *John Ireland*, 127–28 (quotes Ireland in *St. Paul Dispatch*, 23 Jan. 1871); Ellis, *James Cardinal Gibbons*, 2:345; Keane, *Providential Mission of Pius IX*, 13–14.

73. "Ausland," *Katholischer Glaubersbote*, 5 Oct. 1870, 1; "Der Sturz des Papstthums!" *Katholischer Glaubersbote*, 12 Oct. 1870, 4; "Die Ueberfälle der Stadt Rom," *Der Wahrheits-Freund*, 26 Apr. 1871, 299; Kulas, *Der Wanderer of St. Paul*, 69.

74. "The Political Kaleidoscope" and "Results of War," *Northwest Christian Advocate*, 28 Sept. 1870, 308; "Liberal Progress in Europe," *CA*, 22 Sept. 1870, 300.

75. Breed, *Restoration of the Pope*, 2, 4, 20, 23, 24; J. M. Macdon, "The Temporal Power of the Pope," *Princeton Review* 11 (1871): 133.

76. Arthur Coxe to Theodore Roosevelt, 27 Dec. 1870, Ch.J.5.135, Josiah Holland to Roosevelt, 30 Dec. 1870, Ch.B.11.16, and Asa Smith to Roosevelt, Ch.B.8.62, Theodore Roosevelt Papers, 1831–78, Rare Books and Manuscripts Division, Boston Public Library.

77. Vance, *Catholic and Contemporary Rome*, 210 (on Howe); Isaac Hecker to Orestes Brownson, 3 Apr. 1871, in Gower and Leliaert, *Brownson-Hecker*, 302; Orestes Brownson, "Sardinia and the Holy Father," *CW* 13 (June 1871): 289.

78. Jemolo, *Chiesa e stato in Italia*, 243–367; Pollard, *Vatican and Italian Fascism*, 16, 195–96; Halperin, *Separation of Church and State*, 18–39.

79. Chabod, *Italian Foreign Policy*, 5–66, 173–234, 467–95.

80. Martina, *Pio IX*, 3:254–57 (quotation, 257).

81. "The Italian Guarantees and the Sovereign Pontiff," *CW* 13 (July 1871): 567; Prendergast, *Temporal Power of the Pope*, 14, 15.

82. "Italian Rome," *Pilot*, 12 Nov. 1870, 1 (until "this class of men"); "The Seventy-Ninth Birthday of Pius IX," *Pilot*, 17 June 1871, 1. Notwithstanding Catholic claims, the religious vitality of Rome after the conquest of 1870 remain unchanged. See Camaiani, "Motivi e riflessi religiosi," 78–79.

83. Isaac Hecker, "The Outlook in Italy," *CW* 26 (Oct. 1877): 3.

84. Orestes Brownson, "Sardinia and the Holy Father," *CW* 13 (June 1871): 290; "The Italian Guarantees and the Sovereign Pontiff," *CW* 13 (July 1871): 567; *WC*, 10 June 1872, 7; *WC*, 24 Aug. 1872, 1.

85. "Letter from Rome," *CW* 13 (Apr. 1871): 134–39; "From Rome," *WC*, 14 May 1870, 283; "Irreligious Destruction," *WC*, 20 Dec. 1873, 4.

86. *WC*, 24 Aug. 1872, 1.

87. "Mr. Medill's Italian Government," *WC*, 9 Jan. 1875, 4.

88. Shea, *Life of Pius IX*, 3, 287, 161, 162, 417–18. For another popular biography, see O'Reilly, *Life of Pius IX*.

89. "The Rising Generation in Italy," *Milwaukee Catholic Magazine*, 1 Feb. 1875, 59, 58.

CHAPTER TWO

1. Isaac Hecker, "An Exposition of the Church in View of Recent Difficulties," *CW* 21 (Apr. 1875): 117, 121; "The Catholics of the World Own Every Inch of Ground in Rome," *Catholic Times*, 3 Sept. 1881.

2. Cross, in *Emergence of Liberal Catholicism*, claims "American Catholic disinterest" (83) in the temporal power. But he misreads this statement from "The Roman Question—Does It Concern Us?" (*American Ecclesiastical Review* 1 [Nov.–Dec. 1889]): "The very name [temporal power] is uncongenial to [American Catholics], who consider that religion and civil rule have their several fields of actions, almost incompatible with the other." But this sentence was merely rhetorical. The author continues: "Leo XIII recognizes that this struggle for the temporal power is in reality a struggle for the spiritual power" (446). "As a matter of principle [the temporal power] comes very close to us. If the temporal power were yielded, a decided injustice would be done thereby to every Catholic in his faith." The loss of the temporal power "saps the very foundation of public morality and of social stability" (450). Cross also claims Augustine Hewit, a "liberal" Paulist, made "crystal clear how bitterly American Catholics were divided over their obligations to the temporal power." Hewit "could not keep from his articles the basic liberal conviction that the near future would end the Pope's need to concern himself with the powers of a temporal sovereign" (86). In fact, Hewit stated the ideology of the Roman Question without deviation. I am at a loss to understand how Cross came to his conclusions. See Rev. Augustine F. Hewit, "The Temporal Sovereignty of the Pope," *CW* 52 (Dec. 1890): 340–46.

3. M. O'Connell, in *John Ireland*, asserts, "little enthusiasm existed among American Catholics for the temporal power, a political issue which, to most of them, was largely irrelevant" (276). In fact, there was great enthusiasm for the ideology of the Roman Question. In addition to the many citations in chapter 1, see "A Word about the Temporal Power of the Pope," *CW* 6 (Jan. 1868): 528–34; "Pope Pius the Ninth," *CW* 25 (June 1877): 291–317; "A Vision of the Colosseum," *CW* 25 (June 1877): 318–23; "Rome under the Pope and under the Piedmontese," *CW* 28 (May 1879): 754–61; Isaac Hecker, "The Liberty and Independence of the Pope," *CW* 35 (Apr. 1882): 1–10, and "Thomistic-

Rosminian Emersonianism; or 'A Religion for Italy,'" *CW* 38 (Mar. 1884): 808–9; "The Roman Question," *ACQR* 11 (Apr. 1886): 193–210; "The Sacerdotal Jubilee of His Holiness Pope Leo XIII," *ACQR* 13 (Jan. 1888): 42–51; "The Roman Question—Does It Concern Us?" *American Ecclesiastical Review* 1 (Nov.–Dec. 1889): 440–52; Francis Silas Chatard, "The Temporal Power of the Pope," *CW* 50 (Nov. 1889): 213–17; "Our Recent American Catholic Congress and Its Significance," *ACQR* 15 (Jan. 1890): 150–69; "American Catholicity," *ACQR* 16 (Apr. 1891): 396–408; Joseph Shroeder, "American Catholics and the Temporal Power of the Pope," *ACQR* 17 (Jan. 1892): 72–97; Augustine Hewit, "American Catholics and the Roman Question," *CW* 55 (June 1892): 425–36; John Ireland, "The Pope's Civil Princedom," *North American Review* 172 (Mar. 1901): 337–51; William J. D. Croke, "The Situation in Rome," *ACQR* 22 (Apr. 1897): 330–64; and "The Temporal Power," *ACQR* 26 (Oct. 1901): 776–97.

4. Binchy, *Church and State in Fascist Italy*, 35.

5. Chabod, *Italian Foreign Policy*, 147, 394–95; Seton-Watson, *Italy from Liberalism to Fascism*, 98–114; Bosworth, *Italy and the Wider World*, 21–23 (quotes Farini).

6. Chadwick, *History of the Popes*, 286–301; Ward, "Leo XIII and Bismarck," 392–414.

7. Larkin, *Church and State*, 41; Martini, *Studi sulla questione romana*, 25–51.

8. For background for the following paragraphs, see G. De Rosa, *Il movimento cattolico in Italia*, 7–326; Spadolini, *L'opposizione cattolica*; Jemolo, *Chiesa e stato in Italia*, 241–482; Confessore, *I cattolici e la "Fede nella Libertà,"* and *L'Americanismo*; and Agócs, *Troubled Origins*.

9. Agócs, *Troubled Origins*, 97.

10. Caliaro and Francesconi, *John Baptist Scalabrini*, 314–15.

11. Jemolo, *Church and State in Italy*, 71, 72, 73

12. Ibid., 76 (quotation); Duggan, *Francesco Crispi*, 486–93.

13. Francesconi, *Giovanni Battista Scalabrini*; Fonzi, "Scalabrini e la vita politica italiana"; L. De Rosa, "Stato e chiesa," 237–52; Rosoli, *Insieme oltre le frontiere*, 473–520; Trincia, *Emigrazione e diaspora*, 161–228; Confessore, "L'associazione nazionale," 519–36. See Tomasi, *For the Love of Immigrants*, for English translations of Scalabrini's writings on emigration.

14. Confessore, *L'Americanismo*; M. O'Connell, *John Ireland*, 471; John Ireland, "The Pope's Civil Princedom," *North American Review* 172 (Mar. 1901): 337–51.

15. Sullivan, *Mother Cabrini*, 95, 92.

16. Michael Corrigan to Giovanni Simeoni, 9 Oct. 1891, APF, Nuova Serie, 1905, vol. 332, rubr. 153, f. 8–11; Tomasi, *For the Love of Immigrants*, 192 and 195 (quote Rampolla and Scalabrini in 1893).

17. Federico Astorri to Eminenza, 2 Dec. 1897, APF, Nuova Serie, 1905, vol. 332, rubr. 153, f. 81. Zaboglio cited in *Stella d'Italia* (New Haven), n.d., APF, Nuova Serie, 1905, vol. 332, rubr. 153, f. 82.

18. "La vera italianità della nostra scuola," CPA, July 1914, 11, 13.

19. See Browne, "'Italian Problem.'"

20. Joseph Shroeder, "American Catholics and the Temporal Power of the Pope," *ACQR* 17 (Jan. 1892): 94.

21. C. C. Copeland, "The Neglected Italians," NW, 13 June 1903, 10.

22. C. C. Copeland, "The Italians in America," NW, 27 June 1903, 15.

23. "Joliet's New Italian Church," NW, 18 July 1903, 11.

24. Levra, *Fare gli italiani*, 1–80; Tobia, *L'altare della patria*, 17–22; Chadwick, *History of the Popes*, 268–70; Duggan, *Francesco Crispi*, 378–81.

25. Caliaro and Francesconi, *John Baptist Scalabrini*, 131–32; Chadwick, *History of the Popes*, 268–70; "Italy," *Chicago Tribune*, 14 Jan. 1878, 5.

26. Ferdinand Kittell to Professor, 21 Jan. 1878, APF, SOCG, 1878, f. 169–171.

27. "The Italians and Their Late King," *Public Ledger*, 11 Feb. 1878, 1.

28. "Victor Emmanuel," *Chicago Tribune*, 21 Jan. 1878, 8; Morini, *Foundation of the Order*, 126 (Roles); Agostino Morini to Alessandro Carraresi, 21 Mar. 1878, c. 109, no. 133, Morini-Carraresi Correspondence, La Biblioteca Nazionale Centrale di Firenze.

29. Giovanni Mondani to Agostino Morini, 2 Dec. 1878, 26 Mar. 1879, and 13 Feb. 1880, 8–72, 75, 80, Morini Memorial Collection, Western Province Archives, Servants of Mary, Chicago.

30. "St. Louis, 28 January 1878," APF, SOCG, 1878, f. 365–66.

31. "Nuova York, 24 January 1878," APF, SOCG, 1878, f. 366.

32. "Baltimore, 17 January 1878," "Richmond, 17 January 1878," and "Providence, 17 January 1878," APF, SOCG, 1878, f. 367; "The Feeling in America," *Chicago Times*, 18 Jan. 1878, 1.

33. "Cincinnati, 17 Jan. 1878," APF, SOCG, 1878, f. 362–64 (includes John Purcell's speech). On the procession, see "Italy's Dead Monarch," *Cincinnati Daily Times*, 17 Jan. 1878, 4.

34. "*Il Commercial*, 19 Jan. 1878"; "Another Remarkable Sermon," *Chicago Times*, 20 Jan. 1878, 6; "*Times di Chicago*," 20 Jan. 1878, APF, SOCG, 1878, f. 364–65.

35. "A Catholic Discrepancy," *Western Cristian Advocate*, 30 Jan. 1878, 34; "Victor Emmanuel," *CT*, 17 Jan. 1878, 4.

36. John Purcell to Giovanni Simeoni, 20 May 1878, APF, SOCG, 1878, f. 471–73; Simeoni to Purcell, 8 July 1878, APF, Lettere, 1878, f. 344. Thanks to Michael Alexander for translating these two letters.

37. Sebastiano Martinelli to Mariano Rampolla, 3 Aug. 1900, and Rampolla to Martinelli, 4 Aug. 1900, ASV, DAUS, X, fasc. 121 (includes telegrams and letters addressed to Martinelli and his responses).

38. Vitali, *L'Episcopato italiano*, viii, vii; Confessore, *L'Americanismo*, 26–30.

39. Antonio Demo to Sebastiano Martinelli, 1 Aug. 1900, ASV, DAUS, X, fasc. 121.

40. William Byrne to Sebastiano Martinelli, 4 Aug. 1900, ASV, DAUS, X, fasc. 121.

41. "Humbert's Death Mourned," *Boston Evening Transcript*, 31 July 1900, 4 (quotation); "The Peace of King Humbert," *Boston Evening Transcript*, 6 Aug. 1900, 61. PIA recounted numerous funeral masses in the New York metropolitan area in August 1900.

42. Agostino Coglilani to Sebastiano Martinelli, 8 Aug. 1900, ASV, DAUS, X, fasc. 121; "Local Italians Mourn for Humbert," *CST*, 4 Aug. 1900, 1.

43. "The Triple Alliance and the Italian People," *CST*, 4 Aug. 1900, 4. In addition to Umberto, Italian anarchists assassinated President Carnot of France in 1894, the Spanish prime minister in 1897, and Empress Elizabeth of Austria in 1898.

44. "Un intervista con Mons. Doran," *ERI*, 4 Aug. 1900, 1; "Lettera a S. E. Monsignor Martinelli," *ERI*, 11 Aug. 1900, 1; Federico Curzio to Sebastiano Martinelli, 8 Aug. 1900, ASV, DAUS, X, fasc. 121; "La Commemorazione di Umberto I alla Infantry Hall," *ERI*, 18 Aug. 1900, 1.

45. See Duggan, *Francesco Crispi*.

46. Jemolo, *Chiesa e stato in Italia*, 383 (quotation); Duggan, *Francesco Crispi*, 328–32.

47. Duggan, *Francesco Crispi*, 545–47, 584–86; Jemolo, *Church and State in Italy*, 80, 66–

67; Francis Silas Chatard, "The Temporal Power of the Pope," *CW* 50 (Nov. 1889): 214–15 (cites the legislation).

48. Ellis, *James Cardinal Gibbons*, 2:336–40, 340 (describes the hierarchy's letter to Leo XIII, 17 Jan. 1889), 339 (quotes Peter Richard Kenrick to James Gibbons, 26 Nov. 1888).

49. "The Eternal City," *CM*, 19 Jan. 1889, 1 (allocution); "Leo XIII and the Roman Question," *CM*, 12 Jan. 1889, 5 (claims that Crispi suppressed free speech); Bernard O'Reilly, "Restoring the Temporal Power," *CM*, 19 Jan. 1889, 5; "The Duty of American Catholics," *CM*, 19 Jan. 1889, 4.

50. "Premier Crispi's Folly," *CST*, 12 Jan. 1889, 2; "Latest Version of Gladstone's Notions of the Temporal Power," *CST*, 12 Jan. 1889, 4.

51. John O'Shea, "Silvio Pellico to Francesco Crispi," *ACQR* 26 (Oct. 1901): 802, 805, 806.

52. Foa, *Giordano Bruno*, 7–9; Mola, *Storia della Massoneria italiana*, 192–211.

53. Foa, *Giordano Bruno*, 11–18; Chadwick, *History of the Popes*, 302–3, 402–3.

54. Foa, *Giordano Bruno*, 9, 10.

55. Francis Silas Chatard, "The Temporal Power of the Pope," *CW* 50 (Nov. 1889): 216–17 (cites Leo's allocution).

56. "The Eternal City," *CM*, 15 June 1899, 1; "The Giordano Bruno Monument," *CST*, 6 July 1889, 2 ("for the first time"); "The Pope in Rome," *CST*, 3 Aug. 1889, 1–2 ("no person"); "Bruno Affair," *CST*, 13 July 1889, 1 ("Brunomania").

57. Pastoral letter, 22 Sept. 1889, Winand Wigger Papers, II-2-n, University of Notre Dame Archives.

58. "Saints Bruno and Emmanuel," *NW*, 3 Oct. 1903, 16.

59. "Bishop Dunne," *NW*, 25 Oct. 1929, 1; Nelli, "Role of the 'Colonial' Press."

60. "An Anticlerical at Large," *NW*, 25 June 1904, 12 (Dunne quotations); Vecoli, "Prelates and Peasants," 224–25.

61. "The Giordano Bruno Association," *NW*, 29 Feb. 1908, 13; Vecoli, "Prelates and Peasants," 266 (cites "As to Social Settlements," *NW*, 25 Apr. 1908).

62. "Clerical Clash Given Pro and Con," *Chicago Tribune*, 1 Mar. 1908, pt. 1, p. 2.

63. Ibid.

64. Addams, *Twenty Years at Hull-House*, 146–47; Carson, *Settlement Folk*, 102–5.

65. "Clerical Clash Given Pro and Con," *Chicago Tribune*, 1 Mar. 1908, pt. 1, p. 2; "The Giordano Bruno Club and Its Platform," *NW*, 7 Mar. 1908, 11.

66. Raffaele Merry del Val to Delegation, 1 Mar. 1910, and circular, 26 Feb. 1910, ASV, DAUS, I, fasc. 81, f. 3–4, 5–6.

67. "Jane Addams Ignores Protest," *NW*, 27 Feb. 1914, 1; "Hull-House and the Anti-Catholic Propaganda," *NW*, 6 Mar. 1914, 4.

68. Jemolo, *Chiesa e stato in Italia*, 387; Duggan, *Francesco Crispi*, 693–94. For contest see "Solennizzare il XXV Anniversario della Liberazione di Roma," 24 July 1895, ASMAE, SP, b. 31, fasc. "Anno 1895."

69. Leo XIII to Mariano Rampolla, 8 Oct. 1895, Rampolla to Francesco Satolli, 10 Oct. 1895, and Satolli to Richard Olney, 25 Oct. 1895, ASV, DAUS, II, fasc. 18, f. 9, 3, 5–6.

70. Embassy (The Hague) to Alberto Blanc, 16 Sept. 1895, and Embassy (Brussels) to Blanc, 17 Sept. 1895, ASMAE, SP, b. 31, fasc. "Anno 1895."

71. Costantino Nigra to Alberto Blanc, 13 Sept. 1895 (quotes *Bulletin*) and 22 Sept. 1895 ("except for calling"), ASMAE, SP, b. 31, fasc. "Anno 1895"; "Der Österreichische

Episkopat an den Heiligen Vater," *Vaterland*, 22 Sept. 1895, 1 (the Austrian hierarchy's letter).

72. "Vielgeliebte Diöcessanen!" *National Zeitung*, 17 Sept. 1895, 1; Embassy (Berlin) to Alberto Blanc, 10 Oct. 1895, ASMAE, SP, b. 31, fasc. "Anno 1895."

73. Legation (Munich) to Alberto Blanc, 28 Aug. (quotation of speeches) and 19 Sept. 1895, ASMAE, SP, b. 31, fasc. "Anno 1895."

74. Embassy (Madrid) to Alberto Blanc, 27 Aug., 28 Aug., 31 Aug., and 22 Sept. 1895, ASMAE, SP, b. 31, fasc. "Anno 1895." On the protests, see *Epoca*, 26 Aug. 1895.

75. Saverio Fava to Alberto Blanc, 10 Oct. 1895, ASMAE, SP, b. 31, fasc. "Anno 1895." Evidence for the Catholic organization is in ASV, SS, Spogli, Rampolla del Tindaro, b. 5A, fasc. "1895. Di un Associatione negli Stati Uniti per la indipendenza e potere temporale della Santa Sede."

76. "Circular Letter Issued by Cardinal Gibbons," *New York Herald*, 16 Sept. 1895, "The Pope's Deliverance," *New York Herald*, 31 Aug. 1895, and "Prayers for the Pope," *New York Herald*, 16 Sept. 1895, ASMAE, SP, b. 31, fasc. "Anno 1895."

77. "German Catholics Speak," *New York Herald*, 21 Sept. 1895, ASMAE, SP, b. 31, fasc. "Anno 1895"; "Archbishop Corrigan," *CA*, 3 Oct. 1895, 635.

78. Michael Tierney to Francesco Satolli, 7 Oct. 1895, ASV, DAUS, IX Hartford, fasc. 12, f. 3.

79. "Sympathy for the Pope," *Hartford Times*, n.d., "Condoling the Pope," *Hartford Courant*, n.d, and "Pope's Temporal Power," *Hartford Telegram*, n.d., ASV, DAUS, IX Hartford, fasc. 12, f. 4–5 (quotations), 5–7.

80. "New Britain: Catholics Express Sympathy with the Pope," *Hartford Times*, n.d., ASV, DAUS, IX Hartford, fasc. 12, f. 8.

81. John J. O'Shea, "Old Rome and Young Italy," *CW* 62 (Oct. 1895): 104, 113.

82. "Protest," *New Haven News*, 20 Sept. 1895, ASV, DAUS, IX Hartford, fasc. 12, f. 9.

83. Antonio Rozwadowski to Saverio Fava, 17 Sept. and 24 Sept. (quotation) 1895, b. 61, fasc. "Festaggiamenti per le ricorrenze del 20 settembre," ASMAE, LSRD.

84. Antonio Rozwadowski to Saverio Fava, 24 Sept. 1895, ASMAE, LSRD; "Italians in Parade," *Chicago Tribune*, 23 Sept. 1895, 8 (quotations).

85. Tomasi, *Piety and Power*, 144 (quotes John T. Smith).

86. "Italian Unity," *Daily Tribune*, 21 Sept. 1895, and "Italy's Celebration," *New York Sun*, 20 Sept. 1895, ASMAE, SP, b. 31, fasc. "Anno 1895."

87. "Italian Gala Days," *CA*, 26 Sept. 1895, 617; "Archbishop Corrigan," *CA*, 3 Oct. 1895, 635.

88. [Illegible] to Alberto Blanc, 2 Sept. 1895, ASMAE, SP, b. 31, fasc. "Anno 1895."

89. William J. D. Croke, "The Situation in Rome," *ACQR* 22 (Apr. 1897): 334–35.

90. Hibbert, *Rome*, 173–8; Tobia, *L'altare della patria*, 65–66.

91. Hibbert, *Rome*, 274–85; Vance, *Catholic and Contemporary Rome*, 270.

92. Tobia, *L'altare della patria*, 23–60.

93. Charles Collins, "Victor Emmanuel's Monument," *America*, 11 Mar. 1914, 509–10.

94. Vance, *Catholic and Contemporary Rome*, 282–83 (quotes Whiting), 287 (quotes Thayer).

95. Tobia, *L'altare della patria*, 12, 15 (quotations).

CHAPTER THREE

1. "The Protest against Nathan," *America*, 20 June 1914, 221.

2. Macioti, *Ernesto Nathan*, 52–59; Sanfilippo, "La Santa Sede." On Catholic anti-Semitism, see Van Rahden, "Beyond Ambivalence"; and Kertzer, *Popes against the Jews*.

3. "Lettera di Sua Santità Pio PP. X," *Civiltà Cattolica*, vol. 4, fasc. 1447 (24 Sept. 1910): 97–98; Macioti, *Ernesto Nathan*, 52–54; Sanfilippo, "La Santa Sede," 348.

4. Sanfilippo, "La Santa Sede," 347–54; *America*, 29 Oct. 1910, 51, 65.

5. A. Nobili to Antonio di San Giuliano, 28 Oct., 7 Nov., and 9 Nov. (quotation) 1910, and "Ein italienischer Protest," *Bayerische Kürier*, 7 Nov. 1910, ASMAE, SP, b. 34, fasc. "Santa Sede, 1908–1910."

6. Giuseppe Avarna to Antonio di San Giuliano, 7 Nov., 8 Nov. (quotations), 9 Nov., and 11 Nov. 1910, ASMAE, SP, b. 34, fasc. "Santa Sede, 1908–1910." For reactions to Porzer, see "Die Rede des Bizeburgermeisters Dr. Porzer," *Neues Wiener Tagblatt*, 7 Nov. 1910, 4, and "Der Protest gegen Nathan vor der Delegation," *Reichspost*, 10 Nov. 1910, 1, ASMAE, SP, b. 34, fasc. "Santa Sede, 1908–1910."

7. Giuseppe Avarna to Antonio di San Giuliano, 16 Nov. and 29 Nov. 1910, Francesco Tommasini to San Giuliano, 14 Dec. 1910, "Grosse Frauenverfammlung," *Reichspost*, 28 Nov. 1910 ("unworthy"), and *Sankt Bonifatius* 7 (Dec. 1910): 178–79 ("our own government" and "Our Holy Father"), ASMAE, SP, b. 34, fasc. "Santa Sede, 1908–1910."

8. Giuseppe Avarna to Antonio di San Giuliano, 26 Nov. 1910, and Francesco Tommasini to San Giuliano, 15 Dec. 1910 (quotations), ASMAE, SP, b. 34, fasc. "Santa Sede, 1908–1910."

9. Raffaele Merry del Val to Diomede Falconio, 26 Sept. 1910, and "Pope Indignant with Nathan," *Evening Post*, 23 Sept. 1910, 4, ASV, DAUS, II, fasc. 148, f. 3, 4; "The Undying Pope," *America*, 24 Sept. 1910, 610.

10. "The Mayor of Rome," *America*, 1 Oct. 1910, 634.

11. "The Logical Jew," *America*, 5 Nov. 1910, 87. See also Kertzer, *Popes against the Jews*.

12. "Catholic World Resents Insult to Holy Father," *Pilot*, 1 Oct. 1910, 1, 5.

13. "Intolerable Hardihood," *Pilot*, 1 Oct. 1910, 5.

14. "Catholic World Resents Insult to Holy Father," *Pilot*, 1 Oct. 1910, 1, 5.

15. *Dziennik Chicagoski*, 21 Sept. 1910, 7; "Telegramy zagraniczne," *Dziennik Chicagoski*, 27 Sept. 1910, 1; *Naród Polski*, 28 Sept. 1910, 1.

16. John Farley to Pius X, 9 Oct. 1910, James Gibbons to Pius X, 5 Dec. 1910, ASV, SS, 1911, rubr. 66, fasc. 1, f. 49–50, 25; Farley to Diomede Falconio, 10 Oct. 1910, Raffaele Merry del Val to Farley, 21 Oct. 1910, ASV, DAUS, II, fasc. 148, f. 9–10, 19; Sanfilippo, "La Santa Sede," 354.

17. James Flaherty to Diomede Falconio, 2 Dec. 1910, ASV, DAUS, II, fasc. 148, f. 20–21; Sanfilippo, "La Santa Sede," 354–55.

18. Krekenberg to Diomede Falconio, 4 Nov. 1910, ASV, DAUS, II, fasc. 148, f. 12–13. For German responses, see ASV, DAUS, II, fasc. 148, f. 30–47; and ASV, SS, rubr. 66, 1911, fasc. 2 and 5.

19. Nicholas Gonner to Raffaele Merry del Val, 16 Nov. 1910, ASV, DAUS, II, fasc. 148, f. 16–18.

20. Jemolo, *Church and State in Italy*, 111, 146; "Anno di lutto," *Civiltà Cattolica*, v. 1, fasc. 1458 (8 Mar. 1911): 641.

21. John Farley to Rev., 9 Feb. 1911, ASV, DAUS, X, 659A.

22. Gherardo Ferrante to Diomede Falconio, 13 Feb. 1911, and Falconio to Ferrante, 19 Feb. 1911, ASV, DAUS, X, 659A.

23. Raffaele Merry del Val to Diomede Falconio, 28 Jan. 1911, and Falconio to Merry del Val, 13 Feb. 1911, ASV, DAUS, X, 659A.

24. Diomede Falconio to McGrane, 19 Mar. 1911, Falconio to Daniel Toomey, 19 Mar. 1911, Toomey to Falconio, 20 Mar. 1911, Falconio to O'Connell, 21 Mar. 1911, McGrane to Falconio, 21 Mar. 1911, Falconio to Raffaele Merry del Val, 22 Mar. 1911, McGrane to Falconio, 23 Mar. 1911, Toomey to Falconio, 1 Apr. 1911, Merry del Val to Falconio, 3 Apr. 1911, O'Connell to Falconio, 3 Apr. 1911, Falconio to Toomey, 4 Apr. 1911, and Falconio to McGrane, 4 Apr. 1911, ASV, DAUS, X, 659A.

25. "Playing with Fire," *Extension Magazine* 10 (Feb. 1911): 3–4.

26. "Viva Roma!" *America*, 8 Apr. 1911, 615 ("impending bankruptcy"); "Victor Emmanuel's Monument," *America*, 11 Mar. 1911, 510 ("sons of Italy"); Giovanni Bonzano to George Mundelein, 4 July 1911, AAC, 1-1911-M-8.

27. "Il fermo proposito," in Carlen, *Papal Encyclicals*, 37–44; G. De Rosa, *Il movimento cattolico in Italia*, 253–388; Jemolo, *Church and State in Italy*, 84–160; Coppa, "Giolitti and the Gentiloni Pact," 217–28; Formigoni, *L'Italia dei cattolici*, 57–76.

28. De Grand, *Hunchback's Tailor*, 114, 120, 139; Salomone, *Italy in the Giolittian Era*; Mayor to Tommaso Tittoni, 15 Sept. 1908 (on liberalism of Gibbons and intransigent Irish) and 31 Jan. 1909 ("relations"), ASMAE, SP, b. 34, fasc. "Santa Sede 1908–1910"; Mayor to Tittoni, 13 May 1909, ASMAE, SP, b. 361, fasc. "Stati Uniti Affari Politici, 1909."

29. Mayor to Guicciardini, 25 Jan. 1910, ASMAE, SP, b. 361, fasc. "Stati Uniti Affari Politici, 1910."

30. See Macioti, *Ernesto Nathan*; Mack Smith, *Mazzini*, 26, 93, 215–16, 223, 233–34; Carlizza, "Ernesto Nathan," 41 (quotation); and Mola, *Storia della Massoneria italiana*, 255–77; Salvetti, *Società "Dante Alighieri."*

31. See Macioti, *Ernesto Nathan*; Carlizza, "Ernesto Nathan"; Isastia, *Ernesto Nathan*.

32. See Carlizza, "Ernesto Nathan"; De Grand, *Hunchback's Tailor*.

33. Todd, *Story of the Exposition*, 1:216–20, 221–28, 2:36–41; Issel and Cherny, *San Francisco, 1865–1932*, 167–70; *Official Guide of the Panama-Pacific International Exposition*, 14–15.

34. "Is Rome Ruining Panama Exposition?" *Menace*, n.d. (ca. Aug. 1913), BLUCB, PPIE, carton 9, folder 1-21.19, "Complaints."

35. "Why Thus Honor Rome?" *Menace*, n.d. (ca. Aug. 1913), BLUCB, PPIE, carton 9, folder 1-21.19, "Complaints."

36. Koenig to Charles Moore, 9 Sept. 1913, H. W. Moore to Charles Moore, 19 Sept. 1913, and Frank Smith to Charles Moore, 27 Sept. 1913, BLUCB, PPIE, carton 9, folder 1-21.19, "Complaints."

37. N. F. Caufield to PPIE, 16 Oct. 1913, BLUCB, PPIE, carton 9, folder 1-21.19, "Complaints."

38. Brune to Charles Moore, 14 Apr. 1914 (St. Bonifatius Bund), Zarut to Charles Moore, 18 Apr. 1914, and Philipson to Charles Moore, 30 Mar. 1914 ("fair-minded American people"), BLUCB, PPIE, carton 9, folder 1-21.19, "Complaints."

39. W. P. Oliver to Charles Moore, 31 Mar. 1914, and Bushnell to Charles Moore, 16 July 1914, BLUCB, PPIE, carton 9, folder 1-21.19, "Complaints."

40. "Nathan the Delegate," *America*, 18 Apr. 1914, 14; "'Gabby' and Ignorant," *Moni-*

tor, 2 May 1914, 4; "Nathan 'the Jew'," *Tablet*, 13 June 1914, 4; *America*, 25 Apr. 1914, 48 (Knights); "Ungeachtet der Massen-Proteste," *Die Aurora und ChristlicheWoche*, 8 May 1914, 4.

41. Sigmund Livingston to Giovanni Bonzano, 1 June 1914, and Livingston to M. J. Foley, 29 May 1914 (cites "Which Shall It Be? Nathan's Recall or Dead Exposition?" *WC*, 1 May 1914), ASV, DAUS, II, fasc. 148, f. 52–55.

42. Giovanni Bonzano to Sigmund Livingston, 9 June 1914, ASV, DAUS, II, fasc. 148, f. 58. Evidence that Bonzano and the Vatican approved of this campaign against Nathan comes from the fact that, in December 1914, Bonzano strongly endorsed Father Tierney's request for an apostolic blessing for himself and the Jesuits working for *America* magazine. Bonzano wrote, "the eminent [Jesuit] Fathers earned the admiration of all for their strenuous campaign against the coming of Ernesto Nathan as the Italian Commissioner to the Exposition in San Francisco," and for their protests against religious persecution in Mexico (Bonzano to Gasparri, 21 Dec. 1914, ASV, SS, 1915, rubr. 261, fasc. 8, f. 12). Tierney and his fellow Jesuits received the apostolic blessing.

43. M. J. Foley, "The Jews and Nathan," *WC*, ASV, DAUS, II, fasc. 148, f. 70.

44. *Sentinel*, 12 June 1914, 2.

45. "Nathan 'the Jew,'" *Tablet*, 13 June 1914, 4.

46. Herbert Hadley, "The Undesirable Nathan," *America*, 25 Apr. 1914, 37. On Hadley, see "Nathan and the Panama Exposition," *America*, 16 May 1914, 108.

47. "Priests Protest Nathan's Coming," *Tablet*, 16 May 1914, 1 ("heated addresses"); "San Francisco Loses Reunion of American College Alumni," *CST*, 30 May 1914, 4; Alumni Association to James Rolph and Charles Moore, 22 May 1914, California Historical Society Archive, San Francisco, Mayor James Rolph Correspondence, ms 1818, box 11, ser. 1a, folder 92a; "Laymen's League Protests Nathan," *Tablet*, 13 June 1914, 1 (cites resolution).

48. "A Black Eye," *Monitor*, 9 May 1914, 4 ("people of California"); "The Coming of Nathan," *Monitor*, 30 May 1914, 12 ("an insult"); "A.P.A.'s to Welcome Nathan," *Tablet*, 6 June 1914, 2.

49. Thomas N. Page to Charles Moore, 6 May 1914, BLUCB, PPIE, Foreign Office, Italy (May–Dec. 1914), C-A 190. On San Giuliano, see *Tablet*, 18 July 1914, 1; and "Italian Foreign Minister Doesn't Take Opposition to Nathan Seriously," *Sentinel*, 10 July 1914, 17 (San Giuliano quotations).

50. "Anti-Nathan Feeling Growing in Italy," *Tablet*, 3 July 1914, 1 (quotations). On elections, see "Nathan's Power Lessened," *Tablet*, 27 June 1914, 7; and "Ein Wahlsieg der Katholiken in Rom," *Nord-Amerika* (Philadelphia), 18 June 1914, 1.

51. "Ex-Mayor of Rome Awaited," *NYT*, 24 May 1914, 6; "Rousing Welcome to Rome's Ex-Mayor," *NYT*, 26 May 1914, 10; "Nathan Sees President," *NYT*, 27 May 1914, 10; "Marquis Cusani's Notable Services," *Washington Post*, 27 May 1914, 6; "Alla Viglia dell'Arrivo di Ernesto Nathan," *PIA*, 24 May 1914, 1; "Nathan a Nuova York," *PIA*, 25 May 1914, 1; "L'Italia ramingà saluta con l'amore e la gratitudine della Patria E. Nathan," *PIA*, 26 May 1914, 1; "Nathan Has Come," *America*, 6 June 1914, 181; "Nathan's Reception," *America*, 13 June 1914, 206; "Italy," *America*, 1 Aug. 1914, 363.

52. "Nathan Here as Envoy of Italy to Fair," *San Francisco Examiner*, 1 June 1914, 3; "Dedication of Italian Site at Fair," *San Francisco Examiner*, 2 June 1914, 5; "Throng Cheers Italy's Flag on 1915 Site," *San Francisco Examiner*, 3 June 1914, 1 (quotations); "Commissioner Nathan Local Italians' Guest," *San Francisco Examiner*, 5 June 1914, 4; "Envoy Nathan Luncheon Host," *San Francisco Examiner*, 6 June 1914, 6.

53. "Minutes of the PPIE Executive Committee," BLUCB, PPIE, vol. 125, p. 73 (5 May 1914, "a great many letters"), and p. 122 (14 July 1914, "Riordan").

54. "Minutes of the PPIE Executive Committee," BLUCB, PPIE, vol. 125, pp. 138–39 (4 Aug. 1914), p. 189 (13 Oct. 1914), p. 204 (20 Oct. 1914, "resented by all Catholics"), and p. 271 (5 Jan. 1915, on telegram to the league). The Catholic member of the committee was absent from the meetings when Nathan was discussed.

55. *San Francisco Examiner*, 20 and 21 Feb. 1915; "Prayer Opens World's Fair," *Monitor*, 27 Feb. 1915, 1; Edward Hanna to Delegation, 20 Feb. 1915, ASV, DAUS, II, fasc. 148, f. 67–68.

CHAPTER FOUR

1. Wuthnow, *Meaning and Moral Order*, 154–58; Burns, *Frontiers of Catholicism*, 192–96.

2. See Coppa, *Modern Papacy*, 154–69; Ellis, *James Cardinal Gibbons*, 2:204–309; McKeown, *War and Welfare*; Esslinger, "American German and Irish Attitudes"; Cuddy, "Pro-Germanism and American Catholicism"; and Pollard, *Unknown Pope*, 128. Fogarty, in *Vatican and the American Hierarchy*, ignores U.S.-Vatican diplomacy during and immediately after the Great War and claims that the Vatican did not take the United States and its Church seriously as a diplomatic partner until the late 1930s.

3. See Knock, *To End All Wars*; Ambrosius, *Woodrow Wilson and the American Diplomatic Tradition*; Link, *Wilson the Diplomatist*; Walworth, *Wilson and His Peacemakers*; and Zivojinovic, *United States and the Vatican Policies*.

4. G. De Rosa, *Il movimento cattolico in Italia*, 253–388; Jemolo, *Church and State in Italy*, 84–160; Coppa, "Giolitti and the Gentiloni Pact," 217–28; Formigoni, *L'Italia dei cattolici*, 57–76.

5. Pollard, *Unknown Pope*, 7–27; Formigoni, *L'Italia dei cattolici*, 77–98; Jemolo, *Church and State in Italy*, 161–81; Monticone, "I vescovi italiani e la guerra," 627–60; Veneruso, "I rapporti fra stato e chiesa," 679–737; Salvatorelli, *La politica della Santa Sede*, 19–20, 24–25, 59–60; "Pacem, Dei munus," in Carlen, *Papal Encyclicals*, 174.

6. Pollard, *Unknown Pope*, 112–16; Morozzo della Rocca, "Benedetto XV," 542, 544 (quotations).

7. France, England, Italy, and the United States had no diplomatic representation with the Holy See when the war began. Germany and Austria-Hungary, in contrast, were in a favorable position during the war, even after Great Britain established a minister plenipotentiary to the Holy See in late 1914 and France assigned a writer on a semiofficial mission to the Vatican. See Renzi, *In the Shadow of the Sword*, 154–58; Garzia, *La questione romana*, 16–18; Zivojinovic, *United States and the Vatican Policies*, 141–56; and Salvatorelli, *La politica della Santa Sede*, 41–54.

8. Renzi, *In the Shadow of the Sword*, 156–57, 172–75; Zivojinovic, *United States and the Vatican Policies*, 12. Pollard, in *Unknown Pope*, 104–5, claims there is no evidence Gerlach was a spy but acknowledges he may have bribed newspapers. See also Epstein, *Matthias Erzberger*, 118–38.

9. Zivojinovic, *United States and the Vatican Policies*, 6; Pollard, *Unknown Pope*, 90–91.

10. Garzia, *La questione romana*, 18–20; Renzi, *In the Shadow of the Sword*, 166–70.

11. "Ad beatissimi apostolorum," in Carlen, *Papal Encyclicals*, 143–51 (quotations, 144,

150); Garzia, *La questione romana*, 20–33; Zivojinovic, *United States and the Vatican Policies*, 25–26; Veneruso, "I rapporti fra stato e chiesa," 689–90.

12. Garzia, *La questione romana*, 24 (cites Sonnino); Varnier, "Sidney Sonnino."

13. Page, *Italy and the World War*, 166–67.

14. Garzia, *La questione romana*, 34–48; Pollard, "Il Vaticano e la politica estera italiana," 208–11; Zivojinovic, *United States and the Vatican Policies*, 128 (quotes article 15); Veneruso, "I rapporti fra stato e chiesa," 702–5; Seton-Watson, *Italy from Liberalism to Fascism*, 430–36.

15. Benedetto XV to Cardinal Serafino Vannutelli, 25 May 1915, in *Acta Apostolicae Sedis*, 1 June 1915, 253–55. On chaplains, see Morozzo della Rocca, *La fede e la guerra*.

16. Quadrotta, *La chiesa cattolica*, ciii–civ (interview of 21 June 1915 in *La Liberté*); Zivojinovic, *United States and the Vatican Policies*, 48–49 (quotes Page, 31).

17. Quadrotta, *La chiesa cattolica*, cxi (Gasparri interview of 27 June 1915 in *Corriere d'Italia*).

18. Pietro Gasparri to Giovanni Bonzano, 4 Aug. 1915, ASV, DAUS, V, fasc. 68, f. 3–4.

19. Ibid.

20. Garzia, *La questione romana*, 59–61. On the departure of the diplomatic representatives, see *L'Osservatore Romano*, 26 May 1915. Gasparri, in his memoirs, acknowledged the goodwill of the Italian government on this occasion, even though he found the Law of Guarantees inadequate. Spadolini, *Il Cardinale Gasparri*, 171–72.

21. Knock, *To End All Wars*, 15–69; Cassels, *Ideology and International Relations*, 130–36, 146–56; Crunden, *Ministers of Reform*, 225–73.

22. Bruti Liberati, "Santa Sede e Stati Uniti"; Zivojinovic, *United States and the Vatican Policies*; Ellis, *James Cardinal Gibbons*, 2:204–309.

23. Bruti Liberati, "Santa Sede e Stati Uniti," 133–36; Ellis, *James Cardinal Gibbons*, 2: 231–35; Zivojinovic, *United States and the Vatican Policies*, 50–52. For Benedict's letter of 15 May 1916 and Wilson's reply drafted by Lansing, see *Papers Relating to the Foreign Relations*, 1:15–16.

24. Thomas N. Page to Robert Lansing, 22 Jan. and 20 Mar. 1917, *Papers Relating to the Foreign Relations*, 1:750, 761–62.

25. Vincenzo Macchi Di Cellere to Sidney Sonnino, 18 Apr. 1916, ASMAE, GAB, b. 190, fasc. "Trattazione generale, Stati Uniti d'America, Anno 1915–16."

26. See, e.g., Hennesey, *American Catholics*, 224; Gimarc, "Illinois Catholic Editorial Opinion"; Esslinger, "American German and Irish Attitudes"; and Cuddy, "Pro-Germanism and American Catholicism."

27. "Rome on the Potomac: What the Papal Hierarchy Is Doing at the American Capital," *Outlook*, 11 Feb. 1913, 10–12; Nicholas Gonner to Giovanni Bonzano, 9 Jan. 1913, and Bonzano to Gonner, 23 Jan. 1913, ASV, DAUS, IX Dubuque, fasc. 66, f. 3–4, 7. On Gonner, see Gleason, *Conservative Reformers*, 53–54, 77, 81–89, 91, 155, 166, 187, 197.

28. Nicholas Gonner to Giovanni Bonzano, 7 May 1913, ASV, DAUS, IX Dubuque, fasc. 66, f. 11.

29. Pietro Gasparri to Giovanni Bonzano, 17 Jan. 1916, Nicholas Gonner to Bonzano, 14 Jan. 1916, Bonzano to Gonner, 21 Jan. 1916, and Gonner to Bonzano, 23 Feb. 1916 (final quotation), ASV, DAUS, V, fasc. 68, f. 5, 10–12, 13, 9.

30. Nicholas Gonner to Giovanni Bonzano, 14 Jan. 1916, and Bonzano to Joseph Glass, 21 Jan. 1916, ASV, DAUS, V, fasc. 68, f. 10–12, 14.

31. Giovanni Bonzano to Richard Tierney, 21 Jan. 1916, and Tierney to Bonzano, 25 Jan. 1916, ASV, DAUS, V, fasc. 68, f. 15, 16.

32. Kertzer, *Popes against the Jews*, 240–43.

33. Koenig, *Principles for Peace*, 231.

34. Robert Lansing to Woodrow Wilson, 13 Aug. ("emanates from") and 20 Aug. 1917 ("practically goes no further"), *Papers Relating to the Foreign Relations*, 2:43, 44–45; Zivojino-vic, *United States and the Vatican Policies*, 86 (quotes "temporal power" from Lansing's Desk Diary, 21 Aug. 1917); Zivojinovic, "Robert Lansing's Comments."

35. "President Wilson's Reply to the Pope," NYT, 29 Aug. 1917, 1; Jusserand, "Letter to the Editor," 817–19.

36. "Wilson Holds to Policy," NYT, 15 Aug. 1917, 1 ("emanating"); "Pope's Proposals Leave Britain Cold," NYT, 15 Aug. 1917, 1 ("much discussion"); "The Pope's Peace Pro-posal," NYT, 15 Aug. 1917, 8 ("His Holiness"); Zivojinovic, *United States and the Vatican Poli-cies*, 75–96.

37. "Says Rulers Must Hearken to Pope," NYT, 27 Aug. 1917, 1 (quotes Hanna); "Ac-claimed Pope's Plea," NYT, 29 Aug. 1917, 2 (on resolution by Catholic Societies).

38. "Cardinal Gibbons's View," NYT, 16 Aug. 1917, 2; James Gibbons to Giovanni Bon-zano, 17 Aug. 1917, ASV, DAUS, V, fasc. 63 b/1, f. 43–44. On Gibbons's inactivity, see Bruti Liberati, "Santa Sede e Stati Uniti," 138–43; and Ellis, *James Cardinal Gibbons*, 2:243–47.

39. "The Pope's Peace Plea," *Catholic News*, 18 Aug. 1917, 4; "The Pope and Peace," *America*, 25 Aug. 1917, 500; "The President's Reply," *America*, 8 Sept. 1917, 552.

40. "The Pope's Peace Note," *America*, 6 Oct. 1917, 653 ("enenies"); "Rome," *America*, 17 Nov. 1917, 123 (quotes the *Atlantic Monthly*); *Catholic World*, Nov. 1917, 283 (quotes the *New Republic*), 285.

41. Serra, "La nota del primo agosto"; Veneruso, "I rapporti fra stato e chiesa," 723–30; Garzia, *La questione romana*, 154–68 (quotations, 167); Formigoni, *L'Italia dei cattolici*, 86–88; Seton-Watson, *Italy from Liberalism to Fascism*, 477–97.

42. Nigro, *New Diplomacy in Italy*, 11 (quotes Page); "The Pope and the War," *Catholic News*, 1 Dec. 1917, 4 (quotes the *London Morning Post* and the *New York Tribune*); "Rome," *America*, 8 Dec. 1917, 201 (cites *Morning Post*); "The Holy Father's Calumniators," *America*, 8 Dec. 1917, 216–17; "Anti-Catholic Propaganda in the Allied Camp," *America*, 22 Dec. 1917, 278; "Rome," *America*, 19 Jan. 1918, 357 ("unreserved praise"); "The Pope and Capo-retto," *America*, 20 Sept. 1920, 597.

43. Kennedy, *Over Here*, 59–66; Vaughn, *Holding Fast the Inner Lines*, 32–34, 193–200; *Com-plete Report*, 1–7, 92; Creel, *How We Advertised America*, 186, 191–99; Mock and Larson, *Words That Won the War*, 219–20.

44. "The Roman Legion of America," *Il Carroccio* 4 (Apr. 1918): 314–16; Alfonso Arcese to Delegation, n.d., ASV, DAUS, V, fasc. 84, f. 6–8.

45. Dennis Dougherty to Giovanni Bonzano, 9 Sept. 1918, and Bonzano to Dougherty, 10 Sept. 1918, ASV, DAUS, V, fasc. 84, f. 3–5. For the celebration, see "Una grande mani-festazione italo-americano," *PIA*, 19 Sept. 1918, 1; "L'Anniversario Glorioso," *PIA*, 20 Sept. 1919, 1–2; and "XX Settembre," *PIA*, 20 Sept. 1919, 3.

46. *Complete Report*, 104–6, 191–93; Creel, *How We Advertised America*, 227–32; Mock and Larson, *Words That Won the War*, 244, 286–92; Giovanni Bonzano to Pietro Gasparri, 3 Sept. 1918, ASV, DAUS, V, fasc. 91/1, f. 32–33.

47. George Creel to Peter Guilday, 29 Oct 1918, GUA, box 13, folder 9.

48. Peter Guilday to Richard Tierney, 1 Nov. 1918, and Tierney to Guilday, 9 Nov. 1918, GUA, box 13, folder 9.

49. "The Holy Father's Calumniators," *America*, 8 Dec. 1917, 217, prints the inaccurate version that circulated between November 1917 and February 1918.

50. John Wynne to "The Editor," included in Wynne to Giovanni Bonzano, 9 Jan. 1918, ASV, DAUS, V, fasc. 63 b/1, f. 64–65; Pollard, *Unknown Pope*, 128. Bruti Liberati, in "Santa Sede e Stati Uniti," suggests the president pilfered the pope's peace note.

51. John Cowles to Raymond Vermimont, 8 May 1918, GUA, box 14, folder 10.

52. Zivojinovic, *United States and Vatican Policies*, 129–30; Ferrell, "Woodrow Wilson and Open Diplomacy"; Ellis, *James Cardinal Gibbons*, 2:265–76.

53. Zivojinovic, *United States and Vatican Policies*, 127–40, 129 (quotation).

54. "The War Policy of the Pope," *America*, 23 Feb. 1918, 487–88; Giovanni Bonzano to James Gibbons, 26 Jan. [Feb.] 1918 (praise from Bonzano and Benedict), and Pietro Gasparri to Bonzano, 24 Apr. 1918, ASV, DAUS, V, fasc. 63 b/1, f. 74, 79.

55. "Promemoria Orlando del 19 febbraio 1918," in Orlando, *Miei rapporti*, 102–3.

56. Pietro Gasparri to Giovanni Bonzano, 31 July 1918 (for the rewording), and Bonzano to Gasparri, 28 Oct. 1918, ASV, DAUS, V, fasc. 63 b/1, f. 88, 93. At this juncture Gibbons refused to see Wilson about article XV, for fear that the visit would arouse the press against the Church.

57. Sidney Sonnino to Vincenzo Macchi di Cellere, 3 Aug. 1918, ASMAE, GAB, b. 177, fasc. "Vaticano-Modificazione all'articolo 5 della Convenzione di Londra del 1915"; Mosca, "La mancata revisione dell'art. 15," 406 (cites Macchi di Cellere).

58. Zivojinovic, *United States and the Vatican Policies*, 133–37; Ellis, *James Cardinal Gibbons*, 2:272–78; Garzia, *La questione romana*, 201 (quotes Désiré Mercier to Pietro Gasparri, 26 Nov. 1918); Bruti Liberati, "Santa Sede e Stati Uniti," 145.

59. Benedict XV to Woodrow Wilson, 11 Oct. 1918, and Wilson to Benedict XV, 17 Oct. 1918, ASV, DAUS, V, fasc. 63 b/1, f. 96, 103; Zivojinovic, *United States and the Vatican Policies*, 157–75.

60. Patrick Hayes to Giovanni Bonzano, 29 Nov. 1918, and David Walsh to Bonzano, 27 Nov. 1918, ASV, DAUS, V, fasc. 63 b/2, f. 118, 120.

61. Anthony Matre to Giovanni Bonzano, n.d., and William H. O'Connell to Bonzano, n.d. [ca. 3 Dec. 1918], ASV, DAUS, V, fasc. 63 b/2, f. 135–36, 145–46; "Would Put Pope at Peace Table," *Boston Sunday Post*, 24 Nov. 1918, 1, 8, 9.

62. *CW* 108 (Dec. 1918): 429–30.

63. "The Pope and the Peace Conference," *America*, 7 Dec. 1918, 214.

64. Anonymous to Richard Tierney, n.d. [1918], and [Illegible] to Tierney, 20 Oct. 1918, GUA, box 13, folder 6.

65. William H. O'Connell to Giovanni Bonzano, 18 Jan. 1919, Pietro Gasparri to Bonzano, 17 Jan. 1919, James Gibbons to Mercier, 20 Jan. 1919, and O'Connell to Bonzano, 20 Jan. 1919, ASV, DAUS, V, fasc. 63 b/3, f. 155–56, 148, 159–60, 157.

66. On the Catholic press in Allied states, see *America*, 1 Mar. 1919, 515–16, 8 Mar. 1919, 544, 22 Mar. 1919, 599–600, 12 Apr. 1919, 4. For the series, see John C. Reville, "The Origin of the Papal States," *America*, 26 Apr. 1919, 61–63, "The Destruction of the Papal States," *America*, 3 May 1919, 91–93, "Justice for the Pope," *America*, 10 May 1919, 120–21 (quotation), and "The Prison of the Pope," *America*, 24 May 1919, 174–76.

67. Garzia, *La questione romana*, 202–5; *CW* 108 (Jan. 1919): 570.

68. "Evangelical Journalism Again," *America*, 24 May 1919, 179 (quotes the *Herald and Presbyter*); "Senator Sherman and the Vatican," *America*, 12 July 1919, 350–52; Ambrosius, *Woodrow Wilson and the American Diplomatic Tradition*, 139–40; Luigi Cossio to Pietro Gasparri, 21 June and 24 June 1919, ASV, DAUS, V, fasc. 97, f. 3, 5–6.

69. Seton-Watson, *Italy from Liberalism to Fascism*, 505–10, 527–36; House and Seymour, *What Really Happened at Paris*, 112–39.

70. Margiotta Broglio, *Italia e Santa Sede*, 43–57; Spadolini, *Il Cardinale Gasparri*, 233–48; Gaffey, *Francis Clement Kelley*, 233–56; Garzia, *La questione romana*, 206–13; Ellis, *James Cardinal Gibbons*, 2:279–81; Vittorio E. Orlando, "The First Agreement between Italy and the Holy See," *Saturday Evening Post*, 4 May 1929, 12–13, 206.

71. Margiotta Broglio, *Italia e Santa Sede*, 56–71; Sforza, *Contemporary Italy*, 200–207, 333–34; Pollard, *Unknown Pope*, 169.

72. Nigro, *New Diplomacy in Italy*, 56 ("conscious preference"), 88–89 (quotes Mussolini); D. Rossini, *Il mito americano*; Burgwyn, *Legend of the Mutilated Victory*.

73. See Seton-Watson, *Italy from Liberalism to Fascism*, 510–60; and Ledeen, *First Duce*.

74. Pietro Gasparri to Giovanni Bonzano, 23 Feb. 1920, and Bonzano to George Mundelein, 24 Feb. 1920, ASV, DAUS, V, fasc. 101, f. 3, 5.

75. Dennis Dougherty to Giovanni Bonzano, 25 Feb. 1920, and Patrick Hayes to Bonzano, 25 Feb. 1920, ASV, DAUS, V, fasc. 101, f. 6–7, 8–9.

76. Knock, *To End All Wars*, 246–70; Ferrell, *Woodrow Wilson and World War I*, 156–77, 219–30.

77. Dennis Dougherty to Giovanni Bonzano, 27 Feb. 1920, and George Mundelein to Bonzano, 28 Feb. 1920, ASV, DAUS, V, fasc. 101, f. 10–11, 17–18.

78. Giovanni Bonzano to Pietro Gasparri, 9 Mar. 1920, ASV, DAUS, V, fasc. 101, f. 23–28.

79. Ibid.

80. Patrick Hayes to Giovanni Bonzano, 12 Mar. 1920, and Dennis Dougherty to Bonzano, 24 Mar. 1920, ASV, DAUS, V, fasc. 101, f. 29, 31.

81. Fogarty, *Vatican and the American Hierarchy*, 195–209, 216–18, 228–30; Kantowicz, *Corporation Sole*; O'Toole, *Militant and Triumphant*; Morris, *American Catholics*, 165–95.

CHAPTER FIVE

1. Semeria, "Pro-Memoria sui 'Figli d'Italia,'" in Gaetano De Lai to Giovanni Bonzano, 28 Oct. 1920, ASV, DAUS, XII, fasc. 96. On Semeria, see Morozzo della Rocca, *La fede e la guerra*, 11, 15, 83; and Jemolo, *Church and State in Italy*, 164, 203–4.

2. Wuthnow, *Meaning and Moral Order*, 148–49, 159–61.

3. Andreozzi, *Order Sons of Italy in America*, 7–14.

4. De Lai to Giovanni Bonzano, 28 Oct. 1920, ASV, DAUS, XII, fasc. 96.

5. Ibid.

6. Data compiled from ASV, DAUS, II, fasc. 191 a/1–3, b/1–4; and Palmieri, *Il grave problema religioso italiano*. There were probably closer to 400 unincardinated priests because the bishop of Brooklyn did not send a list.

7. Giovanni Bonzano to De Lai, 23 Apr. 1918, ASV, DAUS, II, fasc. 191 a/1.

8. George Mundelein to Diomede Falconio, 22 Dec. 1907, ASV, DAUS, IX, fasc. 72, f. 7–11.

9. For background for the following paragraphs, see D'Agostino, "Clerical 'Birds of Passage.'"

10. This description is a summary of profiles of hundreds of Italian clergy I have compiled from several collections, including ASV, DAUS; APF; APCMR; and the Archivio del Prelato per l'Emigrazione Italiana.

11. Luigi Pozzi to Tarozzi, 25 Oct. 1906, APF, Nuova Serie, 1906, vol. 336, rubr. 5, f. 961–64.

12. Gherardo Ferrante to Giovanni Bonzano, 11 Apr. 1918, ASV, DAUS, II, fasc. 191 b/2; Sartorio, *Social and Religious Life of Italians*, 114.

13. Of the 570 graduates of Chicago's St. Mary of the Lake Seminary between 1926 (its first class) and 1939, 7 were of Italian descent and 1 was a boy born in Italy who came to Chicago as a child. See *Official Catholic Directory*; *NW* (1892–1940); *Ordination Book* of the AAC; Sharp, *Priests and Parishes*; Sexton and Riley, *History of Saint John's*; and Code, *Dictionary of the American Hierarchy*. Formally, the apostolic delegate and the pope were members of the U.S. hierarchy.

14. De Lai to Giovanni Bonzano, 28 Oct. 1920, ASV, DAUS, XII, fasc. 96.

15. Sindoni, "Gli echi della 'Rerum Novarum'"; Borzomati, *I Cattolici e il Mezzogiorno*; Pollard, *Vatican and Italian Fascism*, 52–53.

16. Traniello, *Città dell'uomo*, 141 (quotes Sturzo in Florence in February 1906).

17. Ibid. On Sturzo, see Malgeri, *Luigi Sturzo*.

18. Traniello, *Città dell'uomo*, 152 (quotes Sturzo in Piazza Armerina, Sicily, in 1907).

19. Order Sons of Italy in America, *Costituzione Fondamentale* (1915), 3.

20. Leonardo Marretta to Giovanni Bonzano, 19 Apr. 1913, ASV, DAUS, X, fasc. 699. On Gabbani, see APCMR, 1918 (2), 729/18. In July 1918, Gabbani was still a member of the OSIA.

21. Thomas Hickey to Giovanni Bonzano, 19 Apr. 1913, Bonzano to Hickey, 21 Apr. 1913, and James McFaul to Bonzano, 26 Feb. 1915, ASV, DAUS, XII, fasc. 96.

22. Edoardo Marcuzzi to Delegation, 10 Aug. 1911, Marcuzzi to Luigi Cossio, 19 Nov. 1915 (quotation), and Cossio to Marcuzzi, 25 Nov. 1915, ASV, DAUS, X, fasc. 811; Michael Lavelle to Giovanni Bonzano, 20 Aug. 1917, ASV, DAUS, IX New York (nuova serie), fasc. 73. *L'Italiano in America* (1894–1920) was a weekly; extant copies are in ASV.

23. Edoardo Marcuzzi to Luigi Cossio, 9 Feb. 1916, ASV, DAUS, X, fasc. 811.

24. Giovanni Bonzano to Edoardo Marcuzzi, 17 Feb. 1916, ASV, DAUS, X, fasc. 811.

25. Edoardo Marcuzzi to Delegation, 23 Apr. 1917, ASV, DAUS, X, fasc. 811.

26. *L'Italiano in America*, 1 Apr. 1917, ASV, DAUS, XII, fasc. 96.

27. Ibid.

28. *L'Italiano in America*, 8 Apr. 1917, ASV, DAUS, XII, fasc. 96.

29. Edoardo Marcuzzi to Delegation, 29 Apr. 1917, and Luigi Cossio to Marcuzzi, 1 May 1917, ASV, DAUS, XII, fasc. 96.

30. Edoardo Marcuzzi to Delegation, 14 June 1917, ASV, DAUS, XII, fasc. 96. On the Italian Bureau, see Brown, <u>Churches, Communities, and Children</u>, 94–96. On Ferrante, see Il Carroccio 1 (Dec. 1915): 76–77.

31. Edoardo Marcuzzi to Delegation, 29 Apr. 1917, ASV, DAUS, XII, fasc. 96.

32. Edoardo Marcuzzi to Delegation, 14 June 1917, ASV, DAUS, XII, fasc. 96.

33. Giovanni Bonzano to Gherardo Ferrante, 24 June 1917, ASV, DAUS, XII, fasc. 96.

34. Gherardo Ferrante to Giovanni Bonzano, 30 June 1917, ASV, DAUS, XII, fasc. 96. I

verified the change in the constitution by comparing the two editions of the Order Sons of Italy in America, *Costituzione Fondamentale* published in January 1915 and November 1917.

35. Marcuzzi and Roberto Biasotti, both in the Italian Apostolate, encouraged Cossio to investigate Ferrante. Biasotti, from Annone Veneto on the border of Friuli, shared regional origins with Marcuzzi and Cossio and was in a position to know of Ferrante's abuses because he became, in 1909, the Pallottine Sisters' spiritual director at five of their houses in New York and New Jersey. See APIE, files 510 and 511, which contain a letter from Giovanni Bonzano, 19 Jan. 1922; and Biasotti to De Lai, 13 Feb. 1923, APCMR, 1913 (5), 1604/13.

36. Patrick Hayes to Giovanni Bonzano, 20 Sept. 1917, ASV, DAUS, IX New York (nuova serie), fasc. 75.

37. Ibid. On Sister Edvige, see "Circa Msgr. G. Ferrante, Vicario Generale," n.d., ASV, DAUS, IX New York (nuova serie), fasc. 75.

38. Edoardo Marcuzzi to Giovanni Bonzano, 19 Sept. 1917, and Bonzano to Marcuzzi, 6 Oct. 1917; Circular to Rev. Confratello, n.d. ("indifference"), ASV, DAUS, XIV, fasc. 23.

39. The 260 priests in attendance were primarily from the dioceses of New York, Brooklyn, and Newark but included priests from Buffalo, Boston, Pittsburgh, Philadelphia, Washington, and Springfield, Massachusetts. "Un Congresso di Sacerdoti Italiani dell'East," *L'Italiano in America*, 16 Dec. 1917, 2, ASV, DAUS, XIV, fasc. 23.

40. *Programma pel Primo Congresso Cattolico Italiano*, ASV, DAUS, XIV, fasc. 23.

41 Giovanni Bonzano to Edoardo Marcuzzi, 25 Nov. 1917, ASV, DAUS, XIV, fasc. 23.

42. Edoardo Marcuzzi to Giovanni Bonzano, 7 Jan. 1918, Bonzano to Marcuzzi, 15 Jan. 1918, Marcuzzi to Bonzano, 7 Feb. 1918, Alfonso Arcese to Luigi Cossio, 15 Feb. 1918, and Cossio to Arcese, 20 Feb. 1918, ASV, DAUS, XIV, fasc. 23. *Il Carroccio* 4 (Apr. 1918): 364 notes the publication of the *Acts of the Congress*. I have found no extant copy.

43. Alfonso Arcese to Giovanni Bonzano, 26 Feb. 1918, and Bonzano to Arcese, 2 Mar. 1918, ASV, DAUS, XIV, fasc. 23.

44. Giovanni Bonzano to Alfonso Arcese, 2 Mar. 1918 (Bonzano's version of the speech), Arcese to Bonzano, 18 Mar. 1918, and Bonzano to Arcese, 25 Mar. 1918, ASV, DAUS, XIV, fasc. 23.

45. Edoardo Marcuzzi to Confratello, n.d., ASV, DAUS, XIV, fasc. 23.

46. Bove, *L'Ordine Figli D'Italia*, ASV, DAUS, XII, fasc. 96.

47. "Alle associazione italiane," ERI, 13 Oct. 1917, 1; "Commemorazione del Columbus Day" and "Festa di fondazione," ERI, 20 Oct. 1917, 1, 2; "Lettera aperta ai signori," ERI, 3 Nov. 1917, 1.

48. See D'Agostino, "Scalabrini Fathers."

49. Sebastiani to Giovanni Bonzano, 29 Dec. 1916, Bonzano to Matthew Harkins, 6 Jan. 1917, Harkins to Bonzano, 13 Jan. 1917 (quotation), and Harkins to De Lai, 1 Sept. 1917, ASV, DAUS, IX, fasc. 43. Bove became a monsignor after these events.

50. Antonio Bove to Giovanni Bonzano, 18 Jan. 1918, ASV, DAUS, IX, fasc. 43. On Harkins's withdrawing his reservations, see Matthew Harkins to Bonzano, 11 Nov. 1918, ADP, Msgr. Anthony Bove Papers, folder 2, 3B/1-115. On Bove's medal, see Antonio Vico to Harkins, 9 June 1918, Vico to Bove, 10 July 1918, and Harkins to Benedict XV, 2 Sept. 1918, ADP, Bove Papers, folder 1, 3B/1-114.

51. Giuseppe Silipigni to Michele Cerrati, 15 Feb. 1922, APIE, fasc. 515; *Il Carroccio* 2 (June 1916): 443; *Il Carroccio* 3 (Mar. 1917): 206; *Il Carroccio* 4 (Feb. 1918): 173; Salvemini, *Italian Fascist Activities*, 113–14.

52. Antonio Bove to Giovanni Bonzano, 25 Sept. 1918, and Bonzano to Bove, 27 Sept. 1918, ASV, DAUS, XII, fasc. 96.

53. Bove, *L'Ordine Figli D'Italia*, ASV, DAUS, XII, fasc. 96.

54. Ibid.; "Redhot Battle Rages over the Sons of Italy," *Providence News*, 4 Dec. 1918, 1, 2. The apostate and grand venerable was Vincenzo Cinquegrana, who had assisted Bove at St. Ann's before he left the Church.

55. Bove, *L'Ordine Figli D'Italia*, ASV, DAUS, XII, fasc. 96.

56. Antonio Bove to Giovanni Bonzano, 31 Oct. 1918, and Roberto Biasotti to Bove, 2 Nov. 1918, ASV, DAUS, XII, fasc. 96.

57. "L'iniziazione delle Loggie Fratelli Bandiera e Prata Sannita," *ERI*, 2 Nov. 1918, 1 (quotation); "Cerimonia patriottico-relegiosa [sic]," *ERI*, 9 Nov. 1918, 1.

58. "Coscienza o tornaconto," *ERI*, 16 Nov. 1918, 1.

59. "Voci del pubblico," *ERI*, 23 Nov. 1918, 1.

60. "La Loggia Giordano Bruno risponde" and "Dichiarazione" (Rhode Island Grand Lodge response), *ERI*, 30 Nov. 1918, 1.

61. "Communicazione del supreme oratore," *ERI*, 7 Dec. 1918, 1 (Albano's quotation). For more coverage of the conflict, see "Nota editoriale" and "Nuove Loggie," *ERI*, 7 Dec. 1918, 1; "Grandiosa e patriottica manifestazione," *ERI*, 4 Jan. 1919, 1; and "Redhot Battle Rages over Sons of Italy," *Providence News*, 4 Dec. 1918, 1, 2.

62. "Ancora," *ERI*, 14 Dec. 1918, 1.

63. Michele Albano to Giovanni Bonzano, 3 Dec. 1918, ASV, DAUS, XII, fasc. 96.

64. Giuseppe Silipigni to Giovanni Bonzano, 4 Dec. 1918, ASV, DAUS, XII, fasc. 96.

65. Edoardo Marcuzzi to Luigi Cossio, 14 Dec. 1918, ASV, DAUS, XII, fasc. 96.

66. Giovanni Bonzano to Michele Albano, 11 Jan. 1919, ASV, DAUS, XII, fasc. 96.

67. Roberto Biasotti to Luigi Cossio, 2 Feb. 1919, and Cossio to Biasotti, 7 Feb. 1919, ASV, DAUS, XII, fasc. 96; Executive Committee to Giovanni Bonzano, 10 Feb. 1919 (quotations), ASV, DAUS, XIV, fasc. 23.

68. Giovanni Bonzano to Alfonso Arcese, 11 Feb. 1919, ASV, DAUS, XII, fasc. 96.

69. Ibid. On the dissolution of the unions, see Alfonso Arcese to Giovanni Bonzano, 13 Feb. 1919, and *Bollettino dell'Unione del Clero Italiano* 2 (Mar. 1919), ASV, DAUS, XIV, fasc. 23; Edoardo Marcuzzi to Giovanni Bonzano, 6 Nov. 1918, ASV, DAUS, X, fasc. 811; and De Lai to Bonzano, 17 Nov. 1921 (includes Marcuzzi to Rev. Padre, 6 Nov. 1918), ASV, DAUS, XII, fasc. 96. On the money from Hayes, see Marcuzzi to Bonzano, 31 Dec. 1918, ASV, DAUS, X, fasc. 811.

70. Giovanni Bonzano to Antonio Bove, 24 Feb. 1919 (quotations), Thomas Walsh to Bonzano, 13 Feb. 1920, Bonzano to Walsh, 14 Feb. 1920 (responding to an inquiring bishop), T. Lalli to Bonzano, 13 Oct. 1921, Bonzano to Lalli, 15 Oct. 1921 (directing priests and bishops to consider lodges), Angelo Carpinella to Bonzano, 21 Oct. 1921, and Bonzano to Carpinella, 26 Oct. 1921, ASV, DAUS, XII, fasc. 96.

71. Edoardo Marcuzzi to Giovanni Bonzano, 6 Nov. 1918, ASV, DAUS, X, fasc. 811; Gherardo Ferrante to Luigi Cossio, 13 Aug. 1919, Cossio to Ferrante, 16 Aug. 1919, and Thomas Hickey to Bonzano, 12 Aug. 1921, ASV, DAUS, XII, fasc. 96. Other priests entered the OSIA offices. In 1919 Father Francesco Pannetta was elected New York grand orator.

72. Nelli, "Role of the 'Colonial' Press," 84 ("disgrace"); *NW*, 21 Mar. 1908, 3 ("every intelligent man").

73. For biographical information on Marchello, see Maurice Marchello Papers, Immi-

gration History Research Center, St. Paul, Minn., box 4, folder 33; *Bollettino Parrochiale della Chiesa di Sant'Antonio,* Aug. 1936, 6–7; Maurice Marchello, "The Need for an Italo-American 'Risorgimento' in Chicago Politics," *La Tribuna Italiana Transatlantica,* 27 Jan. 1934; Gambera, "Memorie," typed manuscript at the Center for Migration Studies, New York.

CHAPTER SIX

1. McGreevy, "Thinking on One's Own"; Gleason, *Speaking of Diversity,* 207–11, *Contending with Modernity,* 261–68, and "American Catholics and Liberalism," 60.

2. Diggins, "American Catholics and Italian Fascism," 54 (quotation), and *Mussolini and Fascism,* 182–203; Nazzaro, "L'atteggiamento della stampa cattolico-moderata americana"; W. Smith, "Attitude of American Catholics toward Italian Fascism." Miscamble, in "Limits of American Catholic Antifascism," also claims Diggins exaggerates Catholic anti-Fascism.

3. Diggins, "American Catholics and Italian Fascism," 54.

4. Diggins, *Mussolini and Fascism,* 196.

5. Gleason, *Speaking of Diversity,* 210–11, and *Contending with Modernity,* 266–68; McGreevy, "Thinking on One's Own," 112. For a Catholic critique of liberals on this issue, see McGreevy, "Pragmatism to a Fault?"

6. Giovanni Bonzano to Pietro Gasparri, 20 Jan. (on "invasion of the Vatican") and 3 May 1921, ASV, DAUS, II, fasc. 206, f. 40–41, 59–62.

7. Giovanni Bonzano to Pietro Gasparri, 12 Mar. and 9 May 1921, ASV, DAUS, II, fasc. 206, f. 53–54, 64–65.

8. Giovanni Bonzano to Pietro Gasparri, 5 Mar. 1921, ASV, DAUS, II, fasc. 206, f. 47.

9. For background for the following pages, see Costigliola, *Awkward Dominion;* Schmitz, *United States and Fascist Italy;* Migone, *Gli Stati Uniti e il fascismo;* Iriye, *Globalizing of America;* Cassels, *Mussolini's Early Diplomacy;* and Lyttelton, *Seizure of Power.*

10. Schmitz, *United States and Fascist Italy,* 52, 53.

11. Cannistraro and Sullivan, *Il Duce's Other Woman,* 357–58; Diggins, *Mussolini and Fascism,* 27–28; "R. W. Child Is Dead," NYT, 1 Feb. 1935. On Child's conversion and funeral, see Giuseppe Castruccio to Augusto Rosso, 4 Feb. 1935, ASMAE, AP2, b. 26.

12. Schmitz, *United States and Fascist Italy,* 65 (circular, "emerge from the chaos," and "rejoiced"), 78 ("methods").

13. Cannistraro and Sullivan, *Il Duce's Other Woman,* 350–68, quote on 351; Nasaw, *Chief,* 470–74. Mussolini's salary in 1928 was 32,000 lire, or about $1,685.

14. Salvemini, *Italian Fascist Activities,* 135–38; Patrick Hayes to Thomas Lamont, 5 Mar. 1925, TWLP, box 42, folder 20; Hayes to Martin Egan, 20 Nov. 1925, TWLP, box 43, folder 3.

15. Pietro Fumasoni-Biondi to William H. O'Connell, 26 Oct. 1925, AAB, Chancellor's Office Papers, Apostolic Delegate, 1925; Fogarty, "Cardinal William Henry O'Connell," 142 (quotes Fumasoni-Biondi to Pietro Gasparri, 26 Mar. 1925, on "Coolidge's candidacy").

16. Schmitz, *United States and Fascist Italy,* 67–68.

17. See Canali, *Il delitto Matteotti.*

18. Schmitz, *United States and Fascist Italy,* 67 (quotes Thomas Lamont to Henry P. Fletcher); Chernow, *House of Morgan,* 281; Lamont to Giacomo De Martino, 23 Oct. 1925, TWLP, box 43, folder 2.

19. Costigliola, *Awkward Dominion,* 111–39; Migone, *Gli Stati Uniti e il fascismo,* 45–199; Schmitz, *United States and Fascist Italy,* 89–100; Cassels, *Mussolini's Early Diplomacy,* 262–71.

20. John A. Ryan, "Cancel War Debts and Reparations," *Annals of the American Academy of Political and Social Science* 120 (July 1925): 62–64, and "The International Ledger," *Com,* 2 Dec. 1925, 92–94 (quotations); Broderick, *Right Reverend New Dealer,* 125, 135–36.

21. For background for the following pages, see Malgeri, *Luigi Sturzo,* 97–186; Traniello, "L'Italia cattolica nell'era fascista," 257–80, and *Città dell'uomo,* 141–84; G. De Rosa, *Il Partito popolare italiano;* Jemolo, *Chiesa e stato in Italia,* 563–686; Formigoni, *L'Italia dei cattolici,* 77–132; Margiotta Broglio, *Italia e Santa Sede;* J. Molony, *Emergence of Political Catholicism in Italy;* Webster, *Cross and the Fasces,* 50–128; Wolff, *Between Pope and Duce,* 1–128; Coppa, "Mussolini and the Concordat of 1929"; Kent, *Pope and the Duce;* Rhodes, *Vatican in the Age of Dictators;* Pollard, *Vatican and Italian Fascism,* 1–74; Binchy, *Church and State in Fascist Italy;* Halperin, *Separation of Church and State,* 87–109; Lyttelton, *Seizure of Power;* De Grand, *Hunchback's Tailor,* 229–68, and *Italian Left in the Twentieth Century,* 31–61; Mack Smith, *Italy and Its Monarchy,* 233–74; A. O'Brien, "The *Osservatore Romano* and Fascism."

22. "The Naples Conference," *America,* 15 May 1920, 76; J. P. Conry, "Social Organization of Italian Catholics," *CW* 112 (May 1921): 35–41 (quotation, 41); Giuseppe Quirico, "The Rise of the People's Party in Italy," *CW* 114 (Jan. 1922): 506–15; NW, 4 Aug. 1922, 11.

23. Rhodes, *Vatican in the Age of Dictators,* 27 (quotes Mussolini's novel, the *Cardinal's Daughter*); Schnapp, *Primer,* 6 (quotes "Platform of the Fasci di Combattimento," 6 June 1919); Margiotta Broglio, *Italia e Santa Sede,* 80 (quotes *Il Popolo d'Italia,* 18 Nov. 1919).

24. Margiotta Broglio, *Italia e Santa Sede,* 82 (until "anticlericalism"); Halperin, *Separation of Church and State,* 99 ("Latin and Imperial tradition").

25. Rhodes, *Vatican in the Age of Dictators,* 27 (quotation).

26. Gelasio Caetani to Benito Mussolini, 17 Feb. 1923, Mussolini to Caetani, 25 Feb. 1923, Robert Clegg to Caetani, 14 Mar. 1923, and Caetani to Clegg, 20 Mar. 1923, ASMAE, AMB II, b. 17, fasc. "Fascismo e Massoneria."

27. "The School on Monte Mario," *CA,* 7 July 1921, 876; "Americans Aid in Robbing Italian Youth of Faith," *NW,* 22 June 1917, 2. On Italian Protestants and Waldensians (indigenous pre-Reformation Italian evangelicals), see Ricca, "Le chiese evangeliche," 405–40.

28. "Audience with the Pope," *Columbia,* Oct. 1920, 17 ("Catholic faith"); "Holy Father Asks K. of C. to Offset Methodism in Rome," *Monitor,* 18 Sept. 1920, 1; John B. Kennedy, "For the Land of Columbus," *America,* 3 Sept. 1921, 468–69; Kauffman, *Faith and Fraternalism,* 250 ("anti-Latin"); "Methodist Activities in Rome," *NW,* 3 Sept. 1920, 1.

29. John Burke to John Noll, n.d. [Mar. 1922] (describes O'Connell's speech), and copy of printed sermon of Rev. Bayley of the Methodist Episcopal Church of Hagerstown, Md., ACUA, NCWC, box 9, file: "NCWC: Church: Anti-Catholic Propaganda: Protestants in Italy, 1922–1955."

30. "Protestants in Rome," *CA,* 21 July 1921, 939 (quotes Tipple's letter); "The 'Why' of the Campaign against Methodism's Monte Mario Collegio," *CA,* 11 Aug. 1921, 1023. On the progress of the college, see Tipple, "The Eighth Hill of Rome," *CA,* 2 Mar. 1922, 262–63. On the college opening, see Tipple, "Rome, 1872–1922," *CA,* 15 June 1922, 743–45. On the bishops' resolution, see "The Attack on Monte Mario," *CA,* 20 July 1922, 890. On its approval, see "'I Am Satisfied with Your School,'" *CA,* 23 Aug. 1923, 1036.

31. L. J. S. Wood, "Mussolini and the Roman Question," *CW* 119 (Apr. 1924): 64 (quotation).

32. "With the Fascists in Italy," *CW* 116 (Mar. 1923): 842; L. J. S. Wood, "Mussolini and

the Roman Question," *CW* 119 (Apr. 1924): 65; "Mussolini and the Vatican," *America*, 2 Dec. 1922, 147; "The Crucifix Restored to the Schools," *America*, 23 Dec. 1922, 218; "Fascisti and Masons," *America*, 3 Mar. 1923, 459–60; "The Fascista Government," *Monitor*, 5 Dec. 1922, quoted in W. Smith, "Attitude of American Catholics," 95; *NW*, 1 Feb. 1924, 4.

33. See Malgeri, *Luigi Sturzo*; La Bella, *Luigi Sturzo*; and Papini, *Il Coraggio della democrazia*.

34. L. J. S. Wood, "Mussolini and the Law," *Com*, 19 Nov. 1924, 42–43 (first three quotes), and "Mussolini and History Future," *Com*, 26 Nov. 1924, 74–75 ("Communism and chaos"). Other articles by Wood published in *Com* include "Italian Freemasonry," 4 Mar. 1925, 461–62, "Holy Year in Rome," 17 June 1925, 161–62, "The Fascist Labor Legislation," 16 June 1926, 149–50, "Three Years of Mussolini, I," 18 May 1927, 38–39, and "Three Years of Mussolini, II," 25 May 1927, 68–69. Wood also wrote "Mussolini and the Roman Question," *CW* 119 (Apr. 1924): 64–75. For articles by Harvey Wickham published in *Com*, see "Baiting the Duce," 5 May 1926, 712–15, "The Fascist of Fascism," 29 Dec. 1926, 204–6, "The Renaissance of Machiavelli," 14 Sept. 1927, 435–36, "The Renaissance of Machiavelli," 21 Sept. 1927, 465–67, "The Theatre at Ostia, I: The Restoration," 19 Oct. 1927, 574–76, "The Theatre at Ostia, II: The Greek Plays," 26 Oct. 1927, 605–7, and "Potenziani of the Pilgrim Staff," 16 May 1928, 36–38. On the magazine, see Van Allen, *Commonweal and American Catholicism*, who claims it was neutral on Fascism.

35. "Premier Reforms Fascists," *America*, 2 Aug. 1924, 368 ("progress"); "Premier Mussolini," *America*, 25 Oct. 1924, 28 ("wonderful work").

36. *CW* 120 (Dec. 1924): 405. For similar remarks, see "The High-Handed Mussolini," *CW* 121 (June 1925): 408; and "Mad Mussolini," *CW* 122 (Mar. 1926): 838–39. See also Gribble, *Guardian of America*.

37. Halperin, *Separation of Church and State*, 92 (quotes Gioacchino Volpe).

38. See Jemolo, *Church and State in Italy*, 182–277; and Lyttleton, *Seizure of Power*, 308–32.

39. On awareness in America of a coming reconciliation, see "Mussolini's Popularity," *America*, 6 Feb. 1926, 389; and "The Vatican and Mussolini," *America*, 3 Apr. 1926, 582.

40. See Jemolo, *Church and State in Italy*, 182–277; and Lyttleton, *Seizure of Power*, 269–307.

41. Joseph Tibe to Benito Mussolini, 19 Aug. 1925, ASMAE, AP1, b. 1600, f. 7376 "Miscellanea."

42. Giacomo De Martino to Benito Mussolini, 5 Jan. 1926, Mussolini to De Martino, 9 Jan. 1926, and De Martino to Mussolini, 25 Feb. 1926, ASMAE, AP1, b. 17, fasc. "Fascismo e Massoneria"; Diggins, *Mussolini and Fascism*, 201.

43. L. J. S. Wood, "Italian Freemasonry" *Com*, 4 Mar. 1925, 461–62.

44. Stephen Grayson, "Mussolini and the Masons," *America*, 11 July 1925, 295–96; "Mobbing of Amendola," *America*, 1 Aug. 1925, 366.

45. "Cardinal Lauds Mussolini," *NYT*, 29 Feb. 1924, 4; Benito Mussolini to William H. O'Connell, 4 July 1926, AAB, Cardinal William Henry O'Connell Papers, General Correspondence, box 7, folder 12; Salvemini and La Piana, *What to Do with Italy*, 68 (quotes O'Connell after the award).

46. Salvemini and La Piana, *What to Do with Italy*, 68 (Mundelein), 69 (Dougherty); "Hayes Come Home," *NYT*, 7 Feb. 1926, 2 (quotes Hayes); Dennis Dougherty to Giacomo De Martino, 29 Apr. 1927, Philadelphia Archdiocesan Historical Research Center, Cardinal Dennis Dougherty Collection, 80-4568, shelf D-2, box 2; John Carter, "American Reactions to Italian Fascism," 224–25, quotes Hickey in *NYT*, 3 Oct. 1926.

47. Benito Mussolini to Italian Embassy (Washington), 29 Apr. 1925, Leopoldo Zunini to Giacomo De Martino, 7 May 1925, De Martino to MAE, 9 June 1925, Nicolo De Carlo to Augusto Rosso, 29 May 1925, Agostino Ferrante di Ruffano to De Martino, 7 June 1925, "Local Italians Join," *Boston Herald*, 8 June 1925, and "Italian King's Silver Jubilee Celebrated," *Boston Globe*, 8 June 1925, ASMAE, AMB II, b. 75, fasc. "Giubileo sovrano, 1925."

48. Leopoldo Zunini to MAE, 7 May and 19 June 1926, ASMAE, AP1, b. 1602, fasc. "Vaticano." See Fairman, "Twenty-Eighth International Eucharistic Congress."

49. Leopoldo Zunini to MAE, 21 June 1926, "Religione e patria," PIA, 22 June 1926, and Giuseppe Rossi, "Il Congresso Eucaristico Internazionale a Chicago," *L'Idea*, 17 July 1926 (quotations), ASMAE, AP1, b. 1602, fasc. "Vaticano"; Donovan, *Twenty-Eighth International Eucharistic Congress*, 404–5.

50. "Discorsi del nostro Console Generale Commendatore Zunini," *L'Idea*, 17 July 1926, 3 (on papacy); "Solenne aperatura del Congresso Eucaristico," *Corriere d'America*, 21 June 1926, 1.

51. Leopoldo Zunini to MAE, 25 June 1926, "Religione e patria," PIA, 22 June 1926, "Simposio in onore dei pellegrini," PIA, 25 June 1926 (quotations at the symposium), and Internal Report, Rome, 11 Aug. 1926, ASMAE, AP1, b. 1602, fasc. "Vaticano." On audience with Mario Lauro, see Salvemini, *Italian Fascist Activities*, 163–64.

52. Paolo Emilio Giusti to Benito Mussolini, 4 July 1926, and "La visita del Cardinale Legato," *La Stampa Italiana*, ASMAE, AP1, b. 1602, fasc. "Vaticano"; Mormino, *Immigrants on the Hill*, 156–63.

53. James Gill to Benito Mussolini, 18 July 1926, ASMAE, AP1, b. 1602, fasc. 7389.

54. T. S. Horry to Benito Mussolini, 1 Dec. 1927, ASMAE, AP1, b. 1604, fasc. 7403.

55. Eugene Holgius to Benito Mussolini, 2 Aug. 1926, 16 July 1926, ASMAE, AP1, b. 1602, fasc. 7389.

56. Rhodes, *Vatican in the Age of Dictators*, 28 (quotation); Coppa, "Mussolini and the Concordat of 1929," 91; Traniello, "L'Italia cattolica nell'era fascista," 274–75; Carlen, *Papal Encyclicals*, 293–304.

57. S. Bonaventura, *Vita di S. Francesco*, v, vii–ix; Mussolini to consuls, 2 Dec. 1925 (quotations), ASMAE, AMB II, b. 9, fasc. "Centenario francescano. 1925–1927."

58. Dino Grandi to consuls, 21 July 1926, Valeriano Pianigiani to Giacomo De Martino, 3 Aug. 1926 ("personalities"), De Martino to Pianigiani, 2 Sept. 1926 ("old admirier"), and Italian Embassy (Washington) to MAE, 7 Oct. 1926 (on the celebration), ASMAE, AMB II, b. 9, fasc. "Centenario francescano. 1925–1927."

59. Valerio Valeriani to Giacomo De Martino, 13 Nov. 1926, ASMAE, AMB II, b. 9, fasc. "Centenario francescano. 1925–1927."

60. Agostino Ferrante di Ruffano to Benito Mussolini, 23 Mar. and 9 May (on pontifical mass) 1927, ASMAE, AMB II, b. 9, fasc. "Centenario francescano. 1925–1927"; William H. O'Connell to Pietro Fumasoni-Biondi, 13 Mar. 1928, AAB, Chancellor's Office Papers, Apostolic Delegate, 1928.

61. "Seventh Century of the Death of Saint Francis" (program), Embassy to MAE, 29 Nov. 1926 (includes De Martino's address), ASMAE, AMB II, b. 9, fasc. "Centenario francescano. 1925–1927"; "Quarta grande convenzione della grande loggia O.F.I.," PIA, 30 Nov. 1926, 8.

62. Michael Curley to Carlo Tornielli, 28 Feb. 1927, Tornielli to Giacomo De Martino, 11 Mar. 1927 (quotation), and De Martino to MAE, 16 July 1927, ASMAE, AMB II, b. 61,

fasc. "Mons. Curley. Proposta di onorificenza. 1927." On "Iron Mike," see Spalding, *Premier See*, 353, 345.

63. Giacomo De Martino to Benito Mussolini, 25 Jan. ("sons of Italy") and 8 Mar. ("long conversation") 1928, ASMAE, AP1, b. 1605, fasc. "Rapporti politici, Semestre 1"; "Red Menace Lurks in U.S., Says Envoy," *Philadelphia Ledger*, 25 Jan. 1928; "L'Ambasciatore De Martino a Filadelfia," *Corriere d'America*, 26 Jan. 1928; "Un Discorso dell'Ambasciatore," *PIA*, 26 Jan. 1928; "L'Ambasciatore De Martino Ospite dei Figli d'Italia," *L'Opinione*, 25 Jan. 1928.

64. Sincere Observer to Benito Mussolini, 25 Oct. 1927, ASMAE, AP1, b. 1604, fasc. 7403.

65. "Elenco nominativo dei confidenti dell'OVRA," *Gazzetta Ufficiale della Repubblica Italiana*, 2 July 1946 (supplement), 13. On Pucci, see C. Fiorentino, *All'Ombra di Pietro*, 7–18; ACS, DPP, "Mons. Enrico Pucci."

66. Entries dated 8 Mar. 1930, 44, 14 Aug. 1930, 44, 22 Jan. 1932, no number, and 29 Dec. 1938, 40 (all on Pucci), 20 Aug. 1931, 158 (on Ferretti), and 10 July 1931, 333 (on Interior Ministry), ACS, DPP, "Mons. Enrico Pucci"; Pucci, *La pace del laterano*.

67. C. Fiorentino, *All'Ombra di Pietro*, 13; entries dated 24 Sept. 1930, 40, 25 July 1931, 56, 30 Oct. 1931, 56, 13 Sept. 1940, 40, and 22 Jan. 1932, no number, ACS, DPP, "Mons. Enrico Pucci."

68. C. Fiorentino, *All'Ombra di Pietro*, 12; entries dated 8 Feb. 1930, 44, 24 Sept. 1930, 40, and 9 July 1931, 44, ACS, DPP, "Mons. Enrico Pucci."

69. ACS, MCP, Nupie, b. 32, fasc. 122, "Pucci monsignor Enrico."

70. Entries dated 22 Nov. 1929, 56, 24 June 1930, 44, 9 June 1931, 44, 22 Jan. 1933, no number, 11 Jan. 1933, 38, and 27 Jan. 1933, 44, ACS, DPP, "Mons. Enrico Pucci." For a sampling of Pucci's articles, see "Fascisti Attacks Distress Pope," *NW*, 26 Aug. 1921, 2, "The Roman Question Again," *Com*, 12 Oct. 1927, 546–48, "Two Interesting Incidents Follow Vatican Treaty," *NW*, 17 Jan. 1930, 9, and "Sept. 20, Great Holiday Ends in Italy," *NW*, 17 Oct. 1930, 9.

71. Entries dated 16 Feb. 1932, 56, and 9 Mar. 1941, 726, ACS, DPP, "Mons. Enrico Pucci."

72. Memo, 26 July 1920, ACUA, NCWC, box 31, file: "NCWC News Service, 1920–23" (quotation). See also memo, 12 Mar. 1934, ACUA, NCWC, box 31, file: "NCWC News Service, 1934–35."

73. Justin McGrath to William Russell, 14 Feb. 1921, and Enrico Pucci to McGrath, 1923, box 31, file: "NCWC News Service, 1920–23," ACUA, NCWC; McGrath to John Burke, 27 May 1924, Edward Hanna to John A. Ryan, received 3 June 1924, ACUA, NCWC, box 31, file: "NCWC News Service, 1924–29."

74. Justin McGrath to John Burke, 27 May 1924, ACUA, NCWC, box 31, file: "NCWC News Service, 1924–29."

75. Justin McGrath to John Burke, 31 May and 12 June 1924, and Burke to Edward Hanna, 24 May 1924 (on Wood), ACUA, NCWC, box 31, file: "NCWC News Service, 1924–29."

76. Koon, *Believe, Obey, Fight*, 121–27; Wolff, *Between Pope and Duce*, 48–59.

77. Pollard, *Vatican and Italian Fascism*, 45; Wolff, *Between Pope and Duce*, 55; Koon, *Believe, Obey, Fight*, 125–27.

78. The Whole of America to Benito Mussolini, Mar. 1928, ASMAE, AP1, b. 1607.

79. Le Moyne to Benito Mussolini, 18 Dec. 1928, ASMAE, AP1, b. 1609.

80. Alfredo Rocco, "Political Doctrine of Fascism," in Schnapp, *Primer*, 103–24; John A. Ryan, "The Doctrine of Fascism," *Com*, 17 Nov. 1926, 42–44.

81. John A. Ryan, "Doctrine of Fascism," *Com*, 17 Nov. 1926, 42.

82. John A. Ryan, "Fascism in Practice," *Com*, 24 Nov. 1926, 74, 76.

83. Harvey Wickham, "Baiting the Duce," *Com*, 5 May 1926, 712–15.

84. Harvey Wickham, "The Fruits of Fascism," *Com*, 29 Dec. 1926, 204, 205.

85. "The Doctrine of Fascism," *Com* 15 Dec. 1926, 158 (Kerrish quotation).

86. "The Facts of Fascism," *Com*, 19 Jan. 1927 ("highly-placed"); "The Facts of Fascism," *Com*, 9 Feb. 1927, 385 (Ryan's response and quotation from Pius XI).

87. Luigi Sturzo, "The Mission of Italy," *Com*, 5 Jan. 1927, 234, 235, 236.

88. Luigi Sturzo, "The Problem of Italy," *Com*, 12 Jan. 1927, 262, 264. On Sturzo's difficult relationship with American Catholics, see Malgeri, *Luigi Sturzo*, 249–58.

89. Hearley, *Pope or Mussolini*, 18–21 (Duffy quotation in *New York World*, 1 Apr. 1928, and Kelly quotation in *NYT*, 31 Mar. 1928); "Mussolini Again," *Com*, 11 Apr. 1928, 1280 (Bedford); "This Mussolini," *America*, 14 Apr. 1928, 16–17 (Parsons); John M. Thomas, "Church and State in Italy," *Com*, 30 May 1928, 92–94. On the resolution of the conflict, contrast "The Pope and Italian Youth," *CW* 127 (May 1928): 238–39, with "Catholic Organizations in Italy," *CW* 128 (July 1928): 495.

90. See Miscamble, "Limits of American Catholic Antifascism."

91. Giacomo De Martino to Benito Mussolini, 28 Feb. 1928, ASMAE, AP1, b. 1607; Consul to De Martino, 24 Feb. 1929, ASMAE, AP1, b. 1605, fasc. "Rapporti politici, Semestre 1."

92. John Hearley, "Il Duce Visions a Pope King," *Independent*, 28 Jan. 1928, 87–88, 97.

93. "The Incubus of the Temporal Power," *Atlantic Monthly* 141 (Apr. 1928): 540, 542.

94. Nicolas Norris to Benito Mussolini, 16 Jan. 1929, Anonymous to Mussolini, 1928, and Ex-Catholic to Mussolini, 11 June 1928, ASMAE, AP1, b. 1607.

95. Anonymous to Benito Mussolini, 10 May 1928, Anonymous to Mussolini, 11 June 1928, and Philadelphian to Mussolini, 4 July 1928, ASMAE, AP1, b. 1607.

96. Alfredo Camerano to Benito Mussolini, 20 Feb. 1928, and Michele Speciale to Mussolini, 4 June 1928, ASMAE, AP1, b. 1607.

97. M. J. Foley to Benito Mussolini, 28 Dec. 1928, ASMAE, AP1, b. 1609; David Hickey to Mussolini, 4 Nov. 1928, ASMAE, AP1, b. 1607.

CHAPTER SEVEN

1. Pollard, *Vatican and Italian Fascism*, 49–50, 62.

2. Binchy, *Church and State in Fascist Italy*, 301–16.

3. Coppa, "Mussolini and the Concordat of 1929," 95–96; Binchy, *Church and State in Fascist Italy*, 221–302. All citations to the Lateran Pacts are from Pollard, *Vatican and Italian Fascism*, 197–215 (quotation, 197).

4. See Coppa, "Mussolini and the Concordat of 1929," 81–119; and Binchy, *Church and State in Fascist Italy*, 317–632.

5. Binchy, *Church and State in Fascist Italy*, 377 ("totalitarian state").

6. Pollard, *Vatican and Italian Fascism*, 64–66.

7. Ibid., 108–11 (quotes article 2, 109; quotes "despite this defeat," 110); Ricca, "Le chiese evangeliche," 429; Binchy, *Church and State in Fascist Italy*, 589 (quotes Pius on 30 May 1929).

8. Pollard, *Vatican and Italian Fascism*, 72; Binchy, *Church and State in Fascist Italy*, 108, 205–7 ("Inside the State," 205; "We have not resurrected," 206; "Education must belong to us," 207).

9. Binchy, *Church and State in Fascist Italy*, 212–13 (quotations); Pollard, *Vatican and Italian Fascism*, 72.

10. Binchy, *Church and State in Fascist Italy*, 216–18; Pollard, *Vatican and Italian Fascism*, 73 ("heretical"); Wolff, *Between Pope and Duce*, 95–96 (cites "Rappresentanti in terra").

11. Hearley, *Pope or Mussolini*, x ("boomerang"); Traniello, "L'Italia cattolica nell'era fascista," 280–81 (quotes Salvemini and Ferrari).

12. Enrico Pucci, "September 20, Great Holiday, Ends in Italy," NW, 17 Oct. 1930, 9.

13. "Good News from Rome!" *America*, 16 Feb. 1929, 447; Hubert L. Motry, "Principles of Papal Sovereignty Recognized," *NCWC Bulletin* 10 (Mar. 1929): 3–5 (quotation, 3), 25; Moorhouse Millar, "The Meaning of the Roman Settlement," *Thought* 9 (June 1929): 5–19.

14. "The Independence of the Holy See," *Sign* 7 (Mar. 1929): 451–53.

15. "Sovereignty and Freedom of Pope Guaranteed by the Vatican," *Our Sunday Visitor*, 17 Feb. 1929, 1; "A Historic Settlement," NW, 1 Mar. 1929, 4 ("a historian"); "Mere Justice," NW, 7 Mar. 1929, 4 (Mussolini as pacifier).

16. "Friede zwischen Kirche und Staat in Rom geschlossen," *Nord-Amerika*, 14 Feb. 1929, 1 ("cornerstone"); "Lösung der Römischen Frage und Konkordat," *Nord-Amerika*, 21 Feb. 1929, 1 ("kings"); "Watykan I Kwirynal Na Stopie Pokojowej," *Dziennik Chicagoski*, 11 Feb. 1929, 1; "'Te Deum Laudamus' Rozbrzmiewa Dzis We Wloszech," *Dziennik Chicagoski*, 12 Feb. 1929, 1, 2; "Papiez Blogoslawi Tlum Z 200,000 Osób," *Dziennik Chicagoski*, 13 Feb. 1929, 1.

17. "Once Again the Pope No Politician," CW 129 (July 1929): 483–85; Bishop Shahan, "Lateran Treaty and Italian Concordat," CW (July 1929): 385–95 (quotations, 386, 387, 394–95).

18. Giacomo De Martino to William H. O'Connell, 20 Feb. 1929, AAB, Cardinal William Henry O'Connell Papers, box 7, folder 5; Agostino Ferrante di Ruffano to De Martino, 21 May 1929, ASMAE, AP1, b. 1609.

19. Hearley, *Pope or Mussolini*, 158.

20. Ibid., 163, 164, 165; Joseph Schrembs to Valerio Valeriani, 15 Feb. 1929, ADC, SP.

21. D. O'Brien, *Public Catholicism*, 162 (quotes James Walsh to Peter Guilday, 14 Aug. 1929).

22. American to Benito Mussolini, 4 Mar. 1929 ("You have done"), Anonymous to Mussolini, 23 Mar. 1929 ("my dear Benito"), and Craig Donaldson to Mussolini, 5 Sept. 1929 (Catholic students' letter), ASMAE, AP1, b. 1609, fasc. 7429 "Miscellanea."

23. John Griffin to Benito Mussolini, 3 Oct. 1930, ASMAE, AP1, b. 1611.

24. Irene Di Robilant, "The Italo-Vatican Treaty," Nov. 1929, TWLP, box 43, folder 15.

25. "King Pius XI," *Christian Century*, 21 Feb. 1929, 253, 254, 255.

26. "The More Prince the Less Priest," *Baptist*, 16 Mar. 1929, 343; "Is the Pope Satisfied with the Italian Settlement?" *Baptist*, 30 Mar. 1929, 408.

27. "Mussolini Bargains with the Vatican," CA, 14 Feb. 1929, 196 ("advantage" and "culmination"); H. E. Woolever, "Will Vatican State Have Minister in Washington?" CA, 21 Feb. 1929, 237 (quotes Congressional debates).

28. "The New Papal State," *Zion's Herald*, 13 Feb. 1929, 197.

29. "Pope to Be Temporal Ruler," *Christian Observer*, 20 Feb. 1929, 2.

30. John A. Faulkner, "Temporal Power," *Princeton Theological Review* 27 (July 1929): 458; Samuel W. Irwin, "Monte Mario and the Concordat," *CA*, 30 May 1929, 688 ("new laws"); "Enlarged Religious Freedom," *CA*, 6 June 1929, 708 ("must admire" and "this news").

31. Rev. Alfredo Taglialatela, "The Reconciliation between State and Church in Italy," *CA*, 7 Nov. 1929, 1352–54.

32. For masterful works on these Protestants, see Marsden, *Fundamentalism and American Culture*; Carpenter, *Revive Us Again*; Weber, *Living in the Shadow*; and Boyer, *When Time Shall Be No More*.

33. Rev. L. Sale-Harrison, "Mussolini and the Resurrection of the Roman Empire," *Moody Bible Institute Monthly*, Apr. 1929, 386, 387.

34. O. Smith, *Is the Antichrist at Hand?* 16, 18–19, 38–39.

35. Winrod, *Mussolini's Place in Prophecy*, 5, 6, 7, 16.

36. Holsinger, *Ethiopia and Mussolini*, 10, 16, 15, 21, 24.

37. Bauman, *Light from Bible Prophecy*, 20, 23.

38. "A mother in America" to Benito Mussolini, 18 June 1930, ASMAE, AP1, b. 1611.

39. Margaret Rowen to Benito Mussolini, 25 May 1925, ASMAE, AP1, b. 1600, f. 7376 "Miscellanea"; William Reitmann to Mussolini, 16 Mar. 1929, ASMAE, AP1, b. 1609, f. 7429 "Miscellanea."

40. De Felice, *Jews in Fascist Italy*, 92–99. Binchy, in *Church and State in Fascist Italy*, 605, claims there were 47,485 Italian Jews in the 1931 census.

41. Michaelis, *Mussolini and the Jews*, 10–14 (quotations, 28–29).

42. De Felice, *Jews in Fascist Italy*, 87 (quotation); Michaelis, *Mussolini and the Jews*, 31.

43. D. Kleinlerer, "Jewish Life in Italy Revives," *Sentinel*, 14 Oct. 1927, 8.

44. Charles E. Joseph, "Random Thoughts," *Sentinel*, 14 Oct. 1927, 11 (quotes the *Reflex*); "Mussolini Received Sokolov," *Sentinel*, 16 Nov. 1927, 4.

45. "Apostolic Delegation Does Not Know if Italian Jews Are Affected by Canon Law," *Sentinel*, 22 Feb. 1929, 2; De Felice, *Jews in Fascist Italy*, 90–91 (cites Mussolini's speech and on Pacifici's concerns); Michaelis, *Mussolini and the Jews*, 53 (also cites Mussolini's speech); "The Religious Tolerance of a Dictator," *B'nai B'rith Magazine* 43 (July 1929): 319.

46. Diggins, *Mussolini and Fascism*, 202–3 (cites Jewish editors and *B'nai B'rith Magazine* 48 [Apr. 1934] ("pains to demonstrate"); Augusto Rosso to MAE, 3 June 1936, ASMAE, AP2, b. 30, fasc. "Miscellanea"; Bayor, *Neighbors in Conflict*, 80.

47. "Mussolini's Agreement with Vatican," *Sentinel*, 14 Feb. 1929, 47.

48. De Felice, *Jews in Fascist Italy*, 91 ("after ten years"); Michaelis, *Mussolini and the Jews*, 29 ("the political difference" citing *Israel*), 55 (Michaelis's judgment).

49. Carlton J. H. Hayes, "Italy and the Vatican Agree, I: The Roman Question," *Com*, 27 Mar. 1929, 589, 590, 591; Allitt, *Catholic Converts*, 237–51; Jefferson Carter, "Carlton J. H. Hayes," 15–20.

50. Carlton J. H. Hayes, "Italy and the Vatican Agree, II: The Settlement," *Com*, 3 Apr. 1929, 619, 620, 621.

51. Ibid., 619 ("Cavour's formula" and "put the house"), 620 ("veriest nonsense").

52. Van Allen, *Commonweal and American Catholicism*, 28–32; Charles C. Marshall, "An Open Letter to the Honorable Alfred E. Smith," *Atlantic Monthly* 139 (Apr. 1927): 540; "Catholic and Patriot: Governor Smith Replies," *Atlantic Monthly* 139 (May 1927): 721–28; "Should a Catholic Be President?" *Com*, 13 Apr. 1927, 623; John A. Ryan, "Church, State,

and Constitution," *Com*, 27 Apr. 1927, 680–82; Marshall, *Governor Smith's American Catholicism*.

53. Sforza was introduced as "one of the most intelligent and finest Catholics" (*Vatican-Italian Accord*, 23). On Sforza in the 1940s, see Miller, *United States and Italy*.

54. *Vatican-Italian Accord*, 6, 7, 8.

55. Ibid., 10, 12.

56. Ibid., 15–19.

57. Ibid. For a corrective to Ryan's financial claims, see Binchy, *Church and State in Fascist Italy*, 384.

58. *Vatican-Italian Accord*, 25, 26.

59. Ibid., 27, 31.

60. Parsons, *Pope and Italy*, 25–27, 39–40, 3, 40.

61. Ibid., 78, 77.

62. Hearley, *Pope or Mussolini*, 201, 198.

63. Ibid., 22–24, 32, 62.

64. Ibid., 81, 54–55, 59.

65. Ibid., 169, 171–72.

66. On the Catholic Revival, see Halsey, *Survival of American Innocence*; Sparr, *To Promote, Defend, and Redeem*, 17–62; Gleason, *Contending with Modernity*, 1103–206; Allitt, *Catholic Converts*, 191–236; Southern, *John La Farge*, 219 (quotation); and McDonough, *Men Astutely Trained*, 75–84. La Farge, in a letter to Luigi Sturzo in 1943, acknowledged his own earlier confusion about the relationship between the Fascist corporate state and Catholic teaching. "Father [Charles] Coughlin got a lot of people twisted on this matter, as he got all twisted up himself. My views happen to be pretty definitely against the corporate political notion, since I had been set straight very vigorously when I was in Rome in 1938, and talked to some of the men who had collaborated on the *Quadragesimo Anno*" (John La Farge to Luigi Sturzo, 22 June 1943, FLS, f. 560, c. 51).

67. Chesterton, *Resurrection of Rome*, 10–12, 14–15.

68. Ibid., 22.

69. Ibid., 194, 183, 186, 190, 188, 191.

70. Ibid., 195, 194–95, 195.

71. Ibid., 201, 202, 203.

72. Ibid., 214, 224–25, 226, 234, 226–27, 227, 229, 224–25.

73. Ibid., 263, 265, 269.

74. Webster, *Cross and the Fasces*, 112; Traniello, "L'Italia cattolica nell'era fascista," 277–82.

75. Binchy, *Church and State in Fascist Italy*, 331, 517 (quotation); Koon, *Believe, Obey, Fight*, 132–34.

76. Binchy, *Church and State in Fascist Italy*, 339, 513–22 (quotation, 522); Pollard, *Vatican and Italian Fascism*, 155.

77. Edward Hearn to Martin Carmody, 18 June 1931, Hearn to Ambassador in Rome, 1 June 1931 ("gesture inimical"), John Garrett to Hearn, 15 June 1931, and Pietro Fumasoni-Biondi to Carmody, 21 June 1931 ("presence in Rome"), Archive of the Knights of Columbus Supreme Office, New Haven, Conn., Sc-13-12A; "American K.C. Seeks Protest on Fascist Ban," *New York Herald*, 1 June 1931, 1; Kauffman, *Faith and Fraternalism*, 339–45.

78. Binchy, *Church and State in Fascist Italy*, 522–27; Cooney, *American Pope*, 43–48; Koon, *Believe, Obey, Fight*, 134–36.

79. "Statement," 1 June 1931, ADC, SP; "Caesar Challenges Peter," *Com*, 10 June 1931, 142; *Ave Maria*, 4 July 1931, 23.

80. "Smierc Wrogom!—Mussolini" and "Gratulacje Sowieckie Dla Mussoliniego," *Dziennik Chicagoski*, 4 June 1931, 1, 2.

81. *CW* 133 (July 1931): 491 ("one cannot espouse"); *CW* 133 (Aug. 1931): 611 ("it must be confessed"), 615 ("supernatural reason").

82. *Christian Century*, 6 May 1931, 597.

83. *CA*, 26 Feb. 1931, 263 ("such toleration"); "A Methodist Visits 'Il Duce,'" *CA*, 16 Apr. 1931, 511; "Il Duce and the Pope," *CA*, 11 June 1931, 742 ("not hostile").

84. "Non abbiamo bisogno," in Carlen, *Papal Encyclicals*, 446, 447, 452, 453.

85. Ibid., 446, 452.

86. Ibid., 448, 455, 450, 456.

87. "The War for Liberty," *Com*, 15 July 1931, 272; "When Is the Church in Politics?" *Christian Century*, 15 July 1931, 916.

88. "An Old Question Comes Up," *CA*, 6 Aug. 1931, 972.

89. Pollard, *Vatican and Italian Fascism*, 160–94.

90. Rhodes, *Vatican in the Age of Dictators*, 51–52; "Mussolini Decorated by Pope Pius XI," *NW*, 15 Jan. 1932, 2; "Premier Mussolini Received in Private Audience by Pontiff," *NW*, 19 Feb. 1932, 1 (quotation); "Honors Exchanged between Vatican and Quirinal," *NW*, 11 Mar. 1932, 1.

CHAPTER EIGHT

1. Augusto Rosso to Benito Mussolini, 18 Dec. 1922, and Gelasio Caetani to Mussolini, 22 Mar. 1923, ASMAE, AP1, b. 1598.

2. Gelasio Caetani to Benito Mussolini, 25 May 1923, ASMAE, AP1, b. 1598.

3. Cannistraro, *Blackshirts in Little Italy*, 8–9 (quotes Mussolini, 15 May 1921); Cassels, "Fascism for Export," 709.

4. For background for the following pages, see Cannistraro, *Blackshirts in Little Italy*; Salvemini, *Italian Fascist Activities*; Luconi, *La "Diplomazia Parallela"*; Pretelli, "Fasci italiani"; Fabiano, "I fasci italiani all'estero"; Gentile, "La politica estera del partito fascista"; De Caprariis, "'Fascism for Export?'"; Diggins, *Mussolini and Fascism*, 77–143; Franzina and Sanfilippo, *Il fascismo e gli emigrati*; and Miller, *United States and Italy*, 12–16.

5. Giuseppe Bastianini to Benito Mussolini, 2 Dec. 1926, n.d. [June 1923], and 28 June 1923, ACS, Segreteria Particolare del Duce, Carteggio Riservato, 1922–43, b. 37, "Bastianini, Giuseppe."

6. Santarelli, *Storia del movimento*, 481; Burgwyn, *Italian Foreign Policy*, 57–70; Bosworth, *Italy and the Wider World*, 44; Cassels, *Mussolini's Early Diplomacy*, 377–89.

7. Cannistraro and Rosoli, "Fascist Emigration Policy," 675–89.

8. Giacomo De Martino to MAE, 30 Sept. 1927, ASMAE, AP1, b. 1607.

9. Giacomo De Martino to Benito Mussolini, 2 May 1926, ASMAE, AP1, b. 1602.

10. Ibid.

11. Ottanelli, "'If Fascism Comes to America'"; Gabaccia, *Italy's Many Diasporas*, 142;

Vecoli, "Making and Un-Making of an Italian Working Class" ("discordant coalition"). Vecoli also writes, "anti-Fascists constituted a sizeable minority" of immigrants. Bosworth, in *Italy and the Wider World*, in contrast to Vecoli, claims that "despite some recent myth-making to the contrary, the emigrants from the Italies had been little affected by intellectual Anti-Fascism" (126).

12. Giacomo De Martino to consuls, 19 Nov. 1929 ("tactical errors"), ASMAE, AMB II, b. 64, fasc. "Documenti relativi a rapporti tra fasci e consoli"; Cannistraro, *Blackshirts in Little Italy*, 108 (cites *Il Nuovo Mondo*, organ of the AFANA, 25 Dec. 1929); Ray Tucker, "Tools of Mussolini in America," *New Republic*, 14 Sept. 1927, 89–91; Marcus Duffield, "Musso-lini's American Empire: The Fascist Invasion of the United States," *Harper's Magazine* 159 (Nov. 1929): 661–72.

13. Luigi Sillitti to Giacomo De Martino, 20 Oct. 1925, ASMAE, AMB II, b. 63, fasc. "Fasci Italiani negli Stati Uniti. 1926–1927." On Lauro, see *La Parola del Popolo*, 4 Aug. 1923, FLNF, box 21, I.E; *Chicago Italian Chamber of Commerce*, March 1929 and May 1929, FLNF, box 22, II.B.2.g, III.B.3.a.

14. Salvemini, *Italian Fascist Activities*, 16, 24–26. On diplomats, see *Annuario Diplomatico*.

15. Giuseppe Castruccio to Giacomo De Martino, 12 June 1929, ASMAE, AP1, b. 1609; "Protestant Strategy in Italy," *Christian Century*, 17 Apr. 1929, 312.

16. Carlo Fama to Gelasio Caetani, 11 May 1923, and Caetani to Benito Mussolini, 25 May 1923, ASMAE, AP1, b. 1598.

17. Giuseppe Castruccio to Giacomo De Martino, 2 Sept. 1929, ASMAE, AP1, b. 1609.

18. Giacomo De Martino to Giuseppe Castruccio, 9 Sept. 1929 ("provoke"), ASMAE, AP1, b. 1609.

19. Giacomo De Martino to MAE, 21 June 1929, ASMAE, AP1, b. 1609.

20. "Avvenimenti importanti al Garibaldi Institute," *Vita Nuova*, July–Aug. 1929, 9.

21. Giuseppe Castruccio to Giacomo De Martino, 3 Mar. 1932, ASMAE, AP2, b. 8.

22. Clark W. Cumming to Mario Carosi, 31 Mar. 1936, ASMAE, AP2, b. 30.

23. Giuseppe Castruccio to Giacomo De Martino, 15 Dec. 1930, MAE to Castruccio, 13 Feb. 1931, and Castruccio to MAE, 11 Mar. 1931, ASMAE, AP2, b. 3.

24. Giuseppe Castruccio to Giacomo De Martino, 17 Feb. 1931, ASMAE, AP2, b. 4, fasc. "Commemorazione Lincoln"; Castruccio to Augusto Rosso, 6 Apr. 1933, ASMAE, AP2, b. 19.

25. Giuseppe Castruccio to Augusto Rosso, 7 Sept. 1933, ASMAE, AP2, b. 16.

26. Giuseppe Castruccio to Giacomo De Martino, 27 Nov. 1929, ASMAE, AP1, b. 1608.

27. Giuseppe Castruccio to Giacomo De Martino, 24 Feb. 1931 (on speech and Fascist salute), ASMAE, AP2, b. 1; Castruccio to Augusto Rosso, 14 Feb. 1933 ("speaks Italian"), ASMAE, AP2, b. 18. For coverage of event, see "Regard for Lincoln," *NW*, 7 Apr. 1933, 11.

28. Giuseppe Castruccio to Augusto Rosso, 14 May 1935 ("encouraged"), ACS, MCP, Nupie, b. 447, fasc. "Propaganda italiana a Chicago"; Castruccio to Rosso, 4 Feb. 1935 (on Washburn funeral), ASMAE, AP2, b. 26.

29. Fulvio Suvich to Cesare De Vecchi, 6 Feb. 1933 (quotes Castruccio), and De Vecchi to MAE, 14 Feb. 1933, ASMAE, AP2SS, b. 14; "Bishop Meets Mussolini," *NYT*, 8 July 1932, 17 (quotes Mahoney); *NW*, 22 July 1932, 1.

30. Giuseppe Castruccio to Giacomo De Martino, 8 Apr. 1930, ASMAE, AP1, b. 1611; George Mundelein to Castruccio, 5 Sept. 1935, AAC, Chancery Correspondence, box 29, folder 5.

31. NCWC News Service, 24 July 1933, Loyola University of Chicago Archives, Office of the President, Papers of Samuel Knox Wilson, SJ, box 1, folder 31, and box 2, folder 13.

32. "General Italo Balbo Visits the Sisters at Columbus Hospital," NW, 28 July 1933, 8 (on Stevens Hotel and Columbus Hospital); "Balbo and His Flight," NW, 11 Aug. 1933, 4 ("decaying Catholic nations").

33. Mario Carosi to Fulvio Suvich, 14 Oct. 1936, ACS, MCP, Nupie, b. 451, fasc. "Propaganda italiana all'estero."

34. NW, 18 Dec. 1931, 17; NW, 5 Feb. 1932, 1; Franco Fontana to Augusto Rosso, 10 May 1937, ACS, MCP, Nupie, b. 449; D'Agostino, "Missionaries in Babylon," 375–76.

35. For accounts of these awards published in NW, see 9 Oct. 1925, 3, 6 June 1930, 3, 17 Apr. 1931, 1, 1 May 1931, 3, 14 Aug. 1931, 1, 18 Sept. 1931, 3, 18 Dec. 1931, 17, 5 Feb. 1932, 1, 11 Mar. 1932, 1, and 18 Mar. 1932, 9.

36. Mark Gross to Angelo Cerminara, 19 May 1936, Alessandrini to Mario Carosi, 7 July 1936, ACS, MCP, Nupie, b. 452, fasc. "Marquette University of Milwaukee."

37. Fulvio Suvich to MAE, 29 Jan. 1937 (quotations); "Una laurea ad honorem all'Ambasciatore Suvich," PIA, 26 Jan. 1937, ACS, MCP, Propaganda, b. 441, fasc. "Fordham University."

38. Francis Murphy to Benito Mussolini, 20 Sept. 1936, ASMAE, AP2, b. 30, fasc. 3.

39. Augusto Rosso to MAE, 10 Apr. 1935, ASMAE, AP2, b. 26.

40. Bishop of Fort Wayne to Benito Mussolini, 2 Nov. 1936, ASMAE, AP2, b. 30.

41. "Cincinnati Prelate Rips War-Mad World," Cleveland News, 24 Sept. 1935, ASMAE, AP2, b. 28, fasc. "Discorso dell'Arcivescovo di Cincinnati."

42. Romeo Montecchi to MAE, 1 Oct. 1935, ASMAE AP2.

43. Romeo Montecchi to Italian Embassy (Washington), 23 May 1936, ASMAE, AP2.

44. Ercole Dominicis to Benito Mussolini, 26 Oct. 1936, Consul (Philadelphia) to MAE, 7 Apr. 1937, Emanuele Grazzi to Italian Embassy (Holy See), n.d. (on Hayes during Ethiopian war), Giuseppe Bastianini to Ralph Hayes, 8 Mar. 1938 (award), and Hayes to Bastianini, 16 Mar. 1938 (acknowledges award), ASMAE, AP2, b. 52, fasc. "Missioni e Missionari."

45. Rossi Longhi to MAE, 3 Oct. and 5 Oct. 1936, Fulvio Suvich to MAE, 18 Oct. and 10 Nov. (quotation) 1936, ASMAE, AP2, b. 28, fasc. "Viaggio Card. Pacelli"; Fogarty, Vatican and the American Hierarchy, 246–48.

46. Galeazzo Ciano to Italian Embassy (Washington), 7 Oct. 1936, Consul (Philadelphia) to Fulvio Suvich, 21 Oct. 1936, Mario Carosi to Suvich, 31 Oct. 1936, Consul (Boston) to Suvich, 1936, and Suvich to MAE, 10 Nov. 1936, ASMAE, AP2, b. 28, fasc. "Viaggio Card. Pacelli."

47. Bonifacio Pignatti to MAE, 23 Nov. 1936, ASMAE, AP2, b. 28, fasc. "Viaggio Card. Pacelli"; Pignatti to MAE, 12 Feb. 1937 ("four Princes"), ASMAE, AP2, b. 35, fasc. "Viaggio Cardinale Pacelli; Nunziatura a Washington."

48. Italian Embassy (Washington) to MAE, 30 Dec. 1936, ASMAE, AP2, b. 32.

49. Fulvio Suvich to MAE, 14 Apr. 1938 (quotes Fontana), and MAE to Italian Embassy (Holy See), 3 Jan. 1939, ASMAE, AP2, b. 52. On Hitler, see Keefe, "Mundelein Affair"; and Kantowicz, Corporation Sole, 224–25. On Roosevelt administration, see Schmitz, United States and Fascist Italy, 134–220. The journalist was Anthony Czarnecky.

50. Fulvio Suvich to MAE, 29 Nov. 1937, ASMAE, AP2, b. 42; Miller, United States and Italy, 11 (quotes Ickes). On Kirchway, see ibid., 20–23. On Stone, see Cottrell, Izzy, 12–145.

51. Agent to Franco Fontana, 25 Nov. 1938, Fontana to MCP, 30 Nov. 1938, MCP to Fontana, 23 Jan. 1939, James to Galeazzo Ciano, 20 Nov. 1938, and MCP to Fontana, 4 Jan. 1939, ACS, MCP, Nupie, b. 445, fasc. "Chicago—Pubblicazioni"; Alessandro Savorgnan to consul (Chicago), 14 Jan. 1938 (on Father Kane), ASMAE, AP2, b. 52, fasc. "Missioni e Missionari." On the Church and Fascism, see Allitt, *Catholic Converts*, 219–36.

52. Sincere Friend of Italy to Benito Mussolini, 31 Dec. 1936, ASMAE, AP2, b. 42; Giuseppe Cosmelli to MAE, 20 Oct. 1938, ASMAE, AP2, b. 46.

53. Giuseppe Cosmelli to MAE, 13 Sept. 1938, and Franco Fontana to Embassy, 8 Aug. 1938, ASMAE, AP2, b. 47.

54. Carmela La Valle to Benito Mussolini, 2 July 1937, Anonymous to Mussolini, 27 May 1937, and Max Guggenheim to Mussolini, 12 July 1937, ASMAE, AP2, b. 36, fasc. "Pretesa campagna antisemitica."

55. "Come va l'Italia?" CPA, Jan. 1923, 9, 10.

56. "Il Preti e la Patria," CPA, Feb. 1927, 13, 15.

57. Nelli, *Italians in Chicago*, 138, 173–74 (on IANU); Giuseppe Castruccio to Giacomo De Martino, 22 July 1929 (quotations) and 10 May 1930 (on meeting to stem out-migration), ASMAE, AP1, b. 1609, 1610.

58. Giacomo De Martino to MAE, 20 Apr. 1932, and Cesare De Vecchi to MAE, 25 Apr. 1932, ASMAE, AP2SS, b. 10.

59. *Chicago Italian Chamber of Commerce*, Oct.–Dec. 1928, *Bulletin Italo-American National Union*, Feb. 1929, and *Il Bollettino Sociale*, 15 June 1929, FLNF, box 22, III.H; *Il Corriere Italico*, 1 May 1937, FLNF, box 22, III.B.1.

60. Beniamino Franch to Rafaello Carlo Rossi, 8 June 1937, St. John the Baptist Provincial Archive of the Scalabrini Fathers, Oak Park, Ill., box 22, folder E; Franco Fontana to Augusto Rosso, 10 May 1937, ACS, MCP, Nupie, b. 449.

61. Giacomo De Martino to consuls, 8 Aug. 1932, ASMAE, AP2, b. 13; "Serata della lingua italiana," 1939, OLP, ser. 2, box 14, folder 187.

62. Schiavo, *Italian-American Who's Who*, 165, 308–9.

63. See textbooks in Immigration History Research Center, St. Paul, Minn.; and "Program," 1935, OLP, ser. 2, box 15, folder 187.

64. Antonio Ferme to Riccardo Secchia, 27 Aug. 1930, Secchia to Giuseppe Castruccio, 24 June 1933 and 22 May 1934, OLP, ser. 2, box 15, folder 186.

65. "Parini, Piero," in Cannistraro, *Historical Dictionary of Fascist Italy*, 393–4; Giuseppe Castruccio to Pastors, 5 Mar. 1934, 037, OLP, ser. 2, box 15, folder 186.

66. Checks, Piero Pomante to Pastors, Mother Superiors, and Teachers, 22 May 1935 (quotations), and Pomante to Pastors, 22 May 1935 (invitations to Vesuvio), OLP, ser. 2, box 15, folder 186; Giuseppe Castruccio to Pastors, Mother Superiors, and Teachers, 17 May 1935 (on contest), OLP, ser. 2, box 15, folder 187.

67. *Bulletin Italo-American National Union*, July 1936, and *Bollettino della Chiesa di Sant'Antonio* 2 (Oct. 1935) and 3 (June 1936), FLNF, box 22, II.B.2.f; "Serata della lingua italiana," 1938, 1939, OLP, ser. 2, box 15, folder 187.

68. *Le Mammole della Madre Cabrini* 8:2 (Apr.–June 1938): 53.

69. General Chapter Reports for 1932 and 1938, Archives of the Franciscan Sisters of the Immaculate Conception, Rome.

70. Sanders, *Education of an Urban Minority*, 258.

CHAPTER NINE

1. Gillis edited the *Catholic World* from 1922 until 1948; Ciarrocchi edited Detroit's *La Voce del Popolo* from 1910 to 1954. On circulations, see *Catholic Press Directory for 1932*, 89, 125.

2. Bonifacio Pignatti to Fulvio Suvich, 2 Apr. 1936, and Suvich to Pignatti, 6 May 1936, ASMAE, AP2SS, b. 31, fasc. "Missioni cattoliche all'estero."

3. Bonifacio Pignatti to Fulvio Suvich, 14 May 1936, ASMAE, AP2SS, b. 31, fasc. "Missioni cattoliche all'estero."

4. See Gribble, *Guardian of America*; Broderick, *Right Reverend New Dealer*, 260; Southern, *John La Farge*, 178.

5. Justin McGrath to John Burke, 11 Mar. 1931, and Frank Hall to Burke, 14 Sept. 1931, ACUA, NCWC, box 31, file: "NCWC News Service, 1930–31"; Gribble, *Guardian of America*, 226–28.

6. *Seventh National Eucharistic Congress*, 426. On *Cleveland News* rebuttal, see Joseph Trivisonno to John Harney, 27 May 1936, PFA, SGP.

7. James Gillis (note to himself), 5 Sept. 1935, James Gillis Correspondence, PFA; "The Ambition of Mussolini," *CW* 142 (Oct. 1935): 1, 2, 4, 6, 8.

8. "War Is On, Reason Is Off," *CW* 142 (Nov. 1935): 136, 137, 138; Gribble, *Guardian of America*, 147–48, 291 n 99, 148 (quotes Frank Hall to James Gillis, 24 Jan. 1936).

9. Joseph Trivisonno to James McFadden, 16 Jan. 1936, and McFadden to Trivisonno, 17 Jan. 1936, ADC, Holy Rosary Papers.

10. "The Shame of Italy," *CW* 143 (May 1936): 137, 138.

11. Joseph Trivisonno to John Harney, 27 May 1936, PFA, SGP.

12. John Harney to Joseph Trivisonno, 5 June 1936, PFA, SGP.

13. I have no direct evidence Trivisonno wrote to Rome or to the apostolic delegation. Gillis's articles were, however, in the possession of Bonifacio Pignatti, the Italian ambassador to the Holy See. ASMAE, AP2SS, b. 31, fasc. "Stampa cattolica in Italia, sequestro e sospensioni di giornali opuscoli e Varie."

14. Thomas O'Neill to John Harney, 19 June 1936, PFA, SGP.

15. John Harney to James Gillis, 2 July 1936, PFA, SGP.

16. "Editorials," ASMAE, AP2SS, b. 31, fasc. "Stampa Cattolica in Italia, sequestro e sospensioni di giornali opuscoli e Varie"; Spalding, *Premier See*, 346–47 (on Fitzpatrick but makes no mention of Fascism).

17. Joseph Schrembs to Cesare Gradenigo, 2 Sept. and 4 Sept. 1931, ADC, SP.

18. Romeo Montecchi, radio address, WJAY (Cleveland), Sept. 1935, ASMAE, CLE, b. 98, fasc. "Montecchi, 1935."

19. Piero Parini, Circolare no. 05, 12 Aug. 1935, MAE to consuls, 8 Sept. 1935, ASMAE, CLE, b. 1, fasc. "Vertenza Italo Etiopica; Attività Uffici Consolari"; Romeo Montecchi to agents, 23 Sept. 1935, ASMAE, CLE, b. 89, fasc. "Clero Italiano nella giurisdizione consolare"; Montecchi to agents, 22 Nov. 1935, ASMAE, CLE, b. 89, fasc. "Associazioni Italiane ed Italo-Americane." Montecchi had agents in Columbus, Akron, Steubenville, Louisville, Youngstown, Cincinnati, Lorain, Toledo, and Sandusky.

20. See Norman, "Influence of Pro-Fascist Propaganda," and "Italo-American Opinion"; Kanawada, *Franklin D. Roosevelt's Diplomacy*, 75–89; Luconi, *La "Diplomazia Parallela*," 85–111; Migone, *Gli Stati Uniti e il fascismo*, 350–57; Diggins, *Mussolini and Fascism*, 287–312; and Harris, *United States and the Italo-Ethiopian Crisis*.

21. Montecchi's reports, ASMAE, CLE, b. 1, fasc. "Vertenza Italo Etiopica; Attività uffici consolari." On Cincinnati, see *Itala Gente*, June 1936, ASMAE, CLE, b. 89, fasc. "Western Hills Publishing Co." On New York, see Salvemini, *Italian Fascist Activities*, 208. On Rhode Island, see "Pro Croce Rossa," *ERI*, 24 July 1936, 1. See also Consul (Philadelphia) to Embassy, 21 Aug. 1936, ASMAE, CLE, b. 3, fasc. "Miscellanea"; and "3,000 Italian Couples Here Will be Remarried with Rings Sent from Il Duce," *Chicago Daily News*, 23 Apr. 1936.

22. Augusto Rosso to consuls, 31 Mar. 1936, Romeo Montecchi to agents, 2 Apr. 1936, Montecchi to Olindo Melaragno (*La Voce*), 2 Apr. 1936, Montecchi to pastors, 2 Apr. 1936, Americo Ciampichini to Montecchi, 8 Apr. 1936, Leo Pera to Montecchi, 15 Apr. 1936, Montecchi to Ciampichini, 15 Apr. 1936, and "Preghiera per la Patria," ASMAE, CLE, b. 1, fasc. "Preghiera per la patria."

23. Romeo Montecchi to MAE (quotations), ASMAE, CLE, b. 102, fasc. "Trivisonno Giuseppe"; "Italy Decorates Msgr. Trivisonno," *Cleveland Plain Dealer*, 17 May 1937, and "City Italians Glow Proudly as Order of Crown Is Pinned on 'Little Father,'" *Cleveland News*, 17 May 1937, ASMAE, CLE, b. 102, fasc. "Trivisonno Giuseppe."

24. Romeo Montecchi to Joseph Schrembs, 6 Feb. 1936 (on the Italian Red Cross), ADC, SP; Montecchi to Italian Embassy (Washington), 9 July 1936 (on discounted fare), Montecchi to Tarabotto, 17 July 1936 (on courtesy), M. Farley, "In Bishop Schrembs' Defense," *Cleveland Press*, 14 Aug. 1936, Montecchi to James McFadden, 27 Aug. 1936, McFadden to Montecchi, 29 Aug. 1936, "High Lights," *La Voce del Popolo* (Cleveland), 23 Sept. 1936 (cites *Cleveland Plain Dealer*, 18 Sept. 1936, "only safe country"), and Schrembs to King Vittorio, Christmas telegram, 1936, ADC, SP, b. 102, fasc. "Bishop Joseph Schrembs."

25. Cannistraro, "Fascism and Italian-Americans in Detroit," 31, 34.

26. Ibid., 38.

27. Report, 5 Dec. 1934, ASMAE, AP2SS, b. 37, fasc. "Mons. Giuseppe Ciarrocchi"; Ciarrocchi, ACS, CPC, b. 1328, fasc. 124311.

28. "Giuseppe Ciarrocchi," 5 Dec. 1934, ASMAE, AP2SS, b. 37, fasc. "Mons. Giuseppe Ciarrocchi"; "Avowed Foe of Fascism: Monsignor Ciarrocchi, 75," *Detroit Times*, 29 Sept. 1954, and "Death Halts Busy Life of Msgr. Ciarrocchi," *Michigan Catholic*, 30 Sept. 1954, CP. Ciarrocchi was incardinated into the diocese of Detroit by 1919. Extant copies of *La Voce del Popolo* are in CP; ACS, CPC; and ASMAE, AP2SS, b. 21 and b. 37.

29. Giuseppe Ciarrocchi to Michael Gallagher, 16 Oct. 1934, CP.

30. Cannistraro, "Fascism and Italian-Americans in Detroit," 34–35; Giuseppe Ciarrocchi to Michael Gallagher, 16 Oct. 1934, and Vincent Castellucci to Ciarrocchi, 30 Nov. 1934, CP.

31. "Vigilate continuamente," VP, Sept. 1934.

32. Giacomo Ungarelli to Michael Gallagher, 1 Oct. 1940, CP.

33. Giuseppe Ciarrocchi to Michael Gallagher, 16 Oct. 1934, CP.

34. Michael Gallagher to Giacomo Ungarelli, 2 Nov. 1934, CP; Augusto Rosso to MAE, 5 Dec. 1934, ASMAE, AP2SS, b. 21, fasc. "Attività politica di religiosi all'estero."

35. Augusto Rosso to MAE, 5 Dec. 1934, ASMAE, AP2SS, b. 21, fasc. "Attività politica di religiosi all'estero."

36. "La Voce dei nostri lettori," VP, 30 Nov. 1934.

37. Ibid.; Sturzo, *Italy and Fascismo*, 186. On the historiography of Fascist Italy, see Salomone, *Italy from Risorgimento to Fascism*; and Bosworth, *Italian Dictatorship*.

38. "Scolastica fascista," VP, 23 Nov. 1934.

39. "Una lezioncina a due cari figliuoli," *VP*, 30 Nov. 1934.

40. "Il nostro credo," *VP*, 30 Nov. 1934. *Confino* was banishment and enforced isolation of political prisoners to a southern Italian village or island.

41. "Scolastica fascista," *VP*, 23 Nov. 1934. Sandino's papers can be found at the Immigration History Research Center, St. Paul, Minn.

42. "Tuoni di guerra o bluff per uso interno?" *VP*, 1 June 1934 ("disastrous financial conditions"); "La condanna di Cesare Rossi," *VP*, 21 Sept. 1934; "Spunti ed appunti," *VP*, 23 Nov. 1934 ("principles of the Gospel"); Killinger, *Gaetano Salvemini*, 252.

43. "Amenità della vita," *VP*, 2 Nov. 1934; "Amenità della vita," *VP*, 16 Nov. 1934 (quotation).

44. "Una lezioncina a due cari figliuoli," *VP*, 30 Nov. 1934.

45. "La Voce di nostri lettori," *VP*, 23 Nov. 1934 (quotation); "Echi della nostra filippica," *VP*, 9 Nov. 1934.

46. MAE to Cesare De Vecchi, 29 Dec. 1934, ASMAE, AP2SS, b. 21, fasc. "Attività politica di religiosi all'estero"; Amleto Cicognani to Michael Gallagher, 9 Jan. 1935, CP.

47. Amleto Cicognani to Michael Gallagher, 9 Jan. 1935, CP.

48. Giuseppe Ciarrocchi to Michael Gallagher, 14 Jan. 1935, CP. I have not found Gallagher's reply to Ciarrocchi.

49. "A Detroit il fascismo ricorre alle autorità ecclesiastiche per imbavagliare il Rev. Ciarrocchi," *Stampa Libera*, 5 Feb. 1935, Giacomo Ungarelli to Michael Gallagher, 6 Feb. 1935, and Gallagher to Amleto Cicognani, 6 Feb. 1935, CP.

50. Amleto Cicognani to Michael Gallagher, 9 Feb. 1935, CP.

51. "Il conflitto Italo-Abissino sarà evitato" and "Quel che ha raccolto la commissione McCormack sulla propaganda straniera negli S.U.," *VP*, 15 Feb. 1935; "Il rapporto della commissione McCormack al Congresso," *VP*, 22 Feb. 1935; "A Few Exceptions to an Authoritative Declaration," *VP*, 2 Aug. 1935.

52. Guastone Belcredi to Italian Embassy (Washington), 11 May 1936 (quotes *La Voce* editorials, n.d.), ACS, CPC, b. 1328, f. 124311.

53. Guastone Belcredi to Italian Embassy (Washington), 20 Nov. 1935 (meeting with Gallagher), 11 May (quotes *La Voce* editorials, n.d.), and 19 May 1936 (details of Gallagher's speech), ACS, CPC, b. 1328, f. 124311.

54. Prefect of Ascoli Piceno to Ministry of the Interior, 17 Apr. 1936 (on Ciarrocchi's family), Ministry of the Interior to Prefect of Aquila, 31 July 1936 (on Valente), and "Editor Feels Il Duce's Ire," *Detroit News*, 31 July 1936 (quotations), ACS, CPC, b. 1328, f. 124311.

55. MAE to Bonifacio Pignatti, 13 Aug. 1937, ASMAE, AP2SS, b. 37, fasc. "Attività politica del clero all'estero"; Eugenio Pacelli to Amleto Cicognani, 6 Sept. 1937, CP. See also Pugliese, *Carlo Rosselli*.

56. Eugenio Pacelli to Amleto Cicognani, 6 Sept. 1937, CP.

57. Amleto Cicognani to Edward Mooney, 21 Sept. 1937, and Mooney to Cicognani, 27 Oct. 1937, CP; MAE, 21 Dec. 1937, contains a summary of Pacelli's report dated 23 Nov. 1937, ASMAE, AP2SS, b. 37, fasc. "Attività politica del clero all'estero."

58. M. P. Kelly, "'Lift Embargo'—Catholic Priest," *Daily Record*, 28 Jan. 1939, 2.

59. Edward Hickey to Giuseppe Ciarrocchi, 31 Jan. 1939, and Ciarrocchi to Hickey, 1 Feb. 1939, CP.

60. Luigi Sturzo to Giuseppe Ciarrocchi, 14 Oct. 1940, f. 565, c. 76, FLS; Ciarrocchi to Sturzo, f. 565, 77, FLS.

61. Giuseppe Ciarrocchi to Luigi Sturzo, 25 Jan. 1941, f. 565, c. 82, FLS; Ciarrocchi to Sturzo, 25 Feb. 1941, f. 565, c. 83, FLS.

62. Giorgio La Piana to Luigi Sturzo, 8 Oct. 1940, Scritti inediti, 2; Giuseppe Ciarrocchi to Luigi Sturzo, 25 Feb. 1941, f. 565, c. 83, FLS; Malgeri, Luigi Sturzo, 272–91 (on Sturzo's return to Italy).

63. See Brinkley, Voices of Protest; and Tentler, Seasons of Grace, 315–42.

CHAPTER TEN

1. See D'Agostino, "'Fascist Transmission Belts,'" and "Triad of Roman Authority."

2. McGreevy, Parish Boundaries, 10 ("each parish"); Warner, "Place of the Congregation" (on "de facto congregationalism").

3. See Tomasi, "L'assistenza religiosa"; and Perotti, Il Pontificio Collegio.

4. See Schiavo, Italian Contribution; Pellica and Rocca, Dizionario degli istituti di perfezione; and D'Agostino, "Scalabrini Fathers," and "Italian Ethnicity and Religious Priests."

5. The Official Catholic Directory (1936 and 1940) indicates no Italian worked in Providence diocesan offices. In Cleveland, four Italian religious priests were listed as "translators" in 1940.

6. "Pro Croce Rossa," ERI, 24 July 1936, 1; "Italo-Americans Honor Columbus and Verrazzano," Providence Journal, 12 Oct. 1936, 1, 10; "1500 Persons Hear Praise for Italy," Providence Journal, 19 Apr. 1937, 11.

7. "Italian School Closes Friday," Evening Bulletin, 22 May 1937, 16; "Dr. T. F. Walsh Lauds Italians," Evening Bulletin, 28 May 1937, 28.

8. "St. Joseph's, Natick," Providence Visitor, 30 Apr. 1936, 5. Cormuto had been a prisoner of war imprisoned in Hanover, Germany, where he befriended Lt. Vincenzo Verderosa, vice consul of Providence during these events; see Providence Visitor, 17 Sept. 1936, 3.

9. Pasquale Parente to Francis Keough, 8 Sept. 1936, and Keough to Raffaelo Carlo Rossi, 8 Sept. 1936, ADP, 3F/56-2.

10. Pasquale Parente to Francis Keough, n.d. [1936], ADP, 3F/56-3; Amleto Cicognani to Keough, 10 Sept. 1936, ADP, 3F/56-2; Committee to Excellency, 10 Sept. 1936, ADP, 3F/56-3.

11. For claims Keough suppressed coverage of the event in local newspapers, see "Parish History of the Sacred Heart," ADP. See also "L'agitazione degl'italiani di Natick," ERI, 25 Sept. 1936, 1, 4.

12. "Gli italiani di Natick rivogliono Padre Russo," ERI, 2 Oct. 1936, 1, 4.

13. "Fatti e chiacchere," ERI, 9 Oct. 1936, 4; "Tentativo fallito a Natick di riaprire la chiesa per forza," ERI, 16 Oct. 1936, 3; Francis Keough to Amleto Cicognani, 19 Sept. 1936, ADP, 3F/56-2.

14. Amleto Cicognani to Pietro Pillarella, 1 Oct. 1936, ADP, 3F/56-2.

15. Vincenzo Verderosa to Guido Segrè, 13 Oct. 1936, ASMAE, AP2SS, b. 37; "Tentativo fallito a Natick di riaprire la chiesa per forza," ERI, 16 Oct. 1936, 3.

16. Guido Segrè to Vincenzo Verderosa, 26 Oct. 1936, ASMAE, AP2SS, b. 37.

17. Francis Keough to Amleto Cicognani, 17 Oct. 1936, ADP, 3F/56-3.

18. Pietro Pillarella to Francis Keough, 22 Oct. 1936, ADP, 3F/56-3.

19. Vincenzo Verderosa to Guido Segrè, 3 Nov. 1936, ASMAE, AP2SS, b. 37.

20. Ibid.; Francis Keough to Vincenzo Verderosa, 25 Nov. 1936, ADP, 3F/56-4.

21. Francis Keough to Amleto Cicognani, 7 Nov. 1936, ADP, 3F/56-4.

22. Guido Segrè to Vincenzo Verderosa, 14 Nov. 1936, ASMAE, AP2SS, b. 37.

23. "La chiesa di Natick è stata riaperta," ERI, 13 Nov. 1936, 4.

24. Vincenzo Verderosa to Guido Segrè, 3 Nov. 1936, ASMAE, AP2SS, b. 37; "Nuova associazione formata a Natick," ERI, 27 Nov. 1936, 1; Amleto Cicognani to Francis Keough, 10 Mar. 1937, ADP, 3F/56-5.

25. Francis Keough to Edigio Vagnozzi, 2 Feb. 1937, ADP, 3F/56-5.

26. Francis Keough to Amleto Cicognani, 12 Mar. 1937, ADP, 3F/56-5; "Gli incidenti di Natick definitivamente risolti," ERI, 27 Nov. 1936, 1; "La restituzione delle offerte pro casa parrocchiale di Natick," ERI, 4 Dec. 1936, 1; "Comunicato consolare agl'italiani di Natick," ERI, 11 Dec. 1936, 1; "Casa parrocchiale italiana a Natick," ERI, 11 Dec. 1936, 3, 8.

27. Francis Keough to Amleto Cicognani, 12 Mar. 1937, ADP, 3F/56-5.

28. Ibid.

29. Giovanni Petrarca to Benito Mussolini, n.d., ASMAE, AP2SS, b. 37.

30. "Casa parrocchiale italiana a Natick," ERI, 11 Dec. 1936, 3, 8.

31. "Superba manifestazione in onore dei Padri Cormuto e De Angelis," ERI, 30 Apr. 1937, 1, 3.

32. Vincenzo Verderosa to Guido Segrè, 14 May 1937, AP2SS, ASMAE, b. 37.

33. "Memo for his Excellency," 8 June 1937, Vincenzo Verderosa to Francis Keough, 9 July 1937, and Keough to Verderosa, 30 Aug. 1937, ADP, 3F/56-6.

34. "From the desk of Rev. Charles Mahoney," 10 Aug. 1937 (on dynamite), ADP, 3F/56-6; "The Parish History of the Sacred Heart," 11, ADP.

35. See St. Rocco's Parish; Schiavo, Italian Contribution, 499, 899–902; Hynes, History of the Diocese, 316–17, 325, 341; and "Historical Sketch of Holy Redeemer Church," ADC, HR. Gattuso was born on 6 August 1893 in San Cataldo, Caltanissetta (Sicily).

36. Barton, Peasants and Strangers, 18–21, 49, 58, 83–85; Ferroni, "Italians," 559–61. On the Red Cross, see Cleveland Plain Dealer, 25 May 1936. On the Temple, see Veronesi, Italian Americans and Their Communities, 255–58; and Catholic Universe Bulletin, 4 Aug. 1939, 1, 3.

37. Poluse, "Archbishop Joseph Schrembs," 63; Ferroni, "Italians," 559–60; St. Rocco's Parish; Veronesi, Italian Americans and Their Communities, 216, 249; "Parish Report: Holy Redeemer, 1939," and "Financial Report for 1939," ADC, HR; Cesare Gradenigo to Eugenio Maranecci, 5 May 1930 (given to me by a curious Mercedarian in Rome); Sante Gattuso to Joseph Schrembs, 28 Sept. 1938, ADC, SP, Religious Orders: Men.

38. Romeo Montecchi to Italian Embassy (Washington), 28 Feb. 1940, ASMAE, AP2, b. 70.

39. Sante Gattuso to Joseph Schrembs, 12 Dec. 1939, and Vincent Balmat to Gattuso, 10 Jan. 1940, ADC, HR. Although Schrembs had formal authority over the appointment, his confirmation of a pastor chosen by the superior in a religious congregation was common procedure.

40. "Prelate Brands Riot at Church 'A Mortal Sin,'" Cleveland News, 19 Feb. 1940, 9; "Parish Put under Ban as It Rebels," Cleveland Plain Dealer, 19 Feb. 1940, 7.

41. "Parish Put under Ban as It Rebels," Cleveland Plain Dealer, 19 Feb. 1940, 1 (quotations); "Church Is Closed," Catholic Universe Bulletin, 16 Feb. 1940, 1, 2; "Decree of Interdict Published," Catholic Universe Bulletin, 23 Feb. 1940, 1, 2, 11.

42. Notes of Vincent Balmat, 11 Jan. 1940, ADC, HR.

43. Notes of Vincent Balmat, 19 Jan. 1940, ADC, HR.

44. Notes, 30 Jan. 1940, ADC, HR.

45. "Meeting of Committee from Holy Redeemer Parish," n.d., ADC, HR.

46. Ibid.

47. Ibid.

48. Ibid. Father Loi-Zedda claimed the weekly collection had fallen from $110 to $19.

49. Notes, 9 Feb. 1940, ADC, HR; Begin, "Report of Special Commission to Install Father Vincent Caruso," 13 Feb. 1940 (quotation), ADC, HR.

50. Committee of Fifty to Joseph Schrembs, 20 Feb. 1940, ADC, HR.

51. Theresa Piscioneri to Joseph Schrembs, 20 Feb. 1940, Member to Schrembs, 19 Feb. 1940, Capt. Joseph Grotenrath to Schrembs, 17 Feb. 1940, and Schrembs to Grotenrath, 28 Feb. 1940, ADC, HR.

52. Romeo Montecchi to Joseph Schrembs, 24 Feb. 1940, ADC, HR; Montecchi to MAE, 28 Feb. 1940 (quotations), ASMAE, AP2, b. 70.

53. Montecchi to MAE, 28 Feb. 1940, ASMAE, AP2, b. 70.

54. Floyd Begin to Willam O'Donnell, 28 Feb. 1940 (on Loi-Zedda), Begin to Helen Sanzo, 1 Mar. 1940, and "Interrogatorium proponendum," 4 Mar. 1930 (Marcini's testimony), ADC, HR.

55. Romeo Montecchi to Italian Embassy (Washington), 21 Mar. 1940, ASMAE, AP2, b. 70.

56. Ibid.

57. James McFadden to Joseph Schrembs, 16 Mar. 1940, ADC, HR.

58. Amleto Cicognani to Joseph Schrembs, 15 Mar. 1940, ADC, HR.

59. Ambassador to Romeo Montecchi, n.d., included in Italian Embassy (Washington) to MAE, 31 Mar. 1940, ASMAE, AP2, b. 70; James McFadden to Joseph Schrembs, 18 Mar. 1940, ADC, HR.

60. Joseph Schrembs to Amleto Cicognani, 19 Mar. 1940, ADC, HR.

61. Francesco Contorni to Joseph Schrembs, 18 Mar. 1940, ADC, HR. Schrembs gave St. Rocco in perpetuum to the Mercedarians in 1941. Alfredo Scotti to Schrembs, 18 July 1941, ADC, SP, Religious Orders: Men.

62. Cleveland Press, 20 Mar. 1940, 1, 2; Catholic Universe Bulletin, 22 Mar. 1940, 1, 2. Cicognani approved of the outcome; see Amleto Cicognani to Joseph Schrembs, 29 Mar. 1940, ADC, HR.

EPILOGUE

1. Schmitz, United States and Fascist Italy, 153–71; Diggins, Mussolini and Fascism, 282–83.

2. Schmitz, United States and Fascist Italy, 167 ("dynamic personality"), 184 ("Italian people").

3. Ibid., 193 ("Berlin and Prague"), 202 ("I believe"), 211 (University of Virginia speech). Also see Di Nolfo, Vaticano e Stati Uniti, on Myron Taylor.

4. Fogarty, Vatican and the American Hierarchy, 292.

5. Ibid., 295, 299, 302, 297 (quotation). See also Miller, United States and Italy.

6. Fogarty, Vatican and the American Hierarchy, 302–3 (quotations). See also Miller, United States and Italy.

7. Ginsborg, History of Contemporary Italy, 8–38.

8. Miller, *United States and Italy*, 11–64; Diggins, *Mussolini and Fascism*, 386–94; Killinger, *Gaetano Salvemini*, 294–95; G. Williams, "Professor George La Piana."

9. Salvemini and La Piana, *What to Do with Italy*, 51, 219. On Sturzo, see Malgeri, *Luigi Sturzo*, 235–91.

10. Salvemini and La Piana, *What to Do with Italy*, 44, 265, 277, 279.

11. Luigi Sturzo, "The Vatican and Fascism," *Com*, 17 Dec. 1943, 229 ("psychology" of Pius XI), and "Beyond Salvemini–La Piana," *Com*, 25 Feb. 1944, 468 ("Catholic journalists"). In the 1970 edition of Binchy, *Church and State in Fascist Italy*, Binchy writes: "Among the letters I received after the book was published [in 1941] was one from Don Sturzo who took me very gently to task for exaggerating the resistance of the Vatican [to Fascism]" (v).

12. For the best study on this complex period, see Miller, *United States and Italy*.

13. Ginsborg, *History of Contemporary Italy*, 52–120. See also Domenico, *Italian Fascists on Trial*; and Del Pero, "United States and 'Psychological Warfare.'"

14. McGreevy, "Thinking on One's Own"; Gleason, *Contending with Modernity*, 261–68. The only reference to Fascism or the Lateran Pacts in the work of either is in Gleason, "American Catholics and Liberalism": "Liberals were also uneasy about the Lateran treaty of 1929, which they interpreted as a rapprochement between the Catholic church and fascism" (60).

15. McGreevy, "Thinking on One's Own," 108; Gleason, *Speaking of Diversity*, 209. Gleason, in *Contending with Modernity*, calls Seldes the "liberal scourge of Catholicism" (262–63). Even the committed Catholic, Binchy, in *Church and State in Fascist Italy*, drew upon Seldes's *Vatican: Yesterday, Today, Tomorrow* as the best source on Vatican finances.

16. John P. Delaney, "Il Duce Departs," *America*, 19 May 1945, 128–30; "End of a Dictator," *America*, 12 May 1945, 114 ("poison"); Cannistraro and Aga Rossi, "La politica etnica"; Diggins, *Mussolini and Fascism*, 340–52, 399–421.

17. Arendt, *Origins of Totalitarianism*; Gleason, *Speaking of Diversity*, 210–11, and *Contending with Modernity*, 266–68; McGreevy, "Thinking on One's Own," 112. McGreevy, in "Pragmatism to a Fault?" restates the Catholic apologia.

18. Blanshard, *Communism, Democracy, and Catholic Power*, 296, 55–56; Marty, *One Nation, Indivisible*, 157–61.

19. Ellis, *American Catholicism*, 26–34, 70, 160.

20. Brinkley, *Liberalism and Its Discontents*, 134. Boorstin's pluralist trilogy included Glazer, *American Judaism*, and Hudson, *American Protestantism*.

21. See Herberg, *Protestant-Catholic-Jew*; and Marty, *One Nation, Indivisible*, 277–312.

22. Halsey, *Survival of American Innocence*, 74–76; Gleason, *Contending with Modernity*, 125–30.

23. Dolan, *American Catholic Experience*, 105; Tentler, "Who Is the Church?" 247.

24. Hennesey, "Papacy and Episcopacy," 175.

25. Dolan, *American Catholic Experience*. For exemplars of this internalist, Americanist historiography, see D. O'Brien, *Renewal of American Catholicism*; A. Greeley, *Catholic Experience*, and *Catholic Myth*; Dolan, *In Search of an American Catholicism*; McCann, *New Experiment in Democracy*; and Kantowicz, "Cardinal Mundelein of Chicago." Many of these studies make substantial claims about the Vatican without any investigation of Vatican archives. For a different assessment from my own of this literature, see Tentler, "On the Margins."

26. See Orsi, *Madonna of 115th Street*, and *Thank You, St. Jude*; Tweed, *Our Lady of the Exile*; McGreevy, *Parish Boundaries*; and Kane, *Separatism and Subculture*.

27. Rodgers, "Exceptionalism," 31.

28. Fogarty, *Vatican and the American Hierarchy*, 330 (quotes Giovanni Montini to Francis Spellman, 12 Mar. 1953).

29. J. Clark, in *Language of Liberty*, argues the revolution was a religious war. See also Colley, *Britons*.

30. Binchy, *Church and State in Fascist Italy*, 23, 24, 143.

31. The historiography of immigration has a rich heritage of internationalism and comparativism. See Foerster, *Italian Emigration of Our Times*; Hansen, *Atlantic Migration, 1607–1860*; Thistlewaite, "Migration from Europe"; J. Briggs, *Italian Passage*; Virtanen, *Settlement or Return*; Cinel, *From Italy to San Francisco*; Gabaccia, *Militants and Migrants*; Baily, *Immigrants in the Promised Land*; and Gjerde, *From Peasants to Farmers*.

32. D. O'Brien, "American Catholic Historiography," 89.

Bibliography

MANUSCRIPTS AND ARCHIVAL SOURCES

Berkeley, California
University of California, The Bancroft Library
  Panama Pacific International Exposition Records

Boston, Massachusetts
Archive of the Archdiocese of Boston
  Archbishop John Williams Papers
  Cardinal William Henry O'Connell Papers
  Chancellor's Office Papers
Boston Public Library, Rare Books and Manuscripts Division
  Theodore Roosevelt Papers, 1831–78
Harvard Business School, Baker Library Archives
  Thomas W. Lamont Papers

Chicago, Illinois
Cardinal Joseph Bernardin Archive and Record Center
Loyola University of Chicago Archive
Servants of Mary, Western Province Archives
  Morini Memorial Collection
    Luigi Giambastiani Papers
    St. Philip Benizi Papers
University of Chicago, Regenstein Library
  Special Collections, Foreign Language Newspaper Files

Cleveland, Ohio
Archive of the Diocese of Cleveland
  Holy Redeemer Parish Papers
  Holy Rosary Parish Papers
  Joseph Schrembs Papers

Detroit, Michigan
Archive of the Archdiocese of Detroit
  Giuseppe Ciarrocchi Papers

Florence, Italy
La Biblioteca Nazionale Centrale di Firenze
  Collezione d'Autografi, Lettere, Varie, Morini-Carraresi Correspondence

New Haven, Connecticut
Archive of the Knights of Columbus Supreme Office

New York, New York
Archive of the Diocese of Brooklyn
Center for Migration Studies
  Records of Our Lady of Pompeii, New York

Notre Dame, Indiana
University of Notre Dame Archives

Oak Park, Illinois
St. John the Baptist Provincial Archive of the Scalabrini Fathers

Philadelphia, Pennsylvania
Philadelphia Archdiocesan Historical Research Center
  Archbishop Patrick John Ryan Collection
  Archbishop Prendergast Collection
  Cardinal Dennis Dougherty Collection

Providence, Rhode Island
Archive of the Diocese of Providence
  Msgr. Anthony Bove Papers
  St. Ann's Parish Papers

Rome, Italy
Archive of the Franciscan Sisters of the Immaculate Conception
Archive of the Servants of Mary, General House
Archivio Centrale dello Stato
  Casellario Political Centrale
  Gabinetto
  Ministero della Cultura popolare
    Nuclei Propaganda Italiana all'Estero
    Propaganda
  Ministero dell'Interno
    Divisione Polizia Politica, Direzione generale di pubblica sicurezza
  Segreteria Particolare del Duce, Carteggio Riservato
Archivio della Congregazione "De Propaganda Fide"
  Congressi Collegi Vari
  Lettere
  Nuova Serie
  Scritture Originali riferite nelle Congregazione Generali (America Centrale)
  Udienza
Archivio del Pontificio Consiglio per la Pastorale dei Migranti e Itineranti
Archivio del Prelato per l'Emigrazione Italiana

Archivio Generalizio Scalabriniano
Archivio Segreto Vaticano
    Delegazione Apostolico negli Stati Uniti
    Segreteria di Stato
        Spogli di Cardinali e Officiali di Curia
            Bedini, Gaetano
            Rampolla del Tindaro, Mariano
Archivio Storico Diplomatico, Ministero degli Affari Esteri
    Affari Politici verso gli Stati Uniti d'America, 1915–30
    Affari Politici verso gli Stati Uniti d'America, 1931–45
    Affari Politici verso la santa sede, 1931–45
    Archivio Politico Ordinario e di Gabinetto, 1915–18
    Commissariato dell'Emigrazione
    I Fondi Archivistici dei Consolati in Cleveland
    I Fondi Archivistici della Legazione Sarda e delle Rappresentanze Diplomatiche Italiani
        negli Stati Uniti d'America, 1848–1901
    Fondo Ambasciata a Washington, unprocessed, ca. 1910–1924
    Fondo Ambasciata a Washington, unprocessed, ca. 1920s
    Serie P. Politici, 1891–1915
Biblioteca dell'Archivio di Stato di Roma
    Alessandro Gavazzi, "Diario autobiografico"
Istituto Luigi Sturzo
    Archivio di Luigi Sturzo
        Fondo Luigi Sturzo

San Francisco, California
California Historical Society Archives
    Mayor James Rolph Correspondence

St. Paul, Minnesota
Immigration History Research Center
    Maurice Marchello Papers

Washington, D.C.
Archive of the Catholic University of America
    National Catholic Welfare Conference
Georgetown University Library
    Special Collections Division
        The America Magazine Papers
St. Paul's College
    Paulist Fathers Archive
        James Gillis Correspondence
        Superior General Papers

PRIMARY SOURCES

Addams, Jane. *Twenty Years at Hull-House*. Edited by Victoria Bissell Brown. Boston and New York: Bedford/St. Martin's, 1999.

Annuario diplomatico del regno d'Italia, 1937. Rome: Tipografia del Ministero degli Affari Esteri, 1937.

Bauman, Louis S. *Light from Bible Prophecy: As Related to the Present Crisis*. New York: Fleming H. Revell Co., 1940.

Blanshard, Paul. *American Freedom and Catholic Power*. Boston: Beacon Press, 1949.

———. *Communism, Democracy, and Catholic Power*. Boston: Beacon Press, 1951.

Bonaventura, Saint. *Vita di S. Francisco*. Edited by Guido Battelli. Sancasciano Val di Pesa: Stab. Tipo-Litografico F.lli Stianti, 1926.

Bove, Antonio. *L'Ordine Figli D'Italia di fronte alla coscienza cattolica: Lettera aperta alle associazioni italiane negli Stati Uniti dal Rev. Antonio Bove, parroco della chiesa di S. Anna, Providence, R.I.* Providence: N.p., October 17, 1918.

Breed, William Pratt. *The Restoration of the Pope: A Discourse Preached in the West Spruce Street Presbyterian Church*. Philadelphia: Sherman and Co., 1871.

Carlen, Claudia, ed. *The Papal Encyclicals, 1903–1939*. Vol. 3. Wilmington, N.C.: McGrath Publishing, 1981.

Chesterton, G. K. *The Resurrection of Rome*. New York: Dodd, Mead and Co., 1930.

Child, Richard Washburn. *A Diplomat Looks at Europe*. New York: Duffield and Co., 1925.

Complete Report of the Chairman of the Committee on Public Information. Washington, D.C.: Government Printing Office, 1920.

Creel, George. *How We Advertised America*. New York: Harper and Brothers, 1920.

Donovan, C. F. *The Story of the Twenty-Eighth International Eucharistic Congress*. Chicago: N.p., 1927.

Ellis, John Tracy. *American Catholicism*. Chicago: University of Chicago Press, 1956.

Faber, Frederick William. *Devotion to the Pope*. Baltimore: Murphy and Co., 1860.

Fuller, Margaret. *"These Sad but Glorious Days": Dispatches from Europe, 1846–1850*. Edited by Larry J. Reynolds and Susan Belasco Smith. New Haven: Yale University Press, 1991.

Glazer, Nathan. *American Judaism*. Chicago: University of Chicago Press, 1957.

Gower, Joseph F., and Richard M. Leliaert. *The Brownson-Hecker Correspondence*. Notre Dame: University of Notre Dame Press, 1979.

Hearley, John. *Pope or Mussolini*. New York: Macaulay Co., 1929.

Herberg, Will. *Protestant-Catholic-Jew: An Essay in American Religious Sociology*. New York: Doubleday, 1955.

Holsinger, Paul H. *Ethiopia and Mussolini in Light of Prophecy*. Oakland, Calif.: Grace Tabernacle, 1935.

House, Edward Mandell, and Charles Seymour. *What Really Happened at Paris: The Story of the Peace Conference, 1918–1919*. New York: Charles Scribner's Sons, 1921.

Hudson, Winthrop. *American Protestantism*. Chicago: University of Chicago Press, 1961.

Hughes, Rev. John. *Complete Works of the Most Rev. John Hughes, DD*. Edited by Lawrence Kehoe. 2 vols. New York: Lawrence Kehoe, 1866.

Jusserand, Jean J. "Letter to the Editor." *American Historical Review* 37 (July 1932): 817–19.

Keane, Rev. John J. *The Providential Mission of Pius IX: A Discourse Delivered at the Requiem Mass for Our Holy Father, Pope Pius IX, in the Cathedral of Baltimore, February 18th, 1878*. Baltimore: John Murphy, 1878.

Koenig, Harry C., ed. *Principles for Peace: Selections from Papal Documents, Leo XIII to Pius XII*. Washington, D.C.: National Catholic Welfare Conference, 1943.

Marshall, Charles C. *Governor Smith's American Catholicism*. New York: Dodd, Mead and Co., 1928.

Morini, Austin. *The Foundation of the Order of Servants of Mary in the United States of America (1870–1883)*. Translated by Conrad M. Borntrager. Rome: Edizioni Marianum, 1993.

Names of Contributors to the Collection in Aid of Our Holy Father, Pius IX, Made in the Diocese of Philadelphia. Philadelphia: N.p., 1860.

Official Guide of the Panama-Pacific International Exposition. San Francisco: Wahlgreen Co., 1915.

Order Sons of Italy in America. *Costituzione fondamentale e leggi generali dell'Ordine Figli d'Italia*. New York: Covino Press, 1915, 1917.

———. *Rituale*. New York: R. Paolella Press, 1915.

O'Reilly, Rev. Bernard. *A Life of Pius IX*. New York: P. F. Collier, 1878.

Orlando, Vittorio E. *Miei rapporti di governo con la S. Sede*. Milan: Garzanti, 1944.

Page, Thomas Nelson. *Italy and the World War*. New York: Charles Scribner's Sons, 1920.

Palmieri, Aurelio, OSA. *Il grave problema religioso italiano negli Stati Uniti*. Florence: Sordomuti, 1921.

Papers Relating to the Foreign Relations of the United States: The Lansing Papers, 1914–1920. 2 vols. Washington, D.C.: United States Printing Office, 1939.

Parsons, Wilfred, SJ. "The Church in Contemporary Italy (1919–1931)." *Catholic Historical Review* 16 (April 1932): 1–18.

———. *The Pope and Italy*. New York: America Press, 1929.

Prendergast, J. J. *The Temporal Power of the Pope*. San Francisco: Catholic Truth Society, n.d.

Pucci, Enrico. *La pace del Laterano*. Florence: Libreria Editrice Fiorentina, 1929.

Quadrotta, Guglielmo. *La chiesa cattolica nella crisi universale*. Rome: Casa Editrice Bilychnis, 1921.

Ryan, John A. *Declining Liberty and Other Papers*. New York: Macmillan, 1927.

Sartorio, Enrico C. *Social and Religious Life of Italians in America*. Boston: Christopher Publishing House, 1918.

Schnapp, Jeffrey T., ed. *A Primer of Italian Fascism*. Lincoln: University of Nebraska Press, 2000.

Scoppola, Pietro, ed. *Dal neoguelfismo alla democrazia cristiana: Antologia di documenti*. Rome: Studium, 1963.

Seldes, George. *Sawdust Caesar: The Untold History of Mussolini and Fascism*. New York: Harper and Brothers, 1935.

———. *The Vatican: Yesterday, Today, Tomorrow*. Harper and Brothers, 1934.

The Seventh National Eucharistic Congress: Official Record. Cleveland: Ward and Shaw Co., William J. Raddatz and Co., A. S. Gilman Co., 1936.

Shea, John Gilmary. *The Life of Pius IX*. New York: Thomas Kelly, 1877.

Smith, Oswald J. *Is the Antichrist at Hand? What of Mussolini*. New York: Christian Alliance Publishing Co., 1927.

Spadolini, Giovanni, ed. *Il Cardinale Gasparri e la questione romana*. Florence: Felice Le Monnier, 1973.

Stock, Leo Francis. *United States Ministers to the Papal States: Instructions and Despatches, 1848–1868.* Washington, D.C.: Catholic University Press, 1933.

St. Rocco's Parish, Cleveland, Ohio: Celebrating 75 Years, 1914–1989. N.p, n.d.

Sturzo, Luigo. *Italy and Fascismo.* London: Faber and Gwyer, 1926.

———. *Scritti inediti.* Vol. 3: 1940–1946. Edited by Francesco Malgeri. Rome: Istituto Luigi Sturzo, 1975.

Tomasi, Archbishop Silvano M., ed. *For the Love of Immigrants: Migration Writings and Letters of Bishop John Baptist Scalabrini, 1839–1905.* New York: Center for Migration Studies, 2000.

The Vatican-Italian Accord: Discussed by Count Carlo Sforza, Charles Clinton Marshall, John A. Ryan. Pamphlet 56, ser. 1928–29, 5–31. New York: Foreign Policy Association, April 1929.

Vitali, Luigi, ed. *L'Episcopato italiano in morte si S. M. Umberto I.* Milan: L. F. Cogliati, 1900.

Winrod, Gerald B. *Mussolini's Place in Prophecy.* N.p., 1933.

PUBLISHED SECONDARY SOURCES

Agócs, Sándor. *The Troubled Origins of the Italian Catholic Labor Movement, 1878–1914.* Detroit: Wayne State University Press, 1988.

Allitt, Patrick. *Catholic Converts: British and American Intellectuals Turn to Rome.* Ithaca, N.Y.: Cornell University Press, 1997.

Ambrosius, Lloyd E. *Woodrow Wilson and the American Diplomatic Tradition: The Treaty Fight in Perspective.* New York: Cambridge University Press, 1987.

Anderson, Benedict. *Imagined Communities: Reflections on the Origins and Spread of Nationalism.* New York: Verso, 1983, 1991.

Andreozzi, John, comp. *Guide to the Records of the Order Sons of Italy in America.* University of Minnesota: Immigration History Research Center, 1989.

Appleby, R. Scott. *"Church and Age Unite!" The Modernist Impulse in American Catholicism.* Notre Dame: University of Notre Dame Press, 1992.

———. "If the Church Is Not a Democracy, What Is It?" *Criterion* (Spring/Summer 1996): 13–20.

———. "The Triumph of Americanism: Common Ground for U.S. Catholics in the Twentieth Century." In *Being Right: Conservative Catholics in America,* edited by Mary Jo Weaver and R. Scott Appleby, 37–62. Bloomington and Indianapolis: Indiana University Press, 1995.

Arendt, Hannah. *The Origins of Totalitarianism.* New York: Harcourt, Brace and Co., 1951.

Baily, Samuel L. *Immigrants in the Lands of Promise.* Ithaca, N.Y.: Cornell University Press, 1999.

Barry, Colman J. *The Catholic Church and German Americans.* Milwaukee: Bruce Publishing Co., 1953.

Barton, Josef J. *Peasants and Strangers: Italians, Rumanians, and Slovaks in an American City.* Cambridge, Mass.: Harvard University Press, 1975.

Battelli, G. "I vescovi italiani tra Leone XIII e Pio X. Contributi recenti." *Cristianesimo nella storia* 6 (1985): 93–143.

Bayor, Ronald H. *Neighbors in Conflict: The Irish, Germans, Jews, and Italians of New York City, 1929–1941.* Urbana and Chicago: University of Illinois Press, 1988.

Behnen, Michael. *Die USA und Italien 1921–1933.* 2 vols. Münster: Lit Verlag, 1998.

Bender, Thomas, ed. *Rethinking American History in a Global Age.* Berkeley and Los Angeles: University of California Press, 2002.

Bezza, Bruno, ed. *Gli Italiani fuori d'Italia: Gli emigranti italiani nei movimenti operai d'adozione, 1880–1940*. Milan: Franco Angeli, 1983.

Billington, Ray Allen. *The Protestant Crusade, 1800–1860: A Study of the Origins of American Nativism*. New York: Macmillan, 1938.

Binchy, Daniel A. *Church and State in Fascist Italy*. London: Oxford University, 1941.

Bobbio, Norberto. *Ideological Profile of Twentieth-Century Italy*. Translated by Lydia G. Cochrane. Princeton: Princeton University Press, 1995.

Borzomati, Pietro. *I Cattolici e il Mezzogiorno*. Rome: Studium, 1995.

Bosworth, Richard. *The Italian Dictatorship: Problems and Perspectives in the Interpretation of Mussolini and Fascism*. London: Arnold, 1998.

———. *Italy and the Wider World*. London and New York: Routledge, 1996.

Boyer, Paul. *When Time Shall Be No More: Prophecy Belief in Modern American Culture*. Cambridge, Mass.: Belknap Press of Harvard University Press, 1992.

Briggs, John W. *An Italian Passage: Immigrants to Three American Cities, 1890–1930*. New Haven: Yale University Press, 1978.

Briggs, Kenneth A. *Holy Siege: The Year That Shook Catholic America*. San Francisco: Harper San Francisco, 1992.

Brinkley, Alan. *Liberalism and Its Discontents*. Cambridge, Mass.: Harvard University Press, 1998.

———. *Voices of Protest: Huey Long, Father Coughlin, and the Great Depression*. New York: Vintage Books, 1983.

Broderick, Francis L. *Right Reverend New Dealer: John A. Ryan*. New York: Macmillan, 1963.

Brown, Mary Elizabeth. *Churches, Communities, and Children: Italian Immigrants in the Archdiocese of New York, 1880–1945*. New York: Center for Migration Studies, 1995.

Browne, Henry J. "The 'Italian Problem' in the Catholic Church of the United States, 1880–1900." *Historical Records and Studies* 35 (1946): 46–72.

Bruti Liberati, Luigi. "Santa Sede e Stati Uniti negli anni della grande guerra." In *Benedetto XV e la pace-1918*, edited by Giorgio Rumi, 129–50. Brescia: Morcelliana, 1990.

Burgwyn, H. James. *Italian Foreign Policy in the Interwar Period, 1918–1940*. Westport, Conn.: Praeger, 1997.

———. *The Legend of the Mutilated Victory: Italy, the Great War, and the Paris Peace Conference, 1915–1919*. Westport, Conn.: Greenwood Press, 1993.

Burns, Gene. *The Frontiers of Catholicism: The Politics of Ideology in a Liberal World*. Berkeley and Los Angeles: University of California Press, 1992.

Byrne, Patricia, CSJ. "American Ultramontanism." *Theological Studies* 56 (1995): 301–26.

Caliaro, Marco, and Mario Francesconi. *John Baptist Scalabrini: Apostle to Emigrants*. Translated by Alba I. Zizzamia. New York: Center for Migration Studies, 1977.

Camaiani, Pier Giorgio. "Motivi e riflessi religiosi della questione romana." In *Chiesa e religiosità in Italia dopo l'unità (1861–1878)*, 65–128. Milan: Vita e Pensiero, 1973.

Canali, Mauro. *Il delitto Matteotti: Affarismo e politica nel primo governo Mussolini*. Bologna: Mulino, 1997.

Cannistraro, Philip V. *Blackshirts in Little Italy: Italian Americans and Fascism, 1921–1929*. West Lafayette, Ind.: Bordighera, 1999.

———. "Fascism and Italian-Americans in Detroit, 1933–1935." *International Migration Review* 9 (1975): 29–40.

————. "Gli Italo-Americani di fronte all'ingresso dell'Italia nella Seconda Guerra Mondiale." *Storia Contemporanea* 7 (1976): 855–64.

————, ed., *Historical Dictionary of Fascist Italy*. Westport, Conn.: Greenwood Press, 1982.

Cannistraro, Philip V., and Elena Aga Rossi. "La politica etnica e il dilemma dell'antifascismo italiano negli Stati Uniti: Il caso di Generoso Pope." *Storia Contemporanea* 17 (April 1986): 217–43.

Cannistraro, Philip V., and Theodore P. Kovaleff. "Father Coughlin and Mussolini: Impossible Allies." *Church and State* 13 (Autumn 1971): 427–43.

Cannistraro, Philip V., and Gianfausto Rosoli. *Emigrazione, chiesa e fascismo: Lo scioglimento dell'Opera Bonomelli (1922–1928)*. Rome: Studium, 1979.

————. "Fascist Emigration Policy in the 1920s: An Interpretive Framework." *International Migration Review* 13 (Winter 1979): 673–92.

Cannistraro, Philip V., and Brian R. Sullivan. *Il Duce's Other Woman*. New York: William Morrow and Co., 1993.

Carey, Patrick W. "American Lay Catholics' Views of the Papacy, 1785–1860." *Archivum Historiae Pontificiae* 21 (1983): 105–30.

————. *People, Priests, and Prelates: Ecclesiastical Democracy and the Tensions of Trusteeism*. Notre Dame: University of Notre Dame Press, 1987.

Carlizza, Stefano. "Ernesto Nathan, un sindaco nell'Italia giolittiana." *Giornale di Storia Contemporanea* 4 (June 2001): 36–59.

Carpenter, Joel A. *Revive Us Again: The Reawakening of American Fundamentalism*. New York: Oxford University Press, 1997.

Carson, Mina. *Settlement Folk: Social Thought and the American Settlement Movement, 1885–1930*. Chicago: University of Chicago, 1990.

Carter, Jefferson. "Carlton J. H. Hayes." In *Historians of Modern Europe*, edited by Hans A. Schmitt, 15–35. Baton Rouge: Louisiana State University Press, 1971.

Casella, Mario. "Il Conte Cesare Maria De Vecchi di Cismon, primo ambasciatore d'Italia in vaticano." *Archivum Historiae Pontificiae* 20 (2000): 185–263.

Cassels, Alan. "Fascism for Export: Italy and the United States in the Twenties." *American Historical Review* 69 (April 1964): 707–12.

————. *Ideology and International Relations in the Modern World*. New York: Routledge, 1996.

————. *Mussolini's Early Diplomacy*. Princeton: Princeton University Press, 1970.

Catholic Press Directory. Chicago: J. H. Meier, 1932.

Chabod, Federico. *Italian Foreign Policy: The Statecraft of the Founders*. Translated by William McCuaig. Princeton: Princeton University Press, 1951, 1996.

Chadwick, Owen. *A History of the Popes, 1830–1914*. Oxford, England: Clarendon Press, 1998.

Chernow, Ron. *The House of Morgan: An American Banking Dynasty and the Rise of Modern Finance*. New York: Touchstone, 1990.

Cinel, Dino. *From Italy to San Francisco*. Stanford: Stanford University Press, 1982.

Clare, Loretta. *American Public Opinion on the Diplomatic Relations between the United States and the Papal States: 1847–1867*. Washington, D.C.: Catholic University of America Press, 1933.

Clark, J. C. D. *The Language of Liberty, 1660–1832: Political Discourse and Social Dynamics in the Anglo-American World*. Cambridge, England: Cambridge University Press, 1994.

Clark, Martin. *The Italian Risorgimento*. London: Longman, 1998.

Code, Joseph B., ed., *The Dictionary of the American Hierarchy*. New York: J. F. Wagner, 1964.

Colley, Linda. *Britons: Forging the Nation, 1707–1837*. New Haven: Yale University Press, 1992.

Confessore, Ornella. L'Americanismo cattolico in Italia. Rome: Studium, 1984.

———. "L'associazione nazionale per soccorrere i missionari cattolici italiani, tra spinte 'civilizzatrici' e interesse migratorio (1887–1908)." In Scalabrini tra vecchio e nuovo mondo, edited by Gianfausto Rosoli, 519–36. Rome: Centro Studi Emigrazione, 1989.

———. I Cattolici e la "Fede nella Libertà": "Annali Cattolici" "Rivista Universale" "Rassegna Nazionale." Rome: Studium, 1989.

Connelly, James F. The Visit of Archbishop Gaetano Bedini to the United States of America (June, 1853–February, 1854). Rome: Libreria Editrice dell'Università Gregoriana, 1960.

Cooney, John. American Pope: The Life and Times of Francis Cardinal Spellman. New York: Times Books, 1984.

Coppa, Frank J. Cardinal Giacomo Antonelli and Papal Politics in European Affairs. Albany: State University Press of New York, 1990.

———. "Giolitti and the Gentiloni Pact between Myth and Reality." Catholic Historical Review 53 (July 1967): 217–28.

———. The Modern Papacy since 1789. New York: Longman, 1998.

———. "Mussolini and the Concordat of 1929." In Controversial Concordats: The Vatican's Relations with Napoleon, Mussolini, and Hitler, edited by Frank J. Coppa, 81–119. Washington, D.C.: Catholic University of America Press, 1999.

———. Pope Pius IX: Crusader in a Secular Age. Boston: Twayne Publishers, 1979.

Costigliola, Frank. Awkward Dominion: American Political, Economic, and Cultural Relations with Europe, 1919–1933. Ithaca, N.Y.: Cornell University Press, 1984.

Cottrell, Robert C. Izzy: A Biography of I. F. Stone. New Brunswick, N.J.: Rutgers University Press, 1993.

Cross, Robert D. The Emergence of Liberal Catholicism in America. Chicago: Quadrangle Books, 1958, 1968.

Crunden, Robert M. Ministers of Reform: The Progressives' Achievement in American Civilization, 1889–1920. New York: Basic Books, 1982.

Cuddy, Edward. "Pro-Germanism and American Catholicism." Catholic Historical Review 54 (October 1968): 427–54.

D'Agostino, Peter R. "Craniums, Criminals, and the 'Cursed Race': Italian Anthropology in American Racial Thought, 1865–1925." Comparative Studies of Society and History 44 (April 2002): 319–43.

———. "'Fascist Transmission Belts' or Episcopal Advisors? Italian Consuls and American Catholicism in the 1930s." Cushwa Center for the Study of American Catholicism: Working Paper Series 24 (Spring 1997): 1–39.

———. "Italian Ethnicity and Religious Priests in the American Church: The Servites, 1870–1940." Catholic Historical Review 80 (October 1994): 714–40.

———. "The Scalabrini Fathers, the Italian Emigrant Church, and Ethnic Nationalism in America." Religion and American Culture: A Journal of Interpretation 7 (Winter 1997): 121–59.

———. "The Triad of Roman Authority: Fascism, the Vatican, and Italian Religious Clergy in the Italian Emigrant Church." Journal of American Ethnic History 17 (Spring 1998): 3–37.

Damiani, Claudia. Mussolini e gli Stati Uniti, 1922–1935. Bologna: Cappelli, 1980.

Dante, Francesco. Storia della "Civiltà Cattolica" (1850–1891). Rome: Studium, 1990.

De Caprariis, Luca. "'Fascism for Export?' The Rise and Eclipse of the Fasci Italiani all'Estero." Journal of Contemporary History 35 (2000): 151–83.

De Felice, Renzo. *The Jews in Fascist Italy: A History*. Translated by Robert L. Miller. New York: Enigma Books, 2001.

De Grand, Alexander. *The Hunchback's Tailor: Giovanni Giolitti and Liberal Italy from the Challenge of Mass Politics to the Rise of Fascism, 1882–1922*. Westport, Conn.: Praeger, 2001.

———. *The Italian Left in the Twentieth Century: A History of the Socialist and Communist Parties*. Bloomington: Indiana University Press, 1989.

Del Pero, Mario. "The United States and 'Psychological Warfare' in Italy, 1948–1955." *Journal of American History* 87 (March 2001): 1304–34.

Delzell, Charles F. *Mussolini's Enemies: The Italian Anti-Fascist Resistance*. Princeton: Princeton University Press, 1961.

De Rosa, Gabriele. *Il movimento cattolico in Italia: Dalla Restaurazione all'età giolittiana*. Bari: Laterza, 1970.

———. *Il partito popolare italiano*. Bari: Laterza, 1979.

De Rosa, Luigi. "Stato e chiesa nell'assistenza agli emigrati italiani: L'opera di Scalabrini." In *Scalabrini tra vecchio e nuovo mondo*, edited by Gianfausto Rosoli, 237–52. Rome: Centro Studi Emigrazione, 1989.

Diggins, John P. "American Catholics and Italian Fascism." *Journal of Contemporary History* 2 (October 1967): 51–68.

———. *Mussolini and Fascism: The View from America*. Princeton: Princeton University, 1972.

Dillon, Michele. *Catholic Identity: Balancing Reason, Faith, and Power*. New York: Cambridge University Press, 1999.

Di Nolfo, Ennio. *Vaticano e Stati Uniti, 1939–1952: Dalle carte di Myron C. Taylor*. Milan: Franco Angeli, 1978.

Dolan, Jay P. *The American Catholic Experience: A History from Colonial Times to the Present*. Garden City, N.Y.: Doubleday, 1985.

———. "Catholicism and American Culture: Strategies for Survival." In *Minority Faiths and the American Protestant Mainstream*, edited by Jonathan D. Sarna, 61–80. Urbana and Chicago: University of Illinois Press, 1998.

———. *Catholic Revivalism: The American Experience, 1830–1900*. Notre Dame: University of Notre Dame Press, 1978.

———. *In Search of an American Catholicism: A History of Religion and Culture in Tension*. New York: Oxford University Press, 2002.

———. "The Search for an American Catholicism." *Catholic Historical Review* 82:2 (April 1996): 169–186.

Domenico, Roy Palmer. *Italian Fascists on Trial, 1943–1948*. Chapel Hill: University of North Carolina Press, 1991.

Douglas, Ann. *The Feminization of American Culture*. New York: Avon Books, 1977.

Duggan, Christopher. *Francesco Crispi, 1818–1901: From Nation to Nationalism*. Oxford, England: Oxford University Press, 2002.

Ellis, John Tracy. *The Life of James Cardinal Gibbons: Archbishop of Baltimore, 1842–1921*. 2 vols. Milwaukee: Bruce Publishing, 1952.

Epstein, Klaus. *Matthias Erzberger and the Dilemma of German Democracy*. Princeton: Princeton University Press, 1959.

Esslinger, Dean R. "American German and Irish Attitudes toward Neutrality, 1914–1917: A Study of Catholic Minorities." *Catholic Historical Review* 53 (July 1967): 194–216.

Fabiano, Domenico. "I fasci italiani all'estero." In *Gli Italiani fuori d'Italia: Gli emigranti italiani nei movimenti operai d'adozione, 1880–1940,* edited by Bruno Bezza, 221–36. Milan: Franco Angeli, 1983.

Fairman, Milton. "The Twenty-Eighth International Eucharistic Congress." *Chicago History* 5 (Winter 1976–77): 202–12.

Ferrell, Robert H. "Woodrow Wilson and Open Diplomacy." In *Issues and Conflict: Studies in Twentieth Century American Diplomacy,* edited by George L. Anderson, 193–209. Lawrence: University of Kansas Press, 1959.

———. *Woodrow Wilson and World War I, 1917–1921.* New York: Harper and Row, 1985.

Ferroni, Charles. "Italians." In *The Encyclopedia of Cleveland History,* edited by David D. Van Tassel and John J. Grabowski, 559–61. Bloomington and Indianapolis: Indiana University Press, 1987.

Ffinch, Michael. *G. K. Chesterton.* London: Weidenfeld and Nicolson, 1986.

Fiorentino, Carlo. *All'Ombra di Pietro: La Chiesa Cattolica e lo spionaggio fascista in Vaticano, 1929–1939.* Florence: Le Lettere, 1999.

Fiorentino, Daniele. "Il governo degli Stati Uniti e la Repubblica romana del 1849." In *Gli Americani e la Repubblica romana del 1849,* edited by Sara Antonelli, Daniele Fiorentino, and Giuseppe Monsagrati, 89–130. Rome: Gangemi Editore, 2000.

Foa, Anna. *Giordano Bruno.* Bologna: Mulino, 1998.

Foerster, Robert F. *The Italian Emigration of Our Times.* Cambridge, Mass.: Harvard University Press, 1919.

Fogarty, Gerald P. "Cardinal William Henry O'Connell." In *Varieties of Ultramontanism,* edited by Jeffrey von Arx, SJ, 118–46. Washington, D.C.: Catholic University of America Press, 1998.

———. "Public Patriotism and Private Politics: The Tradition of American Catholicism." *U.S. Catholic Historian* 4 (1984): 1–48.

———. *The Vatican and the American Hierarchy from 1870 to 1965.* Stuttgart: Anton Hiersemann, 1982.

Fonzi, Fausto. "Scalabrini e la vita politica italiana (Piacenza, 1886)." In *Scalabrini tra vecchio e nuovo mondo,* edited by Gianfausto Rosoli, 17–34. Rome: Centro Studi Emigrazione, 1989.

Formigoni, Guido. *L'Italia dei cattolici: Fede e nazione dal Risorgimento alla Repubblica.* Bologna: Mulino, 1998.

Francesconi, Mario. *Giovanni Battista Scalabrini: Vescovo di Piacenza e degli emigrati.* Rome: Città Nuova Editrice, 1985.

Franzina, Emilio. *Italiani al nuovo mondo: L'emigrazione italiana in America, 1492–1942.* Milan: Arnoldo Mondadori Editore, 1995.

Franzina, Emilio, and Matteo Sanfilippo. *Il fascismo e gli emigrati: La parabola dei Fasci italiani all'estero (1920–1943).* Rome-Bari: Laterza, 2003.

Gabaccia, Donna. *Italy's Many Diasporas.* Seattle: University of Washington Press, 2000.

———. *Militants and Migrants: Rural Sicilians Become American Workers.* New Brunswick, N.J.: Rutgers University Press, 1988.

Gaffey, James P. *Francis Clement Kelley and the American Catholic Dream.* Bensenville, Ill.: Heritage Foundation, 1980.

Garzia, Italo. *La questione romana durante la I guerra mondiale.* Naples: Edizioni Scientifiche Italiane, 1981.

Gaustad, Edwin S. *Neither King nor Prelate: Religion and the New Nation, 1776–1826.* Grand Rapids, Mich.: Eerdmans, 1993.

———. *Sworn on the Altar of God: A Religious Biography of Thomas Jefferson.* Grand Rapids, Mich.: Eerdmans, 1996.

Gellner, Ernest. *Nations and Nationalism.* Ithaca, N.Y.: Cornell University Press, 1983.

Gentile, Emilio. *La Grande Italia: Ascesa e declino del mito della nazione nel ventesimo secolo.* Milan: Arnoldo Mondadari, 1997.

———. "La politica estera del partito fascista: Ideologia e organizzazione dei Fasci italiani all'estero (1920–1930)." *Storia Contemporanea* 24 (1995): 897–956.

Giddens, Anthony. *Central Problems in Social Theory: Action, Structure, and Contradiction in Social Analysis.* Berkeley and Los Angeles: University of California Press, 1979.

———. *The Constitution of Society: Outline of the Theory of Structuration.* Berkeley and Los Angeles: University of California Press, 1984.

———. *New Rules of Sociological Method: A Positive Critique of Interpretive Sociologies.* New York: Basic Books, 1976.

Giles, Paul. *American Catholic Arts and Fictions: Culture, Ideology, Aesthetics.* New York: Cambridge University Press, 1992.

Gimarc, Jerry Dell. "Illinois Catholic Editorial Opinion during World War I." *Historical Records and Studies* 43 (1960): 167–84.

Ginsborg, Paul. *A History of Contemporary Italy: Society and Politics, 1943–1988.* New York: Penguin, 1990.

Giorcelli, Cristina. "La Repubblica romana di Margaret Fuller: Tra visione politica e impegno etico." In *Gli Americani e la repubblica romana del 1849*, edited by Sara Antonelli, Daniele Fiorentino, and Giuseppe Monsagrati, 53–88. Rome: Gangemi Editore, 2000.

Giovagnoli, Agostino. "Il neoguelfismo." In *Storia dell'Italia religiosa.* Vol. 3, *L'età contemporanea*, edited by Gabriele De Rosa, 39–59. Bari: Laterza, 1995.

Gjerde, Jon. *From Peasants to Farmers: The Migration from Balestrand, Norway, to the Upper Middle West.* New York: Cambridge University Press, 1985.

Gleason, Philip. "American Catholics and Liberalism, 1789–1960." In *Catholicism and Liberalism: Contributions to American Public Philosophy*, edited by R. Bruce Douglass and David Hollennback, 45–75. New York: Cambridge University Press, 1994.

———. *The Conservative Reformers: German-American Catholics and the Social Order.* Notre Dame: University of Notre Dame Press, 1968.

———. *Contending with Modernity: Catholic Higher Education in the Twentieth Century.* New York: Oxford University Press, 1995.

———. "The New Americanism in Catholic Historiography." *U.S. Catholic Historian* 11 (Summer 1993): 1–18.

———. *Speaking of Diversity: Language and Ethnicity in Twentieth-Century America.* Baltimore: Johns Hopkins University Press, 1992.

Graham, Robert A., SJ. *The Rise of the Double Diplomatic Corps in Rome: A Study in International Practice.* The Hague: Martinus Nijhoff, 1952.

Greeley, Andrew M. *The Catholic Experience.* Garden City, N.Y.: Doubleday, 1967.

———. *The Catholic Myth: The Behavior and Beliefs of American Catholics.* New York: Collier Books, 1990.

Gribble, Richard, CSC. *Guardian of America: The Life of James Martin Gillis, CSP.* Mahwah, N.J.: Paulist Press, 1998.

Halperin, S. William. *The Separation of Church and State in Italian Thought from Cavour to Mussolini.* Chicago: University of Chicago, 1937.

Halsey, William M. *The Survival of American Innocence: Catholicism in an Era of Disillusionment, 1920–1940.* Notre Dame: University of Notre Dame Press, 1980.

Hansen, Marcus Lee. *The Atlantic Migration, 1607–1860.* Cambridge, Mass.: Harvard University Press, 1940.

Harris, Brice. *The United States and the Italo-Ethiopian Crisis.* Stanford: Stanford University Press, 1964.

Haywood, Geoffrey A. *Failure of a Dream: Sidney Sonnino and the Rise and Fall of Liberal Italy, 1847–1922.* Florence: Leo S. Olschki, 1999.

Hearder, Harry. *Cavour.* New York: Longman, 1994.

Heilbronner, Oded. "From Ghetto to Ghetto: The Place of German Catholic Society in Recent Historiography." *Journal of Modern History* 72 (June 2000): 453–95.

Held, David, and John B. Thompson, eds. *Social Theory of Modern Societies: Anthony Giddens and His Critics.* New York: Cambridge University Press, 1989.

Hennesey, James, SJ. *American Catholics: A History of the Roman Catholic Community in the United States.* New York: Oxford University Press, 1981.

———. *The First Council of the Vatican: The American Experience.* New York: Herder and Herder, 1963.

———. "Papacy and Episcopacy in Eighteenth and Nineteenth Century American Catholic Thought." *Records of the American Catholic Historical Society of Philadelphia* 77 (September 1966): 175–89.

Hibbert, Christopher. *Rome: The Biography of a City.* New York: Penguin, 1985.

Hobsbawm, E. J. *Nations and Nationalism since 1780: Programme, Myth, Reality.* New York: Cambridge University Press, 1992.

Hunt, Michael H. *Ideology and U.S. Foreign Policy.* New Haven: Yale University Press, 1987.

Hunter, James Davison. *Culture Wars: The Struggle to Define America.* New York: Basic Books, 1991.

Hutchison, William R. *The Modernist Impulse in American Protestantism.* New York: Oxford University Press, 1976.

Hynes, Michael J. *History of the Diocese of Cleveland: Origin and Growth (1847–1952).* Cleveland: Diocese of Cleveland, 1953.

Iriye, Akira. *Cultural Internationalism and World Order.* Baltimore: Johns Hopkins University Press, 1997.

———. *The Globalizing of America, 1913–1945.* Vol. 3 of *The Cambridge History of American Foreign Relations.* New York: Cambridge University Press, 1993.

———. "Internationalization of History." *American Historical Review* 94 (February 1989): 1–10.

Isastia, Anna Maria. *Ernesto Nathan: Un "mazziniano inglese" tra i democratici pesaresi.* Milan: Franco Angeli, 1994.

Issel, William, and Robert W. Cherny. *San Francisco, 1865–1932: Politics, Power, and Urban Development.* Berkeley and Los Angeles: University of California Press, 1986.

Jemolo, Arturo Carlo. *Chiesa e stato in Italia negli ultimi cento anni.* Turin: Einuadi, 1949.

———. *Church and State in Italy, 1850–1950.* Revised and translated by David Moore. Oxford, England: Basil Blackwell, 1960.

Kalyvas, Stathis N. *The Rise of Christian Democracy in Europe*. Ithaca, N.Y.: Cornell University Press, 1996.

Kanawada, Leo V., Jr. *Franklin D. Roosevelt's Diplomacy and American Catholics, Italians, and Jews*. Ann Arbor: UMI Research Press, 1982.

Kane, Paula M. *Separatism and Subculture: Boston Catholicism, 1900–1920*. Chapel Hill: University of North Carolina Press, 1994.

Kantowicz, Edward R. "Cardinal Mundelein of Chicago and the Shaping of Twentieth-Century American Catholicism." *Journal of American History* 68 (June 1981): 52–68.

———. *Corporation Sole: Cardinal Mundelein and Chicago Catholicism*. Notre Dame: University of Notre Dame Press, 1983.

Kauffman, Christopher J. *Faith and Fraternalism: The History of the Knights of Columbus*. New York: Simon and Schuster, 1992.

Keefe, Thomas M. "The Mundelein Affair: A Reappraisal." *Records of the American Catholic Historical Society* 89 (1978): 74–84.

Kenneally, James. "A Question of Equality." In *American Catholic Women: A Historical Exploration*, edited by Karen Kennelly, CSJ, 125–51. New York: Macmillan, 1989.

Kennedy, David M. *Over Here: The First World War and American Society*. New York: Oxford University Press, 1980.

Kent, Peter C. *The Lonely Cold War of Pope Pius XII: The Roman Catholic Church and the Division of Europe, 1943–1950*. Montreal: McGill-Queen's University Press, 2002.

———. *The Pope and the Duce: The International Impact of the Lateran Agreements*. New York: St. Martin's Press, 1981.

Kent, Peter C., and John F. Pollard, eds., *Papal Diplomacy in the Modern Age*. Westport, Conn.: Praeger, 1994.

Kertzer, David I. *The Kidnapping of Edgardo Mortara*. New York: Vintage Books, 1998.

———. *The Popes against the Jews: The Vatican's Role in the Rise of Modern Anti-Semitism*. New York: Alfred A. Knopf, 2001.

Killinger, Charles. *Gaetano Salvemini: A Biography*. Westport, Conn.: Praeger, 2002.

Kim, Gertrud, OSB. "Roman Catholic Organization since Vatican II." In *American Denominational Organization: A Sociological View*, edited by Ross P. Scherer, 84–129. Pasadena, Calif.: William Carey Library, 1980.

Kloppenberg, James T. *Uncertain Victory: Social Democracy and Progressivism in European and American Thought, 1870–1920*. New York: Oxford University Press, 1986.

Knock, Thomas J. *To End All Wars: Woodrow Wilson and the Quest for a New World Order*. New York: Oxford University Press, 1992.

Koon, Tracy H. *Believe, Obey, Fight: Political Socialization of Youth in Fascist Italy, 1922–1943*. Chapel Hill: University of North Carolina Press, 1985.

Korn, Bertram W. *The American Reaction to the Mortara Case, 1858–1859*. Cincinnati: American Jewish Archives, 1957.

Kulas, John S. *Der Wanderer of St. Paul: The First Decade, 1867–1877*. New York: Peter Lang, 1996.

La Bella, Gianni. *Luigi Sturzo e l'esilio negli Stati Uniti*. Brescia: Morcelliana, 1990.

LaFeber, Walter. "The World and the United States." *American Historical Review* 100 (October 1995): 1015–33.

Larkin, Maurice. *Church and State after the Dreyfus Affair: The Separation Issue in France*. New York: Macmillan, 1974.

Ledeen, Michael A. *The First Duce: D'Annunzio at Fiume*. Baltimore: Johns Hopkins University Press, 1977.

Leetham, Claude. *Rosmini: Priest and Philosopher*. New York: New City Press, 1982.

Levra, Umberto. *Fare gli italiani: Memoria e celebrazione del risorgimento*. Turin: Comitato di Torino dell'istituto per la storia del risorgimento italiano, 1992.

Light, Dale B. *Rome and the New Republic: Conflict and Community in Philadelphia Catholicism between the Revolution and the Civil War*. Notre Dame: University of Notre Dame Press, 1996.

Link, Arthur S. *Wilson the Diplomatist: A Look at His Major Foreign Policies*. Baltimore: Johns Hopkins University Press, 1957.

Lovett, Clara M. *The Democratic Movement in Italy, 1830–1876*. Cambridge, Mass.: Harvard University Press, 1982.

Lowenthal, David. *George Perkins Marsh: Prophet of Conservation*. Seattle: University of Washington Press, 2000.

Luconi, Stefano. *La "Diplomazia Parallela": Il regime fascista e la mobilitazione politica degli italoamericani*. Milan: Franco Angeli, 2000.

Lumley, Robert, and Jonathan Morris, eds. *The New History of the Italian South: The Mezzogiorno Revisited*. Exeter: University of Exeter Press, 1997.

Lyttelton, Adrian. "Creating a National Past: History, Myth, and Image in the Risorgimento." In *Making and Remaking Italy: The Cultivation of National Identity around the Risorgimento*, edited by Albert Russell Ascoli and Krystyna von Henneberg, 27–74. New York: Berg, 2001.

———. *The Seizure of Power: Fascism in Italy 1919–1929*. New York: Charles Scribner's Sons, 1973.

Macioti, Maria Immacolata. *Ernesto Nathan: Il sindaco che cambiò il volto di Roma*. Rome: Newton Cultura Società Servizi, 1995.

Mack Smith, Denis. *Italy and Its Monarchy*. New Haven: Yale University Press, 1989.

———. *Mazzini*. New Haven: Yale University Press, 1994.

Malgeri, Francesco. *Luigi Sturzo*. Milan: Edizioni San Paolo, 1993.

Margiotta Broglio, Francesco. *Italia e Santa Sede dalla grande guerra alla conciliazione*. Bari: Laterza, 1966.

Marraro, Howard R. *American Opinion on the Unification of Italy, 1846–1861*. New York: Columbia University Press, 1932.

———. "The Closing of the American Diplomatic Mission to the Vatican and Efforts to Revive It, 1868–1870." *Catholic Historical Review* 33 (January 1948): 423–47.

Marsden, George M. *Fundamentalism and American Culture: The Shaping of Twentieth-Century Evangelicalism, 1870–1925*. New York: Oxford University Press, 1980.

Martina, Giacomo. "La fine del potere temporale nella coscienza religiosa e nella cultura dell'epoca in Italia." *Archivum Historiae Pontificiae* 9 (1971): 309–76.

———. *Pio IX (1846–1850)*. Vol. 1. Rome: Università Gregoriana, 1974.

———. *Pio IX (1851–1866)*. Vol. 2. Rome: Università Gregoriana, 1986.

———. *Pio IX (1867–1878)*. Vol. 3. Rome: Università Gregoriana, 1990.

———. "La situazione degli istituti religiosi in Italia intorno al 1870." In *Chiesa e religiosità in Italia dopo l'unità (1861–1878)*, 201–24. Milan: Vita e Pensiero, 1973.

Martini, Angelo. *Studi sulla questione romana e la conciliazione*. Rome: Edizioni 5 Lune, 1963.

Marty, Martin E. *The Noise of Conflict, 1919–1941*. Vol. 2 of *Modern American Religion*. Chicago: University of Chicago Press, 1991.

———. *One Nation, Indivisible, 1941–1960.* Vol. 3 of *Modern American Religion.* Chicago: University of Chicago Press, 1996.

———. *Righteous Empire: The Protestant Experience in America.* New York: Dial, 1970.

McCann, Dennis. *New Experiment in Democracy: The Challenge for American Catholicism.* Kansas City: Sheed and Ward, 1987.

McDonough, Peter. *Men Astutely Trained: A History of the Jesuits in the American Century.* New York: Free Press, 1992.

McGreevy, John T. *Catholicism and American Freedom: A History.* New York: W. W. Norton and Co., 2003.

———. *Parish Boundaries: The Catholic Encounter with Race in the Twentieth-Century Urban North.* Chicago: University of Chicago Press, 1996.

———. "Pragmatism to a Fault?" *Commonweal*, 17 August 2001, 22–24.

———. "Thinking on One's Own: Catholicism in the American Intellectual Imagination." *Journal of American History* 84 (June 1997): 97–131.

McKeown, Elizabeth. *War and Welfare: American Catholics and World War I.* New York: Garland, 1988.

Merwick, Donna. *Boston Priests, 1848–1910.* Cambridge, Mass.: Harvard University Press, 1973.

Michaelis, Meir. *Mussolini and the Jews: German, Italian Relations and the Jewish Question in Italy, 1922–1945.* New York: Oxford University Press, 1978.

Migone, Giangiacomo. *Gli Stati Uniti e il fascismo: Alle origini dell'egemonia americana in Italia.* Milan: Feltrinelli, 1980.

Miller, James Edward. *The United States and Italy, 1940–1950: The Politics of Diplomacy and Stabilization.* Chapel Hill: University of North Carolina Press, 1986.

Miscamble, Wilson D. "Catholics and American Foreign Policy from McKinley to McCarthy: A Historiographical Survey." *Diplomatic History* 4 (Summer 1980): 223–40.

———. "The Limits of American Catholic Antifascism: The Case of John A. Ryan." *Church History* 59 (December 1990): 523–38.

Misner, Paul. *Social Catholicism in Europe: From the Onset of Industrialization to the First World War.* New York: Crossroad, 1991.

Mize, Sandra Y. "Defending Roman Loyalties and Republican Values: The 1848 Italian Revolution in American Catholic Apologetics." *Church History* 60 (December 1991): 480–92.

Mock, James R., and Cedric Larson. *Words That Won the War: The Story of The Committee on Public Information.* Princeton: Princeton University Press, 1939.

Mola, Aldo A. *Storia della Massoneria italiana: Dalla origini ai giorni nostri.* Milan: Bompiani, 1992, 2001.

Molony, Deirdre M. *American Catholic Lay Groups and Transatlantic Social Reform in the Progressive Era.* Chapel Hill: University of North Carolina Press, 2002.

Molony, John N. *The Emergence of Political Catholicism in Italy: Partito Popolare 1919–1926.* Totowa, N.J.: Rowman and Littlefield, 1977.

Monsagrati, Giuseppe. "Gli intellettuali americani e la rivoluzione romana del 1848–49." In *Gli Americani e la repubblica romana del 1849,* edited by Sara Antonelli, Daniele Fiorentino, and Giuseppe Monsagrati, 21–52. Rome: Gangemi Editore, 2000.

Monticone, Alberto. "I vescovi italiani e la guerra 1915–1918." In *Benedetto XV, i cattolici e la prima guerra mondiale,* edited by Giuseppe Rossini, 627–60. Rome: Cinque Lune, 1963.

Moore, R. Laurence. *Religious Outsiders and the Making of Americans*. New York: Oxford University Press, 1986.

Mormino, Gary R. *Immigrants on the Hill: Italian-Americans in St. Louis, 1882–1982*. Urbana: University of Illinois Press, 1986.

Morozzo della Rocca, Roberto. "Benedetto XV e il nazionalismo." *Cristianesimo nella Storia* 17 (October 1996): 541–66.

———. *La fede e la guerra: Cappellani militari e preti-soldati (1915–1919)*. Rome: Studium, 1980.

Morris, Charles R. *American Catholics: The Saints and Sinners Who Built America's Most Powerful Church*. New York: Times Books, 1997.

Mosca, Rodolfo. "La mancata revisione dell'art. 15 del Patto di Londra." In *Benedetto XV, i cattolici e la prima guerra mondiale*, edited by Giuseppe Rossini, 401–13. Rome: Cinque Lune, 1963.

Nasaw, David. *The Chief: The Life of William Randolph Hearst*. Boston: Houghton Mifflin, 2000.

Nazzaro, Pellegrino. "L'atteggiamento della stampa cattolico-moderata americana verso il Fascismo prima e dopo la Conciliazione." In *Modernismo, Fascismo, Comunismo. Aspetti e figure della cultura e della politica dei cattolici ne '900*, edited by Giuseppe Rossini, 361–81. Bologna: Mulino, 1972.

Nelli, Humbert S. *The Italians in Chicago, 1880–1930: A Study in Ethnic Mobility*. New York: Oxford University Press, 1970.

Niebuhr, Reinhold. *The Irony of American History*. New York: Charles Scribner's Sons, 1952.

Nigro, Louis John, Jr. *The New Diplomacy in Italy: American Propaganda and U.S.-Italian Relations, 1917–1919*. New York: Peter Lang, 1999.

Norman, John. "Influence of Pro-Fascist Propaganda on American Neutrality, 1935–1936." In *Essays in History and International Relations: In Honor of George Hubbard Blakeslee*, edited by Dwight E. Lee, 193–214. Worcester, Mass.: Clark University, 1949.

O'Brien, Albert C. "*L'Osservatore Romano* and Fascism: The Beginning of a New Era in Church-State Relations, October 1922–July 1923." *Journal of Church and State* 13 (Autumn 1971): 445–63.

O'Brien, David J. "American Catholic Historiography: A Post-Conciliar Evaluation." *Church History* 37 (1968): 80–94

———. *Public Catholicism*. New York: Macmillan, 1989.

———. *The Renewal of American Catholicism*. New York: Paulist Press, 1972.

O'Connell, Marvin R. *John Ireland and the American Catholic Church*. St. Paul: Minnesota Historical Society, 1988.

Official Catholic Directory (1890–1940). New York: P. J. Kenedy and Sons, 1890–1940.

Orsi, Robert A. *The Madonna of 115th Street: Faith and Community in Italian Harlem, 1880–1950*. New Haven: Yale University Press, 1985.

———. *Thank You, St. Jude: Women's Devotion to the Patron Saint of Hopeless Causes*. New Haven: Yale University Press, 1996.

O'Toole, James M. *Militant and Triumphant: William Henry O'Connell and the Catholic Church in Boston, 1859–1944*. Notre Dame: University of Notre Dame Press, 1992.

Ottanelli, Fraser M. "'If Fascism Comes to America We Will Push It Back into the Ocean': Italian American Antifascism in the 1920s and 1930s." In *Italian Workers of the World: Labor Migration and the Formation of Multiethnic States*, edited by Donna R. Gabaccia and Fraser M. Ottanelli, 178–95. Urbana and Chicago: University of Illinois Press, 2001.

Papini, Roberto. *Il Coraggio della democrazia: Sturzo e l'Internazionale popolare tra le due guerre.* Rome: Studium, 1995.

Pellica, Guerrino, and Giancarlo Rocca, eds. *Dizionario degli istituti di perfezione.* 8 vols. Rome: Edizione Paoline, 1974–1988.

Perotti, Antonio. *Il Pontificio Collegio per l'Emigrazione Italiana, 1920–1970.* Rome: Tipografia Italo-Orientale S. Nilo, n.d.

Pizzorusso, Giovanni, and Matteo Sanfilippo. "Il caso Mortara: Due libri e un documento americano." *Il Veltro: Rivista della civiltà italiana* 42 (January–April 1998): 134–41.

Pollard, John F. "'A Marriage of Convenience': The Vatican and the Fascist Regime in Italy." In *Disciplines of Faith: Studies in Religion, Politics, and Patriarchy,* edited by Jim Obelkevich, Lyndal Roper, and Raphael Samuel, 501–17. New York: Routledge and Kegan Paul, 1987.

———. *The Unknown Pope: Benedict XV (1914–1922) and the Pursuit of Peace.* New York: Geoffrey Chapman, 1999.

———. *The Vatican and Italian Fascism, 1929–32: A Study in Conflict.* New York: Cambridge University Press, 1985.

———. "Il Vaticano e la politica estera italiana." In *La politica estera italiana, 1860–1985,* edited by Richard J. B. Bosworth and Sergio Romano, 197–230. Bologna: Mulino, 1991.

Porciani, Ilaria. *La festa della nazione: Rappresentazione dello stato e spazi sociali nell'Italia unità.* Bologna: Mulino, 1997.

Pretelli, Matteo. "Fasci italiani e comunità italo-americane: Un rapporto difficile (1921–1929)." *Giornale di storia contemporanea* 4 (June 2001): 112–40.

Pugliese, Stanislao G. *Carlo Rosselli: Socialist Heretic and Antifascist Exile.* Cambridge, Mass.: Harvard University Press, 1999.

Rahden, Till Van. "Beyond Ambivalence: Variations of Catholic Anti-Semitism in Turn-of-the-Century Baltimore." *American Jewish History* 82 (1994): 7–42.

Renzi, William A. *In the Shadow of the Sword: Italy's Neutrality and Entrance into the Great War, 1914–1915.* New York: Peter Lang, 1987.

Reynolds, Larry J. *European Revolutions and the American Literary Renaissance.* New Haven: Yale University Press, 1988.

Rhodes, Anthony. *The Vatican in the Age of the Dictators (1922–1945).* New York: Holt, Rinehart and Winston, 1973.

Riall, Lucy. *Sicily and the Unification of Italy.* New York: Oxford University Press, 1998.

Ricca, Paolo. "Le chiese evangeliche." In *Storia dell'Italia religiosa.* Vol. 3, *L'età contemporanea,* edited by Gabriele De Rosa, 404–40. Bari: Laterza, 1995.

Rodgers, Daniel T. *Atlantic Crossings: Social Politics in a Progressive Age.* Cambridge, Mass.: Belknap Press of Harvard University Press, 1998.

———. "Exceptionalism." In *Imagined Histories: American Historians Interpret the Past,* edited by Anthony Molho and Gordon S. Wood, 21–40. Princeton: Princeton University Press, 1998.

Rosoli, Gianfausto. *Insieme oltre le frontiere.* Caltanisetta-Rome: Salvatore Sciascia, 1996.

Rossini, Daniela. *Il mito americano nell'Italia della grande guerra.* Bari: Laterza, 2000.

Rumi, Giorgio. *Gioberti.* Bologna: Mulino, 1999.

Salomone, A. William. *Italy in the Giolittian Era: Italian Democracy in the Making, 1900–1914.* Philadelphia: University of Philadelphia Press, 1945.

———. "The 19th-Century Discovery of Italy: An Essay in American Cultural History." *American Historical Review* 73 (June 1968): 1359–91.

Salvadori, Massimo L. *Il mito del buongoverno: La questione meridionale da Cavour a Gramsci.* Turin: Einuadi, 1960.

Salvatorelli, Luigi. *La politica della Santa Sede dopo la guerra.* Milan: Istituto per gli Studi di Politica Internazionale, 1937.

———. *The Risorgimento: Thought and Action.* Translated by Mario Domandi. New York: Harper Torchbooks, 1970.

Salvemini, Gaetano. *Italian Fascist Activities in the United States.* Edited by Philip V. Cannistraro. New York: Center for Migration Studies, 1977.

Salvemini, Gaetano, and George La Piana. *What to Do with Italy.* New York: Duell, Sloan, and Pearce, 1943.

Salvetti, Patrizia. *Immagine nazionale ed emigrazione nella Società "Dante Alighieri."* Rome: Bonacci, 1995.

Sanders, James W. *The Education of an Urban Minority: Catholics in Chicago, 1833–1965.* New York: Oxford University Press, 1977.

Sanfilippo, Matteo. *L'Affermazione del cattolicesimo nel Nord America: Elite, emigranti e chiesa cattolica negli Stati Uniti e in Canada, 1750–1920.* Viterbo: Sette Città, 2003.

———. "La Santa Sede, Ernesto Nathan e le ripercussioni internazionali delle celebrazioni per il 20 settembre 1910." *Archivio della società romana di storia patria* 113 (1990): 347–60.

———. "Tra antipapismo e cattolicesimo: Gli echi della Repubblica romana e i viaggi in Nord America di Gaetano Bedini e Alessandro Gavazzi (1853-1854)." In *Gli Americani e la Repubblica romana del 1849,* edited by Sara Antonelli, Daniele Fiorentino, and Giuseppe Monsagrati, 159–88. Rome: Gangemi Editore, 2000.

Santarelli, Enzo. *Storia del movimento del regime fascista.* Vol. 1. Rome: Riuniti, 1967.

Scaglia, Giovanni Battista. *Cesare Balbo: L'indipendenza d'Italia e l'avvenire della cristianità.* Rome: Studium, 1989.

Schiavo, Giovanni E. *Italian American Who's Who.* New York: Vigo Press, 1936.

———. *The Italian Contribution to the Catholic Church in America.* Vol. 2 of *Italian-American History.* New York: Vigo Press, 1949.

Schmitz, David F. *The United States and Fascist Italy, 1922–1940.* Chapel Hill: University of North Carolina Press, 1988.

Schneider, Jane, ed. *Italy's "Southern Question": Orientalism in One Country.* New York: Berg, 1998.

Serra, Enrico. "La nota del primo agosto 1917 e il governo italiano: Qualche osservazione." In *Benedetto XV e la pace-1918,* edited by Giorgio Rumi, 49–64. Brescia: Morcelliana, 1990.

Seton-Watson, Christopher. *Italy from Liberalism to Fascism, 1870–1925.* London: Methuen, 1967.

Sewell, William H., Jr. "A Theory of Structure: Duality, Agency, and Transformation." *American Journal of Sociology* 98 (July 1992): 1–29.

Sexton, John E., and Arthur J. Riley. *History of Saint John's Seminary of Brighton.* Boston: Roman Catholic Archdiocese of Boston, 1945.

Sforza, Carlo. *Contemporary Italy: Its Intellectual and Moral Origins.* Translated by Drake and Denise De Kay. New York: E. P. Dutton and Co., 1944.

Sharp, John K., ed. *Priests and Parishes of the Diocese of Brooklyn: 1820–1944.* New York: Roman Catholic Diocese of Brooklyn, 1944.

Sindoni, Angelo. "Gli echi della 'Rerum Novarum' nel Mezzogiorno." In *Chiesa e Società nel*

Mezzogiorno: Studi in onore di Maria Mariotti. Vol. 2, edited by Pietro Borzomati et al., 923–37. Soveria Mannelli, Catanzaro: Rubbettino, 1998.

Smith, Timothy L. "Religion and Ethnicity in America." American Historical Review 83 (December 1978): 1155–85.

Southern, David W. John La Farge and the Limits of Catholic Interracialism, 1911–1963. Baton Rouge: Louisiana State University Press, 1996.

Spadolini, Giovanni. L'opposizione cattolica. Milan: Arnoldo Mondadori, 1994.

Spalding, Thomas W. Martin John Spalding: American Churchman. Washington, D.C.: Catholic University of America Press, 1973.

———. The Premier See: A History of the Archdiocese of Baltimore, 1789–1994. Baltimore: Johns Hopkins University Press, 1989.

Sparr, Arnold. To Promote, Defend, and Redeem: The Catholic Literary Revival and the Cultural Transformation of American Catholicism, 1920–1960. Westport, Conn.: Greenwood Press, 1990.

Steinfels, Peter. "The Failed Encounter: The Catholic Church and Liberalism in the Nineteenth Century." In Catholicism and Liberalism: Contributions to American Public Philosophy, edited by R. Bruce Douglass and David Hollennback, 19–44. New York: Cambridge University Press, 1994.

Sullivan, Mary Louise, MSC. Mother Cabrini: "Italian Immigrant of the Century." New York: Center for Migration Studies, 1992.

Taves, Ann. The Household of Faith: Roman Catholic Devotions in Mid-Nineteenth-Century America. Notre Dame: University of Notre Dame Press, 1986.

Tentler, Leslie Woodcock. "On the Margins: The State of American Catholic History." American Quarterly 45 (March 1993): 104–27.

———. Seasons of Grace: A History of the Catholic Archdiocese of Detroit. Detroit: Wayne State University Press, 1990.

———. "Who Is the Church? Conflict in a Polish Immigrant Parish in Late Nineteenth-Century Detroit." Comparative Studies of Society and History 25 (April 1983): 241–76.

Therborn, Göran. Ideology of Power and the Power of Ideology. New York: Verso, 1980.

Thistlewaite, Frank. "Migration from Europe Overseas in the Nineteenth and Twentieth Centuries." In A Century of European Migrations, 1830–1930, edited by Rudolph J. Vecoli and Suzanne M. Sinke, 17–57. Urbana and Chicago: University of Illinois Press, 1991.

Thompson, John B. Ideology and Modern Culture: Critical Social Theory in the Era of Mass Communication. Stanford: Stanford University Press, 1990.

———. Studies in the Theory of Ideology. Berkeley and Los Angeles: University of California Press, 1984.

Tobia, Bruno. L'altare della patria. Bologna: Mulino, 1998.

Todd, Frank Morton. The Story of the Exposition: Being the Official History of the International Celebration Held at San Francisco in 1915 to Commemorate the Discovery of the Pacific Ocean and the Construction of the Panama Canal, 5 vols. New York: G. P. Putnam's Sons and Knickerbocker Press, 1921.

Tomasi, Silvano M., CS. "L'assistenza religiosa agli italiani in USA e il Prelato per l'Emigrazione Italiana, 1920–1949." Studi Emigrazione 19 (June 1982): 167–90.

———. Piety and Power: The Role of the Italian Parishes in the New York Metropolitan Area, 1880–1930. New York: Center for Migration Studies, 1975.

Traniello, Francesco. Città dell'uomo: Cattolici, partito e stato nella storia d'Italia. Bologna: Mulino, 1998.

———. *Da Gioberti a Moro: Percorsi di una cultura politica.* Milan: Franco Angeli, 1990.

———. "L'Italia cattolica nell'era fascista." In *Storia dell'italia religiosa.* Vol. 3, *L'età contemporanea,* edited by Gabriele De Rosa, 257–300. Bari: Laterza, 1995.

———. "Religione, nazione e sovranità nel risorgimento italiano." *Rivista di storia e letteratura religiosa* 28 (1992): 319–68.

Trincia, Luciano. *Emigrazione e diaspora: Chiesa e lavoratori italiani in Svizzera e in Germania fino alla prima guerra mondiale.* Rome: Studium, 1997.

Turner, James. *The Liberal Education of Charles Eliot Norton.* Baltimore: Johns Hopkins University Press, 1999.

Tuveson, Ernest Lee. *Redeemer Nation: The Idea of America's Millennial Role.* Chicago: University of Chicago Press, 1968.

Tweed, Thomas A. *Our Lady of the Exile: Diasporic Religion at a Cuban Catholic Shrine in Miami.* New York: Oxford University Press, 1997.

Van Allen, Rodger. *The Commonweal and American Catholicism: The Magazine, the Movement, the Meaning.* Philadelphia: Fortress Press, 1974.

Vance, William L. *Catholic and Contemporary Rome.* Vol. 2 of *America's Rome.* New Haven: Yale University Press, 1989.

Varnier, Giovanni B. "Sidney Sonnino and la questione religiosa." In *Sidney Sonnino e il suo tempo,* edited by Pier Luigi Ballini, 223–39. Florence: Leo S. Olschki, 2000.

Vaughn, Stephen. *Holding Fast the Inner Lines: Democracy, Nationalism, and the Committee on Public Information.* Chapel Hill: University of North Carolina Press, 1980.

Vecoli, Rudolph J. "Prelates and Peasants: Italian Immigrants and the Catholic Church." *Journal of Social History* 2 (Spring 1969): 217–68.

Veneruso, Danilo. "I rapporti fra stato e chiesa durante la guerra nei giudizi dei maggiori organi della stampa italiana." In *Benedetto XV, i cattolici e la prima guerra mondiale,* edited by Giuseppe Rossini, 679–737. Rome: Cinque Lune, 1963.

Veronesi, Gene P. *Italian Americans and Their Communities of Cleveland.* Cleveland: Cleveland State University Press, 1977.

Virtanen, Keijo. *Settlement or Return: Finnish Emigrants (1860–1930) in International Overseas Return Migration.* Helsinki: Finnish Historical Society, 1979.

von Arx, Jeffrey, SJ. "Cardinal Henry Edward Manning." In *Varieties of Ultramontanism,* edited by Jeffrey von Arx, SJ, 85–102. Washington, D.C.: Catholic University of America Press, 1998.

Walworth, Arthur. *Wilson and His Peacemakers: American Diplomacy at the Paris Peace Conference, 1919.* New York: W. W. Norton and Co., 1986.

Ward, James E. "Leo XIII and Bismarck: The Kaiser's Vatican Visit of 1888." *Review of Politics* 24 (July 1962): 392–414.

Warner, R. Steven. "The Place of the Congregation in the Contemporary American Religious Configuration." In *New Perspectives in the Study of American Religious Congregations.* Vol. 2 of *American Congregations,* edited by James P. Winn and James W. Lewis, 54–99. Chicago: University of Chicago Press, 1994.

Weber, Timothy P. *Living in the Shadow of the Second Coming: American Premillennialism, 1875–1982.* Chicago: University of Chicago Press, 1987.

Webster, Richard A. *The Cross and the Fasces: Christian Democracy and Fascism in Italy.* Stanford: Stanford University Press, 1960.

Williams, George H. "Professor George La Piana (1878–1971), Catholic Modernist at Harvard (1915–1947)." *Harvard Library Bulletin* 21 (April 1973): 117–43.

Wolff, Richard J. *Between Pope and Duce: Catholic Students in Fascist Italy.* New York: Peter Lang, 1990.

Wuthnow, Robert. *Communities of Discourse: Ideology and Social Structure in the Reformation, the Enlightenment, and European Socialism.* Cambridge, Mass.: Harvard University Press, 1989.

———. *Meaning and Moral Order: Explorations in Cultural Analysis.* Berkeley and Los Angeles: University of California Press, 1987.

———. *The Restructuring of American Religion: Society and Faith since World War II.* Princeton: Princeton University Press, 1988.

Yonke, Eric. "Cardinal Johannes von Geissel." In *Varieties of Ultramontanism*, edited by Jeffrey von Arx, SJ, 12–38. Washington, D.C.: Catholic University of America Press, 1998.

Zivojinovic, Dragan R. "Robert Lansing's Comments on the Pontifical Peace Note of August 1917." *Journal of American History* 56 (December 1969): 556–71.

———. *The United States and the Vatican Policies, 1914–1918.* Boulder: Colorado Associated University Press, 1978.

DISSERTATIONS AND UNPUBLISHED PAPERS

Carter, John B. "American Reactions to Italian Fascism, 1919–1933." Ph.D. diss., Columbia University, 1954.

D'Agostino, Peter R. "Clerical 'Birds of Passage' in the Italian Emigrant Church." Paper presented at the annual meeting of the Organization of American Historians, Indianapolis, Ind., 2–5 April 1998.

———. "Missionaries in Babylon: The Adaptation of Italian Priests to Chicago's Church." Ph.D. diss., University of Chicago, 1993.

Madden, William, SJ. "American Catholic Support for the Papal Army, 1866–1868." Ph.D. diss., Gregorian University, 1967.

Mize, Sandra Yocum. "The Papacy in the Mid-Nineteenth Century American Catholic Imagination." Ph.D. diss., Marquette University, 1987.

Nelli, Humbert. "The Role of the 'Colonial' Press in the Italian-American Community of Chicago, 1886–1921." Ph.D. diss., University of Chicago, 1965.

Norman, John. "Italo-American Opinion in the Ethiopian Crisis: A Study of Fascist Propaganda." Ph.D. diss., Clark University, 1942.

Ordination Book, Archdiocese of Chicago. N.p., n.d.

Poluse, Martin Frank. "Archbishop Joseph Schrembs and the Twentieth Century Church in Cleveland, 1921–1945." Ph.D. diss., Kent State University, 1991.

Smith, William B. "The Attitude of American Catholics toward Italian Fascism between the Two World Wars." Ph.D. diss., Catholic University of America, 1969.

Vecoli, Rudolph J. "The Making and Un-Making of an Italian Working Class in the United States, 1915–1945." Keynote address to the Conference on the Lost World of Italian American Radicalism, City University of New York, 14 May 1997.

Index

"Ad beatissimi apostolorum," 108
Addams, Jane, 71–74
Albano, Michele, 154–56
Allies, World War I, 104, 106, 109, 110, 120, 121, 130–31. *See also* England; France; Russia; United States
Altgeld, Peter John, 79
America, 82, 220–21; and Ernesto Nathan, 87–88, 90, 98; and World War I, 112, 114–15, 117, 118, 119–20, 121–22, 124, 126; and PPI, 167; and Fascism, 173, 176, 189, 309; and Lateran Pacts, 202, 214, 219
American exceptionalism, 12, 44–45, 309–15
American Revolution, 44, 136, 141, 314
Angelucci, Federico (OSM), 251–52
Anti-Defamation League, 95–96
Anti-Fascism, 159–60, 173, 187–89, 202, 211, 216, 232, 235, 257, 268, 271, 274, 277–79, 306–9. *See also names of individuals*
Anti-Fascist Alliance of North America. *See* Anti-Fascism
Anti-Semitism, 35–37, 87, 211–14, 223, 249, 250, 251, 257. *See also* Nathan, Ernesto
Antonelli, Giacomo, 28
Apostolic delegation, 6, 10, 53, 61, 65, 73, 136, 143, 144, 162, 247, 282, 283, 310, 337 (n. 13). *See also names of delegates*
Arcese, Alfonso, 118–19, 149
Atlantic Monthly, 117, 190, 216, 219
Austria: and Risorgimento, 1, 19, 22–28, 32, 34, 38, 41, 45; and World War I, 104, 106, 109, 111, 112, 116, 123, 126. *See also* Catholics: in Austria

Balbo, Italo, 168, 174, 201–2, 242–43, 253
Balilla, 186, 254
Baltimore, 4, 63, 181
Barzini, Luigi, Jr., 163
Bastianini, Giuseppe, 232–33
Bedini, Gaetano, 33–35, 313
Beecher, Lyman, 33
Belgium, 56, 75
Benedict XV (pope), 103–31 passim, 132, 148, 151, 158, 331 (n. 42)
Bieberstein, Adolf Marschall von, 75
Binchey, Daniel, 54, 199, 314, 359 (n. 11)
Bismarck, Otto von, 55
Blanshard, Paul, 159, 309–11
Bloom, Sol, 175
B'nai B'rith Magazine, 36, 213, 214
Bocchini, Arturo, 183–84
Bologna, 20, 34, 35, 40, 61
Bonomelli, Geremia, 56–57
Bonzano, Giovanni, 90–91, 95–96, 99, 110, 113–14, 118–19, 121, 123, 124, 127–30, 178–79, 331 (n. 42); and Order Sons of Italy in America, 132–57 passim; and Warren Harding, 162–63
Boorstin, Daniel J., 310
Boston, 46, 58, 66, 177, 181
Bove, Antonio, 150–54
Brady, William, 19
Brinkley, Alan, 310
Brown, Nicolas, 31
Brownson, Orestes, 48
Bruno, Giordano, 67, 68, 70–74, 88, 152–54, 201

Bryan, William Jennings, 98
Buchanan, James, 19, 31, 39
Bülow, Bernhard von, 106, 108
Burns, Gene, 9

Cabrini, Frances, 58, 249
Cabrini Sisters, 58, 254–56
Caetani di Sermoneta, Gelassio, 170, 231–32, 234, 237
Cannistraro, Philip, 164, 267–68
Caporetto, 115, 118, 149, 235
Carosi, Mario, 243, 247, 255
Cass, Lewis, Jr., 31
Cassels, Alan, 232
Castellucci, Vincent, 268, 270, 281
Castruccio, Giuseppe, 236–44, 252–55
Catholic Action, 105, 169, 199, 223–28, 308
Catholic Mirror (Baltimore), 36, 69, 71
Catholic News (New York), 117, 118, 148, 220
Catholics: in Italy who are intransigents, 10, 42, 54, 57, 139; in France, 28, 55; in Italy, 42, 43, 55–56, 91, 118; in Italy who are conciliationists, 42, 56–57; in Germany, 56, 75–76, 85–86, 120–22; in Italy who are Christian Democrats, 56, 139–40, 216, 267–69, 272–73, 308; in Austria, 75, 85–86; in southern Italy, 139–40, 153; under Fascism, 173. See also Catholics, American; Catholic Action
Catholics, American: in support of Vatican and against Liberal Italy, 2, 4, 7, 10, 11, 12, 14, 20, 26, 34–37, 39, 42, 45, 46–47, 50–52, 53–54, 77–78, 86, 88–90, 94, 96–99, 116–17, 121–24; as an American minority, 5, 7, 8, 112–13; in historiography, 6–7, 54, 104, 112, 159–61, 309–15; attitudes toward Mussolini and Fascism, 8, 13, 14, 158, 160, 174–83, 192–93; and Fascist Italy–Vatican relations, 177–79, 202–6, 240–49, 256–57, 261–62, 279–80, 306–7. See also Apostolic delegation; Irish Americans; Italian Americans; Knights of Columbus; Mussolini, Benito: Americans write to; and names of Catholic individuals and Catholic newspapers
Catholic Standard and Times (Philadelphia), 66, 69, 71
Catholic Telegraph (Cincinnati), 26, 28, 65

Catholic Tribune (Dubuque), 113–14
Catholic Universe Bulletin (Cleveland), 261, 262, 267, 302
Catholic World, 48, 49, 78; and World War I, 112, 117, 124, 126; and PPI, 167–68; and Fascism, 172, 173–73; and Lateran Pacts, 203–4; and crisis of 1931, 225–26; and James Gillis, 259–63
Cavour, Camillo Benso di, 12, 38–44 passim, 49, 69, 87–88, 191, 201, 202, 208, 215–18, 237, 306
Central Powers, 104, 106, 109, 110, 112, 118. See also Austria; Germany; World War I
Cerretti, Bonaventura, 126–27, 184
Chadwick, Owen, 43
Charles Albert (king of Piedmont-Sardinia), 27, 37
Chernow, Ron, 166
Chesterton, Gilbert Keith, 13, 220–23
Chicago, 39, 59, 62–63, 71–74, 79, 90; Twenty-Eighth International Eucharistic Congress in, 177–78; Italians in, 231, 236, 237, 238, 251–56; Century of Progress Exposition in, 240, 241, 242–43. See also Loyola University of Chicago
Chicago Tribune, 72–73, 164, 308
Child, Richard Washburn, 163–64, 241, 243
Christian Advocate (New York), 47, 80, 170, 207, 208, 226–28
Christian Century, 206–8, 226–27, 237
Ciano, Galeazzo, 247
Ciarrocchi, Giuseppe, 14, 159, 258, 267–81
Cicognani, Amleto, 245, 247, 271, 275–76, 278, 286–91
Cincinnati, 39, 65–67
Civiltà Cattolica, 31–32, 70, 85, 89, 123, 172–73, 187, 201, 278, 306
Cleveland, 181, 245–46, 282–83, 294–302; Seventh National Eucharistic Congress in, 260–61; and Ethiopian War, 265–67
Colby, Bainbridge, 128–30
Columbus, Christopher, 63, 64, 150, 180, 271, 274, 275, 285
Committee on Public Information (CPI), 118–19, 120, 127, 190. See also Creel, George
Commonweal, 173, 175–76, 185, 187–89, 207, 215–16, 225, 227

Constitution. See *Statuto*; United States:
Constitution of
Consulates, 12, 14, 54, 58, 59, 67, 79, 138,
144, 149, 160, 190; and Agostino Morini
(OSM), 62–63; and Catholic festivals, 177–
78, 181–82; after Lateran Pacts, 197, 205,
230–57 passim, 258, 264, 265, 277, 285,
309; and parish conflicts, 282–303 passim.
See also names of consuls
Coolidge, Calvin, 165, 166
Corrigan, Michael, 58, 77, 80
Cossio, Luigi, 142, 146, 179
Coughlin, Charles, 247, 280, 348 (n. 66)
Council of Vienna, 19–20
Cowles, John, 120–21, 175
Creel, George, 118, 119–20
Crispi, Francesco, 57, 61, 67–70, 74
Croce, Benedetto, 201, 273
Culti ammessi, 198–200, 215, 218
Curley, Michael, 181, 182

Daily Tribune (New York), 30–31, 79–80
D'Annunzio, Gabriele, 126, 128, 134
De Carlo, Pasquale Riccardo, 238–39
De Maistre, Joseph-Marie Compte, 23
De Martino, Giacomo, 165, 175, 180, 181, 182,
190, 204, 234, 235, 238, 252
Demo, Antonio (PSSC), 66, 144
Democratic Party, 12, 166, 304
Detroit, 231, 267–80
De Vecchi di Val Cismon, Cesare Maria, 242,
253, 275
Devotionalism, 4, 32, 37
Diggins, John, 159–61
Dolan Jay, 5–6, 311–13
Dougherty, Dennis, 119, 128–30, 176, 182,
236, 243, 247
Duffield, Marcus, 235, 240–41
Dunne, Edmund, 71–74, 157
Dwight, Theodore, 33
Dziennik Chicagoski, 88, 203, 225

Eccleston, Samuel, 29
L'Eco del Rhode Island, 67, 150–54, 285–87,
292–93
Ellis, John Tracy, 307, 310–11
England, 30, 33–38, 108–9, 112, 121–22, 212,
218, 260–61, 280, 306, 307, 309

Erzberger, Matthias, 106, 108–9
Ethiopian War, 244, 246–48, 259, 260–67,
277, 281, 286, 295, 304
Ewing, Ellen, 46
Extension Magazine, 90, 112

Faber, Frederick William, 37
Falconio, Diomede (OFM), 86–91
Fama, Carlo, 237–38
Farini, Domenico, 55
Farley, John, 88, 89, 90, 148
Fascism, 13, 15; rise of, 80, 103, 127–28, 162,
168–69, 220–21, 251–52; and Blackshirts,
127–28, 152, 167, 174, 175, 185, 232–36,
254, 268, 274; and Fascist League of North
America (FLNA), 178, 233–36; and *fasci
all'estero*, 231–36; in Catholic memory,
309–10. See also Anti-Fascism; Consulates;
Fascist Italy; *and names of individuals*
Fascist Italy, 103, 130, 232, 282–84, 303;
and Lateran Pacts, 3, 13, 14, 158–60, 197–
202, 230, 252–53, 281; Catholic attitudes
toward, 8, 10, 13, 159–60, 171–76, 182,
185–89, 198, 204, 220–23, 230, 240–57,
264–67, 280, 294, 305; U.S. attitudes
toward, 159, 162–63, 183, 206–8, 212–
14, 236–40, 304; monitors U.S. public
opinion, 160, 164, 190, 192–93, 206; war
debts of, 161–66, 175; toward totalitarian state, 174–77, 183–85, 187; awards
American Catholics, 176, 178, 244, 247,
264, 266–67; propaganda, 182, 184, 185,
235–36, 242, 249, 254–56, 277, 285; *culti
ammessi* and American Protestants, 199–
200, 211–14, 216, 218, 236–40; and crisis
of 1931, 223–28; emigration policy of,
233–34; racial laws of, 249–51; Fascist
Social Republic, 306. See also Anti-Fascism;
Balilla; Consulates; Ethiopian War; Fascism; Freemasonry; Italian Americans:
and Fascism; Italy, Kingdom of; Mussolini, Benito; Partito Nazionale Fascista
(PNF)
Fascist League of North America (FLNA). See
Fascism
Fathers of Our Lady of Mercy. See Mercedarians
Fava, Saverio, 76

Ferdinand II (king of the Two Sicilies), 28
"Il fermo proposito," 91
Ferrante, Gherardo, 90, 137–38, 144–47, 156
Ferrante di Ruffano, Agostino, 177, 181, 204
Fiorentino, Carlo, 183–84
Fiume, 109, 126–30, 134
Flaherty, James, 88–89
Fletcher, Henry, 164, 166, 198
Fogarty, Gerald, 332 (n. 2)
Foley, M. J., 95–96, 192
Foley, Thomas, 62
Fontana, Franco, 244, 248, 253
Fordham University, 244–45
France, 27, 28, 32, 35–37, 38, 41, 53, 55, 108,
    113. See also Napoleon, Louis; September
    Convention
Franciscans, 63, 66, 180–81, 284
Franco, Francisco, 15, 230, 248, 279, 308. See
    also Spain
Freeman's Journal (New York), 36, 45
Freemasonry, 93, 98, 109, 182–83, 258, 264,
    314; Catholics against, 2, 40, 59, 70, 72,
    77, 86, 88, 95, 113, 159–60, 172, 173, 175–
    76, 202, 218–19, 222, 245, 247, 251, 261,
    278, 311; Italian, 42, 58, 84, 92; in U.S.,
    120–21, 175; and Order Sons of Italy in
    America, 133, 135, 138–39, 141, 142–44,
    152–57; and Fascist Italy, 168, 170, 175. See
    also Nathan, Ernesto
French Revolution, 4, 44
Fuller, Margaret, 26, 30–31
Fumasoni-Biondi, Pietro, 165
Fuorusciti. See Anti-Fascism; and names of
    individuals

Gabaccia, Donna, 235
Gallagher, Michael, 205, 269–71, 275–76,
    277, 278
Gannon, Robert I. (SJ), 244–45
Garibaldi, Giuseppe, 28, 45, 63, 68, 92, 191,
    202, 275; and Protestants, 12, 33, 41, 238;
    according to Catholics, 30–31, 40, 50, 67,
    69, 72; statue of, 74, 80, 201, 218, 306
Garrison, William Lloyd, 33
Garrison, Winfred, 208
Gasparri, Pietro, 205, 218; World War I and
    postwar settlement, 104, 110–11, 113, 121,
    122–23, 125, 126–30, 163; and Fascist Italy,

169, 172, 197, 228; and Enrico Pucci, 183,
    185
Gattuso, Sante (ODM), 294–302
Gavazzi, Alessandro, 33–34
Gemelli, Agostino, 167, 171, 249
Gerlach, Rudolf, 106, 120–21
German Americans, 8, 36–37, 39, 47, 77, 89,
    94, 112
German Catholic Central-Verein, 89, 113,
    133
Germany, 36, 45, 55; Center Party, 55, 76,
    106, 108; in World War I, 106, 108, 109,
    111, 112, 115; Nazi, 250, 251, 257, 279, 304,
    306. See also Catholics: in Germany
Giambastiani, Luigi (OSM), 252–54
Gibbons, James, 46, 54, 68–69, 76, 91–94,
    117, 119, 121–25
Giddens, Anthony, 8
Gillis, James (CSP), 14, 159, 173–74, 203,
    225–26, 258–67, 280
Gioberti, Vincenzo, 24, 25, 59–60. See also
    Neoguelfism
Giolitti, Giovanni, 91, 92, 167
Gleason, Philip, xi, 159, 308–9
Glennon, John, 178–79
Gonner, Nicholas, 89, 113–14
Gramsci, Antonio, 43
Grandi, Dino, 233
"Graves de communi," 56
Great Britain. See England
Great War. See World War I
Gregory XVI (pope), 21, 23
Greeley, Horace, 19, 30–31, 38
Griffin, James, 241, 243
Gross, Mark (SJ), 244–45
Guglielmotti, Emilio, 134
Guilday, Peter, 115, 119–20, 205

Hanna, Edward, 99, 117, 185, 225
Harding, Warren, 162–63
Harkins, Matthew, 151–53
Harney, John (CSP), 260–63, 281
Hayes, Carlton J. H., 214–16, 309
Hayes, Patrick, 123, 128–30, 146–47, 156, 165,
    176, 204
Hayes, Ralph, 246–47
Hearley, John, 190, 219–20
Hearn, Edward, 224–25

Hearst, William Randolph, 128–29, 164, 259, 261

Hecker, Isaac (CSP), 48, 50, 53

Hennesey, James (SJ), 312

Hickey, Thomas, 142

Hilter, Adolf, 248–49, 250–51, 262, 304

Holstein, Friederich von (Baron), 75

Hoover, Herbert, 163–64, 220

House, Edward, 123

Howe, Julia Ward, 48

Hughes, Charles Evans, 163–64

Hughes, John, 19, 29, 30–31, 32–33, 34

Hull House. See Addams, Jane

Ickes, Harold, 249

Ideology: defined, 8–11; change, 9–10, 103; competition, 10, 13, 132–57 passim; trumps natural law, 159–61, 228–29. See also Liberalism; Natural law; Roman Question (ideology of)

"Ineffabilis Deus," 32

Ireland, 34, 113

Ireland, John, 46, 57, 94

Irish Americans, 8, 32–35, 62, 77–79, 91, 98, 112, 240–41, 243, 259, 280

Iriye, Akira, 7

Italian Americans: diversity among, 12, 13, 34, 54, 63, 67, 71–74, 78–79, 98, 142–43, 149–50, 155–57, 230–32, 235, 267–68; as immigrant Catholic clergy, 12, 13, 58–59, 89–90, 132–43, 148–51, 155–57, 180, 231, 241, 258–59, 270, 279–80, 283–85, 293; migration of, 12, 54, 57–60, 233–34; and Catholic Church, 14, 57–60, 61–67, 71–74, 142, 156–57, 179–82, 197, 231–32, 236, 251–57, 264, 281, 282–303 passim; and Fascism, 14, 177–79, 181–82, 232–39, 250–57, 264–75, 281, 304, 282–303 passim; and Liberal Italy, 38, 59–60, 61–67, 71–74, 78–79, 89–90, 98; images of, 59–60, 162, 235, 257, 281–303 passim, 305. See also Mutual benefit societies

L'Italiano in America, 142–45, 155–56

Italy, Kingdom of, 4, 7, 9, 13, 27, 38, 158; established, 1, 2, 42; Foreign Ministry, 58, 108–9, 122, 177, 182, 206, 231–59 passim, 265–67, 275, 282–83, 299; twenty-fifth anniversary of, 74–80; end of monar-chy, 280, 306–8. See also Fascist Italy; Freemasonry; Liberal Italy; and names of individual kings

Italy America Society, 164–66, 206, 233, 247

Jesuits, 30–31, 35–36, 63, 191–92, 220–21, 236, 244–45. See also Civiltà Cattolica

Jewish Telegraph Agency, 212–14

Jews, 1, 40, 70, 86, 115, 245, 280; American, 3–5, 20, 35–37, 51, 95–96, 197, 229, 250, 251, 280; Italian, 26, 31, 87–88, 92, 211–14, 240, 310–11. See also Anti-Semitism; Nathan, Ernesto

John XXIII (pope), 4

John Paul II (pope), ix

Jusserand, Jules, 116

Kain, John, 77

Keane, John, 46–47

Kelly, Francis, 126

Kelly, Robert (SJ), 242–43

Kenrick, Francis, 34, 35

Kenrick, Peter, 69

Kent, Peter, 230

Keough, Francis Patrick, 282, 286–93

Kertzer, David, 115

Knights of Columbus, 88–89, 94–97, 123, 133, 139, 170–71, 177–81, 191, 224–25, 241, 246–47, 296, 300

Knock, Thomas, 111

Kulturkampf, 55

La Farge, John (SJ), 220–21, 348 (n. 66)

La Guardia, Fiorello, 119

Lamennais, Félicité de, 4

Lamont, Thomas, 163–66

Lansing, Robert, 110–12, 115–16, 123

La Piana, George, 280, 306–9

Lateran Pacts, 3, 13, 158, 184, 193, 197–223 passim, 273, 282, 303, 307–8; and American Catholics, 14, 161, 214–19, 220–23, 256, 309–10; texts analyzed, 198–200; and Italian Americans, 251–57. See also Fascist Italy

Lauro, Mario, 178, 236, 252

Lavelle, Michael, 144, 165

Law of Guarantees: defined, 3, 11, 48–49; and Triple Alliance, 55; Francesco Crispi on, 57, 68; American Catholics criticize, 69, 88, 188, 215; during World War I and postwar unrest, 108–11, 114, 122, 127, 130, 167–68; abrogated by Lateran Pacts, 197, 200, 216. See also Liberal Italy; Pius IX

League of Nations, 104, 126–29, 208, 214, 230, 260

Leo XIII (pope), 53–56, 65, 68–69, 70–71, 74, 79, 145

L'Espérance, Pierre, 286–88

Liberalism, 141, 249, 309; on religion and Roman Question, 1–2, 7–8, 9, 104, 116, 120, 125, 211, 229; and Catholicism, 3–4, 6, 10, 13, 15, 19, 21, 29, 31, 42, 68, 70, 91, 120, 148, 221–23, 148, 158, 159, 161, 169, 187, 188, 220, 222–23, 308, 315; and American exceptionalism, 12, 44–45, 50, 51–52, 215, 311, 314; in Italy, 87, 170, 307, 311, 314. See also Liberal Italy

Liberal Italy (1861–1922): pope in, 1, 2, 4, 11, 12, 20, 48–49, 106, 109, 111, 122, 127, 158; popes and Catholics condemn, 3, 10, 11, 12, 20, 42, 49, 50–56, 59, 70, 74–76, 80–81, 103, 125, 161, 180, 192–93, 203–4, 215, 243, 247; post–World War I crisis and collapse of, 9, 126–30, 157, 161, 167–69; emigration and colonies abroad, 12, 13, 52, 59, 78–79, 90; and Destra, 37–38, 43, 49, 68, 312, 314; Catholic Church in, 42, 45, 62, 231; support in U.S. for, 54, 72–73, 80; architecture in, 80–82; Catholics relax condemnation of, 103–5, 130; in World War I, 108, 119, 123, 127. See also Cavour, Camillo Benso di; Catholics: in Italy; Crispi, Francesco; Nathan, Ernesto

Liberté (Paris), 109–10

Livingston, Sigmund, 95–96

Lombardy, 22, 27, 38, 49, 55–56

Loyola University of Chicago, 236, 240–41, 242–43, 244–45, 253

Lynch, Patrick, 46

Macchi di Cellere, Vincenzo, 112, 122

Mahoney, Bernard, 241–42

Manzoni, Alessandro, 23, 216

Marchello, Maurice, 157

March on Rome. See Fascism

Marcuzzi, Edoardo, 142–50, 153–57

Margotti, Giacomo, 42

Marretta, Leonardo, 141–42

Marsh, George Perkins, 38

Marshall, Charles, 216–17

Martina, Giacomo (SJ), 27, 49

Martinelli, Sebastiano, 65–67, 91

Marty, Martin, 310

Masons. See Freemasonry

Mastai-Ferretti, Giovanni Maria. See Pius IX

Mastrovalerio, Alessandro, 71–73, 157

Matteotti, Giacomo, 165, 172–73, 274

Mayor des Planches, Edmondo, 91–92

Mazzini, Giuseppe, 12, 23, 28, 30–33, 39, 40, 44, 51, 67, 69, 73, 92, 127, 189, 191, 202, 275, 306

McAdoo, William, 128–29

McCloskey, John, 45

McFadden, James, 261–62, 267, 300–301

McFaul, James, 142

McGrath, Justin, 184–85, 260

McGreevy, John, 6, 159, 283, 308–9

McNicolas, John, 245–46, 266

Mellon, Andrew, 164

Menace, 93–94

Mercedarians, 282, 284, 294–302

Mercier, Désiré, 122–23, 125–26

Merriam, Charles, 119

Merry del Val, Raffaele, 73, 85–89, 180

Methodist Episcopal Church (American), 6, 81, 170–71, 208

Metternich, Klemens von, 27

Michaelis, Meir, 214

Miele, Stefano, 144–45

Minzoni, Giovanni, 174, 243

"Mirari vos," 21

Monitor (San Francisco), 93–95, 97, 172

Montecchi, Romeo, 246, 264–67, 295–96, 299–301

Montifiore, Moses, 35

Montini, Giovanni Battista, 184, 313–14

Mooney, Edward, 278, 305

Moore, Charles, 93, 95, 98, 99. See also Panama Pacific International Exposition

Moore, R. Laurence, 5

Morgan, Thomas, 164

Morini, Agostino, 62–63

Morris, Ira Nelson, 98

Morse, Samuel, 33

Mortara, Edgardo, 33–37, 51, 87

Mundelein, George, 90–91, 128–30, 135–37, 178, 242, 243, 247–49

Murray, John Courtney (SJ), 44, 311

Murri, Romolo, 56, 268–69

Mussolini, Benito, 13, 183, 184, 278, 310; and U.S. government, 127, 161–66, 192, 268, 304–5; rise to power of, 156, 167–69, 171, 177; Americans write to, 159, 175, 179, 180, 182, 183, 186, 190–93, 205–6, 211, 245, 250–51, 292; in American religious press, 168, 172, 176, 185–90, 203–6, 208, 215–16, 229; and negotiation and ratification of Lateran Pacts, 170, 174–75, 197–202; and Matteotti crisis, 172–74; celebrated by American Catholics, 178, 180, 181, 203–5, 215–16, 241–43, 246, 261–62, 273; in biblical prophecy, 209–11; on Jews and Zionism, 211–14; meets G. K. Chesterton, 220, 222–23; and crisis of 1931, 223–28; and Ethiopian War, 230, 263, 265–66; *fasci all'estero* and Italian Americans, 231–38, 254, 261–67; according to American intellectuals and journalists, 235, 240–41, 249, 274, 307–9; fall from power of, 305–7. *See also* Anti-Fascism; Fascism; Fascist Italy

Mutual benefit societies, 58, 65–66, 78–79, 133–34, 147–49, 152–54, 178–79, 252, 271, 274

Napoleon, Louis, 27, 28, 32, 38, 40, 43

Napoleon III. *See* Napoleon, Louis

Nathan, Ernesto, 83, 84–99 passim, 172, 202, 331 (n. 42)

Natick, R.I. *See* Rhode Island

National Catholic Welfare (War) Conference (NCWC), 115, 183–85, 202, 260–62

Natural law, 106, 161, 186–87, 223, 226, 229, 260, 309

Neoguelfism, 20–25, 29, 51, 59, 188–89, 216, 221, 272–73

New World (Chicago), 59–60, 71–74, 157, 168, 171–72, 203, 243, 248

New York City, 19, 29, 33–34, 39, 46, 48, 51, 58, 63, 77, 172, 180, 232

New York Times, 98, 116, 117, 164, 176

Nitti, Francesco Saverio, 122, 127–28

Noll, John, 245

"Non abbiamo bisogno," 198, 223, 225–27, 273

Norton, Charles Eliot, 41

O'Brien, David, 315

O'Brien, William, 243–44, 253

O'Connell, Daniel, 64

O'Connell, William Henry, 124–25, 130, 165, 171, 176, 181, 204

Olney, Richard, 74

Opera dei Congressi, 56, 70, 105, 139

Order Sons of Italy in America (OSIA), 13, 132–57 passim, 181, 234, 253, 266, 268, 275, 294–95

O'Reilly, Bernard, 69

Orlando, Vittorio Emanuele, 122, 126–27, 184

Orthodoxy, 67, 106, 113

O'Shea, John, 69–70, 78

L'Osservatore Romano, 110, 169, 171, 187, 198, 201, 223–24, 278

Pacelli, Eugenio, 14, 224, 228, 247–48, 258–59, 263, 272, 275–76, 278, 280, 304–5

"Pacem, Dei munus," 105

Page, Thomas Nelson, 97–98, 109–10, 112, 118

Pallottine Sisters of Charity, 146–47

Palmer, Mitchell, 128

Panama Pacific International Exposition, 85, 93–99

Papal infallibility, 45, 47

Papal States, 1, 2, 9, 10, 12, 20–41 passim, 47, 60, 64, 77, 152, 197, 221

Parini, Piero, 255

Parsons, Wilfred (SJ), 189, 214–15, 218–19, 307, 309

Partito Comunista Italiana (PCI), 167, 308

Partito Nazionale Fascista (PNF), 168–75, 223, 228, 232–33, 249, 254, 273–74

Partito Popolare Italiano (PPI), 13, 105, 130, 139–40, 167–73, 273, 280, 307

Partito Socialista Italiana (PSI), 105, 167

Paul VI (pope). *See* Montini, Giovanni Battista

Peace Note (of Benedict XV), 104–5, 115–18, 120

Peter's Pence, 31, 41–42, 89

Philadelphia, 33, 46, 47, 62, 66–67, 182

Phillips, William, 304

Piacenza, 61
Piedmont-Sardinia, Kingdom of, 22, 24–25, 27, 37–42, 314
Pignatti Morano di Custoza, Bonifacio, 248, 258–59
Pilot (Boston), 28, 29, 41, 88
Pittsburgh, 61–62
Pius IX (pope): and revolution of 1848, 1, 14, 27–29, 32, 308; condemns Kingdom of Italy, Law of Guarantees, liberalism, 2, 31, 42–44, 49, 67, 218–19, 228, 311–12; and American Protestants, 19, 30–31, 47–48; biographical details on, 19–20, 26, 53; as victim like Christ, 20, 29, 32, 37, 50, 88; and American Catholics, 25–26, 29–30, 35–36, 40, 42, 45–47, 49–51, 130, 215; and Catholic devotionalism, 32, 37; and Mortara case, 35–37, 87; loses Papal States and Rome, 38–42, 46; and Cavour and Vittorio Emanuele II, 38, 43, 60–61, 64
Pius X (pope), 56, 85–91, 103, 105
Pius XI (pope), 206, 220, 269, 273, 307; and reconciliation with Fascist Italy, 13, 103, 158, 168–69, 173–75, 178, 189, 192, 202, 249; and Catholic youth, 185–86; and crisis of 1931, 198, 223–29
Pius XII (pope). *See* Pacelli, Eugenio
Pizzardo, Giuseppe, 183, 185, 263
Polk, James, 26
Pollard, John, 186, 200
Pomante, Piero, 254–55
Pope, Generoso, 265–66
Il Popolo d'Italia, 127, 168, 198, 212–13, 232
Porta Pia, 20, 46, 74, 78, 81, 84, 191
Pozzi, Luigi, 137
Il Progresso Italo-Americano, 98, 148, 182, 265
Protestants, 106; support Liberal Italy, 1, 2, 11–12, 20, 24, 33, 43; relations with Catholics, 2, 13, 14, 32–52 passim, 93–94, 105, 113, 126, 162, 309–11, 313, 314; in American religious historiography, 3–6; and Fascist Italy, 14, 170, 179–80, 186, 190; and Italian Americans, 54, 62, 66, 119, 137–38, 236–39, 293; and Waldensians in Italy, 170–71, 208, 237, 238, 308; and Lateran Pacts, 197, 206–11, 214, 229. See also *Culti ammessi*
Providence, 63, 67, 150–54, 291

Pucci, Enrico, 172, 183–85, 202
Purcell, John, 45, 63–65, 67

"Quadragesimo Anno," 224, 348 (n. 66)
"Quanta Cura," 43
Quigley, James, 60
Quirinal Palace, 60–61, 81, 105

Rampolla del Tindaro, Mariano, 55, 57, 58, 74
"Rappresentanti in terra," 201–2
Republican Party, 161–66, 191
"Rerum Novarum," 57, 139–40, 145, 224
Resurrectionist Fathers, 88, 203
Reville, John (SJ), 125
Revolution of 1848, 1, 2, 20, 25, 26–31
Rhode Island, 150–54, 282–83, 285–94
Riordan, Patrick, 99
Risorgimento, 12, 37–52 passim, 135, 152, 208, 254; defined, 3, 11, 15, 19, 20; condemned by Catholics, 14–15, 29, 39, 82, 91–92, 125, 152, 308, 312; Americans' view of, 25, 31, 38–39, 43, 47–48, 96, 162, 218; and Vittorio Emanuele II, 61–64; and Italian liberals, 74, 92, 201, 202, 314; and Jews, 87–88, 211–12; according to Luigi Sturzo, 188–89; Giuseppe Ciarrocchi's vision of, 272–73
"Rite Expiatis," 180
Rocco, Alfredo, 174–75, 187, 211–12, 232
Roddan, John, 28
Rodgers, Daniel, 313
Rolph, James, 93, 97–98. *See also* Panama Pacific International Exposition
Romagna, 38–40
Roman Empire, 2, 24, 29, 206, 209–10, 249
Romano di Avezzana, Camillo, 129–30, 134
Roman Question, 1, 20, 53, 139, 162, 216, 219; and Catholic protest, 2, 3, 7–8, 11, 12, 88, 113, 124, 125, 192; in American historiography, 4, 193, 324 (nn. 2, 3); strategies to resolve and resolution of, 12, 13, 15, 54–57, 103–31 passim, 157, 158, 161, 167, 168, 170, 173, 174, 175, 184–86, 190–92, 197, 201, 203, 205, 251, 257; and World War I, 99, 103–31 passim, 184; and PPI, 167, 169
—ideology of, 13, 19, 309, 311; defined, 3, 5, 7, 9–15; intransigent formulations of,

17–99; created, 19–52; transformation of, 103–93; realization of, 197–303. *See also* Ideology

Rome, 183, 233, 237, 240, 243, 266, 289, 290, 303; papal, 1, 2, 4, 20, 29–33, 35, 43, 45, 47, 53, 61, 64, 67, 76, 81, 83, 92, 161, 170, 258, 268, 305; and revolution of 1848, 1, 14, 27–28, 31; and 20th of September (1870), 1, 20, 45, 58, 64, 77–79, 179; contested status of, 2, 4, 5, 29, 33, 51–52, 54, 70, 82, 84–85, 168, 171; as center of Catholicism and civilization, 4, 7, 33, 40–41, 45, 50, 53, 87, 88, 178, 220–23, 225, 226–27, 228, 237, 246, 247, 249, 260, 262, 263, 267, 270, 272, 313; as capital of united Italy, 43, 68, 75, 78, 82, 84, 88, 89, 91, 164, 175, 176, 177, 203, 226, 229, 258; liberal monuments in, 70–73, 74, 80–83; as destination of pilgrimages, 76, 84, 90, 180, 204; in World War I, 108, 109, 119, 123, 126, 127; Jews in, 213–14; in World War II and Italian republic, 305–7. *See also* Papal States

Roosevelt, Franklin D., 243, 247–48, 249, 259, 265, 270, 280, 304–6

Rosmini, Antonio, 24, 49

Rosselli, Carlo, 277–78

Rosso, Augusto, 214, 241, 243, 245, 266, 270–71, 275, 277, 288, 290

Rozwadowski, Antonio Ladislao, 79

Russia, 106–9, 113, 120

Russo, Francesco, 286–92

Ryan, John A., 128, 166, 186–89, 214–18, 259, 281, 309

Ryan, Patrick, 66

Sacconi, Giuseppe, 81, 83

Sacred Heart, Missionaries of the, 282–83, 286–93

St. Francis of Assisi, 180–81

St. Louis, 39, 63, 177–78, 249

Saint Peter's Cathedral, 61, 89, 148, 169, 221

Salandra, Antonio, 106, 109–10

Salvemini, Gaetano, 202, 274, 280, 306–9

Sanfilippo, Matteo, 7, 85

San Francisco, 93–99

San Giuliano, Antonio, 98

Santucci, Carlo, 169–70

Sarfatti, Margherita, 14

Satolli, Francesco, 74, 76, 77

Scalabrini, Giovanni Battista, 56–58, 61

Scalabrini Fathers, 57–58, 66, 150–51, 243–44, 253, 270, 284

Schmitz, David, 304

Schrembs, Joseph, 163, 181, 204–5, 264, 267, 282, 294–302

Schuster, Ildefonso, 223–24, 277

Seldes, George, 164, 308–9

Sellaro, Vincenzo, 133

Semeria, Giovanni, 132, 134–35, 138–39

Sentinel (Chicago), 96, 213–14

September Accords, 223, 228

September Convention, 43, 45

Servites, 59, 62–63, 251–54, 284

Sforza, Carlo, 216–18

Shahan, Thomas, 181, 203–4

Shea, John Gilmary, 50–51

Sherman, Lawrence, 126

Shroeder, Joseph, 59

Silipigni, Giuseppe, 152, 154–56

Sixtus V (pope), 81

Smith, Al, 14, 189, 216–17, 220, 228

Smith, John Talbot, 79

Sonnino, Sidney, 108–9, 112, 118, 122

Sons of Italy. *See* Order Sons of Italy in America

Southern, David, 259

Spain, 15, 53, 55, 76, 159, 230, 278–79

Spalding, Martin John, 40, 43–45

Spellman, Francis, 225, 305, 313–14

Statuto, 15, 27, 37, 49, 198–99, 200

Sturzo, Luigi, 56, 140, 167, 169, 171–72, 188–89, 269, 273, 279–80, 307, 348 (n. 66), 359 (n. 11)

Suvich, Fulvio, 244–45, 247–49, 259

Swift, George, 79

"Syllabus of Errors," 42–44, 51

Tablet (Brooklyn), 95–98

Taft, William, 93

Taglialatela, Alfredo, 208

Taylor, Myron, 248, 304–5

Temporal power. *See* Roman Question

Tentler, Leslie Woodcock, 312

Thaon di Revel, Ignazio, 178, 233

Thayer, William Roscoe, 82

Tierney, Michael, 77

Tierney, Richard (SJ), 114–15, 119–20, 124–25, 331 (n. 42)

Tipple, Bertrand, 171

Tittoni, Tommaso, 91

Torlonia, Leopoldo, 68, 70

Traniello, Francesco, 23

Treaty of London, 109, 113–14, 118, 120–23, 126

Treaty of Versailles, 127, 129

La Tribuna Italiana Transatlantica, 71–73, 157

Triple Alliance, 54–55, 109

Trivisonno, Joseph, 261–63, 266–67

Tumulty, Joseph, 126, 129

Tuscany, 22, 38

20th of September, 1, 20, 45–46, 58, 72–81, 84–99, 119, 170, 179, 191, 202

Two Sicilies, Kingdom of the, 22, 26–28, 41

"Ubi arcano Dei," 169

"Ubi Nos," 49

Ultramontanism, 24, 44

Umberto I (king of Italy), 55, 60, 65–68, 79

Ungarelli, Giacomo, 267–71, 275–76

United States, 105, 108, 110; government, 30–31, 35, 41, 122, 163–64, 192, 207, 266–67; Constitution of, 44–45, 57, 310, 311, 320 (n. 22); State Department, 111, 162, 163, 164, 166, 198, 247, 249, 304–5; and papal peace Note, 115–16; and European economic reconstruction, 158–66; House of Representatives Un-American Activities Committee (HUAC), 268, 275, 277. See also Committee on Public Information; and names of individual officials

United States Catholic Magazine, 25, 29–30

Valente, Michele, 277

Van Buren, Martin, 19

Vatican, 4, 93–94, 191–92, 201, 203, 214, 310, 313; as modern Calvary, 1, 20, 37; as source of Catholic discipline and authority, 11, 12, 34, 53, 61, 63, 65, 75, 85, 90, 132, 160, 161, 202, 224, 242, 259, 260, 263, 269, 272, 275, 278, 280–86, 294, 300, 303, 312; and Liberal Italy, 12–13, 45–46, 48–49, 66–67, 68–70, 74, 80, 82, 84, 96, 122, 128, 157, 167, 179, 215; in World War I,

104, 106, 109, 112, 119, 121, 122, 123, 128, 130, 141; and Italian migrant clergy, 136–37, 144, 149, 151; and Order Sons of Italy in America, 154, 156; and Fascist Italy, 158–61, 164–65, 168–72, 181, 182, 186, 189–90, 192, 199–202, 223, 228, 283, 285; and United States after World War I, 162, 192, 239, 248; and PPI, 169, 172, 183; and World War II and Italian republic, 305–8. See Apostolic delegation; Lateran Pacts; Law of Guarantees; Pucci, Enrico; Vatican City, State of

Vatican City, State of, 3, 11, 13, 103, 158, 197, 307

Vatican Council, First, 45–46, 323 (n. 69)

Vatican Council, Second, 310–13

Venetia, 22, 27, 38, 41, 45

Veneto, 55–56

Verderosa, Vincenzo, 285–94

Vittoriano, 80–83, 201

Vittorio Emanuele II, 37–38, 40–43, 45, 50, 60–65, 74, 77, 91, 191, 314. See also Vittoriano

Vittorio Emanuele III, 97, 109, 148–49, 267; and Roman Question, 127, 161; and Fascism, 162, 172, 176–77; and American Catholics, 177–78; and ecclesiastical legislation, 199–200; honored by Pius XI, 228; dismisses Mussolini, 305–6

La Voce del Popolo (Detroit). See Ciarrocchi, Giuseppe

Waldensians. See Protestants

Walsh, David (senator from Massachusetts), 123, 128–29

Walsh, David (senator from Montana), 129

Washington, D.C., 4, 46, 177. See also Apostolic delegation

Webster, Richard, 223

Western Catholic (Springfield, Ill.), 95–96, 192

Whiting, Lilian, 82

Wickham, Harvey, 173, 187–88

Wigger, Winand, 71

Wilhelm II (Kaiser), 55

Williams, John, 46

Wilson, Woodrow, 98, 112, 148; and papal diplomacy, 8, 104, 108, 110–11, 114, 115–16, 118, 121, 163; and liberal ideology, 104, 111,

120; and Austria-Hungary, 123; Benedict prays for, 124–25; and Fiume, 126–30
Winrod, Gerald, 209–10
Wise, Isaac Meyer, 35
Wood, L. J. S., 173, 175–76, 185
World War I, 52, 92, 103–31 passim, 190, 241, 269, 294; and papal diplomacy, 8, 80; Catholic attitudes toward, 9, 54, 219, 221–22; and ideological change, 12, 13, 99; and Paris Peace Conference, 120, 123–27, 158
World War II, 172, 184, 267, 303, 304–8
Wuthnow, Robert, 9

Zaboglio, Francesco (PSSC), 58–59
Zionism, 211–14
Zunini, Leopoldo, 177–78